State Dominance in Myanmar

State Dominance in Myanmar

The Political Economy of Industrialization

TIN Maung Maung Than

ISEAS

Institute of Southeast Asian Studies
Singapore

First published in Singapore in 2007 by
ISEAS Publishing
Institute of Southeast Asian Studies
30 Heng Mui Keng Terrace
Pasir Panjang
Singapore 119614

E-mail: publish@iseas.edu.sg
Website: http://bookshop.iseas.edu.sg

ISEAS Library Cataloguing-in-Publication Data

TIN Maung Maung Than.
State dominance in Myanmar: the political economy of industrialization.
1. Industries—Burma.
2. Industrial policy—Burma.
3. Industrialization—Burma.
4. Burma—Economic policy.
I. Title
HD3616 B9T58 2007

ISBN-13: 978-981-230-350-9 (soft cover—13 digit)
ISBN-10: 981-230-350-2 (soft cover—10 digit)
ISBN-13: 978-981-230-371-4 (hard cover—13 digit)
ISBN-10: 981-230-371-5 (hard cover—10 digit)

Typeset by International Typesetters Pte Ltd
Printed in Singapore by Kyodo Printing Co. (Singapore) Pte Ltd

In May 1946, *Bogyoke* declared:

> What we want is full freedom. In the absence of economic freedom, political freedom is nothing but a mockery and an empty show... When we say real freedom, we meant the freedom not only to plan our political destiny but also the economy ... by ourselves.[33]

This essentially represented the sentiments attached to economic independence or self-reliance that seem to have lingered on among Myanmar's leadership circles.

This somewhat inchoate notion of economic independence, which had its roots in the perception of the dependent nature of the colonial economy and exploitation by alien interests, manifested itself in certain measures often labelled as economic nationalism, autarky, or *dirigisme*.[34] On the other hand, one should also note Peter Burnell's comment that "[w]hat national economic independence is and what it would look like if it were attained are rarely made clear".[35]

Evidently, John Wirth's goal for economic nationalism defined as the attainment of "economic power to assure a nation's political independence" is also valid as a goal for economic independence.[36] As such, "national economic sovereignty and control are closely tied to national economic independence"[37] and this was essentially the message conveyed by *Bogyoke*.[38] It may also be seen as a particular economic outlook operating in tandem with the Myanmar leadership's interpretation of socialist principles underpinning the state-led industrial development programme. As the socialist reconstruction process waxed and waned in relation to economic and political exigencies, the notion of economic independence seems to have been perceived as the basis of a complementary strategy of autonomous development.[39]

PLANS AND PLANNING

Plans have been a most persistent instrument of Myanmar's developmental effort, and commitment to some form of national planning is a common feature of all Myanmar governments. The notion that planning is a superior alternative to the market stemmed not only from the negative experiences of the colonial economy but also from the seemingly highly successful experiences of the Soviet economy under Stalin.[40]

The first attempt to introduce a national plan was made by the government of Dr Ba Maw, during the Japanese occupation. He exhorted the immediate implementation of the "New Order Plan", calling for "'One Blood, One Voice, One Command' ... as an appeal for a nation-state–centred sense of loyalty of a kind that the state in Burma had not encouraged before".[41] The plan was geared towards "war-waging and state-making".[42] To him, "planning is concentration, of power and control, of action, of means and ends ... ground-elements in planning are really concentration in one form or another, mass organizations, national unity, mobilization of wealth and labour, collective action, [and] leadership".[43]

Next, the Burma Special Research Commission was formed, in May 1944, to assist in formulating a broad-based plan. The Commission set out immediately for a study tour of countries within the "Co-prosperity Sphere in East Asia".[44] Its interim report contained recommendations, *inter alia*, to form a planning department under the prime minister, to immediately open an applied research institute, to institute state monopoly on foreign trade, to impose state control over commodity distribution, and to expand and reorganize the cooperatives.[45] Before the final report was completed the Japanese retreated, and Ba Maw's government collapsed. Ba Maw's brother, Ba Han, reconstructed the outline of the Myanmar State envisaged by the Commission and, incorporating his observations on the seemingly favourable experience of the Soviet Union, produced a monograph entitled *The Planned State* in July 1946. This treatise, which represented the first attempt to expound the idea of a centrally planned state in the Myanmar context, advocated pervasive state intervention in the production and distribution of commodities, fiscal and monetary controls, control of foreign trade, and social welfare. Ba Han also stressed the significance of electric power for industrialization and stated that "[w]hile a State pursues agricultural production with rapid strides, it should not neglect industrial production".[46]

The exiled British administration based in Simla, India, also made plans in anticipation of the reoccupation of Myanmar.[47] However, it was "suggested that the reconstruction plans ... were unreal, given the resources available in Burma or from Britain".[48] Moreover, they were predicated upon denying self-government to the Myanmar for an extended period of time, which turned out to be politically untenable. The resulting plan for rehabilitation projects were repudiated by the Myanmar nationalists who saw them as means of re-establishing the British economic stranglehold on Myanmar. In the Presidential address delivered to the first AFPFL Congress, in January 1946, *Bogyoke* criticized the British rehabilitation projects as a surreptitious form of "economic fascism in the name of reconstruction".[49] He appeared to have believed that planning would facilitate in "[b]ringing Burma's economic structure closer to a socialist economy" and, in fact, "was necessary in any economic system".[50]

The AFPFL leaders, who became power holders in post-independence Myanmar, apparently regarded planning as essential for economic development.[51] The Governor's Executive Council, effectively the Cabinet, set up a department for national planning and instituted the National Planning Board in early 1947 at the sub-Cabinet level. A step towards coordinated plans was taken on 6 June 1947 when *Bogyoke* (then, Deputy Chairman of the Executive Council) convened a National Rehabilitation Conference at the Sorrento Villa in Yangon. Popularly known as the Sorrento Villa Conference, it was organized into five panels for discussing statistics, planning, finance, ways and means, and co-ordination of the relevant programmes. Unfortunately, *Bogyoke*'s assassination on 19 July cut short the formulation of these ideas into a comprehensive national plan.[52] The National Planning Board was superseded by the Economic Planning Board (EPB), set up in September 1947 "to formulate proposals for a planned economy for Burma for the period 1947–48 to 1951–52".[53] The EPB's task was to formulate:

> a Plan ... that will lead directly to an increase in ... national wealth and extend its benefits to the common man, and at the same time lay down the foundations on a firm and scientific basis for a fully co-ordinated long-term plan of economic development.[54]

The plan was drawn up "in view of the ideal of State Socialism embodied in the Constitution" and was submitted to the Cabinet on December 1947 "in full knowledge of its defects and limitations, but with the firm belief that it will start the country on the road to the full realization of the ideal of a planned economy".[55] The plan, announced on 1 April 1948, reportedly incorporated "most of the valuable material from the 'Sorrento Plans', but not all".[56]

The next forty years saw a succession of plans, many unannounced and some unimplemented. They invariably failed to fulfil the original expectations and, more often than not, fell short of their targets.[57] Yet, planning seemed to have been treated as an article of faith by all those who sought control over the Myanmar state. As a normative attempt "to give substance to aspirations", planning seems to be ideally regarded as "progressing from some authoritative vision of the future ... to a range of ... policies, which are translated into activities through the medium of the plan" creating "the changes envisaged at the outset".[58] As such, it became a symbol of commitment to national economic growth and social welfare as well as a legitimizing factor for the policies and programmes of each successive regime.[59] The following list of plans illustrates the extent of Myanmar's planning continuum within which all national economic policies and programmes were embedded since independence.[60]

(a) *The New Order Plan* (short-term with unspecified time-frame): promulgated c. 1943; implementation unknown.
(b) *Two-Year Plan of Economic Development for Burma* (1948/49–1949/50): promulgated 1 April 1948; unimplemented.
(c) *Comprehensive Eight-Year Economic and Social Development Programme* or *Pyidawtha Plan* or *KTA Plan* (1952/53–1959/60): launched April 1952 and modified late 1953; truncated c. 1955.
(d) *Four-Year Plan* (1956/57–1959/60); internal document; remained as framework for capital budgeting.
(e) *New Four-Year Plan* (1956/57–1959/60): mooted by the Prime Minister, June 1957; incomplete (overtaken by political split of AFPFL).
(f) *Blue Book* (1956/57–1959/60): revised version of (c) prepared by the Robert R. Nathan Associates in June 1957; stillborn.
(g) *Second Four-Year Plan* (1961/62–1964/65): presented to the Parliament, August 1961; practically unimplemented (superseded by military coup, March 1962).
(h) *Sixteen-Year Perspective Plan* (1961/62–1975/76): vague framework for four consecutive four-year plans, c. 1961.
(i) *Military Four-Year Plan* (1966/67–1969/70): internal document? probably implemented as annual plans.
(j) *Military Seven-Year Plan* (1964/65–1970/71): for internal use? implementation unknown.
(k) *First Four-Year Plan* (1971/72–1973/74): announced 1971: truncated March 1974 (to conform with the tenure of the Pyithu Hluttaw or Parliament under the Socialist Constitution of 1974).
(l) *Twenty-Year Perspective Plan* (1974/75–1993/94): endorsed by the ruling BSPP, c. 1973; to be implemented through five four-year plans, i.e. the "Second" through the "Sixth".

(m) *Second Four-Year Plan* (1974/75–1977/78): launched, 1974; implemented.
(n) *Five-Year Development Programme* (1977/78–1981/82): document prepared for donor agencies, February 1978.
(o) *Third Four-Year Plan* (1978/79–1981/82): launched 1978; implemented.
(p) *Five-Year Development Programme* (1980/81–1984/85); continuation of (n); c. 1980.
(q) *Fourth Four-Year Plan* (1982/83–1985/86): launched 1982; implemented.
(r) *Five-Year Development Programme* (1983/84–1987/88); continuation of (p); July 1982.
(s) *Fifth Four-Year Plan* (1986/87–1989/90): launched 1986; truncated mid-1988 (overtaken by events of 1988 leading to the collapse of BSPP rule).
(t) *Five-Year Development Programme* (1986/87–1990/91); continuation of (r); January 1986.

In the major plans of the 1948–61 period, targets remained often unfulfilled but there had been some progress in the learning process for development planning in a mixed economy.[61] However, the plans formulated during the next decade of military rule emphasized public sector investment and seem to have been more influenced by Soviet and East European experiences in central planning than past national experiences.[62] The plans of the Socialist Republic (post-1974) were more elaborate but belong to the same genre as their command-economy predecessors though some elements of Western-style development planning to accommodate external donors were incorporated.

All these efforts at controlling and guiding the national economy by centralized planning reflected the aura and the "peculiar sanctity" attached to the planning process with its accoutrements and paraphernalia, which in turn appear to "give the desired future an illusion of immediacy".[63]

THE SOCIALIST VISION

Ideas and notions on socialism, economic independence, and planning which were received and adopted during Myanmar's independence struggle turned out to be remarkably enduring in the post-independence era.[64] Reformulated and reinterpreted by political elites according to their predispositions and experiences, they have inspired recurring visions of creating a just and prosperous society. As such, they have provided a powerful ideological theme and have had a lasting influence on the economic policy agenda of Myanmar governments.[65]

These entailed a preference for a particular set of policy instruments and at times created blinkers to the "policy-relevant knowledge" deemed necessary to generate appropriate development strategies.[66] As such, the confluence of ideas and notions associated with the *Dobama* socialist tradition, the politico-economic legacy of Aung San, the imperative of economic independence, and the logic of planning constituted a set of predispositions which set the agenda for the persistent "socialist vision" of the post-independence state leaders.[67] Thus, the strategy for economic development and the policy options chosen were influenced by attitudes, preferences, and convictions that had pre-independence roots and were remarkably enduring.[68] These recurring ideas and notions, in turn, channelled post-independence Myanmar towards establishing a self-reliant socialist economy. As elaborated in Chapter 8, this led to the mimicking of a developmental state without the wherewithal to do so and resulted in what "might be described as the bankruptcy of Burma".[69] The first attempt to realize this socialist vision, in the 1948–62 period, is examined in the next chapter.

Notes

1. See, for example, Nicholas Tarling, *Nations and States in Southeast Asia* (Cambridge: Cambridge University Press, 1998), pp. 29–30.
2. Many of them were influenced by "leftist" ideologies, see, for example, Robert H. Taylor, *Marxism and Resistance in Burma, 1942–1945: Thein Pe Myint's "Wartime Traveller"* (Athens, Ohio: Ohio University Press, 1984), pp. 1–7. In fact, even the post-1988 generation of military leaders continue to subscribe to similar nationalist ideals. See, for example, Morten Pedersen, "The World According to Burma's Military Rulers", in *The Illusion of Progress: The Political Economy of Reform in Burma/Myanmar*, edited by David S. Mathieson and R. J. May (Adelaide: Crawford House, 2004), pp. 85–136.
3. For a concise biography of Aung San, see Aung San Suu Kyi, "My Father", in *Aung San Suu Kyi: Freedom from Fear and Other Writings*, edited by Michael Aris (London: Viking and Harmondsworth, 1991), pp. 1–38.
4. Post and Wright listed seventeen points to characterize "the socialist package" (Ken Post and Phil Wright, *Socialism and Underdevelopment* [London: Routledge, 1989], p. 13; also, pp. 11–13).

5. See Allen Fenichel and Azfar Khan, "The Burmese Way to 'Socialism'", *World Development* 9, no. 9/10 (1981): 815.
6. David I. Steinberg, "Economic Growth with Equity? The Burmese Experience", *Contemporary Southeast Asia* 4, no. 2 (1982): 124.
7. The term leftist used here also encompass, apart from Marxism, other influences such as Fabian Socialism, Irish Nationalism, and Indian Nationalism. *Dobama Asiayone* was the pre-eminent political grouping of the day. Its members assumed the prefix *Thakin* (master) to their names. See Maung Maung, *Burma and General Ne Win* (London: Asia Publishing House, 1969), pp. 38–40, 54–55; and Taylor, *Marxism and Resistance,* pp. 3–7. For the Marxist "Indian connection" in Myanmar, see Robert H. Taylor, "The Burmese Communist Movement and Its Indian Connection: Formation and Factionalism", *Journal of Southeast Asian Studies* 14, no. 1 (1983): 95–108. For the diffusion of socialist literature in early twentieth-century Myanmar, see Daw Aye Thida, "1930 Mataing Hmi Myanmar Naingan Twin Tho Hsoshelit Sarpay Pyant Hnant Largyin" [The Diffusion of Socialist Literature into Myanmar before 1930], *Tekkatho Pyinnyar Padeitha Sarsaung* 14, no. 1 (1980): 47–53.
8. "Manifesto of the Dobama Asiayone", reprinted in *The Guardian* (January 1959), pp. 21–26.
9. Robert H. Taylor, *The State in Burma* (London: C. Hurst, 1987), p. 215.
10. Jan Becka, *The National Liberation Movement in Burma during the Japanese Occupation Period (1941–1945),* Dissertationes Orientales, vol. 42 (Prague: Oriental Institute, 1983), p. 38.
11. Maung Maung, *Burma and General Ne Win,* p. 54
12. See, for example, "Socialism ... was an early choice for the freedom movement in Burma ... It was the policy of Burma's architect of independence, *Bogyoke* Aung San", *Working People's Daily* (hereafter *WPD*), 4 January 1966; quoted in Norman Nyun Han, "Burma's Experiment in Socialism", (Ph.D. dissertation, University of Colorado, 1970), p. 100. *Bogyoke*'s (Aung San will, hereafter, be cited as *Bogyoke*) public speeches and writings showed that he had considerable sympathy for the socialist tradition in his eclectic search for approaches towards solving Myanmar's political and economic problems (see, for example, Josef Silverstein, "Introduction", in *The Political Legacy of Aung San,* compiled by Josef Silverstein, Cornell University Southeast Asia Program, Data Paper no. 86 [Ithaca: 1972], pp. 1–12).
13. Jan Becka, "Planning for New Burma: Major-General Aung San's Views of Economic Development", *Archiv Orientalni* 56 (1988): 12–14. For the following discussion, the invaluable contribution of Becka's essay in providing a thematic focus is duly acknowledged.
14. Ibid., p. 13.
15. Ibid. See also H. V. Richter, "The Impact of Socialism on Economic Activity in Burma", in *Opportunity and Response: Case Studies in Economic Development,*

edited by T. Scarlet Epstein and David H. Penny (London: C. Hurst, 1972), pp. 216–39.

16. For Aung San's views and ideas, see, for example, Josef Silverstein, *The Political Legacy of Aung San*; Maung Maung, ed., *Aung San of Burma*, with an introduction by Harry J. Benda (The Hague: Martinus Nijhoff, 1962), pp. 123–42; and Aung San, *Burma's Challenge* (Rangoon: New Light of Burma Press, 1946; reprint, Tathetta Sarpay, 1968).
17. There has been no evidence of his activities within the Communist movement. See Taylor, *Marxism and Resistance*, p. 6.
18. Aung San, "Blue Print for Burma", reprinted in *The Guardian* (March 1957), p. 33–35. The document must be seen in the context of trying to gain the trust and confidence of highly suspicious Japanese militarists as well as the frustrating experiences of politics in a colonial setting. However, the absence of any reference to it in his subsequent pronouncements and discussions suggests that Aung San had discarded such harsh ideas once he got back to Myanmar.
19. Maung Maung, *Burma and General Ne Win*, pp. 299–300.
20. Aung San, "Blue Print for Burma", pp. 33–34.
21. Ibid., p. 34.
22. See Aung San, *Burma's Challenge*, pp. 66–67.
23. Ibid., pp. 67–68. This notion of private capital and the profit motive as the roots of exploitation and inequalities was one of the most persistent ideas influencing the ruling elite of post-independence Myanmar.
24. *AFPFL Convention 1947* (Rangoon: Students Digest Press, n.d.), p. 5. The Burma Socialist Programme Party's (BSPP) 1974 Constitution was premised on the same fundamental principles (see *The Constitution of the Socialist Republic of the Union of Burma* [Rangoon: Ministry of Information, 1974]).
25. *AFPFL Convention 1947*, p. 5. This was, in essence, the approach adopted by the military Revolutionary Council (RC) during the 1964–70 period (see Chapter 5, below).
26. Ibid., p. 6. This policy on trade was the hallmark of all Myanmar governments.
27. Ibid.
28. Becka, "Planning for New Burma", p. 5.
29. Maung Maung, *Burma's Constitution*, 2nd ed. (The Hague: Martinus Nijhoff, 1961), p. 254. It is noteworthy that Nu was then "trying to find accommodation with the Burmese Communists" (U Nu, *U Nu: Saturday's Son*, translated by Law Yone, edited by Kyaw Win [New Haven: Yale University Press, 1975; reprint, Bombay: Bharatiya Vidya Bhavan, 1976], p. 139), who were expelled from the AFPFL in October 1946. The usage of the term "leftist" may be seen contextually as a gesture symbolizing ideological affinity with the Communist Party (ibid., pp. 137–39).
30. Ibid., p. 255.

31. *Burma Independence Celebration* (Rangoon: Department of Information and Broadcasting, 1948), pp. 13, 15.
32. Reginald Herbold Green, "The Role of the State as an Agent of Economic and Social Development in the Least Developed Countries", *Journal of Development Planning*, No. 6 (1974), p. 15.
33. Aung San, *Burma's Challenge*, pp. 137 and 148. More specifically, he emphasized increased rice exports, increased labour productivity, and increased revenue collection rather than borrowing from abroad (see Tin Soe [Bawgagon], *Bogyoke Aung San Ei Seepwayei Amyin* [General Aung San's Economic View] [Yangon: Pyithu Sa-oke Taik, 1974], pp. 108–109, 117–18). This bias against borrowing also had influenced the post-independence leadership's stand on capital formation.
34. For theoretical insights, see, *inter alia*, Peter J. Burnell, *Economic Nationalism in the Third World* (Hemel Hempstead: Harvester/Wheatsheaf, 1986); Dudley Seers, *The Political Economy of Nationalism* (New York: Oxford University Press, 1983); and Harry G. Johnson, *Economic Nationalism in Old and New States* (Chicago: Chicago University Press, 1967). Economic independence may be seen as an organizing principle for measures such as the Burmanization of the economy and the quest for self-reliant industrialization.
35. Burnell, *Economic Nationalism*, p. 34.
36. Quoted in ibid., p. 21. Wirth was referring to the policies involved in Brazilian economic development from 1930 to 1954.
37. Ibid., p. 34.
38. For post-independence consequences, see M. Ruth Pfanner, "Burma", in *Underdevelopment and Economic Nationalism in Southeast Asia*, edited by Frank Golay et al. (Ithaca: Cornell University Press, 1969), pp. 203–65; and James F. Guyot, "Bureaucratic Transformation in Burma", in *Asian Bureaucratic Systems Emergent from the British Imperial Tradition*, edited by Ralph Braibanti (Durham, N.C.: Duke University Press, 1966), pp. 354–443.
39. See Dieter Senghaas, "The Case for Autarky", in *The Political Economy of Development and Underdevelopment*, edited by Charles K. Wilber, 3rd ed. (New York: Random House, 1984), pp. 208–18.
40. See Becka, "Planning for New Burma", p. 7.
41. Taylor, *State in Burma*, p. 225.
42. Ba Maw, "Burma's New Order Plan", *Burma* 1, no. 1 (1944): 107. See also U Tin, "Commentary on the New Order Plan", ibid.: 17–23.
43. Ba Maw, "Burma's New Order Plan", p. 105.
44. See Maung Ba Han, *The Planned State* (Rangoon: Rasika Ranjani, 1947), Appendices.
45. See "Introduction", and Annex A of Ba Han, *The Planned State*; and U Thein, "Economic Development of New Burma", *Burma* 1, no. 1 (1944): 57–66.
46. Ibid., p. 57.

47. For planning efforts by the Myanmar government-in-exile, see Nicholas Tarling, "'A New and a Better Cunning': British Wartime Planning for Post-War Burma, 1942–1943", *Journal of Southeast Asian Studies* 13, no. 1 (1982): 33–59.
48. Ibid., p. 58.
49. Aung San, *Burma's Challenge*, p. 87.
50. Becka, "Planning for New Burma", p. 7.
51. See, for example, U Kyaw Myint, "Drift", *Burma Digest* 1, no. 3 (1946): 50–51.
52. "Foreword", in *Two-Year Plan of Economic Development for Burma* (Rangoon: Government Printing and Stationery, 1948).
53. Chaired by the Prime Minister it included the Ministers for Finance, National Planning, Agriculture and Rural Economy, and Commerce and Supply. See "Document 516: Council of Ministers, Adjourned 7th Meeting, Minute 3", in Hugh Tinker, *Burma: The Struggle for Independence*, vol. 2, *From General Strike to Independence, August 1946 to 4 January 1948* (London: HMSO, 1984) pp. 750–51.
54. "Document 564: Council of Ministers, 16th Special Meeting, Minute 1, Enclosure, Memorandum, Two Year Plan of Economic Development for Burma", in Tinker, *Burma: Struggle for Independence*, vol. 2, p. 822.
55. Ibid. For the reference to planning in the state constitution, see Maung Maung, *Burma's Constitution*, p. 263.
56. "Foreword", *Two-Year Plan*, p. 1.
57. See, for example, Steinberg, "Economic Growth with Equity?"; and Thet Tun, "A Review of Economic Planning in Burma", *Burma Research Society Fiftieth Anniversary Publication* 1 (January 1960): 485–527.
58. A. F. Robertson, *People and the State: An Anthropology of Planned Development* (Cambridge: Cambridge University Press, 1984), pp. 97–98.
59. See, for example, ibid., pp. 106–11; and Taylor, *State in Burma*, pp. 253–54.
60. The list was based on Steinberg's compilation augmented by data from personal contacts with knowledgeable sources within the country who declined to be named; see David I. Steinberg, *Burma's Road Toward Development: Growth and Ideology under Military Rule* (Boulder, CO: Westview Press, 1981), p. 171 (Chart 8.1).
61. See, for example, Frank N. Trager, *Burma: From Kingdom to Republic — A Historical and Political Analysis* (London: Pall Mall, 1966), pp. 153–64.
62. Personal communications with Thet Tun and retired senior officials of the Ministry of National Planning.
63. Hugh Tinker, *Union of Burma: A Study of the First Years of Independence*, 4th ed. (London: Oxford University Press, 1967), p. 126.
64. They were received from abroad in the 1930s mainly in the form of "leftist" literature. Incidentally, in articulating concepts like socialism it was found

to be necessary to introduce a new terminology in the vernacular. See Robert H. Taylor, "Burmese Concepts of Revolution", in *Context, Meaning and Power in Southeast Asia*, edited by Mark Hobart and Robert H. Taylor (Ithaca: Cornell University Southeast Asia Program, 1986) pp. 80–81.

65. See, for example, Post and Wright, *Socialism and Underdevelopment*, p. 9. For ideology as a system determinant, see Stefand Hedlund and Mats Lundahl, *Ideology as a Determinant of Economic System: Nyerere and Ujama in Tanzania*, Scandinavian Institute of African Studies, Research Report, no. 84 (Uppsala, 1989), pp. 6–16.
66. See Stephan Haggard, *Pathways from the Periphery: The Politics of Growth in the Newly Industrializing Countries* (Ithaca: Cornell University Press, 1990), pp. 46–47. On the other hand, political realities and economic exigencies may induce some relaxation in the policy stance to accommodate practices deviating from the original theme. Such setbacks are usually regarded as temporary and the commitment to the original ideas prevents the state leadership from making a radical break with the past to adopt an alternative set of policy options.
67. They belonged to the generation of nationalists whose perceptions of a desirable politico-economic order had been shaped by their personal experiences in the struggle for independence and their interpretations of the colonial economy.
68. Depak Lal attributed the persuasiveness of such ideas in the "south" to their "Janus-faced characteristics" which "combine the 'modern' aspects of the rationalist Enlightenment with those of a partly 'pre-modern' rural nostalgia". See Depak Lal, "Nationalism, Socialism and Planning: Influential Ideas in the South", *World Development* 13, no. 6 (1985): 756.
69. R. H. Taylor, "Disaster or Release? J. S. Furnivall and the Bankruptcy of Burma". *Modern Asian Studies* 29, no. 1 (1995): 46.

Part II

Democratic Experiment (1948–62)

3

Towards a Socialist Welfare State

Leaders of the post-independent Myanmar state embraced parliamentary democracy as the principal political system but continued their fascination with socialist principles as a basis for equitable economic development. As such, the political system exhibited competitive party politics in a democratic setting, state intervention in the economic system was characterized by an indigenous interpretation of economic nationalism with socialist leanings. The prime minister of the day invoked a vision of economic development geared towards a welfare state of sorts that turned out to be illusory.

POLITICS OF THE DISPLACED STATE

After independence, the Myanmar state was "displaced as the creator of political order and economic direction" to the extent that it was "no longer able to determine many of the conditions of social and economic life" in Myanmar.[1] The Anti-Fascist People's Freedom League (AFPFL) government was challenged by various groups seeking power. Although political parties were the major players in the formal political process, the existence of such power seekers and those seeking influence on the conduct of state affairs eroded the incumbent leaders' political hegemony and claim for legitimacy.[2]

Historically, as argued in Chapter 2, "many of the interweaving strands of political and economic developments during these … [post-war] years have [had] pre-war roots".[3] More significantly, there had not occurred any "legitimizing myth which combined a justification for the activities of the modern state with Burmese rather than British notions of justice", with the state failing to provide a "focus of identity" for most of its citizens.[4] In this context, the post-independent political order was an unsuccessful attempt to superimpose the form and structure of parliamentary democracy over an inchoate strata of "socialist" aspirations. However, the political leadership's interpretations of socialism as an organizing principle for the state were impractical and inadequate, thereby necessitating appeals to traditional values, primordial loyalties, and charismatic leadership to perpetuate their hold on state power that eventually led to the demise of the parliamentary system of governance.[5]

The dynamics of industrialization in the parliamentary period can only be understood within this political context which is further elaborated below.

Socialist Aspirations of the Political Leadership

The socialist tradition of the *Dobama Asiayone*, transposed into the legacy of *Bogyoke* Aung San, was enshrined in the Union Constitution of 1947. However, inconsistencies and ambiguities in its exposition by the politicians as well as apparent contradictions in the state's policies and programmes led to "confusion ... over the interpretation of 'state socialism'" as such.[6]

The publicly expressed views of Nu, the first Prime Minister of Myanmar, and Ba Swe, the secretary-general of the Burma Socialist Party (BSP), reflected the socialist aspirations of the League's leadership.[7] Between February 1948, when Nu reminded the Burma Chamber of Commerce that "the policy of state socialism is one from which my government will not be deflected",[8] and December 1953, when he declared that his version of Burmese Socialism was the realization of the Pyidawtha State,[9] Nu's conception of socialism evolved towards a welfare state interpretation.[10] Meanwhile, Ba Swe's position on socialism also moved from a Marxist stance to one that resembled Nu's version.[11]

Thus, Marxist rhetoric and radical metaphors began to lose their attractiveness and relevance in the mid-1950s. Hence, as Rose pointed out, "[t]he general line of Socialist policy in Burma might be summarized as nationalization plus industrialization plus a Welfare State".[12] By 1956, Myanmar Socialists' "doctrinal position ... had brought them much closer to the outlook of the Western [democratic] Socialists".[13] At the Third All-Burma AFPFL Congress in January 1958, Socialism was identified with the "ultimate objective" to be realized in an indefinite future, while the "Pyidawtha (Welfare) State" became the "goal of the AFPFL".[14]

In retrospect, it can be said that the socialist aspirations of the immediate post-independence period, as espoused by the AFPFL leadership, became diluted by the imperatives of realpolitik and economic expediencies, in less than a decade of one-party dominance. It devolved into the Pyidawtha (Welfare) State of Nu which became bogged down in the political and economic quagmire of internecine power struggle and an unsustainable economic development programme.

The AFPFL Government: Decline and Demise

The AFPFL (or the League) dominated Myanmar's politics for more than a decade after independence. It was a broad front consisting of the BSP, the People's Volunteer Organization (PVO), class and mass organizations, and individual members.[15]

During the parliamentary era "the machinery of government and party overlapped to such an extent" that the two seemed to be indistinguishable at times and the political fortunes of the government were intertwined with those of the League.[16] The League's organizational links between the centre and the grassroots were weak, and with the rise of powerful local party "bosses", the government's authority and the party leadership's legitimacy were undermined.[17]

As the tide of insurgency subsided, members and supporters of the ruling party jostled for power and privileges. Within the AFPFL, patronage was widespread and power became personalized. These shortcomings aggravated the centrifugal tendencies brought about by personal rivalries among the ruling elite and led to a decline in the League's popularity.[18]

After a poor showing in the 1956 elections, AFPFL's cohesion began to weaken.[19] Latent mutual suspicions came to the fore and, in the jostling for power, two contending factions emerged with the rift affecting not only party members but also the general public and even the armed forces.[20] Finally, in April 1958 the League split into Nu's Clean AFPFL and the Stable AFPFL jointly led by Ba Swe and Kyaw Nyein.[21]

In the subsequent contest for party leadership, Nu's Clean faction won by an eight-vote majority through the support of the opposition National United Front (NUF) and the ethnic minority groups.[22] Thereafter, the government was virtually under seige in the parliament, and the executive functions of the state were emasculated.[23] In such an atmosphere of political instability and uncertainty the twin spectres haunting the military leadership — the legitimation of the Communist insurgents and widespread election violence — seemed more probable than ever.[24] Finally, General Ne Win, the armed forces Commander-in-Chief, was invited on 26 September by Nu to form a non-partisan government, on the premise of restoring stability and holding of elections within six months.[25]

The general elections, held on 6 February 1960, saw an overwhelming victory by Nu's Clean AFPFL, which formed a majority government in April.[26] Soon, an intra-party feud developed and degenerated into an all-out struggle for the spoils of victory by the middle of 1960.[27]

Meanwhile, simmering demands for greater ethnic autonomy boiled over and the Shans played the secession card to force the government's hand.[28] The military leadership perceived increasing challenges (escalation of ethnic dissent, economic uncertainty, and increasing demands for internal peace) to the state and was alarmed by the possibility of Nu relenting to the minorities' quest for a federal system.[29] Probable involvement of foreign powers in the ethnic issue heightened the tensions and the convening of the Seminar on the Federal Principle on 24 February 1962 seems to have provided the military an opportunity to stage a coup on 2 March 1962.[30]

The Security Imperative and Military Ascendancy

Soon after Myanmar gained independence, the state was in turmoil as ideological and ethnic rebellions broke out and in the maelstrom of civil war the nascent AFPFL government was pushed to the brink of collapse.[31] Communists, factions of the People's Volunteer Organization (PVO), Communist sympathizers in the army, the Karen National Defence Organization (KNDO), and some ethnic minorities rebelled in quick succession.[32]

In waging war with its adversaries, the AFPFL leadership, inevitably, became heavily dependent upon the military for its survival.[33] Both the external threat posed by the cross-border intrusion of retreating Kuomintang (KMT) units and the sustained domestic insurrections made the military an indispensable adjunct to central state power.[34]

The imperatives of national security led to the military assuming administrative functions in areas beyond the central government's administrative reach or where martial law was in force.[35] Meanwhile, the military elite became increasingly contemptuous of politicians who were seen as power-seeking opportunists.[36]

Thus, the military redefined its role to encompass "national politics" and assumed a Praetorian role as the political elite became disunited in the competition for state power.[37] Finally, the military coup ended the role of politicians in governance and development.[38]

ECONOMICS OF THE WELFARE STATE

Influenced by nationalist ideals encompassing *Bogyoke*'s socialist legacy, economic independence, and planning (see Chapter 2), Myanmar's leaders were determined to restructure the economy through state intervention. Spurred by misgivings about the fairness and efficacy of the market mechanism, the socialist vision entailed central planning and what Lal characterized as the "rejection of the entrepreneur while embracing the technologist or engineer".[39] The government's economic agenda comprised Burmanization, nationalization, and industrialization. Though varying in intensity and scope with changing political and economic circumstances, the economics of the welfare state was characterized by the predominance of these three themes within a mixed economy setting.[40]

Ideology of Economic Policy and Development Strategy

"Each new state obviously has its own historical background in which both the general ideology and the particular policies of the colonizing nation" have influenced the "development of its general and economic ideology". Moreover, it has "its own particular economic structure and corresponding economic problems toward which its economic policy and ideology are necessarily oriented".[41] In Myanmar's case, its political leaders believed that the only way to develop Myanmar's backward economy and achieve economic independence was to replace private capital with state-controlled investment. The idea of the state dictating the pace and direction of economic activities had tremendous appeal in the light of negative experiences of the *laissez-faire* economy under colonial rule.

Apparently, the dominant developmental paradigm of the 1950s appealed to Myanmar's political leaders. In particular, they were impressed by the Soviet economic performance ostensibly achieved through rapid accumulation of physical capital stock. Thus, capital investment was seen as the most significant factor for economic growth.[42] Constrained by ideological rivalry with its Communist enemies, the Myanmar political leadership was caught in the conceptual current of mainstream economic thought and standard prescriptions recommended by the economic orthodoxy for a "mixed economy" were found to be equally applicable to Myanmar's Socialist economic strategy. They comprised rapid accumulation of capital through increased savings and investment; exploitation of agriculture surplus for industrial investment; import substitution and import protection; and the state's direction of the development process.[43]

Plans and Policies

On 1 April 1948, the Myanmar government announced a two-year economic plan. Formulated quickly (about two months) and handicapped by lack of up-to-date data, it was "more of an enunciation of the economic aspirations of a newly born state and of the economic principles to guide the process of advancement towards these objectives", than a coherent development plan.[44] The outbreak of insurrections prevented its implementation.

In the first two years, nationalization and indigenization measures together with the state's rice export monopoly and foreign exchange restrictions constituted the state's attempt to control the strategic sectors of the economy.[45] The Land Nationalization Act, promulgated in October 1948, was aimed "more at correcting alleged injustices arising out of the colonial pattern of development than at establishing a sound agrarian basis" for increased crop production.[46] In practice, there was very little progress in land nationalization and redistribution.[47]

In the first half of 1951 a group of Oxford academics were invited, by the government, for a brief visit to present their views on development planning in Myanmar. This was followed by Nu's initiative to engage foreign consultants to conduct a national economic and engineering survey leading to a comprehensive economic development programme.[48] A preliminary report recommending immediate action was submitted to the government in January 1952.[49] It formed the basis of the so-called Pyidawtha (Eight-Year) Plan announced with much fanfare at the Pyidawtha Conference held in Yangon from 4 to 17 August 1952.[50] Retrospectively, it appears to be an overly ambitious attempt at establishing a democratic welfare state, through a state-led strategy of "big push".[51] On the other hand, it may be seen as a necessary (but not sufficient) attempt to improve the people's standard of living that had deteriorated since 1940.[52] As such, the political leaders envisaged "bold decisions" in plan execution and to "initiate work on the basis of preliminary plans and estimates", and the Industry and Mines Minister's identification of "self-reliance" as "essential" for success suggests an ideological dimension as well.[53]

The economic targets were based on the Harrods-Domar growth model employing a fixed incremental capital-output ratio (ICOR).[54] A doubling of the GDP by the end of the plan period, to 7 billion kyat in 1950/51 prices, was envisaged. The aim was to raise the "gross national income" substantially so that the average annual per capita income reached the "pre-war [level] at the earliest possible date".[55] The total net investment required was 7.5 billion kyat over an eight-year period. About one-third of the total investment was to be in foreign currency. No serious constraint on domestic capital formation was foreseen as there would be "increased yields of revenue that may be expected from greater economic activity, reform of ... [the] revenue and fiscal system, and the adoption of a modern monetary policy".[56] It was expected that private capital investment would be forthcoming "almost automatically as soon as peace and security returns to the country and economic activity ... [reaches] a high level". However, the onus was on the state "itself to start a large development programme" to generate "sufficient momentum" for the whole effort.[57] On the other hand, it was assumed that the "bulk" of the foreign exchange requirements "would ... [have] to be borrowed from international sources or from other foreign Governments".[58] On the institutional side four (para-statal) development corporations were envisaged to lead the industrial, minerals, agricultural, and transport sectors.[59]

There were very few dissenting voices against the government's initiative.[60] Barely two weeks after the Conference, Thet Tun, a leading technocrat, lauded the "nationalization, socialization, centralization, controls, [and] regulations" instituted since independence and proclaimed that central planning was "essential".[61] He warned that "[s]trong [private] economic interests, even if they are indigenous, should not be allowed to take root".[62] Most politicians joined the bandwagon, and the ruling party appeared determined to establish "forward legitimacy" through the successful implementation of its development programme.[63] Apart from criticisms by left-wing opposition groups, there were initially no serious questioning of the proposed state-led economic strategy or the premises and assumptions for the economic targets as a whole.[64]

However, in August 1953, doubts about the continuation of a favourable balance of payments were expressed, in a seminar, by a leading Myanmar economist. He predicted that the accumulation of foreign exchange reserves could not continue beyond 1953 and concluded that "unless large amounts of foreign investments are forthcoming, either Burma's economic development programme will have to be cut or controls" for reducing domestic consumption would have to be imposed.[65]

The government was soon confronted with the problem of investment shortfalls. Nu announced an "interim programme" on 1 December 1953 to counter the problems of low productivity, slow investment, and deteriorating balance of payments position, but without much success.[66] The government's statement of 8 June 1955, in which the private sector was invited to invest in a wide range of economic activities except for armaments and major public utilities, may be seen as a tactical retreat from the earlier nationalization policy. Guarantees against expropriation for at least ten years were also given.[67] Further deterioration of the balance of payments in the following years led to a scaling down of the projects requiring substantial foreign exchange. A Three-Year Implementation Programme for the public sector, was formulated in early 1956 with emphasis on cutting back projects requiring large foreign exchange outlays.[68]

In mid-1956, nearly half-way through the plan period, two major premises of the original plan remained unfulfilled, and the political uncertainty associated with the League's unanticipated setback in the elections and the impending rift in its leadership had a depressing effect on the policy environment.[69] In April, before handing over the premiership to Ba Swe, Nu "ordered" the Three-Year Implementation Programme to be converted "into a Four-Year Plan" for fiscal years 1956/57 to 1959/60.[70] In the ensuing months several versions of the proposed Four-Year Plan were drafted by the foreign consultants and the planning bureaucracy. Ba Swe's interim premiership did not improve the confusing policy situation.[71] The Eight-Year Plan was virtually abandoned and what followed could be described as rolling plans grafted onto the annual budgetary process rather than a comprehensive scheme as envisaged in 1952.[72]

On 8 June 1957, Premier Nu admitted publicly that the government had made two major blunders; a failure to concentrate on completely restoring law and order, and the launching of the programme "without first preparing the ground systematically".[73] He stressed the importance of agriculture production and emphasized the need to foster private investment in mining and industrial enterprises, stating that "[f]rom practical experience, I no longer like to see [the] Government's finger in all sort of economic pies".[74] He also gave an outline of measures for improving efficiency and productivity as well as to prevent wastage and corruption. Appended to his statement was a directive on the problems and issues related to the new objectives and priorities.[75]

In a speech to the Parliament on 27 September 1957, Nu reviewed the progress of the development programme and reiterated his call for increased participation by the private sector while confining the state's role to consolidation of the existing state enterprises.[76] He explained that "Socialism and nationalization in every field" were no longer "equivalent terms" in the leadership's thinking.[77] However this Four-Year Plan was not officially sanctioned. Instead, the policy process was overshadowed by the political infighting which led to the AFPFL split. Despite the premier's preoccupation with it, planning practically became synonymous with the annual capital-budgeting exercise.[78]

In July 1958, Nu yet again tried to inspire a consensual national planning effort by convening a seminar on "Union Planning" on a huge scale. It was aimed at introducing a consultative dialogue between the central authorities and the representatives of the general public on matters of national concern. Its outcome was more rhetorical than substantive.[79]

General Ne Win's caretaker government did not introduce any new plans but concentrated on increasing efficiency and accountability in the public sector, while trying to liberalize foreign trade. The main concern appeared to be the suppression of price inflation and black markets. The military-controlled Defence Services Institute (DSI), established in 1951 as an extension of military post-exchange services, rapidly expanded during this period. It developed into the largest business conglomerate in Myanmar by diversifying into retail and wholesale trade, services, banking, transport, construction, and manufacturing.[80] The KTA group of foreign consultants were dismissed in February 1959, seven months before the termination of contract.[81] The Union of Burma Investment Act was enacted by the Parliament in 1959 but the related investment rules were announced only in February 1960.[82] Again, as in 1955, the Act elicited very little response as there were elections in March, and

Nu's government which came to power in April did not follow up the matter seriously.

Nu's government was soon beset by a factional power struggle within the ruling party as well as a host of other problems in politics, economics and national security. Amidst political uncertainty and economic stagnation, Nu mooted the idea of a long-term (sixteen years) plan consisting of a series of four-year plans to double the per capita income by 1977.[83] The Second Four-Year Plan, drawn up by indigenous technocrats, was to be the first of the crop. The Plan envisaged a limited role for the state to be confined to "a few industries", with an increase in foreign and private sector participation. Agriculture diversification, modernization, and mechanization would be supplemented by producers co-operatives. Import-substituting industrialization (ISI) would be complemented by attempts to foster industrial exports. In mining and manufacturing, foreign capital would be actively sought.[84] However, political crises derailed the planning process and the Plan remained an analytical exercise, at best, with the demise of parliamentary democracy in March 1962.

Neither a Socialist nor a Welfare Economy

By 1960, more than a decade of planning and state intervention had resulted in neither socialist production relations nor welfare-generating economic growth. Economic exigencies had resulted in the cessation of nationalization efforts and the truncation of the state-led industrialization programme by the mid-1950s. The state had resorted to joint ventures with foreign partners in developing its mineral resources while attempting to foster indigenization in key sectors.[85]

The land nationalization and redistribution programme was also delayed by unfavourable security conditions and was suspended in 1959 with mixed results.[86] The state's attempt to supply agriculture credit failed to meet the farmers' working capital requirements and exploitative money-lending continued into the 1960s.[87] The state appropriated the surplus from the export of agriculture products, through the State Agricultural Marketing Board (SAMB; established in 1946) which monopolized rice exports. The differential between the export price and the state-controlled purchase price was to be exploited for capital accumulation. This "became a self-reinforcing measure" and was tantamount to the imposition of a heavy tax on major crops.[88] The combined effects of this surplus extraction, the uncertainty of land tenure, and the inadequacy of agriculture credit supply produced a situation whereby the farmers had neither the incentive nor the capital to introduce productivity-improving investments.[89] Eventually, the state's attempt to expand agricultural production and to garner the surplus for its planned investments floundered in the wake of insufficient growth and unfavourable international markets for rice exports.[90]

In 1960, agriculture, accounting for less than 25 per cent of the GDP in constant prices, was dominated by small private holdings.[91] The per capita consumption increased by about 20 per cent between 1953/54 and 1959/60 but the latter was only 87 per cent of the 1938/39 figure.[92]

Although the targeted doubling of real GDP was not achieved, the 52 per cent rise between 1951/52 and 1959/60 was not dismal by regional standards.[93] However, that was from a very low base and it is illuminating to compare the structure of Myanmar's economy in 1959/60 with that for 1938/39.

Table 3.1 compares the sectoral contributions to the GDP (in constant 1961/62 prices) between fiscal years 1938/39 and 1959/60. The share of overall goods production declined from 81 per cent to around 49 per cent. Moreover, the total value of goods produced in 1959/60 achieved only 71 per cent of that in 1938/39. Hence, its contribution

TABLE 3.1
Sectoral Components of GDP
(In constant 1961/62 prices)

Sector	*Fiscal Year 1938/39*		*Fiscal Year 1959/60*	
	million kyat	*(share %)*	*million kyat*	*(share %)*
Agriculture	2,987	(47.3)	1,669	(22.7)
Livestock and fisheries	473	(7.5)	352	(4.8)
Forestry	358	(5.7)	345	(4.7)
Mining	605	(9.6)	68	(0.9)
Manufacturing	359	(5.7)	938	(12.8)
Power	60	(1.0)	23	(0.3)
Construction	277	(4.4)	233	(3.2)
Total goods	5,119	(81.1)	3,628	(49.4)
Trade	705	(11.2)	2,067	(28.1)
Total services	489	(7.7)	1,653	(22.5)
GDP	6,313	(100.0)	7,348	(100.0)

Source: Kyaw Myint, "Industrialization in Burma", (Master thesis, University of Sydney, 1978), Table 1.4, p. 15.

to the GDP, in absolute as well as relative terms, had decreased while the contributions of both trade and services increased. Within the goods component of the GDP, the 45 per cent decline in the value-added output of the primary production sectors more than offset the 161 per cent increase in the manufacturing sector.[94] This failure to attain even the pre-war production level meant that the Pyidawtha programme had not been able to establish a broad economic base to support the envisaged welfare state.

Moreover, the state had yet to attain the envisaged dominant role, despite the expansion of its functions.[95] The vital agriculture sector as well as the livestock and fisheries sector remained under private ownership. In the manufacturing sector, where it had been most active, the state's share of production value was only 5.4 per cent in 1960/61.[96]

Unfulfilled expectations seem to be the manifest failure of the Pyidawtha Plan.[97] Moreover, anti-American sentiments aroused by perceptions of the United States' complicity in the KMT aggression were also directed against the American consultants, thereby discrediting the development programme as well.[98] As one commentator put it, "the failure in planning and development" could be summarized as:

> The "ambitious approach" was one; the plans were often designed for prestige rather than tangible results. The resources were limited, the capacity for sustained endeavour was even more so. The factional warfare within the ruling party was harmful. Spheres of influence developed in the Government under rival Ministers, and artificial controversies were excited, such as in the unnecessary fixing of priorities between industry and agriculture. The foreign ... experts were not wisely and effectively used.[99]

Consequently, Myanmar in 1962 remained a primary product exporter dependent upon low-productivity agriculture.[100] The leaders' socialist vision was not realized by their capital-intensive development strategy predicated upon state intervention and indigenization. The whys and wherefores of the state-led industrialization effort that resulted in such an unsatisfactory outcome is the subject of the next chapter.

Notes

1. Robert H. Taylor, *The State in Burma* (London: C. Hurst, 1987), p. 217. For evidence on this "displacement", see p. 249ff.
2. See, for example, Josef Silverstein, "Burma", in *Governments and Politics in Southeast Asia*, edited by George McTurnan Kahin, 2nd ed. (Ithaca: Cornell

University Press, 1964; reprint, 1966), pp. 99–108; and Moshe Lissak, *Military Role in Modernization: Civil–Military Relations in Thailand and Burma* (London: Sage, 1976), pp. 149–52.

3. Taylor, *State in Burma*, p. 218.
4. Ibid., p. 221.
5. Ibid., pp. 245–49, 285–90.
6. Maung Maung, *Burma's Constitution*, 2nd ed. (The Hague: Martinus Nijhoff, 1961), p. 90. See Chapter 2 for the origins of this socialist legacy.
7. Nu and Ba Swe were, respectively, the president and vice-president of the AFPFL until the party split in 1958. Given the centralized nature of executive decision-making in Myanmar at that time, the relevance of alternatives views in the shaping and functioning of the state would be marginal at best (see Maung Maung Gyi, *Burmese Political Values: The Socio-Political Roots of Authoritarianism* [New York: Praeger, 1983], Chapters 4–5).
8. Speech delivered at the Annual General Meeting on 26 February 1948. See Thakin Nu, *Towards Peace and Democracy* (Rangoon: Ministry of Information, 1949), p. 44. The chamber was the most influential commercial association in Yangon.
9. See U Nu, *Forward with the People* (Rangoon: Ministry of Information, 1955), pp. 74, 77.
10. See, for example, Thakin Nu, *From Peace to Stability* (Rangoon: Ministry of Information, 1951), pp. 86, 87.
11. See, for example, U Ba Swe, *A Guide to Socialism in Burma* (Rangoon: Government Printing and Stationary, 1956), pp. 17–31; John Seabury Thomson, "Marxism in Burma", in *Marxism in Southeast Asia: A Study of Four Countries*, edited by Frank N. Trager (Rand Corp., 1959; reprint, Stanford: Stanford University Press, 1965), pp. 46–49; and Saul Rose, *Socialism in Southern Asia* (Oxford: Oxford University Press, 1959), pp. 117–20.
12. Rose, *Socialism*, p. 125. See, also, Maung Maung, "State Socialism in Burma", *The Guardian* (December 1953), pp. 26–27.
13. Rose, *Socialism*, p. 129.
14. U Nu, *Towards a Socialist State* (Rangoon: Central Printing Office, 1958); see p. 3, passim.
15. Maung Maung Gyi, "An Analysis of the Social and Political Foundations of the Burmese Executive (1948–1956)" (Ph.D. dissertation, Yale University, 1958), p. 166. The Communists, a major element in the League since its inception, were expelled in October 1946.
16. Richard A. Butwell, *U Nu of Burma* (Stanford: Stanford University Press, 1963), p. 147.
17. See, for example, John H. Badgley, "Progress and Polity in Burma" (Ph. D. dissertation, University of California, Berkeley, 1962), p. 130; and *New Burma Weekly* (hereafter *NBW*), 28 June 1958, pp. 4, 5.

18. Total membership, which increased to 0.63 million in 1955 from 0.48 million in the previous year, declined to 0.25 million in 1956 (San Nyein and Myint Kyi, *1958–1962 Myanma Nainganyei* [Myanmar's Politics], vol. 1 [Yangon: Universities Press, 1991], p. 148).
19. For an explanation relating this setback to the subsequent split of the AFPFL, see Thein Pe Myint, *Kyaw Nyein* [in Myanmar], with an introduction by U Kyaw Nyein (Yangon: Shwe Pyi Dan, 1961), pp. 173–82.
20. See, Sein Win, *The Split Story* (Rangoon: The Guardian Press, 1959). For Nu's version of events, see U Nu, *U Nu: Saturday's Son*, translated by Law Yone, edited by Kyaw Win (New Haven: Yale University Press, 1975; reprint, Bombay: Bharatiya Bhavan, 1976), pp. 315–25.
21. See, for example, ibid., pp. 169–73.
22. Ibid., p. 325. The NUF was a coalition of twelve opposition groups.
23. See, for example, Butwell, *U Nu of Burma*, p. 197.
24. Myint Kyi and Naw Angelene, *1958-1962 Myanma Nainganyei* [Myanmar's Politics], vol. 1 (Yangon: Universities Press), pp. 33–64, 78–85, 96–100.
25. Nu, in his memoirs, said that it was a *de facto* military coup (Nu, *Saturday's Son*, p. 327). Brigadier (then a colonel) Aung Gyi later claimed that it was indeed a coup (Myint Kyi and Naw Angelene, *Myanma Nainganyei*, pp. 112–13, 151; and personal communications). The military has, all along, insisted that it was not an imposition but an invitation (Tatmadaw Thar Thutaythi Tit Oo, *1948 Khu Hnit Hma 1988 Khu Hnit Atwin Hpyat Than Lar Thaw Myanma Thamaing Akyin Hnint Tatmadaw Ghanda* [A Concise History of Myanmar and the Armed Forces' Role, 1948–1988], vol. 1 [Yangon: News and Periodicals Enterprise, 1990], p. 33).
26. For subsequent developments, see Frank N. Trager, *Burma: From Kingdom to Republic — A Historical and Political Analysis* (London: Pall Mall, 1966), pp. 192–97.
27. For details, see Kyaw Win, Mya Han, and Thein Hlaing, *1958–1962 Myanma Nainganyei* [Myanmar Politics], vol. 3 (Yangon: Universities Press, 1991), pp. 1–76.
28. See, for example, Mya Han and Thein Hlaing, *1958–1962 Myanma Nainganyei* [Myanmar's Politics], vol. 4 (Yangon: Universities Press, 1991), pp. 1–105, 139–66. There was an upsurge of insurgent activities with Shan and Kachin groups taking up arms, ostensibly in protest against Bamar dominance, the state religion issue (Nu instituted Buddhism as the official religion in August 1961), and the abdication of the traditional feudal chieftains in the Shan States.
29. See Tatmadaw Thar Thutaythi Tit Oo, vol. 1, pp. 56–57. For a different perspective, see Chao Tzang Yawnghwe, *The Shan of Burma: Memoirs of a Shan Exile* (Singapore: Institute of Southeast Asian Studies, 1987), pp. 104–20.

30. See Mya Han and Thein Hlaing, *1958-1962 Myanma Nainganyei*, vol. 4, pp. 226–44.
31. See, for example, Hugh Tinker, *The Union of Burma: A Study of the First Years of Independence*, 4th ed. (London: Oxford University Press, 1967), pp. 41–49. For the official view, see *Burma and the Insurrections* (Rangoon: Ministry of Information, 1949); and *Is it a People's Liberation? A Short Survey of Communist Insurrection in Burma* (Rangoon: Ministry of Information, 1952).
32. The PVO was formed by *Bogyoke* Aung San in 1945 with a core of veterans from the anti-Japanese resistance forces. For summaries of various rebellions, see Martin Smith, *Burma: Insurgency and the Politics of Ethnicity* [London and New Jersey: Zed Books, 1991], pp. 44–48, 50–53, 62–64, 71–87, 110–18. See, also, *KNDO Insurrection* (Rangoon: Government Printing and Stationary, 1949). For a different perspective, see Smith Dun, *Memoirs of the Four-Foot Colonel*, Cornell University, Southeast Asia Program Data Paper no. 113 (Ithaca: Southeast Asia Program, Cornell University, 1980).
33. In April 1949, Lt. General Ne Win became the Deputy Prime Minister in charge of defence and home affairs. Until September 1950 he assumed this "dual" function. See San Nyein and Myint Kyi, *1958–1962 Myanma Nainganyei*, vol. 1 pp. 105–106.
34. For the KMT problem, see Maung Maung, *Grim War Against KMT* (Rangoon: 1953); and Robert H. Taylor, *Foreign and Domestic Consequences of the KMT Intervention in Burma*, Cornell University Southeast Asia Program Data Paper no. 93 (Ithaca: Cornell University Press, 1973).
35. Richard Butwell, "Civilians and Soldiers in Burma", in *Studies in Asia*, edited by Robert K. Sakai (Lincoln: University of Nebraska Press, 1961), p. 75. See, also, Louis J. Walinsky, "The Role of the Military in Development Planning in Burma", *Philippine Economic Journal* IV, no. 8 (1965): 310–26. For a negative view, see Chao-Tzang Yawnghwe, "Ne Win's Tatmadaw Dictatorship" (Master thesis, University of British Columbia, 1990), pp. 110–11, 187–89.
36. See, for example, Colonel Maung Maung's derisive remark quoted in Butwell, "Civilians and Soldiers", p. 74.
37. For the development of the military's ideology, see *The National Ideology and the Role of the Defence Services*, 3rd ed. (Rangoon: Ministry of Defence, 1960). At the commanding officers' conference on 21 October 1958, senior commanders voiced their concerns about the shortcomings of the government in confronting the Communists and reproached the politicians for their weakness and duplicity in dealing with the insurgents (Myint Kyi and Naw Angelene, *1958–1962 Myanma Nainganyei*, vol. 1, pp. 97–99, 102).
38. See ibid., pp. 167–69, 175. It was reported that barely a year after the elections some colonels urged General Ne Win to stage a coup (Maung Maung, *Burma and General Ne Win* [London: Asia Publishing House, 1969], p. 291).

39. Deepak Lal, "Nationalism, Socialism and Planning: Influential Ideas in the South", *World Development* 13, no. 6 (1985): 755.
40. A confluence of three factors apparently shaped the ideology of economic policy in newly independent states: "political nationalism"; "ideas on economic development formed by the economic and intellectual history of the interwar period"; and "relations between the developing countries and the advanced countries, which focus on the questions of development assistance" (Harry G. Johnson, "The Ideology of Economic Policy in the New States", in *Economic Nationalism in Old and New States*, edited by Harry G. Johnson [London: George Allen & Unwin, 1967], p. 126). For Myanmar, the first factor was predominant with the second contributing to the economic strategy adopted, while the third factor was marginal, having decided to rely on its own resources and to exercise a strictly neutral foreign policy.
41. Johnson, "Ideology of Economic Policy", p. 124.
42. See, for example, "Investment Requirements: Note", in Gerald M. Meier, *Leading Issues in Economic Development*, 5th ed. (New York: Oxford University Press, 1989), pp. 173–77.
43. See *World Development Report 1991* (New York: Oxford University Press, 1991), pp. 33–35. For an account of Myanmar's economic development in the 1950s, see Louis J. Walinsky, *Economic Development in Burma 1951–1960* (New York: The Twentieth Century Fund, 1962).
44. Thet Tun, "A Review of Economic Planning in Burma", *Burma Research Society Fiftieth Anniversary Publication*, 1 (January 1960), p. 492. Most of the ideas and recommendations of the plan were incorporated in subsequent plans. For details, see *Two Year Plan of Economic Development for Burma* (Rangoon: Government Printing and Stationary, 1948).
45. It covered forests, riverine transport, public utilities, import and export of "strategic" commodities, and price controls of "essential" goods.
46. Maung Myint, "Agriculture in Burmese Economic Development" (Ph.D. dissertation, University of California, Berkeley, 1966), p. 171. Tenancy laws were also enacted in 1948 and in 1950 to provide the agriculturists with security of tenure and to restrict rental charges for rice lands to twice the land revenue payable.
47. The civil war, local politics, and the lack of administrative resources prevented effective implementation. Another law was enacted in 1954 and implementation resumed from fiscal year 1953/54 until 1959, but the results were far from satisfactory (see, for example, Taylor, *State in Burma*, p. 277). Collective farming was never considered as a serious option in the post-independence plans.
48. The study was funded by the U.S. Technical Cooperation Administration Programme. The New York engineering firm Knappen Tippetts Abbet (KTA) was the principal consultant. Pierce Management, Inc. served as mining consultants while the Washington firm of Robert R. Nathan Associates became economic consultants.

49. Walinsky, *Economic Development*, pp. 83–95.
50. For details, see *The Pyidawtha Conference: Resolutions and Speeches* (Rangoon: Ministry of Information, 1952). The Conference was conducted in a top-down, orchestrated manner (for a critique, see *The Nation*, 20 August 1952, p. 5). The government did not even wait for the completion of the study (the final report was submitted in August 1953) in launching its development programme. See Knappen Tippets Abbett Engineering Co., *Comprehensive Report, Economic and Engineering Development of Burma*, prepared for the Government of the Union of Burma by Knappen Tippetts McCarthy, Engineers in association with Pierce Management, Inc. and Robert R. Nathan Associates, Inc., 2 vols. (1953) (hereafter, *KTA Comprehensive Report*).
51. For critiques see, *inter alia*, Thet Tun, "Review", pp. 510–12, 526–27; Frank N. Trager, *Toward a Welfare State in Burma* (New York: Institute of Pacific Relations, 1954), pp. 54–59; Mya Maung, "The Genesis of Economic Development in Burma: the Plural Society" (Ph.D. dissertation, Catholic University America, Washington, 1961), pp. 240–53; and K. S. Mali, *Fiscal Aspects of Development Planning in Burma, 1950–1960* (Rangoon: Department of Economics, University of Rangoon, 1962), pp. 70–86.
52. The GDP for the fiscal year 1950/51 was estimated as only two-thirds of the GDP in 1938/39 (*Pyidawtha Conference*, p. 35).
53. Ibid., p. 42; and pp. 38–39 for optimism regarding capital formation. For the KTA's assessment of the resource potential, see, *KTA Comprehensive Report*, pp. 3–17.
54. This stylized model relates national income growth to investment in capital stock through a technical parameter known as the capital-output ratio. For elaboration, see Hywel Jones, *An Introduction to Modern Theories of Economic Growth* (London: Thomas Nelson & Sons, 1975), pp. 43–68. When factor inputs other than capital are held constant, ICOR may be defined as the ratio of the investment or the increment in the capital stock (required for an increase in GDP) to the increment in real GDP. Assumption of a constant value for the ICOR over a plan period implies a "freeze" in technological change and the productivity of capital. The ICOR concept does not consider factors such as the efficiency of investment and external economies/diseconomies (see Meier, *Leading Issues*, pp. 174–76). The assumed ICOR for the Pyidawtha Plan was 2.2, which, in practice (ex-post estimate) was nearer to 2.6 (*Second Four-Year Plan for the Union of Burma [1961–62 to 1964–65]* [Rangoon: Government Printing & Stationery, 1961], p. 5). The value of ICOR depends on the method of computation, and the same data set may result in a fairly wide range of values when different methods are used. See, for example, Daw Kyi May Kaung, "Ayin Ahni Hnint Konhtwet Achoe Myar", [Capital-Output Ratios] *Tekkatho Pyinnyar Padeitha Sarsaung* 2, no. 1 (1967): 227–39.
55. *Pyidawtha Conference*, p. 37.

56. Ibid., p. 41.
57. Ibid., p. 39. One of the major premises of the plan was that there would be peace and order in the country within a year.
58. Ibid., p. 41. See, also, Thakin Nu, "Foreign Capital in Burma", in *Burma's Freedom: The Second Anniversary* (Rangoon: Ministry of Information, 1950), pp. 70–73.
59. *Pyidawtha Conference*, p. 41.
60. *The Nation* newspaper, in an editorial, cited recent instances of the government's botched projects, cautioned that "the future of the country should not be entrusted *carte blanche* to any one group of advisers". It concluded that "as long as there is a group of yes-men on the one hand, and a virtual monopoly of power on the other, both the economic assistance and the projects will go down the drain" (*The Nation*, 12 August 1952).
61. Thet Tun, "Outline of a Socialist Economy for Burma", *Journal of the Burma Research Society* (hereafter *JBRS*) XXXVII, 1 (1954): 69; paper presented at the Burma Research Society meeting in September 1952.
62. Ibid., pp. 72–73.
63. For use of the term, see Samuel P. Huntington, "How Countries Democratize", *Political Science Quarterly* 106, no. 4 (1991–92): 605.
64. The government was accused of abandoning the socialist principles of the Sorrento Villa Plan endorsed by *Bogyoke* Aung San in 1947, while the KTA advisers were attacked for advocating "state capitalism" at the expense of socialist principles embodied in the Union Constitution (see, for example, Maung Soo San, *Bama Sipwayei Sittan* [Survey of Myanmar's Economy] [Yangon: 1954], pp. 178–207).
65. U Tun Wai, "Outlook for Burma's Balance of Payments", *JBRS* XXXVII, no. 2 (1954): 40. In contrast, the KTA advisers, in their comprehensive report, took the view that Myanmar's rice exports would be more than sufficient to cater for the foreign exchange requirements of the development programme (Walinsky, *Economic Development*, pp. 118–19).
66. See Nu's speech reproduced in *Burma Weekly Bulletin* (hereafter, *BWB*), 9 December 1953, pp. 282–85, 287.
67. See *BWB*, 23 June 1955, pp. 86, 88. However, follow-up measures such as legislation and procedures were lacking and there was no significant response to it.
68. This programme scaled down public sector investment by about one-third (Walinsky, *Economic Development*, pp. 199–211).
69. The insurgency persisted and export earnings plummeted with the sharp drop in the price of rice after 1954 (ibid., pp. 218–24). See, also, Hpo Kyaw San, *Parliman Demokraysi Sanit Hnint Myanmar Naingan* [Myanmar and the Parliamentary Democracy System] (Yangon: Sanpya, 1970) pp. 59–60.
70. Thet Tun, "Review", p. 513. Nu left the government in July 1956 explaining that it was a prelude to eventual retirement from politics. However, he

reassumed the premiership in March 1957; apparently disconcerted by the jostling for power in his absence (San Nyein and Myint Kyi, *1958–1962 Myanma Nainganyei*, pp. 151–59).

71. See ibid., pp. 513–21.
72. See, e.g., ibid., pp. 520–21, 526–27.
73. "Premier on Burma's 4-Year Plan", *BWB*, 13 June 1957, p. 64.
74. Ibid.
75. *BWB*, 13 June 1957, pp. 64–65; and 20 June 1957, pp. 75, 77. For details of the subsequent "new" four-year plan, see "The Union of Burma: A Group Study", Joint International Business Ventures, Country Study, no. 4, mimeographed (Columbia University, New York, 1959), pp. 13–14.
76. U Nu, *Premier Reports to the People on Law and Order, National Solidarity, Social Welfare, National Economy, Foreign Affairs* (Rangoon: Central Printing Office, 1958).
77. Ibid., p. 27.
78. See, for example, Thet Tun, "Organization of Planning Machinery: Lessons from Burmese Experience", *JBRS* XLVI, no. 1 (1963), pp. 30–32; and Walinsky *Economic Development*, pp. 227–37, 242–43, 249–50.
79. For details, see *NBW*, 26 July 1958, p. 5; and 2 August 1958, pp. 5–6.
80. For a comprehensive account of caretaker government's activities, see *Is Trust Vindicated?* (Rangoon: Director of Information, 1960).
81. The dismissal of these highly paid consultants was in line with the regime's emphasis on austerity measures and streamlining of the government agencies. However, nationalist fervour and the "anti-foreign agent" syndrome which characterized Ne Win's rule could not be ruled out either.
82. For the text of the Investment Act, see Walinsky, *Economic Development*, pp. 650–52. The investment rules (1960) may be found in *Burma* IX, no. 3 (1960), pp. 30–33.
83. See Nu's speech to the Parliament on 15 August 1961 (*BWB*, 21 September 1961, p. 167).
84. See, for example, "Second Four-Year Plan Presented to Nationalities", *BWB*, 5 October 1961, p. 182.
85. The indigenization effort was very marginal in the industries. See, for example, M. Ruth Pfanner, "Burma", in *Underdevelopment and Economic Nationalism in Southeast Asia*, edited by Frank H. Golay et al. (Ithaca: Cornell University Press, 1969), pp. 228–29, 242–43, 245–53, 257–61.
86. For the shortcomings of the land nationalization programme, see *Myanma Leiyar Myei Thamaing* [History of Myanmar's Agricultural Land], vol. 2 (Yangon: Burma Socialist Programme Party, 1971), pp. 196–205.
87. The state's average credit supply between 1952 and 1960 was only about 15 per cent of the estimated requirements and the "question of agricultural credit ... remained largely unresolved" (Maung Myint, "Agriculture", p. 181; also, pp. 178–80).

88. Khin Maung Kyi, "Political Economy of Agricultural Modernization in Burma", unpublished discussion paper, mimeographed (Singapore, 1987), pp. 4–5.
89. Ibid.
90. Maung Myint, "Agriculture", p. 207.
91. In 1961/62, holdings of less than 10 acres formed 79 per cent of the total number of farms and comprised nearly half of the cultivated area (Khin Maung Kyi, "Modernization of Burmese Agriculture", in *Southeast Asian Affairs 1982* [Singapore: Heinemann/Institute of Southeast Asian Studies, 1982], p. 122).
92. Derived from Table 18, in *Second Four-Year Plan*, p. 20.
93. Data from Kyaw Myint, "Industrialization in Burma" (Master Thesis, University of Sydney, 1978), Table 5.2, p. 114. The average annual rate of GNP growth in the ECAFE region for the period between 1953/54 and 1961/62 was estimated as 4.2 per cent, whereas Myanmar achieved 4.8 per cent (p. 23).
94. The primary production sectors are agriculture, livestock and fisheries, forestry, and mining.
95. The total number of state employees increased from 56,400 in 1940 to over 154,000 in 1954 and then to around 300,000 by 1963. (Khin Maung Kyi, "Pattern of Accommodation to Bureaucratic Authority in a Transitional Culture [A Sociological Analysis of Burmese Bureaucrats with Respect to Their Orientations Toward Authority]" [Ph.D. dissertation, Cornell University, 1966], pp. 91–92). The Government's current expenditure grew from 646 million kyat in 1952/53 to 1,039 million kyat in 1959/60 (Mali, *Fiscal Aspects*, Table 11, p. 87).
96. Derived from *Report to the People 1964/65*, Table I, p. 2.
97. See, for example, the ridicule brought about by the allegation that U Nu had promised a car, a house, and a monthly income of 800 kyat per family in his Pyidawtha scheme. For U Nu's clarification, see Nu, *Saturday's Son*, p. 216.
98. The KTA advisers' influence on economic policy-making was also resented by the Myanmar technocrats (Thet Tun, "A Critique of Louis J. Walinsky's Economic Development in Burma 1951–1960", *JBRS* XLVII, no. 1 [1964], pp. 175–77, 179–81). The consultants' emphasis on the termination of the insurgency was also seen as part of the anti-Communist drive by the U.S. Cold War strategy (San Nyein and Myint Kyi, *1958–1962 Myanma Nainganyei*, p. 119.
99. Maung Maung, *Burma and General Ne Win*, p. 237.
100. See, for example, Taylor, *State in Burma*, pp. 259–60.

4

Industrialization and the Economy

Operating within the parliamentary democracy system, the Myanmar Government intervened extensively in the national economy in the 1950s and introduced a strategy of import-substitution industrialization, based on an ambitious master plan known as the Pyidawtha Plan. However, the state-led industrialization effort soon ran into difficulties and faltered within a few years of its inception. Feeble attempts by the government to rectify the shortcomings of its industrial strategy and plans by reducing the state's role in industrial development foundered as political instability and economic uncertainty manifested in the late 1950s, brought about by a series of power struggles within the ruling party (see Chapter 3).

INDUSTRIALIZATION AND THE STATE

The leading role of the state in shaping and controlling the industrial sectors (mining, manufacturing, and power) through an import-substituting industrialization (ISI) strategy is an important characteristic of Myanmar's economy in the period under study.

Myanmar's industrialization was not only driven by a desire to ensure higher productivity and better living standards but also influenced by the trauma of losing its sovereignty to an industrial power.[1] Furnivall made an observation that the success of the colonial economy was "chiefly due to European capital and Indian labourer".[2] In independent Myanmar, which vowed to do away with both alien capital and migrant labour, the imperatives to industrialize led to state action on a broad economic front. The Union Constitution of 1947 provided a general framework for the state to play an active economic role.[3]

Industrial Strategy, Policies, and Plans

When the Two-Year Plan was announced in April 1948 by the Anti-Fascist People's Freedom League (AFPFL) Government, ISI was the standard recipe for "late industrializers".[4] The Two-Year Plan's industrial component was more a wish list of projects than a full-fledged plan. It stressed the importance of state ownership in the industrial sector. Private industries would be "regulated" to ensure "consonance with the interest of the country".[5] It also acknowledged the importance of cottage industries and aimed "to increase ... [their] scope and effectiveness" by enhancing their organizational, financial, technical, marketing, and employment capacities.[6] Agriculture surplus would finance industrial development.[7]

The Economic Council's resolution of 2 March 1949 recommended that "industries solely connected with military defence" and atomic energy should belong to the state. It also delineated industries for which, "until such time as the State can undertake sufficient production", private participation would be allowed "on terms and conditions to be settled with each enterprise".[8] In view of "obvious limitations of technical and administrative skill and dearth of indigenous capital", general "terms and conditions on which foreign capital may be accepted for the rehabilitation or development of industries" were outlined.[9]

However, it was superseded in September by the Report on Industrial Policy, in which the Industrial Development Committee considered measures to increase production levels and to clearly demarcate the boundaries for state and private industrial enterprises.[10] This parliamentary report stressed the urgency of its recommendations, given "the very dangerous and almost desperate" economic situation. Its first objective was to discourage all non-productive expenditures and selectively restrict imports.[11] The second objective was to direct exports towards countries which were potential suppliers of machinery and raw materials for the existing industries. A "buy local" campaign together with state intervention in favour of local products were advocated to help domestic small-scale industries.[12]

It cautioned that the resources of both the state and the private "Burman" would be "inadequate to develop industrial production in Burma". Thus, foreign equity capital would be accepted subject to safeguards that protect "national welfare".[13] However, it was not accompanied by any substantive follow-up measures and elicited very little response from foreign investors.

Finally, the Report echoed the Two-Year Plan's emphasis on developing a skilled and disciplined industrial labour force suitable for "large scale industrial production" and stressed that the country needed foreign enterprises to train indigenous labour.[14]

In early 1951, the Planning Ministry sponsored a conference on "Current Economic Problems".[15] There, it was argued that the "overriding argument" for industrialization was the need to absorb "the annual increment" in the labour force.[16] Appropriate industries should be considered "in the light of the shortage of capital"; although "once the industry" was chosen, "the most modern" technology should be employed to "bring the greatest long run benefits".[17]

The American consultants, engaged in late 1951, produced a preliminary report which formed the basis of the Pyidawtha Plan or the Eight-Year Development Plan or KTA Plan, launched in August 1952. The report recommended industrial development to redress the economy's "excessive dependence" on rice production and export, "to increase per capita productivity and output, to conserve foreign exchange and most importantly to make larger quantities and more varied supplies of goods available" to the public. However, it also cautioned the government against investing in "too large scale enterprises" that would strain the financial resources and were irrelevant to the country's immediate needs.[18]

In its initial formulation, the plan envisaged a doubling of the real gross domestic product (GDP) between 1951 and 1960. It entailed four major power projects, restoration and expansion of mineral production, exploration and development of mineral resources, a large-scale coal mining project, and a master plan for the processing and manufacturing industries based on three regional growth centres.[19]

The aim was to establish import-substituting state industries in regions where natural resources were locally available. The private sector was not incorporated in the ISI master plan, though private and co-operative investment in cottage industries and consumer goods producing light industries were to be encouraged and supported.[20]

The Plan was supposed to be implemented under the existing regime of state control over foreign trade.[21] The latter was seen as an essential element of surplus accumulation and a safeguard against capitalist exploitation.[22]

The Economic and Social Board (ESB) which superseded the Economic Council was responsible for the overall supervision of the development projects. Chaired by the Prime Minister, the ESB was a sub-Cabinet of key economic ministers. On the other hand, the actual planning exercises as well as the technical support and services were to be carried out by the Ministry of National Planning. In practice the functions of these two organizations overlapped and the over-centralization brought about by the Prime Minister's *modus operandi* resulted in confusion and misunderstandings.[23]

The Prime Minister's statement of 1 December 1953, entitled "Our Goal and Our Interim Programme" declared that the economic system must not "extract the maximum profit from" the citizens, and "[u]ltimately all trade and industry must be organized into public corporations and co-operatives". The state enterprises were to be accorded top priority, followed by joint ventures with the state, co-operatives, and private enterprises. On the other hand, he promised to "help" the private sector in carrying out the expected investment in support of the Pyidawtha Plan.[24]

The Plan Implementation Conference of February 1954 introduced a programme that envisaged a larger set of industrial projects than that recommended by the KTA consultants. However, balance of payments (BOP) problems and falling foreign exchange reserves soon led to drastic cutbacks, in fiscal year 1954/55, in project-related expenditures.[25]

On 9 June 1955, the government issued a statement on investment policy that not only included measures to protect and support private investment but also contained an appended list of industrial fields "in which private investment, both domestic and foreign" was solicited.[26] Sufficient foreign exchange allocations for industrial needs were promised, while the state would "[r]ender protection and support of industry by tariffs or other means". The criteria for accepting private participation included: potential to assist national economic development on a "sound and balanced" basis; contribution towards increased productivity; provision of "essential goods and services"; and ability to increase Myanmar's export potential or reduce the needs for imports.[27]

Furthermore, in July 1955, Nu declared that his government was "not going overboard for industrialization" and would not be "building uneconomic industrial facilities whose products would have to be protected by high import duties".[28] This sobering reflection was apparently brought about by fiscal difficulties and poor performance of state industrial enterprises (SIEs).[29]

Nevertheless, a "market-friendly" approach with a policy environment conducive to wealth creation that might have provided the critical impetus for industrial development was not seriously pursued.[30] Nothing concrete in terms of effective policy measures, either to enhance private capital formation in the industrial sector or to raise productivity in agriculture, ensued.

The need to rationalize SIEs' management, to increase their operational efficiency, and to encourage indigenous and foreign private investment, were reiterated in Nu's speech to the Parliament on 27 September 1957.[31] Thereafter, the industrial master plan unravelled and lost its potential for technical complementarity among related projects. The result was a constellation of individual state-sponsored projects run by a multitude of boards and agencies under nominal supervision of Deputy Prime Minister Kyaw Nyein.[32]

Further reorganization of the planning machinery, apparently geared towards centralization at the Prime Minister's Office, did not foster substantial improvements in planning or execution.[33] Meanwhile, the promotion of private industries was mainly affected through industrial licensing and selective technical, financial, and operational assistance. However, as pointed out by the Central Committee of Industrialists, the "Government's lack of proper industrial policy" on the private sector was one of the "main draw-backs in [the] development of private industry in the country".[34]

The caretaker government of General Ne Win, installed in October 1958, applied "a brake to the purchase of more factories" and placed more emphasis on agriculture and forestry. The Investment Act of 1959 was promulgated and the need for a development bank for industrial financing was acknowledged.[35] However, preoccupied with improving the law and order situation, it did not introduce major policy initiatives.

Immediately after his election victory, premier Nu announced that state participation in the economy would be rolled back to a manageable extent and the forthcoming economic plan would strive for a proper balance between industry and agriculture.[36] The emphasis in the Second Four-Year Plan, presented in 1961, was on the promotion of private industries. It was assumed that the state would confine itself to "only a few industries" and that the Plan as a whole would rely "heavily on the private sector" for success.[37] Due to political instability, neither this plan nor the promised industrial policy materialized. All in all, the state-led industrialization effort embodied in the Pyidawtha Plan failed to achieve its objectives.

The Roots of Failure

A variety of reasons were given for the failure of the Pyidawtha Plan and the state's industrialization effort. Walinsky, who was closely involved, identified twelve major implementation problems that apparently absolved the KTA consultants of any major responsibility for the failure.[38] However, Thet Tun, a leading Myanmar counterpart, contended that failure was due to "four false major assumptions": continuation of high rice export price; low current expenditure growth; rapid improvement of security conditions; and high administrative efficiency.[39] He wondered "why advisers with an ideology so divergent from the clients' were hired at all".[40] He also questioned the usefulness of advisers from "commercial firms who acquire vested interests and tend to work to perpetuate their contracts".[41] Moreover, according to a World Bank mission (*c.* 1953):

> The principal limitations of the planning activity so far appears to be a preoccupation with engineering and financial aspects of individual projects without adequate consideration for Burma's limited administrative, managerial, and technical capacities.[42]

Others blamed the failure to secure adequate investment capital (especially foreign exchange) and the poor performance of state-owned enterprises (SOEs).[43] Another shortcoming was the "lack of priorities, phasing and co-ordination" in the programme.[44] Another factor was the slower-than-expected improvement of the security situation. The lack of appropriate manpower resources was another bottleneck and "one of the most significant causes" of failure.[45]

On the other hand, the state-led industrialization effort could only be understood in the context of the state's attempt to foster overall economic growth. This entails examination of sectoral economic performance in relation to investment and resource mobilization.

Sectoral Investments and GDP Growth

The investment structure envisioned in the Pyidawtha blueprint required total net investments (including private investments) of 7.5 billion kyat with a state share of 3 billion kyat. Within the state sector, the percentage shares for manufacturing, mining, and electric power were 7.7, 3.8, and 26 respectively. The transport and communication sector was allotted nearly 50 per cent while irrigation schemes accounted for another 12.3 per cent.[46] As pointed out by Schumacher, it favoured developments with little direct bearing on commodity production.[47]

Capital budget allocations provided some insights into the government's development programme. Despite some sectoral mismatch between the actual capital expenditures and the Plan targets, one may still compare these two sets of data to discern whether there were any significant changes in the balance of sectoral investments during implementation.

In Table 4.1 the corresponding capital expenditures can be taken as proxies for state investments. Apparently, the heavy emphasis placed on electric power and infrastructure development did not materialize.[48]

Expenditures for agriculture did not differ very much from investment targets in both absolute values and relative shares. However, the target was set solely for investment in irrigation, whereas the expenditure was

TABLE 4.1
Investment Targets and Capital Expenditures
(Million kyat)

Sector	*Target 1952/53–59/60*	*Expenditure 1952/53–55/56*	*Expenditure 1956/57–59/60*	*Expenditure 1952/53–59/60*
Agriculture	370.0[a]	154.6	211.8	366.4
	(12.3)	(11.7)	(15.9)	(13.8)
Forestry	n.a.	30.6	24.7	55.3
		(2.3)	(1.9)	(2.1)
Mining	115.0	15.7	8.6	24.3
	(3.8)	(1.2)	(0.6)	(0.9)
Industry	230.0	186.6	187.9	374.5
	(7.7)	(14.1)	(14.1)	(14.1)
Power	780.0	202.6	303.1	505.7
	(26.0)	(15.3)	(22.8)	(19.1)
Infrastructure	1,490.0	731.2	594.0	1,325.2
	(49.9)	(55.3)	(44.7)	(50.0)
Total	2,985.0	1,321.3	1,330.1	2,651.4

Notes: In the target, infrastructure comprised transport and communications only, whereas the expenditure data included construction as well. Figures in parentheses are the ratios (percentage) of sectoral outlays to total investment.
a. Investment for irrigation only.
n.a. = not applicable
Source: Thet Tun, "A Review of Economic Planning in Burma", in *Burma Research Society Fiftieth Anniversary Publication*, vol. 1 (1960), pp. 504–505, 519.

for the entire agriculture sector. Actually, the expenditure on irrigation was less than 10 per cent of investment outlay as the planned large-scale irrigation projects remained unimplemented.[49]

In the mining sector, total expenditure was much less than that envisaged in the original plan because of the decision to establish joint ventures with foreign companies which had dominated the minerals industries.

The industrial sector garnered a much higher share of capital expenditure than planned. Despite the moratorium on new projects in the second period, the average level of investment for industry remained high at around 14 per cent for both periods. Thus, the overall expenditure seems to reveal a bias towards industry. The total capital outlay was over 60 per cent higher than the target value, and the cost of industrial projects appeared to have been grossly underestimated.[50]

There were no sectoral targets for the GDP.[51] Moreover, the state's share cannot be ascertained from the aggregated sectoral composition of GDP. Therefore (government) investment expenditures cannot be directly related to the corresponding sectoral contributions to the GDP. Despite this difficulty, relevant sectors in the overall GDP structure may be chosen so as to reflect the corresponding capital investments. This growth pattern may then be compared to the pattern of budgetary expenditures in the corresponding GDP sectors.

Table 4.2 compares changes in the sectoral structure of GDP (in constant 1961/62 prices) between 1951/52 and 1959/60 for major productive sectors. The poor performance of agriculture and forestry (both excluded from the Pyidawtha Programme) is reflected in their reduced shares. Agriculture growth was less than half of the overall GDP growth. The increase in rice output was less than 53 per cent of the target for 1959/60.[52] Timber extraction was adversely affected by the civil war and the volume of teak production was less than 60 per cent of the pre-war average and only 50 per cent of the target. Hardwood volume also fell by nearly 27 per cent.[53]

Mining's share of GDP was minuscule and the power sector's share was even smaller. Their high growth (100 and 183 per cent respectively) resulted from very low bases.[54]

The manufacturing sector tripled its value-added output while doubling its sectoral share. This, considered in isolation, may give the misleading impression that the state's investment bias in its favour had borne fruit. However, given the fact that the private sector accounted for some 95 per cent of the value of manufacturing output for 1960/61, it

TABLE 4.2
Sectoral GDP in 1961/62 Prices
(Million kyat)

Sector	*Fiscal year 1951/52*	*Fiscal year 1959/60*	*Sectoral increase (percentage)*
Agriculture	1,418 (29.3)	1,669 (22.7)	17.7
Forestry	279 (5.8)	345 (4.7)	23.7
Mining	34 (0.7)	68 (0.9)	100.0
Manufacturing[a]	303 (6.3)	938 (12.8)	209.5
Power	6 (0.1)	23 (0.3)	283.3
Total GDP	4,833	7,348	52.0

Notes: Figures in parentheses are for sectoral shares of GDP.
a. Manufacturing included cottage industries.
Source: Kyaw Myint, "Industrialization in Burma" (Master thesis, University of Sydney, 1978), Table 1.4, p. 15.

is more likely that the state's investments were not very efficient.[55] On the other hand, the failure of the agriculture sector to generate sufficient surplus for industrial investment undermined the entire development programme.

FINANCIAL RESOURCES

For a resource-rich country, one financing option is to exploit the surplus from primary production. Another possibility is to borrow from abroad. External assistance from bilateral and/or multilateral donors in the form of grant aid and/or loans can be solicited or foreign equity capital may be invited.[56]

With state control over foreign trade and currency exchange, Myanmar's leaders initially opted for the self-reliant strategy of financing investments with surplus extracted from primary production. It was believed that rice exports and surpluses from the SOEs could yield a gross fixed capital formation (GFCF) of about 5.2 billion kyat between 1952 and 1960.[57] Foreign borrowing was ruled out by the leaders' aversion to indebtedness and their preference for self-reliance.[58] Similarly, foreign investment was never seriously considered despite occasional references by political leaders to the possibility of mutually beneficial arrangements.[59]

Moreover, measures to integrate private sector capital formation with the plan or to attract private industrial investments were absent. It was assumed that the state's capital formation would have a multiplier effect on the private sector "automatically as soon as peace and security" was re-established.[60] The actual GFCF was 74.8 per cent of the target, whereby the state sector fulfilled 80.1 per cent and the private sector accomplished only 69.5 per cent of the target.[61]

Barely a year after planned investments began, the export price of rice dropped precipitously and the expected rising trend in export earnings failed to materialize.[62] Subsequently, foreign exchange reserves were drawn down not only to compensate for falling export earnings, but also for importing consumer goods to counter demand-pull inflation.[63] The state had to resort to monetary expansion and foreign assistance as stop-gap measures.[64]

Reduction of rice-export earnings also depressed the revenues from tariffs, as imports were decreased to arrest the deteriorating balance of payments (BOP).[65] Attempts to increase tax revenues and raise the savings rate were unsuccessful.[66] Deficit financing was pursued not only to finance the development projects but also to sustain a large defence budget and to support domestic consumption and welfare spending.[67] The resulting cumulative deficit in the budget, during the period 1952/53 to 1959/60, amounted to over 1.5 billion kyat, instead of the expected surplus of nearly 2.2 billion kyat.[68]

On the other hand, the banking sector was dominated by the Union Bank of Burma (UBB) whose role involved "deficit-financing and debenture-financing", whereby it underwrote securities issued by the government "to meet operating deficits" as well as debentures issued by SOEs "to provide additional capital".[69] The principal aim of the monetary policy was to ensure currency stability, and the UBB attempted, especially after 1956, to curb inflation by restricting credit creation and also to conserve foreign exchange through exchange controls.[70]

Foreign Trade

The classic ISI strategy is characterized by trade protectionism. Moreover, export pessimism and the "infant industry argument" reinforced the "inward orientation" of many foreign trade regimes.[71] Myanmar's foreign trade regime not only supported industrialization but also served the objectives of indigenizing and nationalizing economic activities.

Teak and rice exports were nationalized soon after independence. State marketing boards controlled exports of forest produce and agricultural goods. Import controls were introduced in 1947. Licensing was the major policy instrument and was also used to indigenize private import agencies by allocating a minimum of 60 per cent of the annual licences to Myanmar nationals.[72] State agencies imported consumer goods and industrial raw materials.[73] All these together with administered prices for "essential" goods and tight exchange controls were utilized for conserving foreign exchange, controlling price inflation, and protecting local industries.[74]

Tariffs were imposed to preserve scarce foreign exchange.[75] Its revenue-generating function also became important as the volume of imports reached significant levels after 1952.[76] In the early 1950s, with substantial reserves in hand, the government allowed private imports under open general licences (OGL).[77] However, in the mid-1950s the balance of payments deteriorated and import licensing was reimposed, significantly reducing the share of private imports. Thereafter, manipulations of OGL listings and selective allocation of import licences were utilized by the government not only to implement the indigenization of foreign trade but also to throttle foreign exchange expenditures.[78] As the state-owned industries came on stream and the private industrial sector expanded, the high tariffs imposed on competing imports did give some protection to the local producers and the differential tariff structure on products within the same industrial branch also influenced investment decisions in the private sector.[79]

Objectives of the Government's trade policy included:

> Assurance of reasonable prices for ... goods ... Increased production of goods within the country ... Maximum possible export of agricultural produce, timber and minerals ... Encouragement and support to citizens ...[80]

On the other hand, as observed by a business leader, it had been "a compromise between four more or less incompatible objectives"; viz., earning or conserving foreign exchange, lowering living costs, nurturing Myanmar business interests, and substituting state trading for private commerce.[81]

The shortcomings of Myanmar-owned firms in the import trade led to the introduction of joint venture corporations (JVC) in early 1957.[82] This enhanced the indigenization effort, reduced the scope of individual trading firms in general and alien firms in particular, and helped stabilize prices of popular imports.[83]

Unavailability of disaggregated trade data make it impossible to assess the combined impact of state interventions on the private industrial sector. It can only be conjectured, on theoretical grounds, that such a combination of state monopolies, tariffs, licensing, and exchange controls, in all likelihood, must have engendered rent-seeking, degraded the efficiency of overall resource allocation, and introduced price distortions.[84]

There was state control over export of major commodities but no effective export-promoting measures existed. When the export price of rice tumbled after 1953, instead of yielding to market forces, the state resorted to barter deals with East European countries to clear unsold rice stocks.[85] Later, the military caretaker government allowed private exports in cotton, rubber, and agriculture produce, that were previously state monopolies. An export promotion council was instituted and an export incentive scheme, whereby import licences were issued to exporters, was introduced.[86] The latter was continued by Nu's government but had little impact on export earnings.[87]

The overall trade balance, which had been positive since 1946/47, registered a deficit in 1956/57 and, except for a surplus in 1958/59, was negative up to the end of the fiscal year 1960/61.[88] The trend in the composition of imports reflected the nature and tempo of the development programme. The share of imported capital goods registered a rising trend from around 27.1 per cent in 1954 to a peak of 40.8 per cent in 1958, and declined thereafter to 26.4 per cent in 1961.[89] Similarly, machinery imports followed an increasing trend from 1953/54 (over 83 million kyat) to 1957/58 (over 172 million kyat), then levelled off after declining to around 108 million kyat in 1959/60, indicating the delayed effect of the truncation of the Pyidawtha Plan.[90]

International trade as an engine of growth remained under-exploited in Myanmar's state-led ISI strategy. On the other hand, given the low base of industrial activity as well as the virtual absence of institutionalized long-term credit facilities, and, most significantly, the state's ambivalence towards private participation, it is doubtful whether selective interventions *a la* South Korea would have been sufficient to induce rapid development of import-substituting industries.[91]

Aid

In attempting to bridge the deficit, foreign assistance became important during the mid-1950s.[92] Nevertheless, the government's soliciting of foreign loans and grants was dictated by economic exigencies and political expediency.

Since independence, Myanmar had cautiously accepted foreign assistance, provided it did not compromise the state's independence and neutrality. Prime Minister Nu stated, in June 1948, that his government would refuse "any foreign aid which would be detrimental to the political, economic and strategic freedom of Burma".[93] However, Nu stated, in June 1949, that for a "large-scale development" programme "the only suitable course" was to secure foreign loans and foreign investment but only with safeguards to prevent them from establishing "a stranglehold on the economic life of the country".[94]

Hence, in September 1950, grants under the United State's Economic Co-operation Administration (ECA) were accepted.[95] Soon dissatisfaction over aid management and the apparent shortcomings of some projects developed amongst Myanmar officials.[96] More significantly, the enactment of the Mutual Security Act of 1951 by the U.S. Congress was seen as an attempt to "secure an overt or more direct commitment to U.S. concepts of collective security" and soured aid relations during early 1952.[97] The last straw was the Myanmar perception that there was U.S. collusion in the Kuomintang aggression and, in March 1953, Myanmar abrogated the aid agreement.[98]

In the aftermath of the post-Korean War rice price collapse, Myanmar unsuccessfully sought loans from the World Bank and the United States.[99] Myanmar then turned to the People's Republic of China (PRC) and negotiated a "trade and aid" protocol in April 1954 which incorporated provision of technical assistance and commodities in exchange for Myanmar rice.[100] This led to a series of similar barter protocols with East European countries in the mid-1950s. These, together with bilateral and multilateral aid and the loan authorized by the U.S. Agricultural Trade and Development Assistance Act (P.L. 480) did relieve some pressures on inflation and eased the balance of payments in late 1950s.[101] In response to Myanmar's request for a general purpose loan, the United States extended a US$25 million loan for new projects that was accepted in March 1957.[102] However, less than 50 per cent of the approved sum was disbursed by September 1960.[103]

The US$4 million Chinese project loan for a cotton-spinning mill, extended in November 1958, remained unutilized during the parliamentary era. Similarly, the US$84 million interest-free loan extended by China, in January 1961, under an economic and technical agreement, did not materialize until the mid-1960s.[104]

The Agreement for Reparations and Economic Co-operation between Myanmar and Japan, concluded in November 1954 after protracted negotiations, provided Japanese goods and services worth US$20 million in grants and US$5 million in loans (for joint ventures with Japanese firms) annually for ten years.[105] The cumulative disbursement was over US$125 million by the end of 1961 and the most significant project was the Baluchaung hydroelectric plant.[106]

Japanese aid also elicited adverse reactions as the government was accused of selling out to Japanese business interests.[107] There were complaints about over-pricing, poor quality and inappropriately designed goods, as well as the high costs of maintaining Japanese expatriates.[108] Moreover, the joint-venture loan scheme never materialized, mainly because the potential Japanese investors preferred trading to direct investment.[109]

Myanmar's foreign assistance experience of the parliamentary period was less than satisfactory. Sought in a haphazard manner without prioritization or sectoral focus, implementation was often dogged by costly delays and much wrangling between the donor and the recipient. Political factors and bilateral relations probably figured as much as economic considerations.[110]

Resource Mobilization

The mix of sources for public sector investment underwent a change in the mid-1950s. Domestic sources of capital based on "current finance" gave way to "non-current finance" and foreign sources of financing.[111] The absence of an integrated financial plan, with prioritized expenditures led to the subordination of investment programming to budgetary expediencies.[112]

Private investment was treated as a residual, and the state did very little to enhance private capital formation. There were no institutional arrangements that provided long-term industrial capital and the private sector had to rely on either self-financing or the informal "curb" market.[113] In spite of all these obstacles, 3.2 billion kyat in private GFCF were realized. As disaggregated data are not available, the contribution of private capital formation to industrial investment cannot be ascertained.[114]

However, statistics on bank credits do highlight some aspects of private financing. Government loans to the private sector from 1952/53 to 1959/60 amounted to about 300 million kyat, of which the share for industries was less than 10 million kyat.[115] Cumulative commercial bank loans from 1952 to 1959 were over 1.6 billion kyat, from which manufacturing received around 300 million kyat.[116] These aggregate figures (including those drawn for non-investment purposes) when compared with the estimated private sector GFCF during the corresponding period, indicate that the majority of private capital formation lay outside the formal credit system. As such, the state lost (by default) the means to control the financing of private industrial capital.[117]

Apparently, all government efforts were directed towards meeting state sector requirements. The financing of the unplanned private sector remained outside state control. Unlike Korea, the Myanmar state lacked the resources and the institutional mechanism to exploit the credit-based system's potential to "exert influence over the economy's investment pattern and guide sectoral mobility".[118]

LABOUR AND INDUSTRIAL EMPLOYMENT

Industrial labour had been in the forefront of the struggle for independence.[119] Recognizing this, the Union Constitution of 1947 promised to "assist workers to associate and organize" and to "protect" their rights "by legislation".[120] These constitutional assurances formed the basis for new legislation and amendments of existing laws and institutions that were aimed at promoting workers' interests.[121] Most of the important laws were enacted by 1952, setting the stage for marked improvement in working conditions from that under the colonial regime.[122]

The Two-Year Plan envisaged the following:

- creating a harmonious relationship between employers and employees;
- assuring fair wages and reasonable standards of living while providing fair and equitable working conditions (adequate welfare facilities, housing, safety, holiday and leave scheme, and accident compensation);
- instituting adequate machinery for dispute settlement;
- "gradual elimination of unemployment" and optimal "redistribution" of labour force;
- instituting training, education, and manpower planning;
- introducing appropriate "industrial methods and processes"; and
- providing social insurance, including unemployment insurance.[123]

Hence amendments to the colonial acts on trade disputes, factories, mines, payment of wages, and compensation were carried out within the first four years of independence. Similarly, new acts on employment statistics, minimum wages, oilfields (labour welfare), leave and holidays, shops and establishments, and factories were enacted.[124]

The large increase in the cost of living for urban workers since 1940 was not matched by the low level of wages.[125] Despite the Minimum Wage Act of 1949 and the formation of the Minimum Wage Council in 1953, very little progress was achieved in instituting adequate wage levels commensurate with rising costs.[126] The average wage level for blue-collar industrial workers remained stagnant throughout the decade of the 1950s.[127] Generally, wages were "not adequate to conduce health and working capacity" in the workers, "nor [had] they been an incentive to efficiency". As for the potential to compensate for the "disadvantages of some occupations and industries" as well as to "attract workers" to desired industries, the prevailing system did not entail "sufficient differential rates either industry-wise or area-wise to fulfil" it.[128]

Though guidelines for occupational safety, paid leave and holidays, and pecuniary compensation for accidents and disability existed, proper enforcement was hampered by the lack of administrative resources. The labour welfare centre scheme, started in 1951, provided facilities for free outpatient medical care, pre- and post-natal counselling, culture and sport activities, library and reading room, and free tuition for evening classes. By 1958, there were seven such centres in Yangon and ten in the districts.[129]

The Standing Joint Labour Advisory Board, established in 1947, was reconstituted after independence as a tripartite body consisting of representatives from the government, employers, and workers to discuss and coordinate "not only matters of mutual interest, but also on labour policy".[130] A standing court for industrial arbitration and offices for labour affairs were set up as early as 1947.[131] On the other hand, labour-management relations appeared to be "on a makeshift basis" and employment contracts were uncommon "with the exception of a few foreign firms". Private employers usually set up their own employment rules, while state enterprises followed government practice. Generally, only the bare minimum of legal rights were accorded, "while everything ... [else had] to be pressed for separately".[132] Nevertheless, except for political agitations during the AFPFL split, there were no large-scale disruptions in the industrial sector after the enactment of the major legislations (*c.* 1951).[133]

To facilitate skills development, a state-sponsored training scheme for industrial supervisors known as Training within Industry (TWI) was introduced in November 1955, with the technical assistance of the International Labour Organization (ILO). There was no other long-term industrial training programme, and basic training facilities in trades where there had been a shortage of skilled manpower were "admittedly inadequate".[134]

The promulgation of the Social Security Act in October 1954 led to the institution of the social security scheme on 1 January 1956, in Yangon. The scheme, under the Social Security Board, provided insured workers with medical care; sickness, maternity, and injury benefits; survivors' pensions; and funeral grants.[135] The social security scheme was subsequently extended to five more major towns in six years. Its coverage expanded from 915 registered establishments and over 66,000 insured persons in 1955/56, to 2,561 and over 253,000, respectively, in 1960/61.[136] The scheme was designed for self-financing with general insurance contributions by the state, employer, and employee according to a schedule based on wage classes. From 1956 to 1962, annual expenditures under this scheme increased fivefold (to 5.5 million kyat) while annual contributions increased over three times (to 9.4 million kyat), registering surplus throughout the period.[137]

An ILO study in 1964 concluded that the social security scheme had been successful and that there was "no reason to doubt that the beneficial impact of the scheme [had] made itself felt wherever it [was] in operation".[138] Apparently, the Social Security Scheme did enhance the welfare of its members.

All these efforts and measures undertaken by the state had resulted in some improvements in the socio-economic conditions of the urban industrial work force. Though far from ideal, the state was able to ameliorate the hardships, brought about by inflation and relative deprivation, of those who had access to these amenities as well as safeguard the rights of workers to some extent.

Organized Labour

Myanmar trade unionism was different from its Western counterpart in character and purpose. Associated with the nationalist struggle for independence, the unions were politicized and mobilized by the political parties. This led to factionalism with individual union leaders "looking more towards winning political power for themselves through the manipulation" of "ignorant and credulous followers".[139]

The Trade Union Congress (Burma) or TUC(B), controlled by Burma Socialist Party (BSP) leaders from the ruling AFPFL, dominated the unions in the 1950s.[140] Although TUC(B) leader Ba Swe identified the principal tasks of the trade unions as protecting "the interests of the working class" and raising "their standard of living", they became tools of their politicking patrons.[141] When the AFPFL split in 1958, the TUC(B) sided with the losing Stable AFPFL faction, while the victorious Clean faction of Nu formed the Union Labour Organization (ULO). By 1960, there were four confederated unions, including the non-partisan Free Trade Union of Burma (FTUB).[142]

Localized or shop unions were the most common entities and trade or industrial federations were confined to a few major industries like oil and transport.[143] The national-level bodies had regional as well as industrial affiliates. The public sector and the (foreign) joint ventures were the major strongholds of unionism and the government's pro-labour stance was conducive to the acceptance of unions by the management.[144]

Usually, "top national bodies [set] ... the policy to be followed by their affiliates in matters of general interests" and provided guidance in political issues, as well as advice and assistance on matters concerning organization, dialogue with employers, and industrial disputes. There was "little inter-relation ... between unions affiliated to different central bodies and between the central bodies themselves".[145]

The impact of Myanmar unionism on industrial labour was rather limited. Institutional weaknesses and factionalism diluted the power of trade unionism. Negotiations over specific issues and disagreements were the most common bargaining processes involving local unions, and there was very little scope for escalating wage demands. "Joint consultations between unions and management ... [were] not a very widespread practice".[146] In short, the politicized trade union movement was divided, weak, and marginalized.

Employment

Employment creation was "considered essentially as a consequence of the general process of output expansion to be brought about by investment programmes under the plan". There had been no attempts "to spell out clearly, distinctly and logically the employment objectives of development planning in Burma". Neither did the plans "specify ... employment targets" nor targets for "the sectoral distribution of employment". Industrialization "did not make any sizeable impact on the employment situation ... and the employment opportunities lagged far behind the growth in the labor force".[147]

Total employment in the processing and manufacturing industries increased from over 576,000 in 1952/53 to around 720,000 in 1961/62.[148] However, registered establishments accounted for only 140,175 in 1960/61 (113,967 in 1953/54).[149] Mining employment fell from 41,271 in 1953 to 14,245 in 1961 and employment in the power sector was insignificant.[150]

Table 4.3 compares the distribution of employment in significant industrial branches (having at least 1 per cent share) in 1961/62 with that in 1952/53. The distribution of employment in registered industries for 1959/60 is also included. Evidently, there was very little change in both the absolute shares of employment and rankings among the industrial branches between 1952 and 1961.

TABLE 4.3
Share of Employment by Industrial Branches

Industrial Branch	*All Industries*		*Registered*[a]
	1952/53 *% (rank)*	*1961/62* *% (rank)*	*1959/60* *% (rank)*
Food and beverage	25.0 (1)	24.0 (1)	36.4 (1)
Textiles	15.3 (2)	14.3 (2)	18.6 (2)
Wood, bamboo, cork except furniture	12.9 (3)	11.1 (3)	10.4 (3)
Tobacco	11.1 (4)	11.1 (4)	9.2 (4)
Footwear and apparel	9.3 (5)	9.0 (5)	4.4 (5)
Non-metallic product except coal and oil	5.2 (7)	6.7 (6)	4.2 (6)
Chemical and Chemical product	6.8 (6)	6.3 (7)	4.0 (7)
Metal product except machinery and transport equipment	3.1 (8)	3.2 (8)	1.8 (11)
Transport equipment and repair	2.5 (9)	2.9 (9)	3.1 (8)
Non-electrical machinery and repair	0.6 (12)	1.1 (10)	0.3 (n.a.)
Furniture and fixture	1.2 (10)	1.1 (11)	0.3 (n.a.)

Notes: Ranking excluded branches with shares of less than 1 per cent in 1961/62.
a. Those registered under the rules of the Factory Act.
n.a. = not applicable
Sources: M. M. Mehta, *Report on the Manpower Situation in Burma* (Geneva: International Labour Office, 1964), Table 4.1, pp. 100–102; Kyaw Myint, "Industrialization in Burma" (Master thesis, University of Sydney, 1978), Table 5.5, p. 122.

Employment in the corresponding registered industries (cottage industries excluded) show a very similar distribution in ranking though the concentration of employment in the top two industrial branches were markedly higher. Between them, the food and beverage and the textiles groups employed nearly 40 per cent of the industrial labour force, while their combined share for registered enterprises was even higher at 55 per cent. This stable pattern of employment distribution over almost a decade indicates that the differential growth pattern of employment opportunities created by the increase in the total number of enterprises had remained virtually unchanged.

Steps taken to alleviate general unemployment included the ban on migrant workers, indigenization measures, the establishment of employment exchanges, and the formation of Rehabilitation Corps (*c.* 1950) for public works.[151] However, industrial expansion in the state sector created much fewer job opportunities than expected. Thus, the elimination of (urban) unemployment was nowhere nearer to realization in 1962 than in 1952.[152]

PROGRESS IN INDUSTRIAL DEVELOPMENT

The Myanmar state pursued the ISI strategy, regulating private industries while establishing and operating industrial concerns. The Ministry of Industry (formed in 1952), whose principal agencies were the Directorate of Industries (DI) and the Industrial Development Corporation (IDC), was responsible for the processing and manufacturing as well as the power sectors.

Supervising, regulating, protecting, and assisting the private sector were the DI's responsibilities since its formation in 1954. With branches in major industrial towns, it operated small-scale industrial projects before they were transferred to the IDC in 1953. The DI also administered the industrial and the weavers' loan schemes. The industrial loan scheme disbursed an average of 0.64 million kyat per year from 1952/53 to 1959/60.[153] The average annual disbursement for the weavers' loan scheme was 0.62 million kyat for the decade since 1950/51.[154] Another task was to scrutinize and recommend all applications for industrial import licences.[155] It was also involved in importing and distributing raw materials, such as cotton yarn and plain cloth, to ensure adequate supply. The DI, in coordination with producers, formulated costing norms and stipulated profit margins for producers, wholesalers, and retailers of selective products.[156]

In 1959, the Standing Committee for the Development of Private Industries was formed to allocate industrial import licences and handle matters related to industrial protection, restriction of entry into saturated product lines, and state aid for private industries. Protection for local industries was accorded through recommendations for tariffs or quotas or an outright ban for competing imports as well as for reduction of tariffs on inputs.[157] Restriction on new entries or expansion was imposed on products showing signs of market saturation.[158]

Formed in November 1952, the IDC was a high-powered agency to develop and operate SIEs as well as to provide assistance to the private sector.[159] Its industrial loan scheme, launched in late 1955, provided cash loans and facilitated hire-purchases of machinery.[160] It also operated a raw materials retail centre for industries whose requirements were too small to warrant separate import licences.

Altogether eight industrial and five pilot plant projects were developed by the IDC and its subsidiary project boards. It also took charge of four nationalized factories and one factory set up by the Kachin State Government.[161] Only one pilot plant was considered economically viable, and many SIEs under its supervision were running at a loss when the caretaker government came to power.[162]

The SIEs also included a textile factory, a brick and tile factory and a pharmaceutical plant (all under separate project boards) as well as three rice mills and seven saw mills. The only significant new industrial investment by a foreign company was the joint venture for soap production with Britain's Unilevers Ltd.[163]

The poor performance of the state's industrial projects was attributed to, *inter alia*, lack of autonomy and accountability, lack of a consistent pricing policy, management shortcomings, low capacity utilization, inappropriate technology, unpopular products, raw material shortages, cutting corners in investment, absence of a proper cost accounting system, and deference to non-economic factors in the choice of projects.[164] However, no serious attempt was made to rectify these shortcomings.[165]

On the other hand, the private industrial sector made substantial progress despite numerous obstacles such as inadequate financial resources, restrictions on foreign exchange, state control on imports of capital and intermediate goods, technical backwardness, and lack of managerial expertise.[166] In fact, the World Bank Mission's Report on "Current Economic Position and Prospects in Burma" (June 1958) stated that it was "surprised to find ... the manufacturing sector ... larger than and considerably more diversified than it had expected". Moreover, it was pointed out that "there has been a growing movement of capital and people into manufacturing".[167]

The expansion of registered industrial establishments between 1953/54 and 1961/62 was one indicator of industrial growth. In this period, they grew from 2,474 to 2,887 (by 16.7 per cent); the labour force increased by 22 per cent; and the total value-added production increased by nearly 213 per cent. The wage bill, also, increased by 135 per cent.[168]

The three major industrial branches (food and beverage, tobacco, and textiles) still dominated in 1961/62 comprising 63 per cent (down 5.5 per cent from 1953/54) of establishments. However, their combined share of value-added fell from 74.7 per cent to 42.1 per cent.[169]

In the same period, the consumer goods industries' share of 85 and 80 per cent, respectively, for the number of establishments and employment slightly fell to 82 and 77 per cent. Nevertheless, in terms of output value, its share fell from 86 to 55 per cent, while the intermediate goods industries' share increased from 9 to 42 per cent. The capital goods industries' contribution had been insignificant on all counts.[170] In terms of the size of labour force, the proportion of establishments with less than fifty workers decreased to 68 per cent in 1961/62 from 78 per cent in 1953/54.[171] There was some slack in industrial production as many state industrial establishments and a number of private industrial groups were operating below full production capacity.[172]

The ownership pattern for 1961/62 reveals that nearly 91 per cent of the registered establishments were owned by Myanmar nationals (up from 86 per cent in 1953/54), while those under joint ownership increased from 4.5 to 5.5 per cent, thereby reinforcing the indigenization trend set after independence. However, the contribution to total value-added by jointly-owned industrial establishments was still substantial at 37.3 per cent (the Myanmar share was 58.6 per cent).[173]

The mineral industries were characterized by joint ventures between the state and the foreign companies which had been exploiting Myanmar's natural resources since the colonial era. The state's reluctance to nationalize these industries may be attributed to lack of funds for rehabilitation and development, inadequate technical and management expertise as well as business acumen, and lack of international reputation. The Myanmar strategy was to acquire "technical, administrative and commercial knowledge and all other techniques connected with these enterprises", with the aim of nationalizing them when the situation permits.[174] This led to the formation of four major joint ventures in oil and minerals production. They were Burma Corporation (1951) of Bawdwin Mines with 50 per cent equity by the state; Burma Oil Company or BOC (1954), with one-third share; Anglo-Burma Tin Company (1956) with 51 per cent share; and Mawchi Mines (1957) with 50 per cent share.[175] However, these partnerships turned out to be less than satisfactory.[176]

The Mineral Resources Development Corporation (MRDC), formed in 1952, was mainly engaged in three (coal, zinc, and an analysis plant) projects, one exploration project, and one minerals trading concern. Both coal and zinc production turned out to be uneconomic and continued on a much smaller scale than envisaged.[177] The MRDC also operated the nationalized Yadanabon (tungsten) Mine. Production of (mainly) lead, zinc, tin, tungsten, and silver steadily improved throughout the first half of the 1950s, until it was retarded by resource depletion and falling world prices in the late 1950s.[178] Nevertheless, the overall output was below the 1939 level. Total production volume in 1961/62 for five major groups of ores and concentrates (tin, tungsten, tin-tungsten mixture, lead, and zinc) was less than 32 per cent of the corresponding volume for 1939.[179] As a result of lower levels of production, the total export tonnage of these five mineral groups, together with other minor products such as copper, nickel, and antimony, attained only 22 per cent of the export volume for 1939.[180]

Although oil production was recovering quite well, the Myanmar leaders were dismayed by the foreign partners' reluctance to renew exploration and the slow pace of indigenization.[181] The BOC's crude oil production more than tripled between 1954 and 1959 and the total crude oil output from all sources in 1961/62 registered a 246 per cent increase from 1953/54, though it was only 56 per cent of the 1939 figure.[182]

In the power sector, fifty-one private power supply establishments were nationalized between 1948 and 1951. The Electricity Supply Board was formed in 1951 for electric power development. Though several large-scale hydroelectric projects were planned only the Lawpita hydroelectric project materialized. Supply of electricity to towns and villages turned out to be uneconomic and could not be sustained. By 1961/62, the overall electricity production was 300 million kilowatt-hours achieving only 38 per cent of the Pyidawtha target for 1959/60. Similarly, the total installed capacity of 191,000 kilowatts was less than 60 per cent of the corresponding target.[183]

The level of industrialization achieved towards the end of the parliamentary era was modest, when compared to the aims of the

Pyidawtha Plan.[184] State contributions to the economy "remained limited" and "failed to yield expected results, in output, operational efficiency, and profits". On the other hand, the private sector had achieved a high growth rate and had "made a significant contribution to the national income".[185] The employment contribution of industries was not up to expectations, and the problem of widespread underemployment and unemployment remained unsolved. Though the government instituted some measures to enhance the working conditions and welfare of workers, there were still much to be done in extending their coverage as well as improving implementation. On the workers' part, "the tendency ... to demand more and deliver less" seems to be a significant and persistent problem confronting Myanmar's industries.[186]

To the military leaders who controlled Myanmar after the 1962 coup, such a state of affairs was deemed unsatisfactory. Hence, in pursuance of self-reliant industrialization, the state assumed sole responsibility for capital formation, undertook nationalization, and established import-substituting industries. This ambitious endeavour is discussed in the next chapter.

Notes

1. See, for example, Maung Maung, *Burma and General Ne Win* (London: Asia Publishing House, 1969), pp. 1–3.
2. John S. Furnivall, *An Introduction to the Political Economy of Burma*, 3rd ed. (Rangoon: People's Literature Committee and House, 1957), p. 161.
3. See Maung Maung, *Burma's Constitution*, 2nd ed. (The Hague: Martinus Nijhoff, 1961), Appendix VII; sections 218 and 219, p. 297.
4. See, for example, Jaleel Ahmad, "Import Substitution: A Survey of Policy Issues", *Developing Economies* XVI, no. 4 (1978): 355–56. The literature on ISI is extremely large, expressing a variety of views and issues. For a summary of issues and some empirical evidence, see Henry Bruton, "Import Substitution", in *Handbook of Development Economics*, edited by Hollis Chenery and T. N. Srinivasan, vol. II (Amsterdam: North Holland, 1989), pp. 1601–44.
5. *Two-Year Plan of Economic Development for Burma* (Rangoon: Government Printing and Stationery, 1948), p. 21; see, also, pp. 21–23. This plan was part of the "Economic Testament" of the AFPFL (Thet Tun, "A Review of Economic Planning in Burma", in *Burma Research Society Fiftieth Anniversary Publication*, vol. 1 [1960], p. 493).
6. *Two-Year Plan*, pp. 22–23.
7. See the statement of the Minister of Agriculture and Forests in Parliament, on 11 October 1948 (quoted in Maung Myint, "Agriculture in Burmese

Economic Development" [Ph.D. dissertation, University of California, Berkeley, 1966], p. 126).

8. "The Industrial Policy of the Union of Burma", in *Burma's Freedom: The Second Anniversary* (Rangoon: Ministry of Information, 1950), p. 113. See Thet Tun, "Organization of Planning Machinery: Lessons from Burmese Experience", *Journal of the Burma Research Society* (hereafter *JBRS*) XLVI, no. i (1963): 28, for details.
9. "Industrial Policy", pp. 113–14.
10. Ibid., p. 114.
11. Ibid., pp. 114–15; see Schedule A, p. 117.
12. Ibid., p. 115; Schedules B and C, p. 118.
13. The emphasis is original (ibid., p. 116). The accompanying schedule contained terms and conditions.
14. Ibid. p. 117.
15. Thet Tun, "Organization", pp. 28–29. The Conference was held at the Ministry of National Planning (9–11 April 1951) and papers presented by the British advisers were then circulated ("Conference Papers on Current Economic Problems", mimeographed [Rangoon, 1951]). The issues discussed were: inflation, currency reform, fiscal policy, industrialization, economic survey, public accounts, and population.
16. Ibid., p. 4. This advice on employment creation was not heeded.
17. Ibid., p. 5.
18. *KTA Preliminary Report*, p. x, cited in Louis J. Walinsky, *Economic Development in Burma 1951–1960* (New York: Twentieth Century Fund, 1962), p. 91.
19. *Pyidawtha: The New Burma* (Rangoon: Economic and Social Board, 1954), pp. 24–28. For details, see Knappen Tippetts Abbet Engineering Co., *Comprehensive Report, Economic and Engineering Development of Burma*, prepared for the Government of the Union of Burma by Knappen Tippetts Abbett McCarthy, Engineers in Association with Pierce Management, Inc. and Robert R. Nathan Associates, Inc., 2 vols., August 1953. The plan was scheduled for fiscal year 1952/53 but only began in 1953/54 (see *The Pyidawtha Conference: Resolutions and Speeches* [Rangoon: Ministry of Information, 1952], p. 35).
20. *Pyidawtha Conference*, pp. 14, 27–28, 104–105.
21. See, for example, Walinsky, *Economic Development*, pp. 498–99, and Table 23, p. 192.
22. See, for example, Nu's address on 8 June 1957 to Government officials, AFPFL affiliates, and the press on the proposed Four-Year Plan (*Burma Weekly Bulletin* [hereafter *BWB*], 13 June 1957, p. 64); and U Nu, *Towards a Socialist State* (Rangoon: Central Printing Office, 1958), p. 47.
23. See Richard A. Butwell, *U Nu of Burma* [Stanford: Stanford University Press, 1963], pp. 128–31; and Walinsky, *Economic Development*, pp. 469–72).

24. *BWB*, 9 December 1953, p. 283. The Resolution of the Fourth Meeting of the ESB, released together with the speech, recommended tariff protection, tax relief, and similar measures to facilitate the operation of industries (ibid., p. 285).
25. See Walinsky, *Economic Development*, pp. 148, 157–62.
26. *BWB*, 23 June 1955, pp. 86, 88.
27. Ibid., p. 86. It did not elicit favourable responses. In the absence of unequivocal procedural guidelines and proper legislation the investment climate remained unattractive.
28. "Speech to the Far East American Council of Commerce and Industry", in U Nu, *Asian Speaks* (Washington, D.C.: Embassy of the Union of Burma, July 1955), pp. 26–27.
29. For details, see Walinsky, *Economic Development*, pp. 163–216; and pp. 451–60 for the general problems of managing SIEs.
30. It has been suggested that a "developmental state" would succeed if it could "govern" rather than replace the market. See, e.g., Robert Wade, *Governing the Market: Economic Theory and the Role of the Government in East Asian Industrialization* (Princeton: Princeton University Press, 1990), Chapter 10.
31. U Nu, *Premier Reports to the People on Law and Order, National Solidarity, Social Welfare, National Economy, Foreign Affairs* (Rangoon: Central Printing Office, 1958), pp. 24–25. For recommendations by the Economic Committee on cutbacks in state-sponsored industrial and mineral development, see ibid., Appendix 3(a), pp. 97–98, 105; for favourable views on private participation and foreign investments, see pp. 99, 101, 106.
32. Nu's disenchantment with state intervention together with the budget squeeze shattered Kyaw Nyein's vision of state-led ISI in 1956 (Walinsky, *Economic Development*, p. 211, n. 30; p. 227). The latter lamented about the lack of cohesion and co-ordination among the AFPFL's leaders in the industrialization effort. He also accused the KTA consultants of opposing industrial development (Thein Pe Myint, *Kyaw Nyein*, with an introduction by U Kyaw Nyein [in Myanmar] [Yangon: Shwe Pyi Dan, 1961], pp. 189–92).
33. For details, see Thet Tun, "Organization", pp. 30–31.
34. *BWB*, 16 August 1958, p. 4. Thus far, all the industrial policies were concerned with generalizations, in what may be classified as a "non-selective" or "horizontal" policy framework (F. Gerard Adams and C. Andrea Bollino, "Meaning of Industrial Policy", in *Industrial Policies for Growth and Competitiveness*, edited by F. Gerard Adams and C. Andrea Bollino [Lexington, MA: D. C. Heath & Co., 1983], p. 15).
35. *BWB*, 24 September 1959, p. 196; see also p. 192.
36. See Nu's speech to the Chamber of Deputies on 5 April 1960 (*BWB*, 7 April 1960, p. 460).

37. For details, see the speech given by the Minister for Industry, Mines and Labour in Parliament on 25 August 1961 (*BWB*, 5 October 1961, p. 182).
38. For details, see Walinsky, *Economic Development*, pp. 371–562, 585–91. However, it may be argued that the implementation of policy goals are influenced by the content of policy itself as well as the social, political and institutional environments. Therefore, the divergence of outcomes from policy goals cannot be attributed solely to the problems associated with the implementation process. See, for example, Merilee S. Grindle, "Policy Content and Context in Implementation", in *Politics and Policy Implementation in the Third World*, edited by Merilee S. Grindle (Princeton: Princeton University Press, 1980), pp. 3–34.
39. Thet Tun, "A Critique of Louis J. Walinsky's Economic Development of Burma, 1951-1960", *JBRS* XLVII, no. i (1964): 176 and 174–81.
40. Ibid., p. 179.
41. Thet Tun, "Organization", p. 34. For a critique of foreign experts, see Hugh Tinker, *Union of Burma: A Study of the First Years of Independence*, 4th ed. (London: Oxford University Press for the Royal Institute of International Affairs, 1967), pp. 124–25.
42. International Bank for Reconstruction and Development (IBRD), "The Economy of Burma", mimeographed (Washington, D.C., November 1953), cited in Anjali Ghosh, *Burma: A Case of Aborted Development* (Calcutta: Papyrus, 1989), p. 49. The Report observed that the viability of many projects depended on "assumed relationships among projects that may or may not materialize" (ibid.).
43. See, for example, Mya Maung, "The Genesis of Economic Development in Burma: The Plural Society" (Ph.D. dissertation, Catholic University of America, Washington, 1961), pp. 245–49, 251–57, 264–75; and Walinsky, *Economic Development*, pp. 420–30, 448–60, 507–12, 544–45, 598–600.
44. The Statement at the first news conference of the newly installed Prime Minister Ba Swe on 3 July 1956 (*Burma* VI [July 1956], p. 54).
45. K. S. Mali, *Fiscal Aspects of Development Planning in Burma, 1950–1960* (Rangoon: Department of Economics, University of Rangoon, 1962,), p. 83; also, Frank N. Trager, *Toward a Welfare State in Burma* (New York: Institute of Pacific Relations, 1954), pp. 54–59, for a remarkably prescient delineation of the obstacles to the planned programme.
46. See *Pyidawtha Conference*, p. 21.
47. Cited in Thet Tun, "Review", p. 504. E. F. Schumacher was U.N. adviser to the government in early 1955.
48. The planned large-scale hydroelectric schemes, except for the Baluchaung project, were not implemented.
49. See Walinsky, *Economic Development*, Tables 31, and 32, pp. 270–71; and pp. 286–88. Agriculture development belonged to a separate five-year programme.

50. See ibid., pp. 300–302. The total cost for nine manufacturing enterprises was nearly two-thirds of the total sectoral outlay (ibid., Table 37, p. 302).
51. For physical output targets, see *Pyidawtha Conference*, p. 28. For production and investment targets, see Thet Tun, "Review", Table 9, p. 497.
52. Only around 83 per cent of the target for sown acreage was realized (ibid.). Major constraints included lack of working capital, draft cattle, and labour (U Khin Win, *A Century of Rice Improvement in Burma* [Manila: International Rice Research Institute, 1991], p. 47) as well as the incentive-depressing effects of land nationalization and state marketing (Maung Myint, "Agriculture", pp. 201–202, 207). Moreover, the average fertilizer application rate of around 1.4 pound per acre in 1959/60 was less than one-twentieth of the corresponding figure in the late 1970s, when the paddy yield increased significantly (Khin Win, *Century of Rice Improvement*", p. 60).
53. See Thet Tun, "Review", Table 7, p. 490; and Table 10, p. 498. See also *Economic Survey of Burma 1962*, Table 11, p. 21. Apart from poor security conditions, extractive methods were outmoded and inadequate (*Economic Survey of Burma 1957*, p. 75).
54. Due to wartime destruction and poor security conditions, minerals and power production were considerably depressed during the first half of the 1950s.
55. See *Report to the People by the Union of Burma Revolutionary Council on the Revolutionary Government's Budget Estimates, 1964/65* (hereafter *Report to the People*) (Rangoon: Ministry of Finance, 1965), Table I, p. 2. For critiques on the relative neglect of agriculture, see, for example, Mya Maung, "Genesis of Economic Development", pp. 251–53.
56. See, for example, "Sources of Capital Formation: Note", in Gerald M. Meier, *Leading Issues in Economic Development*, 5th ed. (New York: Oxford University Press, 1989), pp. 178–86; and Paul Rosenstein-Rodan, "International Aid for Underdeveloped Countries", *Review of Economics and Statistics* XLIII, no. 2 (1961): 107–38. Foreign equity capital associated with an outward-orientation in industry and trade played a significant role in the success of newly-industrializing countries (Stephan Haggard and Tun-jen Cheng, "State and Foreign Capital in the East Asian NICs", in *The Political Economy of the New Asian Industrialism*, edited by Frederic C. Deyo [Ithaca: Cornell University Press, 1987], pp. 84–135).
57. Thet Tun, "Review", Table 13, p. 501.
58. For example, a senior Budget official reportedly stated, in July 1960, that "foreign credits are undesirable. We have plenty to sell without having to get credit" (Institute of Asian Economic Affairs [Tokyo], *Economic Development in Burma*, translated by U.S. Joint Publications Research Service [JPRS] [Washington, D.C.: JPRS, 1962; New York: CCM Information Corporation, n.d.], p. 625).
59. See, for example, Thakin Nu, "Foreign Capital in Burma", in *Burma's Freedom*, pp. 70–73; and *Asian Speaks*, p. 28.

60. *Pyidawtha Conference*, p. 39. Theoretically, "private investment could be positively correlated to government investment" through external economies and demand creation (U Tun Wai and Chorng-huey Wong, "Determinants of Private Investment in Developing Countries", *Journal of Development Studies* 19, no. 1 [1982]: 20).
61. Thet Tun, "Review", Table 14, p. 502. However, because of price increases in construction materials and the higher costs of Japanese reparation goods that formed a substantial portion of capital goods imports, the actual figures must be "deflated quite significantly to bear comparison with targeted figures" (ibid.). Furthermore, a large portion of the private capital formation was absorbed by residential construction (ibid., p. 506).
62. Ibid., Table 9, p. 497. The rice price "which was assumed not to fall below" 50 sterling pounds per ton dropped to 42 pounds in 1955 and 35 pounds in 1956–57, following a downward trend after peaking in 1953 (Mali, *Fiscal Aspects*, p. 84). The total of rice export earnings from 1952/53 to 1959/60 was only half of the planned earnings of 12.5 billion kyat (Thet Tun, "Review", Table 11, p. 499).
63. See, for example, ibid., pp. 500, 506. The foreign exchange shortage was exacerbated by the higher-than-planned import content of expenditures in the state sector (ibid., p. 506). Foreign exchange reserves "fell continuously" by over 50 per cent between June 1953 and February 1955 (U Tun Wai, "Burma", in *Asian Economic Development*, edited by Cranley Onslow [New York: Praeger, 1965; reprint, 1967], p. 9).
64. See Maung Maung Hla, "Some Aspects of Central Banking in Burma", in *Burma Research Society Fiftieth Anniversary Publication*, vol. 1 (January 1960), p. 151. For details on capital formation, see Mali, *Fiscal Aspects*, pp. 47–54.
65. Taxes on imports, which averaged two-thirds of the total tax revenues in the three years prior to 1953/54, fell to 42.7 per cent in that year and remained below 47 per cent throughout the decade. In absolute terms, its rising trend since independence peaked in 1953/54 and thereafter remained stagnant (ibid., Table 12, pp. 93–95).
66. For taxes and revenues, see Soe Myint, "Financing the Deficit since Independence", *JBRS* XLIV, no. ii (1961): 188, 190. For data on savings, see Institute of Asian Economic Affairs (Tokyo), *Economic Development in Burma*, pp. 118–21.
67. Defence spending averaged 30 per cent of the government's total expenditure between 1952/53 and 1960/61 (Mali, *Fiscal Aspects*, Table 11, p. 87). For details, see Thet Tun, "Review", Table 27, p. 519.
68. See ibid., Table 21, p. 508.
69. Institute of Asian Economic Affairs (Tokyo), *Economic Development in Burma*, p. 595; see, also, pp. 422–31, 595–602. According to one analyst, the UBB was not in a position to exercise "effective policy measures to satisfactorily carry out" the task of "deficit financing for the Government and yet avoid

inflation" (ibid., p. 428). The government-sponsored Industrial Development Bank, which opened in October 1961, had very little opportunity to finance investments before becoming redundant under socialist policies (see U Tu Maung, *Myanma Bun Lokengan Thamaing* [History of Myanmar's Banking] [Yangon: Sabei Oo Sarpay, 1983], pp. 180–83).

70. See Maung Maung Hla, "Some Aspects of Central Banking", pp. 150–53.
71. Arguments for and against this approach, may be found in, Nicholas Stern, "The Economics of Development", *Economic Journal* 99, no. 397 (1989): 630–33.
72. However, many licensees resold their allotments to non-Myanmar traders for a quick profit. See M. Ruth Pfanner, "Burma", in *Underdevelopment and Economic Nationalism in Southeast Asia*, edited by Frank H. Golay et al. (Ithaca: Cornell University Press, 1969), pp. 245, 246.
73. See ibid.
74. See, e.g., Walinsky, *Economic Development*, pp. 498–99; and the Industry Minister's reply to the Chairman's address at the Annual General Meeting (AGM) of the Burma Chamber of Commerce (BCC), on 25 February 1954 (*Burma Chamber of Commerce Annual Reports 1953–1954* [Rangoon: 1954], p. 59).
75. See Mali, *Fiscal Aspects*, p. 97.
76. Tariffs comprised more than 50 per cent of total tax revenues in 1951/52 and 1952/53. The ratio for the rest of the decade remained stable in the 36–40 per cent range (See *Union Bank of Burma Bulletin* [First Quarter, 1962], Table 23, p. 55).
77. See, for example, Nu's speech at the AGM of the BCC, on 26 February 1951, promising trade decontrol while advocating preferential treatment to "nationals" (*Burma Chamber of Commerce Annual Reports 1950–51*, p. 48). For details on the OGL scheme, see *Business Directory and National Trade Register* vol. V (1960–61) (Rangoon: Burma Publicity Services, 1961), pp. 318–21.
78. Exchange controls were also imposed on OGL letters of credit in December 1957 (*Economic Survey of Burma 1958* [Rangoon: Government Printing and Stationery, 1958], p. 46). Under the military caretaker regime, exchange control for OGLs and some state monopolies over popular consumer goods were abolished, while the OGL list was drastically reduced in favour of liberal allocation of licences (*Pyiyei Ywahmu: Pyidaungsu Myanmar Naingandaw Asoeya Ei Hsaungywetchet Myar [1/11/58–6/2/60]* [Undertakings of the Government of the Union of Burma] [Yangon: Directorate of Information, (1960)], pp. 239–42).
79. One example was the development of rayon and nylon industry by textile manufacturers, who found that the differential tariff structure had made synthetics more profitable than cotton fabrics (Mali, *Fiscal Aspects*, p. 121, n. 2). Protected manufactures included cigarettes, alcoholic beverages,

biscuits, and confectionaries, soap, furniture, silk and synthetic fabrics, and cotton knitted apparel. For the 1953 schedule of sales tax and customs duty, see *Burma Trade Directory* 4 (1956): 709–25. Tariffs for most items were further increased in September 1957 (Notice No. 479, *Burma Gazette Extraordinary* [24 September 1957]).

80. See *BWB*, 28 April 1955, p. 20.
81. See the Chairman's speech at the AGM of BCC on 6 March 1959 (*Burma Chamber of Commerce Annual Reports 1958–1959*, p. 48).
82. Up to eleven JVCs with the government holding majority shares were established in the late 1950s (Institute of Asian Economic Affairs [Tokyo], *Economic Development in Burma*, pp. 538–39).
83. Despite the advent of JVCs, the widespread abuse of the preferential system by nationals continued. In fact, the military caretaker regime (*c.* 1958–59) deregistered 1,470 importing firms, out of a total of 3,131. Over 85 per cent of those penalized belonged to indigenous owners. (*Myanmar Naingan Sethmu Lokengan Thamaing Apaing 3: Pyanlehtudaungyei Khit Sethmu Lokengan Thamaing* [History of Myanmar's Industry, Part 3: Rehabilitation Era] [Yangon: Ministry of No. 1 Industry, n.d.], pp. 172–73). Nevertheless, the lucrative practice resumed after the return of civilian government, whereby "[e]ighty five per cent of those receiving import licenses sold them to foreigners" (quoted in Pfanner, "Burma", p. 249).
84. See, for example, David Greenaway and Chris Milner, "Trade Theory and the Less Developed Countries", in *Surveys in Development Economics*, edited by Norman Gemmel (Oxford: Basil Blackwell, 1987), pp. 32–47. For rent-seeking, see Anne O. Krueger, "The Political Economy of the Rent-Seeking Society", *American Economic Review* 64, no. 3 (1974): 291–303; and Stanislaw Wellisz and Ronald Findlay, "Protection and Rent-Seeking in Developing Countries", in *Neoclassical Political Economy: The Analysis of Rent-Seeking and DUP Activities*, edited by David C. Colander (Cambridge, MA: Ballinger, 1984), pp. 141–53. For a broader perspective, see Jagdish N. Bhagwati, "Directly Unproductive, Profit-Seeking (DUP) Activities", *Journal of Political Economy* 90, no. 5 (1982): 988–1002.
85. See Walinsky, *Economic Development*, pp. 498–501. However, the limited availability of exchange goods, high transaction costs, and lack of co-ordination limited the scope of barter trade. The total barter sales from 1954/55 to 1959/60 as percentage of total rice exports were only 13.9 per cent in volume and 14.3 per cent in value terms (derived from ibid., Table 18, p. 169, and Table 19, p. 170).
86. The value of import incentive awarded was to be one-quarter of the corresponding export value. See *Pyiyei Ywahmu*, pp. 229–31.
87. For data on non-rice agriculture exports, see *Economic Survey of Burma 1963*, p. 65.
88. See *Report to the People 1971–72*, Appendix 75, p. 360.

89. See Sang Khup, "Diversification of Economy with Special Reference to Burma" (Diploma paper for the Advanced Course in National Economic Planning, Central School of Planning and Statistics, Warsaw, 1963), p. 58; and ECAFE, *Statistical Yearbook for Asia and the Far East 1971* (Bangkok: ECAFE, n.d.), Table 33, p. 66.
90. See Kyaw Myint, "Industrialization in Burma" (Master thesis, University of Sydney, 1978), Table 9.5, p. 255.
91. Cf., Korea's experience summarized in Nam Chong-Hyun, "Trade Policy and Industrial Development in Korea", in *Strategies for Industrial Development: Concepts and Policy Issues*, edited by Suk Jang-Won (Kuala Lampur: Asian and Pacific Development Centre, 1989), pp. 60–79.
92. The cumulative net flow of foreign assistance between 1955/56 and 1960/61 was over 1 billion kyat. See, for example, Soe Myint, "Financing the Deficit", Table 1, pp. 194–95; and also Tun Wai, "Burma", Table 5, p. 21. The contribution of foreign aid to capital expenditures in 1957/58 was estimated at 46 per cent, whereas the percentages for 1958/59 and 1959/60 were believed to be 74 and 82 per cent respectively (John D. Montgomery, *The Politics of Foreign Aid: American Experience in Southeast Asia* [New York: Praeger, 1962], p. 31).
93. Thakin Nu, *Towards Peace and Democracy* (Rangoon: Ministry of Information, 1949), p. 133.
94. Nu, "Foreign Capital", p. 72.
95. John H. Badgley, "Survey of Burma's Foreign Economic Relations, 1948-58", mimeographed (The Rangoon-Hopkins Center for Southeast Asian Studies, Rangoon, 1959), p. 26. Administrative responsibility was transferred in July 1952 to the U.S. State Department's Technical Cooperation Administration.
96. See ibid., pp. 26–28.
97. Frank N. Trager, *Burma: from Kingdom to Republic; A Historical and Political Analysis* (London: Pall Mall, 1966), p. 316.
98. See, for example, Kyaw Nyein's remark, "we had to fight bandits armed by the same people who gave us the money" and "no self-respecting people can put up with this insidious business" (Tibor Mende, *South-East Asia between Two Worlds* [New York: Library Publishers, 1955], pp. 178–79). The American consultants engaged under the ECA programme were retained with government funding. About US$21 million out of US$31.4 million were disbursed (Trager, *From Kingdom to Republic*, p. 31).
99. See Badgley, "Survey", pp. 32–33.
100. Ibid., p. 34. The Chinese also provided grant aid for the extension of the Thamaing spinning and weaving mill in mid-1956.
101. For details, see Walinsky, *Economic Development*, pp. 508–12, 516–27.
102. See ibid., pp. 519–21.
103. General Ne Win's regime (*c.* 1959) was reluctant to incur further debt and was not satisfied with the conditions imposed by the donor. Some projects

were cancelled, while others were curtailed (see, ibid., pp. 527–31; Table 85, p. 531). For a listing of the U.S. aid up to 1961, see Montgomery, *Politics of Foreign Aid*, Appendix I-A, Table 1, p. 281 and Appendix I-C, Table 1, p. 291.

104. See *Burma* X, no. 2 (1961): 20–21. This aid included infrastructure and industrial projects as well as the provision of experts and technicians.
105. See *BWB*, 17 November 1954. The agreement was provided in accordance with the peace treaty between Myanmar and Japan. It came into force in April 1955.
106. For data, see David I. Steinberg, "Japanese Economic Assistance to Burma: Aid in the 'Tarenagashi' Manner?", *Crossroads* 5, no. 2 (1990), Table 5, p. 92. Japanese reparations accounted for nearly 38 per cent of the cumulative aid disbursed up to September 1960 (Walinsky, *Economic Development*, Table 83, p. 511). Grant aid for the Baluchaung project was about US$24 million (*Pyanlehtudaungyei Khit Sethmu*, p. 287).
107. Sceptics pointed out that the amount was disproportionately small in relation to the immense human and material suffering inflicted. Admitting Japanese capitalists into Myanmar through the joint-venture loan, was also condemned. See, for example, U Ba Nyein, *Gyapun Sit Yawkyei* [Japanese War Reparations] (Yangon: Ahthit Sarpay, 1962), pp. 5–32. For Nu's explanation, see "PM on Japanese War Reparations", *BWB*, 27 October 1954, pp. 226–27. Interestingly, one Japanese analyst pointed out that one of the reasons behind the reparations scheme was to "act as pump-priming to expand future [Japanese] commercial exports". (Institute of Asian Economic Affairs [Tokyo], *Economic Development in Burma*, p. 563).
108. See Walinsky, *Economic Development*, pp. 513–14; and Ba Nyein, *Gyapun Sit Yawkyei*, p. 41.
109. See Walinsky, *Economic Development*, p. 515. Perceptions of political instability might have been the decisive factor in the aftermath of the (1958) split in the ruling party.
110. See, for example, Montgomery, *Politics of Foreign Aid*, pp. 31–35, 52–53, 136–38, 165–66.
111. Current finance encompasses current budgetary surplus and monetary expansion. Non-current finance means drawing of foreign exchange reserves, reparations, and net foreign borrowing (see Mali, *Fiscal Aspects*, pp. 47–48, 53–54).
112. See, for example, Maung Maung Hla, "Some Aspects of Central Banking", p. 151; and Soe Myint, "Financing the Deficit", p. 192.
113. Annualized interest rates in the curb market ranged from 24 to 36 per cent with collateral and up to 60 to 120 per cent for unsecured short-term loans (personal communications with entrepreneurs; and *Second Four-Year Plan for the Union of Burma [1961–62 to 1964–65]* [Rangoon: Government Printing and Stationery, 1961], p. 76). In 1955, a hire-purchase scheme for capital equipment was introduced by the government but there were restrictions

on suppliers (only barter-exchange countries and Japan) and the amount available (for example, 15 million kyat for 1955/56) was relatively small in comparison to sectoral requirements (see, for example, Khin Than Kywe, "Financing the Small Manufacturing Establishments of Burma", *Burma Research Society Fiftieth Anniversary Publication*, vol. 1 [960], pp. 125–42).

114. See Thet Tun, "Survey", Table 14, p. 502. A substantial portion of private investment was expended in urban residential construction (ibid., p. 506).
115. More than 96 per cent went to cultivators, of which the majority was probably for working capital. See *Union Bank of Burma Bulletin* (First Quarter, 1962), Table 24, p. 56.
116. Advances for trade and commerce accounted for over three-quarters of the total credit (ibid., Table 14, p. 42). As for manufacturing, virtually all the loans went to rice millers for working capital (see, for example, Institute of Asian Economic Affairs [Tokyo], *Economic Development in Burma*, p. 621).
117. External resources might have been more forthcoming if the state had instituted clearly defined procedures and regulations to back up its assurances to promote private investments (see Robert Wade, "The Role of Government in Overcoming Market Failure: Taiwan, Republic of Korea and Japan", in *Achieving Industrialization in East Asia*, edited by Helen Hughes [Cambridge: Cambridge University Press, 1988], pp. 131–39).
118. Jung-en Woo, *Race to the Swift: State and Finance in Korean Industrialization* (New York: Columbia University Press, 1991), p. 12; see, also, pp. 7–14.
119. For the colonial-era labour movement, see *Alokethamar Asiayone Thamaing* [History of the Worker's Union], vol. 1 (Yangon: Burma Socialist Programme Party, 1982; reprint, 1984), pp. 48–413.
120. Maung Maung, *Constitution*, p. 262. For specific provisions see section 33, p. 262–63; section 15, p. 259; and section 37, p. 263.
121. For labour laws, see *Alokethamar Asiayone Thamaing*, vol. 2 (Yangon: Burma Socialist Programme Party, 1983), p. 121–22. The labour directorate, formed in 1927, was expanded and placed under the newly formed Ministry of Housing and Labour (see U Myo Htun Lynn, *Labour and Labour Movement in Burma* [Rangoon: Department of Economics, University of Rangoon, 1961], pp. 84–88).
122. For details, see ibid., pp. 74–77.
123. See *Two-Year Plan*, p. 39.
124. See, for example, the list in Myo Htun Lynn, *Labour and Labour Movement*, p. 76; and pp. 78–60.
125. After strikes by workers and civil servants, the government added a cost of living allowance to the basic pay of civil servants in October 1946. It was followed by the establishment of a minimum basic monthly salary of 35 rupees (later replaced by kyat). However, casual workers and private sector employees were excluded. The (average) Consumer Price Index

(CPI) for Yangon which was 30 in 1941 rose to 120.9 in 1949. Thereafter, it followed a downward trend to 88.3 in 1954. In the next three years it climbed up to 103.9 and fluctuated around 100 up to the end of the decade (*Economic Survey of Burma 1962*, Table 49, p. 81; and *Union Bank of Burma Bulletin* [First Quarter, 1962], Table 27, p. 63).

126. See, for example, Myo Htun Lynn, *Labour and Labour Movement*, pp. 126–28. The basic salaries in the civil service were substantially raised in April 1948. Average wages in the private manufacturing sector, during the early 1950s, were roughly on par with state sector salaries. It was reported that the salary of a typical low-income head of household could barely meet food expenses and the latter was worse of than his pre-war counterpart (ibid., pp. 123–25, 130–33).
127. Apparently, the average monthly income of regular workers in 1958 was inadequate to support a Yangon household of 3–4 persons (see *Second Four-Year Plan*, p. 72). In fact, the wage level was the same as that in 1951–52. On the other hand, the (annualized) gold price, which roughly reflects the money value, increased by over 50 per cent between 1952 and 1958 (*Union Bank of Burma Bulletin* [Fourth Quarter, 1958], Table 32, p. 68).
128. *Second Four-Year Plan*, p. 73.
129. See, for example, *Burma Labour Gazette*, October 1958, p. 1.
130. Myo Htun Lynn, *Labour and Labour Movement*, p. 86.
131. "Labour Administration in Burma", *Burma: The Fourth Anniversary* II, no. 2 (1952), pp. 49–50. For an explanation of the statutory machinery for settling disputes, see Myo Htun Lynn, *Labour and Labour Movement*, pp. 81–82.
132. "The Union of Burma: A Group Study", Joint International Business Venture, Country Study no. 4, mimeographed (Columbia University, New York, 1959), p. 45.
133. For details on industrial disputes, see ibid., p. 46; and also, *Second Four Year Plan*, Table 58, p. 71.
134. *Economic Survey of Burma 1963*, p. 62. For a listing of trades in which there was a manpower shortage (*c.* 1962), see ibid., p. 61. For details on TWI, see *Burma: The Fourteenth Anniversary*, p. 154.
135. Industrial establishments with ten or more workers were stipulated to register under the social security scheme. For details, see International Labour Office, "Report to the Government of the Union of Burma on the Further Development of Social Security", mimeographed (International Labour Office, Geneva, 1964), ILO/TAP/Burma/R.28, pp. 16–22. The definition for industrial establishment was taken as those "connected with extraction, transformation, or manufacturing in any form whether using power or not but excluding building construction" (*Burma: The Eleventh Anniversary* [January 1959], p. 345).
136. See *Statistical Yearbook 1961*, Table 41, p. 87; and International Labour Office, "Report to the Government of the Union of Burma", p. 16.

137. See ibid., pp. 32, 34.
138. International Labour Office, "Report to the Government of the Union of Burma", p. 87.
139. Tinker, *Union of Burma*, p. 310. First organized in 1921, the trade union movement assumed a national character when the All Burma Trade Union Congress (ABTUC) was formed on 31 January 1939 (*Alokethamar Asiayone Thamaing*, vol. 1, p. 382).
140. As at October 1948, there were 77 registered unions with a total membership of 35,170. The corresponding figures for March 1942 were 51 and 40,292 respectively. BTUC's affiliated strength was only about one-tenth of TUC(B) (Myo Htun Lynn, *Labour and Labour Movement in Burma*, p. 28). When, in December 1950, TUC(B)'s core leadership left BSP to form the Burma Workers and Peasants Party (BWPP), the latter formed the minority Burma Trade Union Congress (BTUC).
141. *Burma* III, no. 4 (1953), p. 8.
142. See International Labour Office, *The Trade Union Situation in Burma* (Geneva: International Labour Office, 1962), pp. 43–44. On 31 October 1961, there were 173 registered unions with a total membership of 64,521 (ibid., p. 37).
143. The number of workers belonging to small unregistered unions might be larger. For example, while there were only about 40,000 registered union members in 1952, a BTUC survey reported an overall strength of 73,000. Similarly, estimates for 1961 put national membership at around 200,000 or three times the registered figure (ibid., pp. 36–37; and Myo Htun Lynn, *Labour and Labour Movement in Burma*, pp. 26, 30).
144. International Labour Office, *Trade Union Situation*, pp. 36–37, 70.
145. Ibid., p. 41.
146. International Labour Office, *Trade Union Situation*, p. 72; and for accounts of the unions' role in industrial relations, see pp. 50–66.
147. M. M. Mehta, *Report on the Manpower Situation in Burma* (Geneva: International Labour Office, 1964), p. 56.
148. See Kyaw Myint, "Industrialization in Burma", Table 5.5, p. 122.
149. There were seasonal fluctuations, especially in the agro-industries (R. M. Sundrum, "Census Data on the Labour Force and the Income Distribution in Burma, 1953–54", mimeographed, [Rangoon, n.d.], pp. 23–24). For details, see Walinsky, *Economic Development*, Table 50, p. 344; Mehta, *Report on the Manpower Situation*, Table 4.1, p. 100; and *Economic Survey of Burma 1963*, Table 35, p. 55.
150. See ibid., Table 36, p. 55.
151. See Myo Htun Lynn, *Labour and Labour Movement*, pp. 115–17; and *Burma: The Fourteenth Anniversary* (January 1962), p. 153.
152. See *Economic Survey of Burma 1963*, pp. 54–55.
153. The annual allotment was 1 million kyat since 1952. The divisional civil authorities were empowered to grant loans with an upper limit of 4,000 kyat,

while the DI supervised the regional allocation of block disbursements. It required security and had to be repaid within sixteen months. The cumulative repayment ratio was around 55 per cent for 1948/49–1959/60 period (Khin Than Kywe, "Financing the Small Manufacturing Establishments", p. 138; and *Sethmu Lethmu Hnyunkyaryeiwun Htarna Ei 1959-60 Bandardaw Hnit Atwet Hnitpatlei Asiyinkhanzar* [Annual Report of the Directorate of Industries for Fiscal Year 1959–60] [Yangon: Government Printing and Stationery, 1963], p. 37).

154. The maximum amount, with security, was only 150 kyat per applicant repayable in twelve monthly instalments within sixteen months. The cumulative repayment ratio for the period 1945/46–1959/60 was around 49 per cent (Khin Than Kywe, "Financing the Small Manufacturing Establishments", p. 137).
155. In 1959/60, 75.4 million kyat in licences (1429 applicants) and 15.9 million kyat in machinery imports (462 applicants) were awarded (*Hnyunkyaryeiwun Htarna*, pp. 69–70).
156. Price controls for seventeen items were introduced in 1959/60. Profit margins for producers and retailers were set at 10 per cent and that for the wholesalers was 5 per cent (ibid., pp. 44–45).
157. Usually on a case by case basis. For measures taken in 1959/60, see ibid., pp. 18, 26.
158. During 1959–61 entry restrictions were imposed on industries producing cigarettes; biscuits; cotton vests; aluminium ware; cosmetics; soap; Japanese-style rubber slippers; plastics; felt hats; umbrella; matches; zinc-coated buckets; coir and rope (*Pyanlehtudaungyei Khit Sethmu*, pp. 127–57). It was mainly enforced through controls in registration, machinery imports, and raw materials.
159. The board of directors included four ministers (ibid., pp. 176–80).
160. The cash loan was for a minimum of 4,000 kyat and were long-term loans (up to twelve years; twenty years for special cases). The total amount sanctioned by the end of 1958 was about 5.4 million kyat. The corresponding amount sanctioned for the hire-purchase loans was 18.7 million kyat (see Institute of Asian Economic Affairs [Tokyo], *Economic Development in Burma*, p. 296).
161. See *Pyanlehtudaungyei Khit Sethmu*, pp. 225–42; and pp. 266–68.
162. The losing concerns comprised five out of six establishments developed by the IDC. Three uneconomic pilot plants folded and another was never built, while the tea factory was closed down by the caretaker government. However, the two nationalized factories turned out to be more profitable. See ibid., pp. 181–202, 228, 242.
163. The state had one-quarter share in the factory which began operations in 1960 (ibid., pp. 243–45).
164. For specific examples see ibid., pp. 186–88, 251–63; and Walinsky, *Economic Development*, pp. 305–307, 312–14. These complaints are common

to all public enterprises, see, for example, C. E. W. Daniel, "Some Aspects of Organization and Administration of State Enterprises: The Burmese Experience as Compared with that of the United Kingdom, Saskatchewan and Chile", seminar paper, mimeographed (Harvard University Graduate School of Public Administration, Cambridge, Massachusetts, April 1959).

165. See Walinsky, *Economic Development*, pp. 460–64.
166. Between 1953 and 1957, the number of enterprises grew by 49 per cent, employment by 42 per cent, and output value by 144 per cent (ibid., Table 54, p. 348). In the 1957/58–1959/60 period, the total output of private industries increased by 10.5 per cent while the value-added for rice milling increased by 26 per cent (*Report to the People 1963–64*, p. 132).
167. Quoted in Daniel, "Some Aspects of Organization", p. 57.
168. Kyaw Myint, "Industrialization in Burma", Table 5.7, p. 130.
169. 1953/54 data are from Khin Than Kywe, "Financing the Small Manufacturing Establishments", p. 114; for 1961/62 data, see *Statistical Yearbook 1967* (Rangoon: Central Statistics and Economics Department, n.d.), Table 93, p. 239.
170. For this group, both the number of factories and employment fell in absolute as well as percentage terms. Though its total value-added output increased by nearly 99 per cent, its share dropped from 5 per cent to 3 per cent (Kyaw Myint, "Industrialization in Burma", Table 5.7, p. 130).
171. Data derived from ibid., Table 3.4, p. 58; and *Statistical Yearbook 1967*, Table 91, p. 237.
172. For specific examples, see ibid., pp. 30–31. The annual Census of Manufactures for 1960/61 revealed that the average unutilized capacities for selected processing and light manufacturing industries ranged from over 35 per cent to 75 per cent (see ibid., p. 29). These figures are roughly comparable to the average non-weighted unutilized capacity (*c.* 1972) for Malaysia and Philippines (Romeo M. Bautista et al., *Capital Utilization in Manufacturing: Colombia, Israel, Malaysia, and the Philippines* [New York: Oxford University Press, 1981], Table 1–2, p. 7). For common causes of low capacity utilization in developing countries, see ibid., p. 32.
173. Derived from *Statistical Yearbook 1967*, Table 91, p. 237.
174. Nu's speech of 4 August 1952, at the opening of the Pyidawtha Conference (U Nu, *Burma Looks Ahead* [Rangoon: Ministry of Information, 1953], p. 89).
175. These equity ratios were in contravention to the Constitutional stipulations that required a minimum 60 per cent equity and the Government had to pass the Union Mineral Resources (Enabling Act) in 1949 to facilitate the incorporation of joint ventures (*Burma; A Group Study*, pp. 62–63). The state's share in BOC was raised to 51 per cent in late 1960 (*BWB*, 3 November 1960, p. 261).

176. Although the Government's representatives were on the management boards, key investment decisions and operations were usually under the control of foreign partners. Government–foreign firm relations in the long drawn out negotiation processes leading to their incorporation were often quite traumatic, replete with political posturing and bargaining by both sides. For example, in the case of BOC, the British Government was involved through its financial guarantee to the company. Moreover, the issue of valuation was also contentious and the large-scale labour retrenchments arising during the negotiations were also exploited by the parties concerned (T. A. B. Corley, *A History of the Burmah Oil Company, Vol. II: 1924–66* (London: Heinemann, 1988), pp. 171–204; for a different perspective, see *Pyanlehtudaungyei Khit Sethmu*, pp. 335–36).
177. See ibid., pp. 306–14. Compared to the Pyidawtha target of 400,000 tons per year in 1959/60, the actual annual coal production was less than 10,000 tons.
178. The world prices drastically fell in 1956/57, causing the closure of small and uneconomic mines and production cutbacks. The price depression persisted into the decade's end (ibid., pp. 316–17).
179. See Walinsky, *Economic Development*, Table 48, p. 341; and *Economic Survey of Burma 1963*, Table 18, p. 24. Refined silver production achieved only 23 per cent of the 1939 volume (Walinsky, *Economic Development*, Table 48, p. 341; and *Report to the People 1971–72*, Table 64, p. 61).
180. See *Economic Survey of Burma 1963*, Table 19, p. 27.
181. The Myanmar were also unhappy with the continuation of the lucrative trading of petroleum products by the foreign partner. The delays and the improvization (usage of cannibalized parts) involved in the construction of the Syriam Refinery were also seen by the Myanmar as duplicity on the part of the foreign partners (Corley, *History of the Burmah Oil Company*, pp. 198, 204–208).
182. The output in 1961 was 3.51 million barrels (ibid., Table 5, p. 210; pp. 396–97 for production data; and Walinsky, *Economic Development*, Table 46, p. 341 for the 1939 figure).
183. Data for 1961/62 are from *Selected Monthly Economic Indicators* (December 1965). These data did not include power generated by the mining and manufacturing establishments for internal use.
184. For a list of state factories established between 1948 and 1962, see U Ba Chit, "Myanmar Naingan Pyithu Paing Ganda Hma Sethmu Lokengan Myar Tihsaukhmu Atwe Akyon Hnint Twaykhaw Mhyawmyinhmu Myar", [Experiences in and Ideas on the Development of State-Sector Industries in Myanmar], in *Presidential Addresses 1972: Burma Research Congress* (Yangon: Research Policy Direction Board, 1972), Chart 3, pp. 103–5.
185. Kyaw Myint, "Industrialization in Burma", p. 181a; and p. 181c.
186. Maung Maung, *Constitution*, p. 107.

Part III

Direct Military Rule (1962–74)

5

Revolutionary Change

Myanmar under the Revolutionary Council (RC) that came to power through a *coup d'etat* on 2 March 1962 underwent a political and economic transformation.[1] The parliamentary regime was replaced by a military junta, which abolished the Constitution and ruled by decree, removing all vestiges of the *ancien regime*. The populace was completely depoliticized and socialist revolution became the vanguard of state ideology. The mixed economy comprising a nascent private sector and a shrinking state sector was replaced by a state-controlled autarkic economy that stressed self-reliance and equity.

RESTRUCTURING STATE AND SOCIETY

Both the RC, which was the supreme authority, and the Revolutionary Government (RG) of senior military officers were chaired by General Ne Win, the idiosyncratic chief of the armed forces.[2] The RG instituted a hierarchy of Security and Administrative Committees (SACs) to replace the civil service.[3] The SACs' principal function seems "to have been to check on local initiatives and to ensure that central directives were followed".[4]

The RC announced its ideology known as the *Myanma Hsoshelit Lanzin* or the Burmese Way to Socialism (BWS), on 30 April 1962.[5] The BWS, inspired by the socialist tradition of pre-independence nationalists, denounced bureaucracy, repudiated parliamentary democracy, and promised to develop a non-exploitative planned socialist economy as well as a socialist democracy appropriate to Myanmar conditions.[6] Subsequently, the RC formed a cadre party called the *Myanma Hsoshelit Lanzin Parti* (Burma Socialist Programme Party, or BSPP) in July. This was followed by the publication of the BSPP's world-view in January 1963. Entitled "The System of Correlation of Man and His Environment" (SCME), it was an eclectic mixture of Buddhism and Marxism couched in general terms susceptible to a variety of interpretations.[7]

The underlying concept in the RC's attempt to restructure state and society seems to be the idea of "*taw-hlan-yei*" (revolution) in a manner distinct from the previous "dominant notions of Burmese politics". The RC "sought to emphasize the idea of revolution itself as the key to the country's problems of unity, stability, and equity".[8] The aim was to establish "a stable centralized state in order to avoid the anarchy which would otherwise result, given the existence of interests antithetical to the revolution".[9] Moreover, the RC endorsed the idea that "the revolutionary state and its institutions, primarily the revolutionary party, must constantly guide" the ordinary citizen "in the correct direction".[10] Thus, the BSPP was formed as a "transitional political party to carry the leadership in Burma's future politics".[11] With the promulgation of the Law to Protect National Solidarity in March 1964, it became the sole legal political organization.

All institutions that could challenge the RC were dismantled or neutralized while potential dissidents and pressure groups were either co-opted or emasculated through socio-economic and administrative controls.[12] The BSPP proceeded rapidly to build up its party apparatus in anticipation of the forthcoming transformation into a mass-based party.[13] Apart from the ritualized symbolism of mass rallies and orchestrated show of support for the RC, politics was of an exclusionary nature whereby a small coterie of junta members made all the important decisions.[14]

The BSPP was transformed into a mass-based party during the First Congress of 1971. Changes in the Cabinet, public administration, and territorial reorganization were also instituted. The Secretariat system of central administration was replaced by one comprising deputy ministers and ministerial offices in March 1972. In April 1972, General Ne Win and twenty other senior military officers relinquished their military ranks as a prelude to constitutional governance.[15]

After a decade of consolidation, the military leaders initiated the process of transferring power to the BSPP. A national referendum on the

Constitution for a single-party socialist state was concluded with 90.2 per cent approval in December 1973. Elections for the *Pyithu Hlutttaw* and People's Councils at all levels were held from 27 January to 10 February 1974.[16] Direct military rule ended with the promulgation of the socialist constitution in March 1974.

To summarize, the RC's rule was characterized by unprecedented power and autonomy for the state which became synonymous with the ruling military junta. Ruling by decree, the RC was able to impose its authority over the polity and the economy, though, as will be shown in the following sections, the latter led to an unsatisfactory outcome.

FROM MIXED ECONOMY TO AUTARKY

The economic objective of the BWS was to establish a socialist economy that entailed "participation of all for the general well-being in works of common ownership, and planning towards self-sufficiency and contentment of all, sharing the benefits derived therefrom".[17] The aim was to solve the "problem of unemployment" and ensure the "security" of "livelihood for every individual" and the nationalization of "such vital means of production as agricultural and industrial production, distribution, transportation, communications, external trade, etc.".[18] Ultimately, benefits would "be distributed in accordance with the quantity and quality of labour expended".[19] However, the RC realized that under the prevailing conditions "egalitarianism" was "impossible" and that:

> Men are not equal physically and intellectually .... But [since] social justice demands that the gaps between incomes are reasonable, and correct measures will be taken to narrow these gaps as much as possible.[20]

Three productive structures were identified; socialist, small-scale private production, and capitalist.[21] Rapid expansion of the socialist structure was envisaged. Meanwhile, the remaining non-socialist structures would be restricted and regulated. Eventually, they were to be transformed into structures conforming to "socialist production relations".[22]

Major constraints were identified as backwardness in agriculture production, industries, handicrafts, trade, transport, and technology. It was believed that they could be overcome by state action. Self-reliance and economic independence were also stressed as essential elements of a socialist economic strategy.[23]

On the other hand, it was decided that formal planning, though implicit in the economic strategy, was to be deferred until such time as and when an appropriate planning infrastructure was established.[24]

The main thrust of the RC's economic policy was oriented towards establishing state control over the "commanding heights" of the national economy through nationalization and regulation of the private sector, while attempting to considerably expand state-owned enterprises (SOEs) in commerce and industry.

Towards State Control: The First Decade

Initially, the RC assumed a pragmatic policy stance reminiscent of the military caretaker period (1958–60). On 8 March 1962, in a meeting with industrialists and business groups, RC vice-chairman Brigadier Aung Gyi explained that socialism did not mean wholesale nationalization. He promised fair treatment to nationals and foreigners alike, revision of the investment law, and no discrimination over the source of investment capital. He envisaged an export-import bank and urged the business community to reduce its dependence on import trade and to establish industries.[25]

However, the nationalization of the joint-venture Burma Oil Company (BOC) (1954) Ltd, in January 1963, and the ouster of Aung Gyi, in February 1963, signalled a move towards a more rapid assertion of state control over the economy.[26] Subsequently, there were waves of nationalization affecting banking, industry, trade, commerce, and services over the next five years. These, together with the demonetization of large currency notes dispossessed the "capitalists", mopped up liquid assets, and transferred substantial amounts of capital stock from the private sector to the state.[27]

In agriculture, it was acknowledged that the existing private production system could not be changed quickly into a collective system and the main objective was to rid it of exploitative practices. The next step would be to form producers co-operatives.[28] In the meantime, a compulsory delivery system for paddy was instituted in October 1964, ensuring the delivery of the stipulated amount at a fixed price to the government. Land committees to supervise land utilization were formed under the SACs. These measures curtailed the economic freedom of the peasants.[29]

The RC's perception of trade as the arena for struggle between anti-socialist elements and the state led to its preoccupation with the problem of commodity procurement and distribution.[30] In 1964, the state assumed responsibility for country-wide distribution of most commodities. In the following years, while grappling with the problem of ensuring equitable distribution, the state introduced a variety of institutional arrangements and administrative controls which turned out to be inadequate.[31] This attempt to replace the market with a centrally administered system of uniform distribution and standardized prices throughout the country resulted in considerable expansion of state employment in the trade sector. However, due to the complexity of disparate (and mainly private) sources of supply and the fickleness of consumer demand, the state-controlled distribution system floundered.[32] It also suffered from over-centralization, stifling procedures, multiplicity of state agencies, and excessive intervention by local authorities.[33]

During the first decade of its rule, the RC promulgated forty-seven laws (including amendments) and several significant proclamations on organizational and administrative measures to enhance its control over the economy.[34] The most significant one was the 1965 Law to Invest Powers to Construct the Socialist Economy. It authorized the government to set up any enterprise, to nationalize wholly or partly all existing enterprises or to manage or to regulate them, and also allowed the setting of prices for any commodity.[35] However, its stipulated penalties — ranging from cautioning and confiscation of goods to the death sentence — failed to deter the development of an audacious parallel or black market; which by the late 1960s had taken root with linkages not only with the rural hinterland but also extending beyond national borders.[36]

In the last one and a half years of its rule, the RC introduced measures that relaxed its grip on the economy. These included the raising of paddy purchase price by about 40 per cent in March 1973 and the lifting of restrictions over internal rice trade in May which was followed by the notification, in June, that indigenous private rubber plantations would be exempted from nationalization for thirty years. Myanmar joined the Asian Development Bank (ADB) in April 1973 and actively sought substantial project loans from the World Bank.

Prelude to Long-Term Planning

Planning was formally incorporated into the BSPP institutional framework only in October 1967 by the formation of the Socialist Economy Planning Committee chaired by General Ne Win.[37] In 1971, the BSPP was assigned the task of formulating a perspective plan as a "concrete expression of party policy".[38]

The Long-Term Plan Formulation Committee of the BSPP, formed in January 1971, was responsible for preparing the framework for a four-year plan and the basis for a long-term perspective plan. The Committee drew up a document, which included economic plan directives and a report for submission to the First Party Congress.[39] Significant points in the directives included:

- a twenty-year plan consisting of five consecutive four-year plans is envisaged;
- establishment of the basic economic, social, and political structures of the socialist system;
- economic enterprises are classified as belonging to state, co-operative, and private sectors, and a preferred demarcation (by ownership) of the economic structure is to be delineated;
- some enterprises are to be allowed as private concerns, others are to be transformed into co-operatives, and those deemed appropriate are to be transformed into state-owned concerns. This is to be done without adversely affecting ongoing production;
- the private sector comprises highland farmers, and peasants not wishing to participate in the state and co-operative sectors; individual livestock owners; producers of forest products for own use, small enterprises owned by nationals; building construction for own use; transport using animal-powered vehicles and mechanized services where the state is still unable to operate, private enterprises in the service sector; and retail trading outside the purview of state and co-operative agencies; and
- the present economic structure based on one or two (major) products is to be transformed into a multi-faceted structure.[40]

The economic strategy envisaged increased production and export of primary products; the establishment of consumer good industries (utilizing inputs from the primary sectors) as well as import-substituting industries; exploitation of minerals resources; and initiation of heavy industries utilizing minerals as raw materials.[41] Hence, the First Four-Year Plan (FYP) would:

(a) improve and consolidate the existing economic structure in concordance with prevailing conditions; to overcome existing economic difficulties and to anticipate future difficulties so as to minimize their adverse effect;

(b) involve mobilizing the working people, maximum utilization of productive capital, maximum reduction of costs, full application of modern techniques appropriate to Myanmar, minimization of loss and damage, and operating in the simplest and most effective way taking the shortest possible time;

(c) complete existing projects within the Plan period, and undertake new projects only if they are absolutely necessary for the Plan's success.[42]

Overall targets for the First FYP were set for gross output, GDP, consumption, per capita income, and per capita consumption.[43] However, considerations of economic parameters and resource availability in relation to these targets were lacking.

Subsequently, the "Scheme for the Planned Implementation of the Economy of All Nationalities" was approved by the BSPP Central Committee in September. It categorized enterprises and industries in relation to the respective sectors in which they would be allowed to operate.[44] It also specified time tables as well as communication pathways for suggestions, iterative drafting, legislation, reporting, supervision, assessment and analysis for the Twenty-Year Long-Term Plan (TYP), the forthcoming FYPs, and annual plans.[45]

The Economic Plan Implementation Committee was formed on 21 September 1971 at the central, township, and ward/village levels as well as at factory/enterprise/office levels. The First FYP began on 1 October 1971.[46]

Finally, the "Long-Term and Short-Term Economic Policies of the Burma Socialist Programme Party" (LTSTEP) document was formulated by the party secretariat and approved, in September 1972, by the Central Committee. The long-term economic policies were to be used as guidelines after the advent of the Pyithu Hluttaw (in 1974), whereas the short-term economic policies were to be implemented during the interim period.[47]

According to the LTSTEP, the economic strategy during the "transitional period" to Socialism was to substantially raise the level of production. This was to be achieved by fully utilizing the productive forces of the country, ensuring consistency between different parts of the economy, and raising economic efficiency and reducing losses and damages in the state and co-operative sectors.[48]

This document identified fifteen major faults in the prevailing economic system:

- absence of concrete long- and short-term plans;
- lack of economic policy co-ordination among government organizations;
- lack of effective plan implementation;
- running of state economic enterprises along administrative rather than commercial lines;
- slack and weak management in state enterprises;
- failure of labour to accept responsibilities commensurate with their rights;
- increase in misappropriation and losses of public property without effective action and punishment;
- inappropriate financial supervision in state enterprises;
- the system of transferring industrial products to state trading agencies at cost;
- using price mark-ups to overcome financial difficulties;
- falling total investment due to exclusion of private investment;
- widespread unemployment and black market activities due to limited opportunities in the state sector;
- the mismatch between the existing educational system and economic activities due to lack of systematic manpower planning;
- slack in production and high administrative costs due to preference for the administrative aspect over the productive aspect in labour deployment; and
- weak economic links with foreign countries.[49]

Evidently, the long-term policy objectives were aimed at rectifying these shortcomings through consistency, efficiency, accountability, and optimal use of resources.[50] The general economic policies thus enunciated contained several pragmatic points which differ from the autarkic policies of the past decade.[51]

Separate policies for six public affairs sectors were also specified and a list classifying industrial enterprises by ownership was appended to the section on long-term policies. In this classification four types of ownership were stipulated, viz. state or public, co-operatives, private (registered) and private (open).[52]

On the other hand, major short-term problems as at mid-1972 were identified as:

- delays in organizing ward/village and factory/enterprise/office level implementation committees and the appointment of professional staff at the township level;
- resentment among the civil servants in the aftermath of the imposition of the new administration system and hiccups in the latter's implementation;
- problems arising from the failure of the ministries concerned to initiate consultation on policy matters with the BSPP Central Committee Headquarters; and
- deficiencies of party leaders in charge of economic matters in practising collective leadership and lack of co-ordination between upper and lower echelons of the BSPP.[53]

The LTSTEP was essentially the economic manifesto of the BSPP. Although some of the policies outlined in it were redundant, generalized, and vague, others were concerned with minutiae or resembled procedures or intentions rather than policies. Nevertheless, it did represent a change in outlook, given the highly centralized and doctrinaire policies pursued in the previous decade. It acknowledged the importance of economic efficiency and enterprise accountability in addition to control, equity, and socialization. It sought to strike a balance between micro and macro issues, economic imperatives and socio-political goals, pragmatism and ideology, and growth and redistribution. The clarification regarding the demarcation of boundaries between the private and the public sectors was also a major step forward towards harnessing the potential of the private sector. However, it still implied the primacy of the state in economic development and the relevance of the BWS as the overarching paradigm linking state, society and economy. As such, there was a continuity in "embedded orientations".[54]

All in all, it should be seen as an attempt to rationalize and legitimatize the BSPP's role in the policy environment of the post-RC state, rather than a comprehensive policy reform scheme. It was more of a "politics-as-usual" than a "perceived crisis" response entailing significant reforms.[55] The major shortcoming of this exercise was the absence of an overall assessment whereby the entire policy set was examined in its totality in view of resources and constraints. There was a lack of priorities among competing policy objectives that would determine the phasing of policy measures as well as identification of inter- and intra-sectoral policy linkages. On the other hand, one may argue that it was to the interest of the BSPP to keep its policy directions vague and generalized, so that in the event of failure it could absolve itself from direct responsibility. It is also possible that the technical experts involved were "playing safe" and did not volunteer any critique which might be seen as expression of discontent or sabotage.

Economic Performance

The state made substantial gains in expanding its role in the economy but its distributional network was far from efficient and was increasingly undermined by the black market. Despite the efforts of the Ministry of Co-operatives (formed in 1965) and the BSPP's exhortations, the co-operative movement aimed at supplementing the state's endeavours in services and the production and distribution of consumer goods did not develop as envisaged.[56] The unpublished four-year plan (1966/67–1969/70), which emphasized increased rice production performed below expectations.[57] The agriculture sector was essentially in private hands and collective enterprises had not materialized.[58]

The state's contribution to the GDP at 1969/70 constant producers' prices was around 30 per cent in 1971. Its share of constant value-added in trade, even in 1973/74, was only 43.3 per cent, while the corresponding figure for goods production was only 13.8 per cent.[59] The average growth rate of real GDP between 1961/62 and 1970/71 was just over 3.4 per cent, while the per capita income barely grew, registering a compound rate of less than 1 per cent per annum.[60]

The BSPP, in 1972, acknowledged the existence of serious economic problems.[61] Agriculture, the leading sector in terms of employment as well as output and exports, had stagnated partly due to the depressed state of the rice industry.[62] The productivity of rice had been affected partly by unfavourable weather in the mid-1960s but mainly by the prevailing system of low government prices tied to the compulsory delivery system and restrictions on the marketing of the surplus. The trade sector was suffering from the state's inability to solve the distributional shortcomings, losses from its uniform rice pricing policy, falling exports and loss of export markets, loss of consumer confidence in the inefficient co-operatives, and supply bottlenecks.[63] The transport and communications infrastructure was also beset with obsolete, deteriorating, and diminishing capital stock, wastage, misappropriation, and could not keep up with the rising demand for services. It was acknowledged that these deficiencies were "deep and massive".[64]

INDUSTRIALIZATION UNDER AUTARKY

Under the ambit of autarkic economic policies implemented by the RC, the industrialization process proceeded slowly; having to rely heavily on internal resources. Nonetheless, the government did accept aid and technical assistance for industrial projects from both multilateral institutions as well as bilateral donors like Japan and West Germany (see the section on "Aid" below). At the same time the private industrial sector was heavily regulated. On the whole, resource constraints emasculated the state's attempt to foster self-reliant industrialization through state enterprises.

Strategy and Policies

Initially, as expressed by Brigadier Aung Gyi, there was to be a continuation of the import-substituting industrialization (ISI) strategy, as a complement to agricultural modernization. The emphasis was to be on primary product processing industries and light consumer goods industries.[65] This entailed policies aimed at promoting private industries.[66]

All these changed when General Ne Win announced, in February 1963, that expansion of private industries would not be contemplated henceforth and that the existing ones would be eventually nationalized.[67] Thereafter, industrialization was predicated upon nationalization and self-reliant capital mobilization based on surplus extraction from primary production.[68] Industries utilizing domestic raw materials as well as heavy and capital goods industries were envisaged.[69] Like many resource-rich developing countries, resource-based industrialization (RBI) overlaid on the basic ISI concept was pursued throughout the RC period.[70] The aim was to establish industries that:

(a) complement agriculture;
(b) process agricultural raw materials into finished goods;
(c) process natural resources into finished goods;
(d) produce consumer goods;
(e) conserve foreign exchange by substituting imported goods;
(f) process surplus natural resources into finished goods for export;
(g) produce tools and machinery for domestic industries; and
(h) produce and distribute electricity.[71]

Most private industries were spared in the early waves of nationalization (1963–65).[72] Instead, they were subjected to supervisory and management committees (composed of representatives for the state, workers, and proprietors), state procurement in exchange for raw materials, and prohibition of expansion.[73] Later, successive rounds of nationalization in December 1968 and January 1972 affected 168 and 69 industrial establishments respectively.[74] Thereafter, the state no longer exercised the nationalization option but concentrated on developing state industrial enterprises (SIEs) as an integral part of state economic enterprises (SEEs) envisaged in the LTSTEP document.

Accordingly, the main objectives for the short term were identified as laying down the basis for industrial development and preventing the decline of productive capacity in existing SIEs. To this end, the recommendations were:

- top priority for the production of minerals that would bring immediate benefits;
- acceptance of foreign loans and technical assistance for mineral projects if the state could not rely on its own resources;
- allowing private and co-operatives to operate selected mining enterprises under a system of sales contracts with state agencies;
- maintenance of the existing productive capacity of SIEs with expansion if and when feasible;
- employing qualified workers for SIEs and deploying the minimum possible amount of labour;
- resumption of operations for idle SIEs, transferring them to co-operatives if the state could not operate them, and liquidating them if both options were not viable;
- restructuring SIEs to increase efficiency and production; and
- replacement of the system requiring SIEs to sell their products at cost to the state.[75]

For the electric power sector, policies were divided into those concerned with expanding generating capacity and those related to ensuring continuity and security of existing output. All were premised upon state ownership or control over electricity production and distribution.[76]

However, with the exception of the oil industry, there were delays in implementing these policies amidst the heightened political activity associated with preparations for the institution of the one-party socialist state.[77] Thus, the changes towards a less dirigiste form of industrial policies in line with those laid out in the LTSTEP document failed to materialize during the last years of RC rule.

Control and Supervision of Industries

The RG's emphasis was on developing industries aimed at achieving self-sufficiency in important consumer goods, selected intermediate products, and heavy industries.[78] In line with this approach, state agencies were reorganized and measures to supervise and regulate the private sector were undertaken. The Industrial Development Corporation (IDC) was reconstituted in August 1962 under a board of directors chaired by the industry minister. The IDC was to be operated according to commercial principles with responsibility for establishing and expanding industries.[79] The Directorate of Industries (DI) was assigned to regulate and guide private industries. Its main functions included exercising general supervision, providing raw materials, machinery and spares, facilitating marketing, and providing technical assistance to both state and private industries.[80] In April 1962, the Industrial Promotion Board was set up to "assist and encourage industrial development in the country".[81] The State Aid to Industries Act was also amended in November 1962, doubling the maximum amount payable under the state-sponsored industrial loan scheme to 8,000 kyat.[82] A central supervision and administration body for all nationalized industries was formed under the Ministry of Industry in September 1965. Each individual enterprise was run by an enterprise management committee that reported to the respective industrial branch's administrative body.

Between October 1964 and February 1969, the Ministry of Industry also formed a succession of committees to supervise and coordinate industrial production. Meanwhile, SIEs under the Ministry of Industry were further classified into ten branches and operational control of the SIEs were transferred from the IDC to the corresponding (branch) management committee. There were also the Industrial Executive Committee formed in October 1964 as an intra-ministry coordination body concerned with budgetary matters, personnel affairs, and other policy issues and the Industrial Planning Committee that was responsible for supervision of new industrial projects.[83]

In 1965, a hierarchy of supervision and coordination bodies were formed from the divisional level down to the township level to oversee private industrial enterprises.[84] The Joint Consultative Committee (JCC), consisting of employer's and employees' representatives, was formed in establishments having a minimum of fifty workers and was responsible for production and workers' welfare. Later it was replaced by the Joint Co-ordination Body.[85]

Production and distribution of goods from both state and registered private industries were linked through state trading agencies after April 1964, when domestic trading were nationalized. The SIEs were required to sell their products at cost to the state trading corporation. There was no incentive to reduce costs as they were borne by budgetary appropriations. Moreover, the state trading agency could generate profit by just marking up the selling price.[86]

On the other hand, supervisory committees exercised control over private enterprises through the supply of inputs, the pricing of outputs, operational management or a combination of all these measures. In the early stages of RC rule, the private sector responded negatively to government controls by resorting to measures that were perceived by the RC as tantamount to sabotage. These included disinvestment, producing lower quality goods, dismissing workers, reducing capacity utilization, diverting raw materials and intermediate inputs, and closure of factories.[87]

The RC inherited a mining sector dominated by private producers and joint ventures with foreign partners. Subsequently, the government took them over by purchasing the remaining shares or by nationalization.[88] The Petroleum and Minerals Development Corporation (PMDC) was established in October 1962 by amalgamating the Mineral Resources Development Corporation, the Geological Department, and the Mines and Explosives Department. It was responsible for exploitation of minerals (except oil), development of mines, and geological studies for all minerals (including oil). It was reorganized as Minerals Development Corporation (MDC) in September 1965.[89] The "Industrial Minerals Production Central Committee" formed by the Ministry of Mines in February 1966 was assigned to develop non-metallic mineral industries. However, production of some industrial minerals whose demands were small and irregular was contracted out to local co-operatives.[90]

The nationalized oil companies were reconstituted into the People's Oil Industry (POI), which became the Myanma Oil Corporation (MOC) in February 1970. Exploration and exploitation of oil and gas reserves were carried out by this agency under the Ministry of Mines.

In the power sector all commercial production and distribution of electricity was owned and controlled by the state. Some SIEs engaged in mining, processing, and manufacturing operations generated electricity for own use while others relied on the national grid. The sole national agency for electric power supply functioned as an SIE under the Ministry of Industry.

TABLE 5.1
State Industrial Enterprises by Industrial Branch

Industrial Branch	*March 1962*		*March 1974*	
	units	*share*	*units*	*share*
Food and beverages	89	53.3	163	21.8
Wearing apparel	9	5.4	58	7.8
Personal and household goods	2	1.2	30	4.0
Housing and construction materials	11	6.6	106	14.2
Industrial materials	40	23.9	357	47.8
Printing	16	9.6	33	4.4
Total	167	100.0	747	100.0

Notes: Share may not add up to 100 per cent due to rounding. Industrial materials comprised fuels, raw materials, industrial equipment and tools, as well as residuals not classified under other categories.
Source: Tawhlanyei Kaungsi Ei Lokesaunggyek Thamaing Akyingyoke [Historial Summary of the Actions of the Revolutionary Council] [hereafter, *Tawhlanyei Kaungsi*] (Yangon: Printing and Publishing Corporation, 1974), Appendix, Table 1, pp. 13–43.

Expansion of Industrial Enterprises

The number of SIEs increased substantially due to new investments and nationalization.[91] Table 5.1 compares the number of SIEs at the beginning and the end of RC rule.[92] Nearly half the increase was due to nationalization and the rest contained a substantial number of small-scale units.[93]

Table 5.2 shows the change in the composition of private industries between 1963/64 and 1973/74. The large reduction in chemical industries was probably due to their heavy dependence upon imports of raw materials that virtually ceased during this autarkic period. The decline of general industries may be attributed to intense competition from black-market imports.[94]

Investment and Production

In the 1962/63–1972/73 period, the total value of state investments in the processing and manufacturing sector was 1.34 billion kyat. Its 17.5 per cent share of the state's total investment in the economy was nearly twice the agriculture's share of 8.7 per cent, despite the latter being nominally accorded top priority.[95] The annual average investment of 122 million kyat generally fell far short of targets.[96] The majority of

TABLE 5.2
Private Industrial Establishments by Industry Branch

Industrial Branch	*1963/64*		*1973/74*		*Change*
	units	*share*	*units*	*share*	*(%)*
Food and beverages	4,290	18.6	7,955	29.0	+(85.2)
Wearing apparel	9,859	42.8	13,182	48.1	+(33.6)
Metals	1,103	4.8	2,386	8.7	+(116.3)
Ceramics	204	0.9	362	1.3	+(77.5)
Chemicals	1,147	5.0	344	1.3	−(70.0)
General	6,421	27.9	3,192	11.6	−(50.3)
Total	23,024	100.0	27,420	100.0	+(19.0)

Notes: Shares are in percentages.
Sources: Myanmar Naingan Sethmu Lokengan Thamaing Apaing 4: Tawhlanyei Kaungsi Karla Sethmu Lokengan Thamaing [History of Myanmar's Industry, Part 4: Revolutionary Period] (Yangon: Ministry of No. 1 Industry, n.d.), p. 66; *1974/75 Hku Hnit Atwet Pyidaungsu Hsoshelit Thamada Myanmar Naingandaw Bundaryei Sipwayei Luhmuyei Achei Anei Hnint Pathet Thi Pyithu Hluttaw Tho Asiyinkhanzar* [Report to the Pyithu Hluttaw on Financial, Economic, and Social Conditions of the Socialist Republic of the Union of Burma] (Yangon: Ministry of Planning and Finance, 1975), Table 72, p. 105.

this investment was in three heavy industries plants, textile plants, a paper factory, and two fertilizer plants.[97]

Table 5.3 shows (gross) values, in constant 1969/70 prices, of annual production by ownership for the processing and manufacturing sector. Although there were fluctuation in the second half of the 1960s, it increased by over 86 per cent between 1961/62 and 1971/72 and the state's corresponding share rose from 28.6 per cent to 43.5 per cent (the co-operatives share was less than 3 per cent). However, in 1972/73 and 1973/74, the state's production value declined by 7.9 per cent and 1.2 per cent respectively, reflecting the unsustainable nature of autarkic development.

Meanwhile the private sector's production remained stagnant and fluctuated around the 1961/62 level. In general, the slow growth of the agriculture sector effected this sector where agro-based industrial output comprised at least 60 per cent of production value.[98] In particular, the state's controls and restrictions depressed the privately operated processing industries which together with the shortage of spares and machinery led to a vicious cycle of technical obsolescence, decline in quantity and quality of products, low rate of returns to investment, and

TABLE 5.3
Production in Processing and Manufacturing
(million kyat in 1969/70 prices)

Fiscal year	*State*	*Co-operatives and private*	*Total*
1961/62	1,274	3,181	4,455
1962/63	1,613	3,491	5,104
1963/64	1,934	2,553	4,487
1964/65	2,077	3,026	5,104
1965/66	1,949	2,947	4,896
1966/67	1,598	3,033	4,631
1967/68	1,702	3,456	5,159
1968/69	2,065	3,189	5,254
1969/70	2,195	3,214	5,409
1970/71	2,329	3,189	5,517
1971/72	2,373	3,084	5,458
1972/73	1,744	3,282	5,026
1973/74	1,623	3,344	4,967

Note: Figures may not add up due to rounding.
Source: Report to the Pyithu Hluttaw 1976/77, Table 79, p. 89.

little or no investment. Consequently, the increase in overall production value between 1961/62 and 1973/74 was only 11.5 per cent.

Table 5.4 compares the quantum indices of production as well as the relative shares of production (in constant 1969/70 prices) by commodity groups, between the fiscal years 1961/62 and 1973/74. Evidently, the intra-sector industrial structure had not undergone significant changes in this period. In the ranking of production, the top three groups which together accounted for over 82 per cent of total value, retained their positions. The fourth and fifth positions were transposed because of the increased processing of crude oil and the decline in the production of industrial raw materials.

The quantum indices indicate that production in 1973/74 for the top five commodity groups, with a combined share of over 90 per cent of the total output, did not increase substantially from the 1961/62 level. Instead, the second-ranking clothing and apparel group and the fourth-ranking industrial raw materials group suffered production declines. On the other hand, the extremely large increments of the commodity groups at the bottom half of the share rankings were from very small bases and were associated with industries dominated by SIEs.[99] As such,

TABLE 5.4
Industrial Production by Commodity Group

Commodity Group	*1961/62*		*1973/74*	
	Q Index	*Share (rank)*	*Q Index*	*Share (rank)*
Food and beverages	82.4	61.6 (1)	97.9	65.7 (1)
Clothing and apparel	87.4	13.2 (2)	63.5	8.6 (2)
Construction materials	79.5	6.8 (3)	85.6	6.6 (3)
Industrial raw materials	141.7	6.1 (4)	102.2	4.0 (5)
Mineral and petroleum products	71.7	5.8 (5)	85.0	6.2 (4)
Personal goods	75.8	2.6 (6)	70.8	2.2 (7)
Miscellaneous	120.2	2.2 (7)	150.9	2.7 (6)
Printing and publishing	42.6	0.6 (8)	88.4	1.0 (9)
Transport vehicles	18.9	0.4 (9)	84.3	1.5 (8)
Household goods	34.5	0.2 (10)	67.9	0.3 (12)
Electrical goods	25.4	0.2 (11)	104.6	0.6 (10)
Machinery and equipment	67.4	<0.1 (12)	78.3	0.1 (13)
Agricultural equipment	nil	nil (13)	166.2	0.5 (11)

Notes: Q (Quantum) index = 100 for 1969/70. Production shares (%) may not add up to 100 due to rounding.
Sources: Various issues of the *Report to the Pyithu Hluttaw.*

they could not offset the sluggish performance of the major commodity groups. Hence, the poor overall sectoral performance.

In terms of constant value-added, the processing and manufacturing sector registered an average (compound) annual growth rate of 2.1 per cent from 1961/62 to 1973/74. Though modest, this was much higher than the 0.9 per cent figure for production (gross output) value, indicating that there had been some progress towards establishing higher value-added industries.[100] However, the sector's share of GDP (in constant 1969/70 prices) declined from 10.5 per cent to 9.7 per cent in the same period.

The processing and manufacturing sector as a whole failed to live up to expectations, and the SIEs that were supposed to be the vanguard of the state-led ISI strategy performed poorly. The main reasons given by the BSPP for the disappointing performance of the SIEs were:

- lumpiness of capital investments involving long gestation periods;
- shortages of raw material and spares;
- technological obsolescence;

- poor quality of domestic raw materials;
- low capacity utilization;
- lack of appropriate financial supervision;
- disincentives and wastage associated with the system of selling products at cost to state trading agencies;
- management shortcomings due to bureaucratic administration, neglect of commercial principles in operation, and excessive reliance on higher authorities;
- slackness of work discipline;
- and the workers' failure to discharge responsibilities commensurate with benefits provided by the state.

It was acknowledged that the private sector was more adversely affected by the shortage of both domestic and imported raw materials as well as machinery, and spares.[101] This diagnosis of the ills and drawbacks plaguing the processing and manufacturing sector remained relevant throughout the RC era.

In the mining sector, during the mid-1960s the government launched a series of exploration and exploitation programmes. The aim was to achieve self-sufficiency in oil by 1970 and to regain, as soon as possible, pre-World War II production levels in important minerals.[102] The small (mainly tin) mines in southeast Myanmar were allowed to operate either as co-operatives or private claims but were obliged to sell their output to the state. Technical assistance from the United Nations agencies as well as bilateral donors such as the USSR, Federal Republic of Germany, Japan, and Austria were sought to rehabilitate old mines, to develop new mines, for feasibility studies, and for exploration activities.[103] Due to insecurity, cross-border smuggling, long lead times as well as lack of infrastructure, technical expertise, skilled workers, and acute foreign exchange shortages, the minerals sector did not register significant gains, despite discoveries of new ore reserves.[104]

During the RC era, three new oil fields and two gas fields were discovered and brought on stream quickly. Thus, oil production increased steadily in the late 1960s and the output in 1973 at 7.5 million (U.S.) barrels was 70 per cent more than that in 1962, but fell short of the peak pre-World War II production of 7.9 million. Natural gas was utilized for the first time in 1970 as feedstock for fertilizer production.[105] Oil exploration was extended to offshore areas in 1971 with Japanese assistance, in line with the shift in the outlook towards a more pragmatic consideration of "beneficial" foreign assistance. Extensive onshore exploration was

TABLE 5.5
Quantum Indices of Production by Mineral Groups
(1969/70 = 100)

Mineral Group	*1961/62*	*1971/72*	*1972/73*	1973/74
Oil and natural gas	73.3	125.1	129.3	122.5
Lead, zinc, silver and allied products	229.3	110.9	126.3	77.6
Tin, tungsten and scheelite mixed concentrates	247.4	197.1	178.5	142.1
Jade and gem	302.9	345.1	279.3	234.5
Industrial minerals	56.8	106.3	121.0	62.7
Others	38.4	125.4	104.2	105.1
Total	98.3	122.4	127.7	109.3

Sources: Various issues of the *Report to the Pyithu Hluttaw.*

also carried out and six new drilling rigs were purchased with foreign loans. A lube-oil blending and packaging plant was added to the Syriam refinery in 1974, again financed by a foreign loan, and twelve offshore "wildcats" were unsuccessfully drilled in the Gulf of Martaban between January 1972 and December 1974.[106]

State investment in the mining sector during the RC era was 436 million kyat (current prices) or 5.7 per cent of the total.[107] The average value-added growth (in constant 1969/70 prices) rate during the 1961/62–73/74 period, was a disappointing 1.1 per cent annually. Consequently, mining's share in the GDP dropped from 1.4 per cent to 1.1 per cent.[108] Meanwhile, the state's share of minerals production leaped to 85.6 per cent from 1.5 per cent reflecting its virtual monopoly. The poor growth performance of the sector (see Table 5.5) indicates the failure of the RBI strategy. Evidently, except for oil, gas, and industrial minerals, production fared poorly and depressed the overall performance.

The physical output of minerals also fluctuated instead of registering steady growth as envisaged by the planners and only a small fraction of the pre-World War II output was attained. Table 5.6 is self-explanatory in this regard.

Electricity production was one area in which there had been steady progress throughout. The capacity of the Lawpita hydroelectric power plant was doubled by constructing a dam while natural gas as a power source was introduced in the early 1970s.

TABLE 5.6
Indices for Physical Output of Important Minerals
(1939 = 100)

Fiscal Year	*Refined silver*	*Tin concentrate*	*Tungsten concentrate*	*Zinc concentrate*	*Refined lead*
1961/62	23.2	16.5	18.0	24.0	21.5
1962/63	29.5	14.7	1.6	30.8	28.2
1963/64	22.5	14.7	1.4	23.8	21.4
1964/65	19.4	16.7	1.6	23.8	20.3
1965/66	19.2	12.1	3.2	19.4	18.8
1966/67	16.5	11.0	3.7	16.5	17.1
1967/68	12.9	7.3	3.8	13.9	12.2
1968/69	13.3	7.1	3.8	16.4	12.9
1969/70	10.3	7.5	4.5	11.8	8.7
1970/71	12.7	8.7	7.3	11.8	11.3
1971/72	11.1	10.1	15.7	12.6	9.7
1972/73	11.5	6.8	13.4	11.8	12.5
1973/74	4.9	8.3	13.0	10.4	5.9

Source: Indices are derived from various issues of the *Report to the Pyithu Hluttaw.*

The state invested more than 284 million kyat (current prices) in the power sector (3.7 per cent of its total investment) during the 1962/63–1972/73 period, averaging less than 26 million kyat annually.[109]

Between 1961/62 and 1973/74, electricity generating capacity increased by more than 62 per cent to 391 megawatts, and the total installed capacity of the state monopoly (reconstituted as the Electric Power Corporation [EPC] in March 1972) increased by nearly 77 per cent to 334 megawatts. The EPC's annual generation doubled to 659 million kilowatt-hours (kwh) and net consumption, also increased by 118 per cent to 504 million kwh. The industry's share of consumption also rose from 42 per cent to 52 per cent and unit production costs decreased from 0.292 kyat to 0.19 kyat. Moreover, the sectoral value-added (in constant 1969/70 prices) increased by an annual compound rate of around 7.9 per cent.[110]

Although the power sector's achievements were more impressive than both manufacturing and mining, it was not without problems. Power transmission and distribution were characterized by high distribution losses and low availability of firm power. Foreign exchange shortages exacerbated the problem of maintaining obsolete equipment and inefficient distribution networks even as new generating projects (funded by foreign aid) were commissioned. The emphasis on industrial and public sector usage led to the marginalization of private consumers. The annual compound growth rate of overall consumption during the 1961/62–1973/74 period was only 6.7 per cent. The corresponding figure for industrial use was 8.7 per cent, whereas that for domestic use was only 4.9 per cent.[111] In 1973/74 electricity was available in 263 (out of 288) towns and 652 (out of 13,751) villages.[112]

FINANCIAL RESOURCES

The state-led ISI strategy premised on RBI was severely constrained by the autarkic economic policies of the ruling military junta. In particular, the lack of adequate financial resources, especially scarce foreign exchange, hamstrung the RC's effort to achieve economic independence through a strategy of self-reliance. In this respect, one needs to explore the process of mobilizing financial resources for industrialization in particular and economic development in general in some detail in order to understand the nature of the problems and constraints that retarded industrial and economic progress during the RC era.

From 1963 onwards, fiscal policy mainly revolved around the budgetary process with the aim of securing current account surplus, while monetary policy was aimed at maintaining a stable exchange rate and controlling the domestic money supply. The RC's main concerns were to prevent inflation and maintain favourable balance of payments and foreign reserve positions. Meanwhile, there were price fixing, wage freezing, and administrative control over trade and investments. Industrial investments were accorded higher priority and capital formation depended upon extracting as much surplus as possible from the productive sectors while reducing consumption to the barest minimum.[113]

In February 1963, private banking was nationalized.[114] Redesignated as People's Banks, their credit operations with the private sector rapidly diminished in the next few years.[115] In October 1966, the RC decided to withdraw Myanmar's membership from the Sterling Area "in order to secure freedom of action" in protecting its "foreign exchange reserves" in the face of a weakening pound.[116] Following the enactment of the Union of Burma Banking Law of 1967 which established the Union of Burma Bank, a unitary banking system was established in November 1969.[117]

Beginning October 1963, a new system of fiscal control and budgeting in the state sector was introduced in which budgets for central government, constituent states (of the Union), and boards and corporations were consolidated under a single structure. Accounting procedures were also changed to conform with centralized control and a central fund was created. Cash transactions in intra-governmental dealings were replaced by book transfers and loans taken by state agencies were converted to equity capital. A new budget format was prescribed in which revenues and expenditures were differentiated by function rather than by agency. Authority for controlling budgeted expenditures were vested in the ministers.[118] As a result, the SEEs operated under a "soft budget constraint" and developed a tendency to disregard economic efficiency.[119] Finally, in 1972, finance and national planning portfolios were merged to form the Ministry of Planning and Finance.

In this context, trade, aid, and revenues became the principal sources of development financing. However, despite attempts to increase domestic savings, shortcomings in resource mobilization undermined the state's ability to pursue an investment programme commensurate with its goals.[120] Though partly alleviated by foreign aid, the shortage of foreign exchange severely limited the scope and pace of industrialization. It has been suggested that there was decapitalization of existing industries and neglect of maintenance and repairs in infrastructure as well as productive capital, as the state struggled to maintain a relatively high level of investment in new industries.[121]

Trade

The only source of foreign exchange was the nationalized foreign trade sector. Surplus extraction from private agriculture production was essentially the same as that exercised under the previous regime but its scope was considerably expanded due to the state's wide-ranging controls over the production and marketing of rice and other agriculture products.

Private imports were prohibited in October 1963 and private exports forbidden after April 1964. The state's foreign trade monopoly was exercised through the Myanmar Export Import Corporation (MEIC) of the trade ministry. Under this centralized scheme, exports were generally supply-driven while imports were determined mainly by the availability of foreign exchange. From mid-1960s onwards export earnings fell short of expectations and significantly constrained the importation of capital and intermediate goods which in turn undermined the ISI programme.[122]

As illustrated in Figure 5.1, exports declined till 1967/68 and stagnated thereafter. Though recovering in 1970/71, the value for 1972/73 was only 54 per cent of that in 1961/62. This was mainly due to declining rice exports. Hence, the total value of imports were considerably reduced after 1964/65 (Figure 5.2). Apparently, imports of consumer goods had to be drastically reduced to maintain imports of capital and intermediate goods at roughly the 1965/66 level. Thus, by 1972/73, the total value of imported consumer goods was only 15 per cent of that in 1964/65 and its share was reduced from 38 per cent to less than 12 per cent.

The corresponding share for capital goods increased from 22 per cent in 1964/65 to 30 per cent in 1965/66 and averaged 41 per cent over the next seven years.[123] This decline in official imports created new opportunities for the black market, while the SIEs benefited from the highly protected trade regime.

FIGURE 5.1
Domestic Exports

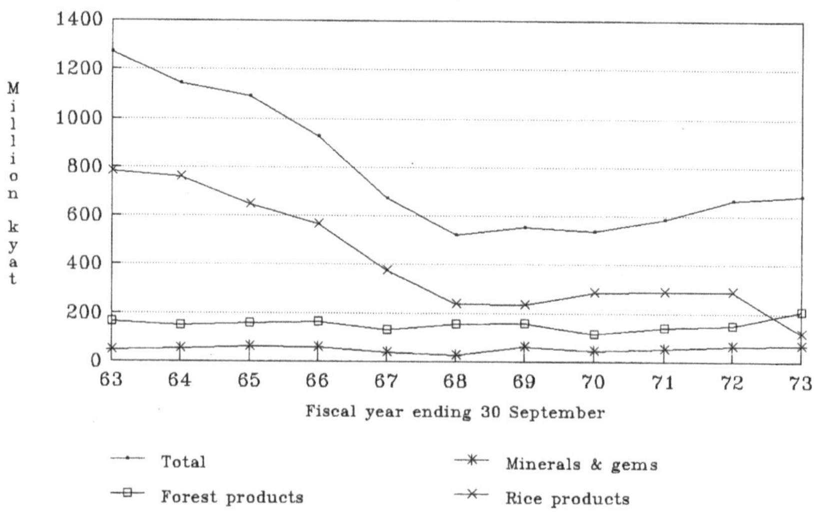

Source: Ministry of Planning and Finance.

FIGURE 5.2
Imports: Value

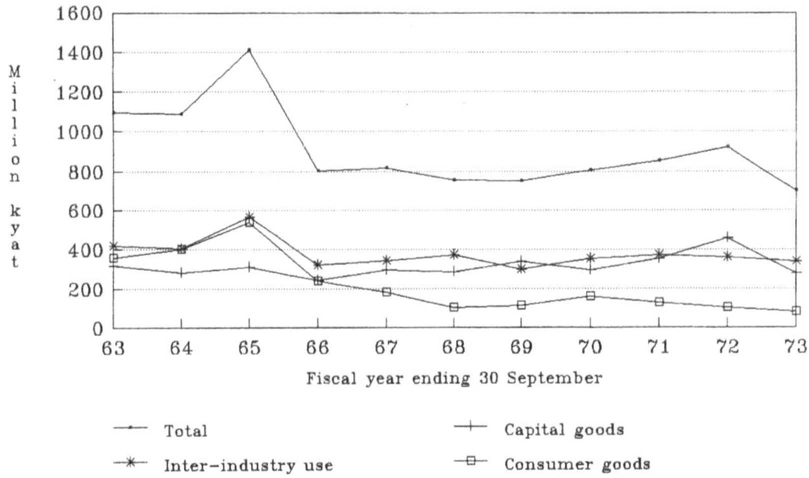

Source: World Bank and Ministry of Planning and Finance.

Aid

Despite the rhetoric of economic self-reliance, the RC continued to solicit technical and financial assistance from the International Monetary Fund (IMF), specialized agencies of the United Nations (UN), sympathetic countries, and country groupings such as the Colombo Plan.

Among the donors, Japan provided the largest amount of official development assistance (ODA) during the RC period.[124] Negotiations for additional Japanese war reparations funds initiated by the previous government was concluded in January 1963 whereby US$140 million (yen equivalent) in grants and US$30 million (yen equivalent) in loans were promised. The grants would be spread over twelve years commencing April 1965, and the loans would be extended for six years after the ratification of the agreement.[125] Together with outstanding disbursements from the 1954 reparations agreement this second-phase agreement resulted in aid averaging around US$21.5 million annually during the 1962–73 period.[126] Of the 47.3 billion yen in grants disbursed under the second phase, approximately 90 per cent were for four heavy-industry projects built in the first phase.[127] For loans provided after 1968, textiles plants and heavy-industry projects were the likely beneficiaries.[128] Additional project loans continued after the promised sum was expended and the processing and manufacturing sector got more than 80 per cent of them.[129]

Chinese (People's Republic of China) aid resulted from the economic and technical cooperation agreement of January 1961. The interest-free loan (for Chinese goods and services) of US$84 million was utilized on infrastructure projects as well as three major plants for manufacturing paper, textiles, and sugar. However, the programme was terminated in July 1967 with some US$55 million unspent, when the relations between the two countries deteriorated after anti-Chinese riots erupted in response to the spilling over of the Maoist Cultural Revolution into Myanmar.[130] It was reinstated in October 1971 but no new industrial projects were undertaken thereafter.

The Federal Republic of Germany (FRG) initially extended a DM35 million loan for five industrial projects and a DM100 million "guaranteed fund" for buying German products.[131] Major projects completed up to 1973 included a textile weaving and finishing plant and a brick factory.

Other donors included the United States whose aid comprised previously undisbursed P.L. 480 loans and a US$30 million grant for the Yangon-Mandalay highway project.[132] Over US$21 million worth of credits were extended by Yugoslavia, Poland, and the Soviet Union for industry and agriculture while Czechoslovakia provided assistance for a tractor plant.[133]

The cumulative net ODA from 1963 to 1973 was estimated at around US$336 million, and Japanese aid probably accounted for roughly half of the 1.34 kyat billion invested in the processing and manufacturing sector during the 1962–73 period.[134] Given the high foreign exchange content (55–60 per cent range for textile and heavy-industry plants) of industrial projects, it is highly likely that the overwhelming majority of new industrial projects would not have materialized without foreign assistance.[135] Thus, ODA, though small in absolute terms, played a highly significant role in developing SIEs during the RC era. Ironically, despite Myanmar's withdrawal from the international economy, ostensibly to enhance economic independence, the state became more dependent upon external assistance. On the other hand, in the choice of projects and implementation there appeared to be a general lack of rigour and donor monitoring. This was especially true in Japanese aid which, as pointed out by Steinberg, was a detached exercise whereby "so much money was promised or pledged and delivered, and then spent" without considering either "how these funds were used" or "the effect of such assistance economically" or otherwise.[136] This kind of donor stance particularly suited the RC which steadfastly adhered to the notion of economic independence and the illusion of autonomy while rejecting policy dialogue with the donors.

In general, ODA inflows partially offset the persistent trade deficits incurred after 1965/66 (see Figure 5.3). However, the relative balance of payments position deteriorated after 1967/68 (Figure 5.4) and this was reflected in the steep drawing down of the foreign exchange reserves.[137]

Revenues

The decline in external trade also effected the state's revenues by reducing custom duties and tariffs. Customs duty as a share of total taxes declined from around 37 per cent in 1960/61 to about 15 per cent in the late 1960s and was less than 16 per cent in 1972/73. Meanwhile, the private sector slipped away from the state's revenue net and the revenue structure shifted gradually from taxes levied on income and profit to those on production and consumption. The former's share declined from around 55–60 per cent in the mid-1960s to about 38 per cent in 1972/73, while the latter's share followed a rising trend from

FIGURE 5.3
Trade Deficit and Net ODA Inflow

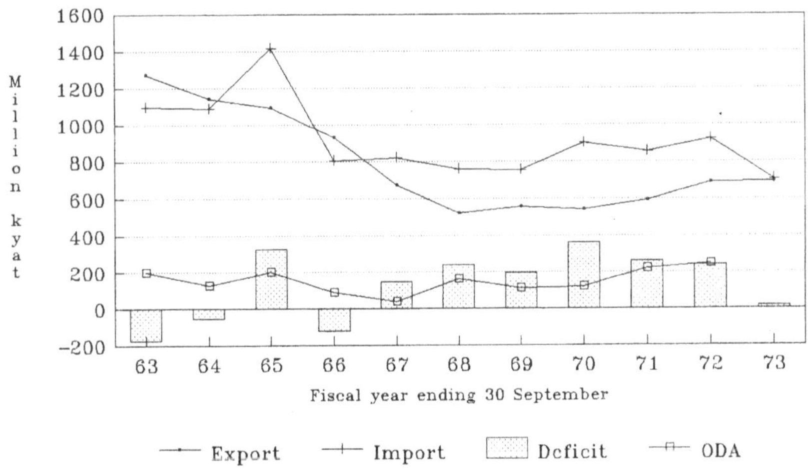

Notes: Net ODA data exclude interest repayments; negative values show surplus.
Source: Union Bank of Burma.

FIGURE 5.4
Cumulative Balance of Payments (BOP) and Foreign Exchange Reserves

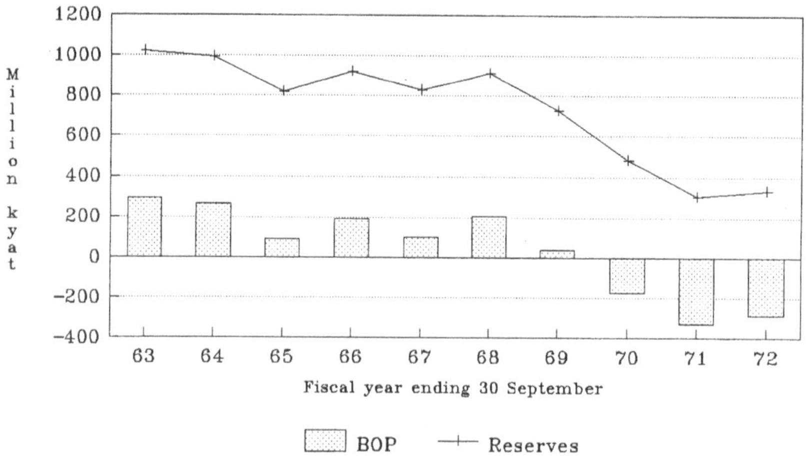

Note: 1962/63 is taken as base year.
Source: Union Bank of Burma.

18 per cent in 1964/65 to 38 per cent in 1972/73.[138] The income tax law was amended in 1963 abolishing the previous system of corporate incentives. Taxable net annual income was set at 4,200 kyat with some provisions for personal deductions. The tax rate for net income or profit exceeding 300,000 kyat was a prohibitive 99 per cent.[139]

This new income tax structure was biased against business profits and aggravated the negative impacts of nationalization and restrictions on private trading and manufacturing. Anecdotal evidence suggests that there was widespread tax evasion. Thus, the share of personal income tax (to total tax) which was less than 6 per cent in 1964/65 further declined to less than 2 per cent in 1972/73. The corresponding share for private corporate tax was less than 1 per cent throughout the late 1960s and the early 1970s.[140]

Tax revenues from the SEEs whose average contribution in the 1966/67–1972/73 period was 42 per cent of total revenues remained stagnant in absolute terms. Long gestation periods of capital-intensive industries as well as inefficiencies in state trading and services appeared to be the main reasons behind SEEs' poor performance. The centralized price-fixing system geared towards uniform pricing and subsidies for "essential items", such as rice and fertilizers, also depressed the earnings of SEEs.[141]

Moreover, overall tax revenues followed a falling trend after 1964 and the total revenue for 1972/73 was 61 per cent less than that in 1964/65. This created a substantial resource gap in financing capital investments throughout the RC period. As shown in Figures 5.5 and 5.6 deficit financing became necessary for capital formation.

LABOUR AND EMPLOYMENT

The RC projected itself as representing the interests of peasants and workers who were portrayed as its natural allies. The government statement on 30 April 1963 promised to "liberate the ... workers from ... exploitation of man by man". It exhorted workers "to actively take part in transforming Burma into a Socialist State" under BSPP leadership and "to re-orientate their outlook" towards "building a socialist economy for the common good".[142]

The RC promised:

- to strive for the earliest realization of the socialist goal by taking unspecified "necessary action" appropriate to the prevailing conditions;

FIGURE 5.5
Consolidated Public Sector Budget Deficit

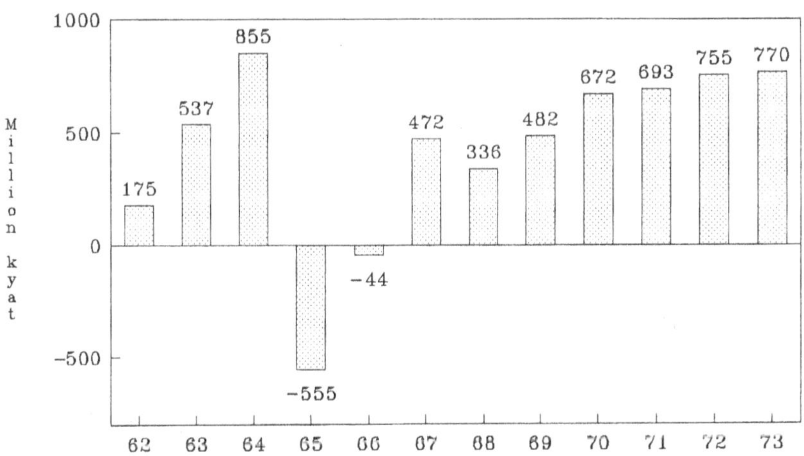

Note: Minus sign denotes surplus.
Source: World Bank.

FIGURE 5.6
Consolidated Public Sector Budget: Ratio of Deficit to GDP

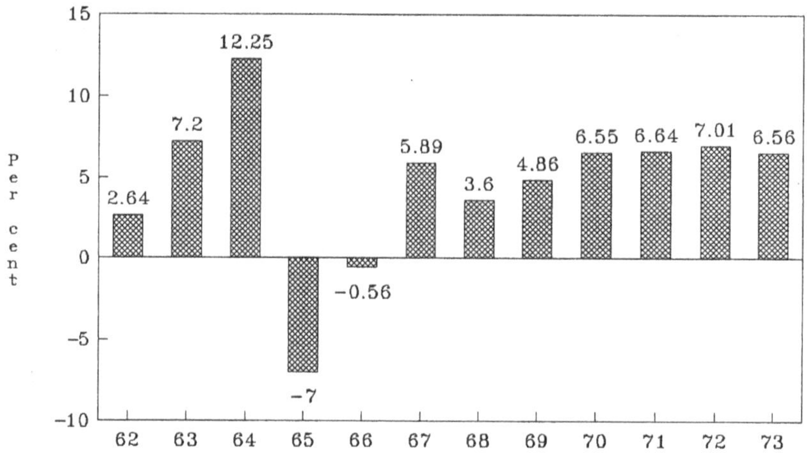

Note: Minus sign denotes surplus.
Source: World Bank.

- to maintain control of production targets while allowing greater participation of workers in managing state and co-operative enterprises;
- to limit the private capitalists' "profit margin" while promoting harmonious "labour-management relations";
- to formulate new labour laws consonant with socialist principles;
- to adopt measures fostering discipline and higher productivity and to dispense benefits commensurate with production gains;
- to safeguard workers unity; and
- to foster "reciprocal aid and co-operation" between workers and peasants.[143]

The Law Defining Basic Rights and Responsibilities of the Workers, promulgated in May 1964, stipulated the following rights:

> (1) employment (2) security of employment (3) leisure (4) education and training (5) maternity leave (6) security when unwell (7) compensations for work-related accidents (8) security when unable to work for other reasons (9) security in old age (10) remuneration proportional to labour and skill (11) regular improvement of living standards (12) cultural developments (13) equality of sexes and (14) congenial conditions of work,

as well as the following responsibilities:

> (1) upkeep of socialist discipline (2) safeguarding the means of production (3) increasing productivity (4) upholding norms (5) promoting workers' unity, and (6) implementation of plans.[144]

Subsequently, the government amended existing laws and regulations, established rules and procedures, and instituted organizational arrangements in line with its professed objectives.[145] However, even in the state sector, there were delays in delivering the stipulated benefits to the workers concerned, whereas those in the private sector benefitted less.[146]

Emoluments of industrial workers barely increased. In the 1962–73 period, the average (male) manufacturing wage increased by 10 per cent. For miners the increment was only 7 per cent.[147] Basic salaries in the state sector remained virtually unchanged until October 1972 when the temporary cost of living allowance (c.l.a.) was incorporated into the basic salary, thereby increasing the lower end scales by 10–22 per cent.[148] However, low salaries were partly compensated by the low rate of inflation. For example, the consumer price index (CPI) for Yangon increased by only 38 per cent between 1962 and 1971.[149] Moreover, for those who enjoyed the social security scheme (see below) as well as employees of large SIEs, especially those that provided housing, the benefits in kind were quite significant.[150]

On the welfare front, the social security scheme's regional coverage was extended to thirteen cities and towns by 1973 and, with effect from January 1970, the institutional coverage was extended to establishments with a minimum of five workers instead of ten.[151] In the 1962–73 period, the number of registered establishments under the scheme increased from 2,843 to 7,392, while membership increased from over 296,000 to over 365,000.[152] In the same period, 35.2 million kyat in cash benefits out of a total contribution income of 123.9 million kyat were disbursed.[153]

Welfare associations for workers were reorganized and placed under BSPP supervision. The government issued, in March 1970, a ministerial directive to restructure them and they were subsequently operated as labour welfare committees.[154] By September 1971, there were 661 associations with over 252,000 members.[155]

Regarding employer–employee relations, the industrial dispute arbitration system was revamped in August 1963. The Industrial Arbitration Court was replaced by the Central Labour Dispute Committee

(CLDC) whose decisions were exempted from judicial intervention. The new hierarchy of sub-committees and appellate committees under it commenced operations in 1964. Township labour supervision committees were also formed to oversee industrial relations as well as labour welfare.[156] The number of disputes brought to them increased rapidly from 1,722 in 1962 to 4,047 and 9,208 in the next two years. Thereafter, it declined continuously to 1,324 in 1971 and remained stable up to September 1973.[157]

Beginning May 1964, township level workers' councils and workers' organizing committees were formed under BSPP supervision. They were further institutionalized, in April 1968, when the Central People's Workers Council (CPWC) was formed at the plenary session of the First People's Workers' Council Conference.[158] The principal aim of this organization was, as pointed out by Taylor, to serve "as a medium for the transmission of the state's policies" while pre-empting the development of autonomous grassroots organization amongst workers. It was also a convenient means for "more" effective control of "productive labour".[159] The organization rapidly expanded, and had recruited over 1.5 million members from 14,053 establishments by February 1972.[160]

Workers participation in management was facilitated by the formation of the Joint Co-ordination Body (JCB) at the enterprises level, in October 1968, under the supervision of the local SAC and the regional labour administration office. Comprising management and People's Workers' Council representatives, the JCB's task involved coordination with management on matters relating to production, welfare, and workers' rights and responsibilities. The JCB scheme was carried out in phases in selected SIEs as well as some establishments in the construction and transport sectors. A total of 284 (28 in the private sector) JCBs were established up to December 1973.[161]

A model worker selection scheme was launched in October 1964 ostensibly to instil the spirit of socialist emulation for higher productivity and better work discipline. Applicable to enterprises with at least 100 workers, the scheme recognized three grades of model workers with the premier grade hailed as "socialist worker". Those who qualified enjoyed a stay at a special holiday camp and were feted by state leaders.[162] Altogether 6,556 model workers, including 360 socialist workers, were honoured up to 1973.[163] There is no evidence to suggest that it had actually contributed towards its professed goals but anecdotal evidence seems to suggest that once the novelty of the scheme wore off most workers tended to become indifferent towards it.

The necessity to establish a uniform code of discipline was recognized and the Directorate of Labour enunciated a model code in January 1970. For implementation, priority was given to enterprises that had formed JCBs. Progress was slow and only 154 establishments adopted work discipline protocols during the RC rule.[164]

Full employment was not explicitly expressed as a policy goal but the right to work was stipulated by law. Existing employment exchanges were reorganized and a central labour appointment and employment office at the capital together with regional offices in major cities and towns were established. Except for professional positions under the purview of the Public Service Commission, all appointments were channelled through these offices. In areas where there were no regional offices, People's Workers' Council assumed the task of co-ordinating job placements. A central employment board was also formed at the Ministry of Labour in December 1969. The total number of job placements from 1962 to 1973 affected through the labour and employment offices came to over 381,000. However, since disaggregated data are not available, the impact of these activities on industrial employment cannot be ascertained.[165] The main problem in the state sector, according to anecdotal evidence, seems to be the lack of skilled technicians and trained personnel.

During the RC period, there was very little increase in industrial employment. At over 804,800 workers (15.3 per cent employed by the state) in 1972/73, its labour force increased by less than 12 per cent in twelve years. The corresponding figure for the mining sector of less than 51,000 (96.3 per cent in state sector) was a huge 250 per cent increase over 1961.[166] Employment in the power sector which stood at around 12,400 (all state employees) in 1972/73 was no different from the 1964/65 figure of less than 13,000. The combined share for all three sectors accounted for only 7.6 per cent of national employment compared to over 66 per cent for the agriculture sector.[167]

However, employment growth among SIEs was more pronounced. Industrial employment as a share of total state employment in 1972/73 was 16 per cent.[168] The increment in state employment for the processing and manufacturing sector in the 1968/69–1972/73 period was more than 66 per cent.[169] In contrast, the more numerous private sector employment decreased by 2.8 per cent. Thus, the average rate of increase in overall industrial employment was below 1.5 per cent and less than the average population growth rate of 2 per cent in the period concerned. As such, the expansion of industrial employment seems to be less than adequate for accommodating the demands of population growth.

RC RULE: A SUMMARY

Politics and economics in Myanmar during the period under direct military rule, characterized by social control and autarkic development was a radical departure from the past. The depoliticization of the citizens and the reassertion of the state was deemed necessary to start afresh with an ideology true to the goals and aspirations of the pre-independence progenitors of socialist ideals. The RC nurtured its alter ego in the form of the BSPP but the rigid military rationale and the "commandism" of its *formateurs* seem to have been retained.[170] The Janus-faced party sired by the political soldiers of the "Anti-Fascist Generation" remained, at best, "soldier politicians" at the beginning of the second decade of its existence.

The economy was characterized by near isolation from the international system and stagnant growth. It was particularly affected by the depressed state of agriculture which was not only the leading sector (in both employment and production) but also provided vital foreign exchange and surplus for industrial capital formation. The First Four-Year Plan for 1971/72–1974/75, truncated in March 1974 to conform with the new financial year (starting 1 April instead of 1 October) and the term of the Pyithu Hluttaw, failed to achieve its annual targets.[171]

The number of SIEs in the processing and manufacturing sector increased substantially under military rule with the state dominating resource-based production and large-scale enterprises.[172] However, these were hampered by the lack of financial and managerial autonomy that degraded their efficiency and deprived them of the ability to generate surplus. Moreover, the emphasis on new projects and capacity expansion resulted in endemic capacity underutilization and technological obsolescence. The private sector was emasculated both by regulations on private ownership and exclusion of the private sector from institutionalized credit and other resources.

The mining sector still suffered from depletion of higher ore grades, lack of technical expertise, and shortage of foreign exchange.[173] Except for oil and gas, production of important minerals were stagnant and way below pre-World War II levels.

Electricity was recognized as essential for industrialization and the private consumer was, by and large, neglected. The capital-intensive and foreign-exchange intensive nature of capacity additions resulted in the relative neglect of distribution networks and end-use facilities for the private customer.

The state expanded and extended the rights of industrial workers and also managed to increase the scope and extent of welfare services. However, most of these improvements were confined to state employees who comprised only a small portion of the industrial labour force. On their part, the workers did not seem to have responded as much as the RC had envisaged, in terms of discipline and productivity.[174] Thus, the conditions of workers as well their commitment to the BWS were far from satisfactory.

However, as the military rule drew to an end there was some optimism that the application of the policies outlined in the LTSTEP document would redress shortcomings and raise the economy to new heights. As such, the long-standing goal of socialist industrialization appeared to be within reach, provided the plans were successfully implemented. The pursuit of this elusive objective during the next fourteen years of BSPP rule is examined in the next chapter.

Notes

1. The military portrayed the coup as an attempt "to set the nation on the path to the socialist goal ... that was almost disappearing from sight" (*Party Seminar 1965: Speeches of the Chairman General Ne Win and Political Report of the General Secretary* [Rangoon: Burma Socialist Programme Party, 1966], p. 31).
2. See, for example, *Tawhlanyei Kaungsi Ei Lokesaunggyek Thamaing Akyingyoke* [Historical Summary of the Actions of the Revolutionary Council] (hereafter, *Tawhlanyei Kaungsi*) (Yangon: Printing and Publishing Corporation, 1974), pp. 254–55.
3. The Central SAC, under the chairmanship of the Minister for Home Affairs, controlled the state/division, district, and township level SACs which were invariably chaired by a military officer. Those at the village/ward level were appointed by township authorities (see ibid., pp. 267–68).
4. Robert. H. Taylor, *The State in Burma* (London: C. Hurst, 1987), p. 314. See also *Tawhlanyei Kaungsi*, pp. 162–65.
5. See Maung Maung, *Burma and General Ne Win* (London: Asia Publishing House, 1969), p. 296.
6. See "Burmese Way to Socialism", in *The System of Correlation of Man and His Environment*, 3rd ed. (Rangoon: Burma Socialist Programme Party [hereafter BSPP], 1964), pp. 43–52.
7. See *The System of Correlation*, pp. 1–39.
8. Robert H. Taylor, "Burmese Concepts of Revolution", in *Context Meaning and Power in Southeast Asia*, edited by Mark Hobart and Robert H. Taylor (Ithaca: Cornell University Southeast Asia Program, 1986), p. 88.

9. Ibid., p. 89.
10. Ibid., pp. 89–90.
11. "The Constitution of the Burma Socialist Programme Party", in *The System of Correlation*, p. 57. See, also, "Specific Characteristics of BSP Party", in *Forward*, 13 September 1964, pp. 4–6. Full membership was accorded to only twenty senior members of the RC and RG during its cadre phase (see Taylor, *State in Burma*, pp. 316–18). Given that it was a creation of the ruling junta and was destined to inherit political power, there were strong instrumental reasons for joining.
12. A general amnesty was announced on 1 April 1963 (see *Forward*, 7 April 1963, pp. 2–3). In July 1963, peace overtures were extended to all insurgent groups (see *Party Seminar 1965*, pp. 46–48). Prominent ex-Communists and Marxists were co-opted as advisors and executives in the expanding state agencies. Some were even admitted into the BSPP (see, for example, Joseph J. Parchelo, "Recruitment of the Burmese Political Elite in the Second Ne Win Regime: 1962–1967" [Master Thesis, University of British Columbia, 1969], p. 84, n. 25). Nationalizations undercut the economic power of the business class in general and foreigners in particular. Controls and restrictions constrained the economic freedom of the private sector. Similarly, restrictions on social and religious organizations were imposed (see, for example, Taylor, *State in Burma*, p. 293).
13. See *Tawhlanyei Kaungsi*, pp. 18–24, for details on the party infrastructure. While the BSPP organization in the military establishment was not allowed to disrupt the command structure (*1968 Parti Hnihnaw Phalei Bwe* [Party Seminar] [Yangon: BSPP, 1968], pp. 165–70), the army's size was continually expanded to counter the growing strength of insurgents (see, for example, Tin Maung Maung Than, "Burma's National Security and Defence Posture", *Contemporary Southeast Asia* 11, no. 1 [1989], pp. 41, 45).
14. There were only two civilians among the twenty-four persons who were RG members at one time or the other (see Tatmadaw Thar Thutaythi Tit Oo, *1948 Khu Hnit Hma 1988 Khu Hnit Atwin Hpyat Than Lar Thaw Myanma Thamaing Akyin Hnint Tatmadaw Ghanda* [A Synopsis of Myanmar's History and the Role of the Armed Forces Across the Years 1948 to 1988], vol. 1 [Yangon: News and Periodical Enterprise, n.d.; reprint, 1990] pp. 229–30). For the military's overbearing style, see Jon A. Wiant, "The Vanguard Army: The *Tatmadaw* and Politics in Revolutionary Burma", in *The Armed Forces in Contemporary Asian Societies*, edited by Edward A. Olson and Stephen Jurika Jr. [London and Boulder, CO: Westview Press, 1986], pp. 253–54).
15. For details, see *Tawhlanyei Kaungsi*, pp. 160–86, 336–37.
16. See ibid., pp. 31–35.
17. "Burmese Way", p. 44.
18. Ibid., p. 45.
19. Ibid., p. 46.

20. Ibid.
21. Here, capitalist structure meant "disconnected and small scale private commercial business" enterprises with capitalist aspirations (see *Pyitwin Yeiyar* [Internal Affairs] no. 3, part 2 [Yangon: BSPP, 1967], pp. 19–20).
22. See ibid., pp. 21–22.
23. Ibid. pp. 62–81.
24. See, for example, *Pyidaungsu Myanmar Naingan Sipwayei Simungain Lanhyunmhu Myar Hnint Asiyinkhanzar* [Union of Burma Economic Plan Directives and Report], unpublished (Yangon: BSPP, 1971), pp. 76–77.
25. Tatmadawthar Thutaythi Tit Oo, p. 100.
26. Interestingly, Aung Gyi had earlier stated, in a press conference, that there was no intention to nationalize the oil industry (cited in T. A. B. Corley, *A History of the Burmah Oil Company, Vol. II (1924-66)* [London: Heinemann, 1988], p. 262; for an account of the events leading to the nationalization, see ibid., pp. 254–70).
27. See M. Ruth Pfanner, "Burma", in *Underdevelopment and Economic Nationalism in Southeast Asia*, edited by Frank H. Golay et al. (Ithaca: Cornell University Press, 1969), p. 250. Nationalization was directed against all business concerns irrespective of ownership. It extended even to the retail sector where 13,469 merchandise shops were nationalized (see *Forward*, 22 March 1964, p. 3). For the list on nationalizations, see Tatmadawthar Thutaythi Tit Oo, pp. 113–15. For a chronology, see David I. Steinberg, "Burma under the Military: Towards a Chronology", *Contemporary Southeast Asia* 3, no. 3 (1981): 244–85. The demonetization of 100 kyat and 50 kyat currency notes in May 1964 not only affected "black" money but also undermined small-scale businesses which usually operated outside the banking system. It was rationalized as a counter-attack against the capitalists who opposed the BWS by hoarding commodities, moving liquid assets beyond the state's reach, and initiating capital flight.
28. See *Pyitwin Yeiyar*, no. 3, part 2, pp. 221–23.
29. In 1963, the RC decreed that peasants be protected from foreclosure and in 1965 promulgated a law to abolish the tenancy rent system. Farmers were allowed the right to work on their respective plots that belonged to the state (see, for example, Mya Than and Nobuyoshi Nishizawa, "Agricultural Policy Reforms and Agricultural Development in Myanmar", in *Myanmar Dilemmas and Options: The Challenge of Economic Transition in the 1990s*, edited by Mya Than and Joseph L. H. Tan [Singapore: Institute of Southeast Asian Studies, 1990], pp. 90–91).
30. See, for example, *Pyitwin Yeiyar*, no. 3, part 2, pp. 187–91, 229–32. The RC Chairman General Ne Win referred to the state's attempt to control domestic trade as akin to getting hold of a tiger's tail (see *Party Seminar 1965*, p. 193).
31. See, for example, *1968 Parti Hnihnaw Phalei Bwei*, pp. 118–21. People's Stores Corporations (PSC) under the trade ministry were established and

were later replaced by twenty-two Trade Corporations formed under the Trade Council. The imposition of state controls over the purchase and transportation of "essential" commodities, affecting 426 items by January 1966, was also unsatisfactory (the state had to relinquish control over thirty-four major items in September and another forty-five in October due to severe bottlenecks).

32. The number employed increased from 17,726 in 1962 to 110,982 in fiscal 1971/72 (*Tawhlanyei Kaungsi*, p. 551 and *1972–73 Khu Hnit Atwet Pyidaungsu Myanmar Naingan Asoeya Ei Bandaryei Sipwayei Luhmuyei Achay Anay Hnint Pathet Ywei Pyithu Tho Asiyinkhanzar* [Report to the People by the Government of the Union of Burma on the Financial, Economic and Social Conditions for 1972-73], [hereafter *Pyithu Tho Asiyinkhanzar*] [Yangon: Ministry of Finance, 1972], Table 6, pp. 14–15).
33. For example, procurement and distribution of raw materials from abroad involved coordination among the supervisory committee of the factory concerned, the relevant industrial branch committee, Trade Corporation No. 18, Central Trade Organization, Ministry of Finance and Revenue, and Myanmar Export Import Corporation (see *Sipwa Yeiyar* [Economic Affairs], No. 7 [Yangon: BSPP], pp. 158–63).
34. See, for example, *Tawhlanyei Kaungsi*, pp. 121–35; and U Aung Than Tun, *Tawhlanyei Khit Oopadei Myar* [Laws of Revolutionary Era], vol. 2 (Yangon: Aunglandaw, 1975), pp. ka-4, ka-9 to ka-17.
35. See idem, *Tawhlanyei Khit Oopadei Myar*, vol. 1 (Yangon: Aunglandaw, 1974), pp. 308–14. This law announced, in October 1965, established the Trade Council. It was amended in 1968 to expand the range of offences covered.
36. See, for example, the interview with Ba Nyein in Carol Goldstein, "Human Errors", *Far Eastern Economic Review* (hereafter *FEER*), 2 January 1969, p. 13–14. The black market took the form of "redistribution of goods from public stores, illegal trading of controlled commodities", illegal border trade, and "smuggling of foreign exchange" as well as performing extra-legal services such as unlicensed private tutoring and acting as go-between to circumvent government regulations (see Kyaw Yin Hlaing, "The Political Economy of Hmaung-kho in Socialist Myanmar", unpublished working paper [Yangon, n.d], pp. 8–14).
37. The planning minister was vice-chairman and all the seven members were ministers, with Ba Nyein (financial adviser) as secretary.
38. This seem to have been informed by the idea of "party-mindedness" and the iterative plan-formulating process in Soviet-type economies (see, for example, Michael Ellman, *Socialist Planning* [Cambridge: Cambridge University Press, 1979; reprint, 1983], pp. 17, 21).
39. For details, see *Simungain Lanhyunmhu Myar*, pp. 77–78.
40. *Tawhlanyei Kaungsi*, pp. 48–49. This is a mixture of particular and general, even somewhat vague, statements on ends and means.

41. See *Simungain Lanhnyunhmu Myar*, pp. 32–34, for the priority scheme.
42. *Tawhlanyei Kaungsi*, pp. 49–50.
43. See *Simungain Lanhnyunhmu Myar*, pp 15–16.
44. This was done for each of the seventeen economic sub-sectors (see *Taingyin Thar Lumyo Myar Arlone Ei Sipwayei Goh Simungain Hpyint Akaung Ahtei Phawyei Simungyet* [Scheme for the Planned Implementation of the Economy of All Nationalities] [Yangon: BSPP, 1971], pp. 14–30).
45. See, for example, ibid., pp. 32–75.
46. See ibid., pp. 54–67.
47. See *Myanma Hsoshelit Lanzin Parti Ei Hnit-Shei Hnit-Toh Sipwayei Muwada Myar* [Long-Term and Short-Term Economic Policies of the Burma Socialist Programme Party] (Yangon: BSPP, 1972), p. 22. This document became the "bible" of Myanmar's planning community.
48. *Tawhlanyei Kaungsi*, pp. 52–53.
49. *Hnit-Shei Hnit-Toh Muwada*, pp. 24–27.
50. For objectives, see ibid., pp. 27–29.
51. For details, see ibid., pp. 29–34.
52. The list covered 24 minerals, 23 non-metallic industrial minerals, 344 items in the processing and manufacturing category, and 4 types of power production. Altogether 282 items were open to the private sector either freely or by registration (ibid. pp. 165–214).
53. The last point illustrates the vexing problem of balance between hierarchy and inner-party democracy common to all Leninist parties, a problem which dogged the BSPP for all its political life (cf. Ken Post and Phil Wright, *Socialism and Underdevelopment* [London: Routledge, 1989], pp. 118–20).
54. For usage of this term, see Merilee S. Grindle and John W. Thomas, *Public Choices and Policy Change: The Political Economy of Reform in Developing Countries* (Baltimore and London: John Hopkins University Press, 1991), p. 31.
55. The nature of such responses usually determine the setting of the policy agenda in most reforms (see ibid., pp. 104–107).
56. For the development of co-operatives, see *Tawhlanyei Kaungsi*, pp. 554–59. The Agricultural and Multipurpose Co-operative (AMPC) scheme was expanded with the number of units doubling between 1961/62 and 1965/66. Thereafter, it stagnated at around 12,500 units (see *Report to the Pyithu Hluttaw on the Financial, Economic, and Social Conditions of the Socialist Republic of the Union of Burma for 1986/87* [Rangoon: Ministry of Planning and Finance, 1986] [hereafter *Report to the Pyithu Hluttaw*], Table 124, p. 233). Producer co-operatives expanded very slowly and by September 1970, there were only eighteen in processing and manufacturing and four in fisheries (*1971 Khu Hnit Pahtama Akyein Parti Nyilargun: Parti Baho Kommiti Okahtagyi Ei Maintgun Myar Hnint Parti Siyoneyei Baho Kommiti Ei Nainganyei Asiyinkhanzar* [1971 First Party Congress: Speeches of the Central Committee Chairman and the Political Report

of the Party Central Organizing Committee] [Yangon: BSPP, 1971], p. 196).

57. See *FEER*, 2 January 1969, p. 13.
58. The private sector accounted for 99.8 per cent of the agriculture value-added in 1973/74 (see *1975/76 Hku Hnit Atwet Pyidaungsu Hsoshelit Thamada Myanmar Naingandaw Bundaryei Sipwayei Luhmuyei Achei Anei Hnint Pathet Thi Pyithu Hluttaw Tho Asiyinkhanzar* [Report to the Pyithu Hluttaw on Financial, Economic, and Social Conditions of the Socialist Republic of the Union of Burma] [Yangon: Ministry of Planning and Finance, 1975] [hereafter *Pyithu Hluttaw Asiyinkhanzar*], Table 10, pp. 30–31).
59. See *Pyithu Hluttaw Asiyinkhanzar 1975/76*, Table 10, pp. 30–31.
60. Data derived from various issues of *Pyithu Tho Asiyinkhanzar*.
61. See *Hnit-Shei Hnit-Toh Muwada*, p. 24 and passim.
62. For a summary on the rice industry in the 1960s, see S. K. Jayasuriya, "Technical Change and Revival of the Burmese Rice Industry", *The Developing Economies* XXII, 2 (1984): 143–45.
63. See *Hnit-Shei Hnit-Toh Muwada*, pp. 64–66, 85–88, 95–98. The annual losses from domestic rice sale averaged 90 million kyat. The state was also saddled with an underemployed trade employees costing around 300 million kyat annually (ibid., pp. 87–88).
64. Ibid., p. 120; also, pp. 111–20.
65. Meeting with foreign correspondents on 7 March 1962; see *Burma Weekly Bulletin*, 15 March 1962, p. 395.
66. Meeting with merchants and industrialists on 8 March 1962; see *Tatmadaw Thar Thutaythi Tit Oo*, p. 100.
67. See the speech delivered on 15 February 1963 to the business community, cited in *Pyitwin Yeiyar*, no. 3, part 2, p. 179.
68. See ibid., pp. 75, 180. Even small-scale and cottage industries would be nationalized in due course while handicraft industries would be co-operatized (ibid., pp. 208–16).
69. See U Thet Tun, "Sethmu Lethmu Phuntbyoyei Mahar Byuhar" [Industrial Development Strategy], in *Presidential Addresses 1971: Burma Research Congress* (Yangon: Research Policy Direction Board, 1971), p. 31.
70. See, for example, Michael Roemer, "Resource-Based Industrialization in the Developing Countries: A Survey", *Journal of Development Economics* 6, no. 2 (1979): 163–202.
71. *Pahtama Akyein Parti Nyilargun*, pp. 74–75.
72. The early targets were large establishments with foreign connections and enterprises with huge debts to the governments or small mines with financial difficulties. Traditional oil production was also nationalized. Between 1963 and 1965 altogether sixteen private factories were nationalized.
73. *Pyitwin Yeiyar*, no. 3, part 2, p. 210.
74. See, for example, ibid., pp. 177–81, 208–209; and Steinberg, "Burma under the Military", pp. 264–65.

75. See *Hnit-Shei Hnit-Toh Muwada*, pp. 236–38.
76. See ibid., pp. 238–40.
77. Offshore oil exploration financed by a Japanese loan and contracted to an American drilling firm began in January 1972. Foreign loans were also utilized for onshore exploration and offshore surveys. See *Petroleum News S.E.A.*, April 1973, pp. 17–19.
78. For details, see U Ba Chit, "Myanmar Naingan Pyithu Paing Ghanda Hma Sethmu Lokengan Tihsauk Hmu Atwe Akyon Hnint Twaykhaw Mhawmyin Hmu Myar" [Experiences in and Ideas on the Development of State-Sector Industries in Myanmar], in *Presidential Addresses 1972: Burma Research Congress* (Yangon: Research Policy Direction Board, 1972), pp. 69–80, 94.
79. See, for example, *Burma: National Economy, 1963–64* (Rangoon: Director of Information, n.d.), p. 49.
80. See ibid., pp. 50, 52.
81. *Burma Weekly Bulletin*, 12 April 1962, p. 431. However, with the marginalization of the private sector, its role was confined to securing repayments of private industrial loans and assisting in the nationalization and supervision of private industries (see *Myanmar Naingan Sethmu Lokengan Thamaing Apaing 4: Tawhlanyei Kaungsi Karla Sethmu Lokengan Thamaing* [History of Myanmar's Industry, Part 4: Revolutionary Period] [Yangon: Ministry of No. 1 Industry, n.d.], pp. 88–89).
82. See Aung Than Tun, *Tawhlanyei Khit Oopadei Myar*, vol. 1, p. 116. It was mainly utilized by cottage industries.
83. See *Tawhlanyei Kaungsi Karla Sethmu*, pp. 88–95, 100.
84. It dealt with registration, industrial relations, raw materials acquisition, production, and distribution (see ibid., pp. 95–99).
85. See *Alokethamar Yeiyar* [Worker' Affairs], No. 5 (Yangon: BSPP, 1969), pp. 36–50.
86. See *National Economy, 1963–64*, p. 51.
87. See *Report to the People by the Union of Burma Revolutionary Council on the Revolutionary Government's Budget Estimates for 1964–65* [hereafter *Report to the People*], p. 3. For government measures, see *Burma News Digest*, 3 April 1963, p. 1; and ibid., 5 June 1963, pp. 9–10.
88. For details, see *Tawhlanyei Kaungsi*, pp. 482–85. The number of state-owned mines grew from four to eighty-nine between 1962 and 1974 (ibid., appendix, p. 12).
89. See ibid., p. 483.
90. For details, see *Myanmar Naingngan Thattu Twin Myar* [Myanmar's Mines] (Yangon: BSPP, 1976), pp. 114–16, 134.
91. See, for example, *Tawhlanyei Kaungsi*, pp. 497, 500; and Ba Chit, "Myanmar Naingan Pyithu", pp. 106–107. For details on the heavy industries that were transferred from the Directorate of Defence Industries (DDI), see *Tawhlanyei Kaungsi Karla Sethmu*, pp. 216–20.

92. Data derived from *Tawhlanyei Kaungsi*, appendix, pp. 14–34, 43.
93. See ibid., pp. 16, 26, 27, 34.
94. General industries included printing presses, workshops, personal and household goods, raw materials, sub-contractors for larger industries, and those not classified under any other group.
95. *Tawhlanyei Kaungsi*, pp. 64, 502.
96. For the 1966/67–1969/70 period the annual industrial (probably including electric power) investment targets were 490 million kyat, 600 million kyat, 700 million kyat, and 800 million kyat, while the actual achievement was (including power) only 107 million kyat, 118 million kyat, 171 million kyat, and 206 million kyat respectively (see ibid.; and *Alokethamar Yeiyar*, no. 4 [Yangon: BSPP, 1968], p. 206).
97. Total cost of these projects was 1.1 billion kyat. For details on investment costs, see *Tawhlanyei Kaungsi Karla Sethmu*, pp. 217–20; *Pyithu Lokengan Sithseiyei Aphwe Ei Pyithu Hluttaw Tho Asiyinkhanzar* [Report to the Pyithu Hluttaw by the Council of People's Inspectors] [hereafter *Lokengan Sithseyei*], unpublished report (Yangon, February 1977), Table 123, p. 262; and *Lokengan Sithseyei* (September 1978), pp. 222–23.
98. Based on estimates for the mid-1960s (data from *Sipwayeiyar* No. 4 [Yangon: BSPP, 1969], Table 1, p. 284).
99. For details on the state's shares in the last six groups depicted in Table 9, see *Pythu Hluttaw Asiyinkhanzar 1975/76*, Table 75, p. 104.
100. Data are from various issues of *Report to the Pyithu Hluttaw*. One indicator of this shift towards a higher level of value-added is the ratio of the value-added or net output to the production value or gross output, which increased from 0.184 to 0.212 in the corresponding period. For data on value-added industries, see U Myat Thein, U Than Aung Yin, and U Maung Maung Lwin, "Sitpyi Khit Myanma Sethmu Htudaungyei Hnint Pyipa Konthweiyei" [Post-War Myanmar's Industrialization and External Trade], paper presented at the Burma Research Congress, Yangon, April 1971, appendix, Table I.
101. *Hnit-Shei Hnit-Toh Muwada*, pp. 49–53.
102. U Aung Khin, "Myanma Yeinan Lokengan" [Myanmar's Oil Industry], in *Presidential Addresses 1966: Burma Research Congress* (Yangon: Research Policy Direction Board, 1966), p. 14.
103. See ibid., pp. 483, 487–88.
104. See, for example, Purita Go, "Burma's Mining Industry", *Asia Mining* (August 1973): 23–26; and *Pahtama Akyein Parti Nyilargun*, pp. 186–89. Major discoveries included iron, copper, nickel, and coal (L. F. Goodstadt, "Burma's Leap", *FEER*, 5 January 1967, p. 26).
105. Production data are collated from *Myanma Yeinan Lokengan* [Myanmar's Oil Industry] (Yangon: BSPP, 1978), pp. 66, 96ff.
106. For reports on exploration, see "Burma Pins Its Hopes on Deep Drilling", in *The Oil and Gas Journal*, 10 April 1972, pp. 85, 87; and "Burma: Production Plus, Refining Minus", in *Petroleum News S.E.A.* (April 1973), pp. 17–19.

107. See *Tawhlanyei Kaungsi*, p. 66. The state's oil industry alone invested nearly 135 million kyat in the 1963/64–1970/71 period (*Myanma Yeinan*, p. 68).
108. Derived from *Report to the Pyithu Hluttaw 1986/87*, Table 8, p. 41.
109. See *Tawhlanyei Kaungsi*, p. 502.
110. Data are derived from various issues of the *Report to the People*. Cost reduction was probably due to the higher share of hydroelectricity and the introduction of gas turbines.
111. Data are derived from various issues of *Report to the People*. In contrast, the average annual growth rate of electricity demand in ASEAN between 1960 and 1973 was 13 per cent (Ang Beng Wah, *ASEAN Energy Demand: Trends and Structural Change* [Singapore: Institute of Southeast Asian Studies, 1986], Table 2.4, p. 29).
112. See *Report to the Pyithu Hluttaw 1986/87*, Table 94, p. 177; and Taylor, *State in Burma*, Table 5.1, p. 307. In most towns and villages, electricity supply was restricted to several hours a day with frequent breakdowns. Brownouts and blackouts were common in all cities including the capital. There were shortages of essential equipment for end users, such as meter boxes and circuit breakers. As such, illegal connections were widespread (especially by cottage industries), resulting in overloading, loss of revenues, and petty corruption among the EPC field staff.
113. It characterized the "one-sided investment emphasis" at the expense of consumption (Post and Wright, *Socialism*, p. 86). This bias towards industrial capital was retained up to the early 1970s. See, for example, *Pyitwin Yeiyar*, No. 7 (Yangon: BSPP, 1971), p. 142.
114. At the end of 1962 there were ten Myanmar banks and fourteen overseas banks (see U Tu Maung, *Myanma Bun Lokengang Thamaing* [History of Myanmar's Banking] [Yangon: Sabei Oo Sarpay, 1983], pp. 188–89).
115. Advances for foreign trade transactions fell from 35 million kyat in 1962 to 7 million kyat in 1963. Similarly, loans for domestic trade dropped from 102 million kyat to 61 million kyat and then to 15 million kyat in 1964 (*Statistical Supplement* [Rangoon: n.p., 1967], Table 55, p. 112).
116. *Forward*, 1 November 1966, p. 3. The Myanmar leaders perceived the sterling-based system as a vestige of colonial hold on the country and an obstacle to economic independence (see the memorandum from the Minister of Finance to the RG dated 21 October 1966, reproduced in Bo Thanmani, *Bah Gyaunt Sterling Ngwekyei Neipei Hma Myanmar Naingngan Hnote Htwet Khe Thalei Bah Dway Gayet Yite Khe Thalei* [Why did Myanmar Withdrew from the Sterling Area and What was the Impact?] [Yangon: News and Periodical Enterprise, 1991], pp. 45–54).
117. See Tu Maung, *Myanma Bun Lokengang Thamaing*, pp. 201–203.
118. See *Burma: National Economy* (Rangoon: Director of Information, 1964), pp. 161–65.
119. This is essentially, a decoupling of "investment from risk" caused by the "passivity of money" in socialist enterprises and a common feature of a

"shortage economy" (Post and Wright, *Socialism*, pp. 101, 104). Capital depreciation was disregarded and the economy suffered "from years of substantial decapitalization in the 1960s and the early 1970s" (World Bank, "Burma: Domestic and External Resource Prospects" [Washington, D.C., South Asia Programs Department, 10 October 1980], Report no. 3098-BA, p. 12).

120. The saving rate in the 1964–73 period fluctuated between 4.7 per cent (1964) and 12.7 per cent (1968) averaging 8.2 per cent (estimated from various issues of Asian Development Bank (ADB), *Key Indicators of Developing Member Countries* [Manila: ADB]).
121. Anecdotal evidence from personal communications with managerial personnel from the SIEs. See also World Bank, "The Economy of the Union of Burma", (Washington, D.C., South Asia Regional Office, 10 November 1972) Report no. SA-34, pp. 30–31.
122. See, for example, *Pahtama Akyein Parti Nyilargun*, pp. 85–86.
123. Data are derived from various issues of *Report to the People*.
124. In the 1963–73 period, the amount of Japanese aid was nearly 70 per cent of the total ODA inflow (derived from David I. Steinberg, "Japanese Economic Assistance to Burma: Aid in the 'Tarenagashi' Manner?", *Crossroads* 5, no. 2 [1990], Table 1, p. 87 and Table 7, p. 95).
125. See *Forward*, 7 February 1963, pp. 6–7. The assistance was tied to Japanese supplies.
126. See Steinberg, "Japanese Assistance", Table 1, p. 87.
127. They were: light vehicle assembly plant (Mazda); large vehicle assembly plant (Hino); agricultural machinery plant (Kubota); and household electrical appliances plant (Matsushita). Although the agreement ended in 1972 these disbursements continued until 1975 (ibid., Table 5, p. 92 and Table 11, p. 100).
128. See ibid., Table 13, p. 103.
129. Estimated from data given in ibid., Table 1, p. 87 and Table 13, p. 103.
130. See Wolfgang Bartke, *China's Economic Aid*, translated by Waldtraut Jarke (London: C Hurst, 1975), pp. 34, 90–93. In July 1967, 412 experts returned to China.
131. An economic and technical cooperation agreement was announced in July 1962. See *Burma: National Economy, 1963–64*, p. 118.
132. The highway project was scrapped by the RG in 1964, apparently for political reasons.
133. See various issues of the *Asia Yearbook* (Hong Kong: Far Eastern Economic Review).
134. Estimated by applying a conversion rate of 360 yen to the dollar and the official exchange rate for dollar (derived from Steinberg, "Japanese Assistance", pp. 100, 103).
135. For the foreign exchange content of investment in textile plants (average 55 per cent), see *Lokengan Sithseyei*, February 1977, Table 123, p. 262. For

the light vehicle assembly and electrical appliances plants (60 per cent), see *Tawhlanyei Kaungsi Karla Sethmu*, p. 221. For urea fertilizer plants (58 per cent), see *Sipwa Yeiyar*, No. 7, pp. 204, 207.

136. Steinberg, "Japanese Assistance", p. 74. See, also, ibid., pp. 74–80 for discussions on the effectiveness of Japanese aid.
137. Foreign exchange reserves which had increased from 821 million kyat (equivalent) in September 1962 to 1,036 million kyat in the following year, declined substantially after 1968 to only 304 million kyat in September 1971 (various issues of *Report to the People*).
138. For details, see Khin Maung Nyunt, "Some Aspects of Public Finance in Burma: 1964-65 to 1979-80" (Master thesis, Institute of Economics, Rangoon, 1980), Table 3-2, p. 85. The figure for 1960/61 was estimated from *Union Bank of Burma Bulletin* (1st quarter 1962), p. 55.
139. For details of tax bands, see *Forward*, 22 October 1963, p. 2.
140. See Khin Maung Nyunt, "Some Aspects of Public Finance", Table 3-4, p. 95.
141. See, for example, World Bank, *Burma* SA-34, pp. 29–30.
142. "Attitude of the Revolutionary Government Towards Labour Problems", *Forward*, 7 May 1963, p. 28.
143. Ibid.
144. "Workers Affairs: A Decade of Socialism", *Forward*, 1 March 1972, p. 12.
145. The most significant measures were the incorporation (October 1963) of temporary workers into the pension, leave, and salary increment schemes enjoyed by permanent staff; and the raising (June 1973) of pensionable age from 55 to 60 as well as the surviving family pension period from ten to fifteen years. See *Aloketharmar Asiayone Thamaing*, vol. 2 (Yangon: BSPP, 1983), pp. 241–46, 257.
146. Even in 1969, some departments had not conferred the rights stipulated in the 1964 Law and had failed to follow the 1963 directive on converting temporary workers to permanent posts. The Fourth Meeting of the Central People's Workers' Council, held in October 1969, found it necessary to mention these shortcomings in its resolutions (ibid., pp. 292–93).
147. Data from various issues of the *Statistical Yearbook for Asia and the Far East* (Manila: ECAFE).
148. The ratio of the top to bottom salary was reduced from 20 to 15 and the 700 different salary scales were reduced to only 20. Pension for the lowest scale was almost doubled (*Aloketharmar Asiayone Thamaing*, pp. 256–67).
149. See World Bank, "The Current Situation and Prospects of the Union of Burma", vol. 1, Main Report (Washington, D.C., Asia Region, 1 June 1973), Report no. 168-BA, annex, Table 9.1. However, the Yangon CPI increased in the following three years by nearly 68 per cent (World Bank, "Development in Burma: Issues and Prospects" [Washington, D.C., South Asia Regional Office, 27 July 1976], Report no. 1024-BA, annex, Table 9.1).

150. For example, in 1970/71 the number of housing units provided was 72,850 compared to 19,529 in 1961/62 (*Alokethamar Asiayone Thamaing*, p. 251).
151. See ibid., pp. 249–50.
152. Both figures included not only industrial enterprises but also those from the service and infrastructure sectors to which the scheme was extended after 1960. For data, see various issues of *Report to the People*.
153. See *People's Workers Gazette* (June 1972), p. 1.
154. The welfare activities included running thrift shops and canteens, redistributing essential food items and basic consumer goods, and agricultural and livestock production (see *Alokethamar Asiayone Thamaing*, pp. 343–45).
155. *People's Workers Gazette* (May 1972), p. 3.
156. See *Alokethmar Asiayone Thamaing*, pp. 243–44, 252–53. Provision was made in 1966 to confiscate the assets of employers who refused to abide by the CLDC's decisions.
157. See *Tawhlanyei Kaungsi Ei Alokethamar Yeiyar Hsaungywetchek Myar* [Revolutionary Council's Activities on Workers' Affairs] (Yangon: BSPP, 1977), p. 78.
158. See *Alokethmar Asiayone Thamaing*, p. 276.
159. Taylor, *State in Burma*, p. 323.
160. See *Alokethamar Asiayone Thamaing*, p. 252.
161. Priority was given to state enterprises employing large numbers of workers and regarded as important production facilities. The figure is from *Tawhlanyei Kaungsi Alokethamar*, p. 88. In practice, the JCBs concentrated on matters such as provision of welfare, socio-cultural activities, and personnel affairs.
162. For details, see *People's Workers Gazette* (November 1969), p. 3; and ibid. (May 1972), p. 3. The holiday was punctuated by lectures, sporting events, sightseeing, and guided tours of factories, government departments, production facilities, and national monuments.
163. See *Tawhlanyei Kaungsi*, p. 463.
164. See *Tawhlanyei Kaungsi Alokethamar*, pp. 92–95.
165. The appointments covered state as well as co-operative and private employers. It is interesting to note that the total number of state employees increased by over 255,000 in roughly the same period (estimated from Taylor, *State in Burma*, p. 311).
166. The 1964/65 figure was also around 51,000 suggesting that mining employment remained stagnant thereafter.
167. All 1972/73 data are from *Pyithu Tho Asiyinkhanzar 1973–74*, Table 5, p. 12. All other employment data are from various issues of the *Report to the People*.
168. This ratio may be distorted because the figure for state sector employment contained a substantial number of casual and part-time workers.
169. See various issues of the *Report to the People*.

170. See, for example, Taylor, *State in Burma*, pp. 298–99; and Wiant, "The Vanguard Army", pp. 253–54.
171. GDP growth targets for the first two years were 5.4 and 8 percentage points but the actual growth rates were only 2.5 and 2.8 respectively (*Thabawtayar Yeiyar* [Theoretical Affairs], No. 11 [Yangon: BSPP, 1977], pp. 105, 150).
172. In 1973/74 the state owned 94 per cent of the 409 industrial establishments employing 100 or more workers. In the 51–100 employee category, the state's share of 644 establishments was 44 per cent. This was in contrast to the state's share of only 5 per cent of the registered total of 29,184 establishments (*Pyithu Hluttaw Tho Asiyinkhanzar 1974/75*, Table 73, p. 106).
173. See, for example, U Soon Sein, "Myanma Thattu Toophawyei Lokengan", [Myanmar's Mining Industry], in *Presidential Addresses 1971: Burma Research Congress* (Yangon: Research Policy Direction Board, 1971), pp. 53–61.
174. See, for example, the discussion by the Minister of Industry and Labour, at the workers' seminar on 30 April 1965 in which he cited instances of gross absenteeism and indiscipline among state workers (*Alokethamar Hnihnawbwe Hmattan* [Workers' Seminar Record] [Yangon: Director of Information, 1965], p. 169); and the ten points listed, as the shortcomings of the workers underlying the fall in productivity, in *Sipwa Yeiyar* No. 4, pp. 226–33.

Part IV

One-Party Socialist State (1974–88)

6

Planned State under Party Guidance

The Burma Socialist Programme Party (BSPP) that was transformed into a mass party prior to the institution of the Socialist Constitution that mandated one-party rule became the supreme economic as well as political authority of Myanmar. The elected government formulated and executed long- and short-term economic plans under the guidance of the BSPP cadres whose supervisory and monitoring functions extended from the centre through the regional hierarchy of party apparatus down to the enterprise and ward/village tract level.

BURMA SOCIALIST PROGRAMME PARTY MONOPOLY

Instituted on 3 January 1974, the Socialist Republic of the Union of Burma was a unitary one-party socialist state led by the BSPP.[1] Electoral representation was based on a four-tier hierarchy consisting of three regional people's councils (ward/village, township, and state/division) and the Pyithu Hluttaw ("Parliament"), held on a quadrennial basis. However, given the BSPP's prerogative of nominating "official" candidates, elections implied confirmation rather than competition.[2]

The locus of all three state powers (executive, judicial, and legislative) was the BSPP-dominated unicameral Pyithu Hluttaw, thereby blurring the demarcation between the party and the state.[3] There were regional and local administrative and judicial bodies under the central organs of state power.[4] The state executive operated under the leadership and guidance of the Central Committee and the Central Executive Committee (CEC) of the BSPP. Similarly, the territorial hierarchy of people's councils were supervised by the corresponding regional party organs.[5] The new political order was predicated upon the BSPP's "centralized control, pervasive authority and sole legitimacy".[6] In this system, as observed by Taylor:

> People seem also to have developed the capacity ... to recognize and accept with resignation the gap that exists between the ideals and goals of the state and the actual behaviour of its institutions and personnel.[7]

Trilateral Affinity: Party, State, and the Military

Though devoid of a formal political role, the military's influence in Myanmar's governance remained undiminished during the BSPP era. In fact, the political leadership comprised the party's military formateurs led by (retired) General Ne Win.[8] Although formally subscribing to the BSPP's political role, the party organization within the armed forces was structured to ensure that the chain of command was not compromised. The latter reflected the command hierarchy with commanders invariably elected to top party posts at all levels. Moreover, the military served as a reservoir of human resources for the party and the state apparatus.[9]

The trinity of institutions managing Myanmar shared a common ethos in their military heritage. As such, politics resembled a "triangle of accommodation" in which the party assumed the pre-eminent position relying on the military for support in realizing its goals through the state apparatus.[10]

However, the unsuccessful coup attempt by the "young turks" in 1976 and the series of public unrest in the mid-1970s, together with the failure to achieve planned economic targets, appeared to have created tensions between the government and the party leadership in the late 1970s.[11] Following severe criticism of the regime's economic performance at the Third Party Congress in February 1977, the Prime Minister was replaced in a major Cabinet shake-up at the March session of the Pyithu Hluttaw, in what was believed to have been the BSPP leadership's bid to reassert control over the state's functions.[12] After a major purge in the BSPP in late 1977,[13] the ruling trinity appeared to have succeeded in maintaining the triangle of accommodation and the

BSPP's pre-eminence in politics and governance remained unchallenged for at least a decade.

Political Sclerosis and BSPP's Dissolution

The BSPP's monopoly in controlling the state meant that the singular route to the control of state resources lay with the party. Increasing bureaucratization resulted in a privileged class, even as more professionals and technocrats were co-opted into the system. Though "inner-party democracy" and "democratic centralism" were the professed guidelines for the *modus operandi* of the BSPP, "centralism" appeared to have prevailed over "democracy" in practice.[14] This led to authoritarian practices and structural rigidities. The centrality of "the idea of a party as a political force committed to the furthering of the interests of the society as a whole" and the "tendency to subordinate to that pursuit the articulation of sectional interests in society" also insulated the BSPP from the socio-political and economic changes occurring beyond the umbra of routinized political exercises.[15] Moreover, the political leaders were unable to "incorporate their own ideological construction", i.e., the Burmese Way to Socialism (BWS), "into their own beliefs" since the latter "had not grown out of political or revolutionary experience" like those of "socialist leaders in China and Vietnam".[16]

On the other hand, the cadre system provided patronizing opportunities and spawned a system similar to the Soviet *nomenklatura*.[17] This became the principal instrument for party control over state and public affairs and its members enjoyed perks and privileges.[18] Although the BSPP system was not as elaborate and pervasive as the Chinese and Soviet systems, its impact in terms of the selection of key functionaries and the rationalization of patronage as well as the cadres' general reaction was similar.[19]

Meanwhile, the state–party–military trinity appeared to have instituted political stability and ensured regime security by consolidating its political superstructure.[20] In reality, the BSPP could not forestall the building up of systemic weaknesses associated with one-party dominance in an authoritarian setting.[21] Though the top political leadership was aware of problems associated with organizational slack, corruption, and poor policy implementation, the root of such shortcoming was attributed to "the personal weakness of individuals".[22] The Party Chairman's adage of preferring "goodness" over "ability" became the party's maxim.[23] By the mid-1980s, some weaknesses in primary party organizations were acknowledged, but the BSPP's self-assessment suggested a positive prognosis, citing overall success and favourable trends in all fronts.[24] As such, the ossification of the *nomenklatura* and the widening of the gulf between the centre and the grassroots were overlooked.

On the other hand, the upbeat party rhetoric belies the fact that the political discourse had been a monologue directed against a depoliticized populace, deprived of alternatives in a "political desert".[25] As an established one party system operating with impunity, the BSPP failed to discern the erosion of its superstructure and the signs of sclerosis through apathy, confusion, complacency, and corruption.[26] Thus, the BSPP leadership was ill-prepared for the explosion of suppressed discontent that engulfed Myanmar in 1988.

As the state's economic drive ran out of steam in the mid-1980s, inflation and shortages of consumer goods brought economic hardship to the populace while the *nomenklatura* enjoyed access to scarce resources. By 1987, the economy was in dire straits. The party's response was more of a hortatory and bureaucratic nature.[27] As such, the party leadership remained ambivalent towards the grim economic situation and the sporadic outbreak of public disorder in the first half of 1988. The turmoil resulting from the cycle of demonstrations, repression and respite (which attracted unprecedented external media attention) that ensued was unparalleled.[28] Amidst uncertainty and apprehension brought about by the sour mood of the public over what was perceived as unduly harsh repression of demonstrations over genuine grievances, an extraordinary session of the BSPP Congress was convened in July 1988. The resulting change in leadership from Ne Win to Sein Lwin aggravated the rapidly deteriorating legitimacy of the BSPP and the state leadership.[29]

The organizational changes and remedies proposed by the post-Ne Win leadership were seen as too little and too late by the agitated polity.[30] The political leadership seemed unable to seize the initiative, reacting legalistically and sluggishly to the mounting populist demands. Subsequently, the elaborate political and administrative superstructure buckled and collapsed. The regional hierarchy of people's councils were paralysed and the BSPP underwent rapid disintegration at the grassroots.[31] It was observed that:

> the weakness of the party was it was born as a party in power and grew up as one. It lacked practical experience in making sacrifices, taking risks, and striving to overcome adversity. Power corrupts, and absolute power corrupts absolutely.[32]

As the tempo of demonstrations, civil disobedience, and agitation for an interim government increased, it was perceived by the military leadership as anarchic with the government rapidly losing control. Latent fears of external intervention resurfaced and the spectre of a divided military reappeared. Finally, on 18 September 1988, Myanmar's armed forces took over state power, in the wake of the abandonment of the BWS and the eventual dissolution of the BSPP.[33] All in all, it seems that the BSPP had not been able to translate its concentrated power into legitimate authority.[34] As such, the party collapsed when confronted with the groundswell of public discontent fuelled by economic crisis; the crisis whose aetiology is the subject of the following sections.

ECONOMIC STRATEGY, POLICIES, AND PLANS

The overall economic strategy, adopted by the BSPP's First Congress of 1971 and elaborated in the party's "Long-Term and Short-Term Economic Policies" (LTSTEP), was to substantially increase commodity production. The aim was to achieve proportional growth under planned production. The Second Party Congress, in October 1973, endorsed the Twenty-Year Plan (TYP) from 1974/75 to 1993/94, constituting five four-year plans (FYPs), as well as the Second FYP that replaced the truncated First FYP (1971/72–1973/74).[35]

The economic policies adopted were in line with the LTSTEP document in which both long-term and short-term policies were specified. The latter was intended for implementation before the advent of the Pyithu Hluttaw in 1974 but many of its objectives remained unfulfilled and had to be retained as guidelines for successive FYPs.[36]

The long-term economic policies contained general objectives as well as specific measures. Mainly directed at the state sector, these included:

- introducing material incentives and commercial principles in operating state economic enterprises (SEEs) with profit as performance indicator;

- expanding management authority and instituting a reward and punishment system based on performance;
- safeguarding state assets against losses and misappropriation;
- establishing financial autonomy for SEEs with the state charging interest for capitalization as well as rents;
- introducing competition between SEEs and co-operatives/private enterprises and amongst SEEs in selected industries;
- limiting excess profit-taking and price escalation of SEEs by emphasizing cost reduction over price mark-up;
- allowing investments by private citizens in selected economic enterprises;
- allowing individuals and co-operative to operate enterprises supporting state economic activities;
- providing an education system relevant to economic activities and manpower needs;
- commercializing external trade;
- soliciting of beneficial external assistance;
- transferring selected enterprises from the state to the co-operative sector;
- minimizing manpower and costs in the administrative services, while giving priority to satisfy the manpower and investment needs of the productive enterprises; and
- striking a balance between political and economic benefits in carrying out economic activities.[37]

The long-term policies for national planning included, *inter alia*:

- accumulating surplus without eroding the prevailing level of consumption;
- allocating investment in the most efficient way;
- delegating operational control over production to the management concerned;
- establishing reciprocal relations between higher and lower coordinating bodies involved in plan formulation and implementation;
- establishing national plan targets at the central level based on targets coordinated at the township level;
- implementing plans through administrative means with the organizational support of the BSPP and its affiliates; and
- reporting of annual plan performance within three months and instituting annual appraisals for investments.[38]

Similarly, for finance, the policies envisaged the following:

- relating cash plans and loans plans to the financial plans of SEEs;
- incorporating enterprise accounts into the consolidated budget to reveal the profit-and-loss situation of each SEE;
- coordinating the budget with the plan to ensure consistency at all times;
- allocating budget through the state-owned banks in accordance with financial plans;
- instituting financial supervision and annual auditing of SEEs;
- applying, wherever possible, cost accounting methods in SEEs;
- minimizing expenditures in the state sector;
- reviewing and reforming the revenue system to foster rapid economic development; and
- soliciting official development assistance (ODA).[39]

The major objectives of the TYP included the transformation from an agricultural economy to an agro-based industrial economy and the development of socialist production relations.[40]

This entailed the doubling of the per capita gross domestic product (GDP), while assuming average annual growth rates of 2.3 per cent for population and 2 per cent for labour productivity.[41]

The TYP growth targets, depicted in Table 6.1, reflected attempts to achieve faster growth of exports over imports and to substantially raise investments. The average GDP growth rate of 5.9 per cent was to be achieved by posting progressively higher average GDP growth in the five consecutive FYPs.[42]

TABLE 6.1
Overall Twenty-Year Plan Targets

Target variables	*Growth Index (1973/74 = 100)*	*Annual Growth Rate (%)*
Net output (GDP)	315	5.9
Consumption	258	4.8
Investment	620	9.6
Imports value	486	8.2
Exports value	790	10.9
Average per capita GDP	200	3.5
Average per capita consumption	164	2.5

Source: Planning Department.

TABLE 6.2
Sectoral Growth Targets of the Twenty-year Plan

Economic Sector	*Growth Index (1973/74 = 100)*	*Annual Growth Rate (%)*
Production	347	6.4
Agriculture	256	4.8
Livestock & fisheries	256	4.8
Forestry	256	4.8
Mining	352	6.5
Processing & manufacturing	607	9.4
Power	607	9.4
Construction	397	7.1
Services	304	5.7
Transportation	425	7.5
Communications	425	7.5
Financial institutions	262	4.9
Social & administrative services	262	4.9
Rentals & others	262	4.9
Trade	262	4.9

Source: Planning Department.

The TYP emphasized production over services and trade. It also envisaged faster growth in infrastructure and industrial development as shown in Table 6.2.

As evident in Table 6.3, in terms of sectoral contributions to GDP, there would be a reduction in the primary sectors' share and substantial increases in the shares of the industrial sectors, with the processing and manufacturing sector almost doubling its share.

The desired pattern for socialist production relations was formulated in terms of targets for outputs by ownership implying a significantly diminished role for the private sector by 1993/94 (Table 6.4). In production, the state's share would be more than doubled and the co-operatives were to quadruple their share while the private sector's share was to be reduced by over 60 per cent. In services and trade, the private sector's share was to decline by 40 per cent. The state's share of GDP would increase by 37 per cent while the co-operatives' share

TABLE 6.3
Targets for Structural Changes in the Economy

Economic Sector	*Share of GDP in 1973/74 (%)*	*Share of GDP in 1993/94 (%)*
Production	51.4	56.5
Agriculture	25.7	20.9
Livestock & fisheries	7.8	6.3
Forestry	2.6	2.1
Mining	1.2	1.3
Processing & manufacturing	11.5	22.1
Power	0.7	1.4
Construction	1.9	2.4
Services	23.6	22.8
Transportation	5.8	7.8
Communications	0.3	0.4
Financial institutions	1.2	1.0
Social & administrative services	9.2	7.7
Rentals & others	7.1	5.9
Trade	25.0	20.7
Total GDP	100.0	100.0

Source: Planning Department.

TABLE 6.4
Targets for Contributions to GDP by Ownership

Economic Sectors	*State*		*Co-operative*		*Private*	
	1973/74	*1993/94*	*1973/74*	*1993/94*	*1973/74*	*1993/94*
Production	18	39	8	33	74	28
Services	58	67	2	9	40	24
Trade	48	54	17	25	35	21
GDP	35	48	8	26	57	26

Note: All figures are in percentage shares.
Source: Planning Department.

more than tripled with a concomitant reduction in private contributions by 54 per cent.

The TYP objectives also included: the elimination of unemployment by the end of the Fourth FYP; establishment of an education system relevant to the economy and supportive of the "socialist mode of production"; narrowing of the differences in the living standards amongst the country's regions, reduction in income disparity; and "steady growth in the accumulation of capital" according to the "law of socialist accumulation of capital".[43]

Consequently, the state would give priority to expanding primary production and exporting the growing surpluses, establishing import-substituting consumer goods industries based on primary products, maximizing minerals output, and initiating investments in heavy industries based on mineral raw materials.[44]

There was no mention of resources and, in contrast to those of centrally planned economies (CPEs), there were no subsidiary plans for investment, human resources, technology, and trade to support it.[45] How the targeted sectoral growth rates would be translated into the desired pattern of production by ownership was never specified and the consistency of the stipulated sectoral growth rates in relation to inter-industry linkages remained untested. Although the share of the private sector in both production (over 60 per cent) and employment (90 per cent) was significant, it was relegated to a residual role in all the plans.[46]

Planning: Institutions and Processes

The BSPP headquarters was responsible for the overall plan guidelines as well as the co-ordination and supervision of plan implementation.[47] The state planning infrastructure, instituted by the reorganization of the state administrative machinery in March 1972, included the Planning Department (PD), the Project Appraisal and Progress Reporting Department (PAPRD), and the Foreign Economic Relations Department (FERD).

The PD headquarters was responsible for sectoral as well as regional planning, whereas the regional offices (state/division and township) had to liaise with the respective people's councils in formulating and monitoring regional plans.[48] The PAPRD scrutinized and evaluated all new projects and monitored ongoing projects. All forms of foreign loans and grants were channelled through the FERD.

Ostensibly, due to organizational and time constraints, the Second FYP was formulated as a top-down exercise, in consultation with various ministries and departments.[49] Subsequent plans were to be formulated and coordinated according to the following procedure.[50]

(a) Laying down of FYP guidelines by the BSPP congress.
(b) Forwarding these guidelines to the Council of State, then to the Council of Ministers, which delegated the task to the Ministry of Planning and Finance.
(c) Setting the format and requesting the ministries to draw up their draft plan targets.
(d) Drafting of plan targets by individual ministries, in consultation with subordinate agencies.
(e) Consolidating the draft plan targets at the Ministry of Planning and Finance after considering their feasibility, sectoral consistency, and concordance to party guidelines. Submitting the consolidated draft plan targets to the Economic Co-ordination Committee (ECC) of the Cabinet and to the BSPP headquarters.
(f) Reformulating the consolidated proposals according to the ECC's recommendations and sending them to the regional (state/division and township) levels.
(g) Coordination of the regional targets between the state/division and township people's councils, based on basic level (factory/enterprise/village) considerations.
(h) Incorporating the feedback from the regional proposals and drawing up the draft plan under ECC's guidance.
(i) Finalizing the draft plan at the ECC in consultation with the chairmen of the state and division people's councils.
(j) Considering the draft plan, submitted by the ECC, at the Cabinet and submitting the final draft to the Council of State and then to the Pyithu Hluttaw.
(k) Approving the draft FYP after deliberations at the relevant Pyithu Hluttaw Affairs Committees and the plenum.
(l) Repeating steps (c) to (k) for the annual plan under the respective FYP framework.

This entailed a continuous planning cycle consisting of overlapping phases of formulation, implementation, monitoring and appraisal.[51] The flow chart for the planning process is illustrated in Figure 6.1.

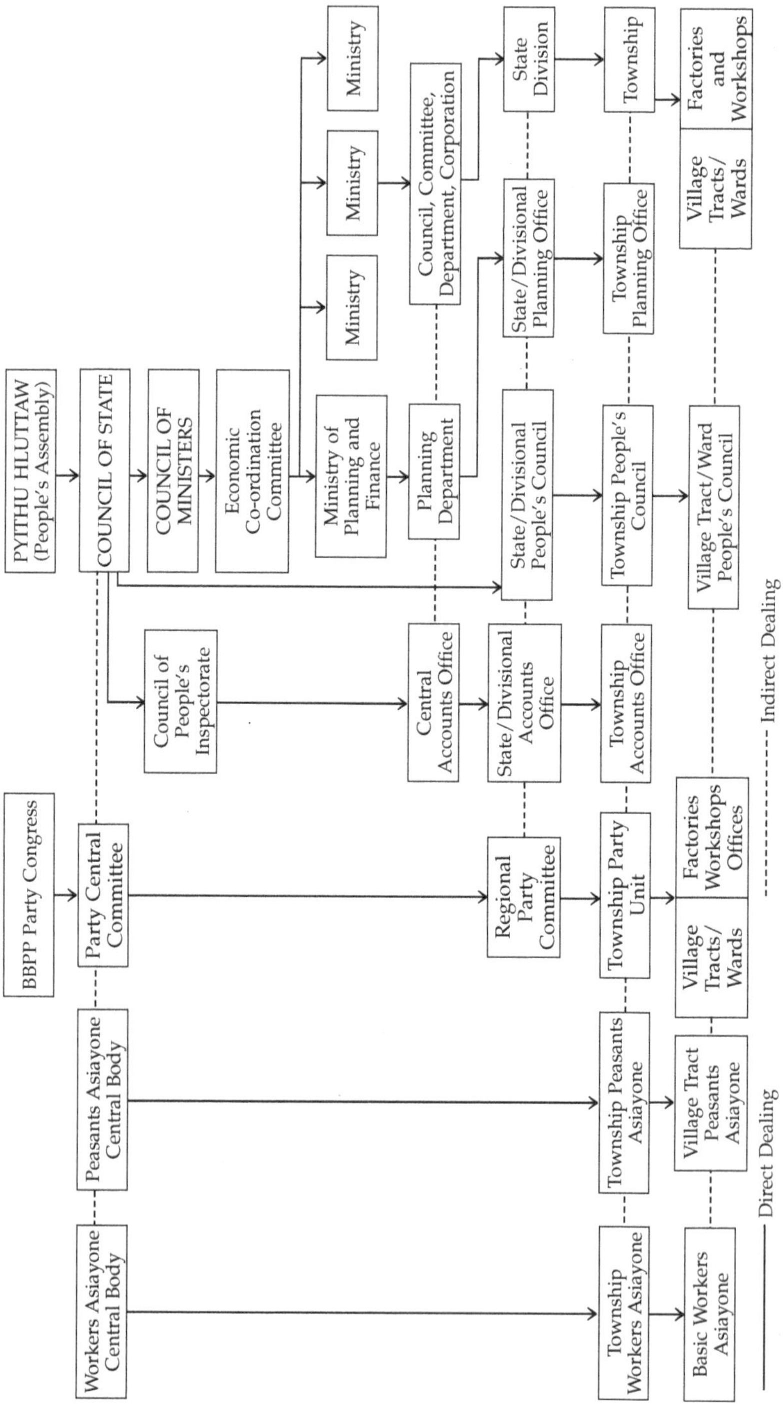

FIGURE 6.1
Planning Procedure in Myanmar

The annual plan targets were endorsed and legislated by the Pyithu Hluttaw for each fiscal year. From 1975/76, annual planning incorporated the "principle of opinion exchange between the central and subordinate organs" and with effect from fiscal 1977/78, the task of proposing township-level plan targets was delegated to the state/division people's councils.[52]

The implementation phase was also meant to be a coordinated effort mobilizing productive, political, and administrative resources. Government agencies were responsible to their respective ministries for sectoral plan implementation and people's councils were entrusted with the task of ensuring that regional targets were met.[53] The BSPP's main role was to supervise and coordinate the annual plans and to provide support and guidance to the implementing agencies.[54]

Four-Year Plans and Annual Plans

The FYPs were endorsed by the BSPP in its quadrennial party congress. Guidelines stipulating objectives, policy measures and quantitative targets for the forthcoming FYP were tabled and usually elicited unanimous acceptance at the plenum. Important FYP guidelines (excluding industrial sectors) established by the successive party congresses are depicted in Table 6.5, together with revisions made by the corresponding Pyithu Hluttaw sessions.[55]

These guidelines were apparently influenced by prevailing economic conditions and experiences gained from previous plans. For example, the dismal performance of the truncated First FYP, whose average (of 2.5 years) annual growth of real GDP was just 1 per cent, was attributed to adverse weather compounded by lack of export growth, low factor productivity, and poor performance of the SEEs.[56] Hence, guidelines for the Second FYP emphasized exports, production efficiency and wastage reduction. The substantial upward revision by the Pyithu Hluttaw of the targeted GDP growth rate reflected not only the government's optimism, but also the political necessity of enhancing "performance legitimacy".[57]

Although the Second FYP was relatively more successful than its predecessor, there were significant shortfalls.[58] As such, the Third FYP guidelines reflected BSPP Third Congress' emphasis on issues of private sector participation, material incentives, and commercialization of SEEs. Here, the large mark-up (by 20 per cent) of the GDP growth target by the Pyithu Hluttaw may be seen as an attempt to rectify the slippage from the TYP growth path.

TABLE 6.5
Four-Year Plan Guidelines

	Policy Objectives and Measures	*Targets*
Second FYP (1974/75–77/78)	To raise exports to the pre-1964/65 level. To fully utilize the country's productive capacities. To achieve steady growth in economic efficiency and labour productivity in the state and co-operative sectors. To substantially reduce material losses in state and co-operative enterprises.	Average GDP growth of 4% (4.5%); K13.3 billion for 1977/78 (13.38) of which goods, 52.1%; services, 23.5%; trade, 24.4% (50.8%, 24.4%, 24.8%). Total investment of K5.81 billion (4.47) Average annual exports of K0.6 billion (0.9). Average labour productivity growth, in net output per worker, of 2% (2.4%).
Third FYP (1978/79–81/82)	To pass laws providing rights, incentives, assistance and encouragement for attracting required private investments. To run state corporations as independent commercial enterprises and practice, a reward and punishment system down to the factory and individual levels.	Average GDP growth of 5.5% (6.6%); K16.1 billion for 1981/82 (16.94) of which goods, 53%; services, 23.3%; trade, 23.7% (52.7%, 23.7%, 23.6%). Total investment of K10.4 billion; 56.49% in the state sector (8.2; 71.92%). Exports of K1.4 billion for 1981/82 (1.24).
Fourth FYP (1982/83–85/86)	To significantly increase the co-operatives' share in production. To ensure smooth production within the plan framework for private enterprises allowed under the Rights of Private Enterprise Law. To apply the reward and punishment system down to the factory and individual levels. To achieve steady growth in savings.	Average GDP growth of 6% (6.2%); K21.1 billion for 1985/86 (21.28) of which goods, 54.2%; services, 23.1%; trade, 22.7% (54.9%, 24%, 21.1%). Total investment of K14.4 billion; 70.1% in the state sector (12.6; 81.9%). Exports of K2 billion for 1985/86 (1.85). Average labour productivity growth of 3.1%.

TABLE 6.5 (continued)

	Policy Objectives and Measures	*Targets*
	To formulate and implement regional development plans for balanced growth and reduction of the gap between urban and rural standards of living. To formulate a manpower plan; to reduce and eliminate unemployment.	
Fifth FYP (1986/87–89/90)	To invest in export projects, with short gestation periods. To raise the output of the state and co-operatives at least to surpass private output, and to significantly increase the co-operatives' share. To expand transportation commensurate with increased production. To favour labour-intensive enterprises. To ensure consistency and balance between economic sectors, enterprises, production and consumption, prices and wages, buying and selling prices in state trading, procurement prices for exempted crops and controlled crops, as well as domestic production and external trade.	Average GDP growth of 6.1% (4.5%); K26.78 billion for 1989/90 (25.22) of which goods, 55.4%; services, 22.9%; trade, 21.7% (54.4%; 25.6%; 20%). Total investment of K14.2 billion (10.3); 70.6% in the state sector (K9.6 billion in the state sector). Exports of K2.1 billion for 1989/90 (1.6). Average labour productivity growth of 3.1% (2.1%).

Note: Figures in parentheses are revisions made by the Pyithu Hluttaw; prices are in constant 1969/70 kyat.

The Third FYP was deemed successful and the party's aim to maintain the growth initiated by the "green revolution" was reflected in the setting of a 6 per cent growth target for the Fourth FYP.[59] On the other hand, concern for the dismal progress in the co-operatives sector towards the desired ownership composition found expression in the call for the co-operatives' accelerated growth.[60] The emphasis on the bonus and penalty systems for greater efficiency was reiterated. The need to raise the level of domestic savings was also recognized.[61] Urban unemployment, especially educated unemployment, was also acknowledged as a serious problem.[62]

In the mid-1980s, negative effects of persistent macroeconomic imbalances began to manifest and the planners set a significantly lower (by nearly a quarter) growth target for the Fifth FYP.[63] Shortage of investment funds and balance of payments difficulties led to exhortations for quick expansion of exports. The continuing lacklustre performance of the co-operatives and the sluggish output of the state sector, that further aggravated the deviation from the TYP norm of the GDP contribution pattern by ownership, were also reflected in the Fifth FYP guidelines.[64] Furthermore, fuel shortages that steadily worsened after 1980 as oil production levelled off led to the call for measures to increase fuel and energy production.[65] The emphasis on labour-intensive projects reflected concerns over unemployment and capital shortfalls.[66]

A rank ordering of sectoral priorities was enunciated in the Second FYP guidelines. Agriculture was first, followed by forestry, mining, transport and communications, livestock and fishery, power, processing and manufacturing, construction, social services, trade, and other services (including financial services).[67] This was meant to "maximize" production "in the shortest possible time" and to contribute towards a "healthier economy as a whole".[68]

Notably, the processing and manufacturing sector was given a lowly seventh position, probably reflecting the bitter experience of the previous decade in which attempts at "heavy" industrialization coupled with relative neglect of the primary products sectors had led to economic stagnation. Trade occupied the second lowest ranking, despite the Plan's aim to "exploit the present favourable export market [for primary products] after fulfilment of domestic requirements".[69] Trade's low priority reflected the leadership's belief that production was more important than exchange and that trade could be effectively "administered".[70]

Each Party Congress passed resolutions on future economic tasks (Table 6.6) which reflected prevailing economic conditions as well as the TYP objectives.[71] The list grew longer with time but the theme of mobilizing the masses was always there. The Third Congress set tasks in line with its emphasis on primary production and ISI strategy. The expansion of the state's economic role was also stressed, while the extremely slow growth of the co-operatives necessitated a reiteration of the need to boost its expansion. Exports promotion was advocated in the context of securing surplus and was reiterated in the Fourth as well as the Fifth Congress, reflecting concerns over poor export performance. The apparent weaknesses of centralization led to the call for effective regional plans. The Fourth Congress also acknowledged transportation bottlenecks and shortages of energy and raw materials that appeared during the Fourth FYP and steadily worsened thereafter.

Unemployment and the low utilization of human resources necessitated resolutions to rectify them. The lack of efficiency among SEEs was also recognized and the Fourth and Fifth Congress resolved to address it. Indications that the green revolution had peaked probably prompted the Fifth Congress to identify the need for reassessing the domestic food situation. Resource constraints, which became more acute towards the end of the Fourth FYP, required due consideration as well.

Each FYP had an overall objective reflecting the political and economic imperatives at hand. Thus, the early optimism of the Second Party Congress was demonstrated by the Second FYP objective specifying "higher production and greater efficiency in all spheres of the economy".[72] However, the principal objective of the Third FYP which was "to regain the original path" of the TYP "by the terminal year" reflected the unsatisfactory performance of the Second FYP in the context of the long-term plan.[73] On the other hand, the aim "to fully implement the targets set forth in [its] guidelines for achieving the principal objectives of the Twenty-Year Plan" and "to accelerate production through streamlining of the existing economic activities and programmes with a view to achieving the objectives of the Long-Term Twenty-Year Plan", emphasized the importance of adhering to the TYP growth path and following its guidelines.[74] This, in turn, became the principal objective of the Fourth and Fifth FYP respectively.

The FYP targets approved by the Pyithu Hluttaw were disaggregated into detailed annual targets within the FYP framework. The annual targets legislated by the Pyithu Hluttaw became the benchmarks for plan implementation and were specified for the corresponding fiscal year.[75]

TABLE 6.6
Resolutions on Future Economic Tasks

Party Congress	*Resolutions*
Second (1973)	To fully utilize people's capabilities for rapid economic development.
Third (1977)	To give priority to formulating and implementing short-term agricultural and animal husbandry projects in annual plans. To satisfy the minimum food and clothing needs through state production of basic foodstuffs and textiles. To fully utilize the people's capabilities. To transform the mode of production including agriculture into state and co-operative enterprises according to plans. To expand and promote export trade. To satisfy the capital requirement for full investment.
Fourth (1981)	To expand agriculture as well as fishery and livestock production. To effectively expand meat and fish production in the co-operatives so as to achieve the ownership ratio envisaged in the TYP. To formulate and implement regional plans ensuring proportionate development and most beneficial utilization of regional resources. To promote exports. To extend transport services commensurate with the planned accelerated production of goods. To ensure adequate supply of raw materials and energy. To formulate and implement a manpower plan for full and effective utilization of human resources. To make systematic arrangements for improving the efficiency of state economic enterprises.
Fifth (1985)	To utilize the people's capabilities in economic movements related to extensively carrying out the tasks for the planned development of a socialist economy in line with the TYP objectives. To assess the balance between population growth and food production capacity and to take necessary anticipatory measures. To continue export promotion and to earn more foreign exchange through private sector services. To increase production of fuels and energy as required by the production and service sectors. To expand formation of state agriculture production organizations and agricultural as well as other production co-operatives. In undertaking planned investments, to take measures for increasing the industrial sector's investment efficiency and expanding production in agriculture, forestry, and livestock and fishery sectors. To systematically assess the plans in relation to the provision of resources required for their implementation. To continuously strive for the reduction and elimination of wastage, loss, and damage in each and every sector. To implement, without fail, regional plans for development and self-sufficiency. To formulate and implement a manpower plan for the full and effective utilization of the people's capabilities.

RESTRUCTURING AND REFORMS

There were institutional restructuring and limited reforms during the mid-1970s.[76] These involved resource mobilization, budgetary control, banking, interest rates, domestic and foreign trade, pricing, distribution, and SEE operations. Although carried out in the context of enhancing overall economic development, they were significant for Myanmar's post-1974 industrialization not only because of inter-sectoral linkages and capital formation, but also in relation to managing SIEs.[77]

Restructuring State Agencies

The new administrative system, introduced in March 1972, empowered the minister to exercise direct control over state agencies, i.e., directorates (regulatory, administrative or planning) or corporations (SEEs). Normally, a deputy minister, responsible to the minister, supervised a cluster of agencies within the ministry.[78] Each ministry had an executive committee chaired by the minister with deputy minister(s) and agency heads as members. It was authorized to exercise collective decision-making in all pertinent matters.[79]

Several sub-Cabinets or ministerial committees were established. The ECC of the Council of Ministers was also reconstituted to oversee economic matters. The Cabinet was responsible to the Council of State.[80] The BSPP formally assumed a leading role in economic policy formulation and overseeing plan implementation. Furthermore, the hierarchy of people's councils was entrusted with the task of controlling virtually all economic activities as well as formulating and implementing regional economic plans.[81] An elaborate committee-based structure was established to deliberate and decide upon the policies, issues, and measures as well as day-to-day administrative matters.[82]

This institutional set-up was aimed at enhancing flexibility and efficiency in planning, production, and distribution, in contrast to the unsuccessful *dirigiste* command authority of the RC era. However, in practice, with the rise of the *nomenklatura*, it turned out to be equally dysfunctional. Entangled lines of authority, the veil of "collective leadership and responsibility", and the practice of blaming adverse externalities for setbacks led to diminished accountability and inefficiency.[83]

Financial Reforms

According to the LTSTEP guidelines on financing and banking policies, financial reforms were undertaken in the areas of taxation and banking.[84]

Tax Reform

The single-schedule tax system was replaced by a progressive income tax system employing multiple schedules in 1974 (Table 6.7).[85] The new system was much more discerning by taking into account the variegated nature of income arising from different sources. Private limited companies were not allowed and the proprietor of a private enterprise had to pay tax as an individual. Those without documentary evidence or suspected of under-reporting income were subjected to presumptive assessment by local tax authorities.[86] The new tax regime was still heavily biased against private business enterprises by imposing a super tax over and above the normal tax rate of 50 per cent for annual incomes above 42,000 kyat.[87] This acted as a disincentive against private initiatives in the economy.

In fiscal 1976/77, a revised tax regime was introduced. The new scheme for profit tax was complemented by the Commodities and Services Tax (CST). Taken together these two measures were expected to improve the state's financial position that had deteriorated for almost a decade.[88]

As evident from Table 6.8, this new regime allowed a relatively higher margin of after-tax profits for private enterprises then the one it replaced. There was a fixed value for tax payable within each income tranche, in contrast to the usual practice of specifying the rate in percentage terms. This introduced an element of inequity within the tranche because the ratio of the tax value to income decreased proportionately from the lower bound to the upper bound. Another feature was that it simplified tax administration by consolidating the non-salaried private income categories and abolishing the relief allowances. The township people's councils were empowered to enforce the collection of profit tax via assessment committees which were entrusted with the task of determining the individual taxpayer's liability.[89]

It was expected that the harsh penalties prescribed by the law as well as close supervision by the people's councils would deter tax fraud and evasion while the relatively more moderate tax rates would encourage private entrepreneurs to be increasingly drawn into the tax net.[90] The capital gains tax set at only 10 per cent for large sums may be seen as extremely generous in relation to the much higher rates for income and business profit.[91]

On the other hand, the CST was tailored to establish a broad tax base by exploiting the anticipated growth in state-controlled merchandise imports as well as the expanding production of the state sector and

TABLE 6.7
Summary of Income Tax System (1974)

Target	*Nature*	*Exemption/Relief*	*Rate*

Resident	On salary, income of co-operatives (industrial co-operatives excluded), and private "entities"; assessed on previous year's income.	Reliefs: first 1,500; 20% of earned income capped at 6,000; 2,000 for wife; age-graduated for child from 400 to 800.
		Exemption up to 10,000 for salary and co-operative income; 8,000 for others.
			Five income categories, viz. (a) salary; (b) professional with short-lived earning potential; (c) professional with steady earning potential; (d) business, property and unspecified (e) co-operatives.
			For (a) to (c) seven income tranches from (1–5,000) to (over 40,000) with levies ranging from 4% for the lowest to 30%, 35%, 40% respectively for the top tranche.
			For (d) six income tranches from (1–5,000) to (over 30,000) ranging from 4%–50%.
			For (e) same as (b) for the first six tranches; 35% to 60% for the next four tranches from (40,001–50,000) to (over 100,000).

Resident	Supertax for private sector for income of more than 42,000.	Excluded capital gains.	(42,001–75,000) at 10% (75,001–150,000) at 20% (150,001–300,000) at 30% (over 300,000) at 45%

TABLE 6.7 (continued)

Target	*Nature*	*Exemption/Relief*	*Rate*
Resident	Tax on capital gains.	Exempted up to 5,000 in profit.	(5,001–25,000) at 20% (25,001–100,000) at 30% (over 100,000) at 40%
Non-resident citizen	Tax on gross foreign income.		10% flat.
Resident alien engaged in state project	Tax on gross income.		25% flat.
Resident alien entity engaged in state project	Tax on gross income of foreign enterprise.		40% flat.
Non-resident alien with income arising in Myanmar	Tax on gross income including capital gains.		60% or tax liable under relevant income schedule; whichever was higher.
State enterprises	Tax on gross income from trade and commerce		50% flat

Note: All values in kyat.
Source: Ministry of Planning and Finance.

TABLE 6.8
Profit Tax for Private Sector (1976)

Nature	*Exemption/Relief*	*Rate*
Tax on business profit	Net income up to 8,000 are exempted. Exemptions: salaried income; co-operatives; foreigner in state-sponsored project; religious or charity groups; income of local municipalities; income from specified savings schemes; receipts in commutation of pension; compensation for death or injury; non-recurring income not being capital gains or receipts from any business undertaking; dividend from partnership, association, company or organization.	Altogether 51 income tranches in three groups: 21 of 2,000 each (up to 50,000); 10 of 5,000 each (up to 100,000); and 20 of 10,000 each (up to 300,000). Value of tax payable was fixed for each tranche: corresponding to 2.4% for the upper bound of the lowest tranche (8,001–10,000) through 36.5% for the median tranche (70,001–75,000) to 66% for the top tranche (290,001–300,000). The marginal rate for profit over 300,000 was 90%. Profits derived from production and transport services enjoyed tax reduction of 10%; profits from cheroot sales subjected to additional 10% charge over scheduled rate.
Capital gains tax on profits from sale, exchange or transfer of land, building, vehicles, and immovable assets	Exemptions: gift, inheritance, donation. Assets valued below 50,000.	The lesser of the two: 10% of net gain or 50% of the difference between the transacted value and 50,000.
Import tax		10% of landed cost.
Entertainment tax		40% of total receipt for movies; 20% on other forms of entertainment.
Tax on salt		0.1 kyat per viss (about 3.6 pounds in weight).

Note: All values in kyat.
Source: Ministry of Planning and Finance.

producers co-operatives.[92] It also covered trade and services performed by the SEEs and producer co-operatives.[93] The CST rate structure involved ten tranches; ranging from zero (covering 59 items) to 60 per cent (increments of five percentage points up to the 30 per cent tranche and ten percentage points each thereon; altogether 281 items were identified as taxable). There were also 27 items subject to *ad valorem* rates ranging from 20 per cent for salt to 170 per cent for petrol and over 200 per cent for alcoholic beverages. For services, the CST was set at 8 per cent on transport fares, 40 per cent on movie tickets, 20 per cent on other entertainment, and 5 per cent on sale proceeds of trade in commodities.

As pointed out by the World Bank, there were some inherent weaknesses in the CST. For example, there could be multiple taxation along the chain of production and marketing and the ultimate result might also significantly deviate from the intended distribution of the consumers' tax burden. On the other hand, exemptions given to many large investment projects to alleviate the CST burden undermined the latter's main objective to raise revenues.[94]

Banking Reform

With effect from 1 April 1976, a centralized system with the Union of Burma Bank (UBB') as the central bank was established.[95] The Myanmar Agricultural Bank (MAB), the Myanmar Economic Bank (MEB), and the Myanmar Foreign Trade Bank (MFTB) were also established.[96] The MEB was meant to play a crucial role in mobilizing and controlling financial resources for the SEEs as well as the non-agricultural private sector. It provided not only domestic funds for all state-sponsored projects, but also channelled foreign credits to government organizations and co-operatives.[97] It also extended term loans, working capital loans, and financial loans to the private sector, subject to approval by the UBB'. Furthermore, its township branches also served as agencies for the MAB where the latter was not represented.[98]

The MAB catered for SEEs and co-operatives engaged in agricultural and livestock production as well as the needs of the individual farmer. It provided annual loans, short-term loans from one to four years, and long-term loans from four to twenty years. Seasonal loans for selected crops and term loans for bullock carts, draught cattle, water pumps, and power tillers were available to village bank members only.[99]

The MFTB conducted foreign exchange transactions. It also maintained clearing accounts under bilateral barter agreements. External credits were used by the MFTB to import goods for the SEEs with repayment denominated in kyat.[100]

The bank rates were revised upwards on 1 April 1975 and again on 1 November 1977. Table 6.9 shows substantial upward revisions

TABLE 6.9
Interest Rates (%)

Account (Bank)	*Before*	*From 1 April 1975*	*From 1 November 1977*
Deposit rates			
Savings certificate: 12-year maturity	4.5	7.6	10.9
Basic rate on savings account	3.5	6.0[a]	8.0[a]
Fixed deposit:			
3-month	0.5	0.5	1.0
6-month	0.75	0.75	1.5
12-month	1.25	1.25	2.5
2-year	2.25	2.25	3.5
Lending rates			
SEEs			
Working capital	3.0	6.0	8.0
Financial loan	n.a.	6.0	8.0
Term loan	n.a.	3.0	5.0
Co-operatives			
Working capital	4.0	6.0	8.0
Term loan	n.a.	7.0	9.0
Private			
To village bank (MAB)	3.0	6.0	8.0
To farmer (village bank)	9.0	12.0	12.0
Car-purchase loan	n.a.	7.0	9.0
House-repair and others	n.a.	8.0	10.0
Small-scale personal loan	n.a.	24.0	24.0

Notes: all rates applied to MEB loans unless indicated otherwise.
a. It entailed a premium of 2 per cent on the three-year minimum balance in addition to this rate.
n.a. = not applicable.
Source: Union of Burma Bank.

of savings rates that were negative in real terms since the late 1960s, indicating a renewed attempt to increase savings, whereas, the extension of loans to SEEs and co-operatives were in line with the new policies of operating SEEs on a commercial basis and to enhance the role of co-operatives.[101] Private loans for cars and home renovations benefited only a small group of government employees and property owners.[102] There was no official credit scheme for financing economic activities in the non-agriculture private sector. Banks, operating as SEEs themselves, made huge profits.[103]

Enterprise Reforms

Beginning with fiscal 1975/76, the "commercialization" of SEEs was introduced in conjunction with a bonus scheme for employees. The idea was that:

> within the framework of socialist economy, central control should be appropriately relaxed and every economic enterprise should be organized in a systematic manner to enable the enterprise to stand on its own. These economic enterprises should be vested with rights to use initiative, innovation and decision-making, and the profit is to serve as an indicator of their success.[104]

Consequently, the Ministry of Planning and Finance formulated a set of detailed guidelines to improve the operational efficiency and the financial position of the SEEs. In essence, the guidelines entailed:

- establishing a chain of responsibility and accountability for the success and failure of economic endeavours at all levels;[105]
- organizing the government agencies into SEEs with their own management bodies in which workers would be accorded one-third representation;[106]
- replacing budgetary allocations for SEEs with bank loans in three phases;[107]
- introducing a system of financial accounts incorporating funds for maintenance and repair, bonus, welfare, enterprise development, and capital depreciation within a regular monitoring regime;[108]
- relaxing (within the plan framework) centralized rigid controls on pricing and operational decision-making and the introduction of legal and contractual obligations into SEE operations;[109]

- establishing profit as the success indicator and the introduction of the operating ratio (current expenditure divided by current receipt) as the single most important performance measure;[110] and
- imposing a system of rewards and punishment with material incentives.

The bonus system for SEEs was assumed to be "the most effective" incentive for the "working people to participate enthusiastically in the establishment of a socialist system". Aimed at improving productivity and product quality and "obtaining maximum benefits from enterprises", it was meant to encourage innovative measures to "minimise wastage, losses, damages and costs" and to satisfy the consumers' demands for new products. Increased production of exportable goods and enhanced import substitution as well as over-achievement of "production norms" by individual workers, were also cited as desirable objectives.[111]

The annual bonus was awarded to the enterprise as a whole, but there were also provisions for awards to outstanding individuals or groups. The "necessary condition for consideration of awarding bonus" was the achievement of the "planned target or the minimum target". Such achievement together with the fulfilment of the "prescribed operating ratio" constituted the "sufficient condition".[112] Out of the total bonus fund, 50 per cent was to be awarded to all employees with lower paid workers receiving a higher relative amount. Another 25 per cent would be disbursed to outstanding individuals, teams/groups and factories/units within the SEE as special bonus. The remaining 25 per cent would also be distributed as special bonus after the relevant accounts had been audited and approved by the relevant council of people's inspectors.[113]

In order to enhance productivity in non-economic organizations that did not qualify for the bonus scheme, the commercialization guidelines also suggested measures such as certificates, vacations, pay increments, promotions, housing, and permission to purchase motor vehicles.[114]

However, these same guidelines did not elaborate on the punishment angle. Instead, there was only a general reference to the requirement for appropriate penalties and actions for losses in connection with the responsibility of the various actors in the chain of accountability (from the workers to the Cabinet) for the SEEs concerned.[115] Similarly, for non-economic organizations it was recommended that "suitable action" should be taken "against those workers" who were "negligent, irresponsible and undisciplined".[116]

Each SEE had to make an annual "contribution" to the state out of its net profit and the balance of the Export Price Equalization Fund (EPEF, established in September 1976 to capture the excess of export prices over domestic costs). In general, it was expected that these measures for decentralization and financial independence together with the bonus scheme would improve SEEs' performance. However, the SEEs, after a short spurt of progress, failed to break out of the typical CPE "soft budget constraint" and floundered in their attempts to raise efficiency and productivity.[117]

Trade Reforms

The long-term pricing policies of the BSPP called for cost cutting, raising procurement prices for agricultural commodities with high supply elasticities, and the co-ordination of prices for agricultural and industrial products to gradually narrow the income differentials between peasants and workers.[118] In line with these guidelines, trade reforms carried out after 1974 included increases in government procurement prices for major agricultural products, price adjustments for SEE products, and the establishment of the EPEF. All these were mainly aimed at inducing higher production of exportable agricultural products. However, until 1988 there was no significant change in the state monopoly on imports and selected exports nor in the extent of state control over the distribution of SEE products and privately-produced basic foodstuff such as rice, cooking oil, onion, chili, beans and pulses.[119]

In agriculture, the substantial disparity between the free market (read black market) and government prices of paddy and important planned crops had been a major disincentive. To address this shortcoming, the procurement price for paddy was raised by some 40 per cent in March 1973. It was again raised by over 50 per cent in July 1974, with provisions for a premium above the prescribed quota.[120] In fiscal 1977/78 and 1980/81, there were minor price increases for quality grades of paddy.[121] Similarly, procurement prices for beans and pulses were raised by 29–46 per cent in 1974/75, over one-third in fiscal 1975/76 and again by 37–108 per cent in the following year. Maize prices were increased by 25, 40, and 43 per cent, respectively.

Corresponding revisions for quality industrial crops resulted in substantial price increments between 1973/74 and 1976/77: jute (88 per cent), cotton (100 per cent), rubber (60 per cent), sugar cane (150 per cent), and Virginia tobacco (100 per cent).[122]

In the case of goods produced by SIEs, the practice was to deliver them at cost to state trading agencies, which then distributed them with a modest mark-up. This system of administered prices negatively affected the SIEs in two ways. First, the cost of capital was not adequately reflected in the ex-factory costing. Second, given the scarcity of manufactured items, the administered prices were generally much lower than free market prices, entailing considerable losses in potential income for SEEs.[123]

All in all, for reasons probably associated with the fear of cost-push inflation and the ideological commitment towards uniformly low prices for basic commodities, the state did not follow up the World Bank's recommendation that "the raising of official prices closer to their clearing levels should be pursued with vigor".[124]

The EPEF, managed by the MFTB, was a form of cross-subsidization amongst exporting agencies, so that local costs could be recovered for exports which were unprofitable at the prevailing exchange rate. Half of the surplus over a 10–12 per cent profit margin could be retained. On the other hand, the EPEF compensated for unprofitable exports by revaluing their export prices to a level based on a 5 per cent profit margin. This was expected to be a temporary measure to boost exports, whereby loss-making SEEs had to ensure that these subsidies did not become a permanent fixture.[125]

Legal Recognition of Private Enterprises

The Rights of Private Enterprises Law, promulgated in September 1977, accorded legal status to private enterprises performing specified economic activities and was meant to enhance economic development through private sector investment and employment. As such, it was a more refined version of the ownership–enterprise matrix delineated in the LTSTEP guidelines.

This law allowed Myanmar citizens to undertake the following economic activities in accordance with existing rules and regulations:

- all forms of cultivation on existing land;
- development of fallow and virgin land;

- offshore fishing;
- inland fisheries not engaged by SEEs or co-operatives;
- fish breeding except pearl oysters;
- extraction, transport, milling and trading of timber and other forest products;
- mechanized road transport;
- mechanized coastal and inland water transport;
- industries in the mining sector and the processing and manufacturing sector which required registration and specified in the list appended to the law; and
- registered wholesale trading of commodities which had not been reserved solely for the SEEs and the co-operatives.[126]

This law differed from the corresponding list in the LTSTEP document in that the former was less restrictive in its scope (see Table 6.10). At the same time, an exclusion list prohibited the private sector from performing specific economic activities (see Table 6.11).

All other economic activities not specified by this law were open to domestic entrepreneurs. Private enterprises, registered accordingly, were guaranteed against nationalization until the end of the TYP in 1994. The law also stipulated that designated crops had to follow the state plan guidelines; designated crops and marine products had to be sold to designated organizations (prices and quotas set by the state); and goods and passengers had to be carried as instructed by relevant authorities from time to time.[127]

Registered private enterprises were required to open bank accounts and were supervised by the people's councils, whose permission was needed for relocation of capital assets and change of premises within the township boundary. Similarly, private transport operators had to seek permission from the respective state/division people's council to change their routes.[128]

Apart from these administrative controls, penalties ranging from fines (up to 10,000 kyat) to prison terms (up to five years) were prescribed for transgressions which included contravening registration rules; misuse of raw materials, machinery, spares, fuel and other material supplied by the state; and relocation and restructuring of the enterprise without permission from the authorities concerned. The penalty for causing price instability was much harsher; imprisonment for three to ten years and confiscation of assets.[129]

TABLE 6.10
Private Economic Activities Requiring Registration

LTSTEP (1972)	*Rights of Private Enterprise Law (1977)*
Earth and earth-based products/materials Altogether 23 items.	*Earth and earth-based products/materials* Reduced to 11 items only.
Processing and manufacturing Altogether 93 items in which registration was mandatory; 111 items in which both registered and unregistered enterprises were permitted.	*Processing and manufacturing* Altogether 90 items, of which 34 were items transferred from the prohibited list in the LTSTEP; 32 items from the LTSTEP list were excised, i.e. they no longer required registration.

Note: The discrepancy between the summation for the processing and manufacturing sector when changes are accounted for in the 1977 list (92 vs. 93) is due to a slight difference in nomenclature of a number of items.
Source: *1977 Oopadei Myar*, pp. 139–44; *Hnit-Shei Hnit-Toh Sipwayei Muwada*, pp. 168–214.

TABLE 6.11
Prohibitions

Field of Activity, Industrial Branch and Enterprise
Mining (25 items)
Extraction and processing of all ferrous and non-ferrous minerals, gems, jade, precious metals, and coal; except earth and earth-based minerals/materials.
Processing and manufacturing (52 items)
Rice bran oil (4 items). Monosodium glutamate. Alcoholic beverages and methylated spirits (9 items). Cigarettes.
Cotton weaving (automatic looms); synthetic cloth weaving.
Cement. Ceramic roofing and wall materials.
Brand-name soap (2 items). Chemical detergent. Matches (wooden). Pharmaceutical industry.
Long-staple cotton ginning. Jute sacks; jute cloth. Industrial chemicals and gases (11 items). Fertilizer.
Exploration, extraction, and processing of oil. Iron works. Telephone and accessories; spark plug; razor blade; hoes.
Electrical machinery and equipment; mechanical machines and equipment; diesel road roller; crane; tractor trailer.
Motor vehicles. Bicycles.
Electric power (4 items)
Large-scale hydroelectric plants. Small-scale hydroelectric plants (generation for own-use exempted).
Large-scale generating plants. Small-scale generating plants (generation for own-use exempted).

Note: Private extraction of tin, tungsten, lead, and mixed ores under contract from state would be allowed.
Source: *1977 Oopadei Myar*, pp. 133–38.

MONETARY AND FISCAL ISSUES

Myanmar's monetary policy was mainly directed at the credit requirements of the state sector.[130] Within the state-owned banking system, interest rates had little impact on the demand for credit by government agencies whose financial needs were usually accommodated in relation to annual plan guidelines. Bank credit to the SEEs dominated the credit expansion since the late 1970s.[131] The rapid growth in gross domestic credit, which averaged 75 per cent annually in the Third FYP period (1978/9–1981/2), on total liquidity was accompanied by the equally fast growth of saving deposits which responded favourably to the higher interest rate structure instituted by the 1977 reforms.[132] Despite the huge credit expansion (1.8 billion kyat in 1977/78 to 31.3 billion kyat in 1984/85 for SEEs), the year-on-year rate of growth of narrow money (currency in circulation) for the 1977–84 period was less than half of that in the 1972–74 period.[133] Thus, this restraint on money creation together with administrative controls over SEEs' pricing kept inflation in check during the Third and Fourth FYP periods.[134] Nevertheless, the average annual growth rate of narrow-money supply was much higher than that of the GDP and was "mainly caused by the fiscal deficits" suffered by the government since 1978.[135]

This seemingly orthodox trend in monetary management was marred by the drastic demonetization measure taken in November 1985, in which roughly one-quarter of the currency was taken out of circulation.[136] Though apparently aimed at exposing tax evaders and undermining black marketeers, the legal provision to recompense innocent individuals turned out to be a loophole exploited by the target groups with alacrity. This action was more a politically inspired punitive measure than an effective monetary instrument to rectify the problem of excess liquidity and illegal trading.[137]

Thereafter, the money supply continued to grow apace and the state yet again resorted to demonetization on 5 September 1987. This time around, there were no provisions for refunds though government employees and pensioners were compensated in the form of an extra-month remuneration. About 56 per cent of the currency was invalidated and both legal and illegal businesses were effected.[138] These two shocks delivered within twenty-two months probably undermined the private entrepreneurs' confidence for the currency.[139]

Myanmar's exchange rate policy after 1975 was predicated upon maintaining a fixed rate pegged to the International Monetary Fund's (IMF) special drawing rights (SDR).[140] Exchange control was administered by the Exchange Control Board through the MFTB. Since foreign trade was under state control the exchange rate played no significant role in balance of payments adjustments.

On the other hand, projects were financed through deficit financing. The renewed push for state-led development, which began in the late 1970s, was characterized by persistent budget deficits. As shown in Figure 6.2, the consolidated public sector (administration, SEEs, and municipalities) budget was continually in deficit after a small surplus in fiscal 1976/77.[141] Figure 6.3 depicts the corresponding trend for the deficit/GDP ratio.

The persistent deficits resulted in the scaling down of the overall public investment programme and to more selectivity in choosing developmental projects after fiscal 1983/84. Additional resource mobilization and intensification of the export promotion drive were also part of the strategy to reduce the deficits but there was little success in that direction.[142]

Simply put, these deficits occurred because revenues failed to keep up with expanding expenditures. The main sources of revenues were taxes and SEEs' contributions to the state (Figure 6.4).[143]

FIGURE 6.2
Consolidated Public Sector Budget Deficit

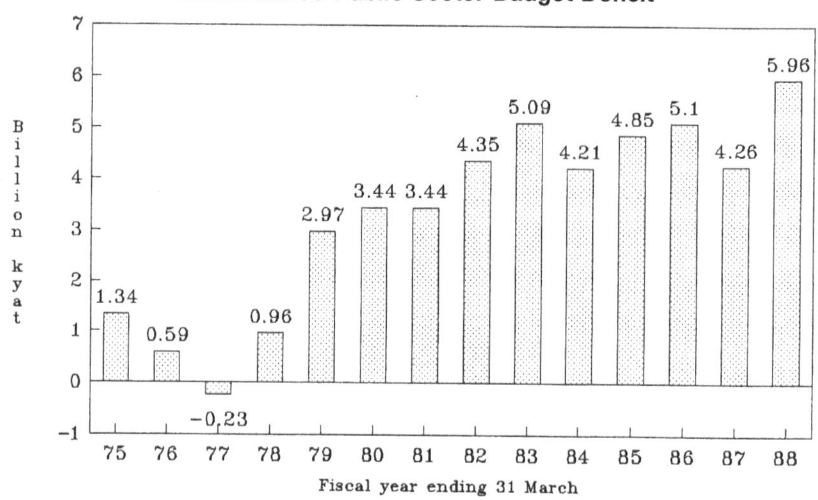

Note: Minus sign denotes surplus.
Source: World Bank.

FIGURE 6.3
Consolidated Public Sector Budget: Ratio of Deficit to GDP

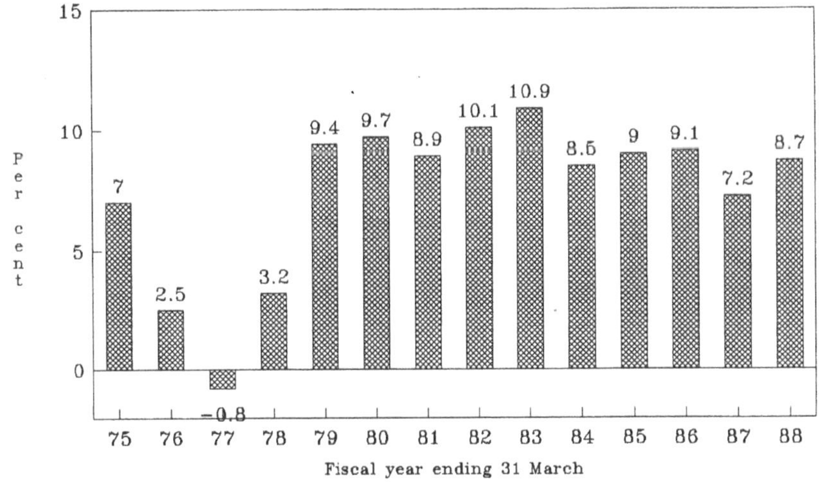

Note: Minus sign denotes surplus.
Source: World Bank.

FIGURE 6.4
Government Current Revenue: Major Components

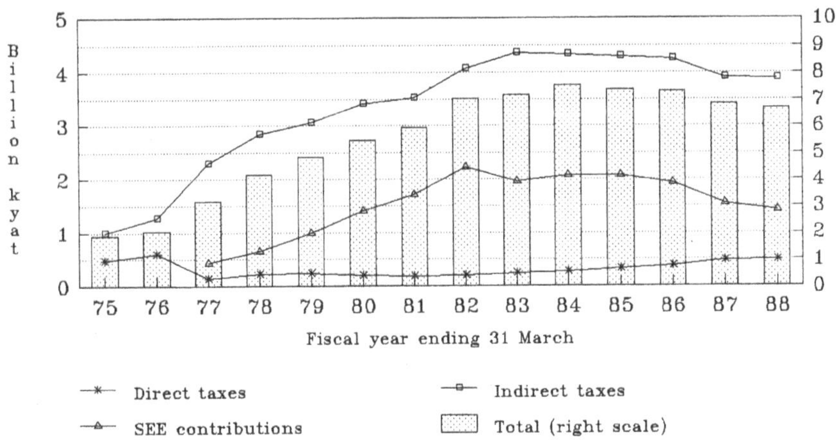

Note: Total includes non-tax revenues.
Sources: Central Statistical Organization and World Bank.

Due to financial reforms, tax revenues doubled between 1974/75 and 1977/78, but its growth slowed down in the next five years before stagnating after 1982/83. In fact, tax revenues as a percentage of GDP stagnated in 1980 at about 10 per cent and declined continuously after 1981/82 reaching 6.4 per cent in 1987/88.[144] Contributions by profitable SEEs also increased by 400 per cent from 1976/77 to 1981/82 and then levelled off afterwards.

As evident from Figure 6.5, the sharp decline in direct-tax revenues after 1976/77 was initially more than offset by the rise in indirect-tax receipts.[145] However, after 1983, indirect taxes stagnated and, though the level of direct taxation substantially improved in the second half of the 1980s, it was not high enough to improve the total revenue position (cf. Figure 6.4).

Reasons for the failure of tax revenues to achieve sustained growth after the initial surge following tax reforms in 1977 may be found in the trends of its components (Figure 6.6). After 1982/83, the cutback in state investments led to the decline of imports. This resulted in falling customs and excise duties whose contribution to total tax receipts had steadily risen to 28 per cent in 1982/83. Similarly, the more significant CST that depended upon imports and SEEs' revenues lost its growth momentum and its declining trend in the share of total taxes could not be arrested (Figure 6.7).[146] There was a steady growth of the tax on incomes and profits after 1982 (see Figure 6.7). However, its income tax component suffered from a narrow and stagnant tax base. Moreover, as

FIGURE 6.5
Government Current Revenue: Shares of Major Components

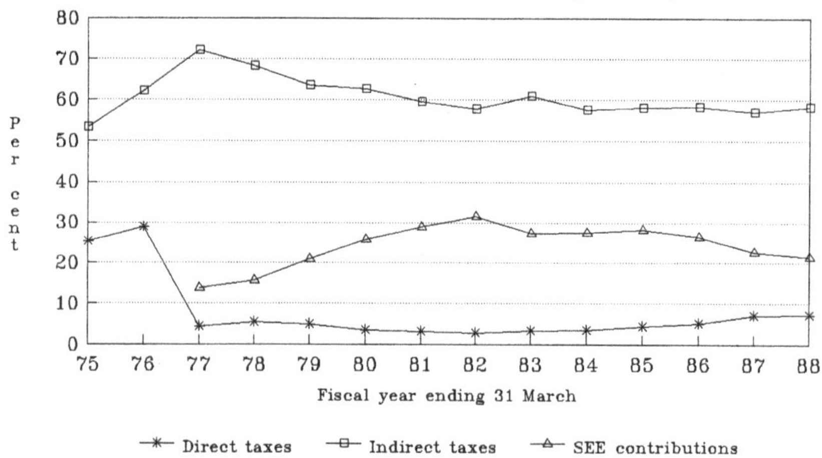

Sources: Central Statistical Organization and World Bank.

FIGURE 6.6
Components of Tax Revenue

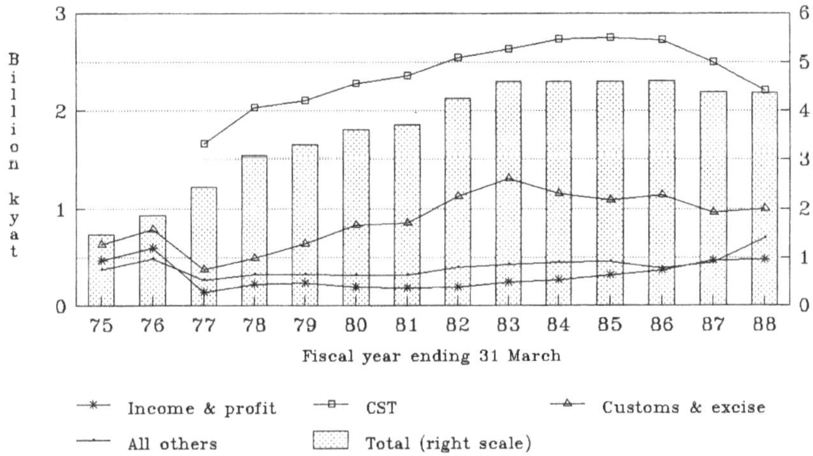

Note: CST = Commodity & Service Tax.
Sources: Central Statistical Organization and World Bank.

FIGURE 6.7
Shares of Major Tax Components

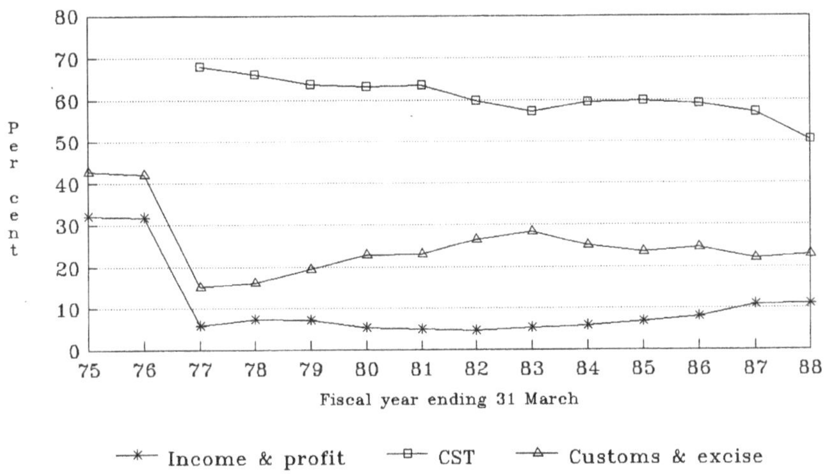

Note: CST = Commodity & Service Tax.
Sources: Central Statistical Organization and World Bank.

the profit tax comprised less than 2 per cent of the private sector valued added (excluding agriculture) in the mid-1980s, the latter's tax potential remained largely untapped.[147] Other taxes remained buoyant but their total contribution was not large enough to make up for substantial reductions in CST receipts.[148]

An important revenue source, the SEE contributions (based on profits and EPEF surpluses), had been adversely effected by their poor performance in both domestic production and exports.[149] Furthermore, given the fixed and overvalued exchange rate, the EPEF balances which depended on international price levels of Myanmar's major exports as well as the volume of exports, suffered from the unfavourable trends in both of these variables.[150]

Hence, "SEEs have been identified as the major source of fiscal deficits" in the 1980s.[151] In the 1977/78–87/88 period, the annual deficit in the overall financial balance of all SEEs doubled in the first two years and then fluctuated between 4–7 billion kyat (Figure 6.8) though its ratio to GDP exhibited a declining trend (Figure 6.9).[152]

As the SEEs failed to establish a consistent overall current account surplus they had to seek ODA and bank financing to plug the deficits (Figure 6.10).[153] The apparent loss of buoyancy[154] in both tax and non-tax revenues after 1982 (see Figure 6.11) did not elicit standard responses aimed at expanding coverage and reducing exemptions to government agencies. It seems that earlier financial reforms were

FIGURE 6.8
All SEE: Financial Balances

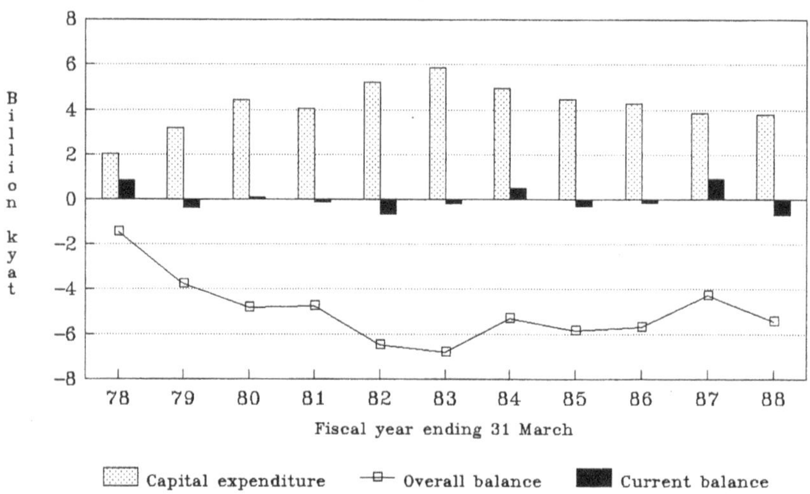

Note: Summation for all ministries.
Sources: Central Statistical Organization.

FIGURE 6.9
All SEE: Financial Balances
(Share of current GDP)

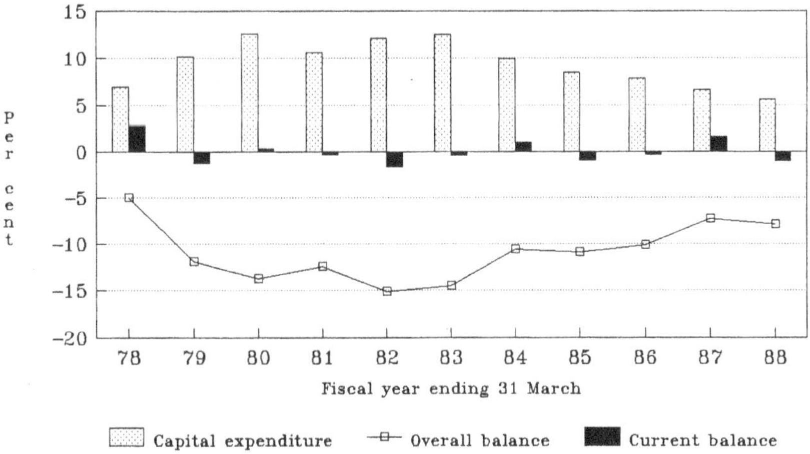

Note: Summation for all ministries.
Sources: Central Statistical Organization.

FIGURE 6.10
SEE Deficit Financing

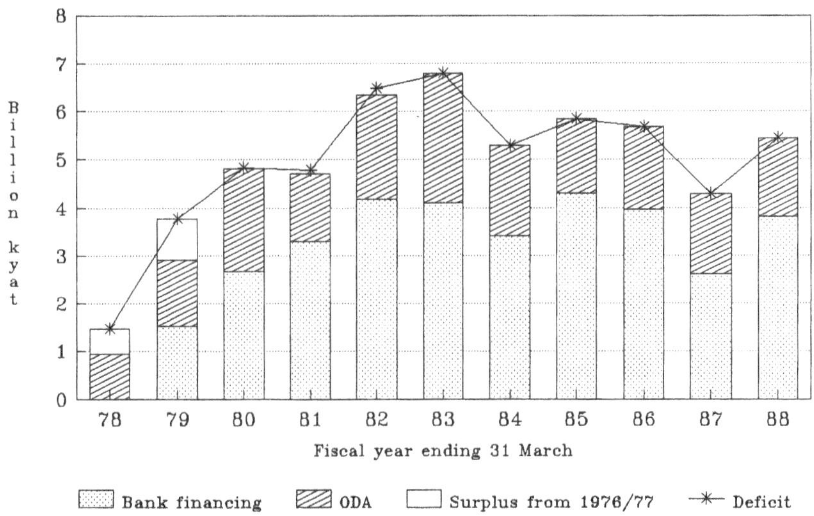

Source: Central Statistical Organization.

FIGURE 6.11
Current Revenue to GDP Ratio

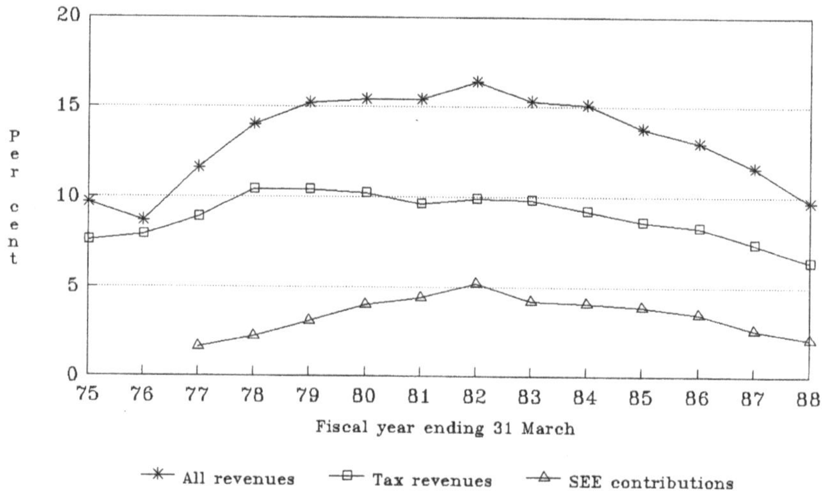

Sources: Central Statistical Organization and World Bank.

viewed as a one-off exercise rather than part of a continuing reform process. The overwhelming desire for price stability also precluded any major upward revision of the SEEs' prices for agriculture products and manufactured goods. As such, the World Bank's recommendations to increase resource mobilization through more extensive tax and price reforms went largely unheeded.[155]

The post-1974 monetary and fiscal policies were aimed at controlling price inflation, financing state-led economic development, and maintaining a favourable balance of payments position. In reality, the financial sector remained undeveloped and the government was unable to prevent persistent budget deficits and recurring balance of payments problems brought about by poor resource mobilization and export stagnation.[156] Though inflation was restrained up to the late 1980s by administrative price controls and substantial increases in saving deposits, there were insufficient funds for development projects.

THE EXTERNAL SECTOR

The TYP envisaged a steadily increasing level of investments in productive sectors as well as large infrastructure outlays, which in turn required substantial foreign currency inputs. Non-convertibility of the kyat and the exclusion of foreign direct investments (FDI), meant that trade and aid were vital sources of scarce foreign exchange for development expenditures. New investments and the maintenance of adequate levels of imports for existing concerns were contingent upon the availability of foreign exchange. Thus, the external sector played a very significant role in development financing.

Foreign Trade

Myanmar's development programme heavily depended upon imports of capital and intermediate goods. Exports were crucial not only for earning scarce foreign exchange to finance such imports but also for extracting surplus from the agricultural sector through differential pricing. Moreover, foreign trade, especially imports, play an important role in generating revenues, directly through tax and duties and indirectly through the state trading monopoly on imported goods.

The long-term policies on external trade envisaged, *inter alia*:

- state control over foreign trade;
- emphasis on capital goods to support industrialization;
- foreign trading through the Myanmar Export Import Corporation (MEIC), though allowing selected SEEs to export directly, while permitting some SIEs and trading SEEs to import directly;
- introducing an international tender system for imports related to new projects;
- raising the level of infrastructure support for export expansion; and
- empowering the trade council to make supply adjustments reflecting international market demands.[157]

The corresponding short-term policies were aimed at "solving the immediate (*circa* 1972) problem of foreign exchange shortages by strengthening the export sector" and promoting "the export of non-primary products".[158]

There were detailed specifications of import requirements by value and product for all line ministries. Scarce foreign exchange was "tightly controlled and centralized in its allocation and utilization" by the Ministry of Planning and Finance "which coordinated and regulated imports by non-trading state agencies".[159]

It turned out that constraints such as weak demand, backward technology, poor infrastructure, inelastic pricing, overvalued exchange rate, over-centralization, over-concentration on a few commodities, bad weather, and population pressure, inhibited export growth.[160]

Hence, the goals of balanced trade and accelerated export growth were not attained. Instead, exports growth could not keep up with rapidly rising imports after 1978 (Figure 6.12). Export earnings consistently failed to achieve annual plan targets after 1980/81.[161] Thereafter, the trade deficit widened to 7 per cent of GDP in 1982/83 before it was checked in 1983/84 (Figure 6.13) by cutbacks in imports.

The share of foreign trade in (nominal) GDP rose from around 10 to over 21 per cent between 1974/75 and 1981/82. However, large deficits in the merchandise account led to cutbacks of imports after 1982/83. Consequently, the share of foreign trade in GDP declined continuously to 8.3 per cent in 1987/88.

As illustrated in Figure 6.14, among the (traditional) principal items, income from timber registered a steadily rising trend up to 1986/87, surpassing rice products as the top export earner in 1984/85. Earnings from rice stagnated after 1981/82 and rapidly dwindled after 1983/84. The rising trend in income from minerals and gems also stagnated in the early 1980s and declined in the second half of the decade. The growth of two previously insignificant exports (fish products and beans and pulses) did not last beyond 1982/83 (Figure 6.15).[162]

FIGURE 6.12
Foreign Trade

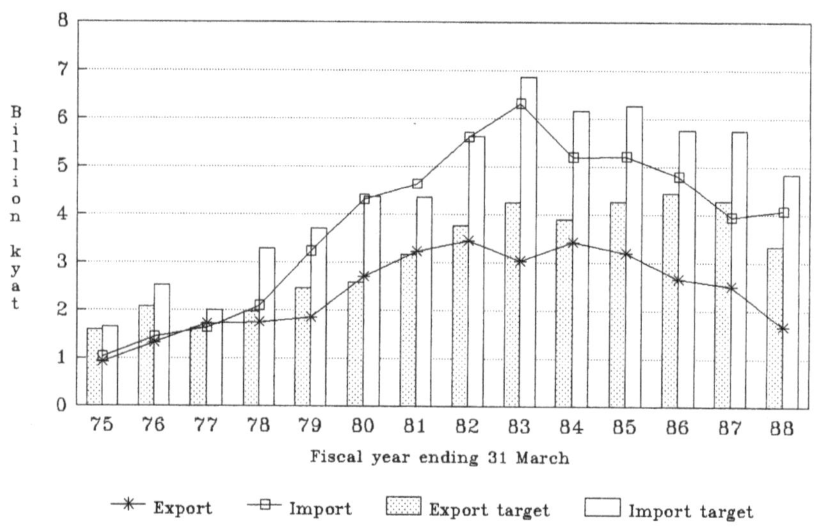

Source: Ministry of Planning and Finance.

FIGURE 6.13
Foreign Trade: Share of GDP

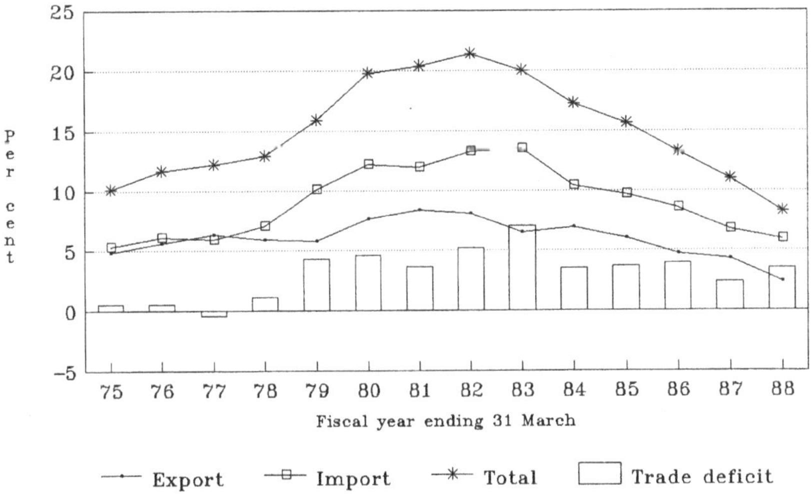

Note: Minus sign denotes surplus.
Source: Ministry of Planning and Finance.

FIGURE 6.14
Domestic Exports

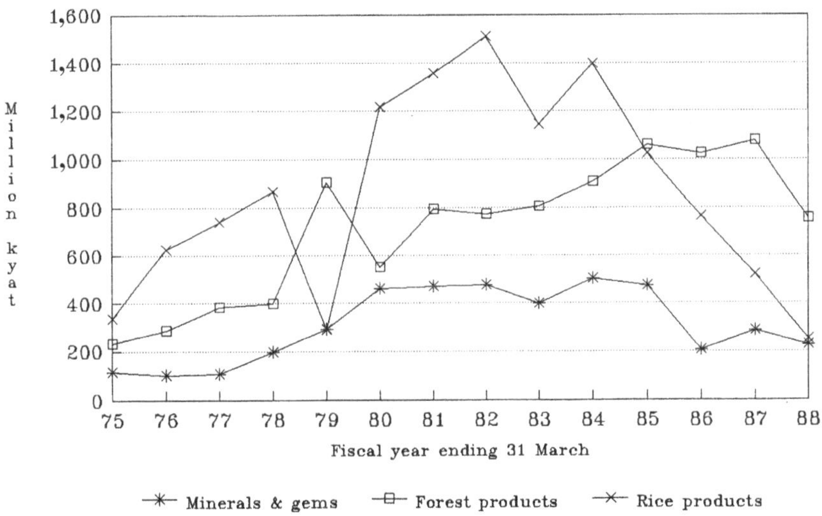

Source: Ministry of Planning and Finance.

FIGURE 6.15
Domestic Exports

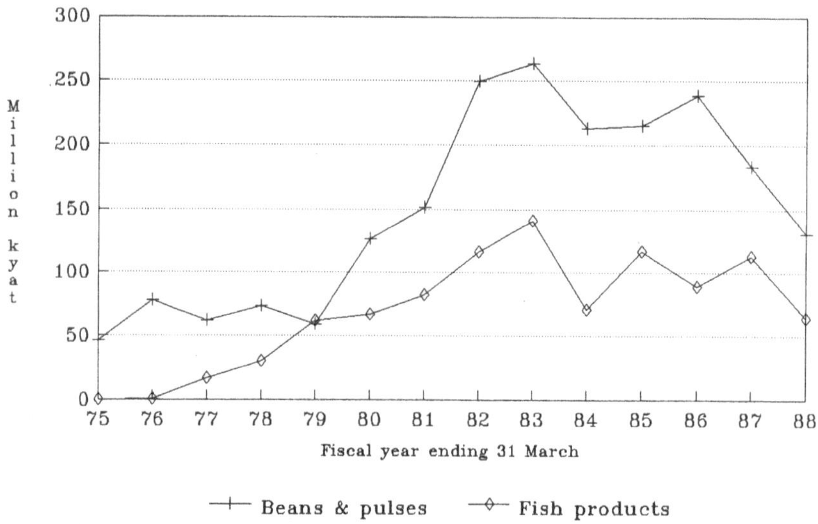

Source: Ministry of Planning and Finance.

Attempts at export diversification had not been successful and heavy dependence on a few principal commodities remained unchanged. As evident from Figure 6.16, the cumulative share of top three commodities in total earnings remained above 70 per cent up to 1986/87. Moreover, shares of new export items such as fish products and beans and pulses stagnated after 1982/83 (Figure 6.17).

The resulting trade gaps were offset by foreign loans and grants (Figure 6.18) which increased considerably after 1977/78.[163] The poor export performance was blamed on falling commodity prices but others have indicated that policy-related supply constraints and shortcomings in marketing and product quality were also responsible.[164] After 1981/82, as evident from Figure 6.19, the trends in import and export price indices moved in opposite directions, and the overall terms of trade deteriorated probably aggravating the problem of trade deficits.

It is found that there had been a marked preference for ODA-funded capital and intermediate goods over consumption goods, as evident in Figures 6.20 and 6.21. After 1982/83 the import volumes of capital and intermediate goods showed declining trends. On the other hand, Figure 6.20 reveals that the volume of consumer goods remained around the 1982/83 level for a few more years.[165] The share of capital goods in total imports rose rapidly from under 30 per cent to 64 per cent between

FIGURE 6.16
Shares of Major Export Items

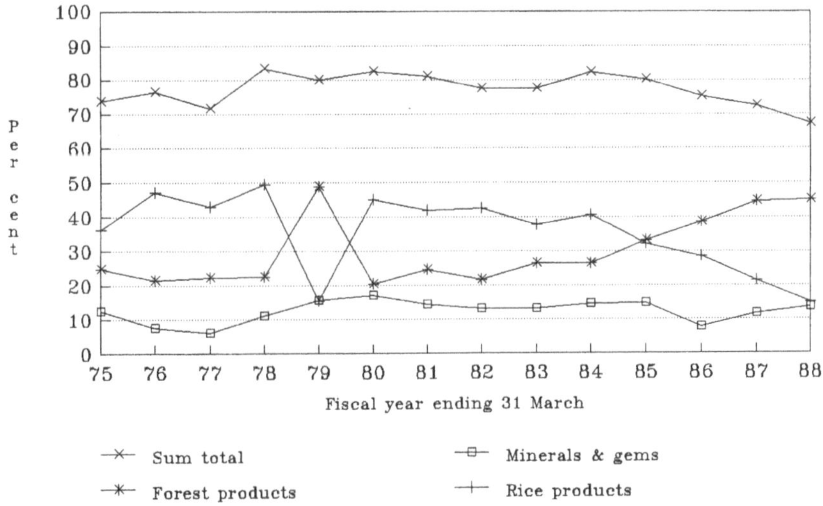

Source: Ministry of Planning and Finance.

FIGURE 6.17
Shares of Major Export Items

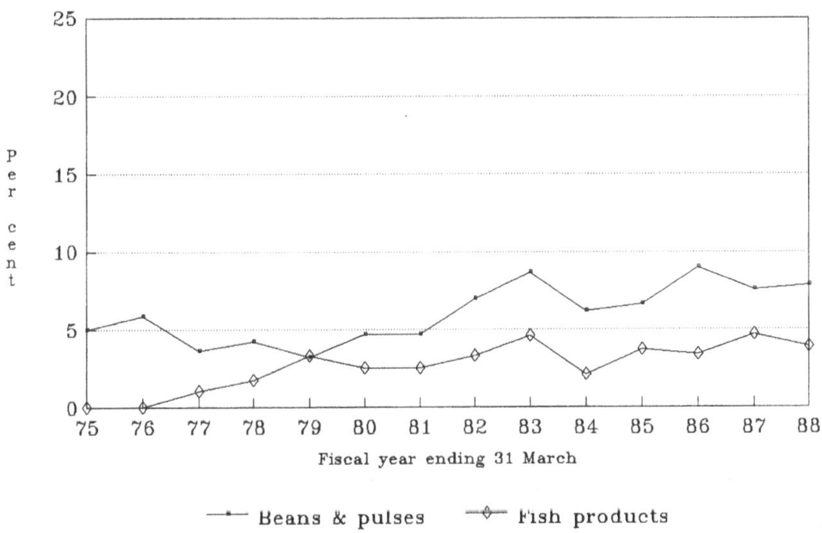

Source: Ministry of Planning and Finance.

FIGURE 6.18
Trade Deficit and Net Foreign Receipts

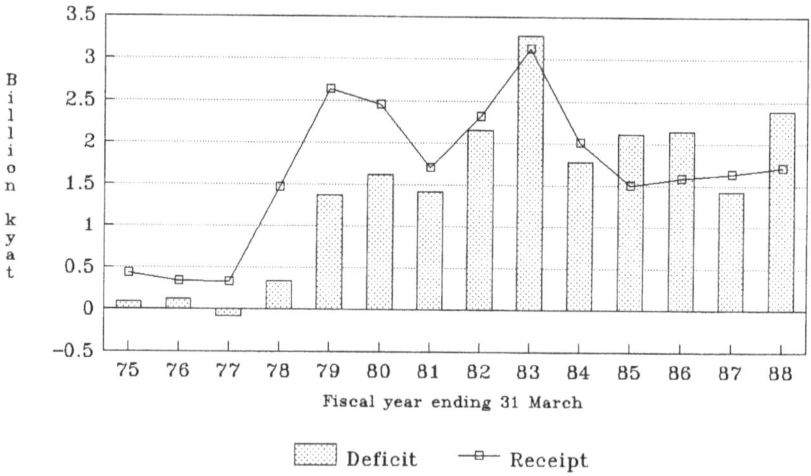

Notes: Net receipts exclude interest repayments; 88 million kyat surplus in 1977.
Source: Ministry of Planning and Finance.

FIGURE 6.19
Terms of Trade: Index (1969/70 = 100)

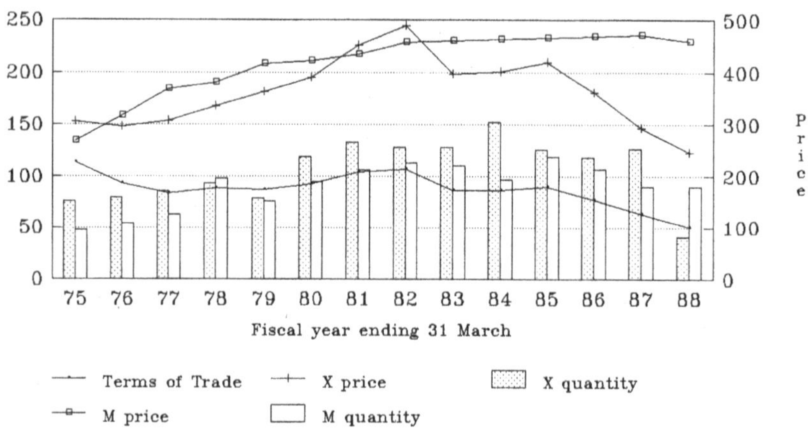

Notes: X = export; M = import; for price indices see right scale.
Source: Ministry of Planning and Finance.

FIGURE 6.20
Imports: Value

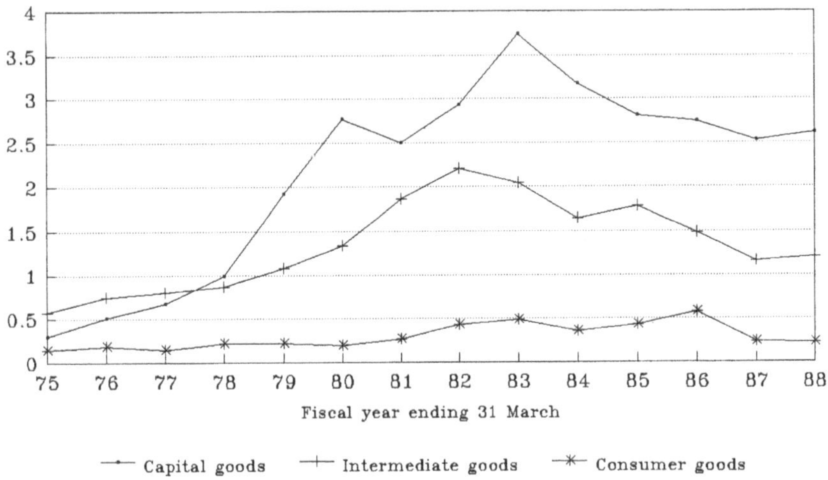

Notes: A small residual of less than 0.7% of total imports remained unclassified.
Source: Ministry of Planning and Finance.

FIGURE 6.21
Imports: Share

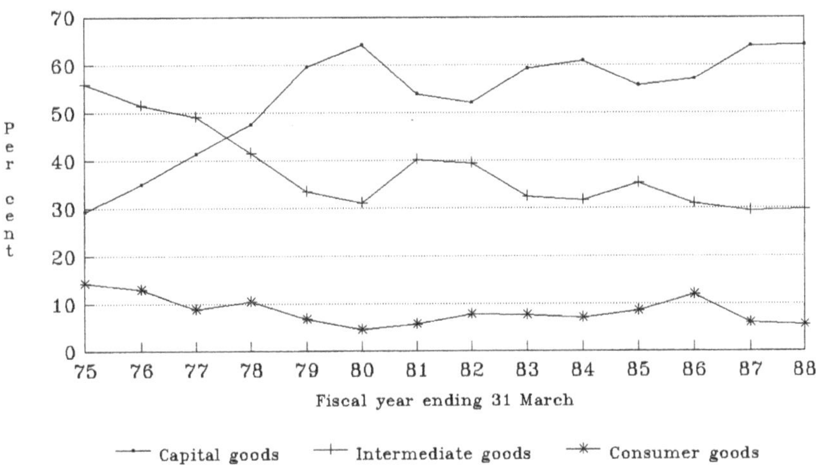

Notes: A small residual of less than 0.7% of total imports remained unclassified.
Source: Ministry of Planning and Finance.

1974/75 and 1979/80, while the consumption goods' share declined from 14 to 4.5 per cent. Contrary to many countries pursuing ISI, the share of intermediate goods declined from 56 per cent to 31 per cent in the same period. However, it can be seen from Figures 6.20 and 6.21 that this changing pattern of import shares occurred in a period of rapid growth of overall imports and a sharp rise in capital good imports.[166]

Illegal Border Trade

Another aspect of Myanmar's external trade was the so-called informal trade that had considerable impact on the overall economy due to its wide scope and huge magnitude.[167] Myanmar's porous borders spawned cross-border illegal trading with India, Bangladesh, China, Thailand, Malaysia, and even Singapore.[168]

The cross-border black market not only deprived the state of substantial tax revenues and trading profits but also undermined its authority in terms of the flouting of socialist principles and huge economic rents for insurgent groups.[169] Nevertheless, the government probably regarded the black market as a safety valve to ameliorate the shortage of consumer goods. As such, retail sales of illegal imports in major cities were generally tolerated though sporadic campaigns to stamp out the big-time operators and wholesale distributors were launched with little or no avail.[170]

Technically, such illegal trade may be characterized as either "trade-diverting" or "trade-creating" or even a mixture of both. In the former, smuggling "diverted" goods that could have otherwise been imported through legal channels, thereby not only reducing government revenues but also consumers' "welfare". On the other hand, the latter made available goods that replace locally produced import-substitutes "at a lower social cost" in a "beneficial trade creation".[171] In the Myanmar case, the state suffered a double blow of the revenue-denying effect of trade diversion and the reduced demand for SEE products as consumers opted for illegal imports that were of higher quality and/or cheaper in price. On the export side there were not only revenue losses but also losses for exporters due to less favourable terms of trade when compared to legal trading.[172]

Thus, while the official trade failed to perform its expected role of financing and providing requisite inputs to the state's industrialization drive, the informal trade served as a potent reminder of the failure of the ISI strategy to satisfy the public's rising demand for manufactures.

Foreign Loans and Aid

Foreign loans and aid became significant only after the Burma Aid Group (BAG) was formed in 1976 under World Bank auspices to channel ODA inflows.[173] Gross foreign loans and grants increased dramatically after fiscal 1976/77 and within two years annual gross receipts quadrupled to US$359 million.[174] Thereafter, it averaged some US$390 million for the next nine years (Figure 6.22).

Figure 6.23 shows that loans with maturity over one year comprised the majority receipts after 1976/77, while grants fluctuated along a slowly rising trend from about US$10 million in 1974/75 to some US$105 million in 1987/88. From 1974/75 to 1987/88, Myanmar received US$857 million in grants and nearly US$3.5 billion in loans; i.e., a cumulative inflow of some US$4.3 billion. When repayments were discounted, cumulative net loans amounted to nearly US$2.4 billion (averaging 69 per cent of gross value), resulting in a net total of over US$3.2 billion. This was a significant sum when compared with the corresponding total export earnings of over US$4.3 billion.[175] As evident from Figure 6.23, the gap between the net and gross values for loans increased after 1978/79 until 1987/88, when Myanmar enjoyed some debt relief.[176]

As such, the ODA constituted the bulk of foreign receipts over the 1974–87 period and was the most significant foreign exchange enhancing

FIGURE 6.22
Foreign Loans Plus Grants

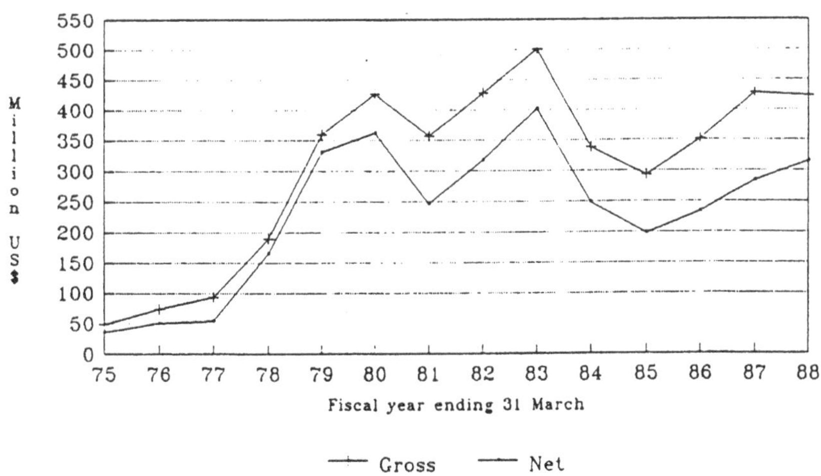

Note: Converted at annual average certified exchange rate from kyat.
Source: World Bank.

FIGURE 6.23
Foreign Loans and Grants

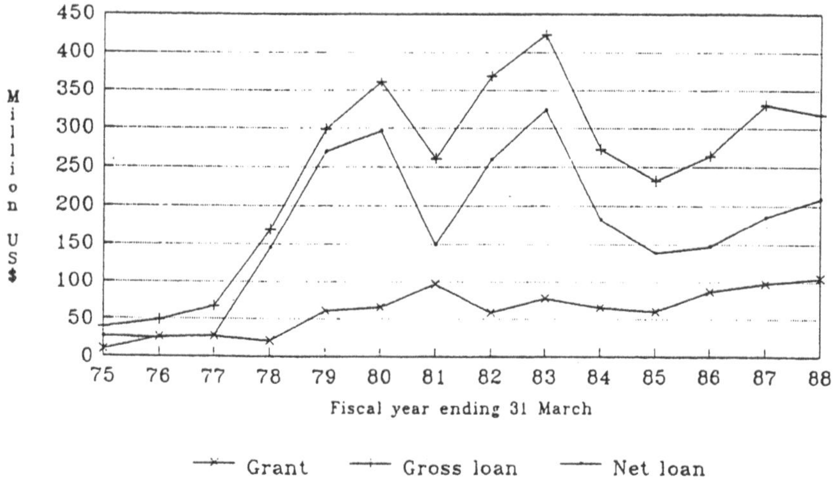

Note: Converted at annual average certified exchange rate from kyat.
Source: World Bank.

factor. The major portion of ODA inflow (averaging over 70 per cent of net inflow) consisted of bilateral assistance. Japan and the Federal Republic of Germany (FRG) were major donors.[177] Loans comprised more than 70 per cent of gross ODA receipts whereby Japan and FRG were top lenders.[178] Most of the concessional loans were from the ADB and the International Development Association (IDA) of the World Bank.[179] Commercial loans and supplier credits were also used for projects that were essential for alleviating bottlenecks or where high returns were anticipated.[180]

IMF credits were also drawn to meet foreign exchange shortfalls. In the late 1970s and early 1980s, Myanmar utilized the Trust Fund facility and stand-by arrangements for credits totalling over SDR 125 million.[181]

The grant component of ODA that also included technical assistance was also dominated (77 per cent) by bilateral assistance.[182] The UNDP, with over US$100 million in grants, topped the list for multilateral sources, comprising mainly of specialized UN agencies. In fact, the United Nations "had come to be regarded as a filler of gaps, and a handler of difficult and diffused jobs".[183]

Thus, virtually all development projects with substantial foreign exchange content were funded by ODA receipts.[184] Throughout the 1980s Myanmar came to rely on ODA receipts not only for capital investment but also for debt relief, programme support, augmenting imports, and securing essential inputs for SEEs.[185] Despite this heavy dependence upon external assistance and deteriorating economic circumstances in the second-half of the 1980s, Myanmar policy-makers were not subjected to donor pressures for major reforms and structural adjustments. There was no evidence of attempts by major donors (either multilateral like the World Bank or bilateral like Japan and FRG) to utilize their aid leverage by linking further assistance to the fulfilment of prescriptive conditions.[186] This may be attributed partly to the deep Myanmar conviction towards policy autonomy and economic independence and partly to the aid policies of major donors.[187] All in all, the relatively large ODA stream was barely enough to temporarily prop up the ailing socialist economy.

Balance of Payments and the Debt Problem

Due to trade imbalances, the annual balance of payments continuously showed current account deficits. Thanks to the ODA inflow, there was a corresponding surplus in the capital account that made up the shortfall. However, the balance of payments position worsened after fiscal 1981/82, resulting in the drawing down of foreign exchange reserves to precariously low levels.[188] This is evident when the cumulative sum of annual net balance of payments position is plotted against foreign exchange reserves at the fiscal year's end (see Figure 6.24). Figure 6.25, which shows the balance of payments items averaged over successive FYPs and the first two years of the Fifth FYP, also illustrates the deteriorating position after 1981/82.

Thus, "the long run underlying chain of causation" could be traced "from [inappropriate] production choices to balance of payments outcome".[189] The government's reaction, from fiscal 1983/84 onwards, had been to curtail SEE capital expenditures "essentially through rephasing and consolidation of their investment programs" which allowed "a cutback in imports".[190]

The amount of total external debt (outstanding on 31 March) rapidly increased from US$35 million in 1976 to US$2.33 billion in 1983. Thereafter, as evident in Figure 6.26, it rose at a faster rate to reach US$4.39 billion in 1987. The gravity of the debt situation after 1981 may be deduced from the steadily rising trend of the percentage of total debt stock to annual exports earning (Figure 6.26), which increased from 297 in 1981 to 1,420 in 1987.[191] In the same vein, the debt service ratio

FIGURE 6.24
Cumulative Balance of Payments (BOP) and Foreign Exchange Reserves

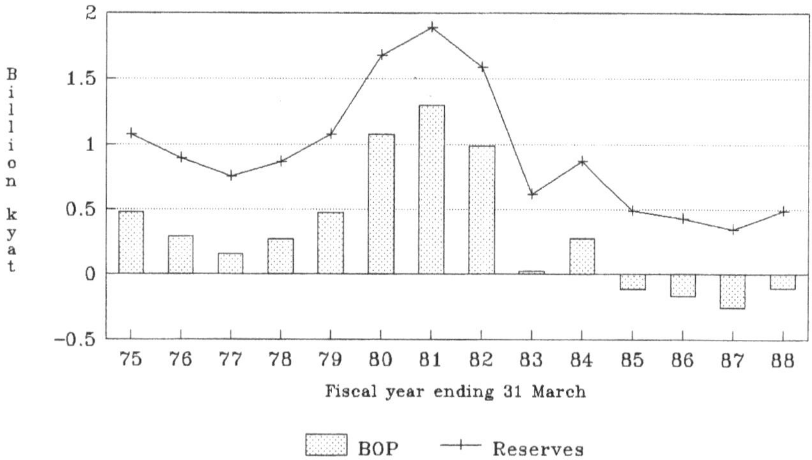

Note: 1974/75 is taken as base year.
Source: Ministry of Planning and Finance.

FIGURE 6.25
Balance of Payments (BOP)

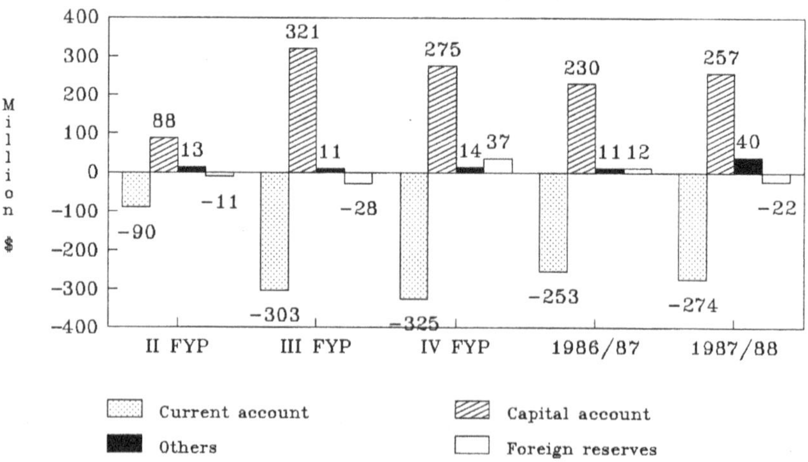

Note: Annual average for FYP; minus sign denotes accumulation of foreign reserves.
Source: Tun Wai (1991), p. 121.

FIGURE 6.26
External Debt Situation

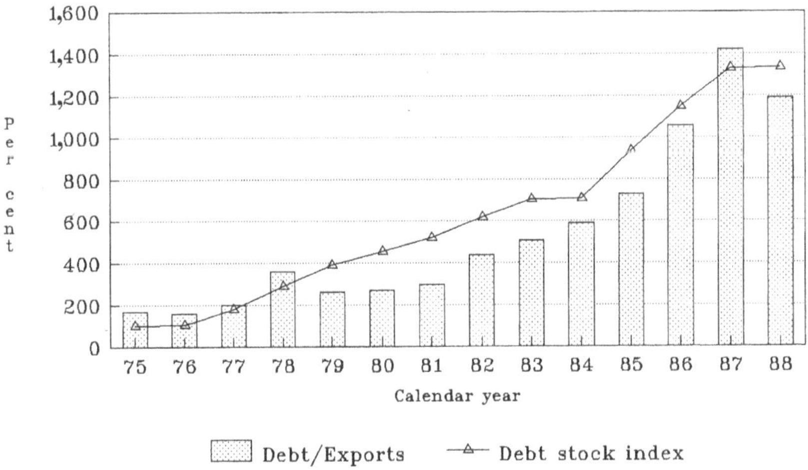

Note: Debt stock as at 31 March; index (1975 = 100).
Source: World Bank, World Debt Tables.

FIGURE 6.27
External Debt Service (debt service/export)

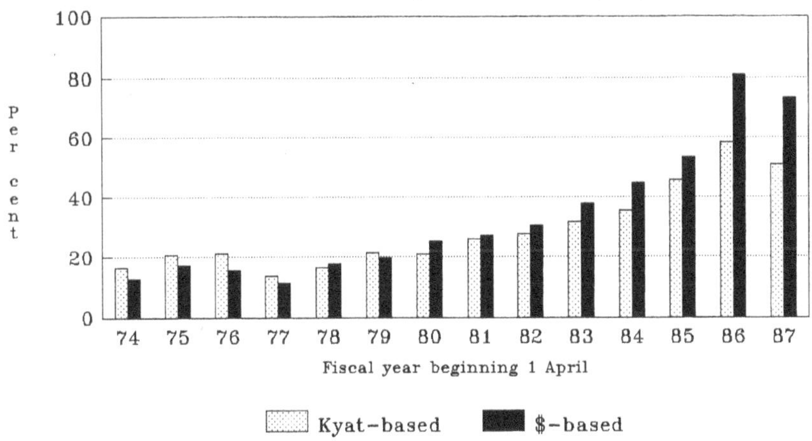

Note: Calendar year for $-based data.
Sources: Khin Saw Oo (1994), p. 244; World Bank, World Debt Tables.

(ratio of amortization and interest payments to export earnings) began to worsen after 1980 as indicated in Figure 6.27 as exports levelled off and debt servicing escalated.[192]

LIMITED GROWTH AND LITTLE STRUCTURAL CHANGE

In line with the TYP guideline to continuously increase state investments, average annual public sector investment rapidly rose from 1.6 billion kyat during the Second FYP (1974/75–1977/78) to 5.6 billion kyat in the Third FYP (1978/79–1981/82), and then to 7.1 billion kyat for the Fourth FYP (1982/83–1985/86). The TYP envisaged an average annual growth of 9.6 per cent for total state investment (in constant prices). This target was surpassed, by some 5 per cent, during the 1974–82 period. "Beginning in 1982/83, however, investment growth slowed and turned negative in almost every year" up to 1987/88.[193]

On the other hand, though the average real GDP growth rate was a credible 4.7 per cent (the target was 4.5 per cent) for the Second FYP, growth rates for the first two years were only 2.7 and 4.1 per cent. There were shortfalls against TYP targets for values of investment, imports and exports by 31, 58, and 43 per cent respectively.[194] Initial setbacks coupled with rising price inflation led to workers' protest in the mid-1970s. Subsequently, there was a major Cabinet reshuffle in March 1977 whereby the Prime Minister and the planning minister were replaced after being severely criticized by the ruling party.[195]

Thereafter, the real GDP growth averaged 6.5 per cent for the Third FYP, which compared favourably with the 6.6 per cent target set by the Pyithu Hluttaw. The public sector investment bolstered by ODA inflows "overachieved by 41 per cent", the TYP target. Still, there were shortfalls of 36 and 46 per cent respectively for imports and exports.[196]

However, by the mid-1980s, the growth momentum which owed its impetus to a conjunction of a surge in agriculture productivity, a favourable trend in prices of primary exports, and substantial ODA receipts, began to falter. The average real GDP growth rate for the Fourth FYP declined to 4.7 per cent and again there were shortfalls against TYP targets in investment, imports, and exports amounting to 36, 63, and 68 per cent respectively.[197] As the Fifth FYP began, the economy regressed and negative GDP growth rates of 1.1 per cent and 4 per cent occurred in 1986/87 and 1987/88.

Since the launching of the TYP, the economy had gone through three phases viz., recovery, growth, and recession. The failure to sustain economic growth beyond the early 1980s may be attributed to the following developments.

Firstly, the growth in agriculture value-added (28 per cent of GDP in constant prices), driven by intensive cultivation employing modern scientific inputs, lost its momentum in the late 1980s (compare Figures 6.28 and 6.29).[198] In 1977/78, the government launched the "Whole Township Special High-Yield Paddy Cultivation Programme" (WTPCP) which entailed high-yielding varieties (HYV), increased subsidized fertilizer application, and close supervision by local authorities (military, BSPP and people's council). This resulted in the doubling of the average yield between 1974/75 and 1982/83, thereby increasing total output by nearly 70 per cent.[199]

Thereafter, rice production stagnated due to saturation in yield and sown acreage (Figure 6.30). As shown in Figures 6.30 and 6.31, growths in production of major crops such as oil seeds, wheat, maize, and sugarcane also became stagnant or declined in the second half of the 1980s.[200] Under the shadow of government controls over marketing and prices, the growth rate in agriculture value-added faltered after 1980/81.[201] After peaking at 12.7 per cent in 1980/81 it consecutively declined to –6.4 per cent in 1987/88.[202] Trade and processing industries that had strong linkages to agriculture were also negatively affected.

Secondly, export prices declined while imports became dearer, worsening Myanmar's terms of trade (see Figure 6.19 above).[203] Moreover, attempts to increase volume and value-added and broaden the export base had not been successful.[204]

Thirdly, recurring budget deficits, cumulating external debts, and deterioration of the balance of payments resulted in reduced essential imports and lower investments as well as fuel/energy and infrastructure bottlenecks.[205]

These adverse developments coupled with rising inflation retarded economic growth and were responsible for the recession in the second half of the 1980s.[206]

The progress in structural changes affecting production and ownership up to 1986/87 — at just over the half-way mark of the plan period — was also unsatisfactory.[207] Shares of the GDP's main components are depicted in Figures 6.32 and 6.33. Agriculture's share increased to 28.6 per cent instead of declining (from the 1973/74) level towards the target of 20.9 per cent. The share of the processing and manufacturing sector hardly increased (9.8 to 9.9 per cent) and was way below the target of 21 per cent. The services' overall share increased to 26.9 per cent instead of being reduced to the targeted 22.8 per cent. Among

FIGURE 6.28
Index of GDP Growth (1974 = 100):
Constant 1969/70 Prices

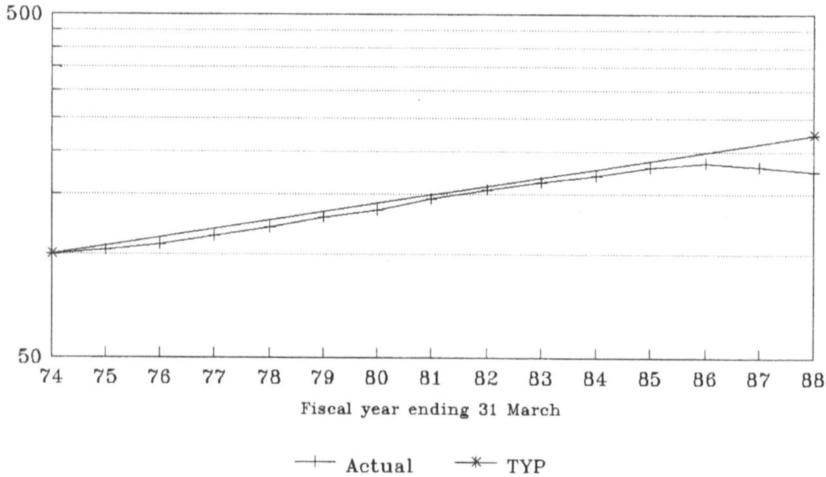

Note: TYP = Twenty-Year Plan trajectory.
Source: Ministry of Planning and Finance.

FIGURE 6.29
Index of Sectoral Growth:
Agriculture (1974 = 100)

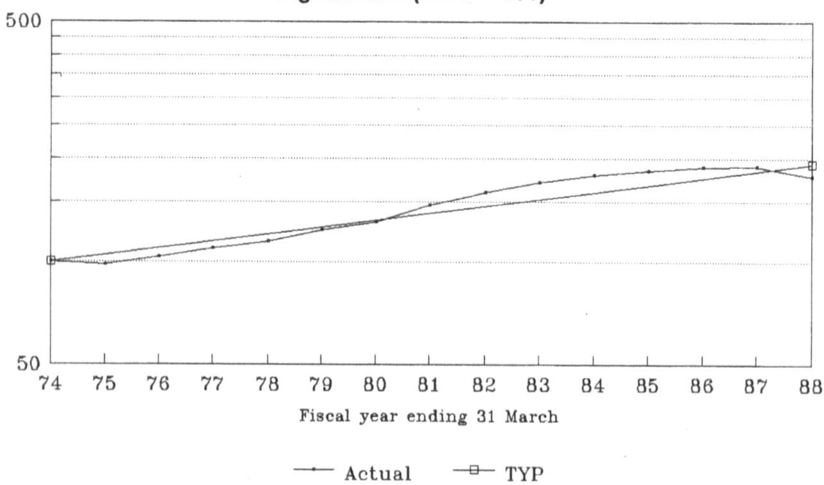

Note: TYP = Twenty-Year Plan trajectory.
Source: Ministry of Planning and Finance.

FIGURE 6.30
Production of Selective Crops: Quantity Index (1969/70 = 100)

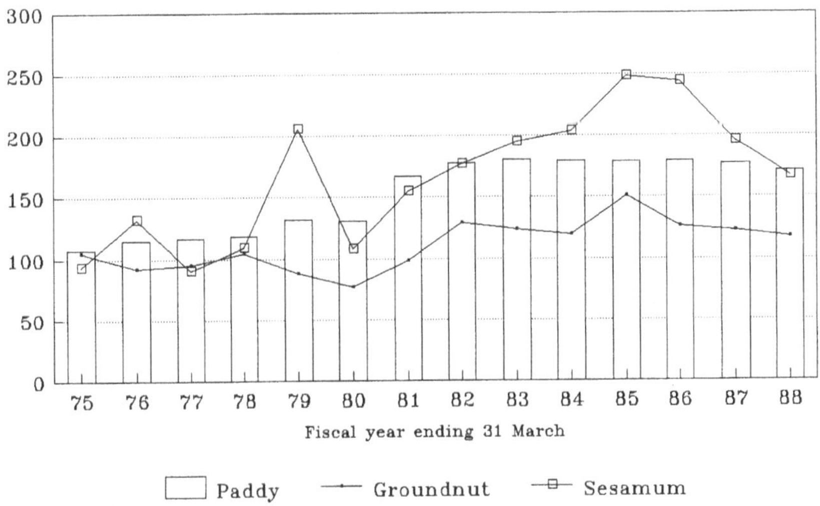

Source: Ministry of Planning and Finance.

FIGURE 6.31
Production of Selective Crops: Quantity Index (1969/70 = 100)

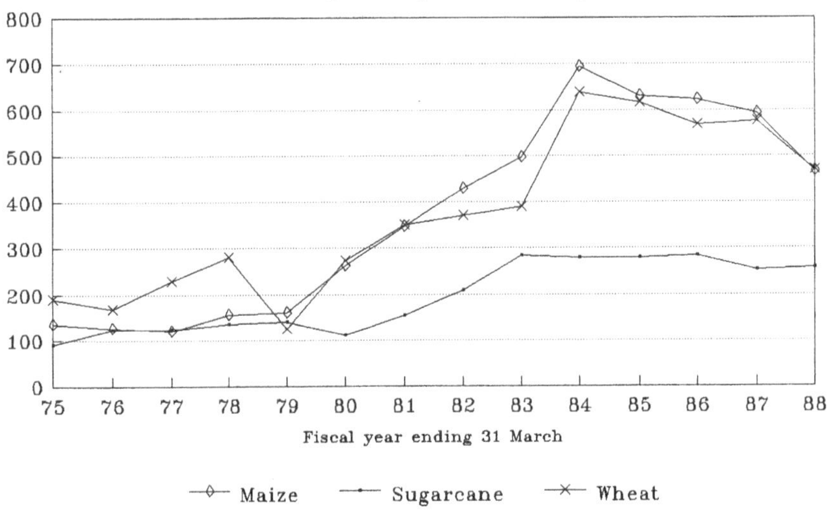

Source: Ministry of Planning and Finance.

FIGURE 6.32
Structural Change: Major Components of GDP
(constant 1969/70 prices)

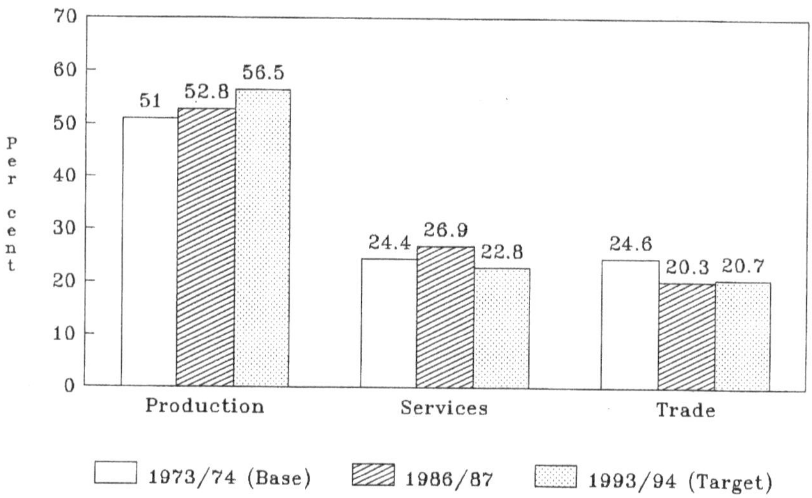

Source: Ministry of Planning and Finance.

FIGURE 6.33
Structural Change: Diverging Sectoral Trends
(constant 1969/70 prices)

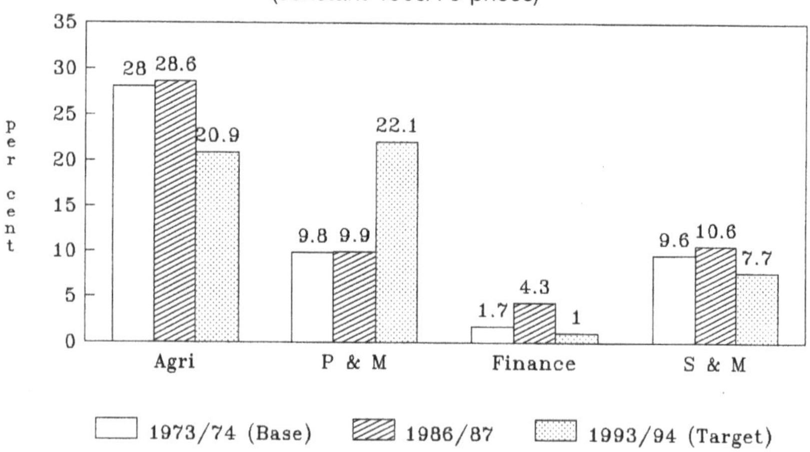

Note: P&M = Processing & Manufacturing; S&M = Social & Administrative Services.
Source: Ministry of Planning and Finance.

the service sectors, the contribution of financial institutions instead of decreasing towards the target of 1.0 per cent increased to 4.3 per cent. Similarly, the share of social and administrative services also grew to 10.6 per cent rather than declining towards the target of 7.7 per cent.

The discrepancy between the achievement and the TYP norm is even more pronounced in the ownership shares for GDP and its components. This is evident in Figure 6.34 which shows the percentage shares in the production component of the GDP by ownership, i.e., state, co-operatives, and private. Given the 1973/74 shares combination of 18:8:74 (state: co-operatives:private), progress had been excruciatingly slow towards the targeted 39:33:28. Though relatively less skewed, the development pattern of GDP shares (Figure 6.35) was also far from satisfactory. Starting out with 35:8:57, the achievement of 37:7:56 was far removed from the desired 48:26:26.

As shown in Table 6.12, the TYP target for the state's share of the services component was achieved even in 1986/87. This meant that the overall target was within reach but for the slow growth of the co-operatives. However, in the trade component, the combination attained in 1986/87 indicates divergence from the targeted pattern; the state's share regressing instead of increasing as envisaged, while the co-operatives' share remained unchanged.

FIGURE 6.34
Distribution of Production (Value-Added) by Ownership

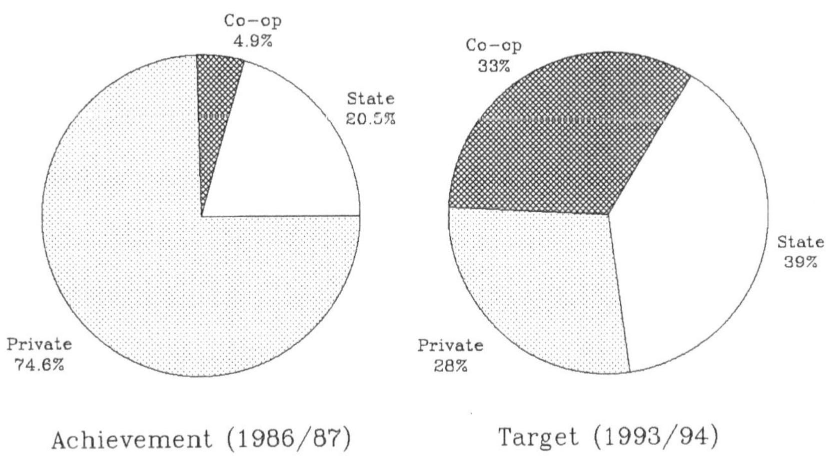

Notes: Based on constant 1969/70 prices; Co-op = Co-operatives.
Sources: Ministry of Planning and Finance.

FIGURE 6.35
Distribution of GDP by Ownership

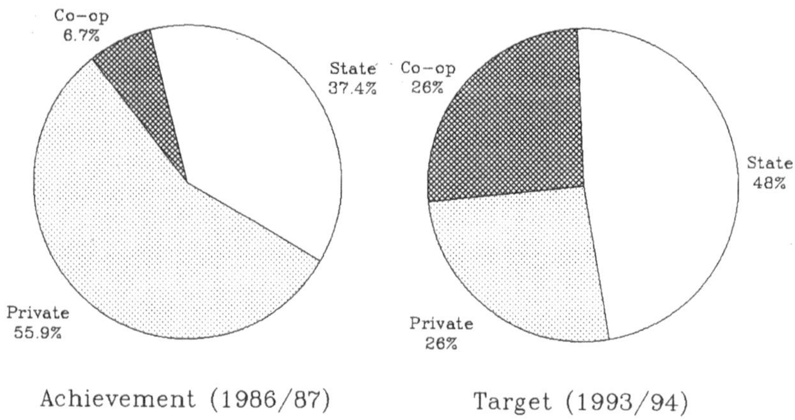

Notes: Based on constant 1969/70 prices; Co-op = Co-operatives.
Sources: Ministry of Planning and Finance.

TABLE 6.12
Ratios of Ownership Shares for GDP Components

	Ratio (state:co-operative:private)		
	1973/74 (actual)	*1986/87 (revised est.)*	*1993/94 (target)*
Services	58:2:40	67:3:30	67:9:24
Trade	48:17:35	42:17:41	54:25:21

Source: Ministry of Planning and Finance.

Due to the extremely weak position of the co-operatives, the TYP targets in ownership shares could not have been realized in the remaining period. Thus, as the planned economy entered its second decade, it not only failed to sustain the moderate growth achieved earlier but also was unable to make substantial progress in eliciting structural change, in line with its socialist aspirations.

Eleventh Hour Reforms: Too Little Too Late

At the Fifth Party Congress in August 1985, the impending economic crisis was not foreseen, though various shortcomings in relation to the Fourth FYP and the TYP guidelines/targets were mentioned in the lengthy report of the Central Committee.[208] The sanguine attitude prevailed throughout the next two years until the BSPP Chairman Ne Win called a high-level meeting of party and state executives on 10 August 1987. He raised the issue of whether "there [was] proper linkage and consistency among the reports [on the country's situation] … submitted since 1974" and counselled that "[f]ailures as well as successes should be thoroughly re-appraised and in submitting reports the entire truth should be submitted without any attempt to hide the facts".[209] Calling for submissions of comprehensive appraisals, he also commented that the present conditions might not be the same as those in 1962 (when the military took power) and in 1974 (when the socialist state was inaugurated). He urged that "changes will have to be made to keep in harmony with the times".[210]

However, the speech was more a philosophical reflection of past experiences than a clarion call for fundamental reforms. In fact, the term economic reform was not mentioned at all in the Chairman's address. Given the ambiguity of his message and the tendency of the party hierarchy to second guess the Chairman's intentions, there was no substantive follow-up.[211] Measures that ensued, such as the decontrol of paddy and some crops, were offset by counter-productive actions such as demonetization.[212]

In another speech delivered at the closing session of the Central Committee meeting on 9 October, Ne Win, again, dwelled upon the theme of dealing with "change". He surmised that both the free-market economies and the centrally-planned economies were suffering from one malaise or another. He expressed concern about Myanmar's economic woes but admitted that no solution was in hand.[213] He said:

> how shall we change? It is necessary for us to change the principles. … We shall have to take into consideration to what extent we should change and how, on the basis of our own experiences as well as the experiences from the world. We must lay down new principles after taking all these into consideration.[214]

On the question of how to bring about the necessary changes, he failed to provide unequivocal guidance for party *apparatchiks*, who had acquired the habit of taking cues from him for major policy decisions.

On the other hand, in the beginning of his address he recalled several instances in the past when foreigners have exploited the gullible

Myanmar whose lack of business acumen was a major liability. He also reaffirmed the need to have "economic independence" in addition to political freedom. In relation to the recent decontrol of major agriculture products, he cautioned entrepreneurs, especially "associate citizens", not to put greed ahead of collective social needs and to be fair towards producers as well as consumers.[215] He urged citizens to acquire business skills ostensibly to be on par with non-citizens who traditionally excelled in entrepreneurship. These remarks, reminiscent of anti-capitalist and nationalist traditions, apparently conveyed a message different from the market-conforming reformist approach warranted by the economic downturn. Given their leader's ambivalence, party and state executives probably adopted a wait-and-see attitude, hoping to muddle through till the next party congress.

At the biannual session of the Pyithu Hluttaw held in the following week, the Council of Ministers reported that the "basic problem" was the "scarcity of foreign exchange" due to falling export earnings which, in turn was attributed to declining commodity prices, narrowing of the export base, and "repercussions of the world's economic, monetary and trade crisis". Remedial actions included stop-gap measures such as forming the "Export Promotion Supervision Committee"; rationing of foreign exchange allocations; substituting, wherever possible, domestic products for imported inputs; utilizing methanol, compressed natural gas, and liquified natural gas as substitute fuels; and to quickly expand the output of the state's offshore fishing industry. The usual refrain calling for "effectively using the natural resources and equipment and mobilizing the strength of the workers so as to minimize the adverse effects" was repeated.[216]

A measure taken to ease financial pressures was Myanmar's successful application, to the United Nations Economic and Social Council, for classification as a least developed country (LDC). When Myanmar attained the LDC status in December 1987 it became eligible for debt relief as well as increased assistance from UN agencies.

However, at the annual session of the Pyithu Hluttaw in March 1988, the complacent mood was still prevalent. The only reform measure was the report that "arrangements have been made so that the co-operative societies and private entrepreneurs may export rice" and "to auction the teak and hardwood in border areas to the foreign" buyers. The platitudinous assurance that the Cabinet was "carrying out its tasks practising collective leadership and taking collective responsibility in accordance with the duties endowed by the Constitution and the principles of socialist democracy" was offered as the closing statement.[217]

It took several months and a spate of civil unrest, public protests, and violent government reactions in the capital and other towns before the ruling party and the legislature responded to the pressing economic issues.[218] In July 1988, at the extraordinary session of the BSPP Congress, a set of measures relating to proposed changes in economic policies was presented and adopted.[219] The Party General Secretary admitted that the economy was caught in a vicious cycle of declining exports, reduced imports, and production decline. He attributed these adverse conditions to a "fall in commodity production, arising [*sic*] of financial problems, inadequacy of foreign exchange, [and] insufficiency of fuel oil supplies". Given the necessity of finding ways and means to "draw" the "growing" volume of private capital "circulating in trading and blackmarketeering activities" into "production enterprises within the framework of the law", he indicated that "positive assurances and proper arrangements must be made ... to encourage enthusiastic and increased private investment".[220]

There was the familiar call for the "fullest use of the productive forces" and that it was "necessary for the entire people to strive with patriotism and with national pride and determination to catch up with the developed countries and developing countries".[221] The Party Congress not only gave the Central Committee the mandate to expedite the measures outlined in Table 6.13 but also authority to change the party constitution as well as the guiding philosophy.[222]

The emergency session of the Pyithu Hluttaw, held two days later, decided to "immediately implement the decisions of the Extraordinary Party Congress in effecting changes in economic policies and guidelines of the State" and authorized the Council of State to expedite the necessary changes.[223]

Apparently, the whole exercise was aimed at allowing some economic space for the private sector, assuming that state and co-operatives sectors would outpace the private sector in value-added growth. Neither was there any indication that the TYP targets for the ratios of GDP shares would be rescinded or revised. Though it was an unprecedented attempt to introduce fairly wide-ranging economic reforms, it was overtaken by rapidly unfolding events that led to the collapse of the socialist order.[224]

TABLE 6.13
Economic Reform Measures (1988)

New opportunities for private and co-operatives sectors

Agriculture: Freedom in choice of crops, production and trading; assurance of the right to work the land brought under cultivation; ownership of industrial crops and orchards geared towards long-term commercial production; permission to buy previously restricted agriculture machinery.

Livestock and fishery: Freedom to exploit inland, coastal and offshore waters; auctioning of the right to work inland fisheries except those reserved by the state for research purposes.

Forestry: Extraction, processing, domestic and external trading of timber and forest products except teak.

Mining: Co-operatives to work small oil wells not worked by the state; exploration, production and trading under state permission of minerals other than pearls, jade and gems.

Processing and manufacturing: Production and trading of all except arms and ammunition.

Power: Production of electricity according to laws, rules and regulations imposed by the state.

Construction: Public works (roads, bridges and other structures) as well as housing.

Transport: Construction, assembly and repair of all modes of transportation other than aviation and railways; domestic transportation services except for aviation and railways.

Trade: Both domestic and external trade; however, for paddy, rice, maize and pulses domestic consumption needs had to be considered before allowing exports; border trading; removal of checks, curbs and hindrances that obstruct commodity flow and restrict commercial activity.

Investment: Joint ventures with local or foreign partners with the state's approval.

Media and entertainment: Publication of newspaper, journal and magazine; construction and operation of cinema halls and screening of movies.

General incentives and facilitating measures

Agriculture: Employ economic incentives including price policies to harmonize costs and prices in an equitable manner.

Finance: Change banking system to gain peoples' confidence and to improve services; change revenue-collecting system to conform with the overall economic changes; draw up loan and cash plans to conform with the changes envisaged.

Trade: Expand private services abroad.

Investment: Make effective arrangements and give guarantees to safeguard business and capital invested by private concerns; Formulate laws and by-laws needed for undertaking mutually beneficial cooperation with foreign investors.

Business legislation: Review and revision of existing laws, rules and regulations on business activities for each business category.

Source: *WPD*, 24 July 1988.

THE ENERVATED STATE

Myanmar was reorganized by the ruling military elite into a unitary state with a new socialist constitution which enshrined the BSPP's exclusive right to lead the country. The Party formulated a long-term plan aimed at establishing a socialist economy at the end of twenty years. Myanmar was to become an agriculture-based industrial country after the implementation of five consecutive FYPs.

Guided by the party, the Pyithu Hluttaw decreed the FYPs and the corresponding annual plans within the TYP framework. The ministries and their line agencies, in coordination with the hierarchy of people's councils, carried out the task of formulating and implementing the annual plans under party supervision.

The severe resource constraints encountered in the decade before 1974 were initially circumvented by more pragmatic policies. With the help of substantial ODA inputs and limited reforms, the state stage-managed an economic recovery in the late 1970s that was followed by almost a decade of agriculture-led growth. However, the economy which, for all practical purposes, resembled a mixed (private/public) regime rather than a centrally planned command system ran into difficulties in the mid-1980, as resource constraints (especially energy, foreign exchange, and government revenues) reappeared and effective policy responses to adverse economic circumstances (unfavourable foreign trade balances and balance of payments, persistent fiscal deficits aggravated by inefficient SEEs) were not forthcoming. Meanwhile, the long-standing problem of illegal or black market trade remained unresolved with corrupt and opportunistic state officials and party cadres becoming increasingly dependent on the support of *hmaung-kho* or illegal business people who not only provided remuneration to them but also financed official events and activities.[225]

Furthermore, vested interests of the *nomenklatura* operating under a rent-seeking economic regime predicated upon a quasi-shortage economy blocked potential avenues for effective reforms. The top leadership, isolated from the grassroots and devoid of alternative opinions, became divorced from reality and revelled in the sanguine projections spawned by distorted statistics.[226]

On the other hand, as will become evident in Chapter 8, the state apparently possessed considerable political autonomy, but unlike successful East Asian developmental states it lacked the capacity to intervene effectively in the economic sphere. The insistence on the primacy of the BWS with its anti-market logic precluded the option of managing the market while, on the other hand, state controls over trade and investment became increasingly vulnerable to both domestic and international market forces. As distorted markets undercut the plans, stasis set in and the economy became hostage to the ideological inertia and political sclerosis of the ruling party. The impending economic crisis, in turn, fuelled the latent fires of popular discontent. Finally, an eleventh-hour attempt by the BSPP and the state executive to institute wide-ranging economic reforms was overtaken by events as the BSPP rule was terminated by a military coup in the wake of an upheaval of unprecedented fury and scope.

In its twenty-six years of governance, two generations of Myanmar military leaders had not been able to establish an enduring and strong state structure that would control the commanding heights of the national economy and fulfil their elusive aspirations of transforming Myanmar into an equitable and prosperous industrialized country. Instead, their legacy had been an enervated state that had denied itself of the opportunities offered by markets as well as the human resources and creative endeavours of its citizens.

Notes

1. See *The Constitution of the Socialist Republic of the Union of Burma* (Rangoon: Ministry of Information, 1974), pp. 2, 4; and Robert H. Taylor, *The State in Burma* (London: C. Hurst, 1987), pp. 307–309.
2. Voting was confined to either accepting or rejecting the BSPP-approved candidate. The public, realizing that "elections are not presented as a possible redistribution of power", rarely attempted to nominate an alternative candidate (Theodore H. Friedgut, *Political Participation in the USSR* [Princeton: Princeton University Press, 1979], p. 72).
3. A BSPP Central Committee meeting was convened before every Pyithu Hluttaw session to determine the agenda and set the stage for the latter.
4. The Council of State, formed with Pyithu Hluttaw representatives, was the highest state authority. The central organs of state power constituted the Council of Ministers (Cabinet), the Council of People's Justices, the Council of People's Attorneys, and the Council of People's Inspectors, whose members were Pyithu Hluttaw representatives selected from a candidature list prepared by the Council of State and approved by the BSPP Central Committee. All central organs of state power were accountable to the Pyithu Hluttaw and, when it was not in session, to the Council of State.

5. The party hierarchy included the Regional Party Committee (RPC; at the state/division level); party unit (township); and party branch, section, and cell (ward/village). Between the quadrennial party congresses the Central Committee was responsible for party affairs but in practice the CEC and the party secretariat were in charge.
6. Donald K. Crone, "Military Regimes and Social Justice in Indonesia and Thailand", in *Civil Military Interactions in Asia and Africa*, edited by Charles H. Kennedy and David J. Louscher (Leiden: E. J. Brill, 1991), p. 97.
7. Taylor, *State in Burma*, p. 372.
8. Although there was no attempt to establish a personality cult, the paramount position of Ne Win in the BSPP (chairman), the state executive (chairman of the Council of State or president), or the military (founding father) was beyond dispute.
9. Senior military officers were Pyithu Hluttaw representatives. Active and retired military personnel maintained an extensive "old boys" network (See, for example, Taylor, *State in Burma*, pp. 316–21).
10. The term was used by Migdal to describe the political process in "weak states" with fragmented social control. See Joel S. Migdal, *Strong Societies and Weak States: State-Society Relations and State Capabilities in the Third World* (Princeton: Princeton University Press, 1988), pp. 247–56. In the Myanmar case, it refers to the power-sharing arrangement affected through selective co-option, into the party hierarchy, of personnel from the state and military establishments. The unabated insurgencies also enhanced the military's role.
11. For the coup attempt, see *Asiaweek*, 3 December 1976 and 4 March 1977; for an explanation, see Jon A. Wiant, "The Vanguard Army: The *Tatmadaw* and Politics in Revolutionary Burma", in *The Armed Forces in Contemporary Asian Societies*, edited by Edward A. Olson and Stephen Jurika, Jr. (London and Boulder, CO: Westview Press, 1986), p. 254. For accounts of the economic malaise and riots, see, for example, Denzil Peiris, "Socialism Without Commitment", *Far Eastern Economic Review* (hereafter *FEER*), 13 September 1974, pp. 27–30; *FEER*, 27 June 1975, p. 20; *FEER*, 8 October 1976, p. 22. For the official version, see *Pahtama Akyein Pyithu Hluttaw Hsahtama Aseeawei Hmattan* [Record of the First Pyithu Hluttaw's Sixth Session] (Yangon: n.p., 1976), pp. 35–38, 363.
12. See, for example, "Burma", in *FEER*, 15 April 1977.
13. See, for example, *FEER*, 23 December 1977, p. 24. Later, the outlawed Burma Communist Party was blamed for sowing dissension via "moles" emplaced during the BSPP's formative stage. See Tatmadaw Thar Thutaythi Tit Oo, *1948 Khu Hnit Hma 1988 Khu Hnit Atwin Hpyat Than Lar Thaw Myanma Thamaing Akyin Hnint Tatmadaw Ghanda* [A Concise History of Myanmar and the Tatmadaw's Role, 1948–1988], vol. 1 (Yangon: News and Periodicals Enterprise, 1990), pp. 230–32.

14. For an elaboration of democratic centralism, see *[1973 Khu Hnit] Dutiya Akyein Parti Nyilargun Parti Baho Kommiti Okahta Gyi Ei Maintgun Myar Hnint Parti Baho Kommiti Ei Nainganyei Asiyinkhanzar* [Second Party Congress 1973: Speeches of the Central Committee Chairman and the Political Report of the Party Central Committee] (Yangon: Burma Socialist Programme Party, 1974), pp. 235–37. Apparently, there was a "two-term relationship between the leadership and the membership of the party, and between the party and the masses" (Michael Waller, *Democratic Centralism: An Historical Commentary* [Manchester: Manchester University Press, 1981], p. 17). An inflexible political structure where central control was emphasized in the name of unity and solidarity also developed.
15. Ibid., p. 111.
16. Robert H. Taylor, "Change in Burma: Political Demands and Military Power", *Asian Affairs* XXII, Part II (1991): 135.
17. See, for example, *The Fourth Party Congress 1981: Party Chairman's Speech and Political Report of the Central Committee* (Rangoon: BSPP, 1985), pp. 115–16. Like the Soviet system it encompassed not only key positions determined by party nominations or requiring the latter's consent but also the functionaries who served in them (see, for example, Michael Voslensky, *Nomenklatura: Anatomy of the Soviet Ruling Class*, translated by Eric Mosbacher [London: Bodley Head, 1984], p. 2).
18. Those on the top tier were entitled to housing, security, official cars, extra petrol rations, (domestic and foreign) medical and travel expenses, as well as access to (scarce) consumer durables (including automobiles) and cheap commodities at controlled prices (enjoying differentials ranging from five to ten times the posted price).
19. The cadres' reaction was characterized by "careerism" and "clientalism" as well as a hypocritical attitude geared towards conformity and avoidance of responsibility (see Voslensky, *Nomenklatura*, pp. 394–96, 413–35; and John P. Burns, "China's *Nomenklatura* System", *Problems of Communism* XXXVI, no. 5 [1987]: 49–51). For an insider's critique, see Tin Aung Hein, "Myanmar Naingan Ei Nainganyei Sipwayei Simunkhantgweyei Luhmuyei Hnint Tayasiyinyei Hsaingyar Keissa Myar Hnint Sutthlyin Ywei Akyanpyu Tinpyagyet Sardan", [Advisory Report on Myanmar's Political, Economic, Administrative, Social, and Judicial Matters], unpublished internal document (Yangon: 2 October 1987), pp. 4–5.
20. See, for example, *Fourth Party Congress*, pp. 114–15; *Pyinsama Akyein Parti Nyilargun Tho Tinthwin Thi Baho Kommiti Ei Nainganyei Asiyinkhanzar* [Political Report of the Central Committee to the Fifth Party Congress] (Yangon: BSPP, 1985), pp. 521–29, 538–40, 581; and Thurein Nyunt "Lanzin Parti Parti Unit Myar Ei Akhan Gandha" [Role of Party Units], *Botahtaung*, 7 August 1988.

21. For systemic shortcomings of one-party systems, see Samuel P. Huntington, "Social and Institutional Dynamics of One-Party Systems", in *Authoritarian Politics in Modern Society: The Dynamics of Established One-Party Systems*, edited by Samuel P. Huntington and Clement H. Moore (New York: Basic Books, 1970), pp. 40–44.
22. See *Fourth Party Congress*, p. 117.
23. See the Chairman's address at the sixth-day session of the Fourth Party Congress, in "The Supplement", *WPD*, 9 August 1981.
24. See *Pyinsama Akyein Parti*, pp. 520, 573–74, 708. For typical self-congratulatory assessments, see Yebaw Than Hlaing, "Ahnauk Ashet Ahant Atar Myar Goh Hpeishar Hpyayshin Yei" [Overcoming Obstacles and Hinderances], *Botahtaung*, 20 September 1987; and Ye Min, "Parti Oohsaunghmu Hnint Pyithu Tatmadaw" [Party's Leading Role and People's Armed Forces], *Botahtaung*, 25 October 1987.
25. The term was used by William Liddle for Indonesia (cited in Crone, "Military Regimes", p. 104).
26. According to the last BSPP-sanctioned President, Dr Maung Maung, the pathology became more acute after U Ne Win relinquished state duties in 1981 (Dr Maung Maung, *The 1988 Uprising in Burma*, Yale University Southeast Asia Studies Monograph 49 [New Haven, Conn.: Yale University Press, 1999], pp. 259, 261–63). See, also, the comment by a former CEC member, quoted in David I. Steinberg, *Crisis in Burma: Stasis and Change in a Political Economy in Turmoil*, ISIS Paper no. 5 (Bangkok: Institute of Security and International Studies, Chulalongkorn University, 1989), p. 42. For an illuminating Myanmar perspective, see Kyaw Yin Hlaing, "Reconsidering the Failure of the Burma Socialist Programme Party Government to Eradicate Internal Economic Impediments", *South East Asia Research* 11, no. 1 (2003): 5–58.
27. See, for example, *WPD*, 11 August 1987 and 10 October 1987; and Tin Maung Maung Than, "Burma in 1987: Twenty-Five Years after the Revolution", in *Southeast Asian Affairs 1988* (Singapore: Institute of Southeast Asian Studies, 1988), pp. 90–92.
28. See, for example, *Burma Communist Party's Conspiracy to Take Over State Power* (Yangon: News and Periodicals Enterprise, 1989); and Bertil Lintner, *Outrage: Burma's Struggle for Democracy* (London and Bangkok: White Lotus, 1990) for a more critical view.
29. *WPD*, 24 July 1988.
30. Sein Lwin was replaced by Dr Maung Maung, a civilian protege of Ne Win, as party Chairman after only eighteen days. Emergency sessions of the Party Congress and Pyithu Hluttaw were convened to endorse economic reforms aimed at opening up the economy to private participation. See *WPD*, 24 July 1988 and 20 August 1988.

31. The BSPP issued a proclamation, on 16 September, permitting the resignation of all government employees from the party.
32. Dr Maung Maung, "Speech at the Extraordinary Party Congress on 10 September 1988", *WPD*, 11 September 1988. On the other hand, one may contend that it was the result of the run-down of an authoritarian system principally organized for exercising control over society. As such, the single apex structure with built-in biases against diversity, flexibility, and sensitivity finally became uncontrollable due to the cumulative effects of the pathological conditions brought about by its obsession with control (Kyi May Kaung, "Theories, Paradigms, or Models in Burma Studies", *Asian Survey* [November 1995]: 1037–38).
33. See John Badgley, "The Burmese Way to Capitalism", in *Southeast Asian Affairs 1990* (Singapore: Institute of Southeast Asian Studies, 1990), pp. 229–39.
34. For the concept of legitimacy based on "legal validity", "justifiability of rules in terms of shared beliefs", and "expressed consent", see David Beetham, *The Legitimation of Power* (Basingstoke and London: Macmillan, 1991), pp. 15–25.
35. The beginning of the fiscal year was changed from 1 October to 1 April with effect from 1974.
36. For details, see *Myanma Hsoshelit Lanzin Parti Ei Hnit-Shei Hnit-Toh Sipwayei Muwada Myar* [Long-Term and Short-Term Economic Policies of the Burma Socialist Programme Party] (Yangon: BSPP, 1972), pp. 29–34, 220.
37. See ibid., pp. 29–34.
38. See ibid., pp. 36–38.
39. See ibid., pp. 38–39.
40. See Ngwe Than Naing, *Sipwayei Simungain Akyaung Thigaungzayar* [Facts about Economic Planning] (Yangon: Sarpay Beikman, 1985), pp. 79–80.
41. See "An Outline of the Discussion for the Twenty-Year Plan and the Second Four-Year Plan", unpublished draft document, Ministry of Planning and Finance (Yangon, 13 December 1973). Labour productivity was measured as GDP divided by labour force.
42. Targets for average annual growth rates (percentage) were: 4, 5, 6, 7, and 7.6 respectively (ibid., p. 4).
43. Ibid., p. 7; and "Hnit-Shei Hnit-Toh Sipwayei Muwada Myar Hnint Simungain Lunhyunhmu Myar" [Long-Term and Short-Term Economic Policies and Plan Guidelines], unpublished document, Planning Department (October 1983), p. 22.
44. See "Outline of Discussion", p. 7.
45. See, for example, M. Kalecki, "Outline of a Method of Constructing a Perspective Plan", in *Socialist Economics*, edited by Alec Nove and D. M. Nuti (Penguin: Harmondsworth, 1972), pp. 213–22.

46. The Declaration 1/73, of August 1973, specified the areas and sectors in which private investment would be allowed in accordance with the stipulations of the LTSTEP document. However, investment and growth parameters for the private sector were not factored into the TYP macroeconomic framework (personal communications with planning staff).
47. This was affected through the Finance and National Planning Affairs Committee of the Cental Committee. See *Baho Yeiyar Kommiti Myar Ei Phwezibon Hnint Lokengan Tarwun Myar* [Organization and Tasks of the Central Affairs Committees], internal document (Yangon: BSPP, January 1971), pp. 15–19.
48. There were units covering the social sector, trade, administrative departments, pricing, commodities, finance, investment, national income, manpower, regional plans, capital equipment, progress monitoring, computing, and research. PD's total staff strength expanded from less than fifty in the late 1960s to several hundred in 1974.
49. The Second FYP was drawn up within three months using the "sectoral balancing" method ("Report on the Second Four-Year Plan", presented to the Pyithu Hluttaw on 11 March 1974 [Yangon, Ministry of Planning and Finance], p. 4).
50. See Ngwe Than Naing, *Sipwayei Simungain Akyaung Thigaungzayar*, pp. 24–35. In practice, the centre dominated the planning dialogue. As such, local feedback, usually resulting from bargaining among those representing party, council, and departmental interests, filtered by the *nomenklatura*, were muted. The role of workers' organizations was overwhelmingly geared towards plan implementation (personal communications with planning personnel).
51. See "Planning Procedures in Burma", unpublished document (Yangon, Planning Department, 23 April 1984).
52. *People's Workers' Gazette* (hereafter *PWG*), May 1975, p. 1. This had resulted in proposals with targets lower than those set by the centre (see, for example, *Pahtama Akyein Pyithu Hluttaw Thatama Aseeawei Hmattan* [Record of the First Pyithu Hluttaw, Seventh Session] [Yangon: n.p., 1977], p. 31; and *Forward*, 1 April 1986, p. 40). Cf., the "minimal plan" tactics practised by Soviet functionaries (Voslensky, *Nomenklatura*, pp. 131–33).
53. Progress reporting was quarterly, whereby reports from the basic level, forwarded via the respective people's councils, were consolidated at the state/division level and thence to the central authorities. For important matters special reports had to be submitted expeditiously to the ECC. See Ngwe Than Naing, *Sipwayei Simungain Akyaung Thigaungzayar*, pp. 203–12.
54. Township party units monitored plan implementation and evaluated projects on a quarterly basis.

55. Each set of FYP guidelines were instituted by the corresponding Party Congress. Table 6.5 was compiled from unpublished documents of the Planning Department.
56. See "Introduction", in *Report to the People by the Government of the Union of Burma on the Financial Economic, and Social Conditions for 1973/74*, Book I (Rangoon: Ministry of Planning and Finance, 1974).
57. For explanation of the term, see John Girling, "Development and Democracy in Southeast Asia", *Pacific Review* 1, no. 4 (1988): 337.
58. In domestic investment, exports, and imports, only 31, 43, and 58 per cent of targets were achieved, respectively. See U Tun Wai, "Economic Reform in Myanmar", mimeographed (Yangon, August 1991), p. 17.
59. See *Fourth Party Congress*, p. 61. The green revolution was initiated by the introduction of "special high yield projects" for cereals and cash crops after 1976.
60. Against the TYP target of 26 per cent the share of the co-operatives sector in GDP had increased from 2 per cent in 1973/74 to only 3.7 per cent by 1981/82.
61. Gross domestic savings was around 17 per cent of the GDP and investment was around 23 per cent (Khin Maung Nyunt, *Foreign Loans and Aids in the Economic Development of Burma 1974/75 to 1985/86*, Institute of Asian Studies, Monograph no. 46 [Bangkok: Chulalongkorn University, 1990], Table 6.1, p. 139).
62. There existed a "major problem" of unemployment among those with secondary and tertiary education which was expected to worsen by 1978 (World Bank, "Development in Burma: Issues and Prospects", Washington, D.C., South Asia Regional Office, 27 July 1976, Report no. 1024-BA, p. 12).
63. At the Burma Aid Group meeting on 14 January 1986, "widespread concerns were expressed over Burma's target of 6.1 per cent growth" in the light of "indications that even ... 4.5% would be difficult to achieve" (World Bank, "Chairman's Report of Proceedings", Meeting of the Burma Aid Group, Tokyo, 14 January 1986, p. 6). This probably prompted its reduction to 4.5 per cent at the subsequent Pyithu Hluttaw. For analysis of the economic decline, see "Summary and Conclusions", in World Bank, "Burma; Policies and Prospects for Economic Adjustment and Growth", Washington, D.C., South Asia Department, 18 November 1995, Report no. 4814-BA.
64. The co-operatives and state shares of GDP in 1985/86 reached only 5.5 and 37.7 per cent respectively.
65. For the fuel problem, see Tin Maung Maung Than, "Burma's Energy Use: Perils and Promises", in *Southeast Asian Affairs 1986* (Singapore: Institute of Southeast Asian Studies, 1986), pp. 89–90.
66. Unemployment was not eradicated by the end of the Fourth FYP. Instead, it was estimated that the level of unemployment in 1983/84 was around

10.6 per cent of the total labour force or 4.6 per cent of the population (*Pyinsam Akyein Parti Nyilargun*, pp. 330–32; see also the section on employment, below).

67. See "An Outline of the Second Four-Year Plan Adopted at the First Pyithu Hluttaw", unpublished document, Planning Department (Yangon, 26 October 1974), p. 2. This ranking remained unchanged thereafter and became the *de facto* priority scheme for the successive FYP.
68. Ibid., p. 3.
69. Ibid.
70. The lingering self-sufficiency dogma diminished the role of foreign trade in economic growth (see, for example, Chairman Ne Win's address to the Fourth Party Congress on 8 August 1981 [*Fourth Party Congress*, p. 188]).
71. These resolutions are collated from newspaper reports.
72. "Outline of the Second Four-Year Plan", p. 9.
73. *Fourth Party Congress*, p. 47.
74. *Report to the Pyithu Hluttaw on the Financial, Economic and Social Conditions of the Socialist Republic of the Union of Burma for 1982/83* [hereafter *RPH*] (Rangoon: Ministry of Planning and Finance, 1982), p. 11; and *RPH 1986/87*, p. 22.
75. The set of annual plan targets stipulated by law constituted 26 (24 before 1977) macroeconomic parameters specifying monetary values (constant 1969/70 prices) and growth rates. The law also identified the corresponding ministries and organizations responsible for the attainment of the respective targets.
76. These reforms occurred within the socialist framework and neither introduced market-based solutions nor reduced the state's hold of the economy's "commanding heights" (cf. Pradumna B. Rana, *Reforms in the Transitional Economies of Asia*, Occasional Paper no. 5 [Manila: Asian Development Bank, 1993]).
77. The processing and manufacturing sector exhibited strong backward linkages with the primary production sectors. Surplus appropriated from the latter and SOEs' contributions were primary sources of funding for industrial investments. Changes in the incentive regime, management modalities, and regulatory measures invariably affected both private industries and SIEs.
78. The number of ministries were reduced from 24 to 19 (Thein Hlaing and Khin Hla Han, *Myanma Nainganyei Sanitpyaung Karla [1962–1974]* [Myanmar's Politics in the Period of Systemic Change], vol. 3 [Yangon: Historical Research Department, 1993], pp. 15–17).
79. Each agency also had an executive committee chaired by the chief executive. Workers' representatives were included but they normally deferred to the chief executive. On the other hand, many issues and matters (such as promotion, transfer or resignation of gazetted officers) were usually referred

to the ministerial executive committee. Many seemingly innocuous matters such as holding research conferences or foreign travel of civil servants had to be submitted to the relevant sub-Cabinet or even the full Cabinet. The hiring and firing of heads of agencies had to be approved by the Council of State. The minister's authority depended upon one's position in the pecking order within the state–party nexus (personal communications with senior ministry officials and personal observations, *c.* 1974–82).

80. The Council of State (29 members including the prime minister) rarely intervened in matters of routine governance. Generally, membership was regarded as a sinecure and many owed their positions to the party elite (personal communications with party personnel).
81. The township people's councils were entrusted with regulating private economic activities, supervising the procurement, allocation, and distribution of restricted commodities as well as control over movement of commodities and personnel within and across their territorial boundaries. The state/division councils provided a broader regional perspective for supervision and coordination of township-level activities and exercised regional authority (personal communications with township-level functionaries).
82. In addition to the executive committees at various levels of BSPP and people's councils, there were also public affairs committees at the BSPP central headquarters as well as in the party and council hierarchies, that ostensibly provided policy inputs and advice in their respective functional areas. In economic affairs, there were committees at the central level for finance and planning; industry and natural resources; co-operatives, agriculture, animal husbandry and forestry; commerce, construction and communications; and science and technology. Similar committees existed at the regional/local levels.
83. The most commonly cited adverse externalities had been the weather and the deteriorating terms of external trade. See, for example, Tin Aung Hein, "Myanmar Naingan Ei Nainganyei"; and Aung Gyi's open letter of 9 May 1988 to the President, Vice President and former RC members (copy in author's possession), pp. 35, 37.
84. See *Hnit-Shei Hnit-Toh Sipwayei Muwada*, pp. 43–44.
85. The old tax schedule comprised 11 income tranches from 1,500–5,000 kyat (7 per cent tax) to 300,001 kyat and above range (99 per cent tax). The tax progression was very steep, reaching 35 per cent at the fourth tranche (5,001–20,000 kyat).
86. The presumptive assessment was based on the individual's tax return and the income estimate provided by the relevant ward/village tract people's council. This became a source of corruption for local tax authorities.
87. Anecdotal evidence suggest that most, if not all, of these enterprises attempted to evade full taxation by guile and graft (personal observation and communications with entrepreneurs and retired income tax officials).

88. "One of the key problems ... is the weak fiscal situation ... reflected in a worsening of the current account position and a growing total deficit" which "has taken place since the mid-1960's but has become much more pronounced since 1972" (World Bank, Report no. 1024-BA, p. 13).
89. The local income tax office liaised with the assessment committee and usually gave technical and staff support to the latter. Reassessment within three years after the current year of assessment though appeals to state/division appellate or central appellate were allowed. The Minister of Finance was empowered to reduce or exempt the tax liability of any taxpayer subject to confirmation by the nearest Cabinet session.
90. The taxpayer had to submit the income declaration form annually and settle the assessment promptly. Fines for late payment or failure to declare taxable income could be up to 10 per cent of tax payable. Prison terms from 3–10 years for tax fraud and 3–7 years for graft together with penalties of 50 per cent over additional liabilities were stipulated. In practice, many resorted to bribery and "creative accounting" to evade what was perceived as unduly high taxes (personal observations). The ratio of personal income tax to total revenue had steadily declined from a peak of some 23 per cent in fiscal 1964/65 to 2.4 per cent in fiscal 1974/75 with the amount collected dropping precipitously from 450 million kyat to 41 million kyat only (World Bank, Report 1024-BA, p. 15; and annex, Table 5.2).
91. It was uncharacteristic of the socialist ethos. Underpricing was rampant due to loopholes in registration procedures and contracts. The rich, civil servants and *nomenklatura* who could travel abroad, and expatriate workers or employees of foreign shipping lines benefited most.
92. They were expected to grow at a faster rate than the private sector as the socialist economy matured and developed.
93. For local products the tax was levied on factory price (cost plus profit margin). The c.i.f. value was used for imports. Tax liability was computed either on the monthly income declaration statement or on the plan-based estimate of average income. At the end of the financial year the balance would be adjusted through an assessment of the annual payable CST based on the annual income declaration statement and report of accounts.
94. World Bank, "Burma: Domestic and External Resource Prospects", (Washington, D.C.: South Asia Programs Department, 10 October 1980), Report no. 3098-BA, Annex B, pp. 3–4. The inflationary implications of the CST as a "tax upon tax" was criticized at the October 1976 session of the Pyithu Hluttaw by representatives in contrast to the normal practice of supporting government legislation on every occasion (see, for example, *Hsahtama Aseeawei*, pp. 264–65, 282–83).
95. The UBB' was empowered to issue currency, manage gold reserves, set exchange rate, determine basic discount rates and interest rates, and supervise state financial investments.

96. See Daw Khin Kyi Kyi, "The Role of Central Banks in Development Finance (Burma)", in *A Collection of Papers Prepared by the Research & Training Department*, vol. 1 (Rangoon: Union of Burma Bank, 1985), pp. 56–63.
97. Projects were evaluated by the Project Review and Evaluation Committee of the Ministry of Planning and Finance before submission to the Cabinet. Apart from deposits, the MEB relied heavily on loans from the UBB' (averaging 57 per cent from 1979/80 to 1983/84). See Daw Khin Kyi Kyi, "The Contribution of Banks to Economic Development", in *Collection of Papers*, pp. 66–71).
98. All applications had to undergo stringent scrutiny at the headquarters and interest rates for term loans were fixed by the central bank. For working capital loans, the interest rate was 3 per cent above the central bank rate. See ibid., pp. 71–74.
99. Paddy was the principal crop for seasonal loans followed by oil seeds. In 1984 there were 29 eligible crops and nearly 12,000 village banks which disbursed credit to the cultivators. For term loans, whatever was bought with it had to be pledged to the bank. See ibid., pp. 74–82.
100. Ibid., pp. 82–83.
101. The proportion of MEB loans to the SEEs which was 47.5 per cent in fiscal 1975/76 became 55.6 per cent in 1977/78 and steadily increased to 95 per cent in 1983/84. The co-operatives share declined from 32.1 per cent in 1977/78 to 3.3 per cent in 1983/84. In the same period, the total value of loans extended by the bank rapidly increased from 3.2 billion kyat to some 27.5 billion kyat.
102. See, for example, *FEER*, 4 April 1980, p. 101. Anecdotal evidence suggests that only a privileged few had access to loans for car purchase and house repairs. Locally assembled cars were allotted to the *nomenklatura* with only a small portion balloted to the civil servants. Similarly, only well-connected members of the establishment were able to secure scarce government housing or build houses.
103. The MEB with an initial capital of 80 million kyat increased its profit from 148 million kyat in 1978/79 to 229 million kyat in 1980/81. The MFTB with an initial capital of 30 million kyat saw its profits jumped from 54 million kyat in 1977/78 to 144 million kyat in 1980/81 (*FEER*, 26 March 1982, p. 96).
104. "Guidelines for Operating on Commercial Lines to be Used by State Economic Organizations in the Various Ministries" (Rangoon, Ministry of Planning and Finance, 1975), pp. 4–5.
105. The Cabinet was responsible for the economic plan; the minister for the relevant SEEs; the managing body for each SEE; the manager for the factory, shop or workplace. Workers organizations at all levels were responsible for motivating workers (ibid., p. 9).

106. Other members were appointed by the parent ministry, with the chief executive of the agency concerned as chairman. Workers' representatives had to be endorsed by the BSPP. See ibid., p. 10.
107. Beginning 1 April 1975, capital expenditures were considered as loans. During the second phase (1978/79–1979/80), new projects had to be financed by bank loans. From fiscal 1980/81 onwards, all SEE expenditures had to be met by bank loans (ibid., pp. 6, 15–17). From fiscal 1977/78, public finance was separated into three sectors, i.e., SEEs, Union Government comprising all other government agencies and organs of state power, and town/city development committees (municipal authorities).
108. Annual after-tax profits were to be allocated into these funds. The SEEs had to prepare monthly, quarterly, half-yearly and annual accounts (ibid., pp. 13–15).
109. See ibid., pp. 7–8, 18–19.
110. SEEs were provided with target operating ratios with the general assumption that it must be less than one. See ibid., p. 23.
111. Ibid., pp. 22–23.
112. Ibid., p. 23.
113. For details, see Ngwe Than Naing, *Sipwayei Simungain Akyaung Thigaungzayar*, pp. 170–72.
114. "Guidelines for Operating", p. 25. In practice, many of these incentives were employed to some degree but there was no concerted effort to change the prevailing individual reward system where seniority, conformity, and loyalty counted most.
115. See ibid., p. 9. There had often been reports in the newspapers of actions taken against corrupt and irresponsible state employees. There had been, virtually, no publicized punishment of any high-level executive for losses and failures suffered by the SEEs. In fact, loyalty to the paramount leader was considered more important than accountability in the *nomenklatura* and the triangle of accommodation also dampened the retributive aspect.
116. Ibid., p. 25.
117. The SEEs could still secure virtually unlimited loans from the state banking system so long as they satisfied planning criteria (Tun Wai, "Economic Reform", p. 53). For a stylized summary of the conditions and consequences of a firm operating under a soft budget constraint, see Janos Kornai, *Economics of Shortage*, vol. B (Amsterdam: North-Holland, 1980), pp. 306–309.
118. *Hnit-Shei Hnit-Toh Sipwayei Muwada*, pp. 44–45.
119. Under the Private Enterprise Law of 1977 registered private enterprises could trade (wholesale) commodities not prohibited by the state. Exports of non-traditional items such as arts and crafts and some marine products were also allowed. Since fiscal 1976/77, the role of state trading corporations was reduced to supplying the goods (wholesale) to co-operatives and retail

distribution of imports and commodities from a few industrial branches. In 1980/81, the distribution of raw materials and capital goods for the private enterprises was handed over from trade corporations to agencies of the ministries concerned.

120. See David I. Steinberg, "Burma Under the Military: Towards a Chronology", *Contemporary Southeast Asia* 3, no. 3 (1981): 270, 273. In fiscal 1974/75, a "compulsory delivery" system was established, whereby paddy must be sold to the government according to fixed quotas, above which could be sold freely or to the government. The quota amount was set by local authorities according to a uniform formula based on size of holding and average yield though family size, and costs in kind were also considered. For details, see Tin Soe and Brian S. Fisher, "An Economic Analysis of Burmese Rice-Price Policies", in *Myanmar Dilemmas and Options: The Challenge of Economic Transition in the 1990s*, edited by Mya Than and Joseph L. H. Tan (Singapore: Institute of Southeast Asian Studies, 1990), pp. 127–28, 136.
121. Ranging from 2 to 7 per cent and 2 to 12 per cent respectively.
122. *RPH 1976/77*, pp. 125–26; and *RPH 1982/83*, pp. 236–37.
123. A World Bank study in 1976 estimated that the total value of the price "gap" amounted to about 3 billion kyat (James Harrison, "Burma's First Steps to Capitalism", *FEER*, 24 December 1976, p. 101). In fiscal 1980/81, automatic price adjustment of SEE products was allowed to compensate for increased costs of imports.
124. World Bank, Report 1024-BA, p. 52; see ibid., pp. 39–44 for the analysis of pricing policies.
125. See Tun Wai, "Economic Reform", p. 15.
126. However, producers who were not brokers and wholesalers with a turnover below the amount stipulated by the relevant authorities did not have to register. See *Pahtama Akyein Pyithu Hluttaw 1977 Khu Hnit Oopadei Myar Nioopadei Myar Hnint Lokehtone Lokeni Myar* [First Pyithu Hluttaw, Laws, By-laws and Procedures, 1977] (Yangon: n.p., 1978), pp. 120–22.
127. Ibid., pp. 123–25.
128. To relocate to another township, permission from the state/divisional people's council was needed. For relocation across state/divisional boundary permission from the relevant ministry was required. See ibid., pp. 123–24.
129. See ibid., pp. 127–29. Inputs supplied by the state were minimal and contingent upon either a contract with the SEE or the availability after satisfying public-sector demands.
130. See Daw Myint Myint Tin, "Financial Structure and the Effectiveness of Monetary Policy", in *Collection of Papers*, p. 153.
131. The SEEs share of total gross credits grew from over 50 per cent in 1977/78 to 90 per cent in 1981/82 and remained above 92 per cent in the 1982–88

period (data derived from World Bank, Report no. 4814-BA, p. 108; and "Myanmar: A Current Assessment" [Washington, D.C.: World Bank, 30 May 1991], Report no. 9209, p. 73).

132. The average annual rate of growth of bank savings (quasi-money) in the 1978–81 and 1982–85 periods was around 39 and 28 per cent respectively (see Khin Saw Oo, "Domestic Resource Mobilization in Myanmar", in *Domestic Resource Mobilization in SEACEN Countries*, edited by Y. M. W. B. Weerasekera [Kuala Lumpur: SEACEN Centre, 1993], Table 8.10, p. 250).
133. See ibid.; and IMF, *International Financial Statistics*, various issues, for data.
134. The consumer price index (CPI) in Yangon increased by only 14 per cent between 1977 to 1983 (*Selected Monthly Economic Indicators* [hereafter *SMEI*] [Rangoon: Central Statistical Organization], various issues). Because free market prices of rationed commodities (many were essential food items) were much higher than their controlled prices, the CPI would have been a poor proxy of price inflation if the proportion of such commodities were misrepresented. However, for government employees, who usually enjoyed some access to controlled commodities, it might well be a fairly reliable indicator of inflationary trends.
135. Myat Thein, "Monetary and Fiscal Policies for Development", in *Myanmar Dilemmas and Options*, p. 74. The growth rate of quasi-money was around 10.8 per cent for the 1978–84 period compared with some 6 per cent for the GDP (estimated from *RPH*, various issues).
136. The withdrawal of top three denominations (100, 50, and 20) was announced on 3 November. Given the circumstances in which the private sector was marginalized and officially frowned upon, private entrepreneurs and ordinary citizens alike developed a strong mistrust of the banking system and preferred cash transactions. The unwieldy and inefficient nature of banking transactions also reinforced this tendency. Having drawn their pay just three days beforehand, most salary-earners were vulnerable. Occurring only two weeks after the conclusion of the quadrennial general elections and on the eve of the very first session of the Fourth Pyithu Hluttaw, its psychological impact could not have been worse.
137. See, for example, Mya Than, "Burma in 1986: The Year of the Snake", in *Southeast Asian Affairs 1987* (Singapore: Institute of Southeast Asian Studies, 1987), pp. 116–17. Subsequently, the amount of circulating currency rapidly climbed back to the pre-demonetization level within six months.
138. 75 kyat, 35 kyat, and 25 kyat notes were invalidated in the notification issued on a Saturday afternoon. Apparently, UBB' top executives and the deputy finance minister were not privy to this decision taken at the highest level of state (personal communications).
139. See, for example, Myat Thein, "Monetary and Fiscal Policies", pp. 57, 60.

140. In January 1975, the Myanmar kyat was effectively devalued by about 30 per cent in relation to major currencies by fixing it at 7.74 kyat per SDR. In May 1977 it was again devalued to 8.51 kyat per SDR.
141. The overall balance was computed from the current account balance and capital expenditures with adjustment for net lending. It does not include foreign grants. For details, see World Bank, Report no. 4814-BA, Table 5.1, p. 102; and idem., Report no. 9209, Table 5.1, p. 67.
142. See U Maung Maung Hla, "The Coordination of Monetary and Fiscal Policies with Special Reference to the Balance of Payments Adjustment (Burma)", in *Collection of Papers*, p. 5.
143. Other minor components were capital income, interest payments, and administrative fees. For data, see Central Statistical Organization (CSO), *Statistical Yearbook 1989* (Yangon: CSO, 1990), Table 15.02, pp. 211–12; and World Bank, Report no. 4814-BA, Table 5.2, p. 103.
144. Derived from data given in Central Statistical Organization, *Statistical Yearbook 1989* (Yangon: Central Statistical Organization, 1990). Cf. the minimum ratio of 12.5 per cent targeted by the government (*Pahtama Akyein Pyithu Hluttaw Thatama Aseeawei Hmattan* [Record of the First Pyithu Hluttaw, Seventh Session] [Yangon, n.p., 1977], p. 40).
145. Direct taxes were levied upon income and profit. Indirect taxes covered CST, customs and excise duties, property taxes, and taxes on use of goods and natural resources.
146. It was attributed to stagnating domestic sales and services, though CST receipts might also have been adversely effected by exemptions and the so-called Special Order Procedure in which imports for priority projects were cleared immediately, deferring the settlement of the necessary tax and duties to a much later date (World Bank, Report no. 4814-BA, pp. 23–24).
147. Income tax applied to less than 20,000 persons and 40 per cent of co-operatives (see ibid., p. 26). The problem of arrears had been quite severe amounting to around 200 million kyat annually during the 1980/81–1985/86 period (*Pyithu Lokengan Sithseyei Aphwe Ei Pyithu Hluttaw Tho Asiyinkhanzar* [Report of the Council of People's Inspectors to The Pyithu Hluttaw] [hereafter *Lokengansit Asiyinkhanzar*], Fourth Pyithu Hluttaw, 4th Session, February 1987, Table 107, p. 355).
148. This included taxes on resource use (land, water, forest products, fish) and miscellaneous fees (lottery, stamp, import duty, motor vehicle use). Taxes on beneficiaries of irrigation and anti-flood schemes were introduced in 1982, but their annual contribution was only around 15 million kyat (IMF report, 16 June 1988, p. 66). The extraordinary surge in the 1987/88 land tax to over 200 million kyat resulted from the Cabinet notification (September 1987) stipulating the payment of land tax in kind, whereby farmers had to surrender a portion of their product, in lieu of cash payment. The total cash value of these crops represented the one-time gain in land tax.

149. The fact that more than half of the total contribution consisted of profits from the monopoly banking system suggests that the poor performance of the non-financial SEEs was masked by the former in aggregated data. See World Bank, Report no. 4814-BA, pp. 24–25. The share of contributions from net profits was raised from 20 to 30 per cent in 1979/80 (World Bank, Report no. 3098-BA, p. 28).
150. These surpluses fluctuated annually around 400 million kyat initially and exhibited a declining trend after 1982 and turned negative in 1986/87. Surplus from rice exports declined after 1982/83 and turned negative in 1986/87. The corresponding balances for minerals and marine products (fourth largest exports after timber, rice, and minerals) had been negative all along. See ibid., p. 103; IMF report (20 May 1987), Table 52, p. 88; and IMF, "Burma: Recent Economic Developments", unpublished report (16 June 1988), pp. 67–85.
151. Myat Thein, "Monetary and Fiscal Policies", p. 79.
152. Foreign grants and loans are excluded in computing the overall balance. For data, see *Statistical Yearbook 1989*, Table 15.01, p. 210.
153. Transport charges, fertilizers, and essential commodities (such as rice, cooking oil) were subsidized; for example, in 1986/87, explicit subsidies amounted to nearly 400 million kyat. Distortions in the exchange rate introduced hidden subsidies for imported goods and depressed export receipts. On the other hand, the availability of relatively cheap financing from the state and the low local cost of imported inputs distorted SEE accounts. The net result of all these price distortions cannot be ascertained but it is clear that they were at odds with the principle of operating SEEs along commercial lines (see, for example, Tun Wai, "Economic Reform", pp. 28–29).
154. Buoyancy relates tax collection to the tax base and coincides with tax elasticity in a fixed tax regime. Buoyancy ratios (growth rate of tax receipts to growth rate of tax base) indicate the potency of tax measures; values greater than one are considered as essential for revenue expansion. For the CST it declined from 1.2 during 1976/77–1979/80 to around 0.4–0.5 in the 1979/80–1984/85 period. For SEE contributions, it deteriorated from 4.9 (1976/76–1979/80) to 2 (1979/80–1981/82) and to –1 (1981/82–1984/85), while the corresponding values for other revenues were 2.4, 1.1, and 0.1 (World Bank, Report no. 4814-BA, Table II-2, p. 23).
155. See World Bank, Report no. 3098-BA, pp. 25–28; and Report no. 4814-BA, pp. 27, 32–34, 53.
156. If the currency ratio (currency/M1; where M1 is the sum of currency and demand deposits) is taken as an indicator of financial development, its extremely high value of 90.8 per cent in end 1975 (before the banking reforms) hardly changed over the next ten years and was 92.8 in end 1986. Such high values (cf. Thailand, 62.7 and 69.7; Indonesia, 50 and 45.7) suggests that the financial sector remained undeveloped (data derived from, Southeast Asian Central Banks [SEACEN] Centre, *SEACEN Financial Statistics*, Money

and Banking, SFS Series No. 1 [July 1991], pp. 12, 75, 189; and SFS Series No. 3 (July 1993), pp. 18, 60, 142. See, also, Myat Thein, "Monetary and Fiscal Policies", pp. 62–63).

157. See Mya Than, *Myanmar's External Trade: An Overview in the Southeast Asian Context* (Singapore: Institute of Southeast Asian Studies, 1992), pp. 53–54.

158. Ibid., p. 54.

159. U Khin Maung Myint, "Burma, Country Paper", presented at the Regional Seminar on Import Management, Pattaya, Thailand, 19–20 February 1981, p. 14; see, also, pp. 13–16. Imports were prioritized in terms of annual plan requirements and the corresponding FYP guidelines. All requisitions to import machinery and equipment, were required to be scrutinized and passed by the central Equipment Control Committee chaired by the Minister of No. 2 Industry. For details on state-owned importing agencies, see ibid., annex B.

160. See Mya Than, *External Trade*, pp. 21–25, 59, 63. For the list of export items and the corresponding state agencies responsible for them, see United Nations Development Programme (UNDP), "Burma: A Brief Review of the External Trade Sector", paper prepared for Burma Donors' Co-ordination Meeting (Rangoon, 2 August 1988), annex 1.

161. In terms of average FYP export targets set in constant 1969/70 prices, the achievement was even worse with fulfilment ratios of only 56, 70, and 57 per cent for the Second, Third, and Fourth FYP respectively. The corresponding ratios for imports were 45, 83, and 73 (Mya Than, *External Trade*, Table 3.16, p. 51). Against the TYP targets, the fulfilment ratios for the last year of FYPs (beginning with the Second) were even worse; achieving only 57, 54, and 32 per cent respectively (Trade Department, internal memo submitted to the Working Group for Compiling Guidelines to Harmonize Domestic Production and External Trade [in Myanmar], c. 1987, p. 30).

162. Receipts for beans and pulses increased from around 60 million kyat in 1978/79 to over 260 million kyat in 1982/83. Earnings from fish products grew rapidly from 0.2 million kyat in 1975/76 to 141 million kyat in 1982/83.

163. Annual net receipts were estimated by subtracting loan repayments from gross receipts of ODA, IMF credit, and commercial loans, though interest payment was excluded.

164. See Mya Than, *External Trade*, pp. 18, 21, 63–64; and UNDP, "Burma: A Brief Review", pp. 8–10.

165. Apparently, the volume of imported consumer goods could not be decreased further without causing undue deprivation to the populace.

166. The ISI strategy usually results in increasing demand for imported fuel, raw materials, spares and intermediate goods (Michael P. Todaro, *Economic Development in the Third World*, 4th ed. [London: Longman, 1989; reprint 1990], p. 438). In the Myanmar case, the absence of such a phenomenon after 1982/83 may be attributed to the relatively faster growth of capital good

imports, low capital utilization, and the diminishing need for petroleum imports as the oil sector developed rapidly.

167. The black market supplied consumption goods as well as raw materials, intermediate goods, machinery and equipment for the private entrepreneurs. For its scope and nature, see, for example, Kyaw Yin Hlaing, "The Political Economy of Hmaung-kho in Socialist Myanmar", unpublished working paper (Yangon, n.d); and Denzil Peiris, "When Survival is Tied to the Blackmarket", *FEER*, 20 September 1974, pp. 34–35; and David Hayes, "Big Border Bonuses", *Focus* (May 1981), pp. 13–14; Japanese field researchers estimated that for 1982/83 the illegal cross-border imports amounted to 1.8 billion kyat (Takamura, S. and T. Mori, *Kokkyo boeki Tonan Ajia kage no keizai* [The Border Trade: A Shadow Economy in Southeast Asia] [Tokyo: Kobundo, 1984], pp. 130–34). It was also reported that between 1974 and 1982, annual two-way cross border trade averaged 16 billion baht, in favour of Thailand by some 3.2 billion baht (Chin Gyar, "*Made in Myanmar Pi Pho Yar*" [To be a True Made in Myanmar], *Kyemon* [19 March 2001]). Another estimate indicated that "two-thirds of illegal imports" in the 1980s came from Thailand (Kyaw Yin Hlaing, "Political Economy", p. 12). Figures as high as US$1.5 billion for China–Myanmar trade had ben cited for the late 1980s after China displaced Thailand as the major exchange partner (Mya Than, *External Trade*, pp. 57–58). Thus, an estimate of the total value of illegal trade as equal to (if not larger than) the official volume (8–9 billion kyat annually in 1980–85 period) seems quite reasonable. In Myanmar's western border with Bangladesh, the illegal trade was estimated at about one-fifth of that with Thailand but was significant at the provincial level (Kyaw Yin Hlaing, "Political Economy", p. 12).

168. Over 0.5 million people were allegedly involved in the black market (Saw Htoo Sein, "Mathudaw Myar Paunghpet Thi Akhar" [When Dissolute People Associate], *Lokethar Pyithu Neizin*, 28 November 1985).

169. Various insurgent groups controlled most of the overland major trading routes along the borders with China and Thailand. Levies from cross-border trade amounted to tens of millions of dollars annually. See, for example, ibid., and "The Jewel in Thailand's Contraband Empire", *SOUTH* (December 1987), p. 15.

170. Despite offers of substantial rewards, sporadic raids of local shops by law enforcement agencies and interdiction by security forces along the smuggling routes (both land and sea), there is little evidence that illegal border trade was seriously disrupted. For example, the sales of confiscated goods during fiscal 1980/81 realized 115 million kyat while the street value of customs seizure in the first half of 1982 came to only 6.5 million kyat (see Aung Kin, "Burma in 1982: On the Road to Recovery", in *Southeast Asian Affairs 1983* [London and Singapore: Gower and Institute of Southeast Asian Studies, 1983], p. 91). The demonetizations of 1985 failed to undermine the financial base of black market operations, while the 1987 demonetization

did paralyse the black market but inflicted more damage to the population at large creating popular discontent that eventually led to the upheaval of 1988 (Kyaw Yin Hlaing, "Political Economy", pp. 34–36).

171. Myat Thein, "A Preliminary Note on Smuggling between Burma and Her Neighbours", discussion paper, Institute of Economics, Rangoon, 23 October 1975, p. 3.

172. Some agriculture products fetched a higher (kyat) price on the black market but in dollar terms the prices of all smuggled commodities were lower than the international prices on the free market. It involved high transaction costs, such as levies of 5 to 10 per cent collected by the insurgents and commissions for transhipment.

173. The Burma Aid Group held its first coordination meeting at Tokyo in November 1976 and met in Paris on 1 February 1978 to endorse Myanmar's proposal for assistance under a five-year development programme (1977/78–1981/82). Initially, it comprised seven donor nations (Australia, Britain, Canada, France, Japan, the United States, West Germany) and the UNDP. Finland, Italy, Norway, Switzerland, the European Community (EC), IMF, and ADB also attended later meetings. The Myanmar government usually submitted five-year development programmes (the last for the 1986/7–90/91 period) to this group highlighting development projects requiring external assistance. For the definition of ODA, see *Geographical Distribution of Financial Flows to Developing countries, 1986/89* (Paris: OECD, 1991), p. 7.

174. The net ODA influx was only US$23 million in 1970, US$67 million in 1974, US$102 million in 1977, and US$274 million in 1978 (Donald M. Seekins, *The Disorder in Order; The Army State in Burma since* 1962 [Bangkok: White Lotus, 2002], Table 1, p. 103). Though denominated in donors' currencies, Myanmar statistics gave equivalent kyat values consolidated as total foreign receipts. To facilitate international comparisons the World Bank converted the country data into U.S. dollar equivalent at the annual average certified exchange rate.

175. Export data were collated from World Bank reports (No. 1024-BA; 4814-BA; and 9209).

176. The ratio of net to gross loans declined annually from about 67 to 41 per cent during the first three years and jumped to a 86–91 per cent range in the 1977/78–1978/79 period as receipts for new ODA projects escalated. Thereafter, it declined (around 55 per cent) due to increased repayments.

177. Japan provided 40 per cent of total net ODA and 57 per cent of total net bilateral assistance. The corresponding figures for FRG were 11 and 16 per cent respectively (derived from Tun Wai, "Economic Reform", p. 122). Substantial bilateral assistance came from non-DAC countries such as China, Czechoslovakia, and Yugoslavia (*Asia Yearbook* [Hongkong: FEER], various issues; and World Bank, Report no. 4814-BA, p. 100).

178. Japan provided 45 per cent (US$1.19 billion) while FRG accounted for 15 per cent (US$407 million) of gross loans (derived from Khin Maung Nyunt, *Foreign Loans and Aid in the Economic Development of Burma 1974/75 to 1985/86*, Institute of Asian Studies, Monograph no. 46 [Bangkok: Chulalongkorn University, 1990], Table 2.6, p. 37; Table 2.12, p. 43; and *Geographical Distribution of Financial Flows to Developing Countries* [Paris: OECD], various issues).
179. Multilateral soft loans totalled over US$900 million and comprised 35 per cent of gross loans (ibid.). For details, see Khin Maung Nyunt, *Foreign Loans and Aids*, Table 2.10, p. 41.
180. Examples were: laying oil pipeline; extension of pulp producing plant; erecting power transmission lines; garments factory for export production; procuring oil rigs; and offshore oil exploration.
181. See Tun Wai, "Economic Reform", p. 124.
182. Japanese aid at nearly US$480 million comprising 42 per cent of total grants was the largest followed by Australia (US$103 million; 9.7 per cent) and FRG (US$81 million; 7.2 per cent). See Khin Maung Nyunt, *Foreign Loans and Aids*, Table 2.13, p. 44 for details.
183. Soe Saing, *United Nations Technical Aid in Burma: A Short Survey*, Research Notes and Discussions Paper No. 69 (Singapore: Institute of Southeast Asian Studies, 1990), p. 50.
184. See, for example, ibid., pp. 64–107.
185. The percentage of ODA-funded imports rose from 52 to 88 between 1982/83 and 1986/87 (IMF, "Burma: Recent Economic Developments", p. 33). See, also, Martin Rudner, "Japanese Official Development Assistance to Southeast Asia", *Modern Asian Studies* 23, no. 1 (1989), Table 9D, p. 104; and David I. Steinberg, "Japanese Economic Assistance to Burma: Aid in the 'Tarenagashi' Manner?", *Crossroads* 5, no. 2 (1990), p. 65 and Table 11, pp. 100–101.
186. Observation based on personal communications with senior planning officials. For a succinct discussion of policy dialogue and conditionality, see Robert Cassen and Associates, *Does Aid Work?* (Oxford: Clarendon Press, 1986; reprint 1988), pp. 69–103.
187. Steinberg, "Japanese Economic Assistance", pp. 67–68.
188. Reserves fell to less than 500 million kyat by 1985 (1.2 months) and plunged to 310 million kyat in March 1987 (under 1 month). These may be compared with the World Bank's "conservative" assumption of maintaining reserves at a level "equal to roughly two months' imports" (World Bank, Report no. 4814-BA, p. 58).
189. Tun Wai, "Economic Reform", p. 42.
190. World Bank, Report no. 4814-BA, p. 17. The annual inflow of non-commercial loans was cut back from an average of US$145 million over the previous three years to some US$25 million for the next two years (ibid.). Its percentage in total external debt increased from 76.4 in 1984 to 79.5, 83.4 and 85.4 in

the following years (*Thailand, Burma: A Country Profile 1991–92* [London: Economist Intelligence Unit, 1991], p. 73).

191. This ratio may be taken as a proxy for the debt burden. Its rising trend was not only caused by the stagnation of exports but also by the unfavourable trend in the exchange rate of the U.S. dollar against the Japanese yen (for details see *Nomura Asia Focus* [June 1989], p. 33) in which 34.7 per cent of the outstanding debt (as at March 1985) was denominated (World Bank, Report no. 4814-BA, Table 4.1, p. 100).
192. Debt servicing increased by 77 per cent between 1982/83 and 1986/87 but decreased by 28 per cent in 1987/88 due to some debt relief accorded by donor countries ("Economic and Social Indicators", unpublished document [Yangon, Ministry of Planning and Finance, March 1990], Table 8.5, p. 22).
193. See Tun Wai, "Economic Reform", p. 20. The decline was some 24 per cent within five years.
194. Ibid., p. 17.
195. See, for example, *Asia 1978 Yearbook* (Hongkong: Far Eastern Economic Review, 1978), p. 146. The economy exhibited unusually high inflation in the plan period with the Consumer Price Index (CPI) in Yangon jumping from 160 in 1972 to 241 in 1974 and then to 408 in 1976 (computation based on various issues of *SMEI*).
196. Tun Wai, "Economic Reform", p. 18.
197. Ibid.
198. In Figures 6.28 and 6.29, the TYP trajectory is plotted as a straight line connecting the stipulated targets for the initial and final years of the TYP, while the curve for actual achievement is based on annual value-added output data. A semi-logarithmic scale is used to reflect the exponential nature of the "time series" with the tangent at any point on the curve representing the rate of growth.
199. See Mya Than, "Agriculture in Myanmar: What Has Happened to Asia's Rice Bowl?", in *Southeast Asian Affairs 1990* (Singapore: Institute of Southeast Asian Studies, 1990), pp. 242–44. Fertilizer subsidies cost some 50 million kyat annually (Tun Wai, "Agricultural Sector Reforms", unpublished draft report [Yangon, n.d.], p. 3). The domestic price of fertilizer remained constant after 1981/82 with the implicit subsidy decreasing from over three to two times the sales price for urea and increasing from 70 to 100 per cent above sales price for triple phosphate between 1982/83 and 1986/87 (IMF, "Burma: Recent Economic Developments", annex, Table 20, p. 55).
200. The exception was the output of beans and pulses which doubled between 1979/80 and 1985/86. However, due to lack of consistent data its trend could not be graphically portrayed.
201. In fact, the "compulsory delivery" system (see n. 120) coupled with price controls administered by the state resulted in not only the underestimation of the value of agriculture products but also acted as a disincentive against

private initiatives towards increasing production (see, for example, Tin Soe and Fisher, "Economic Analysis", pp. 143–46 and World Bank Report no. 4814-BA, pp. 47–48). Other limiting factors were insufficient credit (Tun Wai, "Economic Reform", p. 40); water supply constraints (only 12 per cent of total cultivated area was under irrigation while rain-fed rice constituted over 80 per cent of the overall acreage); high post-harvest losses (estimated at up to 35 per cent for rice; see R. K. Palis and O. J. S. Lazo, "Position Paper on Rice Production in Myanmar", unpublished report [Yangon, 19 September 1992], p. 6); land fragmentation (56 per cent of cultivated area were plots of less than 10 acres); poor quality control in harvesting/milling; the stagnation of total fertilizer input after 1983/84 and its decline by about one-third in 1987/88; shortages of fuels, spares and agricultural machinery; and the continued reliance on production and export of a few staple crops.

202. Data from various issues of *RPH*.
203. For example, the average export price of rice per tonne fell from 2,350 kyat in fiscal 1981/82 to 1,646 kyat in 1984/85 and then to 1,308 kyat, 1,095 kyat and 939 kyat in the following years. Prices of other significant export items such as teak, tin, tungsten, beans and pulses, lead and zinc were also affected by the downward trend in commodity prices (*RPH*, various issues).
204. The associated problems were identified as heavy reliance on a few traditional export products; internationally sub-standard quality of many products; relatively low level of resources allocated to agriculture despite its comparative advantage; lack of institutions and mechanisms for effective export promotion; absence of business acumen and deficiency in legal, contractual and practical aspects of international trading; lack of product/market development, inadequate quality control and poor design/packaging; deficient export infrastructure; lack of appropriate export financing facilities; and an overvalued currency (UNDP, "Burma: A Brief Review", pp. 8–10).
205. See, for example, Liz Carver, "Burma's Socialist Path to Debt Default", *FEER*, 16 April 1987, pp. 74–75; idem., "Lack of Basics", ibid., p. 76; and idem., "The Oil Shortage", ibid., p. 77.
206. The average annual increase in Yangon's CPI which was only 6.4 per cent between 1979/80 and 1982/83 jumped to 19 per cent in the 1982/83–85/86 period and then escalated to 35.1 per cent between 1985/86 and 1987/88 (*SMEI*, various issues).
207. Fiscal 1986/87 was chosen instead of fiscal 1987/88 (the last year of the period under study) because only unreliable provisional estimates were available for the former.
208. The report was long on descriptions and assessments but short on answers and remedies. Apart from exhortations and general guidelines no effective policy initiatives were recommended (*Pyinsama Akyein Parti*, pp. 658–85).
209. *WPD*, 11 August 1987.

210. Ibid.
211. The exception was the report by Tin Aung Hein (see n. 19). It seems that no action was taken, even to discuss the issues raised in his report. Other responses were in the form of sector-wise economic reports which highlighted the economic difficulties being encountered. While blaming adverse international economic conditions, resource constraints, administrative shortcomings, and technical deficiencies, these reports did not advocate wide-ranging economic and political reforms (personal communications with those who had access to these reports).
212. The "21-year old restriction on the free trade of paddy, maize and seven varieties of beans and pulses" was removed in September 1987. However, this was closely followed by two "market-disrupting" measures, viz., demonetization of higher value currency notes without compensation and the collection in kind (a portion of output) of agricultural taxes and profit tax on wholesalers of agriculture products (Mya Than and Nobuyoshi Nishizawa, "Agricultural Policy Reforms and Agricultural Development in Myanmar", in *Myanmar Dilemmas and Options*, p. 109).
213. See *WPD*, 10 October 1987.
214. Ibid.
215. Ibid. Under the Citizenship Law of 1982, an associate citizen is defined as a person who is not of indigenous descent but is eligible for citizenship under the 1948 Union Citizenship Act (see *WPD* 16 October 1982).
216. *WPD*, 13 October 1987.
217. *Guardian*, 15 March 1988. In fact, the decontrol of rice export was announced in February but the highly overvalued exchange rate (roughly six times the official rate) made such exports unprofitable. A border trading agreement was also reached with Yunnan (China) in August 1988. In general, due to administrative red-tape, absence of appropriate legislation, and lack of procedures, these attempts to open up private sector initiatives did not bear fruit during the remaining few months of the BSPP regime.
218. See Lintner, *"Outrage"*, pp. 192–95 for a chronological summary.
219. For example, see ibid., pp. 83–85.
220. *WPD*, 24 July 1988.
221. Ibid. For details of the proposal, see *Naingandaw Ei Sipwayei Hsaingyar Muwada Myar Hnint Lunhnyunhmu Myar Pyupyin Pyaungleiyei Hnint Pathet Ywei Tinpyagyek* [Report on Reforming National Economic policies and Guidelines] (Yangon: Burma Socialist Programme Party, 1988).
222. See *WPD*, 26 July 1988.
223. The restrictive "Right of Private Enterprise Law (1977)" was repealed. See *WPD*, 28 July 1988.
224. The last reform measure enacted by the government was the rescinding on 6 September 1988, of the order (issued on 1 September 1987) stipulating the collection of land tax in kind.

225. See, for example, Kyaw Yin Hlaing, "Reconsidering the Failure", pp. 45–51.

226. Only after the Party Chairman questioned the reliability of economic data in his August 1987 speech did top party and state executives emphasize the importance of correct and consistent statistics in public speeches and in their "guidance" to government officials at ritualistic inspection tours of government agencies. Manipulation of sectoral value-added data to satisfy the party political agenda and to conform to the perceptions of top leadership was also not uncommon in planning circles (personal communications with ex-planners). It has been pointed out that the system resembled a "single apex structure" and was incapable of instituting significant reforms to prevent a system "run-down" leading to an eventual collapse (Kyi May Kaung, "Theories, Paradigms, or Models", pp. 1037–38, 1040).

7

Planned Industrialization in the Socialist Framework

The autarkic approach of the Revolutionary Council (RC) era was modified when the "Long-Term and Short-Term Economic Policies" (LTSTEP) were adopted as the economic manifesto of the Burma Socialist Programme Party (BSPP) that led the Socialist Republic of the Union of Burma after March 1974. However, the state-led import-substituting industrialization (ISI) strategy which had been continuously pursued since Myanmar's independence remained unchanged within the Twenty-Year Plan's (TYP) framework. As such, it entailed acceptance of official development assistance (ODA) and private sector participation in selected industrial activities.

INDUSTRIAL STRATEGY, POLICIES AND PLANS

The aim of Myanmar's industrial strategy in the BSPP framework was to create an industrial base utilizing Myanmar's natural resources and agricultural products for an eventual transformation into an industrialized country. The emphasis was on resource-based industrialization (RBI) while incorporating an "export-substituting" element that entailed increasing the export of value-added (through industrial processing) products.[1] Nevertheless, the legacy of inward-orientation in economic outlook together with restrictive external trade policies foreclosed the EOI (export-oriented industrialization) option.[2]

The long-term policies enunciated in the LTSTEP document were adopted as guidelines for the FYPs and their annual components.[3] Together with the list of ownership vis-à-vis industrial classifications stipulated in the LTSTEP document, the sectoral objectives and policies enunciated in the latter formed the basis of state-led industrialization in the TYP (1974–94) period.[4]

The FYP plan guidelines for the industrial sectors endorsed by the corresponding Pyithu Hluttaw sessions are shown in Table 7.1. They reflected the BSPP's perception on means and ends for transforming Myanmar into an agriculture-based industrial economy by 1994. They also demonstrate the persistence of resource constraints, especially capital and energy shortages, and that each successive FYP encountered essentially the same problems and shortcomings thereby eliciting similar exhortations. These guidelines suggest that underutilization of industrial assets and lack of financial and technological resources were major problems for state industrial enterprises (SIEs) throughout these four FYP periods. Given such constraints, rationalization of the SIEs with less emphasis on new projects and more on full utilization of existing factories should have been carried out from the outset. However, only in fiscal 1983/84 did the state decided to give priority to "completing ongoing projects" and new ones that "were less capital intensive, had short gestation periods, utilized domestic resource base, and had good export potential".[5]

These industrial policies must be viewed in the wider context of the concomitant economic restructuring and reform process as a whole that served either as an enabling or an emasculating policy environment for the former.[6] On this score, their implementation was constrained by the failure to achieve sustained growth of net output in general and exports in particular. Persistent trade deficits and balance of payments difficulties (discussed at length in Chapter 6) plagued the state's RBI drive and the industrial sectors failed to grow significantly despite substantial ODA inputs into them. This unsatisfactory performance manifested not only in the area of production but also in terms of labour welfare and employment generation.

TABLE 7.1
Four-Year Plan Guidelines for the Industrial Sectors

	Policy Objectives and Measures
Second FYP (1974/75–1977/78)	To achieve full utilization of existing industrial capacities.
Third FYP (1978/79–1981/82)	To achieve full utilization of existing industrial capacities. To restrict state-funding to ongoing and new projects approved by the BSPP and the Pyithu Hluttaw. Where capital and technology warrant, to enter, for limited periods, into mutually beneficial co-operation with foreign partners in natural resources development; but without compromising the socialist system.
Fourth FYP (1982/83–1985/86)	To restrict state-funding to essential industries, export-oriented projects and those with short recoupment periods. Where capital and technology warrant, to enter, for limited periods, into mutually beneficial co-operation with foreign partners in natural resources development; but without compromising the socialist system. To institute the requirement for full capacity utilization as an industrial strategy.
Fifth FYP (1986/87–1989/90)	To achieve full utilization of existing industrial capacities. If financial resources are inadequate, preference for increasing capacity utilization over new construction. To invest in projects with short gestation periods for producing basic consumer goods. Where capital and technology warrant, to enter, for limited periods, into mutually beneficial co-operation with foreign partners in natural resources development; but without compromising the socialist system. To expand the construction of hydroelectric, natural gas, and coal power plants.

Source: Planning department and BSPP headquarters.

DEVELOPMENT OF INDUSTRIAL SECTORS

In the industrial field, the important ministries were No. 1 and No. 2 Industry, Mines, and later Energy.[7] Most of the SIEs in the processing and manufacturing sector belonged to these two industry ministries, whereas rice and saw mills came under the trade ministry and agriculture and forest ministry respectively. The mines ministry was responsible for exploration, extraction, and processing of minerals.[8]

At the beginning of the TYP, all SIEs faced two adverse conditions brought about by the autarkic policies of the RC period. The first one was the stagnation of the agriculture sector which was the primary source of investable surplus and with which processing industries had strong backward linkages. Secondly, a legacy of shortcomings and bottlenecks which included inadequate knowledge of resource endowments, poor infrastructure, insufficient supplies of equipment, spare parts and imported raw materials, lack of managerial expertise, and technological obsolescence.[9]

Thus, the processing and manufacturing sector faced problems related to low capacity utilization and unrealistic pricing that led to very low returns on investments.[10] The mining sector had to contend with problems relating to insurgency, technological obsolescence, labour shortage, cross-border smuggling, and the lack of a comprehensive resource inventory.[11] The power sector suffered from distributional bottlenecks resulting from the "low priority given in the past to the construction of distribution and transmission facilities" and there was an underutilization of generating capacities.[12]

Industrial Investments

Despite the assignment of top priority to the agriculture sector in the TYP guidelines, half the cumulative state investments in the 1974/75–1987/88 period were channelled into projects in processing and manufacturing (seventh priority), mining (third priority), and power (sixth priority) sectors.[13] In fact, as evident from Figure 7.1, the combined share of agriculture (the mainstay of the economy) and forestry (second priority; the top foreign exchange earner in the late 1980s) was less than that for processing and manufacturing. At 32.6 per cent the latter received the largest share of total state investments in the period concerned amounting to some 22.7 billion kyat; i.e., more than three times the share of the agriculture sector.[14] Similarly, mining and power garnered respectively 2.9 and 2.6 times the amount invested in the forestry sector.[15]

When compared to cumulative values of annual plan targets (Figure 7.2), it is found that the rank ordering of investment shares for power and mining were reversed due to the underspending of the former and overspending of the latter. Moreover, actual spending fell short of targets

FIGURE 7.1
Cumulative State Investment, 1974/75 to 1987/88
(current prices)

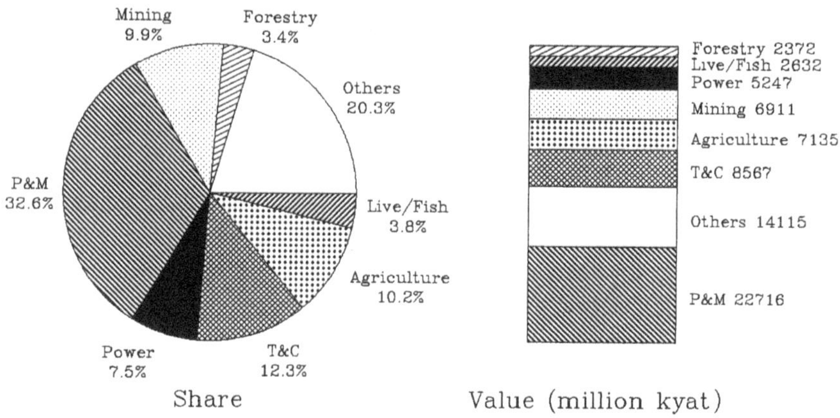

Notes: T&C = Transport & Communications; P&M = Processing & Manufacturing.
Source: Ministry of Planning and Finance.

FIGURE 7.2
Cumulative State Investment Targets, 1974/75 to 1987/88
(current prices)

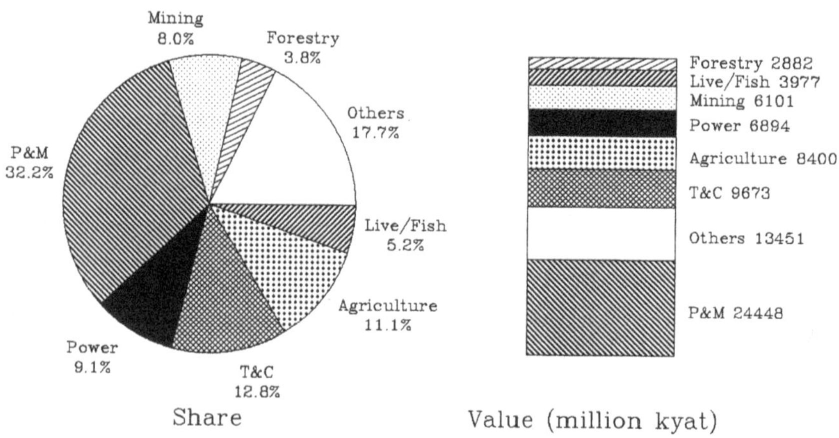

Notes: T&C = Transport & Communications; P&M = Processing & Manufacturing.
Source: Ministry of Planning and Finance.

in total public investment as well as in all productive sectors except for mining.[16] In terms of plan fulfilment the achievements of processing and manufacturing, mining, and power were 92.9, 113.3, and 90.5 per cent respectively, whereas the fulfilment ratio for overall state investments was 91.9 per cent.

Figure 7.3 illustrates the trends in state industrial investments during the implementation of the TYP. After rapidly rising from low bases, investments in mining as well as processing and manufacturing peaked in fiscal 1982/83. However, the power sector enjoyed steady growth reflecting the state's attempt to meet escalating demands for electricity. Industrial investment trends may be compared to the trend of capital goods imports as well as that of overall investments by the state (cf. Figure 7.4). It is apparent that the rapid rise of industrial investments after 1976/77 and their decline after 1982/83 reflected the corresponding trend for overall investments which was highly correlated with that for imported capital goods.[17] On the other hand, investments in the processing and manufacturing sector continued to decline after 1984/85 (Figure 7.3) while both capital goods imports and overall investments levelled off (Figure 7.4). This latter pattern which was reflected in the trends for the mining and power sectors (Figure 7.3) seems to indicate

FIGURE 7.3
State Industrial Invesment
(Current prices)

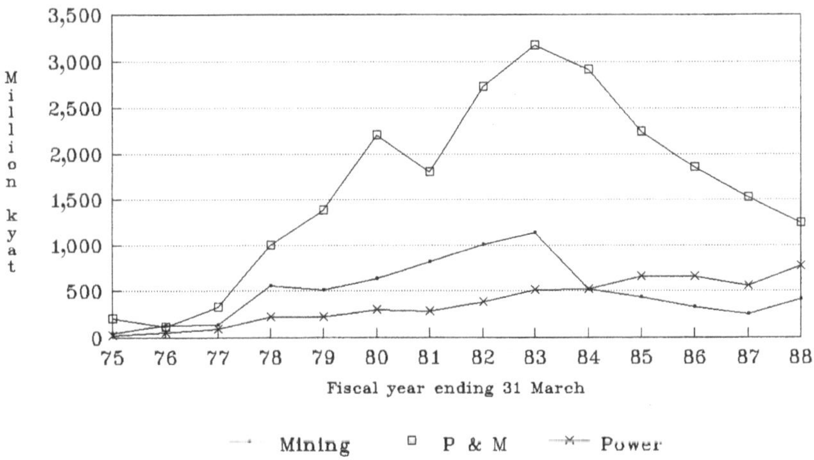

Notes: P&M = Processing & Manufacturing.
Source: Ministry of Planning and Finance.

FIGURE 7.4
Capital Goods Imports and State Investments
(Index: 1974/75 = 100)

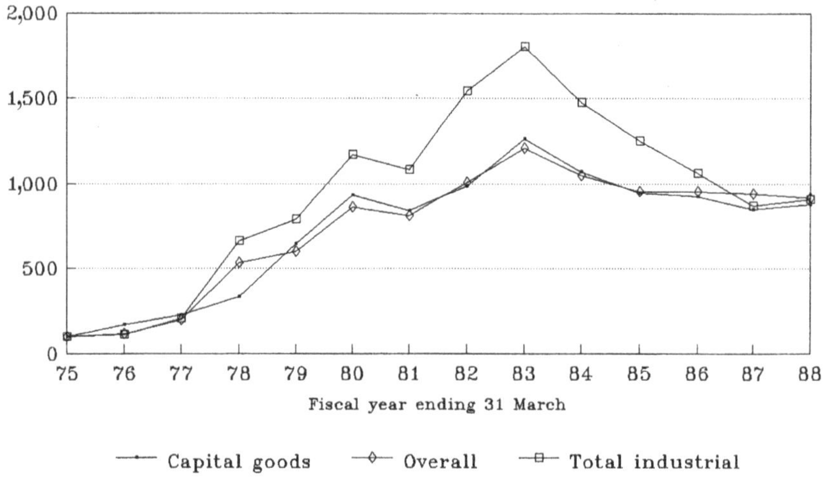

Source: Ministry of Planning and Finance and World Bank.

that, in the face of an overall economic slowdown, the processing and manufacturing sector's investments were substantially cut back in line with the FYP guidelines (see Table 7.1). It appears that the balance shifted in favour of maintaining investments in mining with its short-term export potential and power which was essential to alleviate the electricity bottleneck.[18]

In the mid-1980s, the earlier emphasis on capital-intensive industrial sectors was reduced to realign the state investment profile with the TYP objectives. Table 7.2 shows the changing pattern of industrial investments over successive FYP periods in terms of average annual investments and their corresponding shares in relation to other sectors which were also in competition for limited investment funds.[19]

Annualized investment values (averaged over the FYP period concerned) shown in Table 7.2 reaffirms the pattern observed for the three industrial sectors in the time-series data depicted in Figure 7.3. To a relatively lesser extent, average investment in the three primary product sectors (agriculture, forestry, livestock and fishery) also declined after the Third FYP while their shares remained fairly stable. The modernization and expansion of the long-neglected transport and telecommunications infrastructure resulted in an investment surge

TABLE 7.2
Average State Investment and Share by Sector

Sector	*Second FYP*		*Third FYP*		*Fourth FYP*		*Fifth FYP*[a]	
	K10[6]	*(%)*	*K10*[6]	*(%)*	*K10*[6]	*(%)*	*K10*[6]	*(%)*
Processing & Manufacturing	411	(25.5)	2,031	(36.4)	2,544	(36.0)	1,386	(21.9)
Mining	215	(13.3)	744	(13.3)	605	(8.6)	330	(5.2)
Power	96	(6.0)	294	(5.3)	588	(8.3)	666	(10.6)
Agriculture	158	(9.8)	513	(9.2)	771	(10.9)	684	(10.8)
Forestry	108	(6.7)	203	(3.6)	189	(2.7)	186	(2.9)
Livestock & Fishery	47	(2.9)	362	(6.5)	175	(2.5)	148	(2.3)
Transport & Communications	273	(16.9)	695	(12.4)	623	(8.8)	1104	(17.5)
Others	305	(18.9)	741	(13.3)	1,575	(22.3)	1,815	(28.7)
Total State	1,612	(100.0)	5,583	(100.0)	7,070	(100.0)	6,318	(100.0)

Notes: Average annual investment in kyat (K); sectoral share (per cent in parentheses).
a. Based on the first two years only.
Source: Ministry of Planning and Finance.

during the two years of the Fifth FYP period. Similarly, the aggregated residual sectors classified as "others" also exhibited an upward trend in average investment and significantly raised its share after the Third FYP period.

Sectoral Growth

Notwithstanding the infusion of a relatively large portion of available state investment funds into the three industrial sectors, the resulting growth rates fell short of expectations, as can be seen in Table 7.3.

It is evident from Table 7.3 that the processing and manufacturing sector persistently failed to achieve planned growth rates and also exhibited a downward trend in average growth rate that resulted in a negative value for the 1986/87–1987/88 period. Both the mining and power sectors surpassed the Second FYP targets but were unable to achieve the planned targets in the next two FYPs as the targets were successively revised upwards. However, the mining sector did register respectable growth rates while the power sector achieved double-digit growth in the Third and Fourth FYPs. Nevertheless, for the first two years of the Fifth FYP, despite the substantially scaled-down targets, the

TABLE 7.3
Industrial Growth Targets and Achievements

Sector	*Average Annual Growth (%)*			
	Second FYP	*Third FYP*	*Fourth FYP*	*Fifth FYP*[a]
Processing & Manufacturing	7.5 (7.1)	12.2 (5.3)	9.0 (4.7)	7.7 (–6.4)
Mining	2.4 (6.9)	12.2 (6.0)	18.0 (7.4)	3.0 (–10.3)
Power	9.1 (10.3)	14.3 (12.2)	16.8 (11.3)	7.1 (4.1)

Note: Figures in parentheses are actual growth rates.
a. Based on annual plans for the first two years only.
Source: Ministry of Planning and Finance.

mining sector suffered a double-digit reduction in value-added output while the power sector attained only 58 per cent of the planned target. All these data reflected the sorry state of the national economy, which lost it agriculture-led growth momentum towards the end of the Fourth FYP and regressed thereafter.

The poor performance of the processing and manufacturing sector is also evident in relation to the growth trajectory envisaged in the TYP.[20] As indicated by Figure 7.5, the two trends diverged prominently after 1976/77 and the actual growth trend worsened thereafter.[21]

In both the mining and power sectors, value-added output grew slowly but caught up with the target trajectory in 1977/78 (Figure 7.6). For mining, the actual growth trend kept up with the TYP trajectory up to 1985/86 but faltered and slipped below the latter in the last two years of BSPP rule. Similarly, the growth trend of the power sector surpassed the TYP trajectory by an impressive margin until 1986/87 when it regressed and fell below the TYP path in 1987/88.

On the other hand, the state made substantial progress in enlarging its share of contribution to the sectoral value-added in all industrial sectors. The SIEs contribution to the sectoral value-added (in constant 1969/70 prices) in the processing and manufacturing sector for 1986/87 increased to 52.6 per cent from 33.7 per cent in 1973/74 (TYP base year), while the private sector share dropped to 43.4 per cent from 63 per cent. In the same period, the corresponding SIEs share in mining increased to 88.9 per cent from 83.2 per cent while the SIEs contributed 100 per cent to the value added in the power sector.

FIGURE 7.5
Index of Sectoral Growth: Processing and Manufacturing
(1974 = 100)

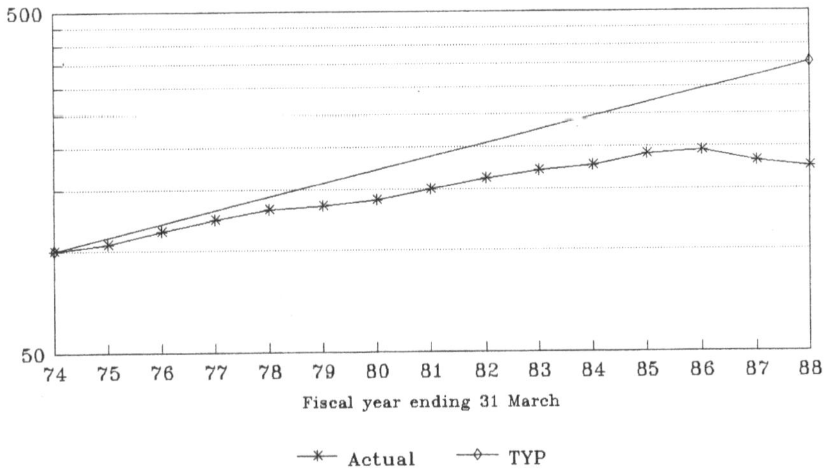

Note: TYP = Twenty-Year Plan trajectory.
Source: Ministry of Planning and Finance.

FIGURE 7.6
Index of Sectoral Growth: Mining and Power
(1974 = 100)

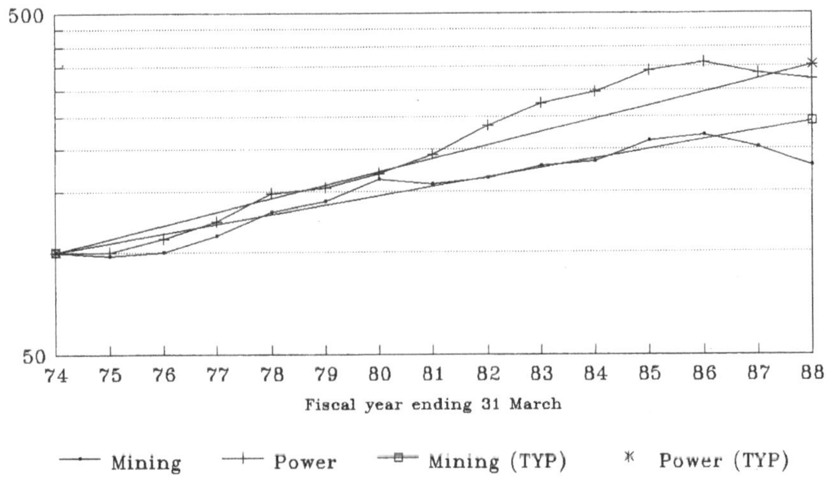

Note: TYP = Twenty-Year Plan trajectory.
Source: Ministry of Planning and Finance.

TABLE 7.4
Number of Industrial Enterprises

Sector	*1974/75*	*1987/88*
State	1,461	1,880
Co-operatives	299	719
Private	27,258	39,059
Total	29,018	41,658

Source: Ministry of Planning and Finance.

Growth of Industries

Given the state's emphasis on investments and the reforms carried out in the mid-1970s that gave some scope for the private sector, the total number of enterprises in the processing and manufacturing increased by 43.6 per cent between 1974/75 and 1987/88. Table 7.4 shows their distribution by ownership.

It follows that, between 1974/75 and 1987/88, the share of state-owned enterprises or SIEs declined from 5 per cent to 4.5 per cent of the total number of industrial enterprises despite 28.7 per cent increase in units. Meanwhile, the co-operatives' share, albeit starting from a very low base, increased from 1 per cent to 1.7 per cent. Numerically, the private-owned enterprises increased by 43.3 per cent and overwhelmingly outnumbered the rest with its share slightly declining to 93.8 per cent in 1987/88 from 94 per cent in 1974/75.

However, there is a huge diversity in the size of industrial enterprises, both in terms of production capacity and workforce. In Myanmar, where light processing industries were dominant and financial and production data were unavailable, the size of workforce is a useful indicator of the scale of industrial enterprises.

It is evident from Table 7.5 that in the 1974/75–1987/88 period, despite the overall growth, the number of mid-size enterprises decreased while that of the largest size remained unchanged. Meanwhile, the smallest-size enterprises increased their numbers as well as their share. The preponderance of small and medium-size industries (SMIs) was apparent and their share increased over the period to nearly 99 per cent in 1987/88.[22] The numerical distribution of enterprises further disaggregated by ownership within each size cohort (see Table 7.6) reveals that private enterprises formed the bulk of small industries while the state sector dominated the medium-size and large-size industries.

TABLE 7.5
Distribution of Industrial Enterprises by Workforce

Size of Workforce	*1974/75*	*1987/88*
	units (% share)	*units (% share)*
Below 10 workers	23,733 (81.8)	38,634 (92.7)
10–50 workers	4,361 (15.0)	2,336 (5.6)
50–100 workers	431 (1.5)	195 (0.5)
Above 100 workers	493 (1.7)	493 (1.2)

Source: Ministry of Planning and Finance.

TABLE 7.6
Distribution of Industrial Enterprises by Workforce and Ownership

Size of Workforce	*1974/75*	*1987/88*
	units (% share)	*units (% share)*
Below 10 workers		
State	269 (1.1)	981 (2.5)
Co-operatives	57 (0.2)	404 (1.0)
Private	23,407 (98.7)	37,249 (96.5)
10–50 workers		
State	514 (11.8)	256 (11.0)
Co-operatives	158 (3.6)	283 (12.1)
Private	3,689 (84.6)	1,797 (76.9)
50–100 workers		
State	267 (61.9)	154 (79.0)
Co-operatives	28 (6.5)	32 (16.4)
Private	136 (31.6)	9 (4.6)
Above 100 workers		
State	411 (83.4)	489 (99.2)
Co-operatives	56 (11.3)	0 (0.0)
Private	26 (5.3)	4 (0.8)

Source: Ministry of Planning and Finance.

The distribution of gross output value (in constant 1969/70 prices) among industrial branches is another indicator of the prevailing structure of industry and Table 7.7 compares the corresponding rank-ordered shares for 1974/75 and 1986/87.[23]

TABLE 7.7
Share of Output Value by Industrial Branches

Industrial Branch	*1974/75*	*1986/87*
	% (rank)	*% (rank)*
Food and beverage	65.0 (1)	62.9 (1)
Textiles	7.1 (3)	6.9 (2)
Industrial raw material	4.3 (5)	6.6 (3)
Construction material	6.7 (4)	5.7 (4)
Minerals	7.5 (2)	4.7 (5)
Transport equipment	1.4 (7)	2.8 (6)
Printing & publishing	1.0 (8)	2.2 (7)
Personal goods	2.6 (6)	1.7 (8)
Others	4.4 n.a.	6.5 n.a.

Notes: n.a. = not applicable; "others" included electrical goods, household goods, agricultural equipment, industrial equipment, workshops and miscellaneous products.
Source: Ministry of Planning and Finance.

It is evident from Table 7.7 that the composition of the top eight industrial branches remained unchanged over the twelve-year period though some changes in rank-ordering had occurred. Food and beverages retained its top position and its huge majority share of output value barely changed. It can be seen that production by light industries overwhelmingly dominated gross output in constant value terms.[24] Moreover, in terms of increasing commodity production that was emphasized by the ruling BSPP, the sector apparently failed to deliver as may be seen in Table 7.8.[25] It can also be seen that per capita production of liquid fuels and most household products decreased. On the other hand, other commodities that registered modest increases over a thirteen-year period — such as sugar, cotton yarn, towel, and blanket — were quantitatively very small in absolute terms. Only cement and fertilizer production increased substantially due to new capacity additions.[26]

In the mining sector where the state had a monopoly over both exploration and extraction, there were attempts to expand output and introduce more higher value-added products. Nevertheless, ore degradation, ageing equipment, lack of modern technology, and scarcity of foreign exchange prevented this sector from realizing its full potential, and as evident from Table 7.3 the sectoral growth rates were disappointingly short of targeted values.[27]

TABLE 7.8
Per Capita Production of Selected Commodities

Item (unit)	*1974/75*	*1987/88*	*Change (%)*
Sugar (kg)	0.71	0.99	39.4
Cotton yarn (kg)	0.21	0.26	23.8
Male *sarong* (piece)	0.15	0.081	(–)46.0
Female *sarong* (piece)	0.031	0.006	(–)80.6
Child *sarong* (piece)	0.022	0.003	(–)86.4
Cotton vest (piece)	0.12	0.045	(–)62.5
Towel (piece)	0.032	0.04	25.0
Blanket (piece)	0.026	0.029	11.5
Mosquito netting (yd)	0.024	0.047	95.8
Umbrella (piece)	0.02	0.0006	(–)97.0
Soap (kg)	1.33	0.7	(–)47.4
Cement (kg)	6.81	10.22	50.1
Aluminium-ware (lb)	0.37	0.22	(–)40.5
Petrol (gallon)	2.13	1.37	(–)35.7
Kerosene (gallon)	2.31	0.0012	(–)99.9
Diesel (gallon)	2.49	1.93	(–)22.5
Fuel oil (gallon)	1.11	0.88	(–)20.7
Fertilizer (kg)	3.93	7.68	95.4

Note: Longyi is Myanmar for sarong; imperial gallon was used for liquid fuels.
Source: Ministry of Planning and Finance.

The oil industry that was regarded as having a high growth potential turned out to be most disappointing, as onshore production faltered in the early 1980s and the offshore ventures with foreign partners from 1974 to 1982 failed to yield tangible results.[28] Crude oil production increased rapidly from 1975 (when pre-World War II level was regained) at a compound growth rate of nearly 12 per cent annually to over 11 million barrels in 1979/80. However, as shown in Figure 7.7, oil output stagnated for the next six years and declined steeply in the remaining two years. This decline was attributed to depletion of known reserves and technological backwardness in exploration/production.[29] Consequently, there was a persistent shortage of gasoline, diesel, and fuel oil, which negatively affected the transport, construction, as well as manufacturing sectors and even agricultural and timber production.[30]

As illustrated in Figure 7.8, the gas industry, whose product was utilized as chemical feedstock as well as for production of thermal and electrical energy, was relatively more successful. Though the gap between plan target and production diverged after 1976/77, gas

FIGURE 7.7
Crude Oil (million bbl)

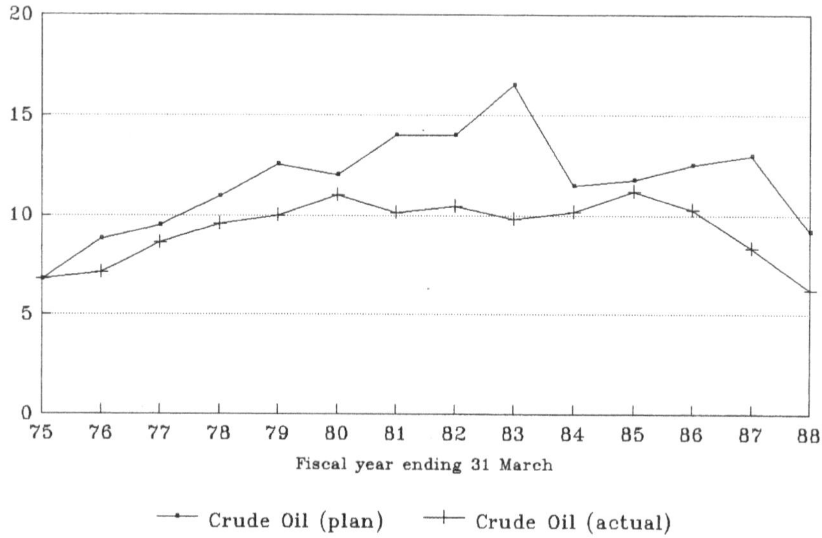

Source: Ministry of Planning and Finance.

FIGURE 7.8
Natural Gas (billion cubic ft)

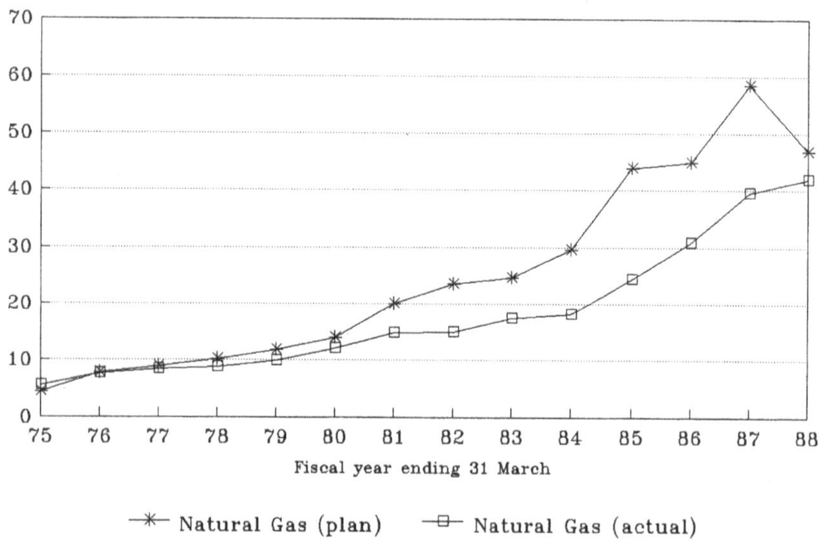

Source: Ministry of Planning and Finance.

output increased from 5.6 billion cu. ft in 1974/75 to 41.9 billion cu. ft in 1987/88, averaging 16.8 per cent annual growth. In the mid-1980s, as oil production faltered, the government took measures to substitute natural gas for liquid fuels in industrial plants and power generators to alleviate the shortage of oil-based liquid fuels. This probably accounted for the rapid growth of natural gas supply after 1983/84.[31]

Electricity generation, which was the state's prerogative also progressed substantially but still fell short of both industrial and consumer demands.[32] Net output of commercial electricity increased at an annual average rate of 9.1 per cent in the 1974/75–1987/88 period. In the same period, industrial power consumption grew by 9.8 per cent with its share slightly up from 52.6 to 57.2 per cent of total consumption. Meanwhile, total generating capacity in this capital-intensive and foreign-exchange dependent sector increased from 386 to 960 megawatts. Despite its high growth rates in output and substantial capacity additions, power supply could not keep up with electricity demand and there were frequent brownouts and blackouts in urban areas throughout the 1980s.[33]

Apparently, most of the shortcomings of the three industrial sectors described in the foregoing were associated with extensive state intervention in them. Given that the state had exclusive control over mining and power production and had channelled a major portion of available resources into SIEs in the processing and manufacturing sector while marginalizing the private sector, a closer examination of SIEs would be useful for understanding the problems of state-led industrialization during the BSPP era.

State Industrial Enterprises

Development of SIEs under the TYP were largely financed by foreign loans and aid.[34] Most SIEs in the processing and manufacturing sector enjoyed a monopoly position in domestic production but had to compete with illegal imports from China, Bangladesh, India, Thailand, and even Singapore. Anecdotal evidence suggest that in many industrial branches, such as textiles, food and beverages, pharmaceuticals, household goods, and personal goods, black-market goods not only supplemented the inadequate supply of SIE products but also competed with them. The latter were regarded as inferior to illegal imports in terms of quality as well as variety.[35] On the other hand, items which were in high demand were persistently in short supply and subject to some form of rationing or priority scheme (often favouring the military and government officials).

Attempts to expand manufactured exports were also unsatisfactory as they accounted for only around 6 per cent of total value of exports in the late 1980s. Main export products were sugar, cement, cotton, cotton seed, garments, sheet glass, animal hide, rice bran, bran residue, glycerine, bamboo pulp, petroleum coke and naphtha.[36] As evident from Figures 7.9 and 7.10, exports from the Ministry of No. 1 Industry — which can be taken as representative of light manufacturing industries — fluctuated over the years and had little impact on the external trade situation which deteriorated after 1976/77 (see Figure 6.13).[37] In fact, the total amount of foreign exchange earned during 1976/77–1986/87 was only 23.3 per cent of foreign exchange expenditures in the current account.[38]

Another feature of investments by SIEs in the Ministry of No. 1 Industry was their heavy dependence upon foreign exchange that averaged 37.6 per cent over the 1976/77–1986/87 period. The problem was equally acute for current expenditures and only 44 per cent of the amount requested by the ministry for current outlays were allotted in the same period. After 1982/83, this gap between requirements and allocations became more pronounced as indicated by the decreasing trend in the ratio of allocation to request. The latter decreased from

FIGURE 7.9
Ministry of No. 1 Industry's Export: Total Value

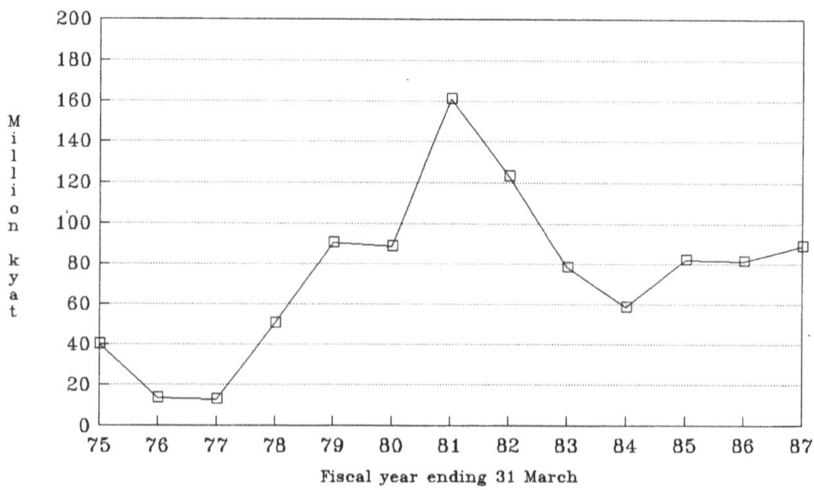

Source: Ministry of No. 1 Industry and Ministry of Planning and Finance.

FIGURE 7.10
Ministry of No. 1 Industry's Export: Share of All Exports

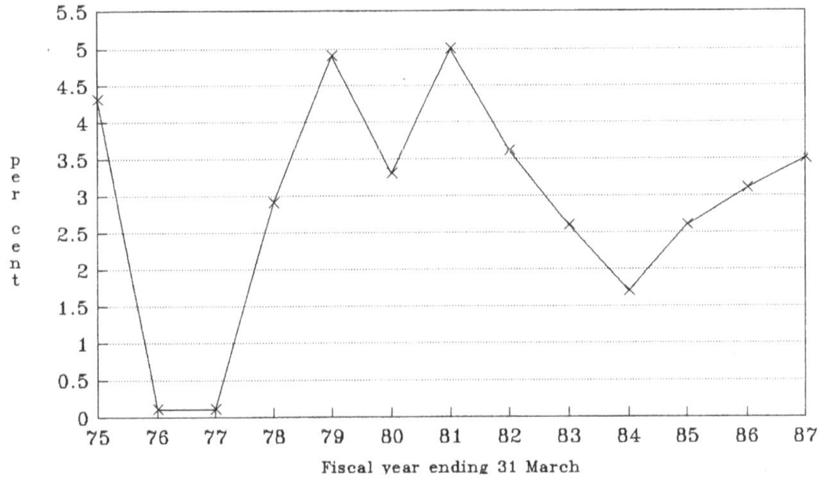

Source: Ministry of No. 1 Industry and Ministry of Planning and Finance.

75.2 to 47.1 per cent in 1983/84 and declined every year to reach 22 per cent in 1986/87.[39]

In the oil and gas sector there was a state monopoly. Self-reliant approaches to both onshore and offshore exploration and downstream production resulted in poor assessment of potential fields and wastage of scarce foreign exchange as well as a foreclosure on finance, technology, and expertise essential for success.[40] One of the biggest miscalculations on the refining side was the building of the 25,000 barrels/day refinery with a US$120 million Japanese ODA loan in an area where the oil output begun to decline once the plant came onstream in 1982.[41] Domestic prices of refined products were extremely low in comparison to international prices and did not reflect their scarcity value entailing extremely high opportunity costs and foregone revenues.[42]

Almost all SIEs in mining were geared towards exports. As illustrated in Table 7.9 their physical output exhibited rising trends before stagnating in the mid-1980s and declining thereafter (except for Group III).[43] Nevertheless the total value of mineral exports (see Figure 6.14) stagnated after enjoying steady growth up to 1979/80.[44]

TABLE 7.9
Minerals Production Quantum Index
(1969/70 = 100)

Fiscal Year	*Group I*	*Group II*	*Group III*
1974/75	69.7	148.8	102.2
1975/76	36.3	147.8	123.7
1976/77	40.5	101.0	133.1
1977/78	68.8	110.0	183.8
1978/79	73.6	227.5	172.0
1979/80	77.6	303.5	209.3
1980/81	86.3	342.3	179.9
1981/82	111.6	341.2	180.7
1982/83	104.5	390.4	199.2
1983/84	102.4	419.0	207.7
1984/85	87.5	438.5	218.1
1985/86	85.9	348.1	245.8
1986/87	80.1	278.1	323.5
1987/88	56.3	218.6	226.1

Note: Group I comprised lead, zinc, silver and allied products; Group II contained tin, tungsten and scheelite mixed concentrates; Group III included industrial minerals.
Source: Ministry of Planning and Finance.

The Electric Power Corporation (EPC) was the only SIE in the power sector. It was heavily dependent upon ODA for generation as well as transmission, and since the mid-1970s, it had relied increasingly upon natural gas-fired thermal units.[45] The major inefficiency in electricity supply was the high losses incurred between generation and consumption that averaged 27.3 per cent during 1974/74–1979/80 and worsened during the 1980s, averaging 31.9 per cent in the 1980/81–1987/88 period. Electricity tariffs also did not reflect the fact that there was suppressed demand and remained practically unchanged throughout the 1980s, depriving EPC of the potential to raise revenues.[46] Illegal connections and malpractice by consumers were quite common entailing revenue losses through corruption and evasion of charges.[47]

Despite the introduction of partial reforms for state economic enterprises or SEEs (that affected SIEs as well) in the mid-1970s (see Chapter 6), the SIEs failed to generate necessary current surpluses even for their own investments. Figures 7.11 and 7.12 illustrate the unsustainable nature of deficits incurred by the bulk of SIEs.[48]

FIGURE 7.11
SIEs: Financial Balances

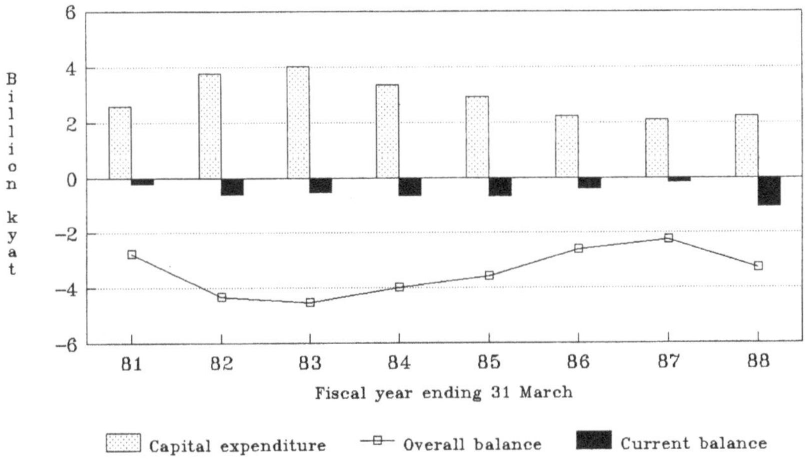

Note: Summation for industry, mines and energy ministries.
Source: Central Statistical Organization.

FIGURE 7.12
SIEs: Financial Balances
(Share of current GDP)

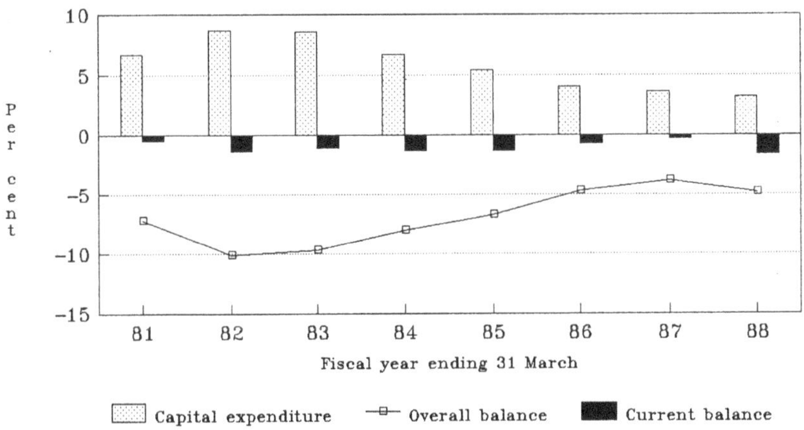

Note: Summation for industry, mines and energy ministries.
Source: Central Statistical Organization.

Evidently, the current account balance was negative all along and the deficit trend in overall balance followed the corresponding trend in capital expenditures which were cut back by nearly one-half within three years after peaking in fiscal 1982/83. This poor performance characterized all SEEs in the 1980s and may be attributed to the following deficiencies:[49]

- use of SEEs as an instrument of social and political control over society;
- though ostensibly operating autonomously along so-called commercial lines, they were still under considerable centralized control imposed by the party and the government;
- the existence of inconsistent multiple objectives;
- the operating ratio used as the efficiency measure did not reflect true financial costs such as amortization;
- administrative pricing was prevalent and price adjustments were too cumbersome or inadequate to be effective;
- some underlying investments of the SEEs were inappropriate while in others financial constraints had resulted in under-investment;
- inefficient management and poorly motivated workers; and
- as foreign exchange shortages became acute, necessary spares and intermediate goods were not sufficiently provided leading to a vicious cycle of production decline and revenue losses which was further aggravated by the penchant for new projects at the expense of sustaining existing ones.

Moreover, all SEEs were affected by the soft budget constraint, whereby "there was no budget constraint or refusal of loans by [state] banks provided the SEEs were carrying out investments in accordance with the Plan".[50]

Besides the aforementioned general malaise common to all SEEs, the most serious deficiencies for SIEs was capacity underutilization. The average capital utilization ratio for the processing and manufacturing sector, which was in the 50–55 per cent range in the mid-1970s, steadily increased to 65–70 per cent in the late 1970s. As can be seen in Figure 7.13, it started to decline after 1981/82 and dipped below 50 per cent in 1986/87.[51] Figure 7.14 indicates that the post-1981/82 overall decline was mainly due to the deteriorating trend for SIEs under the Ministry of No. 1 Industry. The reasons for low capacity utilization were:[52]

- ageing equipment and technological obsolescence;
- inadequate maintenance, and lack of spare parts;
- shortage of raw materials and intermediate goods;

FIGURE 7.13
Capacity Utilization Ratio: Processing and Manufacturing Sector

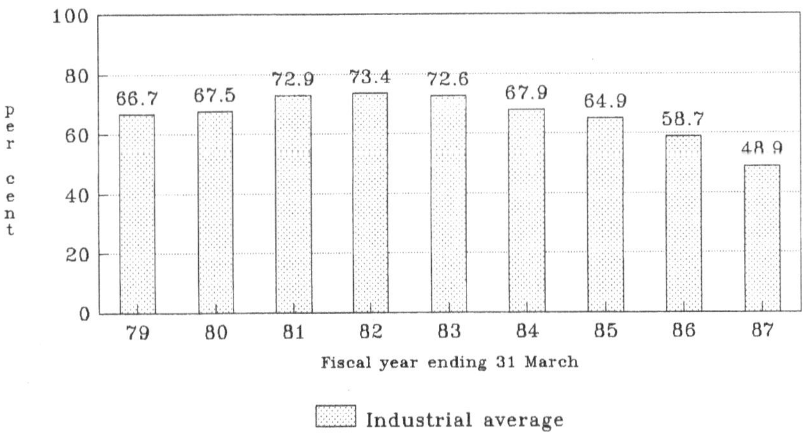

Source: IMF, "Burma", 1987, annex, p. 59; idem., 1988, annex, p. 57; and RPH, various isues.

FIGURE 7.14
Capacity Utilization Ratio: Processing and Manufacturing Sector

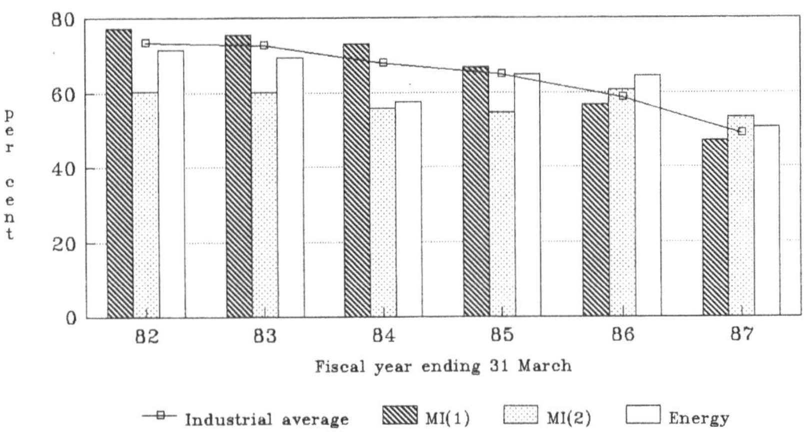

Note: MI(1) = Ministry of No. 1 Industry
MI(2) = Ministry of No. 2 Industry
Source: Ibid.

- shortage of qualified workers;
- shortage of fuel and electricity;
- lack of demand; and
- lack of storage due to distributional bottlenecks.

In the second half of the 1980s, acute shortage of foreign exchange together with lower fuel availability and electricity supply problems exacerbated the underlying problems of organization, pricing, financing and distribution, severely depressed the capacity utilization ratios of SIEs in the processing and manufacturing sector. The resulting production decline, in turn, slowed down the growth in sectoral value-added (see Figures 7.5 and 7.6) and triggered a recession in the last two years of BSPP rule.

LABOUR AND EMPLOYMENT

The BSPP continued the Revolutionary Council's claim of furthering the workers' cause and exhorted the latter to wholeheartedly participate in the country's industrial development.[53] Hence, there were refinements and extensions of existing measures and mechanisms relating to the welfare, discipline, and motivation of workers in general and industrial workers in particular. On the other hand, the BSPP reorganized the hierarchy of existing People's Workers Councils in 1977 and renamed it as *Aloketharmar Aseeayone* (workers organization). The latter, constructed as a multi-tiered structure replicating the Leninist hierarchy of the BSPP, held its first national congress in August 1977 which adopted a programme to promote organization, production, discipline, and welfare.[54]

Organizational work was primarily focused on drawing workers into the BSPP fold and mobilizing them into activities organized by the various tiers of the *Asiayone* under BSPP guidance. The implication was that workers themselves would take charge of their own affairs and relevant issues but in reality the *Asiayone* was run by BSPP cadres and state executives strategically placed at different tiers of the organization's executive committees.[55]

The drive for increasing production was carried out through on-the-job training programmes, campaigns to reduce wastage and losses, and attempts to encourage innovation and research. The existing model workers scheme was extended gradually to cover more establishments and increase the number of recipients.[56]

The main thrust of instilling work-site discipline was through the SEE management committees formed according to the BSPP guidelines for enterprise reforms (*c.* 1975) and the introduction of contracts between management and employees for observing disciplinary rules at establishments. This measure implemented by the Directorate of Labour in coordination with *Asiayone* Central Headquarters resulted in an increase in the number of establishments with such contracts from 232 in December 1978 to 467 in September 1987.[57]

Generally, the BSPP-led government's actions were aimed at expansion and improvement of measures introduced by its predecessor for the workers' well-being. In the area of legislation and regulations relating to workers' rights, entitlements, safety, and dispute settlement, there were no major changes as the focus was on streamlining the prevailing laws and rules in accordance with the administrative reforms of 1972 and enterprise reforms of 1975.[58]

The Social Security Scheme remained the backbone of labour welfare, though it had to be supplemented by various institutional and ad hoc measures to alleviate the hardship suffered by low-income workers in the face of inflationary pressures. Its coverage increased from twenty-three towns to sixty-one and the size of membership increased by 42.6 per cent to 360,000 for individuals and by 78.3 per cent to 14,443 for establishments, during 1974/75–1987/88. In 1978/79, medical care was transferred to the Scheme from the health ministry and the ratio of pecuniary benefits (given to claimants) to receipts (from subscriptions) jumped from around 20 per cent to over 45 per cent in the next five years.[59]

Workers welfare associations were reorganized in November 1977 and they expanded from around 1,158 to 3,610 between 1978 and 1987. Their membership increased from over 207,000 to nearly 649,000 in the same period. It was reported that some associations had been successful in generating income through agriculture and animal husbandry.[60]

There was no major adjustment in the salary structure of state-sector personnel in the BSPP period, but following the "doubling of consumer prices between 1973/74 and 1983/84, wages" increased by "10 per cent on average with a greater increase for low paid workers".[61] Moreover, the daily minimum wage was raised from 3.85 kyat to 5.4 kyat and then to 6.5 kyat.[62] In 1976 a special arrangement was initiated to sell seventeen basic commodities (most of them rationed) at controlled prices to state employees drawing the salary scale of 350 kyat and below.[63] Later, this was extended to the next higher scale and as production faltered in the late 1980s the items were reduced to five. In addition, occasional emergency loans were extended through co-operative credit societies and many SIEs allowed their workers to purchase selected products directly from their factories.[64] These somewhat cushioned the impact of inflation on their wages which continuously fell in real terms throughout the 1980s.[65]

In a way, these ad hoc arrangements as well as the reorganization of workers organization in 1977 may be seen as state responses to workers' frustrations over rising costs of living that led to riots in mid-1974. These unprecedented incidents — that elicited harsh repression by security forces and the imposition of martial law in Yangon and other affected areas — were attributed to the "economic problem and the high rice price" as well as "subversives" amongst the workers.[66] On the other hand, all these measures taken together could not prevent the disenchanted workers from joining forces with the dissidents in the popular uprising of 1988, during a severe economic downturn.[67]

The employment creation potential of the processing and manufacturing sector was not fully realized due to its low rate of growth.[68] Overall employment in this sector grew annually at an average of 4.1 per cent during 1976/77–1987/88. This was much higher than the 2.4 per cent average growth of the 15–59 age cohort which served as a proxy for Myanmar's labour reserve. The sector's share of total employment increased from 7.1 to 8.7 per cent. The average growth rate of state employment was only 2.3 per cent compared with 4.4 per cent for the combined rate of private and co-operatives. Mining's corresponding growth rate was nearly 3 per cent and its share rose from 0.5 to 0.6 per cent. However, the state component grew by only 1.7 per cent, and its share within the sector was reduced to 84.6 from 97 per cent. The power sector employed the smallest workforce which increased by 42.8 per cent in the same period, with its share of total employment rising from 0.11 to 0.13 per cent. Since the combined share of total employment by the processing and manufacturing, mining, and power sectors remained below 10 per cent, it may be concluded that the industrialization effort in the BSPP was not very significant in terms of labour absorption.

CONCLUSION

In the reconstituted Socialist Republic of the Union of Burma, the BSPP defined the boundaries and set the parameters of economic activities to be carried out by the state, co-operatives, and the private sectors. The state attempted to replace the private entrepreneur with centralized planning. In this context, the state assumed a dominating role in the country's economic development and pursued a state-led ISI strategy. The latter emphasized state investments towards the realization of the RBI potential of Myanmar's natural resources. However, "entrepreneurship requires combining technological and marketing knowledge, a vision of the future, a willingness to take risks, and an ability to raise capital", all of which were absent in the BSPP era in contrast to the successful interventionist states of East Asia.[69] As evident in the foregoing discussions, the utilization of its agricultural, timber, and mineral resources did not bring about the desired results in terms of either growth or structural change that characterize successful industrial development.[70]

Lacking indigenous technological capability, Myanmar's industrial development was based on an investment-driven approach that was undermined by the state's self-imposed straitjacket of relying only on government revenues and ODA. These turned out to be inadequate even for the investments envisaged under the TYP. Generally, the "initial RBI investment assumes the character of a 'hurdle' which must be overcome" and requires "additional investments [that] will unlock the ... scale and linkage proliferation benefits". As such, the resulting "dynamic scale economies impart a Verdoon effect (a virtuous circle of growth related-efficiency gains)" and this "combination of initial entry hurdle and prospective Verdoon effect yields the characteristic muted and lagged RBI economic stimulus". This did not occur in the Myanmar case because resource constraints barely allowed the SIEs to clear the initial "'sinking' of capital in the ... in the first stage RBI plant" and not much more as the overall investment effort diffused and attenuated across the industrial branches.[71]

While the SIEs engaged in the production of mineral ores, oil and gas, and wood-based industries failed to maintain high capacity utilization rates, the private sector SMIs which were less capital intensive were suffering from the effect of decades of marginalization under state-centric policies.[72] The private sector which was the major supplier of consumer goods for the masses suffered from severe constraints in financing, raw material acquisition, transportation, technology transfer and marketing as the state allocated scarce resources to the state and co-operatives sectors and suppressed market-based activities.[73]

At the national level, the denial of market forces and the marginalization of the private sector impaired the economy's robustness for sustained growth. As the agriculture-led growth spurt of the 1978–83 period faltered, a vicious cycle of low growth–low investment–low returns set in. The slow progress of the processing and manufacturing sector, which had absorbed one-third of state investments and yet whose labour productivity was below the national average, aggravated the problems of economic stagnation in the second half of the 1980s.[74] As will be argued in the next chapter, the failure of the state's ISI strategy during the BSPP era reflected the broader shortcoming of Myanmar's attempt to achieve economic development by mimicking the developmental state without the necessary means available to other successful developmental states of East and Southeast Asia.[75]

Notes

1. This approach was aimed at complementing the ISI strategy of primary producers. See Hla Myint, *Southeast Asia's Economy: Development Policies in the 1970s* (New York: Praeger, 1972), p. 61.
2. Cf. Hans Linnemann, ed., *Export-Oriented Industrialization in Developing Countries* (Singapore: Singapore University Press, 1987), pp. 173–75.
3. For details, see *Myanma Hsoshelit Lanzin Parti Ei Hnit-Shei Hnit-Toh Sipwayei Muwada Myar* [Long-Term and Short-Term Economic Policies of the Burma Socialist Programme Party] (Yangon: BSPP, 1972), pp. 54–61.
4. Industrial policies were mainly for the state sector. The private sector was regarded as a residual and received very little policy attention.
5. International Monetary Fund (IMF), "Burma: Recent Economic Developments", Washington, D.C., 20 May 1987, p. 2. It seems that the notion of continuously expanding the state's role in industry by increasing its share of productive capacity had prevailed and the political leadership was attempting to have the cake and eat it as well.
6. In a broad sense industrial policy "is understood to subsume a wide array of policies that affect production and trade" as well and can be taken "as a generic term for the spectrum of policies that may be relevant to furthering ... industrial development" (World Bank, *Korea: Managing the Industrial Transition, Vol. I, The Conduct of Industrial Policy* [Washington, D.C.: World Bank, 1987], p. 100).
7. No. 1 Industry was concerned with planning and regulatory functions and operated SIEs in textiles, foodstuff, pharmaceutical, household goods, ceramics, and general industries. Jute as well as paper and chemicals were added in the mid-1980s. No. 2 Industry was formed in March 1975 for conducting industrial research and initially covered technical services; heavy equipment and consumer durables; paper and chemicals; oil exploration; petrochemical products; petroleum products distribution; and electric power. The energy ministry was formed in April 1985 to specialize in fuels and electricity development.
8. This included oil and gas until the advent of the energy ministry.
9. See World Bank, "Development in Burma: Issues and Prospects", Washington, D.C., South Asia Regional Office, 27 July 1976, Report no. 1024-BA, pp. 30–34.
10. See ibid., Table 1, p. 5; Table 11, p. 31; pp. 30, 32, 40–41.

11. See ibid., pp. 34–35, 37–38. "No significant new mines have come into operation for nearly 40 years. Production of minerals for export is in volume about 10% of its pre-war level." (ibid., p. 34).
12. Ibid., p. 37.
13. Those classified as "others" comprised construction, trade, social and financial services, administration and municipalities, while transport and communications represented the economically significant infrastructure investments. Projects in processing and manufacturing seem to emphasize capacity expansion and new plants rather than on consolidation and efficiency-improvement of existing ones as recommended by the World Bank (ibid., pp. 33, 35, 37, 46).
14. Most investments in agriculture were for flood prevention and irrigation. These accounted for 1.8 billion kyat in completed projects from 1974/75 to 1988/89 (*Review of the Financial, Economic and Social Conditions for 1989/90* [Rangoon: Ministry of Planning and Finance, 1989], p. 38; hereafter *Review*). One may argue that there could be private sector investments in agriculture. However, evidence from various longitudinal and cross-sectional rural surveys suggests that the peasants had committed very little capital for cultivation purposes (personal communications with a Myanmar researcher who had conducted extensive field work in Myanmar during the 1975–86 period).
15. Both mining and power sectors were highly capital intensive and required substantial foreign exchange inputs.
16. The mining sector exceeded the target because of higher-than-anticipated investments in oil exploration and minerals extraction.
17. Total industrial investment was computed by summing sectoral investments for mining, processing and manufacturing, and power. Overall investment was the sum of investments for all sectors of the economy.
18. For assessment, see, for example, World Bank, "Burma: Policies and Prospects for Economic Adjustment and Growth", Washington, D.C., South Asia Programs Department (18 November 1985), Report 4814-BA, pp. 3–6, 17, 63. It should also be noted that these industrial investments were heavily dependent upon the availability of ODA funds (see, for example, Khin Maung Nyunt, *Foreign Loans and Aid in the Economic Development of Burma 1974/75 to 1985/86*, Institute of Asian Studies, Monograph no. 46 [Bangkok: Chulalongkorn University, 1990], pp. 64–107 where funding sources of projects in the 1974/75–1985/86 period may be found).
19. Second FYP = 1974/75–1977/78; Third FYP = 1978/79–1981/82; Fourth FYP = 1982/83–1985/86; and Fifth FYP = 1986/87–1989/90 (truncated after fiscal 1987/88 when the BSPP regime collapsed). Note that the rising trend for overall investment was reversed in the last period reflecting the deteriorating balance of payments position and the general economic downturn.

20. The time-series data are plotted on a semi-logarithmic scale so that the slope or gradient of the connecting line between any two points represents the growth rate achieved during the corresponding period. The sectoral value-added output in constant prices are shown as indices in terms of the figure for 1973/74 which was the base year of the TYP. This allows comparison of growth trends for different industrial sectors.
21. "Except for a spurt in 1984/85" the growth rate "declined in every year since 1982/83" and registered negative growth in the last two years due to "fuel shortage and scarcity of foreign exchange" (IMF, "Burma: Recent Economic Developments", Washington, D.C., 16 June 1988, p. 11).
22. Definitions of categories for scale or size are usually designed to fit the range of empirical data depending on the nature of the size structure of industries in the country concerned. In one definition, "small enterprises include those with 1–49 employees, medium those with 50–99 workers and large those with 100 or more employees". (Richard Hooley and Muzaffer Ahmad, "Small and Medium-Size Enterprises and the Development Process in Four Asian Countries", in *The Role of Small and Medium-Scale Manufacturing Industries in Industrial Development: The Experience of Selected Asian Countries* [Manila: Economics and Development Resource Center, Asian Development Bank, 1990], p. 8). On the other hand, the group of "firms with 1–9 workers" may be "referred to as 'household industry' and fall outside the SMI designation" (ibid.).
23. It should be noted that the absolute values of output (in constant prices) for all industrial branches increased over the period. Those branches that were lumped together in the "others" category had shares of less than 1 per cent each.
24. If industrial raw material, construction material, minerals, transport equipment, agriculture equipment, and industrial equipment are taken as proxy industrial branches for heavy industries their combined share in 1974/75 and 1986/87 came to only 20.3 and 20.4 per cent respectively.
25. The government's annual report on the national economy included data on production (physical units) of what was described as "important commodities". The last report of the BSPP era issued in April 1988 listed thirty-nine such commodities and seventeen of these were selected to represent the basic commodities which were essential for household use, construction, and transportation. Per capita figures were based on population estimates for the year 1974/75 and 1987/88; 29.8 and 38.6 million respectively (*Review* [1990], Table 1, p. 14).
26. Overall production growth for cement and fertilizer were 94 and 153 per cent respectively. These two products benefited from capacity additions financed by ODA funds and uninterrupted supply of natural gas. Yet, these production levels still fell short of consumer demand as suggested by the existence of a thriving black market for cement and the low level of

fertilizer application in Myanmar agriculture (personal communications with personnel from the construction industry and agriculture economists).

27. Note these comments: "By most accounts the country is considered to have a varied and favourable *mineral endowment* but large tracts of potentially mineral rich areas have not been geologically surveyed or prospected in detail" (United Nations Industrial Development Organization [UNIDO], "Industrial Development Series: Burma", Vienna, 16 December 1987, PPD.65, p. 40); "No new large mining operations involving new deposits have taken place over the past decades" (ibid.).
28. For details of these "production sharing relationships" based on the "service contract system" and joint exploration efforts, see *Petroleum News* (January 1977), p. 9–10; and Doug Harvey, "JNOC Makes an Offer to Explore Deep Oil Reserves in Burma", *Asian Oil & Gas* (October/November 1986), pp. 16–17. Interestingly, in the post-BSPP era, when foreign direct investment has been allowed, two major offshore gas deposits (one of which was discovered in 1982) are being developed at a cost of over US$1 billion (*Bangkok Post*, 17 June 1996).
29. See, for example, World Bank, "Myanmar: Energy Sector Investment and Policy Review Study", Country Department 2, Asia Region, 16 March 1992, Report no. 10394-BA, pp. 28–29.
30. See, for example, Tin Maung Maung Than, "Burma in 1987: Twenty-Five Years after the Revolution", in *Southeast Asian Affairs 1988* (Singapore: Institute of Southeast Asian Studies, 1988), pp. 88–89; and IMF, "Burma" (1988), p. 10.
31. The fact that natural gas was cheaper than equivalent liquid fuels also made fuel substitution measures attractive (IMF, "Burma" [1988], p. 14).
32. See, for example, World Bank, 10394-BA, p. vi.
33. For reasons, see ibid., pp. 48, 51.
34. See, for example, *Petroleum News* (November 1979), p. 21, for examples of external financing in the oil and power industries.
35. Based on recollection of author's observations made in Yangon and Mandalay during the 1973–83 period and annual visits to Myanmar thereafter. For example, it was estimated that nearly two-thirds (in volume) of textiles fabric consumed in 1982/83 were from the black market with official imports accounting for only 8.5 per cent of the total (Mya Than, "A Brief Survey on Burma's Textiles Industry", mimeographed, Institute of Economics, n.d., p. 15).
36. Data from UNIDO, PPD.65, p. 20; and an unpublished internal study by the Ministry of No. 1 Industry completed in late 1987 (in author's possession; hereafter referred to as MI1/87).
37. The value of exports from the Ministry of No. 1 Industry averaged 77.8 million kyat/year during 1982/83–86/87 and comprised 25 items (MI1/87, Table 3, p. 12). The corresponding figure for the 1976/77–1981/82 period

was 87.8 million kyat (ibid., Table 8, pp. 20–21). Export of petroleum coke which was outside the purview of the Ministry of No. 1 Industry, averaged 3.9 million kyat annually during 1975/76–1979/80 and averaged 10 million kyat annually in the next five years (*Pyithu Lokengan Sithseyei Aphwe Ei Pyithu Hluttaw Tho Asiyinkhanzar* [Report of the Council of People's Inspectors to the Pyithu Hluttaw] [Yangon: Office of the Council of People's Inspectors, 30 September 1981; hereafter *RCPI*], p. 77; and *RCPI* [12 September 1985], Table 27, p. 67).

38. It was reported that the export drive failed due to poor quality control, inflexible supply response, marketing deficiencies, and high production costs. In some products the ministry suffered financial losses at the prevailing exchange rate (MI1/87, pp. 35–36).
39. See ibid., Table 5, pp, 13–14; Table 12, pp. 31–32; and Table 18, p. 55. Industrial plants in the Ministry of No. 2 Industry which produced transport vehicles, agriculture equipment, electrical appliances, industrial equipment, and liquid fuels were likely to be even more capital intensive. Anecdotal evidence suggest that their operational requirement for foreign exchange was probably higher than that for the light industries as they were heavily dependent upon imports of components, intermediate goods, tools and spares (personal communications with production personnel in these plants).
40. The former was exemplified by the announcement in November 1981 by the prime minister of the discovery of "giant" oil reserves in central and southern Myanmar which turned out to be unrecoverable (see, for example, *Working People's Daily* [hereafter *WPD*], 7 November 1991). Examples of the latter was the syndicated loan, of tens of million U.S. dollars, taken in 1977 and 1978 from commercial banks to buy drilling rigs (*Petroleum News*, November 1979, p. 21) and the buying, in 1984, of second-hand jack-up offshore rig to drill for wildcats along the continental shelf (*Petromin*, November 1984, p. 2).
41. Tin Maung Maung Than, "Burma's Energy Use: Perils and Promises", in *Southeast Asian Affairs 1986* (Singapore: Institute of Southeast Asian Studies, 1986), p. 77.
42. In mid-1985, the black market price in the capital was reported to be six times the official price of rationed petrol and was even higher in the countryside (*Asian Business*, June 1985, p. 29). In April 1988, it was twenty-two and twenty-eight times the official price in Yangon and Mandalay respectively (IMF, "Burma" [1988], p. 14).
43. The poor showing of Group I minerals whose index remained below the 1969/70 level for eleven out of fourteen years was due to ore degradation and ageing equipment (see UNIDO, PPD.65, p. 24).
44. The main reason was the decline in their world prices. Exports based on a buy-back scheme for small-scale private and co-operative enterprises were negligible and all exports could be attributed to SIEs.

45. In addition to lower operating costs, their modular nature was also convenient for capacity additions in phases, given the persistent foreign exchange shortage. The natural-gas component of EPC's total capacity increased from 16.4 to 42.8 per cent between 1974/75 and 1987/88. For ODA in this sector, see Tin Maung Maung Than, "Burma's Energy Use", pp. 84–85.
46. See World Bank, Report no. 10394-BA, p. 87 for analysis.
47. Field personnel usually colluded with consumers to make illegal connections or tamper with meter readings.
48. Although there were SIEs in other ministries, those under the two industry ministries, mines ministry, and energy ministry constituted the majority of them. Data for years before 1980/81 are unavailable. When compared to Figures 6.8 and 6.9 which depict the financial balances of all SEEs, Figures 7.11 and 7.12 show that the SIEs followed the pattern set by the former. In fact SIEs were worse off than the SEEs as a whole which managed to register a current account surplus in four out of eleven years (1977/78 to 1987/88).
49. See, U Tun Wai, "Economic Reform in Myanmar", unpublished draft report, Yangon, August 1991, p. 13; Khin Maung Kyi, "Problems of Socialist State Enterprise in International Economy: A Case Study of Competitiveness of Public Enterprise in a Trade-Dependent Developing Country", Discussion Paper, Singapore, n.d., pp. 23–25. The human resources problem was aggravated by the widespread practice of appointing active and retired military officers to SEEs as executives and the existence of a tacit reserved quota for military personnel in new industrial projects (personal communications with senior SIE executives).
50. Tun Wai, "Economic Reform", p. 53. "Industrial SEEs are the largest users of bank credit" in the 1980s (IMF, "Burma" [1988], p. 26).
51. Data up to 1980/81 are from various issues of the annual *Report to the Pyithu Hluttaw on Financial, Economic, and Social Conditions of the Socialist Republic of the Union of Burma* (Rangoon: Ministry of Planning and Finance; hereafter *RPH*). The rest are from IMF, "Burma" (1987); and IMF, "Burma" (1988).
52. See, for example, *RCPI*, 1979; and UNIDO, "UNIDO Industry Sector Review Mission to Myanmar, 12-19 June 1989: Report". Vienna, Regional and Country Studies Branch (12 October 1989), PPD/R.30., pp. 24–26.
53. See, for example, the May Day message of BSPP chairman and the Republic's first President Ne Win (*WPD*, 1 May 1974).
54. *Alokethamar Aseeayone Thamaing* [History of the Worker's Union], Vol. 2 (Yangon: Burma Socialist Programme Party, 1983), pp. 370–78; 379ff.
55. See, for example, Robert H. Taylor, *State in Burma* (London: C. Hurst, 1987), p. 325. The *Asiayone* membership stood at nearly 2.04 million (1.34 million in September 1978) in 275 townships on 30 September 1987 (*Alokethamar Aseeayone Thamaing*, Vol. 2, p. 379; and *Lokethar Jarnei* 1 [1988], p. 11).

56. Altogether 8,410 model workers including 722 socialist workers were selected during 1974/75–1986/87 (ibid., p, 16; and *Botahtaung*, 17 March 1988).
57. Ibid., p. 14; and *Alokethamar Aseeayone Thamaing*, Vol. 2, p. 398.
58. See ibid., pp. 399ff.
59. However, this ratio slowly declined thereafter due to faster rate of increases in receipts against benefits. The membership actually declined from the 1973 figure of 365,000. This was believed to have been due to the redefinition of coverage to exclude persons who were not "active" members. All data are derived from various issues of the *Statistical Yearbook* published by the government.
60. Nearly 86 per cent of the associations and 85 per cent of the members were in the state sector and 4.4 per cent and 3.5 per cent respectively were in the co-operatives sector. See *Alokethamar Aseeayone Thamaing*, Vol. 2, p. 390; *Lokethar Jarnei* 1 [1988], p. 17; and *Botahtaung*, 3 April 1988.
61. IMF, "Burma" (1988), p. 16.
62. *Lokethar Jarnei* 11 (1987), p. 11.
63. *Alokethamar Aseeayone Thamaing*, Vol. 2, p. 415.
64. *Lokethar Jarnei* 10 (1987), p. 8. Most sold their entitlements at a profit to private merchants through intermediaries who were moonlighting workers.
65. Annual inflation remained at 5–6 per cent from 1982/83 through 1985/86 and rose to double digit rates thereafter (IMF, "Burma", p. 16).
66. See, for example, President Ne Win's speech at the opening of the Central Committee Meeting on 1 July 1974 (*People's Worker's Gazette* [August 1974], pp. 2–3; and Taylor, *State in Burma*, pp. 335–36).
67. See, for example, James Guyot, "*Burma in 1988: Perestroika* with a Military Face", in *Southeast Asian Affairs 1989* (Singapore: Institute of Southeast Asian Studies, 1989), pp. 117–21, 125.
68. The estimated sectoral employment elasticity of manufacturing with respect to changes in real output was 0.736 for 1988/89; compared to 0.515 for social and administrative services, 0.501 for mining, 0.277 for agriculture, and 0.2 for power (Tun Wai, "Economic Reform", p. 22). Because there was very little structural change these figures could be taken as proxies for employment potentials of the corresponding sectors for the 1980s as well. All employment data were derived from estimates given by various issues of the *RPH*. Data before 1976/77 were incompatible with the practice, adopted since then, of classifying administrative personnel from SIEs as belonging to the category for administration and other services.
69. Joseph E. Stiglitz, "Some Lessons from the East Asian Miracle", *World Bank Research Observer* 11, no. 2 (1996): 162.
70. In fact, one observer after studying cases of RBI in the oil and gas sector concluded that "a sound macro-economic environment [is] an important prerequisite for RBI investments" and "so demanding are the overall requirements for RBI, most developing countries might be well advised

to eschew such a strategy" (R. M. Auty, *Resource-Based Industrialization: Saving the Oil in Eight Developing Countries* [Oxford: Clarendon Press, 1990], p. 255).

71. Ibid., p. 253.
72. See, for example, UNIDO, PPD.65, pp. 27, 45–46.
73. See ibid., p. 23. In fact, 95 per cent of the country's rice-milling capacity was in the private sector.
74. The value-added per worker (in constant 1969/70 prices) grew by only 10.2 per cent in the processing and manufacturing sector during 1976/77–84/85 whereas the corresponding growth for the whole economy was 34 per cent. The amount of negative growth in the remaining years up to the end of the BSPP rule was also larger for the former when compared to the latter (based on data from various issues of *RPH*).
75. See, for example, Stiglitz, "Some Lessons", pp. 156–74.

8

The End of the Socialist Era

The socialist era in Myanmar, though usually identified with the rule of the Burma Socialist Programme Party (BSPP), had roots that predated the 1974 Constitution which formally instituted one-party rule under the ideological ambit of the Burmese Way to Socialism. One could say that it began with the rise of young nationalist *thakin* politicians in colonial Myanmar (see Chapter 2). Consequently, the socialist vision of successive Myanmar political leadership had influenced the strategies and policies for economic development and industrialization since independence, culminating in the BSPP-planned socialist economy with its twenty-year long-term plan that promised to transform Myanmar into a modern industrialized state through growth with equity. This failed to materialize as the state faltered and stumbled near the three-quarters mark of its self-professed journey. It was a story of developmental failure, brought about by self-imposed resource constraints and state over-reach, compounded by the pathology of one-party authoritarian system, that ended the socialist era in 1988.

DEVELOPMENTAL FAILURE

Despite ambiguities in defining "economic development" as such (see Chapter 1), most would agree that economic growth is a necessary (but not sufficient) condition for developmental success. Hence, following Kuznet's concept of a general economic transformation identified as "modern economic growth", Syrquin's interpretation of "long-term economic growth" as "intrinsically a process of [economic] change" serves a useful conceptual anchor in assessing Myanmar's achievement after four decades of state intervention. According to Syrquin, long-term economic growth entails a "rise in [national] income" associated with "changes in composition of demand, international trade and factor use, all of which interact with the pattern of productivity growth, availability of natural resources and government policies" to "determine the pace and nature of industrial growth".[1] Such changes may be reflected in the output and employment structures of the economy over the period concerned.

In the case of Myanmar it is worthwhile to look for signs of changes in economic structure as well as economic growth and compare the results with those of more successful Asian states (hereafter referred to as HPAEs or high-performing Asian economies); countries that registered high growth rates and substantial structural changes between the 1960s and the late 1980s by following export-oriented industrialization strategies (EOI).[2] When Myanmar's economic structure is examined over two chronological periods divided by the 1962 coup, one finds very little structural change in terms of relative contribution by major sectors to the gross domestic product (GDP). This is illustrated in Figures 8.1 and 8.2.[3] It is evident that the share of the trade sector decreased as the services sector gained ground

FIGURE 8.1
Sectoral Share of GDP
(constant 1961/62 prices)

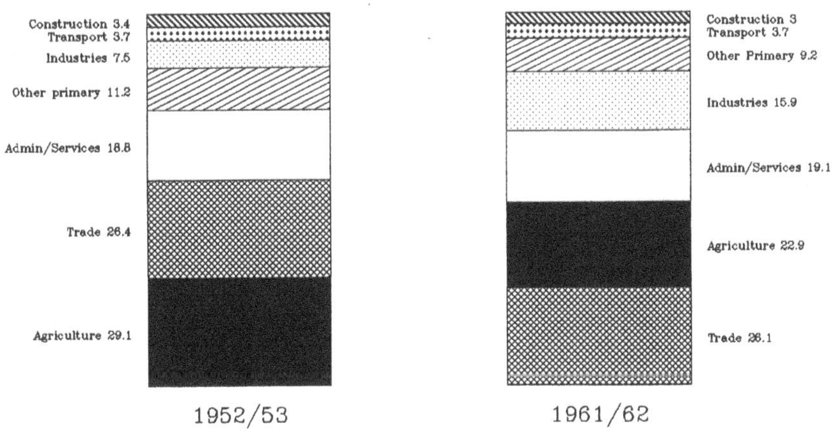

Source: Ministry of Planning and Finance.

FIGURE 8.2
Sectoral Share of GDP
(constant 1969/70 prices)

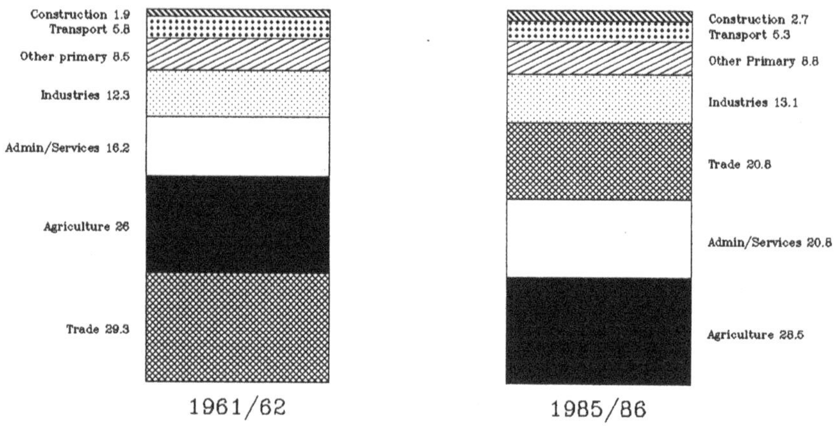

Source: Ministry of Planning and Finance.

due to the state's post-1962 policies that had generally been market-hostile and trade-inhibiting.[4]

The processing and manufacturing sector, which was the locus of import-substituting industrialization (ISI), failed to increase its sectoral share in two decades since 1957. As evident in Table 8.1, Myanmar fared poorly after 1960 when compared with selected HPAEs.[5]

TABLE 8.1
Percentage Share of Manufacturing in GDP

Year[a]	*Myanmar*	*Taiwan*	*Korea*	*Thailand*	*Malaysia*
1957	10.6	—	—	—	11.0
1963	10.5[b]	24.9	14.7	11.7[c]	—
1970	10.7	—	—	16.0	13.0[d]
1981	10.2	40.2	29.2	21.7[e]	—
1987	9.9	42.5	30.3	22.2	23.0

Notes:
a. Fiscal year for Myanmar (end before 1974 and beginning thereafter);
b. fiscal year 1961/62;
c. for 1960;
d. for 1968;
e. for 1980.
Sources: Ministry of Planning and Finance (Myanmar); Balassa (1991), Table 3.2, p. 58 and 5.2. p. 107 (Korea and Taiwan); Narongchai (1991), Table 2.1, p. 10 (Thailand); and Ariff (1991), pp. 24, 25 (Malaysia).

TABLE 8.2
Share of Employment in Major Economic Sectors

	1931 (%)	*1987/88* (%)
Agriculture	66.4	62.5
Livestock & fishery	2.3	1.4
Forestry	0.9	1.2
Mining	0.6	0.6
Processing & manufacturing	9.1	8.7
Construction	1.6	1.7
Transport & communications	3.5	3.3
Social services	3.9	2.9
Administration	0.8	3.8
Trade	9.0	9.8
Others	1.9	4.3

Note: The values may not add up to 100 due to rounding errors.
Sources: Robert H. Taylor, *The State in Burma* (London: C. Hurst, 1987), Table 5.7, p. 344; and Ministry of Planning and Finance.

Similarly, as evident from Table 8.2, the employment distribution among major economic sectors hardly changed over more than five decades from that ascertained in the 1931 Census. Most significantly, the employment share of the agriculture sector remained virtually unchanged.

The employment share of the processing and manufacturing sector that reached only 8.7 per cent in 1987/88 was much less than those of Taiwan (22 per cent) and Korea (13 per cent) in 1971.[6] The average annual growth rate of manufacturing employment achieved during the 1964/65–1985/86 period was around 2.8 per cent and was considerably lower than that achieved by Taiwan (5.2 per cent; 1952–60) during the latter's ISI phase.[7]

It is not possible to determine Myanmar's productivity growth because of serious deficiencies in the data on factor inputs.[8] However, if the value of net output per worker is taken as a proxy it can be seen from Figures 8.3 and 8.4 that the progress achieved over two decades since the mid-1960s was rather modest. During the 1964/65–1985/86 period, the real GDP (at constant 1969/70 prices) per worker increased at an average annual rate of 1.76 per cent while the corresponding growth rates for the agriculture and the processing and manufacturing sectors were 1.81 and 0.67 per cent respectively.[9]

FIGURE 8.3
Sectoral Net Output per Worker: Index
(1969/70 = 100)

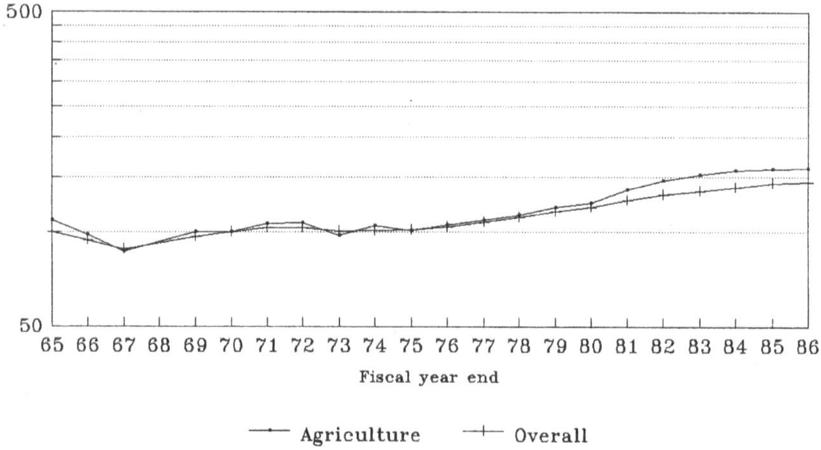

Note: Fiscal year ending September till 1973 and March thereafter.
Source: Ministry of Planning and Finance.

FIGURE 8.4
Sectoral Net Output per Worker: Index
(1969/70 = 100)

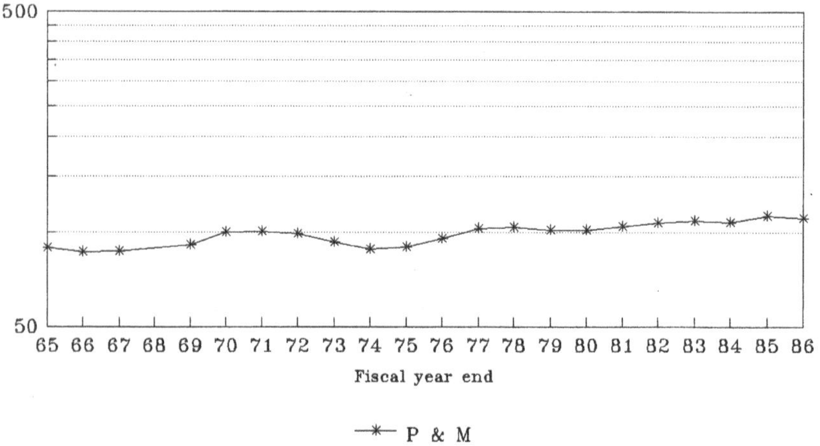

Note: Fiscal year ending September till 1973 and March thereafter.
Source: Ministry of Planning and Finance.

Examination of long-run economic growth trends, in terms of indices of annual growth for GDP and its major components for the same two periods, reveals that, while the overall GDP grew faster than that of the agriculture sector during the pre-1962 period they were closely correlated in the post-1962 period (Figures 8.5 and 8.6).[10] This is not

FIGURE 8.5
Sectoral Value-Added Index
(1955/56 = 100)

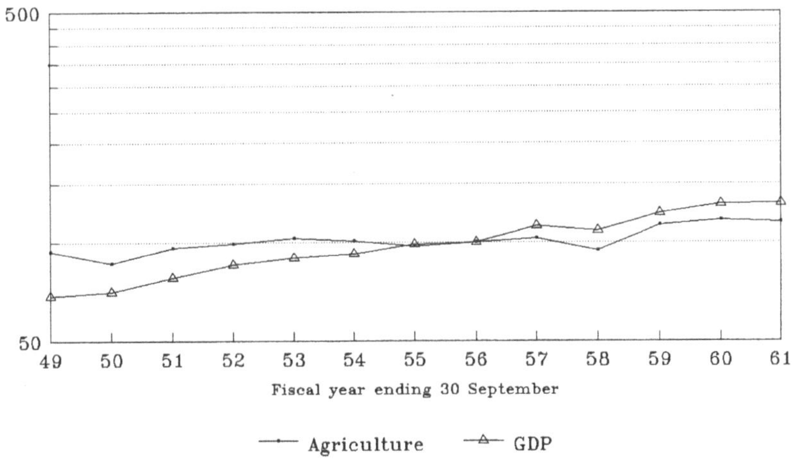

Note: Constant 1961/62 prices.
Source: Kyaw Myint (1978), p. 15.

FIGURE 8.6
Sectoral Value-Added Index
(1969/70 = 100)

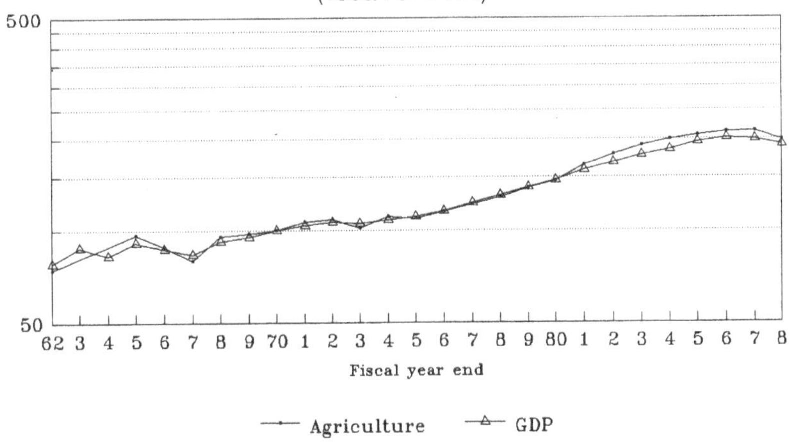

Note: Fiscal year ending September till 1873 and March thereafter.
Source: Ministry of Planning and Finance.

surprising since agriculture remained the leading sector in Myanmar's economy throughout the post-coup era.

In fact, Myanmar's average GDP growth rate during the 1950s, albeit starting from a different base, was quite respectable when compared with the corresponding figures for Thailand and Korea.[11] This is evident in Table 8.3, while the corresponding trends for GDP growth are illustrated in Figures 8.7 and 8.8.

TABLE 8.3
Real GDP Growth Rates: Period Averages

	1951 to 1961 (%)	*1953 to 1961 (%)*
Myanmar	5.3	—
Korea	—	4.0
Thailand	5.8	—

Sources: Kyaw Myint (1978), p. 15 (Burma); *International Financial Statistics Yearbook 1980* (Washington, D.C.: IMF, 1981) (Korea); James C. Ingram, *Economic Change in Thailand 1850–1970* (Stanford: Stanford University Press, 1971), Table XVII, p. 222 (Thailand).

FIGURE 8.7
Comparative Real GDP Growth: Index
(1956 = 100)

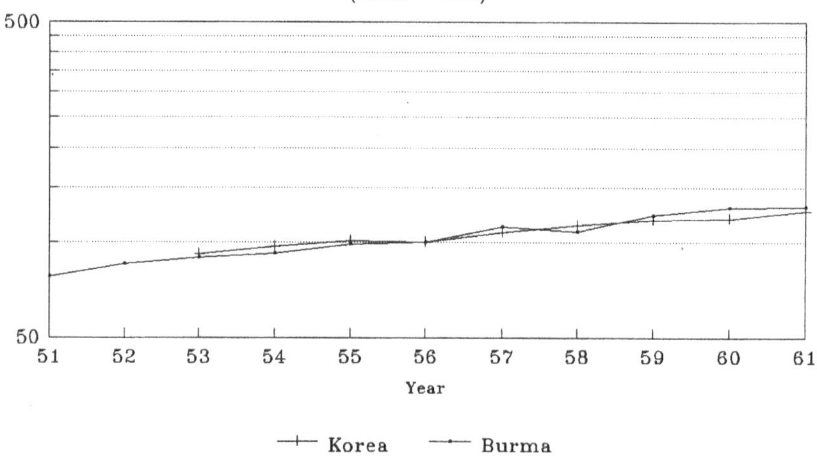

Note: Constant 1961/62 prices for Burma; 1975 prices for Korea.
Source: Kyaw Myint (1978), p. 15; IMF.

FIGURE 8.8
Comparative Real GDP Growth: Index
(1956 = 100)

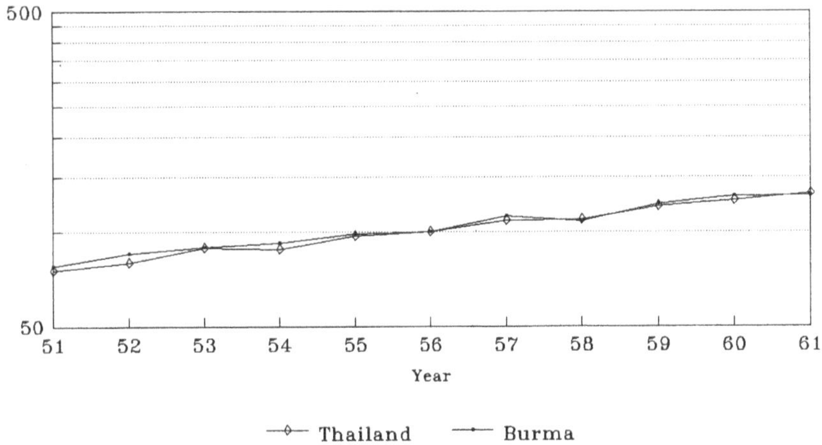

Note: Constant 1961/62 prices.
Source: Kyaw Myint (1978); Ingram (1971), Table XVII, p. 222.

FIGURE 8.9
Comparative Real GDP Growth: Index
(1970 = 100)

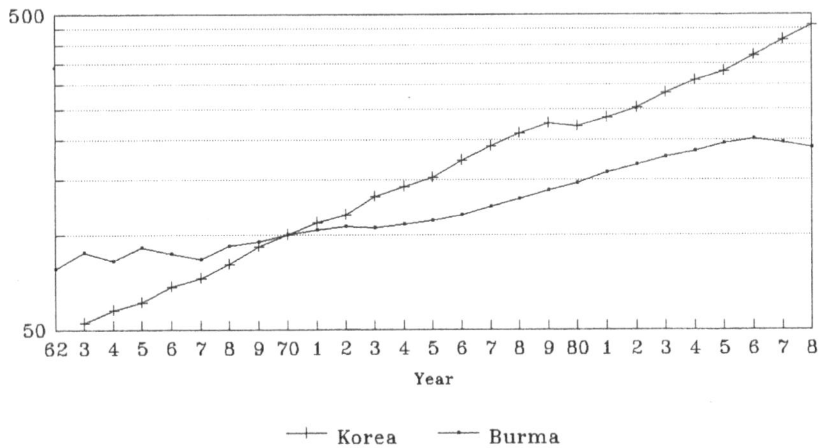

Note: Constant 1969/70 prices for Burma; 1985 prices for others.
Source: Burmese Government and IMF.

However, during the 1961/62–1987/88 period, as indicated by Figures 8.9 and 8.10, Myanmar's growth lagged considerably behind HPAEs.[12] In fact, it was more in tune with that of India and Pakistan, which had

FIGURE 8.10
Comparative Real GDP Growth: Index
(1970 = 100)

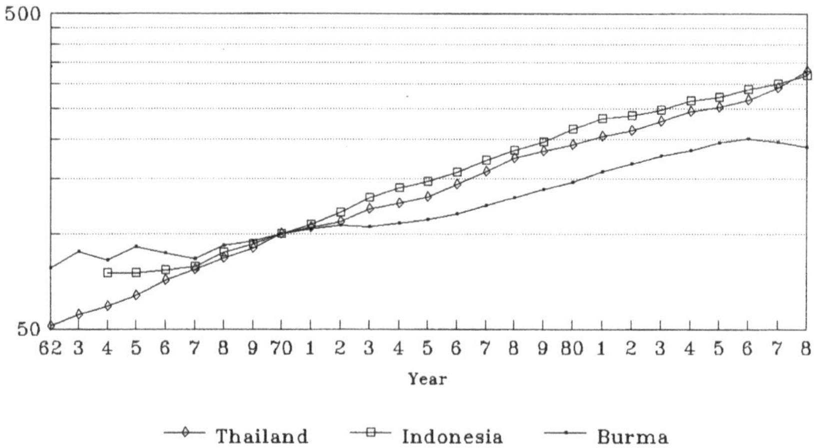

Note: Constant 1969/70 prices for Burma; 1985 prices for others.
Source: Burmese Government and IMF.

inward-looking mixed economies (Figures 8.11 and 8.12). This is evident in Table 8.4 in which average annual growth rates for the GDP and the manufacturing value-added are compared.[13]

TABLE 8.4
Real Growth Rates: Period Averages
(%)

	GDP 1962–1988	*Manufacturing value-added*	
		1970–1980	*1980–1988*
Myanmar	3.5	3.6	3.2
Taiwan	—	12.0	9.5
Korea	9.1	17.0	11.2
Thailand	7.4	10.5	6.3
Malaysia	6.2[a]	12.0	6.7
Indonesia	5.7[b]	14.5	7.9
India	4.0	4.6	8.3
Pakistan	4.9	5.4	8.2

Notes:
a. For 1970–88;
b. for 1964–88.
Sources: Ministry of Planning and Finance (Myanmar; GDP); *International Financial Statistics Yearbook 1991* (others; GDP); ESCAP, *Economic and Social Survey of Asia and the Pacific 1991*, Part 2 (Bangkok: ESCAP, 1992), Table II.8, p. 165 (manufacturing value-added).

FIGURE 8.11
Comparative Real GDP Growth: Index
(1970 = 100)

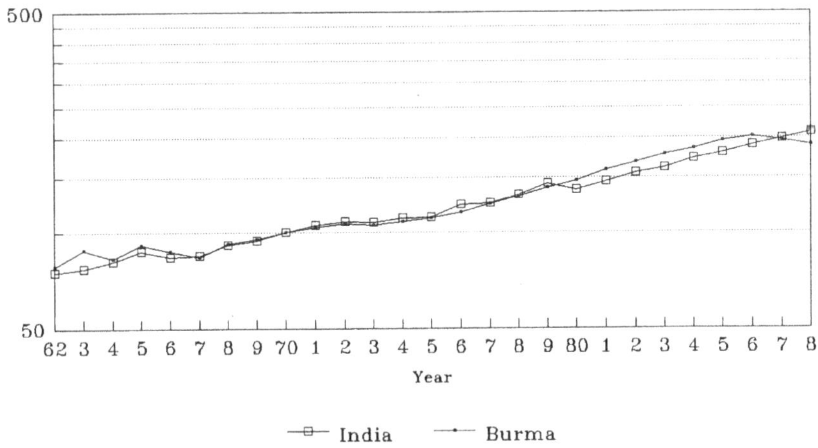

Note: Constant 1969/70 prices for Burma; 1985 prices for others.
Source: Burmese Government and IMF.

FIGURE 8.12
Comparative Real GDP Growth: Index
(1970 = 100)

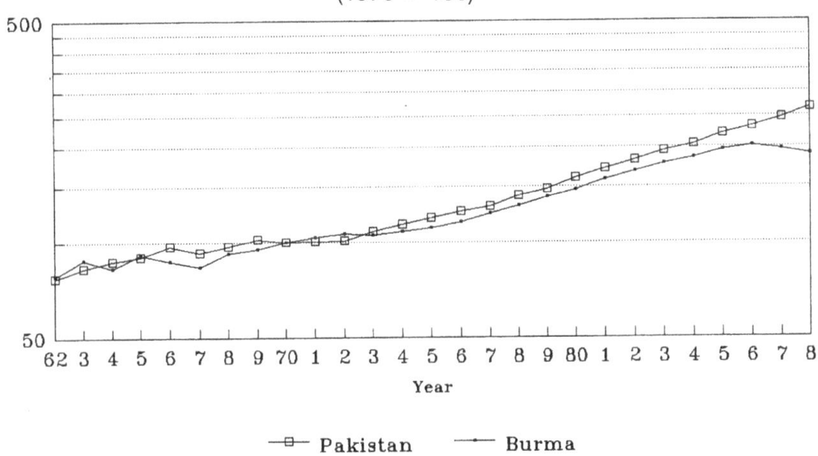

Note: Constant 1969/70 prices for Burma; 1985 prices for others.
Source: Burmese Government and IMF.

The divergence in the growth trajectories between Myanmar and the HPAEs became significant in the early 1960s when Myanmar closed its economy for nearly a decade. Myanmar reverted to accepting official development assistance (ODA) in the early 1970s but the average growth rate of 5.7 per cent achieved during 1975–85 turned out to be unsustainable.

The trends in the net output (in constant prices) of the processing and manufacturing (P&M) sector can be seen from Figures 8.13 and 8.14. Though it grew at a faster rate than the GDP during the parliamentary period due to its extremely low base the sector fell behind and failed to match the moderate GDP growth achieved during the 1976/77–1985/86 period.

Investment–Output Link: A Stylized Model

This poor long-term performance of the Myanmar economy should be viewed in the context of the overall thrust of the Myanmar developmental effort. In formulating and implementing a succession of development "plans", capital investment had been emphasized throughout. Though the preferred means for capital accumulation varied over the four decades since independence, Myanmar's leaders seem to have adopted a strategy of investment-driven growth informed by a structuralist approach to industrialization.[14] Investments figured prominently in the quantitative guidelines for Myanmar's major economic plans.[15]

Sources of economic growth may be identified with factor inputs such as labour, capital and technology.[16] Stylistic growth models emphasized domestic savings and subsequent investment as a necessary (but not sufficient) "basic condition" for a "take-off into continuous self-sustained growth".[17] One such model developed by Tsiang and empirically tested on selected HPAEs is applied here to examine whether such a basic condition was satisfied in the period under study.[18]

In this model, "the excess of savings per capita over the requirement of capital investment" (per capita) "to maintain the existing capital/labour ratio in the face of population growth may be regarded as the basic condition for the take-off".[19] In other words, "the average propensity to save should be greater than the average capital/output ratio times the rate of population growth".[20] Thus, the following function that may be called the "take-off margin" must be positive.

$$(S/Y) - (I/dY)(dL/L)(1/100)$$

Here, (S/Y) is the percentage of national income saved; (I/dY) is net annual investment as a ratio of annual increment of real national income; and (dL/L) is the annual rate of increase of population.[21]

FIGURE 8.13
Sectoral Value-Added Index
(1955/56 = 100)

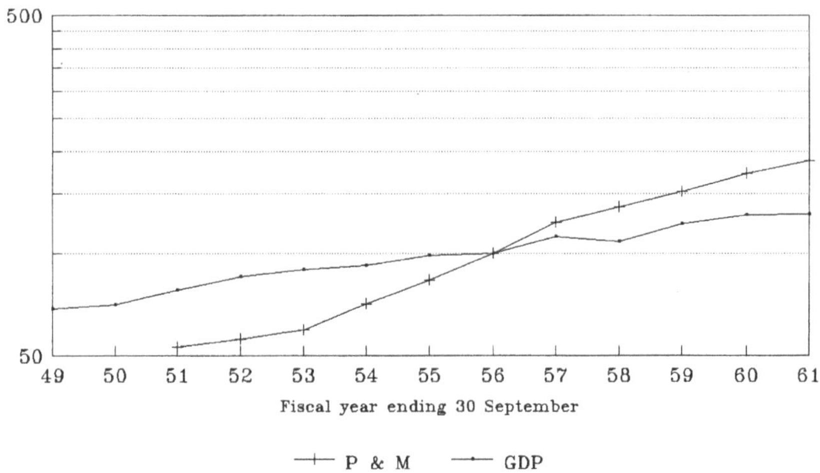

Note: Constant 1961/62 prices.
Source: Kyaw Myint (1978), p. 15.

FIGURE 8.14
Sectoral Value-Added Index
(1969/70 = 100)

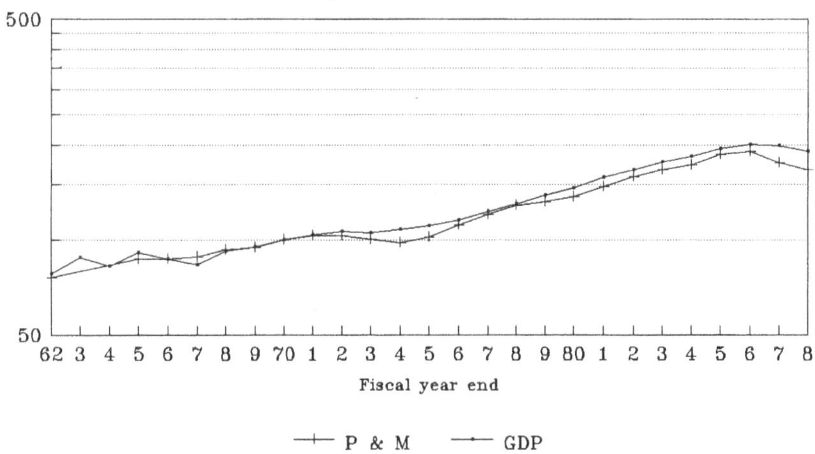

Note: Fiscal year ending September till 1973 and March thereafter.
Source: Ministry of Plannng and Finance.

FIGURE 8.15
Take-off Margin: Burma
(1952/53–1959/60)

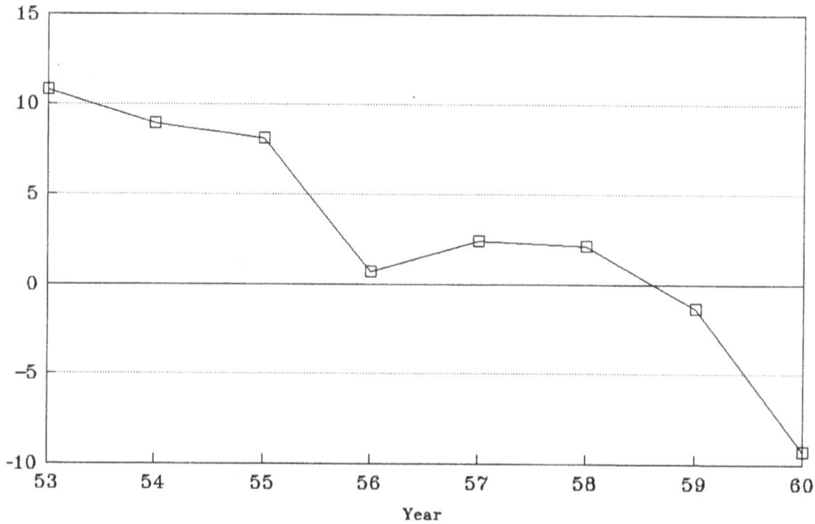

Source: Ministry of National Planning.

Figures 8.15 and 8.16 show the results of applying Tsiang's analysis to Myanmar, which when compared with Figures 8.17 and 8.18 for Taiwan and Korea, showed the inadequacy of Myanmar's savings and investment efforts to satisfy the take-off margin stipulated in the model.[22] Empirical evidence from successful countries suggests that in and around the "approximate take-off years" the take-off margin became positive and increased steadily to reach a double digit value within a few years and remained large thereafter.[23] Myanmar in the 1953–60 period exhibited a declining trend while during the 1975–83 period it registered a barely positive value that fluctuated without any distinct sign of a rising trend.[24]

A False Trail

Since independence, Myanmar had followed a false trail of investment-driven growth without ever satisfying even the basic condition for take-off. Myanmar governments had all along been very much concerned with high inflation, yet they had resorted to deficit financing by monetary expansion when revenues were unable to support investment expenditures.[25]

FIGURE 8.16
Take-off Margin: Burma
(1972/73–1983/84)

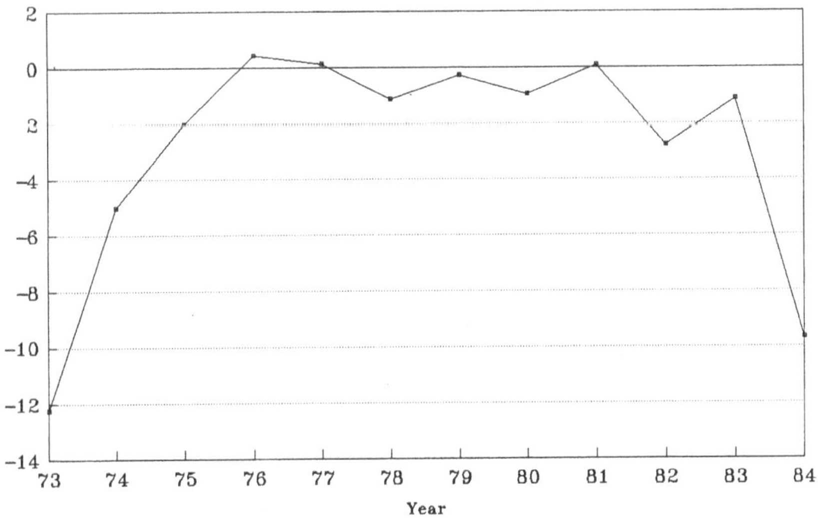

Source: Ministry of Planning and Finance.

FIGURE 8.17
Take-off Margin: Taiwan

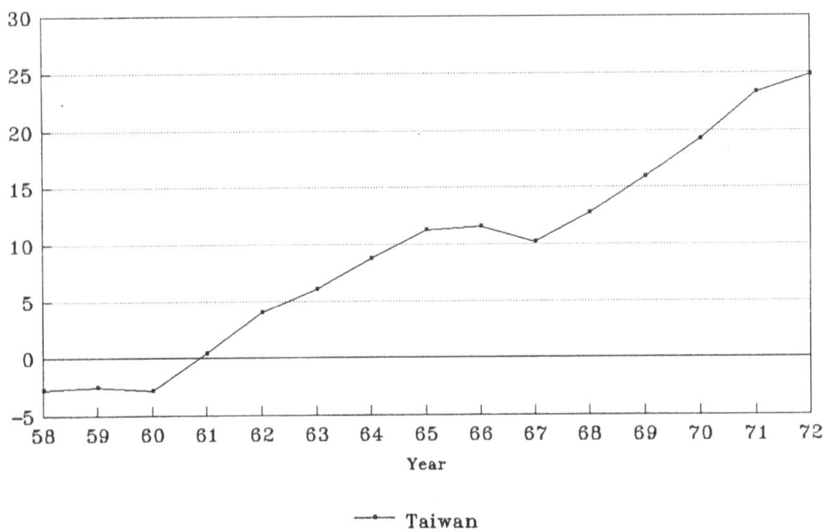

Source: Tsiang (1989), p. 26.

FIGURE 8.18
Take-off Margin: Korea

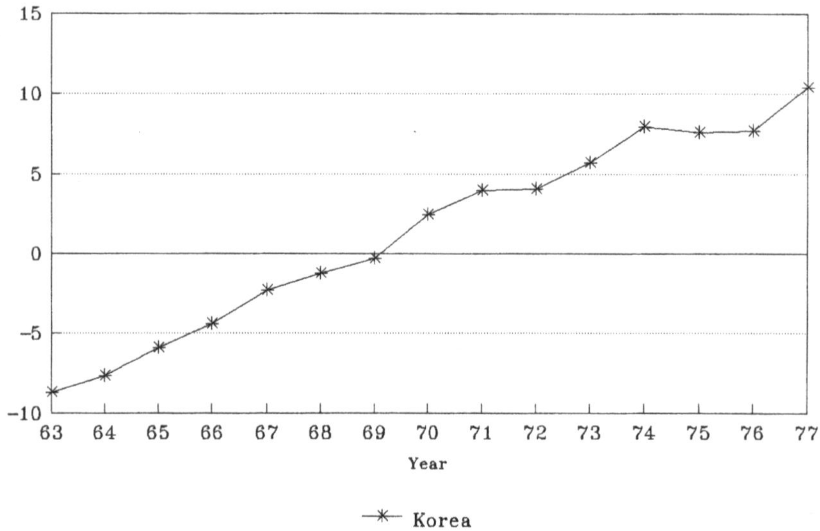

Source: Tsiang (1989), p. 31.

As illustrated in Figure 8.19 the government managed to bring down the relatively higher growth rate of currency increase to the level of real GDP growth in the later half of the 1950s and the tight-money policy held down the monetary expansion throughout the 1960s. However, after the launching of the Twenty-Year Plan (TYP), with its attendant high ODA inflows and public expenditures, the divergence between the currency and GDP growth rates quickly set in (Figure 8.20). To curb the escalating monetary expansion and the increasing leakage of money to black market operations, the government went to the extreme by demonetizing the large-value currency notes twice within two years in the late 1980s.[26]

The inevitable inflationary pressures accompanying such a monetary expansion was somewhat ameliorated by administrative price controls on essential commodities (like rice and cooking oil) and products of state economic enterprises (SEEs).[27] Nevertheless, the divergence between wages and the cost of urban living widened considerably leading to increasing relative deprivation and creeping discontent among the wage earners of the state sector; especially industrial labour. Figures 8.21 and 8.22 illustrate the widening gap between wage income and (urban) consumer prices as the TYP unfolded.[28]

FIGURE 8.19
Real GDP and Currency Growth: Index
(1955/56 = 100)

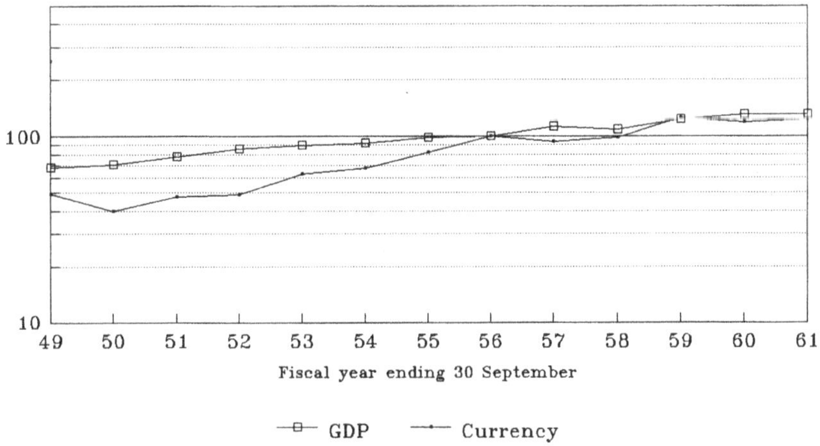

Note: GDP in constant 1961/62 prices.
Source: Kyaw Myint (1978), p. 15; Ministry of Planning and Finance.

FIGURE 8.20
Real GDP and Currency Growth: Index
(1969/70 = 100)

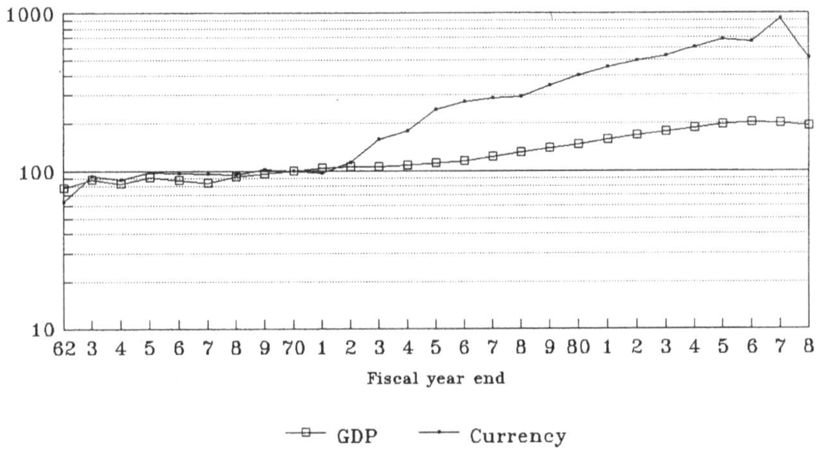

Note: Fiscal year ending September till 1973 and March thereafter.
Source: Ministry of Planning and Finance.

FIGURE 8.21
Wage Index and CPI
(1953 = 100)

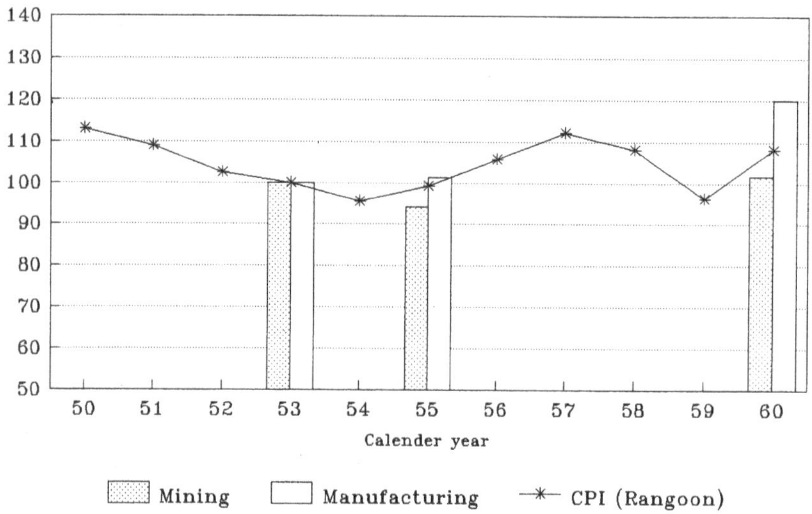

Note: Central Statistics and Economic Department.

FIGURE 8.22
Male Wage Index and CPI
(1960 = 100)

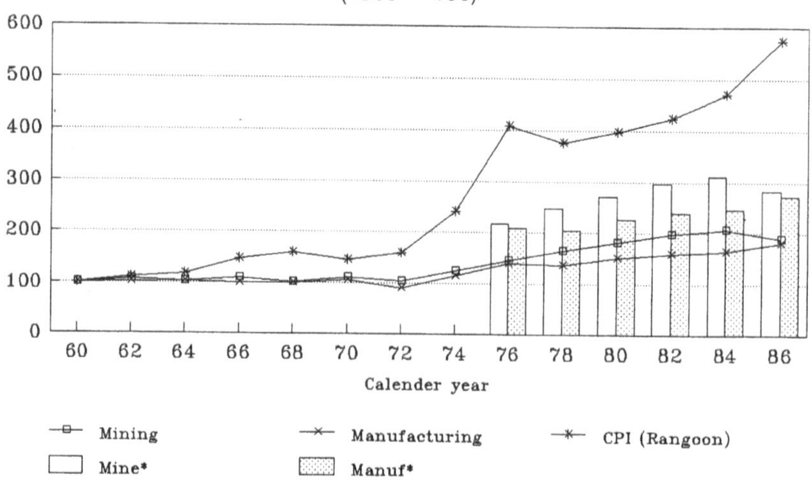

Note: * denotes values compensated for state subsidies on essential goods.
Source: ESCAP (Bangkok).

Another serious problem affecting deficit financing was the persistent balance of payments (BOP) problem caused by the perennial trade deficit in the absence of foreign direct investments (FDI). The BOP problem worsened in the mid-1980s despite the cutback on imports that effected the SEEs in particular and further fuelled illegal imports that further undermined the financial and ideological underpinnings of the socialist system. The gap that remained after the current account deficit had been balanced by the capital account surplus was met by drawing down the foreign exchange reserves that plummeted to an extremely low level after 1983 and never recovered. These trends in the major determinants of the BOP situation are depicted in Figures 8.23 and 8.24 for two periods; the first preceding the TYP and the second beginning with the first year of the TYP.

The two pillars of Myanmar's investment drive were the agriculture surplus and the ODA inflow. While the former's export potential was never realized, the substantial inflow of ODA — averaging nearly US$400 million annually in the 1979/80–1987/88 period — played a significant part in financing state-sponsored investment projects and in deferring the BOP crunch by providing commodity loans and other essential imports as well.

FIGURE 8.23
Balance of Payments: Current Account Deficit, Capital Surplus and Gross Reserves

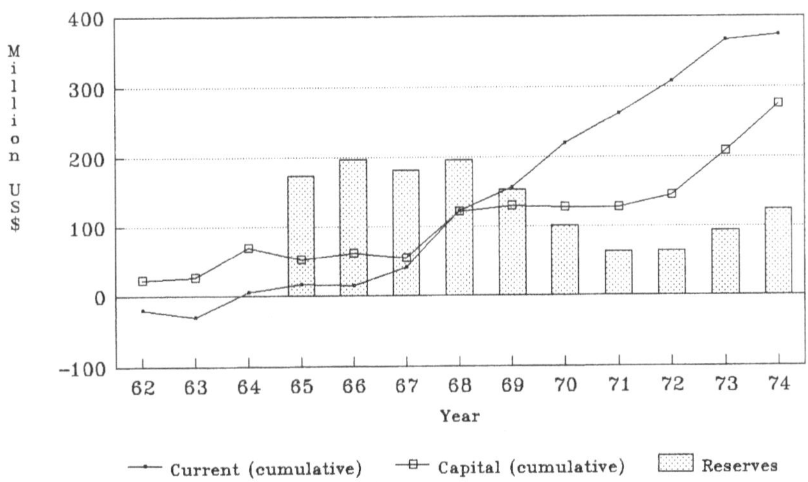

Source: IMF and Union of Burma Bank.

FIGURE 8.24
Balance of Payments: Current Account Deficit, Capital Surplus and Gross Reserves

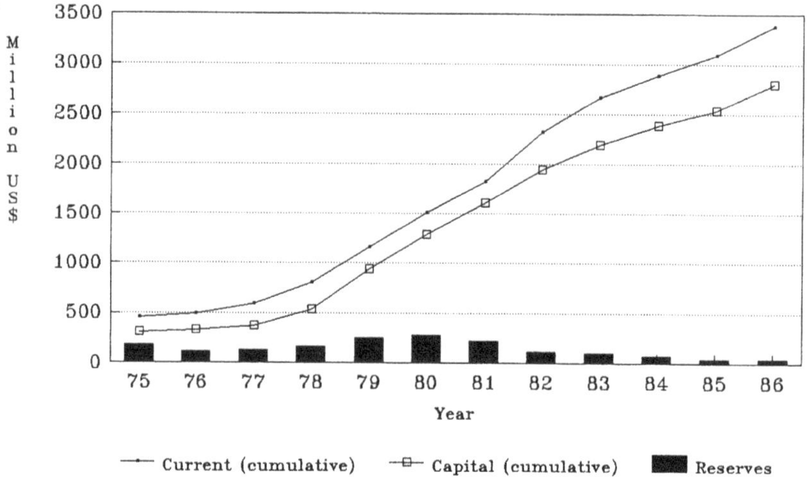

Source: IMF and Union Bank of Burma.

However, the investment-driven growth became unsustainable as the two legs on which it stood weakened and faltered in the mid-1980s. Agriculture production stagnated after 1983 and the ODA inflow began to lose its effectiveness at about the same time as mounting debt servicing became increasingly burdensome (see, for example, Figures 6.22 and 6.27). As the end of the decade approached, the Myanmar economy regressed and tottered on the edge of financial bankruptcy.

Indeed, as pointed out by Taylor, the upheaval in 1988 that ended the socialist era was the result of the "underlying systemic and structural weaknesses which might be described as the bankruptcy of Burma".[29] This notion of bankruptcy referred to not only meant financial bankruptcy that led to Myanmar's admission (in 1987) into the least developing country (LDC) club but also policy bankruptcy which denied Myanmar of means to overcome the inexorable slide towards economic and political crisis.

Perhaps with the benefit of hindsight, it can be summarized that Myanmar had followed a self-defeating resource-based ISI strategy riding on the back of a state-led developmental approach, which in turn was severely constrained by the denial of private participation and neglect of market forces. As a result, the overextended weak state was driven to the point of bankruptcy. The puzzle that needs explaining in this context is why Myanmar adopted the particular set of policies. A plausible explanation may be arrived at by taking a historical perspective on state-centred responses to the perceived problem of underdevelopment. As such, the highly interventionist Myanmar state is identified as the locus of developmental impulses and consequently treated as the focus of analysis.

MIMICKING THE DEVELOPMENTAL STATE: PATHWAY TO BANKRUPTCY?

In August 1988 Myanmar erupted in a spasm of popular protest marred by violence and repression. It was precipitated by the bankruptcy of the state. The performance legitimacy, sought by the framers of the Burmese Way to Socialism (BWS), failed to materialize. Instead, the economy regressed and the self-imposed constraints of the political leadership, aggravated by the ossification of the one-party (Burma Socialist Programme Party or BSPP) system, deprived the ruling elite of bold and innovative options for rectifying the economic decline.

Although the economic debacle that doomed the BSPP-led state appears to have vindicated both the proponents of the "state failure" paradigm and the critics of the dysfunctional authoritarian one-party state,[30] its roots lie beyond the much-maligned BSPP era. In essence, what transpired was but a climax of the long-standing effort since independence by Myanmar's ruling elite to establish a developmental state of sorts. This involved a long iterative process that was triggered by historical events that may be traced much further back in the distant past spanning nearly a century.[31]

After World War II, the only successful Asian late industrializers besides Japan were a handful of East and Southeast Asian states collectively known as NIEs (newly industrialized economies). Many of them exhibit a strong state role in economic development and are classified as "developmental states".[32] A successful developmental state may be characterized as one:

- where there is either *de facto* or *de jure* one-party governance with the ability to "concentrate ... political power at the top" thereby "enhancing political stability and continuity in policy";
- dominated "by purposeful and determined developmental elites, which have also been relatively uncorrupt" while their coherence

"have been enhanced by a dense traffic [of elite circulation and interaction] between the top levels of the civil and military bureaucracy and high political office";

- where there exists a *"relative autonomy* of the developmental elites and the state institutions which they command";
- where "[e]lite determination and the relative autonomy of the state has helped to shape very powerful, highly competent and insulated economic bureaucracies with authority in directing and managing" socio-economic development;
- where "civil society has experienced weakness, flattening or control at the hands of the state";
- where "power, authority and relative autonomy of the state were established at an early point in ... development history, well before national or foreign capital became important or potentially influential" thereby enhancing state capacity against "private economic interests"; and
- exhibits "endurance" that may be attributed to its ability to "deliver" economic goods to its citizens.[33]

In this context, the developmental state may be functionally defined as:

> [A state] whose politics have concentrated sufficient power, autonomy and capacity at the centre to shape, pursue and encourage the achievement of explicit developmental objectives, whether by establishing and promoting the conditions and directions of economic growth, or by organising it directly, or a varying combination of both.[34]

To be successful, "developmental states must be immersed in a dense network of ties that bind them to societal allies with transformational goals".[35] It follows that in the course of industrial development, the developmental state and civilian enterprises "both ... need each other", meaning that "each side *uses* the other in a mutually beneficial relationship to achieve developmental goals and enterprise viability."[36]

A variety of factors such as historical circumstances, ideological predisposition of the ruling elite, the inherited objective conditions at independence, and the complex dynamic interactions between agencies and structures, all contributed towards producing a milieu which may or may not be conducive to the establishment of such an entity. In Myanmar, all the regimes since independence had tried, albeit unsuccessfully, to fashion a centralizing unitary state that controlled the commanding heights of the economy and played a leading role in development. Myanmar's developmental failure may be attributed to the shortcoming in this mimicking of the developmental state.

In his survey of developmental states, Leftwich stressed the primacy of politics in the emergence of such states and pointed out that:

> Their provenance is everywhere traceable to the socio-economic structures, histories and especially political struggles which constituted the formative processes of these states, ... And their ability to deal both with civil society and with particular local and foreign interests highlights the centrality of politics and state capacity in shaping mutually advantageous economic relationships.[37]

Hence, in Myanmar's case a similar approach is taken to examine first the initial setting conditioned by the colonial legacy and the country resource endowment and then assess the state's role in terms of attributes identified with the developmental state.

The Initial Setting: Historical Experiences

In one interpretation of NIEs' success, it is argued that

> A developing country's policy space and its performance over time are constrained by the initial conditions bestowed upon it by nature and the economy's colonial past.[38]

In a similar vein, it can be said that the Myanmar ruling elite's response to the problems of state building and economic development were largely influenced by the historical experience of Myanmar's first encounter, under British rule, with modernity and the international political economy. Interpretation of these experiences by the leadership coupled with optimism regarding Myanmar's resource endowment formed the initial setting from which attempts to fashion a reified Myanmar state emerged.

As outlined in Chapter 2, reactions to mercantilism and colonial administration significantly gave rise to the ardent nationalism of Myanmar political activists who appropriated the vanguard role in the quest for national independence and contributed to a predilection for a particular socialist vision.

Two features of the colonial state had lasting influences on post-independence economic organization and governance. The first was the transformation of a traditional society subject to what Taylor called "social" governance into, what Furnivall called, a "plural society" operating under the principle of "administrative" governance and *laissez faire* economics.[39] The second was the "generation of new and antagonistic concepts of ethnicity and cultural customs and traditions, each with claims to unique and non-negotiable rights".[40]

The emergence of the plural society with its economic stratification and functional differentiation among the mixed community of natives and aliens resulted in "simmering racial hostility and periods of violent resistance", especially in times of economic recession (like the Great Depression in the 1930s).[41] Colonial Myanmar during the late nineteenth century achieved sustained growth in per capita output but Myanmar received very little economic benefit.[42] Instead, a barrier developed between Myanmar and the modern world of commerce and administration imposed by the colonial rulers who affected "indirect rule" through India and Indians.[43] This barrier added insult to injury and considerably retarded the emergence of an indigenous middle class and the associated "sprouts of civil society".[44]

The reaction to misery and perfidy suffered by Myanmar under colonial rule was the rise of passionate nationalism which vowed to redress the real and perceived injustice by doing away all the vestiges of colonialism. The strident nationalism and the subsequent diffusion of "leftist" ideologies had far-reaching ramifications for independent Myanmar. The nationalist leaders' predilection for a strong self-reliant state was reinforced by the depravations and ignominy suffered by Myanmar during World War II and under Japanese occupation. The anti-Japanese resistance movement and the subsequent struggle for independence heightened the nationalist fervour and accorded the youthful nationalist leaders unprecedented prestige and legitimacy to set the nationalist agenda for independent Myanmar.

The anti-capitalist stance, the notion of self-reliance, aversion to foreign investment and mistrust of the free play of international economic forces, economic nationalism, and the great emphasis placed on state ownership and control of means of production, natural resources and external trade, had all been the hallmark of independent Myanmar. Propelled by the twin logic of a "rationalist planning mode" and a "defensive reaction mode", Myanmar's developmental approach led to an inevitable clash of the logic of nationalism and the logic of economics that culminated in the bankruptcy of the state.[45]

On the other hand, the ascriptive elevation of ethnicity to the forefront of communal relations and the administration separation of the centre and the periphery under colonial rule distorted the "original non-political and non-determinate" perception of ethnicity.[46] The Myanmar nationalists' attempt to mobilize the populace through emphasis on race, language, and religion, might have also accentuated the sense of alienation amongst the other racial groups.[47] Consequently, ethnic differences were politicized and reified to the extent that the option of integrating disparate "nations" into a unified nation-state was foreclosed. During World War II some (British) loyalist ethnic groups found themselves at odds with the Myanmar nationalists who sided with the Japanese invaders. All in all, there was little opportunity for the indigenous racial groups to develop a sense of belonging and bonding culminating in an "imagined community" of sorts.[48] The result was a persistent refusal to acknowledge the legitimacy of the central state.

The enduring ideas and lingering notions carried over from the anti-colonial nationalist struggle shaped the vision of the ruling elites, who believed that a unique blend of nationalism, socialism and statism would dismantle the plural society and replace it with a modern, prosperous and integrated society. They succeeded too well in the first task but failed in the second.

The socio-political legacy of the colonial experience was not the only "boundary condition" at the initial stage of Myanmar's founding moment influencing its developmental direction. The other factor was the country's resource base. Natural resources may be regarded as both an opportunity and a constraint. While some economists have suggested that "a country's development prospects may well be inversely proportional to its natural resource endowment",[49] the Myanmar perception seem to have been that the supposedly rich resource endowment would facilitate rapid development once independence is attained. This had significant bearing upon the attitude among Myanmar's top leaders towards the pace and nature of the state-led industrialization effort.

Dubious Autonomy, Weak Capacity, Illusory Power and Elusive Legitimacy

The nationalist leaders of the ruling party, the AFPFL (Anti-Fascist People's Freedom League) embraced socialism without clarifying its meaning and endorsed it as the "dominant ideology" while interpreting it expediently (see Chapter 3).[50] The military Revolutionary Council (RC) that seized state power in the 1962 coup as well as the BSPP, its progeny, both reinterpreted socialism in the form of the BWS. All along, Myanmar socialism had to contend with Communism whose proponents had taken up armed struggle. Having forsworn Marxism as its philosophical basis, the dominant ideology found itself drawing political capital and ideological sustenance out of the anti-capitalist, anti-foreign, and *dirigiste* strands.

Driven by nationalism and a socialist vision, the post-independence Myanmar leaders, in attempting to achieve economic development through industrialization, strove to emulate the developmental state. In the following sections, the Myanmar state is assessed in terms of the following six attributes that characterize the developmental state.[51]

(a) a committed developmental elite;
(b) assurance of the relative autonomy of the state and concomitant high state capacity for policy implementation;
(c) existence of a competent and impartial economic bureaucracy insulated from sectional interests;
(d) a weak civil society subordinated to a strong state;
(e) effective management of non-state economic interests;
(f) strong coercive power to maintain order and stability combined with credible performance legitimacy.

It is argued in the following sections that, with the exception of the marginalization of non-state economic interests, the Myanmar state was found wanting in all the interrelated attributes which characterize successful developmental states.

The Developmental Elite

Usually, a core group of politicians and technocrats committed to economic development, often led by a visionary leader who maintains a strong grip over the centralized decision-making and is predisposed to an explicit developmental agenda, is "instrumental in establishing the developmental regime".[52] Moreover, in most cases, these elites managed to forge a strong and mutually respected relationship with the civil service or bureaucracy that shares a common developmental goal with them.[53] This kind of "developmentalism" may be regarded as an "ideology or world view that accords industrialization a higher priority than other societal roles and gives the state a leading role in promoting it."[54]

Myanmar did have a core group of political elites during the parliamentary era (1948–62) who were keen to develop the country through economic planning and state-led industrialization. They shared similar generational experiences during the independence struggle and had endured the challenge posed by the protracted civil war that ensued after independence. They also had a charismatic leader, Nu, who by his own account was a reluctant politician thrust upon the political centre stage by extraordinary circumstances. However, this idiosyncratic political leader, who became increasingly preoccupied with religion, apparently lacked the sustained developmental fervour of those successful developmentalists such as Korea's President Park Chung Hee or Singapore's Prime Minister Lee Kuan Yew.[55] Moreover, elite cohesion started to unravel in the mid-1950s and deteriorated thereafter to the extent that the military leaders saw a reason to intervene in 1958. When the politicians resumed power after U Nu's party won the 1960 general elections, developmental commitment became severely attenuated amongst the incumbent leadership, who were increasingly constrained by the ongoing internecine power struggle. To sum up, the political elites of the parliamentary era were found to be wanting in terms of both clear perception of developmental means and ends as well as in unity and cohesion.[56]

The subsequent era of direct military rule saw a ruling elite fashioned from a select group of senior officers led by their supreme commander General Ne Win. There were some hiccups in elite cohesion during the first few years of the RC rule when some members of the group fell by the wayside in the process of a radical restructuring of the socio-economic environment. By the mid-1960s, the ruling elite had consolidated their unity under the domineering personality of General Ne Win. However, their commitment and energies were mainly focused on replacing the old socio-political order with a new self-reliant socialist order, leaving little room for developmental initiatives. Hence, this group did not constitute a developmental elite as such and very little economic progress was achieved.

On the other hand, the state that was reconstituted in 1974 and led by the BSPP leadership did have tangible developmental goals. The party elite pushed for industrial development through planned growth and structural change. They employed quantifiable parameters of economic progress that followed the norms and practices of international development agencies like the World Bank. While their methods might be unorthodox when compared with East Asian developmental states, the ruling elite of the BSPP era was, by and large, development oriented. Though there were several "purges" in the Leninist-style party, the top BSPP elites were rather cohesive in their commitment towards development through the TYP. Nevertheless, the Achilles heel of the ruling elite's developmentalism turned out to be the idiosyncratic personality of their "paramount leader", who had attained such stature that he commanded almost absolute power. He was highly nationalistic, inward-looking, and extremely averse to integration with the international economy.[57]

Relative Autonomy and State Capacity

Following Crone, it can be said that the concept of the relative autonomy of the state in relation to society can be translated as the state elites' "varying degree of independence [insulation] from" pressures exerted by powerful social actors as well as from "the wider social base".[58] In developmental states, this autonomy is utilized by state elites to override class, regional or sectional interests in pursuit of economic development.[59] Thus, a high degree of autonomy "is believed to work as a necessary, not sufficient, prerequisite for restructuring and policy effectiveness.[60] However, state autonomy does not mean isolation from societal concerns and aspirations. Instead, it "is an autonomy embedded in a concrete set of social ties that bind the state to society and provide institutionalized channels for the continual negotiation and renegotiation of goals and policies".[61] As such, state elites have to "become embedded in a progressively dense web of ties with non-state and other state actors (internal and external)" so as to enable the state "to co-ordinate the economy and implement developmental objectives".[62]

On the other hand, for successful development, autonomy must be coupled with state capacity, i.e., sufficient capability to "maintain effective control of the commanding heights of decision-making and the policy-making process" and to be "able to manage the various competing special interests" so as to maximize the developmental gains.[63] It requires putting "autonomy and embeddedness together".[64] In fact, "capacity describes the limits to autonomy".[65]

Apart from effective control of natural, financial, human, and symbolic resources, state capacity depends upon the nature of state-society relationship. It follows that "the development of state capacity is influenced by the manner in which power is aggregated and exercised"; especially in the form of control exercised by the state over the society at large.[66]

The state during the 1948–62 period evidently had lower relative autonomy than the typical developmental state. Moreover, the crucial element of "embedded autonomy" was missing as embeddedness borders on "capture".[67] The dominance of the AFPFL over other parties and its co-option of trade unions and mass organizations created some autonomy but within the ruling party there were sectional interests that compromised the state managers' autonomy. As for foreign pressures, the state managed to preserve its political autonomy by circumventing the geopolitics of the Cold War through strict neutrality and non-alignment.

The state's autonomy and its capacity to formulate and implement an effective economic development programme were mainly eroded by political instability and insurgency brought about by persistent problems related to unresolved issues in leadership succession and national security.[68] Hence, despite the initial adoption of a developmental agenda, the state lacked the capacity to mobilize sufficient material and human resources for its successful execution. The leaders' socialist convictions and *dirigiste* proclivities precluded the state from co-opting the private sector into a strategic coalition and to fashion links with external capital for industrial development.[69]

The RC period saw an unprecedented rise in state autonomy as the military junta ruled by decree. However, it was a dubious autonomy because it was accompanied by disengagement between state and society. There was no embeddedness at all. In its attempt to replace the "dispersed domination" of the parliamentary state with "integrated domination" and establish an "overarching hegemony", the revolutionary state embraced autarky and undermined its own capacity by denying itself the potential sources of strength from within and without the country. Thus, private capital, entrepreneurship, and direct links to the international economy with its modern management practices and advanced technology were precluded.[70]

The BSPP socialist state also achieved a high degree of relative autonomy and managed to rely less on coercive measure for social control when compared with the RC period. Nonetheless, the BWS lacked embeddedness as such with the polity highly depoliticized. Consequently, state capacity was constrained by the relative isolation from societal interests and the regime's refusal to welcome FDI. Myanmar under one-party rule somewhat resembled China in that "networks of personal relations and reciprocal obligations" existing at various levels of the party-state and at the juncture between state and society, thereby eroding state capacity as "patron–client factionalism and localist deception" became the "main ingredients in the *real* politics".[71] The state's capacity to marshal financial resources was low because of its suppression of market forces and denial of private initiatives. The state was also burdened with inefficient SEEs. It ended up with "the worst combination" viz., a "soft maximal state" with weak capacity and high state intervention.[72]

Economic Bureaucracy

State-led development is a non-starter if there is no competent, loyal, and impartial economic bureaucracy or civil service to implement development policies. Observers have pointed out that successful developmental states are blessed with capable and powerful economic bureaucracies that enjoy the confidence and trust of the highest political authorities and are insulated from societal pressures. In some cases, such as in Korea and Indonesia under the New Order, the technocrats themselves were given ministerial positions to guide and oversee economic development in general and industrialization in particular.[73] In the case of Myanmar, the "appointive bureaucracy" syndrome inhibited bureaucratic efficiency.[74]

Myanmar developed a planning bureaucracy very early in its developmental quest and, in the parliamentary era, the prime minister or the deputy prime minister usually assumed the chair in the successive bodies in charge of national economic development. However, in practice, political considerations tended to dictate development planning and implementation.[75] Moreover, the large number of reorganizations undergone by the planning machinery seems to suggest that a stable institutional configuration, conducive to long-term planning, was lacking.[76]

As for the civil service, it lacked self-confidence as the politicians rode roughshod over them with contempt and disdain, with the entire system regarded as the legacy of colonial rule. There was also disunity among the bureaucratic elite as competent but seemingly arrogant veterans from the colonial era were increasingly at odds with newcomers, some of whom took advantage of their personal relationship with the AFPFL leadership. They all reputedly worked in fear under the spectre of the powerful Bureau of Special Investigations (BSI), which, at times, seemed to exercise its powers overzealously. Moreover, technocrats with developmental competence in the hierarchy were too few to constitute a critical mass. Above all, the civil service imbued with an administrative mindset did not empathize with its political masters on developmental issues.[77]

Under the RC rule, the military elites viewed the entire bureaucracy with suspicion. Many top bureaucrats were replaced by party cadres or military officers, while others were required to toe the revolutionary line. The civil service as a whole became demoralized and cynical. The economic bureaucracy's function was reduced to carrying out ministerial directives.[78] Thus, no competent economic bureaucracy in the developmental sense functioned at that time.

The BSPP era saw the rapid expansion of the economic bureaucracy in line with the onerous tasks of implementing and monitoring the various plans and its components. The planning bureaucracy was staffed by a new generation of people, many of whom were trained in the Soviet Union and Eastern Europe, supervised by senior bureaucrats who had survived the transition by pledging allegiance to the socialist order. As such, it had no authority, little power, and dubious competence to implement economic policies dictated by the BSPP guidelines.[79] The economic bureaucracy that existed under the one-party socialist state had little say in the developmental agenda. It was a mere follower of the party bureaucracy whose goals were more political than developmental. As such it compared very poorly with those of the successful developmental states.

Civil Society

Civil society may be described as a "web of all privately-organised interests and groups, above the family level but below the state".[80] If "parochial associations that do not evince an interest beyond their immediate concerns" and "groups that do not have a concept of the state independent of their own aims"[81] are excluded, Myanmar in the 1950s appeared to be lacking in one. There were few or no mediating structures in the "middle ground between the communal groups and state structures".[82] Societal formations that existed were either intimidated or co-opted by the state. Moreover, the existence of powerful local strongmen patronized by the political elite also lend support to the "general weakness" and the "flattening" of societal formations.[83] The civil war, apathy amongst indigenous races towards one another's problems, and political instability in the second half of the 1950s were not conducive towards the emergence of a viable civil society. The incongruence between different nationalisms of the indigenous ethnic groups and the inherited state institutions, based on principles which were diametrically opposed to the very essence of nationalism, created an untenable situation that inhibited the forging of a strong civil society out of the "peoples" who inhabited independent Myanmar.[84]

The RC-era state obliterated all existing societal institutions and suppressed the disparate elements that survived. Only organizations affiliated to the BSPP were allowed to operate under party guidance and control.[85] In this context there was no room for civil society at all.

Following the adoption of the 1974 Constitution, commissioned by the BSPP, the latter — the sole legal party allowed — played the leading role in all matters pertaining to politics, economics and public affairs. The Myanmar state was reconstructed as a reification of the symbiotic relationship among the party, the state executive and the military with the party assuming the paramount position (see Chapter 6). Therefore, there was no place for civil society that encompasses social groups which "are separate from but address the state".[86] Thus, it can be assumed that civil society, necessary for developmental success, practically did not exist during the BSPP era.

Non-State Economic Interests

Effective management of non-state economic interests, which may hinder economic development, is related to state power and autonomy. It has been observed that, in many cases, the developmental state was able to cope with the demands from such interests and could impose its will upon them.[87]

In Myanmar, local and foreign economic interests preceded independence and continued thereafter. During the decade of the 1950s, the state's ISI strategy and protective tariff structure proved beneficial to a select group of industrial capitalists and traders. While foreign economic interests were circumscribed by the regime's predilection for economic nationalism, just like in some African states, local capital "tended to remain weak not only because" the state "monopolized potentially lucrative economic activities" but also because those who had the ability "to promote their business interests were often absorbed into" the regime's "patronage networks".[88] On balance, it can be said that the state's nationalization and Burmanization policies, limited the scope and power of foreign non-state economic interests. The general weakness of private capital, being dependent upon the state for protection and support, limited its influence on the state.

In the RC period, given its overt coercive power and self-reliant autarkic policies there was no room for non-state economic interests to influence state policies, aimed at suppressing the market and denying the role of private capital in the economy.

In the BSPP era, the state delimited the role of the private sector and discouraged private initiatives through a host of rules and regulations. Private economic activities went underground, and the black market economy became the expression of non-state economic interests. Nevertheless, the state managers did not take into consideration those interests in its developmental agenda. Such interests were deemed irrelevant to policy-making and implementation, mistakenly believing that eradicating them would be a matter of time through sustained suppressive measures.

Power, Order and Legitimacy

Many of the successful ex-colonial developmental states have been labelled as authoritarian by Western observers. It seems that their ruling elites were not averse to using its coercive power in enforcing discipline, soliciting compliance and maintaining public order. They do not take challenges to their authority lightly and their treatment of opposition borders on contempt.[89]

However, they do enjoy high legitimacy in terms of both the nation-state itself and the regime that controlled it. Much of this could be attributed to what is commonly identified as performance legitimacy, brought about by the ability of the regime to deliver economic benefits to the population at large. Thus "[l]egitimation occurs from the state's achievements, not from the way it came to power."[90]

In Myanmar, the concept of the nation-state itself was contested from the very beginning. Furthermore, the legitimacy of successive regimes from Nu's AFPFL government to General Ne Win's BSPP government were questioned and challenged by a motley array of armed groups ranging from Communists to drug-trafficking warlords. While the RC rationalized its rule in terms of the military's "historic duty" to prevent the dissolution of the state itself, its legitimacy was contentious. The BSPP legitimated its one-party rule through the 1974 Constitution and the system of elected "people's representatives". Despite considerable efforts by the BSPP to legalize and institutionalize its rule, societal acquiescence was mainly due to resignation and lack of choice that did nothing to enhance its legitimacy. This was borne out by the 1988 upheaval in which its own rank and file abandoned the party in times of need.[91]

In contrast to successful developmental states, performance legitimacy was never established throughout the four decades of sovereign nationhood. Indeed, as outlined in the first part of this chapter, the state's economic performance declined so precipitously in the late 1980s that it suffered a legitimacy crisis that led to its near-collapse in August 1988.

DENOUEMENT: BANKRUPTCY?

Development strategies usually "guide or facilitate the process of developmental change".[92] Such strategies may be defined as "sets of government policies" shaping "a country's relationship to the global economy" and affecting "the domestic allocation of resources among industries and major social groups".[93] Thus, the nature of the adopted development strategy — which may be identified by its orientation (along the continuum of inward to outward outlook) and relative weight given to the role of state and market (along the spectrum from *dirigisme* to *laissez faire*) — influences the corresponding developmental pathway of the country.

According to current conventional wisdom, informed by neoclassical doctrine, there is only one pathway towards sustained economic growth. That is the path of international competition through private initiatives in which states yield to the logic of the market and internationalization of factor inputs. This means a liberal trade regime, EOI (export-oriented industrialization) strategy, and attracting FDI through a mutually beneficial relationship with multinationals. The role of the state is more of an arbiter and facilitator rather than an actor. As the risks of "state failure" far more outweigh that of "market failure" the state is supposed to prepare the ground, set fair and impartial rules, and stay away from the playing fields.[94]

On the other hand those who read the "facts" associated with the rise of East and Southeast Asian NIEs differently, contend that the state has a distinct and pivotal role in the success of these countries. They subscribe to the developmental state model in general and reject the free-market approach to development.[95]

There is also a broadly constituted constellation of "middle-of-the road" analysts who stressed the importance of pragmatism and flexibility in policy-making and acknowledge the "market-conforming" role of the state.[96] According to them:

> The extreme version of the statist as well as the neo-classical models of East Asian success lack analytical and empirical credibility. One must move away from the idea that the "strong developmental state" in East Asia produced error-free policies. Equally, one must move away from the naive notion that East Asian success vindicates the efficacy of *laissez faire* policies. The truth probably lies in a synergetic interaction between the state and the market ... [97]

Yet others advocate flexibility as the key to sustained economic development. In their view, "a flexible economy" is "one in which individuals, organisations and institutions efficiently adjust their goals and resources to changing constraints and opportunities".[98]

Myanmar experience seems to be at odds with the criteria specified by all three approaches. What Myanmar had gone through from 1948 to 1988 neither conformed to the neoclassical paradigm nor the flexibility recommendations. The overambitious state intervention by the state in trade and production, the execution of the state-led ISI strategy, the financial repression and the ambivalent stand on FDI, all at odds with neoclassical fundamentals were present during the parliamentary era.[99] The prolonged winding down of the Pyidawtha Plan and the attenuation of the ISI effort over the same period showed the lack of policy flexibility and presence of a strong inertia inhibiting timely changes. The RC's record points to an approach that clearly violated the neoclassical model's prescriptions and that period under direct military rule was characterized by rigidity in policy-making. The BSPP era, despite its socialist flavour, saw policies informed by the neoclassical bent of the multilateral lending institutions and donor states (Japan and Germany in particular). Nevertheless the policy options were circumscribed by the denial of a significant role for the private sector that eventually turned to the black market for profit and sustenance. The ODA was no substitute for private capital and only served to prolong the agony of the hobbled state. Flexibility that would have brought about timely economic reforms before it was too little too late seemed to have been absent.

If we look at the developmental state model, it is evident from the foregoing discussions that the state during the parliamentary era was too weak to emulate the former. Crucial elements such as high relative autonomy and capacity, legitimacy, as well as a competent and confident economic bureaucracy were missing. Above all, the ruling elite was disunited and its understanding of developmental goals and means was too diffuse to be effective.

The state under the RC rule exhibited a very weak affinity to the developmental state. The developmentalist ethos was eclipsed by the exigencies of consolidating power and suppressing adversaries. Moreover, the state's capacity was limited by autarky and there was no viable economic bureaucracy.

As for the BSPP era, there were indeed some elements resembling the characteristics of a developmental state; especially the nature of the regime that was similar to what Cummings aptly called "bureaucratic authoritarian industrializing regimes".[100] The TYP was a clear indicator of the elite's developmental commitment. There was considerable policy autonomy but this was at the expense of effective interaction with society as well as the world at large. The state apparently wielded considerable power in relation to a weak society. Such power was illusory because its coercive dimension did not lend itself to be translated into effective authority. Non-state economic interests were suppressed to the point that they went underground, thereby frustrating the state's best efforts to control the economy. All in all, the BSPP regime's developmental goals were never realized because state capacity was not up to the mark and its legitimacy was fragile.[101] In short, it can be said that in attempting to mimic the developmental state without sufficient capacity and legitimacy Myanmar took a pathway that led to bankruptcy and the collapse of the socialist one-party state.

Still, Myanmar's tragedy begs the questions, why did the state not introduce sufficient and timely reforms to avoid such a debacle and maintain its hegemony? What about the demonstration effect of successful neighbours who became NIEs during the 1980s?

To shed light on this puzzle we need some elaboration in relation to the flexibility argument of the pragmatists who suggest that:

> economic flexibility depends crucially on policy adaptability ... [defined] as the capacity to change the policy framework within which the economy operates, whether in detail or in overall direction, rapidly, efficiently and effectively, and without undue social or political friction. Policy adaptability is a function both of the character and ethos of the government and the bureaucracy ... and of their degree of insulation from the immediate pressures of the political arena ... which is possible only if the relationship between the policy-making process and the wider political economy permits the effective regulation of both the "state" and "civil society" within certain broadly acceptable parameters.[102]

One must go back to Myanmar's colonial past for an understanding of the self-imposed constraints on policy adaptability that had persisted amongst Myanmar's ruling elites. These leaders were conditioned by their collective historical experience under colonial rule which when reinterpreted became an indictment against capitalism and free markets. It should be noted that the same generation of nationalistic leaders had led Myanmar from 1948 to 1988 and their conservative nationalism had also rubbed off on their younger followers. To Myanmar's top leaders market failure is a catastrophe when compared to state failure; an eventuality deemed to be improbable.[103]

As pointed out in Chapter 2, ideological currents of the nationalist movement lingered on for nearly half a century. Though "ideology does not define the [economic] system in any clear-cut once-and-all fashion ... it does establish taboos, constraints, and biases which have important influences on the nature and the evolutionary path of the economy."[104] Similarly, the Myanmar political elites' ideological prejudices against markets and private capital and preference for equity and economic independence produced self-imposed constraints that circumscribed policy options even during the parliamentary era in a mixed economy setting. Thereafter, under military rule, a set of tacit taboos that forbade currency devaluation, foreign exchange convertibility, FDI, and price-based incentives manifested. The ruling elite also developed an affinity for self-reliance, economic planning, and what Hirschman called "an innate preference for ... self — or internal — financ[ing]" of investments".[105] The underlying "transforming vision" of the RC military elites engendered a development programme under the BSPP leadership that was more than economic and bordered on the "ideological".[106] Most significantly, as the "primary function of ideology" seems to be "to attack, change, or destroy existing systems" and it is purportedly "far better in this role than in that of building a new order" the socialist vision of all Myanmar leaders (both civilian and military) apparently failed in the latter aspect.[107]

On the other hand, it has been argued that "economic ideology" and the "strategic goal orientation" of the state leadership "sets the direction of economic policies".[108] Economic ideology may be defined in terms of a "relative stance" along the "continuum" between two polar extremes of *laissez faire* and "economic nationalism", and the strategic goal orientation "is conceived as a particular preference on the economic growth-stability-equity spectrum" (G-S-E in short).[109]

If Myanmar is analysed along these lines it is evident that the economic ideology stayed at the nationalist end of the spectrum and the strategic goal orientation had been prioritized in terms of equity first; stability second; and growth third; i.e. E-S-G in symbolic representation. The leaders' overall perspective it seems to have been E-S-G all the way for four decades since independence. This form of rigidity in orientation sustained by nationalistic convictions made it extremely difficult for top leaders to switch strategies in mid-stride; especially if the change represents a U-turn.

Moreover, it should be noted that the switching from the ISI to EOI and the changing over from inward to outward orientation occurred among the Asian NIEs during the late 1960s. As such, there was no demonstration effect yet to be emulated during the parliamentary era when the state-led ISI strategy informed by the intellectual currents of immediate post-World-War II period was adopted in the early 1950s.[110] Hence, the following discussion on factors that inhibits timely economic reforms will be confined to the BSPP era when such an opportunity was sorely missed.

It has generally been accepted that centrally planned economies (CPEs) exhibit "the deleterious effects of seeking to over-institutionalise economic activity" thereby resulting in "large systemic rigidities".[111] It seems that "the stability value of socialism turned out to be an immobility burden in the end".[112] In socialist Myanmar, despite the limited reach of the state and the weak nature of central planning embedded in a mixed economic setting, systemic rigidities which plagued Soviet-type economies were present and at the micro-level the problem of reforming SEEs remained as intractable as they had been in CPEs.[113] However, the success of economic reforms in the People's Republic of China (PRC) reminds us that it is possible for a Leninist one-party state to introduce radical economic reforms by controlling the transition process.

Drawing lessons from actual practice, Grindle identifies the following enabling conditions for successful reforms:[114]

(a) a perceived economic crisis;
(b) commitment of political leadership to follow through proposed reform measures;
(c) existence of political institutions playing a key role in consensus-building, negotiating, and bargaining among all effected groups;
(d) key role for technocrats in formulating, packaging, disseminating and implementing policy reforms; and
(e) strong state capacity and regime legitimacy.

On the other hand, much of the success depends upon the regime's ability to manage the implementation of reform measures to overcome the "problems of bureaucratic capacity, resistance, and compliance".[115] Moreover, "successful economic policy reform does not necessarily mean economic recovery" as such, reforms are not panacea to achieving sustained growth and prosperity.[116]

In the Myanmar case, partial reforms, mooted around 1970 and introduced in the mid-1970s, were prompted by inflationary pressures and slow economic growth. The reform measures included material incentives for state employees, administrative restructuring, management reforms in SEEs, reform of financial institutions and tax reforms. They were, however, carried out under the ambit of the TYP and the long-term and short-term economic policies of the BSPP (Chapter 6). The inward trade orientation and the ISI strategy remained unchanged. As such, these partial reforms did not address the fundamental limitations of the socialist orientation and shortcomings of the TYP guidelines.

In the more comprehensive reforms adopted by the emergency congress of the BSPP in July 1988, the incorporation of the domestic and foreign private sector into the national economy was considered for the first time since 1963. It included liberalization of production, trade and services in all economic sectors and legalization of the informal border trade. Most significantly, legal procedures to facilitate joint ventures between local (state, co-operatives, private) and foreign partners were promised.[117]

In this eleventh-hour proposal to rescue the failing economy, it is evident that Grindle's first two conditions were present but the institutional component of the third condition was missing, given that the BSPP was the only institution in place. Moreover, the virtual absence of the fourth condition and the rapidly eroding legitimacy in the face of overwhelming popular pressures rendered the regime impotent as events overtook its feeble responses.

Most significantly, the presence of an acute sense of crisis is crucial for obstinate regimes to change track. In the case of Myanmar, the BSPP leaders did not seem to realize the enormity of the crisis, until the last few weeks of their rule. They had, all along, believed that they could prevail with palliative measures, some coercion, and perhaps a little bit of luck. Their nationalist pride and self-righteous ideological conviction prevented them from discerning the slide to bankruptcy in the last few years of their rule as well as the sclerosis of the party and the ossification of the state. They neglected societal aspirations and failed to acknowledge the gap between ideology and reality.

Given that Myanmar was receiving a relatively large amount of ODA during the 1980s, one may also wonder whether multilateral lending agencies such as the World Bank or donor countries could have any influence over Myanmar's policy orientation that would have facilitated effective reforms. In this respect, one could say that the political leaders' deceptively sanguine interpretation of Myanmar development performance was aided by the reassuringly "mild" advice given by the World Bank which served as the principal link to the donor community. Despite its stated preference for the market over government intervention, the Bank, which "has repeatedly said ... that it respects every country's right to adopt the political system of its choice", did not press for wide-ranging reforms.[118] Both the IMF and the World Bank decided not to challenge the very foundations of Myanmar's development strategy, which was intertwined with the political structure and the ideology of the ruling party. They only offered technical advice on sectoral and developmental issues; either in their occasional review and assessment of Myanmar's economy or in the context of Burma Aid Group coordination meetings.[119]

As for ODA donor countries, given the Myanmar government's aversion to any suggestion that would imply an encroachment of national sovereignty, they avoided exerting any peer pressure on Myanmar or imposing conditionality on their ODA provisions. In formulating ODA projects, they generally deferred to the government's policy agenda.[120] Moreover, Myanmar leaders' conflation of economic with political issues and the practice of delinking external relations from internal affairs left donors with no options to pursue policy dialogues.[121] Even Japan, with which the Myanmar government had the most comfortable relationship and which probably had the highest leverage among donor states (by way of consistently high levels of ODA commitment throughout the last decade of BSPP rule), was reticent about proffering policy prescriptions until it was too late.[122] According to Steinberg, the Japanese government did press for unspecified but "substantive economic reforms" to justify further economic assistance in March 1988, when the Myanmar economic economy was at its nadir. This "remonstrance" probably moved the Myanmar leadership to formulate the belated reforms of July 1988.[123]

Grindle's fourth condition was not satisfied because there existed very little "policy space" for establishment planners/technocrats to explore alternative market-conforming approaches under centralized one-party socialist rule. On the other hand "outside expertise" had been "mainly used to add the weight of international prestige to domestically favoured policy options" or conveniently disregarded citing unique local circumstances.[124]

The absence of the fifth condition was all too apparent when the regime unravelled within a few weeks after the adoption of reforms by the Pyithu Hluttaw.

All in all, in the Myanmar situation the most important factor for or against change seems to be the role and attitude of Ne Win, the paramount leader. By the 1980s, there existed a huge deferential gap between the topmost tier of the policy hierarchy and Ne Win himself. Though he withdrew from active governance in 1981, it was widely believed that no major political and economic decisions were made without his approval.[125] Throughout the BSPP era (and the RC rule before that) "he was systematically shielded from mundane unpleasant realities" by his subordinates.[126]

Over time, as he became aware of the economic difficulties faced by Myanmar, Ne Win mooted the need for changes in outlook and approaches. Yet, he seems to be ambivalent towards change even as he spoke about changing with the times when he said:

> ... how shall we change? It is necessary for us to change the principles ... We shall have to take into consideration to what extent we should change and how, on the basis of our own experiences as well as the experiences from the world. We must lay down new principles after taking all these into consideration.[127]

Given his domineering position in the hierarchical relationship with the rest of the BSPP leaders, there was no possibility of a dialogue or exchange of views on such an occasion. In fact, the "top down pyramidal control structure" set up by Ne Win himself resembled a "single apex structure" that was impervious to feedback and highly inflexible.[128] As such, his general and vague remarks did not elicit any responses that called for a major rethink of the goals, orientation, and strategies, which, in turn, could lead to effective reforms. As such, an opportunity to bring about reforms of the scale and scope necessary for reversing the rapidly deteriorating economic situation was lost.[129]

It is tempting to compare Ne Win with Indonesia's Soeharto in the context of "the political choices of the key policy maker in the system". However, as pointed out by Liddle such choices do not "take place in a vacuum" and the "political considerations" of policy-makers must be connected in a "situationally specific way with the structural, cultural, domestic, and international contexts". These two sets are linked through the "policy-makers' perceptions, goals and calculations".[130]

Both the context and the links were different when we compare the situation in which the two leaders found themselves in power. Indonesia was economically and politically bankrupt under the mercurial Soekarno regime. Soeharto assumed power decisively but not immediately after the abortive Communist uprising that created chaos and mayhem and elicited a traumatic anti-Communist backlash. In Myanmar, despite Nu's idiosyncratic style and the problem of possible ethnic secession the political crisis was not compounded by a severe economic crisis. Ne Win assumed power in a coup that hardly affected the polity at that time.

In Indonesia, leftist and Communist ideologies lost their legitimacy and became anathema to the ruling elites whereas in Myanmar the "revolution" was portrayed as a return to socialist principles of the nationalist movement for independence. To Ne Win and his lieutenants it was a rare opportunity to "reassert" the state that was "displaced". They could afford to be less pragmatic than Soeharto in policy choice because they perceived that the parameters of performance legitimacy were based not on growth but equity. Moreover, because of their credentials as nationalist freedom fighters prior to independence it was believed that further legitimization lay in the direction of self-reliant socialism.

Once different and divergent pathways were chosen at the juncture where each of them assumed power, what followed was based on their convictions reinforced by their patrimonial leadership style and their own measures of progress filtered through the prisms of their world view.[131]

Thus, Myanmar's developmental experience can only be understood in the context of "social, political and economic structures" that impinged upon the state without excluding "the individual agency and the single person's power of self-determination".[132] In short, one could conclude that it is this curious interplay between personality, agency, and structure informed by particularistic interpretations of historical experiences that led to Myanmar's path towards bankruptcy through the failure of its state-led industrialization effort.

Notes

1. Moshe Syrquin, "Flexibility and Long-Term Economic Development", in *The Flexible Economy: Causes and Consequences of the Adaptability of National Economies*, edited by Tony Killick (London: Routledge, 1995), p. 34.
2. The term HPAEs became popular with the publication of the World Bank study *The East Asian Miracle* in 1993 (*The East Asian Miracle: Economic Growth and Public Policy* [New York and Oxford: Oxford University Press, 1993]). Examples given here are Taiwan, Republic of Korea, Thailand, Malaysia, and (whenever data are available) Indonesia. Taiwan and Korea represent countries that had pursued state-led industrialization policies. Of course, there have been arguments that Southeast Asian HPAEs and Northeast Asian HPAEs had different initial conditions and different kinds of state interventions that had influenced their economic growth trajectories but such arguments do not rule out comparing their economic performance altogether. See, for example, Anne Booth, "Initial Conditions and Miraculous Growth: Why is South East Asia Different From Taiwan and South Korea?",

World Development 27, no. 2 (1999): 301–21. Thailand, which is similar to Myanmar in terms of resource endowment, size and population, had not had any consistent state industrial policies. Malaysia is an example of another resource-rich country that had followed an intermediate trajectory between the statist pattern of Taiwan/Korea and the market-driven path of Thailand. Indonesia (under President Soeharto) was similar to post-1962 Myanmar in terms of its *de facto* one-party system of governance and a strong military participation in governance as well as the presence of a state-led industrialization strategy. However, all of them differed from Myanmar in that they all allowed a substantial role for the private sector and courted FDI.

3. There was a reclassification of GDP sectors in the early 1970s and a change of the base year for constant prices. Hence, it is not possible to directly compare the sectoral GDP structure for the pre- and post-1962 periods. The fiscal year 1952/53 was taken as the initial year for comparison in Figure 8.1 because it was the base year for the Pyidawtha Plan. Similarly, fiscal 1961/62 had been the benchmark year for all official statistics up to 1988, while 1985/86 was the last year before the economic recession set in. Interestingly, the market-orientation pursued by the military junta that assumed power after the Socialist state collapsed did not bring about significant structural change after a decade either (see Figure 9.5 below).
4. With the exception of financial services, the services sector was less regulated than other sectors, with easier entry and exit options for private entrepreneurs. Moreover, it had links to the "informal sector" and served as a residual for activities not classified under trade or (goods) production. Moreover, it was characterized by a tremendous diversity in terms of "size, market orientation, factor proportions" as well as financial and organizational attributes. It is usually associated with low and erratic income, job insecurity, harassment by local authorities, a mixture of flexibility and vulnerability and an opportunity to evade taxation and reap high profit margins (Hal Hill, *Southeast Asian Economic Development: An Analytical Survey*, Economic Division Working Papers No. 93/4 [Canberra: Research School of Pacific Studies, 1993], p. 31).
5. Myanmar's Pyidawtha Plan was, more or less, truncated in 1957. Taiwan and Korea shifted to EOI in the early 1960s (Stephen Haggard, *Pathways from the Periphery: The Politics of Growth in the Newly Industrializing Countries* [Ithaca: Cornell University Press, 1990], pp. 25, 74; and Bela Balassa, *Economic Policies in the Pacific Area Developing Countries* [Basingstoke and London: Macmillan, 1991], pp. 58, 106). Thailand and Malaysia embarked upon the EOI path at about 1970 and 1968 respectively (Narongchai Akrasanee, "The Role of Policy Research in the Trade and Industrial Reforms of Thailand", in *Authority and Academic Scribblers: The Role of Research in East Asian Policy Reform*, edited by Sylvia Ostry [San Francisco: ICS Press, 1991], pp. 10, 12;

and Mohamed Ariff, "Managing Trade and Industry Reforms in Malaysia", in *Authority and Academic Scribblers*, p. 25). Finally, 1987 was the year before Myanmar's socialist system collapsed.

6. Values for Taiwan and Korea are from Anis Chowdhury and Iyanatul Islam, *The Newly Industrializing Economies of East Asia* (London: Routledge, 1993), Table 6.3, p. 90.
7. The Myanmar growth rate could not be determined accurately because there was a change in public sector employment data after fiscal 1975/76, whereby administrative personnel were excluded. Other data are from Haggard, *Pathways from the Periphery*, Table 9.7, p. 242.
8. In fact, there are no data on private sector investments and capital depreciation. Data on public sector investment are also problematic due to inconsistencies in the level of aggregation as well as in the determination of price deflators (personal communications with planning officials).
9. The long-term overall growth target envisaged in the TYP was 2 per cent.
10. The time-series data are plotted on a semi-logarithmic scale so that the slope of the connecting line between any two points represents the growth rate for the corresponding period. In this way, growth and retrogression are prominently displayed. There was a discontinuity between the pre- and post-1962 data (see note 3). The pre-1962 data used in this chapter are taken from Kyaw Myint, "Industrialization in Burma" (Master thesis, University of Sydney, 1978), p. 15.
11. Myanmar's per capita income in 1952 was about US$40 while Korea's figure was around US$30. Thailand's 1957 figure was about US$70. By 1960 Myanmar attained US$60 while Korea's nominal figure went down to less than US$12 due to the massive devaluation (by over 1,000 per cent) of its currency. The corresponding figure for Thailand was about US$86 (All these figures are derived from data given in IMF, *International Financial Statistics, Supplement to 1965/66 Issues* (Washington, D.C.: IMF, n.d.).
12. As in the case of India, it could be that the "real economy, perhaps" had "not done so badly as" had the "measured economy" because "much economic activity" was in the black market (Ronald J. Herring, "Embedded Particularism: India's Failed Developmental State", in *The Developmental State*, edited by Meredith Woo-Cummings [Ithaca and London: Cornell University Press, 1999], p. 310).
13. The average compound growth rate for HPAEs are computed from data given in *International Financial Statistics Yearbook 1991* (Washington, D.C.: IMF, 1992).
14. The structuralist approach may be identified by the following central features: scepticism about the benefits of the free market; the need for structural change; importance of deciding who owns and controls national resources; technology is seen as a key dynamic input for development and its mastery is imperative; capital accumulation is deemed to be essential for growth

and structural change which will bring about an economic transformation (See Tom Hewitt, Hazel Johnson and Dave Wield, *Industrialization and Development* [Oxford: Oxford University Press and The Open University, 1992], p. 137). Myanmar planners derived investment requirements from assumed incremental capital-output ratios (ICOR) applied to desired growth rates. As pointed out by Toye, the "significance of investment spending depends on whether it is merely" an accounting figure or expenditure used in "purchasing assets which will actually be productive of income streams more valuable than the assets' costs, when suitably discounted" (John Toye, *Dilemmas of Development*, 2nd ed. [Oxford: Blackwell, 1993], n. 6, p. 177).

15. See, for example, *Pyidawtha: The New Burma*, (Rangoon: Economic and Social Board, 1954), pp. 20–23; *Second Four-Year Plan for the Union of Burma (1961–62 to 1964–65)* (Rangoon: Government Printing and Stationery, 1961), pp. 29, 32–39; and Chapter 6, Table 6.5.
16. See, for example, G. K. Shaw, "Policy Implications of Endogenous Growth Theory", *Economic Journal* 102, no. 412 (1992): 611–21. Human resources have also been identified as a source of economic growth (see, for example, *The East Asian Miracle*, pp. 43–47).
17. S. C. Tsiang and Rong-I Wu, "Foreign Trade and Investment as Boosters for Take-off: The Experiences of the Four Asian Newly Industrializing Countries", in *Foreign Trade and Development in the Newly Industrializing Asian Countries*, edited by Walter Galenson (Madison: University of Wisconsin Press, 1985), p. 306. The point here is that the criterion is a minimal requirement in terms of capital formation as a precondition for investment-driven growth.
18. This model is relevant for Myanmar for the following reasons: (1) The Myanmar economy since independence, except for an autarkic period (1964–70), resembled a mixed economy with heavy state intervention rather than a Soviet-type command economy. (2) There was a large agriculture sector that was never collectivized and an equally huge service sector that existed outside the formal planning framework. (3) There was also a pervasive parallel or informal economy. (4) The state had, by and large, relied on policy instruments and measures (fiscal, monetary, regulatory, and direct investment) which were not dissimilar to those employed by HPAEs. In fact, the language and terminology used in the elaboration and assessment of the plans since independence were those of mainstream development economics (see the foregoing chapters and various World Bank country studies/reports for Myanmar).
19. Tsiang and Wu, "Foreign Trade and Investment", p. 306.
20. Ibid., p. 307.
21. See Sho-Chia Tsiang, *Success or Failure in Economic Takeoff*, Chung-Hua Institute for Economic Research (CIER) Research Monograph Series no. 26 (Taipei: CIER, 1989), p. 31.

22. For Myanmar, five-year moving averages were used for all variables. All data for the 1953–60 period except those for population growth rates were from *National Income of Burma 1958* (Rangoon: Government Printing and Stationery, n.d.) and *National Income of Burma 1963*. The population growth rate for the entire period was assumed to be 2.5 per cent throughout because no data was available. Even if it was lower, the declining trend would not have changed significantly. All data for the period 1973–85 were derived from various issues of the annual *Report to the Pyithu Hluttaw on Financial, Economic, and Social Conditions of the Socialist Republic of the Union of Burma* (Rangoon: Ministry of Planning and Finance). HPAEs data were taken from Tsiang, *Success or Failure.*
23. See ibid., p. 39.
24. The estimated value for 1984/85 was (–)21.9 per cent which indicated a declining trend after 1982/83.
25. Econometric studies of developing countries have not found any conclusive evidence that deficit financing is detrimental to economic growth as such. However, it was also pointed out that "[w]hat the deficit financing is used for in the economy is important" (Michael A. Nelson and Ram D. Singh, "The Deficit Growth Connection: Some Recent Evidence from Developing Countries", *Economic Development and Cultural Change* 43, no. 1 [1994]: 184).
26. These were in November 1985 and September 1987.
27. Newly industrialized economies of Southeast Asia have demonstrated that "low growth of money supply has been associated with low inflation and the converse" (Hill, *Southeast Asian Economic Development*, p. 46).
28. The bar graph in Figure 8.22 represents the average wage augmented by 50 per cent to account for the provision of basic commodities at controlled prices. The 50 per cent figure was estimated from the average profit obtained for a typical monthly ration for factory workers (based on personal observation during the 1980s).
29. R. H. Taylor, "Disaster or Release? J. S. Furnivall and the Bankruptcy of Burma". *Modern Asian Studies* 29, no. 1 (1995): 46.
30. For arguments supporting the state-failure thesis, see, for example, Deepak Lal, "Industrialization Strategies and Long-Term Resource Allocation", in *Development Strategies for the 21st Century*, edited by Teruyuki Iwasaki, Takeshi Mori, and Hiroichi Yamaguchi (Institute for Developing Economies, 1992), pp. 480–507. For Myanmar, see David I. Steinberg, *Crisis in Burma: Stasis and Change in a Political Economy in Turmoil*, ISIS Paper no. 5. (Bangkok: Institute of Security and International Studies, Chulalongkorn University, 1989.)
31. It is important to note that the core groups of Myanmar's ruling elites who were responsible for choosing the developmental path in both the civilian era and the military-socialist era were of the same generation and shared similar historical experiences under colonial rule. They belonged either to

the nationalist *thakin* movement or the anti-Japanese resistance movement of 1945. The leading personalities were Nu, Myanmar's first premier and General Ne Win.

32. Taiwan, Korea, Singapore, and Hong Kong are regarded as first tier NIEs with Malaysia, Thailand, and Indonesia in the second tier. See, for example, Adrian Leftwich, "Bringing Politics Back In: Towards a Model of the Developmental State", *Journal of Development Studies* 31, no. 3 (1995): 400–27. The development of the concept of the "capitalist" developmental state was attributed to Chalmers Johnson, who utilized it in his study of the historical role of Japan's Ministry of Trade and Industry (MITI) in the country's post-World War II economic success. For a reflection on this concept, see Chalmers Johnson, "The Developmental State: Odyssey of a Concept", in *The Developmental State,* edited by Woo-Cummings, pp. 32–60.
33. Adrian Leftwich, "Governance, the State and the Politics of Development", *Development and Change* 25, no. 2 (1994): 378–80. For another perspective on the attributes, see Christopher M. Dent, "The New International Political Economy of East Asia and the Developmental State", in *Developmental States: Relevancy, Redundancy or Reconfiguration?* edited by Linda Low (New York: Nova Science Publishers, 2004), pp. 80–81.
34. Leftwich, "Bringing Politics Back In", p. 401. For a critique of the concept, see Mark Beeson, "The Rise and Fall(?) of the Developmental State: The Vicissitudes and Implications of East Asian Interventionism", in *Developmental States,* edited by Low, pp. 29–40.
35. Peter Evans, *Embedded Autonomy: States and Industrial Transformation* (Princeton: Princeton University Press, 1995), p. 248. For the failures of the developmental state in the era of globalization, see, for example, Cal Clark and Steve Chan, "What Can One Learn from the Asian Flu? Implications for the Developmental State", in *Developmental States,* edited by Low, pp. 41–56. For a more sympathetic view towards the continued relevance of the concept, see Anis Chowdhury and Iyanatul Islam, "The East Asian Crisis: A Political Economy Explanation", ISEAS Working Papers, Visiting Researchers Series No. 1 (Singapore: Institute of Southeast Asian Studies, 2001).
36. Johnson, "Developmental State", p. 60.
37. Leftwich, "Bringing Politics Back In", p. 421. For an overview of the Southeast Asian NIEs experience in the developmental state context, see, for example, K. S. Jomo, "Southeast Asian Developmental States in Comparative Perspective", in *Developmental States,* edited by Low, pp. 57–77.
38. Gustav Ranis, "Another Look at the East Asian Miracle", *World Bank Economic Review* 9, no. 3 (1995): 510.
39. Robert H. Taylor, "Perceptions of Ethnicity in the Politics of Burma", *Southeast Asian Journal of Social Science* 10, no. 1 (1982): 12; and idem, "Disaster or Release?", pp. 51–56.

40. Ibid., p. 59.
41. Ibid., p. 54.
42. See, for example, Lloyd G. Reynolds, "Government and Economic Growth", in *From Classical Economics to Development Economics*, edited by Gerald M. Meier (Basingstoke and London: Macmillan, 1994), p. 227.
43. The British incorporated Myanmar as part of British India and implemented a "cost-effective way of governing an empire with few personnel" from Britain thereby utilizing Indian as intermediaries (Tony Killick, "Economic Inflexibility in Africa: Evidence and Causes", in *The Flexible Economy: Causes and Consequences of the Adaptability of National Economies*, edited by Tony Killick [London: Routledge, 1995], p. 183).
44. The term was used to describe social organizations in contemporary China (Vivienne Shue, "State Power and Social Organization in China", in *State Power and Social Forces: Domination and Transformation in the Third World*, edited by Joel S. Migdal, Atul Kohli and Vivienne Shue [Cambridge: Cambridge University Press, 1994], p. 83).
45. Herring, "Embedded Particularism", pp. 316–19. See also, Taylor, "Disaster or Release?", pp. 55, 56, 60, 62.
46. Ibid., p. 58. Under the traditional system in which patrimonial authority was personalized, racial differences did not figure prominently in communal relations.
47. The nationalist movement was dominated by Bamar activists who portrayed nationalism as the conflation of three "national" attributes: Bamar race; the Myanmar language; and Buddhism. Taken together this trinity could be interpreted as masking a hidden agenda for racial dominance by the majority Bamars.
48. See Benedict Anderson, *Imagined Communities: Reflection on the Origin and Spread of Nationalism*, rev. ed. (London: Verso, 1991; reprint 1993).
49. F. Gerard Adams and Inger Marie Davis. "The Role of Policy in Economic Development: Comparisons of the East and Southeast Asian and Latin American Experience", *Asian-Pacific Economic Literature* 8, no. 1 (1994): 15.
50. Here ideology is used "in the sense of a moderately consistent set of ideas and beliefs arising from within a society and accounting for its socio-economic phenomena and containing also some guidance for action". (Comment by Albert O. Hirschman on Alexander Gerschenkron's essay, "Ideology as a System Determinant", in *Comparison of Economic Systems: Theoretical and Methodological Approaches* [Berkeley: University of California Press, 1971, reprint 1973], p. 290). Dominant ideology is the term employed by Hirschman to describe that belonging to the class of "*official*" or "*pro-status quo* ideologies" in contrast to the "*insurgent* or *advocate* ideologies" (ibid.).
51. This is a slight modification of Leftwich's six-point listing (Leftwich, "Bringing Politics Back In", p. 405).

52. Ibid., p. 405.
53. Ibid., p. 406.
54. Ben Ross Schneider, "The *Desarrollista* State in Brazil and Mexico", in *The Developmental State*, edited by Woo-Cummings, p. 283.
55. See, for example, U Nu, *U Nu: Saturday's Son*, translated by Law Yone, edited by Kyaw Win (New Haven: Yale University Press, 1975; reprint, Bombay: Bharatiya Bhavan, 1976), pp. 85–86, 114, 316–25. For the rise of the military as a powerful contender for state power, see Mary Callahan, *Making Enemies: War and State Building in Burma*. (Ithaca: Cornell University Press, 2003), Chapters 5–7.
56. See, for example, Louis J. Walinsky, *Economic Development in Burma, 1951–1960* (New York: The Twentieth Century Fund, 1962), pp. 566–67, 575–77.
57. See, for example, *Myanma Hoshelit Lanzin Parti Okahta Gyi Ei Khitpyaung Tawhlanyei Thamaingwin Maintgun Baungyoke* [Compendium of Historic Revolutionary Speeches by the Chairman of the Burma Socialist Programme Party]. No. 1 (Yangon: Burma Socialist Programme Party, 1985), pp. 416–17, 432–35, 443–44.
58. Donald K. Crone, "State, Social Elites, and Government Capacity in Southeast Asia", *World Politics* XL, no. 2 (1988): 255–56.
59. Leftwich, "Bringing Politics Back In", p. 408.
60. Jei Guk Jeon, "The Comparative Politics of Economic Development in East Asia: A Conceptual Mapping", *Pacific Focus* IX, no. 1 (1994): 69.
61. Evans, *Embedded Autonomy*, p. 59. For elaboration, see ibid., pp. 234–35. More specifically, Woo-Cummings argues that "[f]inance is the tie that binds the state to the industrialists in the developmental state" (Meredith Woo-Cummings, "Introduction: Chalmers Johnson and the Politics of Nationalism and Development", in *The Developmental State*, edited by Woo-Cummings, p. 10).
62. Leftwich, "Bringing Politics Back In", p. 408.
63. David Seddon and Tim Belton-Jones, "The Political Determinants of Economic Flexibility, with Special Reference to the East Asian Nics", in *The Flexible Economy*, edited by Killick, p. 355.
64. Evans, *Embedded Autonomy*, p. 73.
65. Michael Bratton, "Peasant-State Relations in Postcolonial Africa: Patterns of Engagement and Disengagement", in *State Power and Social Forces*, edited by Migdal, Kohli and Shue, p. 236.
66. Crone, "State, Social Elites", p. 256. He contends that collaborative means of social control is more efficient than coercive means (see ibid., pp. 257–58). For a broader perspective on weak states and low capacity, see Francis Fukuyama, *State-Building: Governance and World Order in the 21st Century* (Ithaca: Cornell University Press, 2004), Chapter 2.
67. Evans, *Embedded Autonomy*, pp. 50, 60.

68. There were not only welfare losses and opportunity costs, brought about by insecurity in areas that happened to be where most of Myanmar's natural resources were located, but also undermining of the state's economic policies by the emergence of the black market trade with bordering countries.
69. Cf. the experience of the Asian NIEs outlined in Frederic C. Deyo, "Coalitions, Institutions, and Linkage Sequencing: Toward a Strategic Capacity Model of East Asian Development", in *The Political Economy of the New Asian Industrialism*, edited by Frederic C. Deyo (Ithaca and London: Cornell University Press, 1987), pp. 227–47.
70. Joel S. Migdal, "The State in Society: An Approach to Struggles for Domination", in *State Power and Social Forces*, edited by Migdal, Kohli and Shue, p. 27.
71. Shue, "State Power and Social Organization", p. 71; emphasis is original. For a penetrating insight of BSPP politics, see Tin Aung Hein. "Myanmar Naingan Ei Nainganyei Sipwayei Simunkhantgweyei Luhmuyei Hnint Tayasiyinyei Keissa Myar Hnint Sutthlyin Ywei Akyanpyu Tinpyagyet Sardan" [Advisory Report on Myanmar's Political, Economic, Administrative, Social, and Judicial Matters], unpublished report, Yangon, 2 October 1987, pp. 3, 4, 16–17.
72. Keun Lee, *New East Asian Economic Development: Interacting Capitalism and Socialism* (New York: M. E. Sharpe, 1993), p. 19. A soft budget constraint is the situation in which state enterprises operated under budgetary support from the central government that obviates the need to be financially robust and independent.
73. See, for example, Seddon and Belton-Jones, "Political Determinants of Economic Flexibility", pp. 355–60; and Mari Pangestu, "Managing Economic Policy Reforms in Indonesia", in *Authority and Academic Scribblers: The Role of Research in East Asian Policy Reform* (San Francisco: ICS Press, 1991), pp. 93–120.
74. See, for example, Schnieder, "The *Desarrollista* State", pp. 291–97.
75. See, Walinsky, *Economic Development in Burma*, pp. 218–36.
76. See, for example, Institute of Asian Economic Affairs [Tokyo], *Economic Development in Burma*, translated by U.S. Joint Publications Research Service (Washington, D.C.: Joint Publications Research Service, 1962; reproduction, New York, CCM Information Corporation, n.d), pp. 56–57.
77. See, for example, Khin Maung Kyi, "Patterns of Accommodation to Bureaucratic Authority in a Transitional Culture (A Sociological Analysis of Burmese Bureaucrats with Respect to Their Orientations Toward Authority)" (Ph.D. dissertation, Cornell University, 1966), pp. 91, 95–96, 103–106, 112–16, 124.
78. See, for example, San Nyein and Mya Han, *Myanma Nainganyei Sanitpyaung Karla (1962-1974)* [Myanmar's Politics in the Period of Systemic Change], Vol. 2 (Yangon: Historical Research Department, 1993), p. 16.

79. Personal experience of the writer during his stint at the office of the deputy prime minister cum planning minister (1973–79).
80. Leftwich, "Bringing Politics Back In", p. 415.
81. Naomi Chazan, "Engaging the State: Associational Life in Sub-Saharan Africa", in *State Power and Social Forces*, edited by Migdal, Kohli and Shue, p. 256. It is sometimes argued that such elements should be included in the definition for Myanmar and also pointed out they could evolve and/or transform into social movements under propitious circumstances. See, for example, Kyaw Yin Hlaing, "Burma: Civil Society Skirting Regime Rules", in *Civil Society and Political Change in Asia*, edited by Muthiah Alagappa (Stanford, CA: Stanford University Press, 2004), pp. 389–418.
82. Ibid., p. 255.
83. Leftwich, "Bringing Politics Back In", p. 416. For Myanmar, see Taylor, *State in Burma*, pp. 267–68.
84. See Taylor, "Disaster or Release?", pp. 60–61.
85. For details, see Mya Han, et. al. *Myanma Nainnganyei Sanitpyaung Karla (1962-1974)* [Myanmar's Politics in the Period of Systemic Change], Vol. 1 (Yangon: Universities Press, 1993), pp. 51–56, 138–280.
86. Chazan, "Engaging the State", p. 278. For a case study on the absence of civil society in Myanmar, see David I. Steinberg, "A Void in Myanmar: Civil Society in Burma", in *Strengthening Civil Society in Burma: Possibilities and Dilemmas for International NGOs*, edited by Tom Kramer and Pietje Vervest (Chiangmai: Silkworm Books, 1999), pp. 1–14.
87. Leftwich, "Bringing Politics Back In", p. 416.
88. Catherine Boone, "States and Ruling Classes in Postcolonial Africa: The Enduring Contradictions of Power", in *State Power and Social Forces*, edited by Migdal, Kohli and Shue, p. 129.
89. See, for example, Leftwich, "Bringing Politics Back In", pp. 418–19.
90. Johnson, "Developmental State", p. 53.
91. See, for example, James Guyot, "*Burma in 1988: Perestroika* with a Military Face", in *Southeast Asian Affairs 1989* (Singapore: Institute of Southeast Asian Studies, 1989), pp. 125, 129–30.
92. Gary Gereffi, "Paths of Industrialization: An Overview", in *Manufacturing Miracles: Paths of Industrialization in Latin America and East Asia*, edited by Gary Gereffi and Donald L. Wyman (Princeton: Princeton University Press, 1990), p. 22.
93. Ibid., p. 23.
94. There is a vast and expanding literature that extols the virtues of "free markets", "right prices", liberal trade regimes, and EOI. A short summary of this so-called "Washington consensus" (named after the World Bank and the IMF, its principal advocates) may be found in Danny M. Leipziger and Vinod Thomas, "Roots of East Asia's Success", *Finance and Development* (March 1994): 6–9.

95. This topic generated a fast expanding body of writings that blossomed in the late 1980s. The first wave of studies was concerned with the policy processes in Japan, Taiwan and Korea. Studies of Southeast Asian states appeared in the second wave with no end in sight. A summary of the main arguments in the form of a critique of the neoclassical stand may be found in Research Institute of Development Assistance (RIDA), the Overseas Economic Cooperation Fund (OECF), *The World Bank's East Asian Miracle Report: Its Strengths and Limitations*, OECF Discussion Papers No. 7 (Tokyo: RIDA/OECF, 1995).
96. See, for example, Ranis, "Another Look at the East Asian Miracle".
97. Chowdhury and Islam, *Newly Industrializing Economies*, pp. 55–56; quoted by Killick in RIDA/OECF, pp. 126–27.
98. Tony Killick, "Relevance, Meaning and Determinants of Flexibility", in *The Flexible Economy*, edited by Killick, p. 18.
99. This suppression of financial markets and excessive central control over financial services is not uncommon in post-colonial regimes of countries which had undergone colonial exploitation (see Hill, *Southeast Asian Economic Development*, p. 35).
100. Bruce Cummings, "Webs with No Spiders, Spiders with No Webs: The Genealogy of the Developmental State", in *The Developmental State*, edited by Woo-Cummings, p. 70.
101. All this came to a head in 1988 when the deterrence of coercive power broke down in the absence of performance legitimacy.
102. Seddon and Belton-Jones, "Political Determinants of Economic Flexibility", p. 325.
103. This observation is based on conversation with senior citizens and military officers who were close to those at the power centres of all three periods.
104. Hirschman, "Ideology as a System Determinant", p. 292.
105. Ibid., p. 293.
106. Cf. Stephen A. Quick, "The Paradox of Popularity: Ideological", Program Implementation in Zambia", in *Politics and Policy Implementation in the Third World*, edited by Merilee S. Grindle (Princeton: Princeton University Press, 1980), p. 42.
107. Hirschman, "Ideology as a System Determinant", p. 297.
108. Jei, "Comparative Politics of Economic Development", p. 71.
109. Ibid., pp. 69–70. Here stability means price stability.
110. For elaboration of the dominant views in developmental thinking during the 1945–70 period, see, for example, Reynolds, "Government and Economic Growth", pp. 233–37. In fact, premier Nu became disenchanted with *dirigisme* by the late 1950s but he neither had the political will nor the time to redress the situation as internecine struggles erupted in the ruling party and political instability ensued (see, for example, Nu, *Saturday's Son*, pp. 218–19).

111. Alexander Neuber, "Adapting the Economies of Eastern Europe: Behavioural and Institutional Aspects of Flexibility", in Killick, *The Flexible Economy*, p. 118.
112. Attributed to Oliver Williams, quoted in ibid.
113. See, for example Barbara Lee and John Nellis, *Enterprise Reform and Privatization in Socialist Economies*, World Bank Discussion Paper, no. 104 (Washington, D.C.: World Bank, 1990).
114. See Merilee S. Grindle, "The Political Economy of Economic Policy Reforms: Lessons for Policymakers", *Strategic Papers* (Institute for International and Strategic Studies, Manila) 4 no. 4 (1992), pp. 4–6.
115. Ibid., p. 6.
116. Ibid., p. 7.
117. For details, see Chapter 6; and *Naingandaw Ei Sipwayei Hsaingyar Muwada Myar Hnint Lunhnyunhmu Myar Pyupyin Pyaungleiyei Hnint Pathet Ywei Tinpyagyek* [Report on Reforming National Economic Policies and Guidelines] (Yangon: Burma Socialist Programme Party, 1988).
118. Toye, *Dilemmas of Development*, p. 86. See also p. 69.
119. See, for example, *FEER*, 8 October 1982, pp. 79–80; World Bank, "Burma: Policies and Prospects for Economic Adjustment and Growth", Washington, D.C., South Asia Programs Department (18 November 1985), Report no. 4814-BA, pp. 27, 33–34, 39–53, 63; and International Monetary Fund (IMF), "Burma: Recent Economic Developments", Washington, D.C. (20 May 1987), passim.
120. Personal communications with planning officials.
121. It is doubtful whether even a concerted attempt by donors to exert pressure for radical policy changes would have succeeded in the face of government intransigence. An adverse reaction in which Myanmar would forgo the ODA and resume its isolationist stance was equally likely. See, for example, Steinberg's comment on the leadership style of Ne Win (David I. Steinberg, "Japanese Economic Assistance to Burma: Aid in the 'Tarenagashi' Manner?", *Crossroads* 5, no. 2 [1990]: 82) whose contempt for any foreign interference is well known.
122. Contrary to other Japanese aid recipients with more open economies Myanmar's inward-oriented socialist economy did not avail itself the opportunity for Japan to reap benefits in terms of expanded trade and investments. Nevertheless, "the Japanese aid program accounted for a major element in Japanese exports to Burma" (ibid., p. 77).
123. Ibid., p. 67; see, also, pp. 68–69, 82.
124. Edgardo Boeninger, "Economic Policy Change and Government Processes", in *Managing Policy Reform in the Real World: Asian Experiences*, edited by Geoffrey Lamb and Rachel Weaving (Washington, D.C.: World Bank, 1992), p. 15; see also pp. 18–19.
125. Anecdotal evidence suggests that the 1987 demonetization was instigated by him (The deputy finance minister and the central bank chairman were

reportedly unaware of the announcement; personal communications with knowledgeable observers). His extreme aversion to currency devaluation and mistrust of private entrepreneurs were also well known among Myanmar's policy circles.

126. See, for example, Steinberg, "Japanese Economic Assistance", p. 82.
127. See his speech to the BSPP Central Committee (*WPD*, 10 October 1987).
128. Kyi May Kaung, "Theories, Paradigms, or Models in Burma Studies", *Asian Survey* (November 1995), pp. 1037–38.
129. It is doubtful whether even if a reform package similar to the one of July 1988 were to be announced by the end of 1987, it would have saved the socialist regime *a la* China. It took the next regime seven years to regain 1984/85 real GDP even after abandoning the BWS and instituting an "open door" policy. Perhaps a better timing would be at the beginning of the Fifth Four-Year Plan in early 1986.
130. R. William Liddle, "Soeharto's Indonesia: Personal Rule and Political Institution", *Pacific Affairs* 58, no. 1 (1985): 404.
131. The fall of Soeharto in May 1998 and the concomitant Indonesia economic crisis do not negate Indonesia's sate-led developmental achievements in the 1980s and early 1990s. The problem seems to be that Indonesia in the mid-1990s increasingly regressed from a developmental state orientation towards a quasi-predatory state model under a "Sultanist" regime. See, for example, Hadi Soesastro, "Governance and the Crisis in Indonesia", in *Reform and Recovery in East Asia: The Role of the State and Economic Enterprise*, edited by Peter Drysdale (London: Routledge, 2000), pp. 120–46; Evans, *Embedded Autonomy*, pp. 12, 50; and H. E. Chehabi and Juan J. Linz, "A Theory of Sultanism: A Type of Nondemocratic Rule", in *Sultanistic Regimes*, edited by H. E. Chehabi and Juan J. Linz (Baltimore: John Hopkins University Ptress, 1998), pp. 3–25.
132. Toye, *Dilemmas of Development*, p. 146.

Part V

Military in Charge

9

Dual Transition under Military Rule: The State Prevails

> The weak state combined with competitive markets is James Buchanan's heaven; the strong state combined with atomistic markets is Deepak Lal's heaven; the weak state combined with monopolistic markets is Mancur Olson's hell; the strong state combined with monopolistic market[s] is Douglas North's hell.[1]

The political system of Myanmar had changed four times during the twentieth century. In 1948 it changed from a colonial political system that allowed limited "home rule" to a parliamentary democracy system of majoritarian rule that mimicked the Westminster model. After the military coup of 2 March 1962, the country was ruled by decree as the ruling Revolutionary Council (RC) assumed executive, judicial, and legislative powers. From January 1974 until the military coup of 18 September 1988, a one-party socialist system that professed "democratic centralism" was in place. Thereafter, Myanmar's political system reverted back to that in which the military junta known as the State Law and Order Restoration Council (SLORC) exercised executive, legislative, and judicial powers. The military regime which has been conflated with the state appears to be determined to "bring the state back in" to play a domineering role after the latter's near-collapse in the upheaval of 1988.[2]

In this latest round of regime change, the ruling military junta (re-established as the State Peace and Development Council, or SPDC, on 15 November 1997) has been managing a dual transition towards "multi-party electoral democracy" and a market-oriented economic system. A challenging task made more difficult because the junta's legitimacy and authority have been contested, since its inception, not only by the legally constituted political opposition and a constellation of illegal or unlawful organizations, insurgents, and expatriate groups, but also by some Western states and non-governmental organizations (NGOs) as well.[3]

THE ONGOING POLITICAL TRANSITION

After over six weeks of public demonstrations, which turned violent at times, the state apparatus became paralysed as unrest spread from Yangon to major cities and towns all over the country.[4] In the words of Dr Maung Maung, the last President and Party Chairman of the BSPP era, the "government, being defunct, was redundant" as central administration broke down.[5] In the evening of 18 September the military stepped in and took over state power by forming a junta of senior commanders led by the defence minister cum armed forces chief General Saw Maung.[6] Restoration of law and order, preserving peace and tranquillity, facilitating smooth transportation and communications, and providing decent livelihood for the public were the professed objectives of the junta which promised to hold "multi-party democracy general elections" once these objectives had been accomplished.[7]

The four political objectives enunciated by SLORC have been adopted by the SPDC as well. They entail:

- stability of the state, community peace and tranquillity, prevalence of law and order;
- national reconsolidation;
- emergence of a new enduring state constitution; and
- building of a new modern developed nation in accordance with the new state constitution.

The realization of the fourth objective appears to have been premised upon the attainment of the first three goals. Thus, the politics should be subordinate to these four objectives that represent higher national objectives, in contrast to what is perceived as narrow self-serving "party politics" that characterized political parties.[8]

In the subsequent restructuring of the state by SLORC/SPDC in the context of the establishing "multi-party democracy", the junta which is playing the role of the *formateur* of democratic transition has envisaged a symbiotic relationship between the Tatmadaw (Myanmar's armed forces) and the state under the forthcoming constitution.

The Tatmadaw, as the most powerful and enduring institution in independent Myanmar, has played a dominant role in shaping the political contours of Myanmar and has developed an ethos not dissimilar to the Praetorian tradition. The 1945-generation of military leaders led by (retired) General Ne Win, who made their mark during the anti-fascist revolution against the Japanese in 1945, had fashioned a military tradition extending beyond national defence requirements and bordering on the political. This inculcation of the dual function concept within the Myanmar military that incorporates both the security and the public affairs dimensions has enabled it to assume a corporate identity as the guarantor as well as the embodiment of state authority. It entails that the Tatmadaw be not only an instrument but also a determinant of state power. The military's penchant for perceiving stark dichotomies in critical issues and its natural affinity towards unity, order, stability and conformity, have probably led its current leaders (belonging to the post-1945 generation) to view the path of democratic evolution in the first decade of Myanmar's independence as chaotic and retrogressive. As such, it has conceived its role as safeguarding the state not only from those committed to destroy Myanmar but also from the perceived folly of the politicians whose ineptitude and disunity ostensibly present a clear and present danger.[9]

Upholding the tradition of the Tatmadaw as national saviour, the military junta is determined to ensure that the transition to democratic rule would not compromise the three principal "main national causes" that it had professed to safeguard under all circumstances. Defined as "non-disintegration of the Union, non-disintegration of national [i.e. multi-racial] solidarity, and perpetuation of national sovereignty", these formed the framework for the overwhelming emphasis on controls and regulations to ensure unity, order and stability in the context of a "strong state". Furthermore, a "firm" constitution is deemed to be a precondition for a stable multi-party political environment, in which indigenized rules of "multi-party democracy" presumably appropriate to Myanmar's conditions can be formulated according to the military's vision of the Myanmar state.[10]

Towards Elections

After the coup, SLORC Chairman General Saw Maung stated that the military would not "cling to state power for a long period". On the other hand SLORC Secretary 1, Major General Khin Nyunt declared on 12 April 1990 that "the military would remain in office after the elections until a new constitution was drafted and a 'strong' government was formed".[11] A large number of political parties emerged, numbering 235 at the close of registration on 28 February 1989.[12] The Pyithu Hluttaw Election Law was promulgated by SLORC on 31 May 1989, and the election commission that was established on 11 September 1988 by the parliament of the BSPP era was retained by SLORC to oversee the elections.

Although 492 single-seat constituencies were established, only 485 were contested in the elections held on 27 May 1990, because of logistical and time constraints in the seven remaining constituencies. There were 2,209 candidates representing 93 parties and 87 independants.[13] The turnout was 72.6 per cent and 12.3 per cent of the total votes became null and void due to irregularities. The independants won six seats while 27 parties won 479 seats in what was generally agreed to be tightly controlled but fair elections. The National League for Democracy (NLD) won 392 seats and claimed victory.[14]

While election results were being meticulously processed, the victorious parties led by NLD pressed for a prompt power transfer. SLORC responded by announcing its Declaration No. 1/90 on 27 July 1990 that precluded immediate power transfer.[15] In essence, the junta's declaration meant that there would be no transfer of power until a proper constitution was drafted and ratified and the role of the successful election candidates was not to form a government but to participate in the National Convention (NC) that would draft an "enduring" constitution. As such, the 1990 elections did not lead to the formation of a government by the winning party and the implementation of the election results has become a bone of contention between the junta and its political detractors.[16]

Aftermath: The Impasse

The deliberations of the National Convention (NC) commenced on 9 January 1993. The NC's objectives include instituting the military "to participate in the national political leadership role of the future state". They also entail the upholding of the trinity of "main national causes".[17]

After several recesses the NC reached a conclusion regarding the fundamental outlines of the constitutional principles. Principles underlying state structure, administrative configuration, and political representation were subsequently distilled by the junta-appointed steering committee from the various proposals put forward during the proceedings. By September 1993, a detailed set of 104 "basic principles" endorsed by the National Convention Convening Committee (NCCC) had been established as a basis for future deliberations.[18]

The NLD party, which became the embodiment of its secretary-general Daw Aung San Suu Kyi's ideas and goals (as the latter rapidly gained widespread popularity helped by the image of her father General Aung San, who was the hero of the independence movement and the "founding father" of the Myanmar armed forces), initially took part in the NC. The party's delegates walked out of the convention in November 1995, ostensibly due to dissatisfaction with the conduct of the proceedings, and were subsequently expelled for breach of discipline. Thereafter, relations between the government and the NLD leadership became fraught with difficulties thereby resulting in a political impasse that remains until the present day. The NC went into an eight-year recess after April 1996 though the steering committee continued to sit frequently for deliberations. No official explanation was given but there have been hints that the inability to reach a consensus on the issue of autonomy for national races had been the main reason.[19]

Until late 2000, the top leadership of the NLD remained uncompromising in its challenge to the ruling SPDC. This continued despite the fact that many of its township organizing committees had publicly declared their dissolution and individual members had resigned from the party, ostensibly over the confrontational stance and intransigent attitude of the party leadership. Tens of thousands of members had reportedly left the party and scores of townships executive committees had ceased to exist. It appeared that neither admonitions by advocates of human rights and democracy (including the UN Commission for Human Rights), limited sanctions and arms embargo by certain Western states and groupings (prominently, the United States, the European Union, the Scandinavian countries, and the International Labour Organization) and withholding of development assistance (by the World Bank, Asian Development Bank, Japan and Britain, among others) nor friendly persuasion by regional states and intercession of the UN Secretary General (who appointed a special envoy), managed to break the impasse between the military regime and the NLD.

However, a glimmer of hope dawned in January 2001 when it was revealed that secret talks between the NLD leader Daw Aung San Suu Kyi, who was under virtual house arrest, and representatives of the junta had been going on since October 2000. Apparently, the UN special envoy Mr Razali Ismail had been instrumental in breaking the ice.[20] Despite occasional rumours that the talks had broken down, both sides had maintained throughout 2001 that the dialogue process was continuing.

The ruling junta promoted its members just after the fourteenth anniversary of the coup (18 September 1988) that brought back direct military rule in Myanmar. The junta vice-chair and army chief General Maung Aye was promoted to a newly created rank of deputy senior general, Secretary-1 and military intelligence chief Lt. General Khin Nyunt was upgraded to full general, while the ten junta members who had relinquished their regional commands in November 2001 became Lieutenant Generals. Many more command and staff positions were upgraded in rank as well. Commentators interpreted this promotion exercise as indicating an attempt to ensure corporate loyalty within the military leadership during an important phase in the regime's programme of managed political transition. Optimists viewed it as a positive step towards ensuring unity of purpose for the professed political reforms while pessimists saw it as further consolidation of the military's grip and the enhancement of the top leader's authority.

The release of the *de facto* opposition leader Daw Aung San Suu Kyi from 19 months of house arrest on 6 May 2002 was hailed by all those who were interested in the unfolding political events in Myanmar. The military regime (without referring to Daw Aung San Suu Kyi's release) portrayed that day as marking the "turning of a new page" and promised to allow "citizens to participate freely in" Myanmar's "political process" albeit with priority given to "national unity, peace and stability". Daw Aung San Suu Kyi herself took a conciliatory stance in the first press conference on the very same day and stated that the confidence-building phase was over and a channel had been opened. In the four months after her release she made several unprecedented visits to aid projects sponsored by NGOs and NLD offices in Yangon and its environs as well as three trips to other towns and cities. She was allowed to meet the visiting foreign ministers from Japan and Australia in the following few months. Meanwhile, dozens of NLD activists and other dissidents were released from prisons in several batches and there were some more reopenings of the NLD offices (virtually all closed down during the 1998–2000 period but were allowed to reopen since June 2001). Those developments gave rise to widespread speculation in the first few weeks of her freedom that a breakthrough in reconciliation between the junta and the NLD would soon be forthcoming which did not happen.

Apparently, no further "dialogue" between Daw Aung San Suu Kyi and the government seemed to have occurred in the second half of 2002, with various government spokesman and ministers indicating that the government was in no hurry to resume the secret talks.

On the other hand, Daw Aung San Suu Kyi called for the release of all political prisoners and insisting that substantive discussion of policy matters must begin soon. Though she repeatedly promised that she would be flexible and was willing to cooperate with the government for the good of the polity she also insisted that without changes that would benefit the people her release amount to nothing. She insisted on accelerated change and she appeared to be holding a position still at odds with the junta's perspective on a managed political transition.

As this "dialogue process" became the locus of Myanmar's political transition and the focus of attendant international attention, a series of tactical moves by the government and the NLD to outwit each other in the political game ensued. This resulted in a political impasse that persisted throughout the second half of 2002 and continued into the first quarter of 2003. Meanwhile the frustrated NLD leaders shifted their focus to organizing tours of the countryside by Daw Aung San Suu Kyi soon after her release. Consequently, tensions between NLD supporters and pro-government detractors rose rapidly in the course of these tours which increasingly seemed to resemble boisterous NLD campaign rallies. Unfortunately, Daw Aung San Suu Kyi's tour of upper Myanmar in May 2003 was violently interrupted in a deadly confrontation between her entourage of activists and supporters and a mob of detractors on the night of 30 May 2003 in Depeyin Township. As a result, Daw Aung San Suu Kyi and the accompanying party leaders were taken into protective custody while many of her supporters were also detained.

There was an international outcry led by the exiled opposition groups and Western governments over the so-called Black Friday clash and the subsequent incarceration of the NLD leaders and followers in general and Daw Aung San Suu Kyi in particular. Although the government was able to disprove the rumour that Daw Aung San Suu Kyi was hurt and explained that her detention at an undisclosed location was of a "temporary" nature to safeguard her, calls for immediate release of the NLD leadership ensued from the international community, with the exception of China (which refused to comment on "internal affairs" of a sovereign state). Even ever-friendly ASEAN (the Association of Southeast Asian Nations; that has disavowed interfering in the internal affairs of its member states), in the joint communiqué of the 36th ASEAN Ministerial Meeting (16–17 June 2003), mentioned that "recent political developments in Myanmar, particularly the incident of 30 May 2003" were discussed at the forum and "urged Myanmar to resume its efforts of national reconciliation and dialogue among all parties concerned leading to a peaceful transition to democracy". Many ASEAN members were concerned that as a consequence of Western hostility to the regime in relation to what the latter perceived as untoward repression of the NLD and gross injustice against Daw Aung San Suu Kyi, ASEAN's collective image would suffer and the "Myanmar issue" would become a "distraction" impeding ASEAN's close cooperation with its Western dialogue partners. Western nations roundly condemned the junta and the United States (which had already banned new investments since 1997) imposed further punitive measures on Myanmar that included an imports ban and financial restriction on state-owned banks while the European Union (EU) expanded the visa ban on state officials.

The junta seemed to be oblivious to international criticisms and manifold appeals by friends and foe alike to release Daw Aung San Suu Kyi and her colleagues. It took the apparent crisis in stride and turned it into an opportunity to raise the tempo of its moribund process of managed transition towards a "disciplined democracy" by instituting a major Cabinet shakeup in which the junta Secretary-1, General Khin Nyunt was appointed as the prime minister, a position previously held by the SPDC Chairman Senior General Than Shwe (who retained his defence portfolio). Though there were much speculation over whether this was a "demotion" or "promotion" for the General widely regarded as the third-ranked leader of Myanmar (later seen by some in the West as an enlightened "moderate") it may, in fact, be regarded as a *de jure* confirmation of what has all along been a *de facto* situation in the political governance of Myanmar.

The Road Map

In the wake of economically damaging sanctions and adverse media publicity in the West, the junta launched a strategic offensive against its detractors by revealing the "road map" as the major thrust of the "future policies and programme of the state". Prime Minister General Khin Nyunt announced a seven-point road map on 30 August 2003 in an address on "Developments and Progressive Changes in Myanmar Naing-Ngan" to a large assembly of state executives, academics and representatives of academia and NGOs. General Khin Nyunt, in his speech that delineated the contours of the road map, blamed the opposition NLD (which walked out of the NC in November 1995 apparently in protest against alleged orchestration of and interventions in the proceedings by the authorities concerned) for carrying out a plan "aimed at destroying" the NC by placing "the attitude and wishes of an individual" and putting the party's own "interests" "above the national cause", as a consequence of which "efforts for political development have faltered at half-way point." (*New Light of Myanmar* [hereafter cited as *NLM*], 31 August 2003). He promised that the government would implement a seven-step "political programme" for "building the nation" which entails:

- Reconvening the NC.
- After successful conclusion of the NC, "a step by step implementation of the process necessary for the emergence of a genuine and disciplined democratic system".
- Drafting a new constitution according to the basic principles and details "laid down" by the NC.
- A national referendum to adopt the constitution.
- Holding of "free and fair elections" for a hierarchy (national and regional) of legislative bodies or Pyithu Hluttaws (people's assemblies) as per the new constitution.
- Convening of the Hluttaw as per the constitution.
- "Building a modern, developed and democratic nation by the state leaders elected by the Hluttaw" together with the "government and other central organs [of state power] formed by the Hluttaw". (ibid.).[21]

Not surprisingly, the regime's detractors were dismissive of this road map, pointing out that it had no time line and argued that it was a stalling tactic, whereby the junta's old political line was repackaged and rescheduled to deflect criticisms from its detractors and allay the fears of the neighbouring states and ASEAN who had been concerned about the regional repercussions of a protracted political crisis in Myanmar.

Although many critics tended to think that the recent Cabinet changes and this idea of a road map (hailed by China and Thailand) were reactions by the junta to the domestic and international repercussions of the Black Friday clash, it seemed more likely that they were part of a well thought-out sequence to prepare the military for the long haul in managing Myanmar's political transition towards a unitary state dominated by the military establishment. A process of military leadership renewal, which is integral to the aforementioned end, that began with the major Cabinet reshuffle in November 2001 and the subsequent military reshuffle that brought all regional commanders who were also SPDC members to Yangon with promotions was further instituted by appointing the Adjutant General as SPDC's Secretary-2 in February 2003 and his elevation to Secreatry-1 upon Khin Nyunt becoming prime minister on 25 August 2003 together with the appointment of the Quartermaster General to the post of Secretary-2 appear to be part of this process as well.

Subsequently, the NCCC (with Secretary-2 as Chair) was established in September 2003. As the first step of the road map, the National Convention (NC) assigned with the task of drafting the detailed principles of a new state constitution was reconvened with much fanfare on 17 May 2004 after an eight-year suspension.

Despite earlier indications that the party would be willing to participate provided the NC started on a clean slate and the detained General Secretary Daw Aung San Suu Kyi as well as Vice-Chairman U Tin Oo were released, the NLD boycotted the NC, claiming that its demands were not met by the government. The Shan National League for Democracy (SNLD, a key NLD ally that won the second largest number of seats in the 1990 election) and the United Nationalities Alliance (UNA, a grouping constituting elected ethnic representatives whose parties were deregistered) also stayed out of the NC. The Shan State Kokang Democratic Party was also absent.

Nevertheless, 1,076 out of the 1,088 registered delegates attended the opening session, representing eight officially designated groupings: viz., political parties, elected representatives (from the 1990 general election); national races (ethnic groups); peasants; workers; intellectuals and intelligentsia; public service personnel (including military); and "other invited" persons (mainly from twenty-three ceasefire groups). The expanded roster of the NC (55 per cent more than that in the last sitting from 1993 to 1996) and the large proportion of ethnic representatives (nearly 60 per cent of the delegates and nearly thrice the strength of the cohort in the last sitting) was lauded by the government's supporters who hailed the NC was hailed as a "historic milestone" in Myanmar's political history. On the other hand, detractors in the opposition camp deplored the absence of the NLD and its ethnic allies and alleged that the NC was a "sham" exercise replete with gag orders, restrictive regulations and top-down "instructions" to guide the process. Those hoping for a *tabula rasa* approach were also disappointed to hear, in the opening speech of the NCCC Chairman, Secretary-2 of the junta, that the current NC was a continuation of the work done in the last exercise that had laid down the much-maligned set of "104 basic principles" that were perceived by the opposition as undemocratic and heavily biased in favour of the military's continued dominance.

The NC was adjourned on 9 July after all the delegate groups had tabled their respective proposals in response to the detailed principles on the sharing of legislative, executive and judicial powers drawn by the National Convention Convening Work Committee (NCCWC). The Chief Justice, in his capacity as the NCCWC Chairman, stated in his closing speech that the recess would enable the delegates to "carry out their business and social tasks" left unattended when they joined the NC, while the "panel of alternate chairmen" processed their proposals. No firm date for the resumption was initially given except for some references to an "open season" and conclusion of harvesting (*NLM*, 10 July 2004). The authorities concerned stated that "positive results" were achieved before recess. Meanwhile, opposition circles claimed that a caucus comprising a significant number of ethnic ceasefire groups had called for more transparency in the proceedings and a better deal for them in terms of autonomy and resource allocations, thereby creating some turbulence that marred the smooth sailing anticipated by the authorities.

When General Khin Nyunt abruptly retired citing "health" reasons on 19 October followed by revelations from the ruling circle that "insubordination", corruption and dereliction of duty were the real reasons, many observers opined that NC and the seven-point road map to "disciplined democracy", which appeared to be his brainchild, would be compromised. However, the new prime minister (previously the junta's Secretary-1) as well as the newly promoted (from Secretary-2) Secretary-1 who was also the NCCC Chair had quickly asserted that both the NC and the road map stemmed from the SPDC's collective decision-making and would continue to serve their purpose.

Some ministers and deputy ministers believed to be close to the deposed prime minister were also dismissed and the military intelligence apparatus commanded by General Khin Nyunt was quickly dismantled and its top officers were prosecuted. It was eventually replaced by a new bureau for military security affairs under the command of an army commander from outside the intelligence community.[22]

The NC resumed again on 17 February 2005 and went into recess on 31 March 2005. The NCCC Chair, in his concluding address, gave the following reasons for the adjournment "until the end of [the] year": to give the members of the panel of chairmen "enough time to compile their studies", to "enable the delegates to continue their businesses and attend to social affairs" and because "the weather is getting hot" (*NLM*, 1 April 2005).

Meanwhile, the NLD, displaced from the mainstream political process and deprived of the top leadership, has resorted to the traditional liberal democratic tactics of signature campaigns (to free its leaders), issuing demands (to the authorities), articulating appeals (to the UN and advanced democracies of the West) and organizing commemorative gatherings that cut no ice with the authorities and have little impact on the polity. It is increasingly being marginalized and is in danger of being overtaken by events in the near future unless it could find creative solutions to increase capacity, enhance credibility, and renew its ageing leadership, in the face of massive constraints.[23]

On the international front, the United States and EU remain unconvinced that Myanmar had progressed in the areas of human rights, forced labour, human trafficking, religious freedom, child soldiers, and narcotics eradication, despite the government's immense efforts to prove otherwise. Furthermore, the continued detention of Aung San Sun Kyi and alleged persecution of the NLD remain a most contentious issue, and Western sanctions have been extended and bilateral and multilateral official development assistance (ODA) continue to be denied by the United States, EU, Japan and influential Western governments.

However, regional cooperation and support have more than compensated for the negative impact of Western sanctions, which, thus far, remained unabated. The military regime appeared to be confident that it could ride out the storm of Western sanctions with the help of neighbouring states and increased exploitation of its natural resources. Ironically, Myanmar's fledgling modern market-oriented urban sectors such as manufacturing, banking and external trading are bearing the brunt of those sanctions. On the other hand, Myanmar still has sufficient counterpoise in the form of food security, relatively productive rural agricultural sector, natural resources and the informal sector that enables the economy to subsist at a low level of equilibrium. This, in turn, allows it to withstand the overall impact of Western punitive measures. Possessing a very high pain threshold, it is highly unlikely that the regime would give in to the West's pressures in the near future. It may even be counterproductive, as the self-reliance mentality would be further reinforced. As for the road map, the junta (as of mid-2005) appeared to be ready to forge ahead at its own pace and if its explanation for forfeiting the right to take the ASEAN Chair in 2006 could be taken at face value, it seemed determined to move forward to the next phase of writing the new constitution in 2006 and stage a referendum in the near future.[24]

Whether Myanmar's military rulers could successfully manage the political transition towards constitutional governance in accordance with their professed road map and achieve an enduring national unity would, by and large, depend upon how the following issues could be amicably settled amongst all the stakeholders:

- equitable centre–periphery relations;
- rebirth of civil society and institutional pluralism;
- growth of alternative avenues of political and social mobility;
- furtherance of impersonal and impersonally administered (rule of) law;
- dispute settlement and adjudication by an independent judiciary; and
- unfettered intellectual inquiry and elimination of mandated orthodoxy.[25]

Given the asymmetric power and resource relationships between the regime and its detractors, which considerably favour the former, the eventual political change is likely to occur through a slow process of "regime transformation" as suggested by Steinberg[26] rather than "regime change" as advocated by the military's opponents.

THE ECONOMY IN TRANSITION

The economy inherited by SLORC when it came to power was in a recession but the structural conditions were very much different from the typical centrally planned economy in which agriculture was collectivized and the state's penetration of industrial society was almost total. Hyperinflation was not present and foreign debt was not unmanageable though the national currency (kyat) was not convertible.[27]

Myanmar did not have a huge ailing state-owned industrial sector, whose restructuring would deprive the livelihood of a substantial portion of the nation's labour force. Nor did it have an elaborate command economy — with its maze of state-controlled input-output linkages, subsidies, and distributive networks — which on dismantling would result in unacceptable deprivation leading to social unrest. As depicted in Chapter 6, the Myanmar economy, for all practical purposes, had been a financially repressed mixed agriculture-based economy with state-controlled foreign trade (albeit with considerable leakage through the black market) and no formal role and little economic space for private enterprises. The government was dependent on ODA for much of its developmental expenditures. On the other hand, the state had been committed to central planning and the steady expansion of the public sector. Its preference for administrative and regulatory policy instruments had created distorted macroeconomic conditions and its neglect of microeconomic principles had resulted in misallocation of resources, inefficiency and low productivity. Short of technology and capital, private enterprises had managed to survive by relying on the parallel or informal economy, whereby the value of its (illegal) foreign trade component alone was estimated to be on par with official trade.[28] The agriculture sector, dependent on small private holdings for production, remained stagnant despite the state's provision of fertilizer subsidies, cultivation loans, rural infrastructure and extension services.

This rather grim economic situation in 1988, seemed amenable to rapid rectification once socialism is abandoned as the organizing principle, the economy is opened up to private initiatives, the bureaucracy is revamped, and the state decides to withdraw its onerous interventions in the economic domain.[29] However, the political economy of market reforms in Myanmar is such that straightforward solutions advocating the primacy of the market and "getting the price right" are not applicable *carte blanche*. Given the nationalist legacy, their interpretation on the nature of the crisis that led to the collapse of the socialist order and the subsequent unsettling political situation, the state managers have been rather weary of relinquishing control over economic functions perceived as essential for maintaining order and stability. On the other hand, the realization that the old system was untenable seems to have created a sense of inevitability and relief in officially embracing the market economy. The result has been a somewhat inchoate notion of the market as a solution to economic ills, at times, bordering on the naivete and a not inconsiderable trepidation towards the ramifications of such a transition. The lingering image of the self-centred private entrepreneur and mistrust of private capital as an instrument of non-state power have manifested in an ambivalent attitude towards the private sector as a whole. The absence of a comprehensive and consistent set of economic reforms in which the role of the state in the new economic setting is clearly delineated in both operational and legal terms exemplified the expediency and opportunistic nature of the transition process in Myanmar. Crucial issues whose resolution should have been an integral part of a well-laid transition programme have not been tackled as a whole at the highest level of authority in a manner befitting their importance in determining the outcome of the ongoing economic transformation. Instead, some have been considered piecemeal by different state agencies with varying levels of influence in the policy-making process while others have been deferred or neglected, resulting in conflicting measures or uncoordinated actions. Issues concerning the form (marketization, corporatization, privatization), pace (gradual, rapid) and direction (in terms of sectors, areas, economic functions) of the economic transition to a market-economy have yet to be delineated, analysed and prioritized.[30]

In reducing state control over the economy, the order and sequencing in the switching of policy instruments from those relying on highly distortionary administrative/discriminatory measures to those associated with less distortionary market-oriented/non-discriminatory measures are important. Similarly, the modalities of substituting opaque discretionary/arbitrary/exclusionary controls, regulations, and procedures with transparent legally constituted/rule ordered/ inclusionary business-oriented rules remain to be clearly spelt out. All of them must be worked out by taking into consideration their social and economic costs as well as their implications on the administrative and decision-making structures of the state. Moreover, as pointed out by a Myanmar economist, "political stability plays an important role in Myanmar's economic and social development", and that requires a compromise non-zero sum solution to the political impasse that has persisted far too long.[31]

At the centre, the same bureaucratic structure responsible for the BSPP's plans had been formulating the annual and short-term (four- and five-year plans) and a thirty-year perspective plan, whose objectives and quantitative targets would be fulfilled by "[m]ass participation and co-operation of the organizations concerned".[32] Meanwhile, civil servants and citizens are constantly exhorted to strive towards plan fulfilment while being vigilant against "subversion" and "the malevolence of neocolonialists". Farmers, traders, and industrialists have been continuously reminded of their obligation to the state and are warned to refrain from excessive greed and profiteering.

Myanmar's economy may be stylistically characterized as a double dual economy. The formalized economy is split into two transaction circuits: one a kyat-based exchange regime and the other a U.S. dollar–denominated regime with the latter influencing the former's supply decisions as well. The informal or parallel component comprises the extensive rural-based quasi-subsistence exchange circuit and the illegal black market sector based mainly on transactions involving gold, precious stones, opium, timber, and other scarce and restricted commodities. They are, of course, interconnected by the cross-flows of money, goods and services with each driven by a different economic logic and operating within different parameters that sometimes overlap. The state is concerned mainly with the formal part and despite occasional forays by the state to control it the informal part generally lies beyond the umbra of state authority, undermining the latter's attempts to manage the transition process.

The formal economy is apparently suffering from the negative consequences of devaluation without actual devaluation since all private sector transactions involving internationally tradable commodities are geared towards the black market rate of exchange (usually pegged to the U.S. dollar). This, in turn, induces high transaction costs for exports while pushing up the price of imports. Prices of domestic products also tend to follow the inflationary exchange rate. Myanmar suffers the worst of both worlds, having denied of the benefits of outright devaluation as well. Inflation is also fuelled by the government's deficit spending that included significant amounts for economic infrastructure as well as non-productive expenditures and for beautification and modernization of the urban landscape and dwellings. Opportunity cost of capital for productive investments, especially in export-oriented manufacturing, is high and most, if not all, potential investors are tempted to pursue short-term gains and to invest in areas beyond the reaches of the tax net. Entrpreneurs are not risk averse but have little confidence in the domestic currency and are anxious about the uncertainty of private sector's future relations with the state.[33] Where political legitimacy is contested, corruption is near endemic, differential privileges are accorded through "connections" rent-seeking is widespread, rent-avoiding is profitable, and ersatz capitalism looms on the horizon, long-term investment in depreciating assets — subject to controls and regulations by the state — seems simply not worth the while for many potential investors.

Reforms and Restructuring: Market Orientation?

It can be said that Myanmar's economic transition process started with the operationalization of cross-border trade that was legalized by the BSPP government in 1987. The promulgation of a rather liberal foreign investment law in December 1988 was the next major step towards liberalization.[34] The former measure was an *ex-post facto* act to plug the considerable drain of revenue and instil some discipline into the rampant black market trade. The latter was an attempt to redress the capital deficiency caused by the cessation of official development assistance (ODA) flows (caused by donor states reaction to the martial law regime following the coup) and to "jump start" the economy through foreign direct investment (FDI).[35]

A slew of institutional, legal and administrative reform measures were introduced over the next fifteen years (see Table 9.1) to expand the private sector, reduce or dismantle state monopolies in the economy, broaden the tax base, improve financial and banking services, streamline state-owned enterprises, and institute privatization.[36] These included the revoking of restrictions in agricultural trade and the relaxing of restrictions on production, milling, storing, transport, marketing, and pricing of major crops. Private foreign trade under licence was allowed, with the exception of several products reserved for state trading.[37] Other measures included: reformulation of corporate procedures; revision of regulations and procedures on domestic and foreign trade; reactivation and reconstitution of chambers of commerce and business associations; and transforming municipal authorities into development committees.

However, earlier reform measures seem to have stopped short of redressing serious shortcomings (see Tables 9.2 and 9.3). There have also been some backsliding since the late 1990s, such as export, import and foreign exchange restrictions, revoking of foreign exchange licences from private banks and expansion of state industrial projects.[38] After warning in 2000 that "unless badly needed reforms are undertaken, the economy will continue to depend heavily on ad hoc policies", the Asian Development Bank stated, in 2005, that the "economy underperforms [in 2004] because of macroeconomic imbalances and structural problems".[39]

TABLE 9.1
Significant Reform Measures In Myanmar

Year	Measure
1988	introduction of Union of Myanmar Foreign Investment Law
1989	decontrol of commodity prices introduction of Fishing Rights of Foreign Vessels Law revocation of the 1965 law that established the socialist economic system regularization of border trade introduction of State-Owned Economic Enterprises Law on the scope of the state sector
1990	introduction of Myanmar Tourism Law allowing 100 per cent retention of exports earnings introduction of Private Industrial Enterprise Law introduction of the Central Bank of Myanmar Law introduction of Financial Institutions of Myanmar Law introduction of Myanmar Agricultural and Rural Development Law introduction of Commercial Tax Law introduction of Myanmar Marine Fisheries Law
1991	initiation of industrial zones in Yangon announcement of the Central Bank of Myanmar Rules and Regulations introduction of Freshwater Fisheries Law introduction of Forest Law introduction of Promotion of Cottage Industries Law reestablishment of Myanmar Chamber of Commerce and Industry
1992	announcement to lease inefficient state-owned factories announcement of denationalization of nationalized saw mills announcement of the establishment of four private banks introduction of Tariff Law introduction of Savings Bank Law
1993	introduction of U.S. dollar–denominated foreign exchange certificate (FEC) introduction of Myanmar Hotel and Tourism Law introduction of Myanmar Insurance Law
1994	introduction of Myanmar Citizens Investment Law introduction of Myanmar Mines Law licensing of representative offices of 11 foreign banks introduction of Science and Technology Development Law

TABLE 9.1 (continued)

1995	announcement of the formation of Privatization Committee announcement of permission for joint-venture between local private banks and foreign banks opening of the licensed foreign exchange centre for FEC trading in Yangon
1996	permission given for local private banks to conduct foreign exchange business and to pay interest on foreign currency deposit establishment of Myanmar Securities Exchange Centre Co. Ltd., a joint venture between Japan's Daiwa Securities and the state-owned Myanma Economic Bank introduction of Computer Science Development Law introduction of Insurance Business Law official rate of exchange for levying custom duties changed to 100 kyat per U.S. dollar (raised to 450 kyat in 2004) accompanied by reduction of tariffs to a fraction of previous values
1997	announcement of paddy procurement through a tender bid system; but never implemented.
1998	announcement of leasing of fallow and virgin land for paddy and cash-crop cultivation or livestock breeding by private entrepreneurs including foreigners
1999	introduction of Law Relating to Overseas Employment
2000	across the board increase of public sector salaries by 5–6 times to be in line with private sector wages; but no official announcement was made.
2003	scrapped compulsory delivery scheme of selling paddy to the state

Note: The data was collated from various issues of state-owned newspapers and relevant government announcements and from *Index of Laws and Rules, Enacted and Promulgated by the State Law and Order Restoration Council and The State Peace and Development Council (1988–1999)* (Yangon: Attorney-General Office, 2000).

TABLE 9.2
Macroeconomic Reforms

1. Fiscal reforms	Weak
Tax reforms	Existing system strengthened
Modern tax system	Several taxes and a narrow tax base; widespread evasion
Subsidies reform	Subsidies continues on a lesser scale; mainly for state employees
2. Monetary reform	Weak
Interest rates liberalization	Some adjustments but administered rates continue with negative real values; central bank rates reduced by 20% in April 1999
Banking system	Central bank under finance ministry; state banks and local private banks; the latter dominated by a few big players
Capital market	Practically non-existent
Exchange rate	Multiple rates exist; grossly overvalued official rate; quantitative controls imposed in 1998; foreign exchange licence of private banks revoked in 1998
3. Trade reforms	Weak
Export/imports controls	Government monopoly of rice, teak and mineral exports; licensing system for private sector; foreign trade restrictions imposed in 1998
Replacement of quantitative restrictions and tariff reductions	Little action on the former but joined ASEAN CEPT

Source: Modified from Pradumna B. Rana and Wilhelmina Paz, "Economies in Transition: The Asian Experience", in *From Reform to Growth: China and Other Countries in Transition in Asia and Central and Eastern Europe*, edited by Chung H. Lee and Helmut Reisen (Paris: OECD, 1994), p. 129, Table 1.

TABLE 9.3
Microeconomic Reforms

1. Price reforms	Moderate adjustments since 1988; controlled prices for staples and raw materials; drastic increase in charges for public utilities, post and telecommunications
2. Agriculture reforms	Moderate; never collectivized; procurement quota reduced since 1988 but continues
3. Non-agri enterprise reforms	Weak
Corporate governance	Weak; low transparency; inadequate and out-of-date data
Promotion of non-state enterprises	Some progress since 1988 but uneven
Privatization of small enterprises	Ongoing; fairly widespread
4. Reforms of the legal framework	Moderate but piecemeal
Corporate law	Pre-war legacy; modified
Property law	Pre-war legacy; little action
Bankruptcy law	Pre-war legacy; little action
Anti-monopoly law	Little action
Foreign investment law	Since November 1988; no major revision
Labour law	Socialist legacy; law for overseas employment introduced but enforcement is weak.

Source: Ibid.

Privatization and State-Owned Enterprises

In many countries (especially post-communist states) privatization of state-owned enterprises (SOEs) "has long been promoted in the belief that it fosters greater economic efficiency and stimulates economic growth"[40] through "the discipline of private ownership as well as to raise revenue without raising taxes".[41] Depending on the overall political and economic environment, modalities of privatization, quality of decision-making and clarity of objectives, varying degrees of success or failure have been observed. However, according to a study done by the Adam Smith Institute in the late 1990s "privatization, in the vast majority of cases" appeared to be "a very successful and beneficial reform for developing and post-communist countries."[42]

In Myanmar, privatization was also introduced, in the early 1990s, as part of the reform package to transform the command economy to a market-oriented system. It began with the leasing of SOEs (known as SEEs or state economic enterprises in Myanmar) to foreign private entrepreneurs and inviting them to form joint ventures with state agencies. This resulted in the leasing of 121 and forming of 18 joint ventures out of the total of 1,767 existing SEEs during the period up to June 1994.[43]

In January 1995, the Myanmar Privatisation Commission (MPC) was formed with Secretary-1 of the ruling SLORC as Chairman and the Minister for National Planning and Economic Development as Secretary and comprising twelve other ministers, attorney-general, auditor-general, and four senior civil servants (SLORC Notification No. 10/95, 9 January 1995). On the same day, the MPC announced that fifty-one SEEs under five ministries would be privatized as the first phase of a systematic privatization programme.[44] Later eight sawmills belonging to the Ministry of Forestry were added to the list for the first phase.

The MPC was vested with wide-ranging powers to facilitate the "transfer of" factories, business enterprises, and other state-owned assets (such as business premises that had been nationalized during the Socialist era) "to the private sector in an orderly phase by phase manner". At the same time, it would "help the private entrepreneurs to acquire business skills", while promoting "the emergence of national economic enterprises in the hands of the national entrepreneurs".[45] It was also mandated to "prevent the monopolization by a private group in the distribution of national wealth" and "to carry out privatisation in the basis of patriotic spirit".[46]

The list of privatization candidates were supplied by the relevant ministries to the MPC which vetted the list and those selected for privatization were then evaluated by a pricing committee (chaired by a deputy minister). Finally, the list would be made public together with floor prices for competitive bidding. In implementing the privatization programme for nationalized enterprises, the "first priority was to 'give back' companies to their original owners when possible".[47] The second priority was to encourage "groups of people or companies to band together to bid for state-owned business",[48] and "[o]nly after this stage could foreign involvement be considered".[49]

Nevertheless, progress in privatization of SEEs was slow and towards the end of the SLORC era (in late 1997), only seven had been sold to the private sector and three more leased out, with twenty-eight transferred to different ministries, and twenty-one remained to be privatized.[50]

When SPDC was formed, in November 1997, to supersede SLORC, the MPC was revitalized and a privatization list of another forty-two factories belonging to four ministries, together with two livestock breeding farms and seventy-six cinema halls, was announced in January 1998. The MPC Chairman, Secretary-1 of the SPDC, called for an effort to "expedite" the process.[51] In the next three years several lists of candidates for privatization (mainly cinema halls, small processing plants, and nationalized business premises) were announced by the MPC. Up to early 2001, altogether "138 assets from eight ministries" had been privatized, thereby "generating more than 2 billion kyat" for the government.[52]

It is noteworthy that 87 out of the total of 138 state assets privatized, in six years since the formation of the MPC, were cinema halls and it also included (an unspecified number of) nationalized business premises. Given that the actual number that had been privatized was still very small in relation to the overall figure of nearly 1,800 SOEs in the mid-1990s the privatization programme appeared to have slowed down towards the end of the century.[53] Furthermore, the absence of a properly functioning share market probably has had negative implications on the distributive aspect of such transfer of assets. In fact, according to Brigadier-General (B.G.) Abel, then Minister of the SPDC Chairman's Office, "identifying and evaluating the worth of" SEEs "that [could] be sold is a laborious process". Moreover, "one of the key challenges was the lack of local entrepreneurs' technical and technological skills to come in, take over a state-run company, and turn it around to operate profitably".[54] On the other hand, "the real value of" the privatization "process lies in its contribution to the establishment of an entrepreneurial culture."[55]

In August 2002, eight more cinemas were put up for auction while the joint secretary of the MPC hinted that the successful bidders might be allowed to redevelop the premises if the current line of business (before privatization) turned out to be commercially unviable.[56] By early 2003, the number of privatized state assets reached 180 (out of some 600 enterprises identified by 18 ministries) with a total sales value of 2.87 billion kyat. B.G. Abel, secretary of the MPC, explained that the process "must proceed slowly because" of the lack of "management expertise" and "financial capacity" in the private sector and most "potential buyers" also "lack the hard currency required to upgrade and operate" the privatized enterprise. He also explained that the government was concerned about employment losses through downsizing and wanted to avoid price increases by the new owners.[57] All in all, it seems that a significant success in the ongoing privatization programme in Myanmar remains to be seen.

"Attempts to professionalize" SEE "management by giving them greater independence, and some realignment and reorganization of enterprises" were "part of the reforms introduced by the SLORC government."[58] Administrative price controls were abolished and price increases to reflect market conditions were "approved more readily than before".[59] On the other hand, the swapping in April 1989 of existing SEE debt for government (zero-interest) bonds, and incorporating SEE accounts into the government's central State Fund Account appears to be a retrograde step in efficiency/accountability terms. Under this system, "an individual SEE can have its deficit covered automatically, but cannot retain a surplus."[60] Moreover, the continued access of foreign exchange (albeit limited by its scarcity) by SEEs at the official exchange rate (that had been increasingly discounted in value from around one-twentieth of the open-market rate to about one-sixtieth throughout the 1990s and further to one-in-one hundred by the turn of the century) allowed SEEs a cost advantage over private enterprises that had to import raw materials, equipment, and spares at market rates. Meanwhile, the government resumed an ambitious building programme of industrial SEEs in the late 1990s as well as a renewed expansion into the retail sector by initiating "bazaar boats" to ply the Ayeyarwady River and opening Win Thuzar retail shops (numbering forty-seven up to July 2005), selling products from SEEs, all over the country (*NLM*, 19 July 2005).

In general, the astute observation concerning the problem of Myanmar SEEs made in the early 1990s by a veteran Myanmar economist appears to hold true well into the millennium. He identified several factors, "including nonviability of the original investments (resulting from inappropriate government strategy), inefficient management, low labor productivity" and "reduced capacity utilization".[61] A Japanese study in late 1998, pointed out "the lack of corporate vitality" and "management resources", as well as "heavy intervention by the government" as some of "the many areas" that "need improvement".[62] Consequently, huge deficits in the SEEs overall budget persisted throughout the decade despite reforms.[63] As such, the problem of loss-making SEEs remains to be resolved satisfactorily, either through divestiture or restructuring.

Economic Strategies and Plans

In the first few months of its rule, SLORC concentrated on the immediate task of restoring law and order, reconstructing public administration and re-establishing transportation and communication networks that had been disrupted by the 1988 upheaval, which had "adversely affected the economic activities for nearly 9 months".[64] In the next three years (ending with fiscal 1991/92) the state's economic strategy appeared to be geared towards "recovery and stabilization of the economy" from the recession that set in after 1986.[65] As such, the government quickly introduced market-oriented measures to bring in FDI and liberate the agriculture and trade sectors from extensive state controls. The economic strategy after 1992 seemed to be premised upon achieving substantial growth, through expanded infrastructure development, increased production of agricultural commodities, extensive exploitation of marine resources, acceleration of tourism and FDI-driven natural resource extraction.[66] By the late 1990s, following harsh economic sanctions imposed by Western states (*c.* 1997) and the onset of the Asian financial crisis (*c.* 1998), more emphasis was put on food security, self-sufficiency and self-reliance.[67]

In the 1989/90–1991/92 period, the planning cycle was confined to annual plans under the so-called Stabilization Programme. Next, a "Short Term Four-Year Plan (1992/93–1995/96)" was formulated with "special focus" on "enhancement of production, especially agriculture, and export promotion".[68] Proclaiming that plan targets for the first Four-Year Plan had been surpassed,[69] the government announced the launching of the "Short Term" Five-Year Plan (known as the Second Short-Term Plan, or SSTP) in early 1996 to cover the period from 1996/97 to 2000/2001.[70] The professed primary objectives of the SSTP were: "to further consolidate the gains achieved in recent years and to lay firm and stable foundations for a modern, peaceful and market-oriented economy."[71] The plan was geared towards the realization the four national economic objectives stipulated by the junta as:

- Development of agriculture as a base and all-round development of other sectors of the economy as well.
- Proper evolution of the market-orientated economic system.

- Development of the economy inviting participation in terms of technical know-how and investments from sources inside the country and abroad.
- The initiative to shape the economy must be kept in the hands of the State and the national peoples.

In formulating the SSTP, the Ministry of National Planning and Economic Development had stipulated (overall and sectoral) quantitative targets (volume and/or value) for growth rates, output of goods and services, external trade, investment, budget and balance of payments, as well as structural changes in terms of ownership shares (for state, co-operative and private sectors). Moreover, sectoral priorities (in descending order of importance) were also set as:

1. Agriculture.
2. Livestock and fisheries.
3. Mining with special emphasis on exploration and production of crude oil, natural gas, gems and jade.
4. Transportation and energy.
5. Processing and manufacturing with special emphasis on the development of value-added industries and agro-based industries.
6. Export of goods and services.

The government, again claiming that targets were exceeded, launched another Five-Year Plan (the Third Short-Term Plan, or TSTP) for the period 2001/02 to 2005/06 to boost the economy to the take-off stage for sustained growth. The objectives of the TSTP were more detailed and ambitious:

- To establish agro-based industry [*sic*] and other required industries as a first step in order to set up an industrialized nation.
- To develop electric power and energy sectors to be in line with the expansion of industry.
- To expand agriculture, livestock and fishery sectors for self-sufficiency and export promotion.
- To carry on afforestation works and greening of nine arid zones.
- To expand the educational and health service for the development of human resources.
- To develop the rural area.
- To undertake for all-round development of other sectors.

- To retain the firm foundations of economic and financial situation by:
  - performing high economic growth rate;
  - reducing budget deficit gradually and to gain surplus starting from the third year of the Plan;
  - reducing the rate of inflation;
  - reducing the current-account deficit [of the balance of payments] and to gain surplus starting from the fourth year of the Plan.[72]

Economic Performance: Little Structure Change

The plans formulated and implemented by the military government were complimented by policy reforms in areas such as finance, banking, production, trade and services as well as in sectors such as agriculture and industry.[73] Myanmar's macroeconomic policy under SPDC rule is "to strive for sustained, stable high growth of the economy through provision of infrastructure facilities and creating more diversified economic structure for emergence of agro-based industrial country", that would result in an "industrialized economy within the context of market-oriented economic system."[74]

According to government figures, the economy gradually recovered from the recession of the earlier period and gained momentum during the first half of the 1990s. The growth rate of GDP (at constant 1985/86 prices) surpassed the targeted 5.1 per cent figure by a wide margin, achieving an average of 7.5 per cent over the First Four-Year Plan period. Government data showed that the growth rate slowed substantially in the early years of the SSTP Plan that followed, but regained double-digit growth rates towards the end of the plan period (see Figure 9.1). Furthermore, using a different base year (2000/01) for constant prices the authorities claimed that the first three years (2001/02, 2002/03, and 2003/04) of the TSTP registered impressive growth rates of 11.3, 12.0, and 13.8 per cent respectively, thereby surpassing the planned average target of 11.3 per cent.[75]

As can be seen from Figure 9.2, the growth of the agriculture sector was closely correlated with GDP growth, the former being the largest productive sector in the economy contributing over one-third of the GDP throughout the 1990s.[76] The agriculture sector managed to grow at an average of 4.7 per cent throughout the decade of the 1990s. The average growth rate (in constant 2000/01 prices) for the three-year period from 2001/02 to 2003/04 was reportedly 7.3 per cent and was much less than the corresponding value of 12.3 per cent attained by the GDP. This sectoral growth was enhanced by an increase of over one-third in net sown area between 1988/89 and 2002/03. The irrigation ratio of net sown area also increased from 12.6 per cent in 1988/89 to 19 per cent in 2002/03.[77] These achievements were attributed to a massive building programme for irrigation infrastructure as well as reform measures that decontrolled prices of agricultural products and facilitated multiple cropping (summer paddy in particular).[78]

However, there were also criticisms that the government's agricultural policies had failed to raise productivity and that recent (from 1998 onwards) attempts to employ extensive commercial farming by local entrepreneurs as a means to raise output was misguided and inefficient. Problems associated with small farm sizes (averaging 5.6 acres only), shortage of working capital, lack of fertilizers, and the prevalence of restrictive practices in marketing had also been pointed out as serious constraints affecting sustainable growth.[79] Although the rural agriculture sector is expected to respond rapidly and benefit most from market liberalization (like in Vietnam and the People's Republic of China) Myanmar's trend is not very encouraging. It seems to be constrained by the scarcity of scientific and technological inputs, infrastructure deficiencies, poor water management, high transportation costs, and the state's continued claim over the property rights for agriculture land. A significant portion of agricultural produce might have been diverted towards border trading and the resulting diminished supply together with escalating transportation costs and administrative bottlenecks, in all likelihood, were behind the price inflation of food items in urban Myanmar during the decade of the 1990s.[80] After the three-decades old compulsory delivery system that compelled rice farmers to deliver a portion of the crop (at below-market prices) to the government was dismantled in early 2003 and the banning of private rice exports was relaxed, the rice market situation apparently improved.[81] Nevertheless, most of the aforementioned problems remained unresolved and the full potential of Myanmar's agriculture had not been realized.[82]

Although real (in constant prices) GDP growth rates were higher than those achieved during the 1980s, it took some time for the level of real GDP in per capita terms to surpass the highest level attained during the BSPP era. This is evident from Figure 9.3. In fact, it was only in fiscal year 1996/97 that the per capita GDP surpassed the level achieved in fiscal year 1985/86.

FIGURE 9.1
Real GDP Growth Rate
(in constant 1985/86 prices)

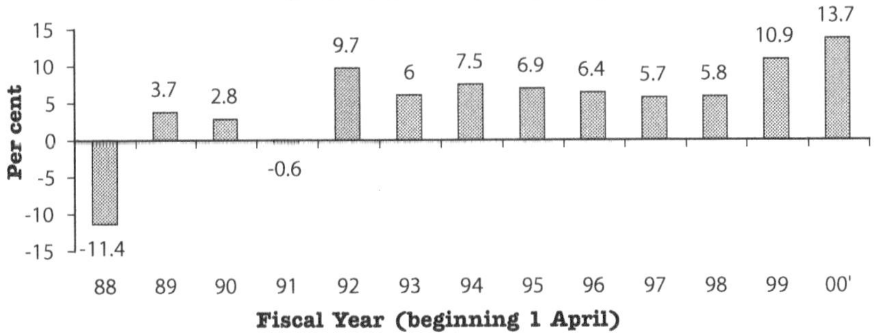

Source: Ministry of National Planning and Economic Development.

FIGURE 9.2
Real Growth Rates of GDP and Agriculture
(in constant 1985/86 prices)

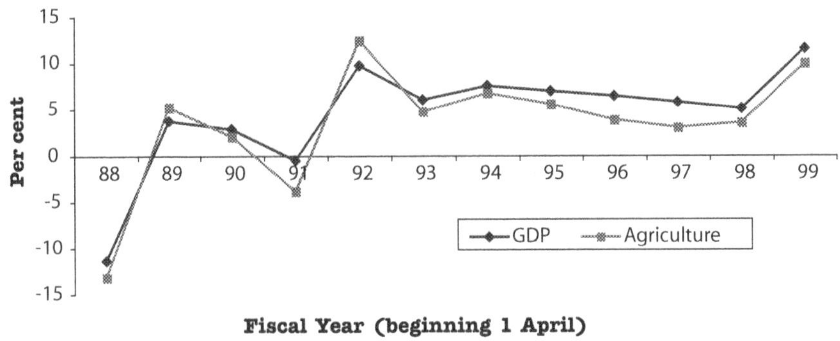

Source: Ministry of National Planning and Economic Development.

FIGURE 9.3
Real Per Capita GDP
(in constant 1985/86 prices)

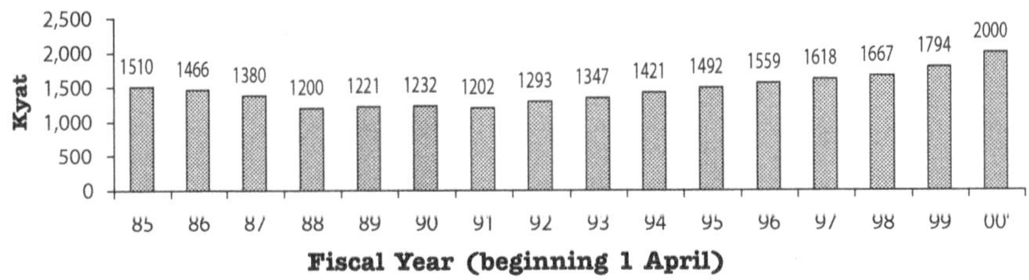

Note: The 2000 figure is provisional.
Source: Ministry of National Planning and Economic Development.

TABLE 9.4
Percentage Share of Employment in Major Economic Sectors

	1987/88	*1997/98*
Agriculture	62.5	62.7
Livestock & fishery	1.4	2.2
Forestry	1.2	1.0
Mining	0.6	0.8
Processing & manufacturing	8.7	9.1
Power	0.1	0.1
Construction	1.7	2.2
Transport & communications	3.3	2.7
Social services	2.9	3.3
Administration	3.8	4.8
Trade	9.8	9.7
Others	4.2	1.5

Note: The values may not add up to 100 due to rounding errors.
Sources: Ministry of National Planning and Economic Development.

On the other hand, the structural composition of the GDP (in constant prices) either by sector, or by ownership did not undergo any significant changes in the period under military rule (Figures 9.4 and 9.5).[83] In terms of employment structure, the pattern in fiscal year 1997/98[84] did not vary substantially from that in 1987/88 (see Table 9.4). Partial reforms carried out by the state to expand private sector involvement in the economy and induce a bigger role for the market had not yielded substantial structural change in the national economy.

Policies to foster greater and more efficient mobilization of financial resources had limited success only and major problems in the form of budget deficits, monetary overhang, foreign exchange shortage and low savings and investment rates remained unresolved throughout the decade of the 1990s.[85] Most Myanmar economists subscribed to the view that investment is a "fundamental factor for economic growth" and held the opinion that "Myanmar lagged behind the more successful Asian countries" due to its "poor performance" in "domestic resource mobilization".[86]

The SLORC/SPDC government's financial policies that evolved during the 1990s had been aimed at reducing the persistent fiscal deficits and inflation as well as raising savings and investment to achieve

FIGURE 9.4
Structural Change of GDP by Sector

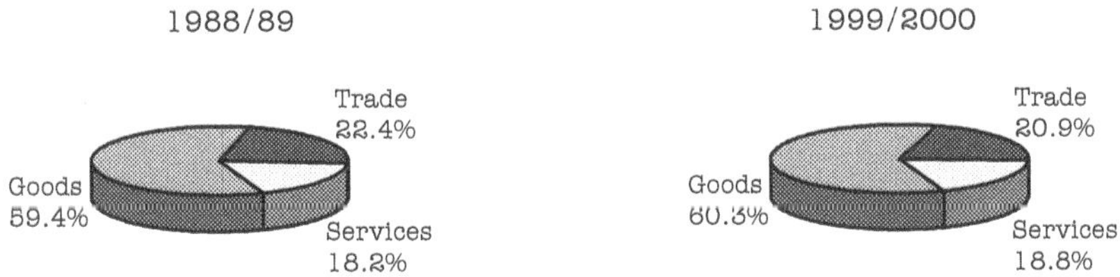

Source: Ministry of National Planning and Development.

FIGURE 9.5
Structural Change of GDP by Ownership
(at 1985/86 constant prices)

Source: Ministry of National Planning and Development.

sustainable growth. Policy instruments involved covered taxation, banking, interest rates, and foreign exchange.

In the past decade, Myanmar had utilized deficit financing for its investment requirements. Nevertheless, there had been indications that "the current [late 1990s] national budget is only able to meet 30 per cent of the capital needs of the state sector".[87] As Myanmar leaders placed great emphasis on self-reliance, domestic resource mobilization was important for that matter. While revenues (mainly through taxes and SEEs contributions) had been increasing in absolute terms, its ratio to GDP had been deteriorating since the early 1990s and was around 5 per cent by the turn of the century (see Figure 9.6).[88] Meanwhile, the tax component of the revenue was steadily declining as a ratio of GDP as well as of total revenues.[89] On the other hand, the rising trend in budget deficit as a proportion of nominal GDP was arrested by cutting back government expenditures (see Figure 9.7).[90]

FIGURE 9.6
Government Revenue as a Proportion of GDP

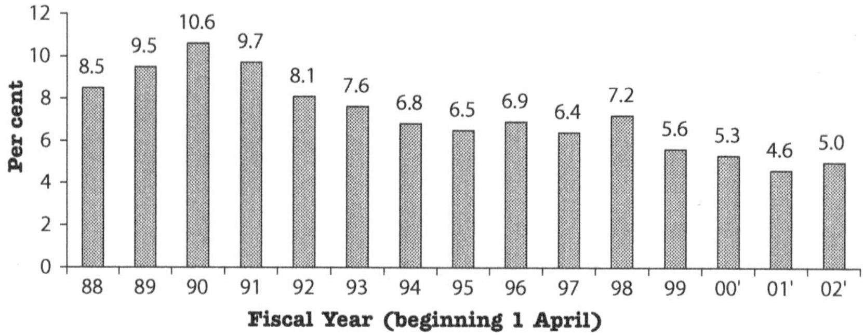

Source: *International Financial Statistics*, various issues.

FIGURE 9.7
Budget Deficit as a Proportion of GDP

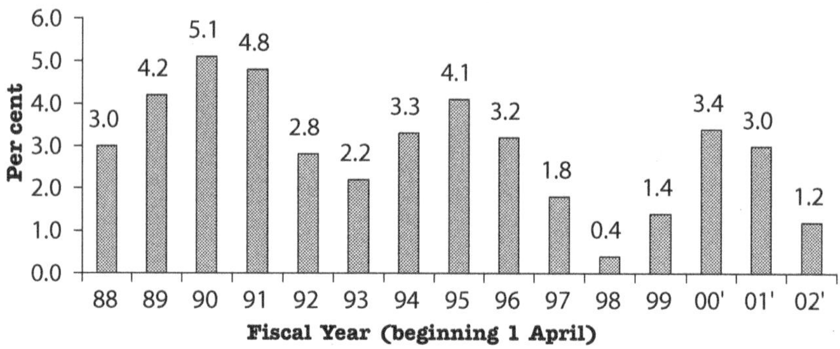

Source: *International Financial Statistics*, various issues.

Annual inflation, as measured by the (urban) consumer price index (CPI) was also increasing at double-digit rates during most of the decade of the 1990s (see Figure 9.8).[91] This was not only due to monetary expansion (see Figure 9.9),[92] but also due to demand-pull factors, such as government-led massive infrastructure expansion and unbridled competition in sourcing scarce export commodities (mainly by the private sector) in the face of declining open-market value of the local currency vis-à-vis the U.S. dollar.[93]

Given that government revenues were inadequate and FDI inflow had been rather low and narrowly concentrated (see below), "[d]omestic

FIGURE 9.8
Consumer Price Index in Yangon
(Index = 100 for 1986)

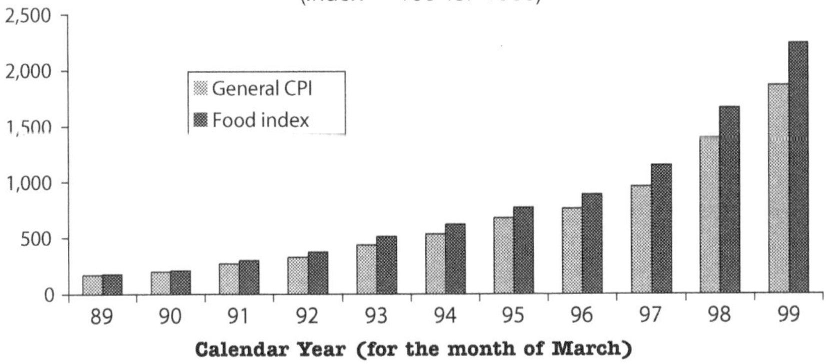

Source: Central Statistical Organization.

FIGURE 9.9
Annual Growth Rate of Money (M1)

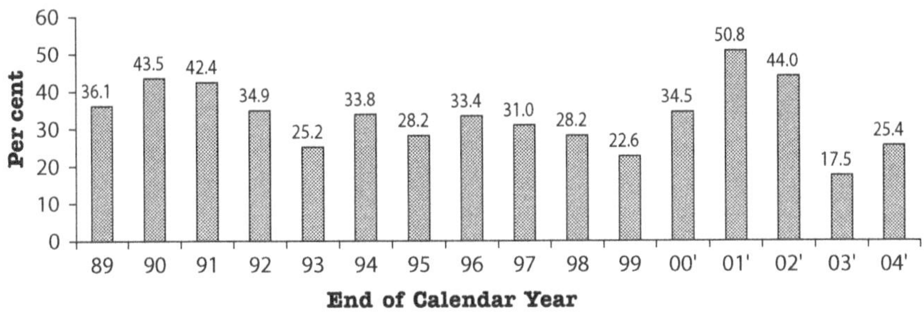

Source: *International Financial Statistics*, various issues.

savings mainly contributed by private sector savings with banks" had provided "the bulk of investment in Myanmar since mid-1990s".[94] However, despite the high growth of savings from a very low base, the overall level was still low as a proportion of GDP. The lingering mistrust of the banking system (a legacy from the Socialist era) and high inflation rates leading to negative real interest rates that prevailed throughout the decade of the 1990s appeared to have depressed the propensity to save.[95] As such, the ratios of both savings and investment to GDP were rather low in Myanmar during the 1990s, as illustrated in Figure 9.10.

FIGURE 9.10
Gross Domestic Savings and Investment

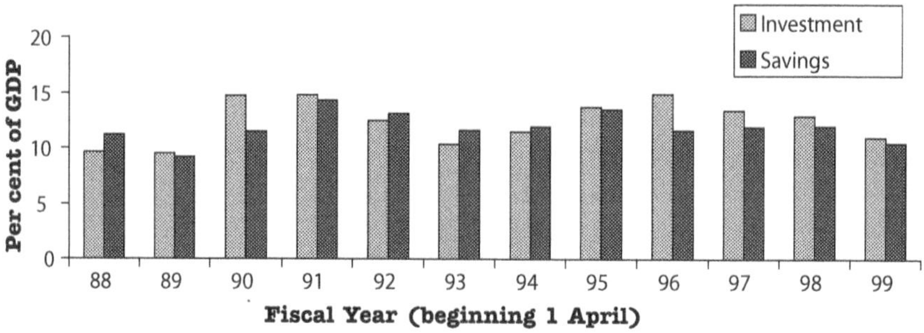

Source: Ministry of National Planning and Economic Development.

FDI has been regarded as a promising source of investment capital that would bring in much-needed foreign exchange, as ODA (that used to cater for state industrial investments during the BSPP era) inflows have been drastically reduced after 1988, as a result of a moratorium imposed by Japanese and Western bilateral donors, as well as by multilateral aid agencies like the World Bank and the Asian Development Bank.[96] Myanmar's FDI receipts sputtered in the early 1990s after an initial surge but recovered strongly in the mid-1990s (se Figure 9.11).[97] However, the FDI inflows were drastically reduced in the late 1990s as the Asian financial crisis set in and the investment climate was soured by Western sanctions and dissident pressures on corporate investors.[98] Notwithstanding cheap labour, a widespread comprehension of English and a fairly large domestic market (a population of 53 million in 2004), there have also been several factors deterring potential foreign investors, such as lack of "regular and consistent" supply of electricity, delays and inefficiencies in ports, and inadequate modern communication facilities, as well as complex rules and regulations compounded by a diverging dual exchange rate and lack of a clear dispute settlement mechanism.[99] Nonetheless, as indicated in Figure 9.12, the majority of the approved FDI (US$7.76 billion up to 31 January 2005) were in the (mainly offshore) oil and gas sector that began to generate an income stream, after the turn of the century, bringing in substantial amounts of scarce hard currency through natural gas sales to Thailand.[100] However, the tourism sector, among the earliest beneficiary of FDI, had yet to fulfil expectations.[101]

FIGURE 9.11
FDI Approvals

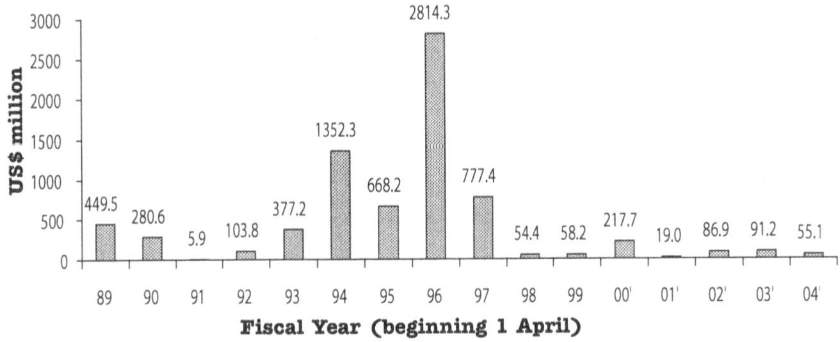

Source: Ministry of National Planning and Economic Development.

FIGURE 9.12
Approved Foreign Direct Investment by Sector
(as of 31 January 2005)

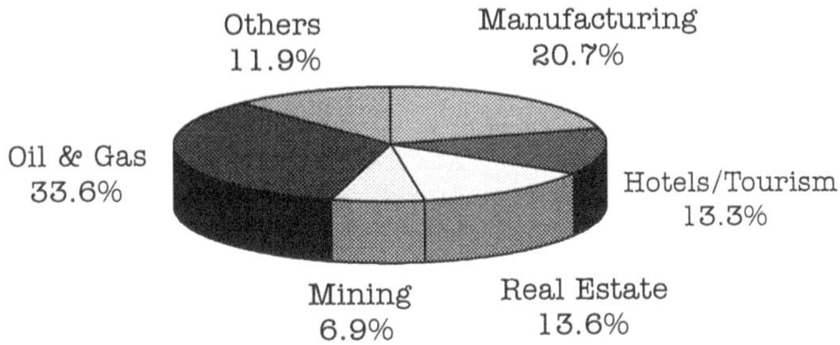

Note: Others include Transport and Communications, Livestock and Fisheries, Industrial estate, Construction Agriculture and other services (in descending order of share).
Source: Ministry of National Planning and Economic Development.

When market-oriented reforms were introduced in 1988 and 1989, exports picked up quickly and imports surged in 1990. However, both collapsed in the following year (see Figure 9.13). In the next three years, both exhibited strong growth but again slowed down in the second half of the 1990s, with exports performing worse than imports. The rising imports were fuelled by the mini construction boom of the mid-1990s, private sector demand, and also by state-sponsored infrastructure developments. This had led to increasing trade deficits (see Figure 9.14) and imports were reined in by a slew of government restrictions on foreign exchange access, import restrictions and reduced quotas (through

FIGURE 9.13
Growth Rate of Exports and Imports

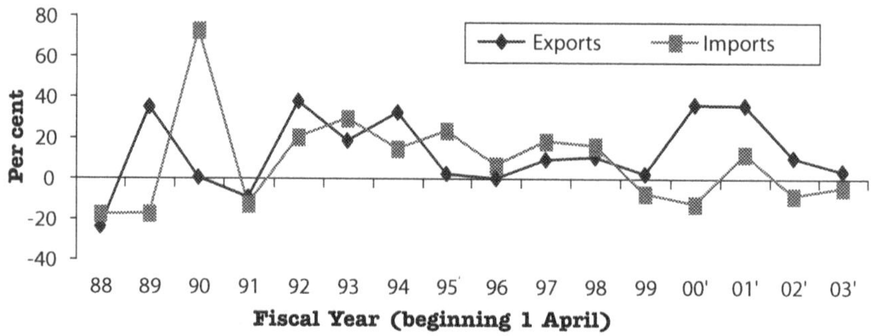

Source: *Asian Development Outlook*, various issues.

FIGURE 9.14
Mechandise Trade Deficit

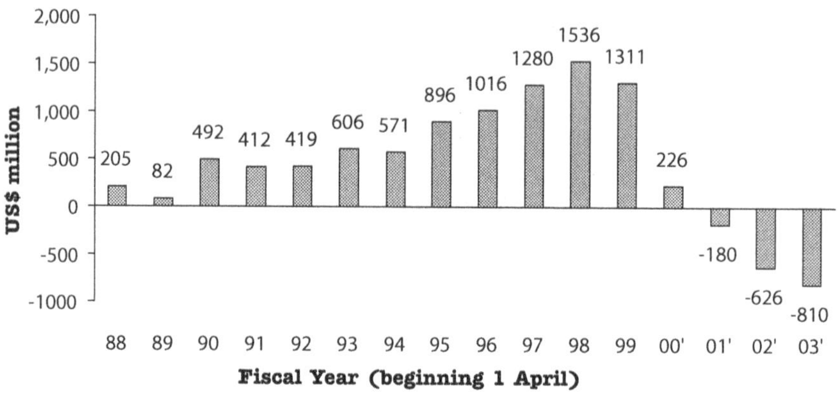

Note: Negative value denotes surplus.
Source: *Asian Development Outlook*, various issues.

control over licensing) that began in late 1997 and culminated in the imposition of a prioritized import scheme by the commerce ministry in March 1998.[102] Subsequently, imports registered negative growth from 1999 to 2003, except for 2001. Meanwhile export growth recovered strongly in 2000 and 2001 but the momentum slowed down substantially in 2002 and exports registered negative growth in fiscal year 2003/04. In fact, the SSTP export target of 15.8 billion kyat for 2000/01 (the plan's last year) was not met, achieving only 12.7 billion kyat.[103] On the other hand, due to export recovery and substantial cutbacks in imports the balance of trade had registered a surplus since 2001.[104]

The export pattern had undergone some changes since 1989/90 in which the top five commodities (teak, rice, fish and prawns, bean and pulses, and hardwood in descending order) constituted some 49 per cent of the total export value. In 2002/03, the top five exports (natural gas, garments, beans and pulses, teak, and rice in descending order) took up nearly 64 per cent of the total value. In terms of destination, exports to the top five countries (China, Thailand, India, Singapore, and Hong Kong in descending order by value) comprised some 71 per cent of the total value of exports in 1989/90, whereas in 2002/03, the top five destinations (Thailand, China, India, the United States, and Singapore in descending order by value) made up over 76 per cent of the total value. Significant earnings from garment exports to the United States and natural gas exports to Thailand in 2002/03 were responsible for the observed change in the pattern of exports between those two years. The corresponding geographical pattern for imports exhibited some changes as well. In 1989/90, imports from the top five sources (Japan, EU, Thailand, China, and Singapore in descending order by value) constituted 85 per cent of total value, while in 2002/03 the top five countries (Singapore, China, Malaysia, Thailand, and Japan in descending order by value) took up around 78 per cent of the total value.[105]

Myanmar's foreign exchange reserves were in a precarious position at the end of 1988 but recovered in the following year as exports picked up and the FDI started to flow in. Though peaking in 1995, in the second half of the decade this persistent deficit in the merchandise account, falling FDI, and declining balances in service and transfer accounts (mainly caused by the Asian financial crisis) aggravated the balance of payments situation, thereby putting pressure on the free market exchange rate of the kyat (local currency) and foreign exchange reserves as well (see Figures 9.15 and 9.16).[106] However, after the turn of the century, the reserves position improved steadily as the balance of trade turned positive and exports (boosted by natural gas sales) surged again. Nevertheless, as Figure 9.16 shows, its relative value as a proportion of imports was still weak despite the fall in imports (compare Figure 9.13).

The Myanmar currency (kyat) is non-convertible and holding foreign currency has been illegal for the last four decades. Nonetheless, a black market for foreign currency (mainly U.S. dollars and Thai baht) has existed all along. As such, even before the introduction of foreign exchange certificates (FEC; denominated in U.S. dollar equivalent) in 1993,

FIGURE 9.15
Foreign Exchange Reserves

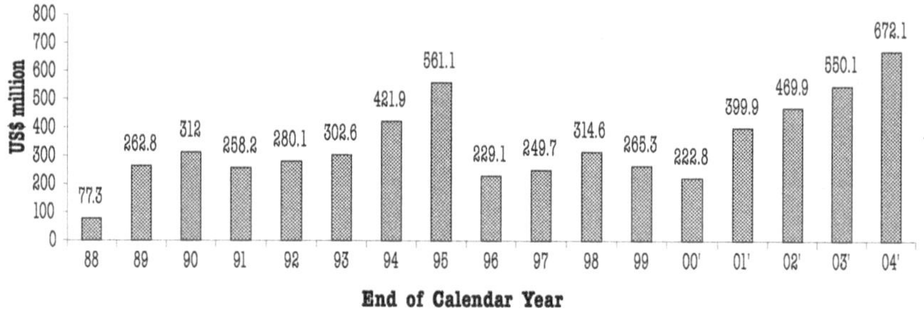

Source: *International Financial Statistics*, various issues.

FIGURE 9.16
Ratio of Foreign Exchange Reserves to Imports
(in equivalent months)

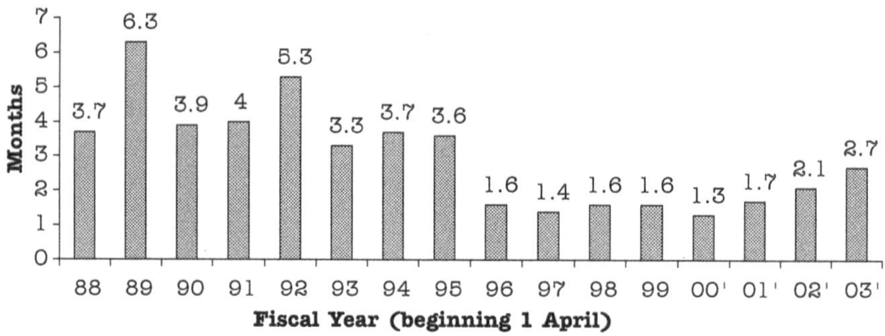

Source: *Global Development Finance: Country Tables*, various issues.

a complicated multi-tiered exchange rate system existed in Myanmar.[107] Thus, "the scope of the official exchange rate [pegged, since 1977, to IMF Special Drawing Rights or SDR at 8.51 kyats to one SDR]" was "reduced and … narrowed to public sector transactions such as repayment of foreign debts and SEEs" foreign transactions "as well as evaluation of foreign direct investment".[108]

Most of the foreign debts were incurred during the 1970s and early 1980s. Total debt outstanding as at March 2003 was reported to be around US$6.6 billion, of which some 82 per cent was long-term public debt with the rest in the form of short-term debt. Japan, the largest bilateral donor, had extended several debt-relief grants worth some 65 billion yen between late 1987 to March 2000.[109] The World Bank had "approved no new lending for Myanmar since 1987" and, as at mid-2005, regarded the country as "currently in arrears to the World Bank" (http://web.worldbank.org/WBSITE/EXTERNAL/COUNTRIES/EASTASIAPACIFICEXT/MYANMAREXTN/0,,menuPK:332674~pagePK:141159~piPK:141110~theSitePK:332668,00.html). Myanmar was also classified as a heavily indebted poor country (HIPC) belonging to the group of eleven countries in the "pre-decision point" stage in terms of eligibility to debt relief under the HIPC Initiative (launched in 1996 as a joint IMF and World Bank project) (http://siteresources.worldbank.org/NEWS/Resources/HIPC_glance.pdf).

To sum up, it appears that Myanmar was nowhere nearer to becoming an open market economy a decade after forming the Privatization Committee and still lacked the "'development fundamentals' necessary for sustained development".[110] The "expansionist policies" (both fiscal and monetary) had achieved spurts of high growth and created employment but "at the expense of macroeconomic stability" with "all its ramifications". This, aggravated by Western economic sanctions, was "not only affecting medium-term growth prospects" but also "making future reform efforts more and more unattractive" if left unrectified.[111]

Industrialization

The state-sponsored import-substituting industrialization (ISI) strategy of the BSPP era had given way to a strategy of industrialization that encourages the domestic private sector as well as FDI to engage in establishing and expanding both export-oriented and import-substituting industrial enterprises. During the early stage of reform and restructuring, the South Korean model of industrialization under President Park appeared to have been perceived as relevant to Myanmar's industrial development.[112] Subsequently, the state appeared to be playing a leading role, both in terms of guidance and planning as well as in setting up supporting institutions to foster technological development as well to cater for financial needs. In planning to establish "the national industrial sector through the three-pillar system — the state sector, the local privates sector and foreign investment", the "[n]ational entrepreneurs are regarded as the new economic forces".[113] The slogans "To Leap Over Era with Industrial Might" and "Support Domestic Products" regularly carried by state-owned newspapers for the past few years suggest that industrialization is seen as an important task in economic development. The junta chairman had given the following guidelines for Myanmar's industrial development:[114]

- An industrialized nation must be established for modernization;
- Necessary industries must be established simultaneously based on agricultural development;
- Only when entrepreneurs and industrialists gather at suitable places will the government be able to provide support conveniently;
- National industrialists are required to submit their requirements properly and acquire the government support.

He also promised "to provide basic needs for development of the industrial zones". For financing needs "assistance will be provided not only in kyat but also in foreign currency" and taxes "which have been a burden to the industrialists will be scrutinized and exemptions given".[115]

In July 1995, the junta formed the Myanma Industrial Development Committee (MIDC; comprising twelve members and including nine ministers), chaired by the Minister of Agriculture and Irrigation (it was reconstituted in January 1998 with the Minister of Industry-1 as chair) and the Myanma Industrial Development Working Committee (MIDWC; comprising forty members that included deputy ministers, department heads, and chief executives of SEEs), chaired by the Minister of Industry-2, to pursue the following objectives.[116]

- to develop agro-based industries;
- to raise the quality and quantity of industrial products;
- to produce new machinery items;
- to produce machines, parts and tools for industries; and
- to obtain [*sic*] good foundations for turning the country into an industrialized nation.

In May 1999, the junta established a high-powered committee for "central guidance and supervision of state-owned industrial enterprises". Called the "Central Committee for Industrial Development (CCID), and chaired by the Vice-Chairman of SPDC, the committee was formed with the three junta secretaries, one deputy prime minister and six ministers. The minister who chaired the MIDC was the secretary to CCID.[117] It professed to implement policies "calling for extensive application of

[a] mechanized farming system, extension of establishment of [*sic*] new factories, boosting production by operating factories at full capacity and development of industrial zones".[118]

In the second half of the 1990s, with limited progress in the privatization process, the state's focus for its processing and manufacturing SIEs became increasingly oriented towards an ISI strategy aimed at self-sufficiency and self-reliance. A significant number of new industrial projects were undertaken by the state since 1988 and there was no sign of reduction in the state's direct involvement in the industrial sector.[119] The private sector was also encouraged to set up import-substituting industries. In fact, the MIDC even went to the extent of promoting the emergence of a private automobile industry, which, hitherto, had been the preserve of the Ministry of Industry-2.[120] It strongly encouraged the "national industrialists" to take up the challenge of locally producing motor vehicles, assuring that "the government would provide financial, technological and material support", and revealing that "plans are underway" to secure "markets" for motor vehicles manufactured at various industrial zones.[121]

As mentioned above, the establishment of "industrial zones" (IZs) is accorded a high priority in the state's policies for industrialization. The IZ concept was probably conceived in the initial phase of the reform process as a means to attract manufacturing FDI by providing a designated precinct with adequate infrastructure. The Department of Human Settlement and Housing Development (DHSHD) began in 1989 to develop IZs around Yangon's suburbs. Later, the clientele was expanded to include local enterprises not only to improve their operating environment but also as part of the master plan to beautify the city and enhance the well-being of its residents. The professed objectives of the IZs were:

- providing employment opportunities; especially in newly established urban townships;
- promoting new industries;
- raising living standards; and
- promoting regional development.[122]

The IZ scheme was then further extended to other cities and major towns throughout the country. By 1997 there were eighteen IZs in six states and divisions, which expanded to twenty-two by 2001. Among them one in Yangon (near the airport) and another in Thanlyin-

Kyauktan (across the river form Yangon) were joint ventures between foreign partners and the government, while the rest were developed by DHSHD. Each industrial zone is under ministerial supervision and the IZs have become showcases for the state's promotion of private industries.[123] Furthermore, the junta had designated fiscal year 2004/05 as the year for development of the industrial sector, and the MIDC had been emphasizing the setting up of foundries and metal-working shops, with government support, in three major IZs and enhancing the role of IZs in converting petrol- and diesel-engine vehicles to compressed natural gas (CNG) run vehicles.[124]

As mentioned in the earlier chapters, Myanmar's industrialization is taken to encompass the processing and manufacturing sector as well as mining, electric power, and energy sectors. As such, developmental trends in each of those sectors are presented in the following sections.

The Processing and Manufacturing Sector

The processing and manufacturing sector in Myanmar employed around 1.7 million workers in fiscal year 1998/99, which constituted only 9.3 per cent of total employment. Its contribution to GDP at constant prices was only around 9.4 per cent in fiscal year 1999/2000 and 10.2 per cent in 2000/01.[125] As such, it can be said that its contribution to the development of Myanmar's economy was rather modest in sectoral terms.

In terms of sheer numbers of enterprises, Myanmar's processing and manufacturing sector has always had a preponderance of private establishments, even during the BSPP era. As can be seen in Figure 9.17, there had been not much change in the respective shares by way of ownership as the number of registered establishments increased from over 42,300 in 1988/89 to nearly 64,400 in 2002/03. The share of SIEs had shrunk substantially from 4.4 per cent of the total to 1.3 per cent, and in terms of absolute numbers there was a decrease of nearly 53 per cent (down from 1,854 to 867). The co-operative establishments also shrunk by some 78 per cent (from 717 to 160), while the number of the private enterprises increased by over 59 per cent (from 39,802 to 63,328).[126]

In terms of the size of labour force, the sector has been characterized by the dominance of small-scale enterprises employing fewer than ten workers. For example, statistics for the fiscal year 1997/98[127] showed that 93.8 per cent of the total consisted of establishments with fewer than ten workers. As illustrated in Figure 9.18, state firms dominated the segment of larger enterprises employing more than fifty workers.

FIGURE 9.17
Share by Ownership of Factories and Industrial Establishments

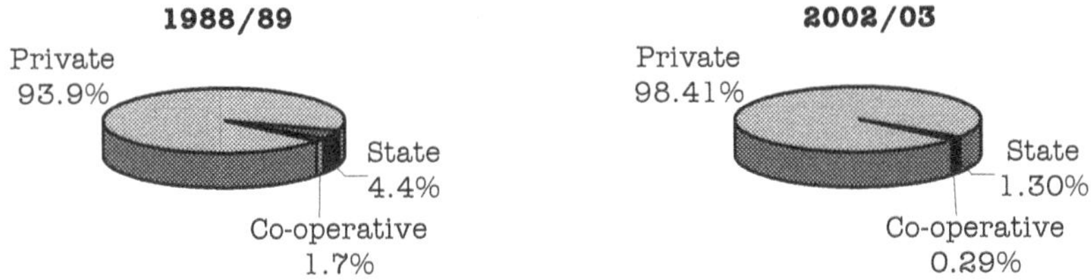

Source: Ministry of National Planning and Economic Development.

FIGURE 9.18
Share by Ownership According to Size of Work Force

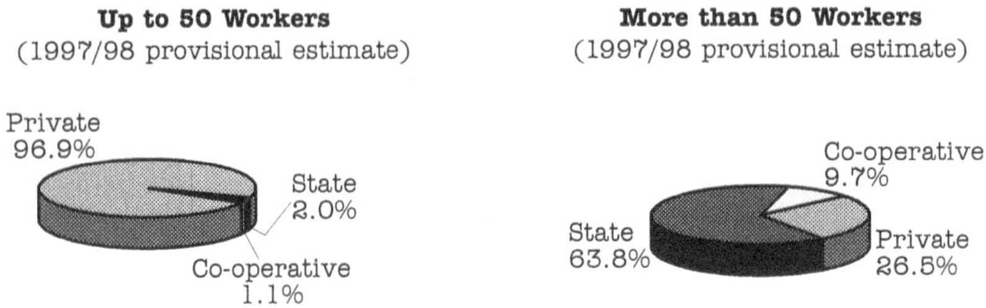

Source: Ministry of National Planning and Economic Development.

However, the state sector did have a substantial number of small industrial establishments as well. In the state sector small firms (fewer than ten workers) comprised roughly half the total as indicated in Figure 9.19. On the other hand, nearly 96 per cent of the private industrial establishments were small firms.

Most of the private industrial establishments were in light manufacturing and processing with food and beverage firms comprising the largest segment at 63 per cent, in late 1998. This was followed by motor workshops at 8.1 per cent and textiles at 6.6 per cent. Each of the remaining industrial branches had a share of less than 2 per cent.[128] As such, the majority of Myanmar's industrial firms may be classified as belonging to the small and medium enterprises (SMEs) category and were essentially geared towards import substitution.[129]

On the other hand, SIEs were spread over nine ministries and include heavy industries such as power plants, oil refineries and petrochemical plants, sugar mills, cement, paper and fertilizer plants, ferrous and non-ferrous mineral processing plants, dockyards, and transport and agricultural equipment factories, as well as a plethora of

FIGURE 9.19
Share by Size of Industrial Work Force According to Ownership

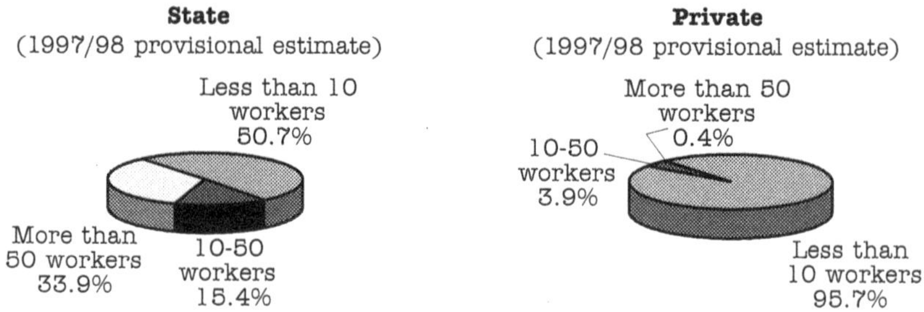

Source: Ministry of National Planning and Economic Development.

light manufacturing plants such as those producing textiles and apparel, an assortment of household consumer goods, construction material, wood products, agriculture products, processed food, edible oil, electrical goods, and spare parts for electrical and mechanical equipment.[130]

The performance of the processing and manufacturing sector, up to the century's end, had not been impressive. Although it was reported to have achieved an average annual real growth rate of 6.1 per cent during the 1990s, the quantum index of production regained the 1985/86 level only after 1993/94 and its level in 1997/98 was only 30 per cent above that for 1985/86. A similar trend could be seen in the growth of sectoral value-added as illustrated in Figure 9.20 (abbreviated as P&M in the figure), with the overall growth index at 140.3 in fiscal year 1999/2000 compared with the base year 1985/86. This was because the sector regressed during the last years of the BSPP period and the recovery was slow in the first few years of SLORC rule. In the first half of the 1990s, the capacity utilization rates also remained low in the 30–50 per cent range.[131]

There could be several factors behind this relatively modest achievement of the processing and manufacturing sector in the decade of the 1990s.[132] For SIEs, it could be attributed to, *inter alia*, foreign exchange shortage that compounded the problem of maintenance and imported inputs, technological obsolescence, problems in the supply of fuel and power, inefficient resource allocation and constraints imposed by non-commercial imperatives derived from security and political considerations.

Although the private sector had grown faster and picked up part of the slack, that had been more than a few constraints that prevented

FIGURE 9.20
Index of Sectoral Value-Added
(1985 = 100)

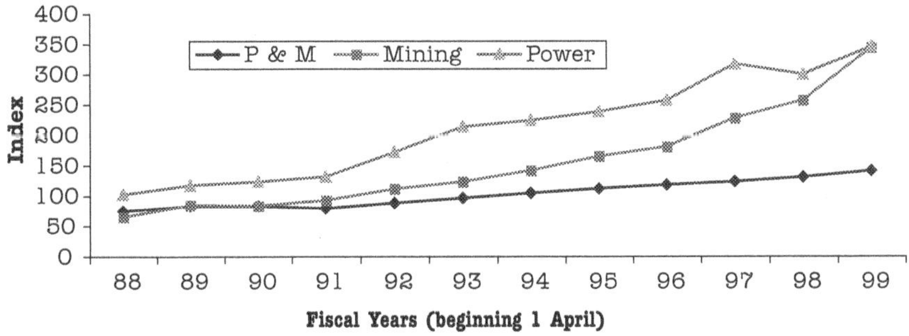

Source: Asian Development Bank.

it from achieving its full potential. Many of them were common to all industrial establishments in most developing countries, while others are probably unique to Myanmar due to its particular socio-economic and political situations. A survey of 132 selected enterprises (106 private firms, 17 foreign joint ventures, 6 SIEs, 2 local joint ventures, and one co-operative enterprise; small, medium and large enterprises, with the number of employees ranging from 5 to over 2,300 and capital ranging from 1 million to 3 billion kyat) conducted in 1997 and 1998 at Yangon and Mandalay (the second largest city in central Myanmar) revealed that "shortage of electricity" appeared to be "the greatest obstacle to productivity".[133] Other obstacles were identified as infrastructure deficiencies (sewage, drainage, space, telecommunications and transportation). Financial "barriers" such as lack of capital and foreign exchange shortage and production "barriers" such as shortage of spares and raw materials, low technological level, and inadequacy of machines and equipment were also mentioned.[134] The "difficulty of hiring skilled labour" had also been identified as one of the "major obstacles to SME business operations" in the industrial sector.[135] A veteran Myanmar industrialist (an octogenarian) who had worked in both public and private sector also added to the list of constraints, factors such as "insufficient market intelligence and marketing skills" and "[a]dministrative procedures, rules and regulations".[136] Meanwhile, a major industrialist with vast experience in both trade and industry, opined that a series of constraints inhibiting Myanmar's industrial development had been: obsolete imported technology and defective imported facilities; lack of hi-tech components; exchange rate instability; rising labour costs; low brand image; low disposable income of customers; absence of sales network and reliable after-sales services; and lack of customer loyalty.[137]

However, according to official figures the processing and manufacturing sector registered double digit growth since 1999/2000, thereby achieving a 10.7 per cent average growth rate over the SSTP (1996/97 to 2000/01) and went on to register 21.8, 26.8, and 22.6 per cent respectively for the first three years of the TSTP (2001/02 to 2005/06).[138]

Mining

Mining is another industrial sector in Myanmar. It incorporated the energy sub-sector until the fiscal year 1997/98, when the latter was accorded a separate sectoral classification by Myanmar's planning ministry. It contributed around 2 per cent (0.5 per cent by the energy sub-sector) of the real GDP in 1999/2000 compared with some 0.7 per cent in 1988/89. As can be seen in Figure 9.20, its sectoral value-added output recovered rapidly after 1991/92, so that its index surpass the 1985/86 figure (of 100) and accelerated to reach an index of 343 in 1999/2000. Its rapid ascent after 1996/97 was probably propelled by the development of private gem and jade mines and the rapid growth of the energy sector that registered an average annual real growth rate of 20.9 per cent in the five years of the SSTP.[139] The average for the first three years of the TSTP was reported to have slackened to 14.1 per cent. On the other hand, significant amounts of FDI, bringing in much-needed technology and hard currency, had not been forthcoming (except in copper extraction) as expected, despite the liberalization of mining laws in the mid-1990s. Investors appeared to be waiting for more favourable regulatory environment and less (perceived) political uncertainty.[140]

Electric Power

Electric power is a necessary but insufficient requirement for industrial development and it also contributes to industrial growth by itself. The government claimed that it had substantially increased the generating capacity of power plants by adding extensions to existing gas turbines, introducing combined cycle technology in thermal power plants, and constructing mini-hydro plants in the countryside. The average real growth rate for the decade of the 1990s was reported to be 11.4 per cent.[141] Its contribution to real GDP remained steady at around 1 per cent from the mid-1990s to the end of the decade. In the first three years of the TSTP, from 2001/02 to 2003/04 the sectoral growth rate averaged 8.1 per cent according to official figures.

Starting from a higher base than both processing and manufacturing and mining, the index of sectoral value-added output for electric power followed a rising trend throughout the 1990s except for the fiscal year 1998/99 when it dipped down (see Figure 9.20). The dent in 1998/99 was due to an abnormally low rainfall in the previous year, that affected Myanmar's largest hydroelectric power plant. Nevertheless, its value-added output index in 1999/2000 reached 345 and was almost identical with the level achieved by the mining sector. The generating capacity increased by 66 per cent between 1988/89 and 1999/2000 and the amount that was generated also doubled. Meanwhile, demand had also been rising rapidly with the advent of economic liberalization. At the same time, the provision of electricity by the state-owned MEPE (Myanma Electric Power Enterprise) coverage had extended to 323 towns and 1,101 villages by fiscal year 2001/02; up from 279 towns and 722 villages in 1985/86.

Although the national grid was supplied by the MEPE under the Ministry of Energy, state agencies under twenty-three other ministries also produce electricity for its own use. In fiscal year 1997/98 (the last year of published data) the combined generating capacity installed by those agencies was equivalent to 35 per cent of MEPE's total capacity and the corresponding electricity production was equivalent to some 14 per cent of that produced by MEPE.

Despite such impressive growth, the power sector had been beset with technical and financial problems. The rate of electricity loss at over 30 per cent throughout the decade was unsatisfactory. Blackouts and brownouts had been recurrent problems since the early 1990s. These were mainly due to technological obsolescence in both generation and distribution parts. The price of electricity had been heavily subsidized for decades since the 1960s and only in 1999 did the government raise the price to be more in line with escalating costs.[142] Shortage of foreign exchange constrained attempts to repair, upgrade and expand deteriorating networks, modernize ageing power plants, and built new plants. There were also irregularities, such as improper and illegal use of electricity that deprived the government of revenues and distorted load distribution.[143]

To overcome supply constraints the government had relaxed its rules and allowed co-operatives and some private consortia to set up local generating plants (mini- and micro-hydro and small thermal plants), while building major multi-purpose dams that include those integrated with hydro-power schemes.[144]

On the other hand, the electric power sector appeared to be the major beneficiary of ODA from the People's Republic of China (PRC), which had contributed the most in terms of value in the absence of ODA from the West and multilateral financial institutions. Apart from the US$120 million loan approved by the Bank of China in September 2000 to pay for Chinese equipment contracted by the 280-megawatt hydroelectric project completed in late 2004 (after six years of construction), equipment and technical expertise provided by the PRC for many mini hydroelectric projects and transmission projects are believed to be funded by Chinese ODA.[145]

All in all, the government appeared to be concentrating on adding new capacities through large and medium hydroelectric schemes with Chinese assistance and may well succeed in achieving its targeted generating capacity by the end of the TSTP. However, inefficiencies in transmission and distribution associated with an ageing and deteriorating network infrastructure could still be a serious problem as the government seemed to lack financial capacity (especially with the continued denial of ODA by multilateral and bilateral donors) for renovations and rebuilding new ones. As such, timely and sufficient provision of electricity for industrial development in general and IZs in particular may remain unfulfilled for the near term.

Energy

The energy sector's value-added output picked up momentum in the late 1990s (buoyed by escalating natural gas output) and achieved an average growth rate of some 27.2 per cent in the SSTP, after registering negative growth of –0.4 per cent on average during the preceding four years. In the TSTP it averaged 13.8 per cent during the first three years from 2001/02 to 2003/04. Meanwhile, domestic oil production had declined steadily from 1992/93 till the decade's end (see Figure 9.21). Though a slight upward trend began in 2000, the production was far below domestic demand. This had inevitably led to huge expenditures of scarce foreign exchange on imports of fuel and crude oil to satisfy the rising demand from industry and transport.[146]

FIGURE 9.21
Output of Crude Oil

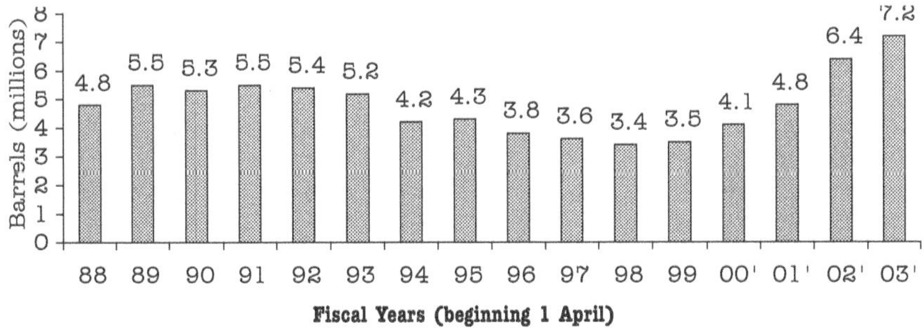

Source: Central Statistical Organization.

As may be seen in Figure 9.12, the oil and gas sector received the largest share of FDI in terms of cumulative approved pledges, and almost all went to the development of the two giant offshore gas fields in the Moatama (Martaban) Gulf. The first of them came on stream in late 1998 and the second after the turn of the century. The income stream from them through gas sales to Thailand was initially delayed by Thailand's reluctance due to the Asian economic crisis. On the other hand, until recently, utilization of offshore natural gas for domestic use and onshore exploration was hindered by lack of capital, infrastructure and technology, and some industrial observers believed that potential investors were still reluctant to commit deeply in the oil and gas sector in general.[147] A new offshore gas field with significant commercially exploitable results was found in the Bay of Bengal in early 2004 eliciting a lot of interest from India. Meanwhile there was a flurry of activities in onshore exploration as well as joint ventures and production sharing contracts with foreign firms yielded some positive results in old and new fields. Twenty years after the Ministry of Energy was established, Myanmar's energy officials and the local media appeared to have embraced the notion that a gas bonanza is there in Myanmar's waters waiting to be exploited to the country's advantage.[148] Whether this optimism would be justified remains to be seen.

The Private Sector

The private business sector regained some role in the national economy under SLORC/SPDC rule as legislative and administrative reforms swept away many of the restrictions and discriminations against the private

TABLE 9.5
Number of Registered Business Enterprises

	End April 1991	*End June 2005*
Exporters/Importers	2,813	19,494
Business Representatives	504	2,363
Partnership Firms	576	1,272
Myanmar Companies Ltd.	855	14,346
Foreign Companies/Branches	87	1,469
Joint Venture (Local & Foreign)	33	148
Chambers & Associations	5	41
Total	4,873	39,133

Source: *Trade News* (7 September 2005); and Khin Maung Oo, "Myanmar's Market Policy and External Economic Relations Policy," In *Myanmar-Korea Economic Cooperation*, edited by Than Nyun and Dalchoong Kim (Seoul: Yongsei University, 1993), p. 115.

sector in production, trade and services; those that had been imposed by the previous regime in the name of socialism. As a result, th number of private business establishments drastically increased during the 1990s to over 39,000 by June 2005 (Table 9.5). Although the increases in exporters and importers as well as private limited companies were impressive their numbers are still low for a country with an urban population of around 16 million in 2005.[149] Such an observation taken together with the low figures for joint ventures and foreign companies point mean there is much room for further development.

The expansion of private participation in the economy was especially prominent in the external trade sector where private exports were almost negligible and imports by private entrepreneurs were virtually non-existent during the Socialist era from the mid-1960s to the late 1980s.[150] From Figures 9.22 and 9.23, it can be seen that in fiscal year 2003/04, the private sector's share exceeded the state sector's share by 11 per cent and the private sector's advancement in imports was even more pronounced. Therefore, the private sector had become the major exporter/importer in value terms.[151] In fact, in the overall trade sector, the private sector's sectoral value-added for 1997/98 (at constant prices) was 3.5 times that of the state sector, whereas this ratio was 2.7 in 1988/89. Interestingly, in the goods production sector there was a decline in the corresponding ratios from 8.8 to 6.5. However, in the construction sector,

FIGURE 9.22
Exports by Ownership

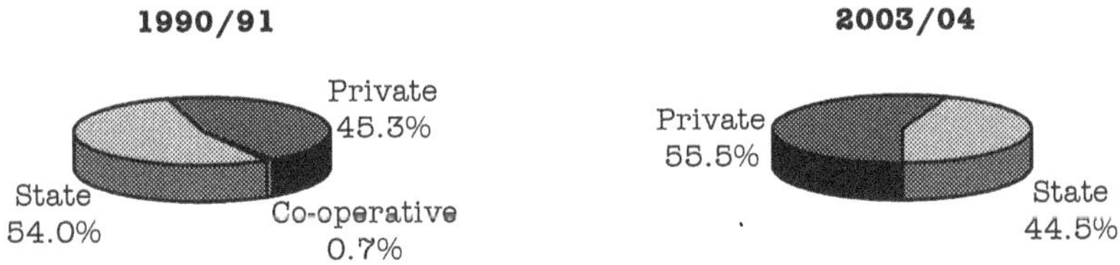

Note: In fiscal year 2003/04, the co-operative sector's contribution was negligible.
Source: Ministry of National Planning and Economic Development.

FIGURE 9.23
Imports by Ownership

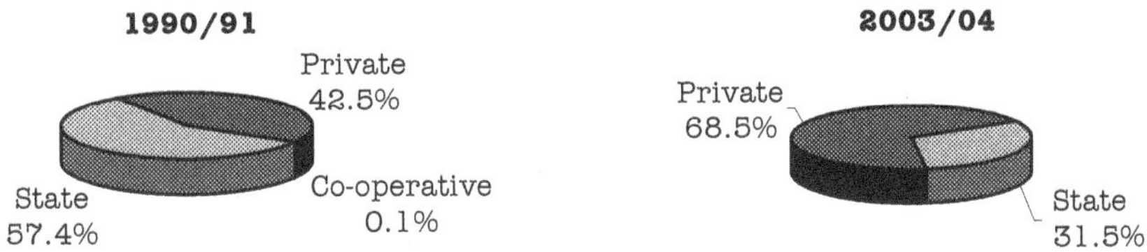

Note: In fiscal year 2003/04, the co-operative sector's contribution was negligible.
Source: Ministry of National Planning and Economic Development.

the private sector's share of sectoral value-added, though still lagging behind the state sector's contribution, rose from 13.3 per cent to 31.4 per cent in the same period. Meanwhile, in the financial services sector, the private sector's share of the sectoral value-added reached 22.8 per cent in 1997/98 from zero in 1988/89.[152]

After the passing of the Myanmar Citizens Investment Law in March 1994, the scope for private domestic investment became well defined. The incentive system (similar to those given to foreign investors in the Foreign Investment Law of 1988) provided by this Law had created favourable conditions for local investors, who, in the past, had complained that they were unduly disadvantaged in relation to foreign investors. As a result some 120 billion kyat worth of investment projects were successful in getting approval from the government under this Law (see Figure 9.24).[153]

In the area of business institutions, the government allowed the moribund (since the early 1960s) chambers of commerce to be revived

FIGURE 9.24
Approved Myanmar Citizens' Investment by Sector
(share as of 31 December 2004)

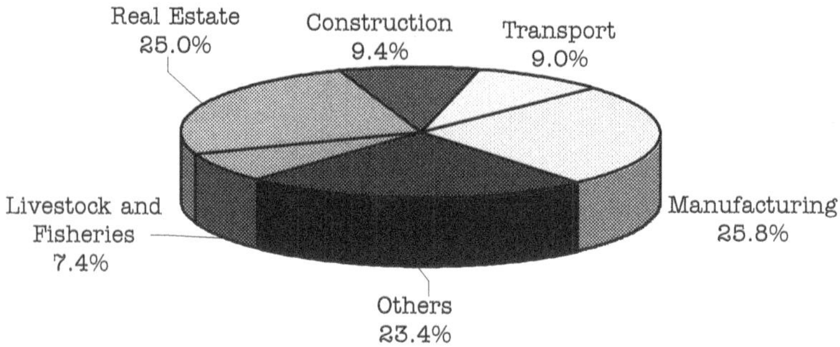

Note: Total value was 120.4 billion kyat.
Source: Ministry of National Planning and Economic Development.

and registered as NGOs under the guidance of the trade (later renamed commerce) ministry. In January 1989, the Union of Myanmar Chamber of Commerce and Industry, the first of many such associations under the new regime, was re-established in Yangon by a trade ministry notification. It was restructured in 1996 into the Union of Myanmar Federation of Chambers of Commerce and Industry (UMFCCI) and became a member of the ASEAN Chambers of Commerce and Industry (ASEAN-CCI) after Myanmar joined ASEAN in July 1997. In the 1990s other chambers pertaining to different regions and/or lines of commercial activity (rice milling, fisheries, etc.) were established and became linked to the UMFCCI after its formation.

The UMFCCI acts as a focal point for private business interests and by mid-2006 its membership consisted of 9,955 Myanmar companies, 766 foreign companies, 159 co-operatives and 2,644 individual members. As for institutional members, there were sixteen state/division chambers of commerce and industries, nine border trade associations, and nineteen other associations.[154]

The private banking sector emerged after a law allowing the establishment of private financial institutions was passed in 1990. The fledgling industry grew rapidly from May 1992, when the first batch of banking licences were issued by the Central Bank of Myanmar, with the total capital growing from 1.1 billion kyat in 1995 to 16.5 billion kyat in 2001. Deposits also grew from 4.3 billion kyat to 350 billion kyat in the same period while loans increased from around 6 billion kyat to 210 billion kyat,[155] By the end of October 2001, twenty domestic private banks were in operation, providing commercial banking services with over 200 branches in major cities, as well as in border areas. Some had introduced modern facilities such as credit cards in local currency, hire-purchase schemes for properties and selected consumer goods, automatic teller machines, and point of sales system machines, call deposit accounts, safe deposit boxes, trust funds, gift cheques, and travellers cheque services.

Just as it seemed to be gaining confidence from the private business sector and the public at large, the fledgling banking sector suffered a major setback in early 2003 when it suffered its first crisis. It appeared that the "immediate trigger" was the "collapse of a succession of informal financial enterprises through the second half of 2002".[156] Those operated like a pyramid scheme linked to highly speculative financial investments that became unsustainable after some time. The contagion effect of those failures in which many people lost their nest eggs hit the formal banking sector through rumours and innuendos (about liquidity problems, money laundering, financial improprieties, among others) creating panic among depositors, big and small. By February 2003 the run on six of the biggest private banks started snowballing despite assurances by the bank executives and Central Bank authorities. Administrative measures such as imposing withdrawal limits, banning account transfers and finally recalling substantial portions of loans further exacerbated the situation and created negative fallout in the private trading and industrial community. The Central Bank had to restrict operations at the six banks affected by the crisis and put them under close supervision.[157] Meanwhile, the Central Bank imposed strict regulations limiting the amount of receivable deposits (seven times the paid-up capital) and loans extendable (70 per cent of deposits), prohibiting call deposits and credit cards and requiring banks to set aside 25 per cent of the net profit in a special reserve fund.[158] In February 2004, three of the six banks were allowed to resume normal operations in conformity with the aforementioned new regulations.[159] Thereafter, the return of badly eroded confidence was slow and the new regulations imposed by the Central Bank had dampened the buoyancy of private banking.[160]

Another setback in the financial sector was the United States' imposition of additional sanctions on 28 July 2003 that affected financial transactions involving the United States.[161] This virtually closed down U.S. dollar transactions in trade and finance denominated in U.S. dollars and a cessation of international credit card usage in Myanmar. The affected parties had to resort to cumbersome and costly alternatives like switching to the euro and financial transactions through third-party guarantors and facilitators.[162]

On the other hand, despite the apparent support given by the authorities in favour of private sector development, the private business community sector seemed to be still viewed with some suspicion and even a bit of derision by the "powers that be".[163] Some government-imposed "market-hostile" measures remains to be changed. Many of the firms established in the euphoric wave of business registrations failed to capture profitable business deals in the lucrative foreign trade sector and have been lying dormant, partly due to the regional environment after the Asian financial crisis and partly to the constraints posed by existing rules and regulations. Lack of capital, expertise, and more importantly, "right connections" inhibit the would-be entrepreneur in the oligarchic business structure of contemporary Myanmar. The military-owned and -operated conglomerates, Union of Myanmar Economic Holdings and Myanmar Economic Corporation, have become a major force in the private sector and are engaged in banking, external trade, manufacturing and gems and jade business, among others. Often state monopolies were replaced by private monopolies when divestiture of SEEs is carried out and new economic organizations are created.[164] The *nouveau riche* of Myanmar also include ethnic rebel chieftains who recently came back to the "legal fold" and have been accorded leadership status with regards to the corresponding "national race" they purportedly represent. Given quasi-autonomy in their respected areas, they were able to employ enormous sums of legalized earnings to further their business interests. Their business concerns are dominant in the construction and banking sectors.[165] All of these developments may crowd out small entrepreneurs in capital and technology intensive areas of business.

Factor markets are either distorted or non-existent. Prospective entrepreneurs have to excruciatingly account for their capital funds. Newly enforced municipal zoning laws forbidding productive activities in build-up areas, fuel, electricity and water shortages, escalating rentals and property prices, high cost of labour in relation to productivity, as well as high inflation have made "entry" into manufacturing difficult. Thus, most are inclined to trading and selected services in the urban economy.

Despite some rationalization of taxes and introduction of new laws and procedures for private business, the potential entrepreneur is still hampered by deficient infrastructure, lack of capital, the complexity and apparent instability of rules and procedures, as well as high transaction costs.[166]

The ambiguous lines of state authority are aggravated by the existence of powerful authorities at both at the centre and in the locality. The high cost of business in Myanmar is mainly due to inflation, considerable increases in the state monopolies' charges for public utilities, postal services, and transportation, and high charges by the quasi-autonomous municipal authorities. Various contributions solicited for the state's religious, cultural, sports, and welfare activities constitute a seasonal cycle of "donations" for the firms, raising their operating costs. The private business sector is being squeezed between the rising costs of factor inputs which have been freed to the market forces and the glass ceiling on earnings imposed by the overvalued exchange rate, the state's "discouragement" of "excessive profits", and a high tax burden aggravated by ambiguous taxation procedures.

CONCLUSION: STATE AND MYANMAR'S DEVELOPMENT

There is no doubt that the military will ensure that the state prevails in the politics of Myanmar in the foreseeable future. The ruling junta is seeking a political configuration which would institutionalize its role in "national politics" as a solution to the perceived problem of dysfunctional "party politics".[167]

Thus, it is eminently clear that the nature of governance and constitutional politics in future Myanmar will not emulate the orthodoxy suggested by liberal democratic traditions. It is ostensibly tailored for Myanmar conditions as perceived by the military leaders who are not prepared to leave the fate of the future Myanmar state in the hands of political parties. The Indonesian New Order State appears to be an attractive model for Myanmar's forthcoming political configuration despite its collapse after Soeharto's resignation.[168] To the junta, a strong state led by a nationalistic political leader acceptable to them is deemed not only desirable but also essential for national unity as well as economic development. It follows from the dictum that the Tatmadaw must play a leading role in national politics. Although societal aspirations for participation and representation may somewhat be assuaged through a multi-party electoral process, the military's institutionalized political role will prevent the dominance of political parties in defining the national interest and setting the policy agenda. This could ultimately lead to the delinking of state power from political power.[169] To that end, the military leadership will see to that the political transition remains under its control. This view is exemplified by the junta chairman's speech, on 27 March 2001, at the parade to commemorate the Armed Forces Day in which he stated that "[i]n the world today you will see a number of developing countries facing all kinds of trouble and misery for having tried to make too hasty a transition to ... democracy without first building the necessary foundations."[170] From the military's standpoint, the firm foundations mentioned in the speech, in all likelihood, meant a strong state controlled by the "praetorian guard".

In general, the introduction of market forces and the opening up of the economy to local and international private initiatives could eventually lead to the erosion of the central state's authority and control over the polity. The ramifications of economic liberalization extend beyond the narrow confines of the economic domain into the political sphere, whereby issues relating to political legitimacy and social justice come into focus.[171] Moreover, Western democracies' insistence on linking trade and aid to political liberalization put additional pressures on states attempting to control the pace and direction of their own developmental processes.[172] Nevertheless, given those aforementioned proclivities for a strong state under military supervision, the role of the state in Myanmar's economic development in general and industrialization in particular will likely to remain pivotal.[173]

As such, the role of the state in Myanmar will not be confined to just providing public goods and the rule of law conducive to market interactions but is expected to be more proactive in defining the parameters of development through industrial, trade, and investment policies. Policy measures thus employed would be expected to be more market friendly than in the past but one cannot rule out direct interventions reminiscent of *dirigisme* in areas perceived by the military as essential to maintain control over state and society.[174]

The common threads that ran through the increasing interventionist role of the state in Myanmar from 1948 to 1988 had been the notions of self-reliance, the principle of state ownership of the means of production, and the ideals of planned economic development. As such, the primacy of the state's role in relation to (the almost non-existent) non-state institutions and the society at large was taken for granted by the ruling elite who tended to project themselves as the embodiment of the "state qua state". This statist legacy remains and has made the present attempts by SLORC/SPDC to institute a market economy open to private initiatives extremely problematic.[175] In fact, the self-reliance paradigm and penchant for planning continue to remain relevant as underlying principles for the current *modus operandi* of the military government. This is especially true in the context of industrialization. The new role of the state in Myanmar's development is contingent upon the military leaders' refashioning of the state–society relationship according to their own interpretation of Myanmar's history and political culture in response to what they perceive as imminent and latent threats to Myanmar's territorial integrity and national sovereignty.

It follows that in significant part of the demand–supply nexus, one sees the state's hand instead of the invisible hand of the market. Like in India of the early 1990s, "the discipline of the market is resisted even as its superiority is celebrated."[176] The state still plans following the same methods used during the Socialist era. External trade is being controlled by a maze of licences, rules, regulations, and procedures that keep changing, as the state encounters what it perceives as challenges by domestic and foreign business interests. Prices of essential commodities such as rice, cooking oil, and meat are still "regulated" and Committees for Reduction of Consumer Prices chaired by senior military commanders endeavour to suppress price inflation through restrictive administrative measures. Diverging trends in the official and the free market exchange rates are, more often than not, tackled by administrative measures against currency traders.[177]

On the other hand, the problem of Myanmar's economic transition is not only getting the macroeconomic fundamentals right but also a matter of changing the microeconomic behaviour of individuals; be they consumers or producers or service providers.[178] Moreover, in the context of Myanmar's state-led development, there is also the important issue of state capability related to its capacity to fuse political, financial, and technical resources into an effective developmental thrust.[179] This is closely linked to the bureaucratic capacity of the civil service,[180] which, in turn, is related to the overall potential for human resources development (HRD) in Myanmar. The negative impact of the gaps in the continuity of tertiary education and the trauma of the state-student confrontation since 1988 could frustrate the state's developmental thrust unless they are rectified in a socially meaningful manner.[181]

Yet, current trends suggest that the SPDC is determined to institute a political order where state control over society is exercised in conjunction with some form of electoral representation while allowing greater private sector participation in the economy. The military leadership seems to have perceived that retaining control over the price of rice and staple foods, foreign exchange rate, banking and insurance, as well as, economic activities in areas such as electric power, minerals, energy and fuels, land use, teak extraction, communications including mass media, and strategic industries in defence and manufacturing, is essential for economic development and maintenance of social stability. This entails that the state will still play a major role in the economic development of Myanmar despite its commitment towards the market economy. The likelihood is that Myanmar will continue along the slow path towards the market-oriented economy under military guidance in which the state's direct economic role is gradually reduced in relative terms but the state will retain strategic control over the private sector.

The question of whether Myanmar can succeed in this state-building exercise will depend upon how well the military can manage the dual task of political and economic transition to a "democratic" state whose economy is organized along market principles.[182] Notwithstanding the unexploited and presumably uncharted natural resources, the seemingly convoluted trends in market development does make it difficult for Myanmar's economy to industrialize, as it is being deprived of development funds by the Western embargo on bilateral and multilateral assistance. Despite the military's best efforts a viable and vibrant private sector in Myanmar will take more time and energy predicated upon a consistent and comprehensive programme of transition in which macro- and microeconomic measures are integrated and the role of the state properly defined and mapped out. Tighter fiscal discipline, closer co-operation as well as co-ordination among ministries and state agencies and a transparent structure of authority with clearly defined executive functions are needed. The state would have to introduce measures that restore confidence on the state's monetary policies as well as those which reflect the state's genuine acceptance of the private sector as a valued partner rather than its handmaiden. The fundamental question of how to establish an efficient and sufficient domestic resource mobilization mechanism compatible with the new market-orientation cannot be deferred any longer. Market-friendly economic institutions have to be established. An impartial and efficient civil service enjoying sufficient remuneration and where meritocracy rather than loyalty counts for career advancement needs to be established.[183] Finally the unpleasant task of tackling the issue of corruption and graft that has come to the fore since the economic "opening" has to be undertaken by the highest authorities of the state. Unlike Vietnam and China, this problem have never been officially acknowledged in the context of economic reforms and the loosening of central controls.[184]

Although it may be, as some have argued, that Myanmar's economic reform is not a "hostage to political reform", Myanmar's transition to the market economy is largely contingent upon underlying political factors which essentially determine its pace and direction.[185] The military's role in the new political order being forged by the SPDC will influence the nature of state–society relationship that will, in turn, define the broad parameters of the emerging political economy. As such, the outcome of the present military's attempt to resurrect the Myanmar state in institutional symbiosis with itself will determine the future of Myanmar's development but whether it will ensure enduring stability and foster economic development remains to be seen. The odds are probably less favourable than what the military leadership would like to believe. Nevertheless, given the paucity of alternative institutions and the military's concerted efforts to perpetuate state hegemony over the polity, it is difficult to envisage a scenario in which the state will not play a major role in Myanmar's development for the next decade or so. Peter Evans discerns "patterns of state involvement in terms of roles" and posits four archetypes, viz., "custodian" (regulating), "demiurge"(producing), "midwifery" (facilitating and promoting), and "husbandry" (cajoling and assisting).[186] The actual development will, in all probability, be in the form of a mixture of "husbandry" and "midwifery" that does not rule out shades of "demiurge". In short, if current trends in Myanmar's political economy continue (there are currently no indications that it would not) the state will prevail rather than wither away under the onslaught of market forces, civil society, and globalization.[187]

Notes

1. Attributed to Lance Taylor by Paul Streeten. See Paul Streeten, "Against the Minimalist State", *World Development* 21, no. 8 (1993), note 7, p. 1296.
2. For an account of the 1988 upheaval from the dissidents' viewpoint, see, for example, Bertil Lintner, *Outrage: Burma's Struggle for Democracy* (Bangkok: White Lotus, 1990). For the military's point of view, see, Tatmadaw Thar Thutaythi Tit Oo, *1948 Khu Hnit Mha 1988 Khu Hnit Atwin Hpyat Than Llar Thaw Myanma Thamaing Ahkyin Hnint Tatmadaw Ghanda* [A Brief History of Myanmar and the role of the Tatmadaw between 1948 and 1988], Vol. 1 and 2 (Yangon: News and Periodicals Enterprise, 1990).
3. For elaboration, see Tin Maung Maung Than, "Myanmar: Military in Charge", in *Government and Politics in Southeast Asia*, edited by John Funston (Singapore: Institute of Southeast Asian Studies, 2001), pp. 203–51.

"Myanmar Export/Import Rules and Regulations for Private Business Enterprises, 1997" (Yangon: Ministry of Commerce, 1997).

4. The cycle of protest and violence was triggered by a tea-shop brawl on 12 March 1988 between engineering students and local youth. Thereafter, student demonstrations, communal violence and sporadic attacks against security forces occurred intermittently in Yangon and some major towns and cities. The tempo of protest and violence intensified at the end of July. For an annotated chronology, see Lintner, *Outrage*, pp. 192–204.
5. Maung Maung, *The 1988 Uprising in Burma*, Yale University Southeast Asia Studies Monograph 49 (New Haven: Yale University Press, 1999), p. 221.
6. According to Dr Maung Maung, the coup was "practically forced on" the military by "grave provocations" that took place on 16 and 17 of September, whereby unruly mobs threatened to storm the defence ministry and forced a platoon of soldiers to give up their arms in central Yangon, respectively (ibid., p. 243; see, also, pp. 223–26).
7. SLORC Declaration No. 1/88, dated 18 September 1988.
8. See, for example, Lt. Col. Hla Min, *Political Situation of Myanmar and Its Role in the Region*, 17th ed. (Yangon: Office of Strategic Studies, Ministry of Defence, 1999), pp. 32–33.
9. For the military's political vision of Myanmar, see, for example, Nawrahta, *Destiny of the Nation* (Yangon: The News and Periodicals Enterprise, 1995).
10. SLORC member and Home Minister, Lt. General Myo Nyunt's address to the National Convention on 7 June 1993 (*The New Light of Myanmar* [hereafter *NLM*], 8 June 1993).
11. Robert Taylor, "Myanmar 1990: New Era or Old?", in *Southeast Asian Affairs 1991* (Singapore: Institute of Southeast Asian Studies, 1991), p. 201.
12. The National League for Democracy (NLD) which was co-founded by Daw Aung San Suu Kyi, the daughter of national hero *Bogyoke* Aung San, emerged the front runner in the run-up to the elections. However, Daw Aung San Suu Kyi was placed under house arrest in July 1989 and was only released in May 1995.
13. See *Taingkyo Pyipyu 1988–1991* [Nation-Building Endeavours 1988–1991], (Yangon: Printing and Publishing Sub-Committee on the Historical Records of Endeavours made by the State Law and Order Restoration Council, 1991), pp. 490, 495.
14. The NLD won 80.8 per cent of the total seats, but it secured only 59.9 per cent of the total votes cast, whereas the National Unity Party (NUP; which was the reincarnation of the BSPP) won only ten seats (2.1 per cent) but garnered 25.1 per cent of the votes. In contrast, the Shan National League for Democracy (SNLD; an ethnic-based party allied to NLD) which won twenty-three seats in the Shan region managed to capture only 1.7 per cent of the votes (Taylor, "Myanmar 1990", p. 204).

15. SLORC has insisted that a constitution need to be formulated before a transfer of power can be affected. For its arguments, see SLORC Proclamation 1/90 dated 27 July 1990 (*Working People's Daily* [hereafter *WPD*], 28 July 1990).
16. SLORC Chairman Senior General Saw Maung was "retired" on medical grounds in April 1992 and replaced by his deputy General Than Shwe. This leadership change did not affect the junta's stand on politics.
17. Address by Lt. General Myo Nyunt on 7 June 1993.
18. For details on the more significant points, see Tin Maung Maung Than, "Myanmar: The Dilemma of Stalled Reforms", ISEAS Trends in Southeast Asia no. 10 (Singapore: Institute of Southeast Asian Studies, 2000), pp. 8–9.
19. Chief Justice U Aung Toe, Chairman of the working committee of the NC, was reported to have said that the NC would be reconvened once the discussions, on basic detailed guidelines regarding separation of powers between the legislative, executive, and judiciary at different levels were completed (*NLM*, 1 September 1998).
20. See, for example, James East, "Myanmar Junta Showing Signs of a Rethink", in *Straits Times*, 15 January 2001.
21. For an elaboration of the "road map", see, for example, Khin Maung Win, "Myanmar Road Map to Democracy: The Way Forward", in *Seminar on Understanding Myanmar*, Yangon, 27–28 January 2004 (Yangon: Myanmar Institute of Strategic and International Studies, n.d.), pp. 6–26.
22. For details, see, for example, Kyaw Yin Hlaing, "Myanmar in 2004: Why Military Rule Continues", in *Southeast Asian Affairs 2005* (Singapore: Institute of Southeast Asian Studies, 2005), pp. 232–38.
23. For an analysis of the NLD's actions and its predicament, see ibid., pp. 239–44.
24. In the statement by the ASEAN Foreign Ministers released in Vientiane on 26 July 2005, it was stated that "Myanmar had decided to relinquish its turn to be the Chair of ASEAN ... because it would want to focus its attention on the ongoing national reconciliation and democratisation process". It was further elaborated that "2006 will be a critical year and the Government of Myanmar wants to give its full attention to the process" ("Statement by the ASEAN Foreign Ministers, Vientiane, 25 July 2005", at http://www.aean.org/17590.htm, accessed on 30 July 2005).
25. Selected from David I Steinberg, "Myanmar: The Roots of Economic Malaise", in *Myanmar: Beyond Politics to Societal Imperatives*, edited by Kyaw Yin Hlaing, Robert H. Taylor and Tin Maung Maung Than (Singapore: Institute of Southeast Asian Studies, 2005), p. 105.
26. Ibid., p. 111.
27. Annual inflation represented by the CPI in the capital was around 25 per cent between 1986 and 1988. Repayment of foreign debt, estimated at around

US$4.5 billion with 90 per cent in soft loans, had received a reprieve due to Myanmar's LDC status.

28. See, for example, Mya Than, *Myanmar's External Trade: An Overview in the Southeast Asian Context* (Singapore: Institute of Southeast Asian Studies, 1992), pp. 56–59.
29. In fact, Brigadier David O. Abel, then Minister of Planning, Finance and Trade, remarked that "the changes affected in the economic policy have now reached the right path ... the country, which is rich in natural resources, could become an economically developed nation within 5-10 years". (*WPD*, 27 July 1989; quoted in Richard Vokes, "Burma and Asia-Pacific Dynamism: Problems and Prospects of Export-Oriented Growth in the 1990s", in *Myanmar Dilemmas and Options: The Challenge of Economic Transition in the 1990s*, edited by Mya Than and Joseph L. H. Tan [Singapore: Institute of Southeast Asian Studies, 1990], p. 219). For a detailed wish list of reform measures suggested by one long-time Myanmar watcher, see David Steinberg's memorandum to the World Bank, dated 5 November 1988, reproduced in David I. Steinberg, *Burma: The State of Myanmar* (Washington, D.C.: Georgetown University Press, 2001), pp. 315–20.
30. For an illuminating discussion on the probable causes of Myanmar's failure to institute rational economic reforms, see Steinberg, "Myanmar: The Roots of Economic Malaise", pp. 86–116.
31. See Mya Than, "Recent Developments in Myanmar: Impact and Implications of ASEAN Membership and Asian Crisis", in *Burma/Myanmar: Strong Regime Weak State?* edited by Morton B. Pederson, Emily Rudland and Ronald J. May (Adelaide: Crawford House, 2000), p. 161.
32. *Review of the Financial, Economic and Social Conditions for 1992/93* [hereafter referred to as *Review*] (Rangoon: Ministry of Planning and Finance, 1992), p. 23.
33. See, for example, Mya Maung, "Burma's Economic Performance under Military Rule", *Asian Survey* (June 1997), pp. 503–24.
34. Subsequently, the Myanmar Investment Commission (MIC) was formed as the sole authority for scrutinizing and authorizing investments by both foreign and local investors. The chairman of the MIC as at mid-2005 was the Minister of Science and Technology.
35. See Mya Than, "The Union of Burma Foreign Investment Law: Prospects of Mobilizing Foreign Capital for Development?", in *Myanmar Dilemmas and Options*, pp. 186–218.
36. For an account and critique of significant reforms up to 1991, see U Tun Wai, "Myanmar", in *From Centrally Planned to Market Economies: The Asia Approach-Volume 3, Lao PDR, Myanmar and Vietnam*, edited by Pradumna B. Rana and Naved Hamid (Hong Kong: Oxford University Press, 1996), pp. 151–331. For an analysis of banking and financial reforms, see "Banking and Financial Reforms in Myanmar", *Myanview* 1, no. 3 (1995), Supplement. These two studies covered almost all the significant reforms in Myanmar.

37. For details on private participation in external trade, see "Myanmar Export/Import Rules and Regulations for Private Business Enterprises 1997" (Yangon: Ministry of Commerce, 1997).
38. See, for example, "Government's Policy Response to the Regional Crisis." *Myanview* 5, no. 4 (1999): 2–3. Cf., the following comment attributed to a World Bank Study: "liberalization has stalled in recent years, ... there has even been some recent reversals in these reforms" (Thomas Crampton, "Burma's Growing Debt is Pushing Economy to the Brink, Bank Warns," *International Herald Tribune*, 15 November 1999). See, also, *Country Profile 2004 Myanmar (Burma)* (London: EIU, 2004), pp. 24–25.
39. Asian Development Bank, *Asian Development Outlook 2000* (New York: Oxford University Press, 2000), p. 106; and Asian Development Bank, *Asian Development Outlook 2005*, online electronic version at http://adb.org/Documents/Books/ADO/2005/mya.asp, accessed on 29 July 2005.
40. Peter Young, "Lessons of Privatization", *Economic Reform Today*, No. 1 (1998): 1.
41. William M. Megginson, "The Impact of Privatization," *Economic Reform Today*, No. 1 (1998): 12.
42. Young, "Lessons of Privatization", pp. 6–7.
43. Su Su Khin, "*Puggliga Tho Hlwepyaung Lokekain Ne Thaw Setyon Mya Ei Lokengan Hsaungywet Hmu Achei Anay Goh Leilar Sisit Chin*" [Analysis of Operational Situation at Factories Transferred to the Private Sector] (unpublished Master thesis., Commerce Department, Institute of Economics, Yangon, June 1996), p. 3.
44. Those included 18 factories under the Ministry of No. 1 Industry (textiles and apparel, leather, paints, matches, biscuit, noodles and seasoning powder); 3 engineering plants and 1 dry cell plant under the Ministry of No. 2 Industry; 2 farms and 2 food processing plants under the Ministry of Livestock Breeding and Fisheries; 4 rice bran oil mills under the (then) Ministry of Trade; 21 cinemas under the Ministry of Information (ibid., appendix 3).
45. For an interesting discussion on entrepreneurship in post-1988 Myanmar, see, for example, Chapter 1 in Toshihiro Kudo, ed., *Industrial Development in Myanmar (2): Prospects and Challenges*, ASEDP No. 64. (Chiba: IDE/JETRO, 2002), pp. 1–42.
46. *Nation-Building Endeavours, Volume III: Historical Records of Endeavours Made by the State Law and Order Restoration Council (From 1 April 1995 to 14 November 1997)* (Yangon: Printing and Publishing Sub-Committee, Historical Records of Endeavours made by the State Law and Order Restoration Council: Yangon, 1999), p. 84.
47. "Privatising in Myanmar", *Myanmar Times and Business Review* (hereafter *MT*), 4–10 September 2000. This mainly applied to cinemas, light industries and business premises.
48. Ibid. An example of this type of transaction was the leasing of the only steel mill in Myanmar (for ten years) to a group of Myanmar entrepreneurs whose previous experience was in the construction sector.

49. Ibid.
50. *Nation-Building Endeavours, Volume III*, p. 86. The fact that twenty-eight factories on the initial list were reverted back to the state, albeit under different ministries, may be seen as a retrograde process. However, it is not surprising given that the operational guidelines of the MPC leave room for non-economic considerations as well (for details, see Su Su Khin, "*Puggliga Tho Hlwepyaung Lokekain*").
51. *NLM*, 25 August 1998.
52. "Creating Right Environment the Key to Privatisation, Says Abel", *MT*, 5–11 February 2001. Nine were leased and 129 were sold outright.
53. "The Ministries want to hang on to state enterprises even though they are not profitable. They may be afraid to loose them" (alleged to be one of the many remarks made by deputy planning minister Brigadier General Zaw Tun at a postgraduate economic seminar in July 2000; he was sacked from his position for such scathing criticism on the government's running of the economy [Internet posting to the newsgroup, soc.culture.burma, on 6 August 2000]).
54. "Privatising in Myanmar", *MT*, 4–10 September 2000.
55. Also attributed to B. G. Abel in "Creating Right Environment", *MT*, 5–11 February 2001.
56. See Win Kyaw Oo, "Eight Government Properties listed for Privatisation", *MT*, 19–25 August 2002. This was a relaxation of the condition set by the MRC, whereby the private investor was required to continue with the same line of business with no retrenchment of existing employees.
57. See Win Kyaw Oo, "Minister Urges Gradual Pace with Privatisation Process," *MT*, 10–16 March 2003.
58. Tun Wai, "Myanmar", p. 258.
59. Ibid., p. 263.
60. "Current Situation of the Myanmar Economy and Its Future Development Strategy", Study Group on the Myanmar Economy, Institute of Fiscal and Monetary Policy, Ministry of Finance, Japan (June 1999), p. 17.
61. Tun Wai, "Myanmar", pp. 197–98.
62. "Current Situation", p. 18.
63. For example, in the 1998/99 budget estimates the SEE sector's deficit of 42 billion kyat was nearly 15 per cent of the sector's total receipts. In the 1999/2000 budget, the deficit of 58 billion kyat was some 20 per cent of overall receipts. See "The 1998/99 Budget," *Myanview* 4, no. 2 (1998), pp. 7–8; "The 1999/2000 Budget," *Myanview* 5, no. 2 (1999), p. 9. See also Myat Thein, *Economic Development of Myanmar* (Singapore: Institute of Southeast Asian Studies, 2004), Table 5.6, p. 145 and pp. 145–48.
64. "*Review 1989/90*", p. 1.
65. "An Outline of the Five Year Plan of Union of Myanmar (1996/97 to 2000/2001)", unpublished document, Yangon, Ministry of National Planning and Economic Development, May 1996, p. 1. The real GDP shrunk by 1.1,

4, and 11.4 percentage points respectively in fiscal years 1986/87, 1987/88, and 1988/89.

66. Major infrastructure projects of the military government involved building bridges and an assortment of irrigation projects, such as dams, weirs, channels. Between 1988 and mid-2000, the construction ministry had built 111 "major" bridges (length of 180 feet or longer) costing over 305 billion kyat and nearly US$109 million (Tekkatho Tin Kha, "Victories of the State, the People and the *Tatmadaw*", *NLM*, 16 July 2000). Another 72 bridges were completed by the government during the next five years (see Construction Ministry website at www.myanmar.com/Ministry/Construction/bridge_act.htm, accessed on 30 July 2005). Similarly, the agriculture and irrigation ministry had completed, up to end if January 2001, 117 irrigation projects worth some 27 billion kyat (Kyi Myint Hein, "*Naignant Ah Mahn Hse Taman-2* [Reservoirs and Dams, the Strength of the Country], *Kyemon*, 19 February, 2001). Furthermore, an additional 53 irrigation projects were completed by the government, up to February 2005 (for detailed information, see Ministry of Agriculture and Irrigation website at www.myanmar.com/Ministry/agriculture/waterresources.htm, accessed on 30 July 2005).
67. See, for example, "Self-Sufficiency is Key to Success", Perspective [editorial], *NLM*, 19 January 2000.
68. "An Outline of the Five Year Plan".
69. The government attributed the success to "the ability to mobilize relatively high levels of investments ... coupled with the ability to more than doubled the value of exports" (ibid.)
70. Despite the absence of Socialist rhetoric and guidelines imposed by the ruling party, there appeared to be little change in the modalities of planning between the BSPP regime and the SLORC/SPDC government. In fact, the format and contents of the annual economic "Review" published by the planning ministry remained the same, save for the change in title (until it ceased publication after the 1998 edition). The BSPP legacy of planning hierarchy comprising central, regional and local units essentially remains intact, except for some adjustments to comply with changes in the public administration hierarchy. Despite the adoption of the market orientation, the planning bureaucracy probably expanded rather than shrunk during the late 1990s. For example, a notice from the Ministry of National Planning and Economic Development, dated 4 November 1996, called upon university graduates to apply for 250 vacancies in the state/division and district planning offices (*Kyemon*, 5 November 1996).
71. "An Outline of the Five Year Plan," p. 2.
72. Untitled pamphlet produced by the Ministry of National Planning and Economic Development, Yangon, March 2003; in author's possession.
73. See, for example, the section on "Policy Reforms", in *Country Presentation by the Government of Myanmar,* Third United Nations Conference on the Least Developed Countries. Brussels, 14–20 May 2001, pp. 12–13.

74. Ibid. p. 12.
75. Personal communications, Yangon, June 2005. These high growth rates were questioned by some quarters whose estimates were much lower. For example, the Economist Intelligence Unit (EIU), estimated that the growth rates (in per cent) for fiscal years beginning 1999, 2000, 2001, and 2002 as only 5.7, 6.2, 5.4, and 5.3 respectively (*Country Profile*, various years). For 2004, the IMF estimated a growth rate of only 3.6 per cent (cited in the "Asia Economic Monitor", Asian Development Bank, August 2005, p. 36, online edition at http://aric.adb,org/aem/aug05/regionalaug05.pdf.)
76. However, agriculture's share of GDP in constant 1985/86 prices had been falling steadily from 38.5 per cent in 1988/89 to 33.6 per cent in 2000/01 (untitled pamphlet, March 2003).
77. Ibid.
78. See, for example, Myat Thein, "Economic Growth, Poverty, and Development Policy in Myanmar", unpublished paper presented at the Symposium on Food Policy in Indochina and Myanmar, Hanoi, March 1999, pp. 12–13.
79. See, for example, Peter G. Warr, "The Failure of Myanmar's Agricultural Policies", in *Southeast Asian Affairs 2000* (Singapore: Institute of Southeast Asian Studies, 2000) pp. 219–38. For a more positive and optimistic view, see "Agriculture: Where to Go and How to Tackle the Challenge," *MT*, 28 August–3 September 2000.
80. Based on Yangon CPI (*Selected Monthly Economic Indicators* [Yangon: Central Statistical Organization], various issues; hereafter cited as *SMEI*).
81. The paddy production in the fiscal year 2003/04 increased by 6.1 per cent as compared to a negative growth of 0.5 per cent in the previous season. The fall in the retail price of rice in the cities by more than 25 per cent in the first half of 2004 also seemed to suggest that the liberalization of rice marketing had led to a higher supply of rice in the domestic market. This was probably due to the positive response from the farmers who were expecting higher income from an increased demand for export. However, exports in the first nine months of 2004 amounted to only 12 per cent of that in the corresponding period in 2003 with little or no private exports, probably leading to an over-supply in the domestic market (data from *SMEI*, various issues).
82. See, for example, Min Htet Myat, "Lifting Rice Controls: More Questions Than Answers", in *Irrawaddy* (May 2003) online edition at www.irrawady.org, accessed on 11 June 2003; and Ardeth Maung Thawnghmung, "Agricultural Implementation Processes in Burma/Myanmar: Problems and Limitations", in *The Illusion of Progress: The Political Economy of Reform in Burma/Myanmar*, edited by David S. Mathieson and R. J. May (Adelaide: Crawford House, 2004), pp. 200–22.
83. More recent data for, 2003/04, saw a marked increase in the goods sector to 65.5 per cent at the expense of the services sector that went down to 11.1 per cent (untitled pamphlet produced by the Ministry of National

Planning and Economic Development, Yangon, March 2005; in author's possession). However, those were calculated using constant prices pegged to a different base year (2000/01) and as such are not compatible with the 1988/89 data (based on constant 1985/86 prices) portrayed in Figure 9.4.

84. The fiscal year 1997/98 was the last available year for sectoral employment data. There is no evidence to suggest that the pattern had significantly changed in the next few years.
85. See, for example, Myat Thein, "Improving Domestic Resource Mobilization in Myanmar", ISEAS Working Papers on Economic and Finance No. 1 (Singapore Institute of Southeast Asian Studies, January 1999).
86. Mya Than and Myat Thein, "Mobilization of Financial Resources for Development in Myanmar", in *Financial Resources for Development in Myanmar: Lessons form Asia*, edited by Mya Than and Myat Thein (Singapore: Institute of Southeast Asian Studies, 2000), p. 4. This view was generally supported by almost all Myanmar economists and policy-makers whom the present author had communicated with in the past two decades.
87. Ibid. As at early 2005 no developed capital markets existed in Myanmar. Although a security firm was set up in 1996 as a joint venture between the government's Myanmar Economic Bank and a Japanese research company up the end of 2000, there had been only one client for over-the-counter stock trading. See, for example, "Current Situation", p. 27.
88. The revenue/GDP ratio came to some 12 per cent even in the last year of BSPP rule. For details, see Mya Than and Myat Thein, "Mobilization of Financial Resources", pp. 10–11.
89. Ibid; and *Statistical Yearbook 2002* (Yangon: Central Statistical Organization, 2002), pp. 328–29. The lottery tax was the only component that exhibited a rising trend in both absolute and relative terms. Between 1990/91 and 1999/2000, the volume of lottery tax multiplied twelve times, while its proportion to GDP increased from 0.28 per cent to 0.32 per cent (data derived from "State Lottery Introduces a K30 Million Monthly Prize", *MT*, 29 May–4 June 2000). One reason given for low tax revenues was that the tax on agriculture was very low at around 1 per cent of total tax revenue. Moreover, the implicit tax on agriculture garnered through price controls (during the BSPP era) was also largely diminished after price and marketing reforms were introduced in 1989. See "Current Situation", p. 16.
90. Ibid., p. 17. Myanmar's Minister for Finance attributed the budget deficits to expenditure on development of infrastructure "in the absence of external financial assistance" using "its own resources" ("Statement by the Hon. Hla Tun, Governor of the Bank for Myanmar at the Joint Annual Discussion" at the IMF/World Bank Group 2004 Annual Meetings, Press Release No. 11, 3 October 2004).
91. The general CPI for Yangon (1986 as base year with the index at 100) increased from 168 to 1967 between 1989 and 2000 (for March) while the corresponding index for food went up from 174 to 2,369 (*SMEI*, various

issues). More recent data (from *SMEI*) are not compatible for longitudinal analysis as the base year was changed to 1997 and the CPI data for Yangon were discontinued towards the end of 2000.

92. This was to cover the budget deficit. According to government statistics, the ratio of currency in circulation to M1 was very high, at around 90 per cent, from 1992 to 1997 (the latter was the last available year for such data in the *SMEI*, published by the Central Statistical Organization). Moreover, since "the establishment of private banks in the early 1990s, the percentage share of quasi money to GDP and also to total liquidity" had been "rising" ("Country Presentation", p. 14).
93. See "Current Situation", p. 20; and Mya Than and Myat Thein, "Mobilization of Financial Resources", p. 13.
94. "Country Presentation", p. 14. Interestingly, despite the government's reduction of Central Bank rates by three and two percentage points respectively in April 1999 and 2000 (apparently to ease the financial burden of local entrepreneurs who were encouraged by the government to engage in investment-heavy agricultural projects on wetlands and fallow land, many of whom were saddled with huge debts after the real estate "bust" of the late 1990s), the rising trend in people's savings had not been aversely affected. The total cumulative savings grew by 44 per cent and 53 per cent on a yearly basis between April 1999 and April 2001 (*SMEI*, various issues). The main reason could be the fact that small business entrepreneurs utilize saving deposits to "park" working capital because of aversion to hold cash and there were still far few avenues for small depositors to invest in (personal communications with knowledgeable observers in Yangon; end 1999 and mid-2000).
95. Myint Myint Tin, "Creating Domestic Investment via the Banking System in Myanmar", in *Financial Resources for Development in Myanmar*, edited by Mya Than and Myat Thein, pp. 81, 84, 85.
96. The donors held back ODA, despite's Myanmar's LDC status, on account of allegations that the military regime had condoned human rights abuses and suppression of the democracy movement. During the decade from 1991 to 2000 Myanmar received just US$641 million worth of ODA from friendly bilateral donors and around US$339 million from multilateral agencies (the largest from the United Nations Development Programme or UNDP). See *Myanmar: Country Economic Report* (Manila: Asian Development Bank, 2001), Table 26, p. 66.
97. This was in contrast to Vietnam (another transition economy of Southeast Asia), which garnered an annual average FDI of US$1.37 billion in the five years from 1999 to 2003 (*Asian Development Bank Key Indicators 2004* [Manila: Asian Development Bank, 2005], p. 331). For an assessment of Myanmar's FDI potential, see, for example, *Myanmar: Trade and Investment Potential in Asia*, ESCAP Studies in Trade and Investment 19 (New York: United Nations, 1996).

98. See, for example, Mya Than, "Recent Developments in Myanmar", p. 153; and Min Zin, "Sanctions Revisited," *Irrawaddy* (May 2001), pp. 15–16. It should be noted that the data in Figure 9.11 are sums approved by the MIC based on pledges by investors. The actual amounts invested are unknown and depend on the nature of the project and its scheduling.
99. U Zaw Min Win, "Analysis of FDI in Myanmar", Third Myanmar–Japan Economic Conference, Yangon, 6–7 December 1999, mimeographed, p. 12; Mats Nystrand and Robert Rupar, *Foreign Direct Investment in Myanmar (Burma)*, Working Paper No. 30, European Institute of Japanese Studies, Stockholm School of Economics (Stockholm, April 1997), p. 74; and personal communications with foreign investors and entrepreneurs (*c.* 1998, 2000).
100. See, for example, Tin Maung Maung Than, "Myanmar's Energy Sector: Banking on Natural Gas", in *Southeast Asian Affairs 2005* (Singapore: Institute of Southeast Asian Studies, 2005), pp. 265–67, 281–83; and for estimates of the probable income stream, see "How Much does Rangoon get from the Gas?", *Irrawaddy* (November 2004), online edition at www.irrawaddy.org, accessed on 1 August 2005.
101. See, for example, Tin Maung Maung Than, "Myanmar (Burma) in 2000: More of the Same?", *Asian Survey* (January/February 2001), p. 149; and EIU *Country Profile*, various years.
102. For details of the scheme that entailed two lists classified as essential goods (A) and consumer goods (B), whereby a minimum of 80 per cent of total imported value must consist of (A) listed goods, see, for example, "Priority import product announced", *Myanview* (July 1998), p. 3. This scheme was abolished in July 2005 (*7 Day News* [in Myanmar] 28 July 2005, p. 1).
103. See "Current Situation", p. 54 and *SMEI* various issues. It is believed that smuggling of commodities with neighbouring countries still accounted for a substantial volume of imports and exports until the crackdown that followed the purge of corrupt intelligence and border security personnel in the last quarter of 2004.
104. The trade surplus may be unsustainable unless export momentum is regained because holding down imports seemed to be untenable in the near future as it had retarded the expansion of the private sector through shortage of imported raw materials, intermediate goods and capital equipment as well as consumer goods (private communications with entrepreneurs and analysts, Yangon and Bangkok, January and February 2004 and January 2005).
105. All data were collated and calculated from *SMEI*, various issues. For imports, commodity-wise comparison was not possible due to discrepancies caused by incompatible border trade data.
106. "Current Situation", pp. 14–15.
107. According to government statistics, the volume of FECs issued as at March 1997 amounted to the equivalent of US$400 million, which exceeded the reserves that stood at around US$250 million. Thereafter, the government

stopped publishing data on FECs. The situation was further complicated by the existence of a separate exchange rate for valuation of customs duties since 1996, which had further devalued the kyat from 100 to a dollar to 180 towards the end of 1998 and then to 450 in 2004. See, for example, ibid., p 32.

108. Ibid. The official exchange rate was around 6 kyat per dollar in the early 1990s and fluctuated around that (depending upon the SDR and U.S. dollar exchange rate). The average open market value of kyat to the U.S. dollar was around 40–60 in the late 1980s; 120 in 1995; 240 in 1997; 355 in 2000; and 960 in 2003 (EIU *Country Profile*, various years). The corresponding exchange rate for the FEC was normally about a few percentage points less.
109. See *Asian Development Bank Key Indicators 2004* (Manila: Asian Development Bank, 2005), p. 223; and also, "Country presentation", p. 24.
110. Myat Thein, *Economic Development of Myanmar*, p. 169.
111. Ibid., p. 242. For plausible reasons behind the unwillingness of the military leaders to institute far-reaching economic reforms, see ibid, p. 243; and also, Steinberg, "Myanmar: The Roots of Economic Malaise", pp. 96–97.
112. "The Asian Economist: An Interview on Regional Economic Issues", *Asian Wall Street Journal*, 24 December 1992.
113. Theimm Htut, "To Exert All-Out Efforts for Industrial Development", *NLM*, Sunday Supplement, 5 September, 1999.
114. Based on "Excerpts from Senior General Than Shwe's Address", *NLM*, 3 August 1999.
115. Ibid.
116. "Country Presentation", p. 40. There are nine sub-committees under MIDWC. For details, see Chit So, "Industrial Development and Reforms in Myanmar", in *Industrial Development and Reforms in Myanmar: ASEAN and Japanese Perspectives*, edited by Minoru Kiryu (Bangkok: White Lotus, 1999), p. 136.
117. SPDC Notification No. 27/99, dated 6 May 1999. Although the mandate of CCID focused on the state sector, a subsequent report on its "work coordination meeting" no. 1/99 suggests that its scope covers the private industrial development as well (see *NLM*, 16 June 1999).
118. Ibid.
119. The Ministry of Industry-1, responsible for light industries, built 30 factories (in the following industrial branches: textile, foodstuff, pharmaceutical, ceramic, paper and chemical, and general and maintenance) between 1988 and 2001 costing 5.5 billion kyat, US$67.7 million and some 7.5 billion yen. Under the TSTP, beginning with fiscal year 2001/02, the same ministry would be building 56 new factories (in all six industrial branches previously mentioned) at a cost of 45 billion kyat and US$1.2 billion (Myat Thein, *Economic Development of Myanmar*, pp. 260–64). Other economic ministries, like Ministry of Industry-2 (responsible for heavy industry), Ministry of

Agriculture and Irrigation, Ministry of Forestry and Ministry of Livestock and Fisheries were also building new SIEs, though on a smaller scale.

120. Ministry of Industry-2 had been engaged in small-scale production of Mazda passenger cars and Hino commercial vehicles from the 1960s and 1970s till 1988 under license from their Japanese parent companies. Thereafter, it continued to produce several hundred jeep-type vehicles a year as well as heavy trucks and buses in three factories under its own brand. Myanmar Automobiles and Diesel Industries, under the same ministry, had been assembling Suzuki passenger and light good vehicles since 1998 in a joint venture with a Myanmar subsidiary of the Japanese parent company. Myanmar Economic Holdings (a private company controlled by the military) had also entered into a joint venture with Isuzu motors for assembling small cars and light trucks. On the other hand, a market survey by the Union of Myanmar Federation of Chambers of Commerce and Industry (UMFCCI) had shown that though there was a huge demand for motor vehicles in Myanmar, the local vehicle-component supply industry was undeveloped and lacked technical know-how. It observed that as "a car has over 6,000 separate components, many of which are precision items and production based on the latest technology, it would be extremely challenging for Myanmar to develop any supporting industry" ("Findings and Recommendations", in UMFCCI, "Myanmar: Demand Survey on Automotive Components" [Yangon, November 2002]). Nevertheless several IZs had produced hundreds of jeep-type vehicles, light pick-up trucks, and light trucks that look like Jeep Wranglers, Mitsubishi and Toyota Sports Utility Vehicles (SUVs), Isuzu, Toyota and Nissan pickups and light trucks in the last few years. Engine blocks and major motive parts, electrical components, drive trains and chasis were imported from Thailand and China and manual assembly had been the hallmark of those vehicles. Meanwhile, it was revealed that inspections made in early 2005 found only 116 out of 439 vehicles made at IZs were found to be in line with MIDC regulations, while the rest had breached the local content rule or contained illegally imported parts or turned out to be slightly modified illegal imports (see Zin Min, "Over 300 Vehicles Denied Registration", *MT*, 13–19 June 2005, p. 4).
121. News reports of the MIDWC-sponsored Coordination Meeting No. 1/2000 on production of motor vehicles, in *NLM*, 8–9 November, 2000.
122. See, Kudo, *Industrial Development in Myanmar (2)*, p. 265.
123. For details, see Zaw Min Win, "Analysis of FDI in Myanmar", pp. 8–9, 14–16; and Kudo, *Industrial Development in Myanmar (2)*, p. 266–67. In the year 2000, there were nearly 4,700 registered private enterprises in the IZs, of which over 98 per cent were small-scale industries and 39 per cent were food processing industries. (Kudo, *Industrial Development in Myanmar (2)*, p. 70). By early 2004, the number had increased to some 6,800. For a list of minsters/deputy ministers assigned to supervise the IZs, see, Myat Thein, *Economic Development of Myanmar*, p. 259.

124. See, "Work Coordination Meeting No. 1/2004 on Myanmar Industrial Development Held", *NLM,* 21 April 2004; and "Coordination Meeting No. 4/2004 on Industrial Development Held", *NLM,* 17 September 2004.
125. See, Myat Thein, *Economic Development of Myanmar,* p, 206; and untitled pamphlet produced by the Ministry of National Planning and Economic Development, Yangon, March 2002; in author's possession.
126. See, untitled pamphlet produced by the Ministry of National Planning and Economic Development, Yangon, March 2003; in author's possession. It was estimated that in early 2004, there were altogether some 101,000 private industries (including unregistered establishments) in the whole country employing around 2 million workers ("Work Coordination Meeting No. 1/2004").
127. Fiscal year 1997/98 was the latest year for which detailed statistics were available for Myanmar's national economy.
128. Dr Kyaw Htin, "SME Development in Myanmar: Policies and Strategies," unpublished working paper, Yangon (*c.* 1999), pp. 7–8.
129. For a Myanmar definition of SME, see ibid., p. 6. There are a number of relatively large private industrial establishments (both in terms of employment and capital investment), such as those producing beer and hard liquor, soft drinks and other beverages, cigarettes, garments, plastic products, batteries, cement, paints, beauty soap, instant noodles, and canned food. See, for example, a cover story on 50 Myanmar industrial products in *Living Color* (November 2000) pp. 23–72. The most prominent export-oriented private industry was garments, whose main destination was the United States. Its export value more than tripled between 1992/93 and 1997/98 to reach some 7 per cent of total export value or around US$70 million (Thet Khaing, "Korean Firms Doubles Staff to 2000 in Search of Profits", *MT,* 1–7 May 2000). Exports further increased to average around US$500 million in the 2000–2002 period (*SMEI,* various issues). However, following the imposition of U.S. sanctions in August 2003, banning imports from Myanmar, garment exports fell drastically leading to a closure of 160 garment factories and retrenchment of over 80,000 workers, including over 70,000 females. Employers had reportedly paid compensation of over 1.2 billion kyat and over 80,000 FECs to the workers who lost their jobs (see "Ayeyawady Division Organization for Women's Affairs Organized A Ceremony to Mark Myanmar Women's Day", *NLM,* 8 July 2005).
130. See, for example, Chit So, "Industrial Development and Reforms", p. 141.
131. Ibid. pp. 133, 145; and "Country Presentation", p. 6.
132. In terms of cumulative FDI approvals the processing and manufacturing sector was second only to the oil and gas sector (Figure 9.12). However, of the US$1.5 billion in approved pledges, over 80 per cent were made in fiscal years 1996/97 and 1997/98 and it is likely that some of them had not yet materialized due to the Asian financial crisis and even those that

did come in, there would be time lag before the results show up in value-added output.

133. Nu Nu Yin, "A Survey of Selected Manufacturing Firms in Myanmar", in *Industrial Development and Reforms in Myanmar*, edited by Kiryu, pp. 35, 63, 65–81.
134. Ibid., p. 63.
135. Minoru Kiryu, "Introduction", in *Industrial Development and Reforms in Myanmar*, edited by Kiryu, p. 3. For a detailed analysis of the problem of human resources in the industrial sector, see Dr Daw Than Toe, "Human Resources Development in Myanmar with Special Reference to Vocational Training for Industrial Development," unpublished working paper, Yangon (*c.* 1998).
136. Kyaw Htin, "SME Development in Myanmar", p. 8.
137. U Thein Tun, *Myanmar Naingan Hnint Sethmu Lokengan Yeizeegyaung* [Myanmar and Industrial Current], paper presented at the economic education seminar organized by the Myanmar Women Entrepreneurs Association, Yangon, 18 December 1999, p. 14.
138. See "Work Coordination Meeting No. 1/2004". Taken at face value, it was a remarkable achievement, given that electricity shortages, import restrictions and fuel rationing, still plagued the private industrial sector. On the other hand, it could indicate that higher capacity utilization had been achieved and higher value-added goods had been produced when compared to the 1990s. It could also be that IZs had attained some maturity with improved linkages (forward and backward) in the industrial sector.
139. "Country Presentation", p. 5.
140. Shawn Crispin and Bertil Lintner, "Burma's Buried Booty", *Far Eastern Economic Review*, 9 December 1999, p. 45.
141. "Country Presentation", p. 6.
142. The price hike was ten times for high-end users in homes and industries. Though it was justifiable in commercial terms, the sudden hike caused consternation among consumers and the business community who had been used to getting cheap electricity. Affected SMEs' business costs suddenly escalated as well. See, for example, "Myanmar Reels under Huge Electricity Price Hike", AFP Report, 3 August 1999 (Internet edition).
143. See, for example, Win Kyaw Oo, "More Inputs are Needed to Power a Hydro Future", *MT*, 4–10 June 2001.
144. See, for example, Win Kyaw Oo, "Promising Power Sector Attracts Private Investment", in Review 2002, *MT*, 23–29 December 2002, p. 14. Some enterprising businessmen and industrialists had also been selling electricity to the local community in the capital city's outskirts and in nearby outlying townships. See Yin Min Tun, "Media Roundup: Power Supply" in *MT*, 2–8 February 2004, p. 6.
145. In January 2003, China offered a US$200 million soft loan. For details of the US$34.7 million project, see "China, Myanmar Sign Contract on Power

Transmission", *People's Daily Online*, 10 October 2003, at http://english.peopledaily.com.cn/, accessed on 2 December 2004. All nine megawatt-scale hydropower projects completed before 2000 used Chinese equipment, together with another five plants with capacities ranging from 150 to 600 kilowatts. See http://www.mynmar.com/build/electricity/0.htm, accessed on 2 December 2004.

146. Myanmar reportedly imported 1.3 million tonnes of crude oil in 1999. See EIU *Country Report, Myanmar (Burma)*, February 2001, p. 22.
147. See, for example, "Myanmar's Upstream Sector hobbled by Pipeline Controversy and Poor R&D Results", *The Oil and Gas Journal*, 26 June 2000, posted in the Internet newsgroup soc.culture.burma on 20 August 2000.
148. See, for example, Nyi Nyi Aung, "Golden Export Outlook for Natural Gas", *MT*, 22–28 March 2004, p. 1; and Kyaw Thu, "Myanmar Biggest Gas Exporter in Asia, Says Minister", *Asia Times* (29 November–5 December 2004), p. 7.
149. Estimate based on the 1983 census and population trends. See, for example, *Statistical Yearbook*, various issues.
150. See, for example, U Maung Maung Yi, "Trade and Investment Situation in Myanmar", unpublished paper presented at the Workshop on Myanmar-Japan Cooperation for the Structural Adjustment of the Myanmar Economy, 25–26 June 2000, Yangon, Myanmar.
151. Data before 1990/91 were not available.
152. Data are not available for (fiscal) years beyond 1997/98.
153. Like in the case of the FDI inflow, no data were available on how much of the approved amount had actually been invested.
154. See Theimm Htut, "UMFCCI to Work with Patriotism and National Outlook", *NLM*, 6 May 2001 and www.umfcci.com.mm/.
155. See U Wint Kyaw, "Ban Akyaung Ngwe Akyaung [On Banks and Money]", *Dhana* (January 2002), pp. 30–32.
156. Sean Turnell, "Myanmar's Banking Crisis", *ASEAN Economic Bulletin* 20, no. 3 (2003): 274.
157. For a detailed account, see ibid., pp. 272–82.
158. See U Than Maung, Pyanlei Know Hta Lar Thaw Puggliga Bangyi Myar [Revival of the Big Private Banks]", *Living Color* (March 2004), p. 73.
159. Eventually, two (Myanmar Mayflower Bank and Asia Wealth Bank) of the three left under supervision were closed down in March 2005 for contravening banking regulations. The third was also closed down in the first week of August 2005.
160. Even by July 2004, the total amount of saving deposits in the private banks came to only 70 per cent of that in January 2003, while for time deposits the total amount received was less than 12 per cent.
161. See Office of the Press Secretary, 28 July 2003, "Executive Order: Blocking Property of the Government of Burma and Prohibiting Certain

Transactions", at BurmaNet News archive www.burmanet.org/bnn_archives/2003/20030729.txt, accessed on 9 August 2004.

162. See, for example, Tun Aung, "Thwinkon Htokekon Lokengan Myar Euro Phyint Asinpyay [Convenience with Euro for Imports/Exports Business], *Living Color* (October 2003), pp. 23–24. It was reported that Myanmar authorities had established links with Belgian-based SWIFT (Society for Worldwide Interbank Financial Telecommunication) group to facilitate financial transactions billed in euros (Nick Mathiason, "Banks bust Burma trade ban", *The Observer*, dated 18 January 2004, posted on the Internet in BurmaNet News, [17–20 January 2004]). The two-way SWIFTNeT FIN traffic (an indicator of usage) for Myanmar in 2004 was 161,000 (comparable to Cambodia's 206,000) messages (SWIFT web site at www.swift.com).
163. See, for example, the news item entitled, "Merchants warned of consequences of raising commodity prices", *NLM*, 19 October 1993; and "Information Committee of State Peace and Development Council holds Press Conference No. 4/2005", *NLM*, 16 May 2005.
164. This occurred in the lucrative cigarette and beer industries. The Union of Myanmar Economic Holdings Ltd (MEH), formed in February 1990 as a joint venture comprising the Ministry of Defence (both in-service and retired) military personnel, and military units portends to be the largest single economic conglomerate in the corporate sector. Its authorized capital of 10 billion kyat (40 per cent of capital shares to be subscribed by the defence ministry) is on par with the entire public sector savings that same year. It has been engaged in securing significant shares in FDI ventures in the services and the manufacturing sectors as well as setting up domestic business concerns in both trade and services.
165. See, for example, Martin Smith, "Ethnic Conflict and the Challenge of Civil Society in Burma", in *Strengthening Civil Society in Burma: Possibilities and Dilemmas for International NGOs*, edited by Tom Kramer and Pietje Vervest (Chiangmai: Silkworm Books, 1999), p. 15; and "Ruby Dragon: A Successful Business Enterprise in Myanmar", in *Business Tank* (June 2004), online edition, www.myanmar.com/Business_Tank/ruby.html, accessed on 6 July 2004.
166. See, for example, Kudo, *Industrial Development in Myanmar (2)*, pp. 1–42, for an illuminating account of entrepreneurship in Myanmar based on survey results on "young entrepreneurs" conducted in the year 2000.
167. *NLM*, 8 June 1993.
168. Foreign Minister U Ohn Gyaw's remarks to the press during his visit to Jakarta with the delegation led by SLORC Secretary-1 Lt. General Khin Nyunt in December 1993 (*Jakarta Post*, 23 December 1993).
169. See, for example, Professor Chai-Anan Samudavanija's explanation of the problem of "state power" in an interview with Kanjana Spindler (*Bangkok Post*, 19 June 1992).

170. "'Peace, Democracy' in Tatmadaw Day Address", *MT*, 2–8 April 2001.
171. See, for example, David Shambaugh, "Losing Control: The Erosion of State Authority in China", *Current History* (September 1993): 253–59; Julian Schweitzer, "Transition in Eastern Europe: The Social Dimension", *Finance and Development* (December 1990): 6–8; and Joan M. Nelson, "The Politics of Economic Transformation: Is Third World Experience Relevant in Eastern Europe?", *World Politics* 45, no. 3 (1993): 433–63.
172. See, for example, Adrian Leftwich, "Governance, Democracy and Development in the Third World", *Third World Quarterly* 14, no. 3 (1993): 605–24.
173. More often than not, some form of political transformation is also concomitant with economic reforms, but even in states undergoing the so-called democratic transition, it is highly unlikely that the state would cease to play a major role in the socio-economic transformation of these societies. See, for example, James Cotton, "The Limits to Liberalization in Industrializing Asia: Three Views of the State", *Pacific Affairs* 64, no. 3 (1991): 311–27; Tony Killick and Christopher Stevens, "Eastern Europe: Lessons on Economic Adjustment from the Third World", *International Affairs* 67, no. 4 (1991), pp. 689–90; William E. Odom, "Durable Democracy Requires a State That Works", *International Herald Tribune,* 14 February 1992; and Yi Feng, "Political Foundations of Economic Management: An Interpretation of Economic Development and Economic Crisis in East Asia", in *The East Asian Development Model: Economic Growth, Institutional Failure and the Aftermath of the Crisis* (Basingstoke: Macmillan, 2000), pp. 71–96.
174. For a similar view, see Steinberg, "Myanmar: The Roots of Economic Malaise", pp. 107–109.
175. For similar views in the context of a longitudinal survey of Myanmar's "developmental disaster" since independence, see Anne Booth, "The Burma Development Disaster in Comparative Historical Perspective", *SOAS Bulletin of Burma Research* (online e-journal) 1, no. 1 (2003), pp. 1–23.
176. Ronald J. Herring, "Embedded Particularism: India's Failed Developmental State", in *The Developmental State*, edited by Meredith Woo-Cummings (Ithaca and London: Cornell University Press, 1999), p. 328.
177. See, for example, "Burma Said Revoking Money-Dealing Licenses in Bid to Stabilise Currency", AFP Report, dated 24 June 2001, posted on the Internet in BurmaNet News (25 June 2001); and *Country Profile 1999-2000, Myanmar (Burma)* (London: EIU, 1999), pp. 34, 39, 40.
178. See, for example, Raymond M. Duch and Harvey D. Palmer, "It's Not Whether You Win or Lose, but How You Play the Game: Self-Interest, Social Justice, and Mass Attitudes Towards Economic Transition", *American Political Science Review* 98, no. 3 (2005): 437–52.
179. See, for example, Donald K. Crone, "State, Social Elites, and Government Capacity in Southeast Asia", *World Politics* XL, no. 2 (1988): 252–68; and

Joel S. Migdal, *Strong Societies and Weak States: State-Society Relations and State Capabilities in the Third World* (Princeton: Princeton University Press, 1988), pp. 10–24, 260–86.

180. See, for example, Alex Mutebi, "'Muddling Through' Past Legacies: Myanmar's Civil Bureaucracy and the Need for Reform", in *Myanmar: Beyond Politics to Societal Imperatives*, edited by Kyaw, Taylor and Tin, pp. 140–60. For a theoretical perspective linking delegation, policy-making and bureaucratic capacity, see John D. Huber and Noland McCarty, "Bureaucratic Capacity, Delegation, and Political Reform", *American Political Science Review* 98, no. 3 (2005): 481–94.
181. For the HRD approach in analysing NIE success, see Wong Poh Kam and Ng Chee Yuen, eds., *Human Resource Development and Utilization in the Asia-Pacific: A Social Absorption Capacity Approach* (Singapore: Institute of Southeast Asian Studies, 1992), especially Chapters 1 and 7. The present measures relying on providing educational infrastructure, indoctrination of teachers and students, and assuring conformity and acquiescence through coercion of both parents, teachers, and students may not be sustainable in the long run and will be counterproductive to human resources development.
182. The military has been engaged in state building, based on its own interpretation of history and corporate culture, since the 1950s. See, for example, Mary Callahan, *Making Enemies: War and State Building in Burma* (Ithaca: Cornell University Press, 2003), pp. 217–27.
183. See, for example, Khin Maung Kyi et al., *Economic Development of Burma: A Vision and A Strategy* (Stockholm: Olof Palme International Center, 2000), Chapters 11 and 12.
184. State leaders have all along urged service personnel to avoid bribery and corruption (see SLORC's Secretary-1 Lt. General Khin Nyunt's address to members of the judicial and legal branches on 29 July 1993; in *NLM*, 31 July 1993). There have been occasional forays by the state intelligence agencies to bring the perpetrators to book. However, it is common knowledge that corruption is not uncommon within the administrative hierarchy.
185. Paul Cook and Martin Minogue, "Economic Reform and Political Change in Myanmar (Burma)", *World Development* 21, no. 7 (1993): 1153.
186. Peter Evans, *Embedded Autonomy: States and Industrial Transformation* (Princeton: Princeton University Press, 1995), p. 13.
187. See, for example, Linda Weiss, *The Myth of the Powerless State: Governing the Economy in a Global Era* (Cambridge: Polity Press, 1998).

Bibliography

LOCAL PERIODICALS AND NEWSPAPERS

Botahtaung (daily).
Burma (quarterly).
Burma Labour Gazette (monthly).
Burma News Digest (weekly).
Burma Weekly Bulletin.
Forward (bi-monthly).
Guardian (bi-monthly).
Kyemon (daily)
Lanzin Thadin (bi-monthly).
Living Color (monthly)
Lokethar Jarnei (monthly).
Lokethar Pyithu Neizin (daily).
Myanmar Times and Business Review (weekly).
New Burma Weekly.
New Light of Myanmar (daily).
People's Workers Gazette (monthly).
Working People's Daily.

YEARBOOKS, STATISTICAL PUBLICATIONS, AND REPORTS

Asia Yearbook. Hong Kong: Far Eastern Economic Review.
Asian Development Outlook. Oxford and New York: Oxford University Press for the Asian Development Bank.
Asian Development Bank Key Indicators. Manila: Asian Development Bank.
Burma: The National Economy. Rangoon: Director of Information.
Burma Business Directory and National Trade Register. Rangoon: Burma Publicity Services.

Burma Chamber of Commerce Annual Report. Rangoon: Burma Chamber of Commerce.

Burma Trade Directory. Rangoon: Burma Commerce.

Country Economic Report Myanmar, Volume 1: Main Report. Manila: Asian Development Bank, December 2001.

Country Presentation by the Government of Myanmar. Third United Nations Conference on the Least Developed Countries. Brussels, 14–20 May 2001.

Country Profile Myanmar (Burma). London: EIU, annual.

Country Report, Myanmar (Burma). London: EIU, annual.

Economic and Social Survey of Asia and the Pacific. Bangkok: Economic and Social Commission for Asia and the Pacific (ESCAP).

Economic Survey of Burma. Rangoon: Government Printing and Stationery.

Geographical Distribution of Financial Flows to Developing Countries. Paris: Organization for Economic Co-operation and Development (OECD).

Global Development Finance: Country Tables. Washington, D.C.: World Bank.

International Financial Statistics. Washington, D.C.: International Monetary Fund.

Key Indicators of Developing Member Countries. Manila: Asian Development Bank.

Myanmar: Trade and Investment Potential in Asia. ESCAP Studies in Trade and Investment 19. New York: United Nations, 1996.

National Income of Burma. Rangoon: Government Printing and Stationery.

Nomura Asia Focus. Tokyo: Nomura Research Institute.

Pyidaungsu Hsoshelit Thamada Myanmar Naingandaw Bundaryei Sipwayei Luhmuyei Achei Anei Hnint Pathet Thi Pyithu Hluttaw Tho Asiyinkhanzar [Report to the Pyithu Hluttaw on Financial, Economic and Social Conditions of the Socialist Republic of the Union of Burma]. Rangoon: Ministry of Planning and Finance.

Pyidaungsu Myanmar Naingan Asoeya Ei Bandaryei Sipwayei Luhmuyei Achay Anay Hnint Pathet Ywei Pyithu Tho Asiyinkhanzar [Report to the People by the Government of the Union of Burma on the Financial, Economic and Social Conditions]. Rangoon: Ministry of Planning and Finance.

Pyithu Lokengan Sithseyei Aphwe Ei Pyithu Hluttaw Tho Asiyinkhanzar [Report of the Council of People's Inspectors to the Pyithu Hluttaw]. Rangoon: Office of the Council of People's Inspectors.

Report to the People by the Government of the Union of Burma on the Financial, Economic and Social Conditions. Rangoon: Ministry of Planning and Finance.

Report to the People by the Union of Burma Revolutionary Council on the Revolutionary Government's Budget Estimates. Rangoon: Ministry of Finance.

Report to the Pyithu Hluttaw on Financial, Economic and Social Conditions of the Socialist Republic of the Union of Burma. Rangoon: Ministry of Planning and Finance.

Review of the Financial, Economic and Social Conditions. Rangoon: Ministry of Planning and Finance.

SEACEN Financial Statistics. Money and Banking, SFS Series no. 1. Kuala Lumpur: Southeast Asian Central Banks (SEACEN) Centre.

Selected Monthly Economic Indicators. Rangoon: Central Statistics and Economics Department; later, Central Statistical Organization, Rangoon.

Statistical Supplement. Rangoon: n.p.

Statistical Yearbook. Rangoon: Central Statistics and Economics Department; later, Central Statistical Organization.

Statistical Yearbook for Asia and the Far East. Bangkok: Economic Commission for Asia and the Far East (ECAFE).

Thailand, Burma: A Country Profile. London: Economist Intelligence Unit (EIU) (annual supplement).

Trade News. Yangon: Ministry of Commerce, (bi-monthly).

Union Bank of Burma Bulletin. Rangoon: Union Bank of Burma.

World Economic and Social Survey 2000: Trends and Policies in the World Economy. New York: United Nations, 2000.

BOOKS AND MONOGRAPHS

Adas, Michael. *The Burma Delta: Economic Development and Social Change in an Asian Rice Frontier, 1852–1941*. Madison: University of Wisconsin Press, 1974.

AFPFL Convention, 1947. Rangoon: Students Digest Press, n.d.

Ahmad, Nafis. *Economic Resources of the Union of Burma*. Natick, MA: U.S. Army Natick Laboratories, Earth Sciences Laboratory, 1971. Technical Report 71-61-ES.

Anderson, Benedict. *Imagined Communities: Reflections on the Origin and Spread of Nationalism*. London: Verso, 1983; reprint, 1990.

Andrus, James Russel. *Burmese Economic Life. Foreword by John S. Furnivall.* Stanford: Stanford University Press, 1948; reprint, 1957.

Ang Beng Wah. *ASEAN Energy Demand: Trends and Structural Change*. Singapore: Institute of Southeast Asian Studies, 1986.

Aung San. *Burma's Challenge*. Rangoon: New Light of Burma Press, 1946; reprint, Tathetta Sarpay, 1968.

Aung Tun Thet. *Burmese Entrepreneurship: Creative Response in the Colonial Economy*. Stuggart: Steiner-Verl., Weisbaden, 1989.

Auty, R. M. *Resource-Based Industrialization: Saving the Oil in Eight Developing Countries*. Oxford: Clarendon Press, 1990.

Ba Han, Maung. *The Planned State*. Rangoon: Rasika Ranjani, 1947.

Ba Swe, U. *A Guide to Socialism in Burma*. Rangoon: Government Printing and Stationery, 1956.

Balassa, Bela. *Economic Policies in the Pacific Area Developing Countries*. Basingstoke and London: Macmillan, 1991.

Bartke, Wolfgang. *China's Economic Aid*. Translated by Waldtraut Jarke. London: C. Hurst, 1975.

Bautista, Romeo M. et al. *Capacity Utilization in Manufacturing: Colombia, Israel, Malaysia, and the Philippines*. New York: Oxford University Press for the World Bank, 1981.

Baxter, James. *Report on Indian Migration*. Rangoon: Government Printing and Stationery, 1941.

Becka, Jan. *The National Liberation Movement in Burma during the Japanese Occupation Period (1941–1945)*. Dissertationes Orientales, vol. 42. Prague: Oriental Institute, 1983.

Beetham, David. *The Legitimation of Power*. Basingstoke and London: Macmillan, 1991.

Binns, B. O. *Agricultural Economy in Burma*. Rangoon: Government Printing and Stationery, 1948.

Burnell, Peter J. *Economic Nationalism in the Third World*. Hemel Hempstead: Harvester/Wheatsheaf, 1986.

Butwell, Richard A. *U Nu of Burma*. Stanford: Stanford University Press, 1963.

Callahan, Mary. *Making Enemies: War and State Building in Burma*. Ithaca: Cornell University Press, 2003.

Cassen, Robert and Associates. *Does Aid Work?* Oxford: Oxford University Press, 1988.

Chakravarti, N. R. *The Indian Minority in Burma: The Rise and Decline of an Immigrant Community*. With a foreword by Hugh Tinker. London: Oxford University Press for the Institute of Race Relations, 1971.

Chao Tzang Yaunghwe. *The Shan of Burma: Memoirs of a Shan Exile*. Singapore: Institute of Southeast Asian Studies, 1987.

Chowdhury, Anis and Iyanatul Islam. *The Newly Industrializing Economies of East Asia*. London: Routledge, 1993.

———. "The East Asian Crisis: A Political Economy Explanation". ISEAS Visiting Researchers Series No. 1. Singapore: Institute of Southeast Asian Studies, 2001.

Corley, T. A. B. *A History of the Burmah Oil Company, Vol. II: 1924–66*. London: Heinemann, 1988.

Donnison, F. S. V. *Public Administration in Burma*. London: Royal Institute of International Affairs, 1953.

Ellman, Michael. *Socialist Planning*. Cambridge: Cambridge University Press, 1979.

Evans, Peter. *Embedded Autonomy: States and Industrial Transformation*. Princeton: Princeton University Press, 1995.

Fenichel, A. H. and W. G. Huff. *The Impact of Colonialism in Burmese Economic Development*. McGill University, Centre for Developing Area Studies, Occasional Paper no. 7. Montreal: Centre for Developing-Area Studies, 1971.

Friedgut, Theodore H. *Political Participation in the USSR*. Princeton: Princeton University Press, 1979.

Fukuyama, Francis. *State-Building: Governance and World Order in the 21st Century*. Ithaca: Cornell University Press, 2004.

Furnivall, John. S. *An Introduction to the Political Economy of Burma*. 3rd ed. Rangoon: People's Literature Committee and House, 1957.

Ghosh, Anjali. *Burma: A Case of Aborted Development*. Calcutta: Papyrus, 1989.

Grindle, Merilee S. and John W. Thomas. *Public Choices and Policy Change: The Political Economy of Reform in Developing Countries*. Baltimore and London: John Hopkins University Press, 1991.

Haggard, Stephan. *Pathways from the Periphery: The Politics of Growth in the Newly Industrializing Countries*. Ithaca: Cornell University Press, 1990.

Harrison, David. *The Sociology of Modernization and Development*. London: Unwin Hyman, 1988.

Hedlund, Stefand and Mats Lundahl. *Ideology as a Determinant of Economic System: Nyerere and Ujama in Tanzania*. Scandinavian Institute of African Studies, Research Report no. 84. Uppsala: n.p., 1989.

Hewitt, Tom, Hazel Johnson, and Dave Wield. *Industrialization and Development*. Oxford: Oxford University Press and The Open University, 1992.

Hill, Hal. *Southeast Asian Economic Development: An Analytical Survey*. Economic Division Working Papers no. 93/4. Canberra: Research School of Pacific Studies, 1993.

Hill, Hal and Sisira Jayasuriya. *An Inward-Looking Economy in Transition: Economic Development in Burma since the 1960s*. Occasional Paper no. 80. Singapore: Institute of Southeast Asian Studies, 1986.

Hla Min, Lt. Col. *Political Situation of Myanmar and Its Role In the Region*. 17th ed. Yangon: Office of Strategic Studies, Ministry of Defence, 1999.

Hla Myint. *Southeast Asia's Economy: Development Policies in the 1970s*. New York: Praeger, 1972.

Htin Aung, Maung. *The Stricken Peacock: Anglo-Burmese Relations, 1752–1948*. The Hague: Martinus Nijhoff, 1965.

Hunt, Diana. *Economic Theories of Development: An Analysis of Competing Paradigms*. Hemel Hempstead: Harvester/Wheatsheaf, 1989.

Ingram, James C. *Economic Change in Thailand, 1850–1970*. Stanford: Stanford University Press, 1971.

International Labour Office. *The Trade Union Situation in Burma*. Geneva: International Labour Office, 1962.

Ishihara, Yoichiro. *Quantitative Analysis of Crisis: Crisis Identification and Causality*. World Bank Policy Research Working Paper 3598, May 2005.

Johnson, Chalmers. *MITI and the Japanese "Miracle": Growth of Industrial Policy, 1925–1975*. Stanford, CA: Stanford University Press, 1982.

Johnson, Harry G., ed. *Economic Nationalism in Old and New States*. Chicago: Chicago University Press, 1967; reprint, London: Allen & Unwin, 1968.

Jones, Hywel G. *An Introduction to Modern Theories of Economic Growth*. London: Thomas Nelson & Sons, 1975.

Khin, U. *Fisheries in Burma*. Rangoon: Government Printing and Stationery, 1948.

Khin Maung Gyi. Pagan U. *Memoirs of the Oil Industry in Burma (1905 A.D.–1980 A.D.)*. Rangoon: n.p., 1989.

Khin Maung Kyi et al. *Economic Development of Burma*. Stockholm: Olof Palme International Center, 2000.

Khin Maung Nyunt. *Foreign Loans and Aid in the Economic Development of Burma 1974/75 to 1985/86*. Institute of Asian Studies, Monograph no. 46. Bangkok: Chulalongkorn University, 1990.

Khin Win, U. *A Century of Rice Improvement in Burma*. Manila: International Rice Research Institute, 1991.

Kitching, Gavin. *Development and Underdevelopment in Historical Perspective*. Rev. ed. London: Routledge, 1989.

Kornai, Janos. *Economics of Shortage*. Vol. B. Amsterdam: North Holland, 1980.

Kudo, Toshihiro. *Industrial Development in Myanmar (2): Prospects and Challenges*. ASEDP No. 64. Chiba: IDE/JETRO, 2002.

Kuznets, Simon. *Modern Economic Growth*. New Haven: Yale University Press, 1966.

Lee, Barbara and John Nellis. *Enterprise Reform and Privatization in Socialist Economies*. World Bank Discussion Paper no. 104. Washington, D.C.: World Bank, 1990.

Lee, Kuen. *New East Asian Economic Development: Interacting Capitalism and Socialism*. New York: M. E. Sharpe, 1993.

Leeson, P. F. and M. M. Minogue, eds. *Perspectives on Development*. Manchester: Manchester University Press, 1988.

Linnemann, Hans, ed. *Export-Oriented Industrialization in Developing Countries*. Singapore: Singapore University Press, 1987.

Lintner, Bertil. *Outrage: Burma's Struggle for Democracy*. Bangkok: White Lotus, 1990.

Lissak, Moshe. *Military Role in Modernization: Civil–Military Relations in Thailand and Burma*. London: Sage, 1976.

Mabro, Robert and Samir Radwan. *The Industrialization of Egypt, 1939–1973: Policy and Performance*. Oxford: Clarendon Press, 1976.

Mali. K. S. *Fiscal Aspects of Development Planning in Burma, 1950–1960*. Rangoon: Department of Economics, University of Rangoon, 1962.

Maung Maung. *Grim War Against KMT*. Rangoon: n.p., 1953.

———. *Burma's Constitution*. 2nd ed. The Hague: Martinus Nijhoff, 1961.

———. *Burma and General Ne Win*. London: Asia Publishing House, 1969.

Maung Maung, Dr. *The 1988 Uprising in Burma*. Yale University Southeast Asia Studies Monograph 49. New Haven, CT: Yale University Press, 1999.

Maung Maung, U. *From Sangha to Laity: Nationalist Movements of Burma, 1920–1940*. Australian National University, Monographs on Southeast Asia no. 4. New Delhi: Manohar, 1980.

———. *Burmese Nationalist Movements, 1940–1948*. Edinburgh: Kiscadale, 1989.

Maung Maung Gyi. *Burmese Political Values: The Socio-Political Roots of Authoritarianism*. New York: Praeger, 1983.

Maung Shein. *Burma's Transport and Foreign Trade (1885–1914)*. Rangoon: Department of Economics, University of Rangoon, 1964.

Mehta, M. M. *Report on the Manpower Situation in Burma*. Geneva: International Labour Office, 1964.

Meier, Gerald M., ed. *Leading Issues in Economic Development*. 5th ed. New York: Oxford University Press, 1989.

Mende, Tibor. *South-East Asia between Two Worlds*. New York: Library Publishers, 1955.

Migdal, Joel S. *Strong Societies and Weak States: State-Society Relations and State Capabilities in the Third World*. Princeton: Princeton University Press, 1988.

Montgomery, John D. *The Politics of Foreign Aid: American Experience in Southeast Asia*. New York: Praeger, 1962.

Morehead, F. T. *The Forests of Burma*. Burma Pamphlets no. 5. London: Longman Greens & Co., 1944.

Mya Than. *Myanmar's External Trade: An Overview in the Southeast Asian Context*. Singapore: Institute of Southeast Asian Studies, 1992.

Myat Thein. "Improving Domestic Resource Mobilization in Myanmar". ISEAS Working Papers on Economic and Finance Series No. 1. Singapore Institute of Southeast Asian Studies, 1999.

———. *Economic Development of Myanmar*. Singapore: Institute of Southeast Asian Studies, 2004.

Myo Htun Lynn, U. *Labour and Labour Movement in Burma*. Rangoon: Department of Economics, University of Rangoon, 1961.

Nawrahta. *Destiny of the Nation*. Yangon: The News and Periodicals Enterprise, 1995.

Nordlinger, Eric. *On the Autonomy of the Democratic State*. Cambridge, Mass.: Harvard University Press, 1981.

Nu, Thakin. *Towards Peace and Democracy*. Translation of selected speeches by the Honourable Thakin Nu, Prime Minister of the Government of the Union of Burma. Rangoon: Ministry of Information, 1949.

———. *From Peace to Stability*. Translation of selected speeches by the Honourable Thakin Nu, Prime Minister of the Union of Burma, delivered on various occasions from 15 April 1949 to 20 April 1951. Rangoon: Ministry of Information, 1951.

Nu, U. *Burma Looks Ahead*. Translation of selected speeches by the Honourable U Nu, Prime Minister of the Union of Burma, delivered on various occasions from 19 July 1951 to 4 August 1952. Rangoon: Ministry of Information, 1953.

———. *Forward with the People*. Translation of selected speeches of the Honourable U Nu, Prime Minister of the Union of Burma, delivered on various occasions between 19 February 1953 and 1 June 1954. Rangoon: Ministry of Information, reprint, 1955.

———. *Asian Speaks*. A collection of speeches made by U Nu, Prime Minister of Burma, during a visit to the U.S.A. in June/July 1955. Washington, D.C.: Embassy of the Union of Burma, 1955.

———. *Premier Reports to the People on Law and Order, National Solidarity, Social Welfare, National Economy, Foreign Affairs*. Translation of the Speech delivered by the Honourable Prime Minister U Nu in the Chamber of Deputies on September 27, 1957. Rangoon: Central Printing Office, 1958.

———. *Towards a Socialist State*. Translation of the Speech delivered on 29 January 1958 at the Third All Burma Congress of the AFPFL. Rangoon: Central Printing Office, 1958.

———. *U Nu: Saturday's Son*. Translated by Law Yone, edited by Kyaw Win. New Haven: Yale University Press, 1975; reprint, Bombay: Bharatiya Bhavan, 1976.

Nystrand, Mats and Robert Rupar. *Foreign Direct Investment in Myanmar (Burma)*. Working Paper no. 30, European Institute of Japanese Studies, Stockholm School of Economics. Stockholm, April 1997.

Post, Ken and Phil Wright. *Socialism and Underdevelopment*. London: Routledge, 1989.

Prakash, Vinod. *Statistical Indicators of Industrial Development: A Critique of the Basic Data*. Economics Department Working Paper no. 189. Washington, D.C.: World Bank, 1974.

Rana, Pradumna B. *Reforms in the Transitional Economies of Asia*. Occasional Paper no. 5. Manila: Asian Development Bank, 1993.

Ranis, Gustav and Syed Akhtar Mahmood. *The Political Economy of Development Policy Change*. Oxford: Blackwell, 1992.

Rees, Judith. *Natural Resources: Allocation, Economics, and Policy*. 2nd ed. London: Routledge, 1990.

Research Institute of Development Assistance (RIDA), The Overseas Economic Cooperation Fund (OECF). *The World Bank's East Asian Miracle Report: Its Strengths and Limitations*. OECF Discussion Papers no. 7. Tokyo: RIDA/ OECF, August 1995.

Rivlin, Paul. *The Dynamics of Economic Policy Making in Egypt*. New York: Praeger, 1985.

Robertson, A. F. *People and the State: An Anthropology of Planned Development*. Cambridge: Cambridge University Press, 1984.

Rose, Saul. *Socialism in Southern Asia*. Oxford: Oxford University Press for the Royal Institute of International Affairs, 1959.

Rothchild, Donald and Naomi Chazan, eds. *The Precarious Balance: State and Society in Africa*. Boulder, CO: Westview Press, 1988.

Seekins, Donald M. *The Disorder in Order: The Army State in Burma Since 1962*. Bangkok: White Lotus, 2002.

Seers, Dudley. *The Political Economy of Nationalism*. New York: Oxford University Press, 1983.

Sein Win. *The Split Story*. Rangoon: The Guardian Press, 1959.

Silverstein, Josef. *The Political Legacy of Aung San*. Compiled with an introductory essay by Josef Silverstein. Cornell University Southeast Asia Program, Data Paper no. 86. Ithaca: Cornell University Southeast Asia Program, 1972.

Smith Dun. *Memoirs of the Four-Foot Colonel*. Cornell University Southeast Asia Program, Data Paper no. 113. Ithaca: Cornell University Southeast Asia Program, 1980.

Smith, Martin. *Burma: Insurgency and the Politics of Ethnicity*. London and New Jersey: Zed Books, 1991.

Soe Saing. *United Nations Technical Aid in Burma: A Short Survey*. Research Notes and Discussions Paper no. 69. Singapore: Institute of Southeast Asian Studies, 1990.

Steinberg, David I. *Burma's Road Toward Development: Growth and Ideology under Military Rule*. Boulder, CO: Westview Press, 1981.

———. *Crisis in Burma: Stasis and Change in a Political Economy in Turmoil*. ISIS Paper no. 5. Bangkok: Institute of Security and International Studies, Chulalongkorn University, 1989.

———. *Burma: The State of Myanmar*. Washington, D.C.: Georgetown University Press, 2001.

Steinberg, David J., ed. *In Search of Southeast Asia: A Modern History*. Rev. ed. Honolulu: Hawaii University Press, 1987.

Takamura, S. and T. Mori. *Kokkyo boeki Tonan Ajia kage no keizai* [The Border Trade: A Shadow Economy in Southeast Asia]. Tokyo: Kobundo, 1984.

Tarling, Nicholas. *Nations and States in Southeast Asia*. Cambridge: Cambridge University Press, 1998.

Taylor, Robert H. *Foreign and Domestic Consequences of the KMT Intervention in Burma*. Cornell University Southeast Asia Program, Data Paper no. 93. Ithaca: Cornell University Southeast Asia Program, 1973.

———. *Marxism and Resistance in Burma, 1942–1945: Thein Pe Myint's "Wartime Traveller"*. Athens, Ohio: Ohio University Press, 1984.

———. *The State in Burma*. London: C. Hurst, 1987.

Tin Maung Maung Than. "Myanmar: The Dilemma of Stalled Reforms". Trends Series in Southeast Asia 10. Singapore: Institute of Southeast Asian Studies, 2000.

Tinker, Hugh. *Union of Burma: A Study of the First Years of Independence*. 4th ed. London: Oxford University Press for the Royal Institute of International Affairs, 1967.

Tinker, Hugh. ed. *Burma: The Struggle for Independence 1944–1948*. Vol. 2, *From General Strike to Independence, 31 August 1946 to 4 January 1948*. London: HMSO, 1984.

Todaro, Michael P. *Economic Development in the Third World*. 4th ed. New York and London: Longman, 1989; reprint 1990.

Toye, John. *Dilemmas of Development*. 2nd ed. Oxford: Blackwell, 1993.

Trager, Frank N. *Toward a Welfare State in Burma*. New York: Institute of Pacific Relations, 1954.

———. *Burma: From Kingdom to Republic — A Historical and Political Analysis*. London: Pall Mall, 1966.

Tsiang, Sho-Chiah. *Success or Failure in Economic Takeoff*. Chung-Hua Institute for Economic Research (CIER) Research Monograph Series no. 26. Taipei: CIER, 1989.

Tun Wai, U. *Economic Development of Burma from 1800 till 1940*. Rangoon: Department of Economics, University of Rangoon, 1961.

Voslensky, Michael. *Nomenklatura: Anatomy of the Soviet Ruling Class*. Translated by Eric Mosbacher. London: The Bodley Head, 1984.

Wade, Robert. *Governing the Market: Economic Theory and the Role of the Government in East Asia Industrialization*. Princeton: Princeton University Press, 1990.

Walinsky, Louis J. *Economic Development in Burma, 1951–1960*. New York: The Twentieth Century Fund, 1962.

Waller, Michael. *Democratic Centralism: An Historical Commentary*. Manchester: Manchester University Press, 1981.

Weiss, John. *Industry in Developing Countries: Theory, Policy and Evidence*. Beckenham: Croom Helm, 1986.

Weiss, Linda. *The Myth of the Powerless State: Governing the Economy in a Global Era*. Cambridge: Polity Press, 1998.

Wong Poh Kam and Ng Chee Yuen, eds. *Human Resource Development and Utilization in the Asia-Pacific: A Social Absorption Capacity Approach*. Singapore: Institute of Southeast Asian Studies, 1992.

Woo, Jung-en. *Race to the Swift: State and Finance in Korean Industrialization*. New York: Columbia University Press, 1991.

World Bank. *Industry: Sector Working Paper*. Washington, D.C.: World Bank, 1972.

———. *Korea: Managing the Industrial Transition*. Vol. I, *The Conduct of Industrial Policy*. Washington, D.C.: World Bank, 1987.

———. *World Development Report 1991*. New York: Oxford University Press for the World Bank, 1991.

———. *The East Asian Miracle: Economic Growth and Public Policy*. New York and Oxford: Oxford University Press, 1993.

ARTICLES

Adams, F. Gerard and C. Andrea Bollino. "Meaning of Industrial Policy". In *Industrial Policies for Growth and Competitiveness*, edited by F. Gerard Adams and C. Andrea Bollino, pp. 13–30. Lexington, MA: D. C. Heath & Co., 1983.

Adams, F. Gerard and Inger Marie Davis. "The Role of Policy in Economic Development: Comparisons of the East and Southeast Asian and Latin American Experience". *Asian-Pacific Economic Literature* 8, no. 1 (1994): 8–26.

"Agriculture-Where to Go and How to Tackle the Challenge". *Myanmar Times and Business Review*, 28 August–3 September 2000.

Ahmad, Jaleel. "Import Substitution: A Survey of Policy Issues". *The Developing Economies* XVI, no. 4 (1978): 355–72.

Ariff, Mohamed. "Managing Trade and Industry Reforms in Malaysia". In *Authority and Academic Scribblers: The Role of Research in East Asian Policy Reform*, edited by Sylvia Ostry, pp. 23-44. San Francisco: ICS Press, 1991.

Athukorala, Prema-chandra. "The Malaysian Experiment". In *Reform and Recovery in East Asia: The Role of the State and Economic Enterprise*, edited by Peter Drysdale, pp. 169–90. London and New York: Routledge, 2000.

"Attitude of the Revolutionary Government Towards Labour Problems". *Forward*, 7 May 1963, pp. 27–28.

Aung Kin. "Burma in 1982: On the Road to Recovery". In *Southeast Asian Affairs 1983*, pp. 87–101. London and Singapore: Gower/Institute of Southeast Asian Studies, 1983.

Aung San. "Blue Print for Burma". Reprint. *The Guardian*, March 1957, pp. 33–35.

Aung San Suu Kyi. "My Father". In *Aung San Suu Kyi: Freedom from Fear and Other Writings*, edited by Michael Aris, pp. 1–38. Harmondswoth: Viking, 1991.

Aye Hlaing. "Trends of Economic Growth and Income Distribution in Burma, 1870–1940". *Journal of the Burma Research Society* XLVII, no. i (1964): 89–148.

Ba Maw. "Burma's New Order Plan". *Burma* 1, no. 1 (1944): 104–109.

Badgley, John. "The Burmese Way to Capitalism". In *Southeast Asian Affairs 1990*, pp. 229–39. Singapore: Institute of Southeast Asian Studies, 1990.

"Banking and Financial Reforms in Myanmar". *Myanview* 1, no. 3 (1995), Supplement.

Becka, Jan. "Planning for New Burma: Major-General Aung San's Views of Economic Development". *Archiv Orientalni* 56 (1988): 1–15.

Beeson, Mark. "The Rise and Fall(?) of the Developmental State: The Vicissitudes and Implications of East Asian Interventionism". In *Developmental States: Relevancy, Redundancy or Reconfiguration?* edited by Linda Low, pp. 29–40. New York: Nova Science Publishers, 2004.

Bhagwati, Jagdish N. "Directly Unproductive Profit-Seeking (DUP) Activities". *Journal of Political Economy* 90, no. 5 (1982): 988–1002.

Boeninger, Edgardo. "Economic Policy Change and Government Processes". In *Managing Policy Reform in the Real World: Asian Experiences*, edited by Geoffrey Lamb and Rachel Weaving, pp. 1–25. Washington, D.C.: World Bank, 1992.

Boone, Catherine. "States and Ruling Classes in Postcolonial Africa: The Enduring Contradictions of Power". In *State Power and Social Forces: Domination and Transformation in the Third World*, edited by Joel S. Migdal, Atul Kohli and Vivienne Shue, pp. 108–40. Cambridge: Cambridge University Press, 1994.

Booth, Anne. "Initial Conditions and Miraculous Growth: Why is South East Asia Different From Taiwan and South Korea?".*World Development* 27, no. 2 (1999): 301–21.

———. "The Burma Development Disaster in Comparative Historical Perspective". *SOAS Bulletin of Burma Research* (online e-journal) 1, no. 1 (2003): 1–23.

Bratton, Michael. "Peasant-State Relations in Postcolonial Africa: Patterns of Engagement and Disengagement". In *State Power and Social Forces: Domination and Transformation in the Third World,* edited by Joel S. Migdal, Atul Kohli and Vivienne Shue, pp. 231–54. Cambridge: Cambridge University Press, 1994.

Bruton, Henry. "Import Substitution". In *Handbook of Development Economics,* edited by Hollis Chenery and T. N. Srinivasan, Vol. II, pp. 1601–44. Amsterdam: North Holland, 1989.

"Burma: Production Plus, Refining Minus". *Petroleum News S.E.A.* (April 1973), pp. 17–19.

"Burma Pins Its Hopes on Deep Drilling". *The Oil and Gas Journal,* 10 April 1972, pp. 85–87.

Burns, John P. "China's *Nomenklatura* System". *Problems of Communism* XXXVI, no. 5 (1987): 36–51.

Butwell, Richard. "Civilians and Soldiers in Burma". In *Studies in Asia,* edited by Robert K. Sakai, pp. 74–85. Lincoln: University of Nebraska Press, 1961.

Carver, Liz. "Burma's Socialist Path to Debt Default". *Far Eastern Economic Review,* 16 April 1987, pp. 74–75.

———. "Acute Lack of Basics". *Far Eastern Economic Review,* 16 April 1987, p. 76.

———. "The Oil Shortage". *Far Eastern Economic Review,* 16 April 1987, p. 77.

Chang, Ha-Joon. "The Economic Theory of the Developmental State". In *The Developmental State,* edited by Meredith Woo-Cummings, pp. 182–99. Ithaca and London: Cornell University Press, 1999.

Chazan, Naomi. "Engaging the State: Associational Life in Sub-Saharan Africa". In *State Power and Social Forces: Domination and Transformation in the Third World,* edited by Joel S. Migdal, Atul Kohli and Vivienne Shue, pp. 255–89. Cambridge: Cambridge University Press, 1994.

Chehabi, H. E. and Juan J. Linz. "A Theory of Sultanism: A Type of Nondemocratic Rule". In *Sultanistic Regimes,* edited by H. E. Chehabi and Juan J. Linz, pp. 3–25. Baltimore: John Hopkins University Press, 1998.

Chit So. "Industrial Development and Reforms in Myanmar". In *Industrial Development and Reforms in Myanmar: ASEAN and Japanese Perspectives,* edited by Minoru Kiryu, pp. 123–56. Bangkok: White Lotus, 1999.

Clark, Cal and Steve Chan. "What Can One Learn from the Asian Flu? Implications for the Developmental State". In *Developmental States: Relevancy, Redundancy or Reconfiguration?* edited by Linda Low, pp. 41–56. New York: Nova Science Publishers, 2004.

Cook, Paul and Martin Minogue. "Economic Reform and Political Change in Myanmar (Burma)". *World Development* 21, no. 7 (1993): 1151–61.

Cotton, James. "The Limits to Liberalization in Industrializing Asia: Three Views of the State". *Pacific Affairs* 64, no. 3 (1991): 311–27.

Crampton, Thomas. "Burma's Growing Debt is Pushing Economy to the Brink, Bank Warns". *International Herald Tribune,* 15 November 1999.

"Creating Right Environment the Key to Privatisation, Says Abel". *Myanmar Times and Business Review,* 5–11 February 2001.

Crispin, Shawn and Bertil Lintner. "Burma's Buried Booty". *Far Eastern Economic Review*, 9 December 1999, p. 45.

Crone, Donald K. "State, Social Elites, and Government Capacity in Southeast Asia". *World Politics* XL, no. 2 (1988): 252–68.

Crone, Donald. "Military Regimes and Social Justice in Indonesia and Thailand". In *Civil Military Interactions in Asia and Africa*, edited by Charles H. Kennedy and David J. Louscher, pp. 96–113. Leiden: E. J. Brill, 1991.

Cummings, Bruce. "Webs with No Spiders, Spiders with No Webs: The Genealogy of the Developmental State". In *The Developmental State*, edited by Meredith Woo-Cummings, pp. 61–92. Ithaca and London: Cornell University Press, 1999.

Dent, Christopher M. "The New International Political Economy of East Asia and the Developmental State". In *Developmental States: Relevancy, Redundancy or Reconfiguration?* edited by Linda Low, pp. 79–99. New York: Nova Science Publishers, 2004.

Deyo, Frederic C. "Coalitions, Institutions, and Linkage Sequencing: Toward a Strategic Capability Model of East Asian Development". In *The Political Economy of the New Asian Industrialism*, edited by Fredric C. Deyo, pp. 227–47. Ithaca: Cornell University Press, 1987.

Duch, Raymond M. and Harvey D. Palmer. "It's Not Whether You Win or Lose, but How You Play the Game: Self-Interest, Social Justice, and Mass Attitudes Towards Economic Transition". *American Political Science Review* 98, no. 3 (2005): 437–52.

Dunn, John. "The Economic Limits to Modern Politics". In *The Economic Limits to Modern Politics*, edited by John Dunn, pp. 1–13. Cambridge: Cambridge University Press, 1990.

East, James. "Myanmar Junta Showing Signs of a Rethink". *Straits Times*, 15 January 2001.

Emmerson, Donald K. "Rediscovering the State: Political Institutionalization in Southeast Asia". In *Asian Political Institutions*, edited by Robert Scalapino, Seizaburo Sato, and Jusuf Wanandi, pp. 138–56. Berkeley: University of California Press, 1986.

Fenichal, Allen and Gregg Huff. "Colonialism and the Economic System of Independent Burma". *Modern Asian Studies* 9, no. 3 (1975): 321–35.

——— and Azfar Khan. "The Burmese Way to 'Socialism'". *World Development* 9, no. 9/10 (1981): 813–24.

Freeman, Nick J. and Denis Hew. "Introductory Overview: Rethinking the East Asian Development Model". *ASEAN Economic Bulletin* 19, no. 1 (2002): 1–5.

Gereffi, Gary. "Paths of Industrialization: An Overview". In *Manufacturing Miracles: Paths of Industrialization in Latin America and East Asia*, edited by Gary Gereffi and Donald L. Wyman, pp. 15–31. Princeton, N.J.: Princeton University Press, 1990.

Girling, John. "Development and Democracy in Southeast Asia". *Pacific Review* 1, no. 4 (1988): 332–40.

Go, Purita. "Burma's Mining Industry". *Asia Mining* (August 1973): 23–26.

Goldstein, Carol. "Human Errors". *Far Eastern Economic Review*, 2 January 1969, pp. 13–14.

Goodstadt, L. F. "Burma's Leap". *Far Eastern Economic Review*, 5 January 1967, pp. 26–27.

"Government's Policy Response to the Regional Crisis". *Myanview* 5, no. 4 (1999): 2–3.

Green, Reginald Herbold. "The Role of the State as an Agent of Economic and Social Development in the Least Developed Countries". *Journal of Development Planning*, no. 6 (1974): 1–39.

Greenaway, David and Chris Milner. "Trade Theory and the Less Developed Countries". In *Surveys in Development Economics*, edited by Norman Gemmel, pp. 11–55. Oxford: Basil Blackwell, 1987.

Grindle, Merilee S. "Policy Content and Context in Implementation". In *Politics and Policy Implementation in the Third World*, edited by Merilee S. Grindle, pp. 3–34. Princeton: Princeton University Press, 1980.

———. "The Political Economy of Economic Policy Reforms: Lessons for Policymakers". *Strategic Papers* 4, no. 4, (1992): 3–7.

Guyot, James F. "Bureaucratic Transformation in Burma". In *Asian Bureaucratic Systems Emergent from the British Imperial Tradition*, edited by Ralph Braibanti, pp. 354–443. Durham, N.C.: Duke University Press, 1966.

———. "Burma in 1988: *Perestroika* with a Military Face". In *Southeast Asian Affairs 1989*, pp. 107–33. Singapore: Institute of Southeast Asian Studies, 1989.

Haggard, Stephan and Tun-jen Cheng. "State and Foreign Capital in the East Asia NICs". In *The Political Economy of the New Asian Industrialism*, edited by Frederic C. Deyo, pp. 84–135. Ithaca: Cornell University Press, 1987.

Harrison, James. "Burma's First Steps to Capitalism". *Far Eastern Economic Review*, 24 December 1976, pp. 100–102.

Harvey, Doug. "JNOC Makes an Offer to Explore Deep Oil Reserves in Burma". *Asian Oil & Gas* (October/November 1986): 16–17.

Hayes, David. "Big Border Bonuses". *Focus* (May 1981): 13–14.

Herring, Ronald J. "Embedded Particularism: India's Failed Developmental State". In *The Developmental State*, edited by Meredith Woo-Cummings, pp. 306–44. Ithaca and London: Cornell University Press, 1999.

Hill, Hal. "Industrialisation in ASEAN: Some Analytical and Policy Lessons". *The Economic Development of Southeast Asia*, vol. IV, edited by Hal Hill, pp. 121–96. Cheltenham: Edward Elgar, 2002.

Hirschman, Albert O. "Comment". In *Comparison of Economic Systems: Theoretical and Methodological Approaches*, edited by Alexander Eckstein, pp. 289–97. Berkeley: University of California Press, 1971; reprint 1973.

Hooley, Richard and Muzaffer Ahmad. "Small and Medium-Size Enterprises and the Development Process in Four Asian Countries". In *The Role of Small and Medium-Scale Manufacturing Industries in Industrial Development: The Experience of Selected Asian Countries*, pp. 1–64. Manila: Economics and Development Resource Center, Asian Development Bank, 1990.

Huber, John D. and Noland McCarty. "Bureaucratic Capacity, Delegation, and Political Reform". *American Political Science Review* 98, no. 3 (2005): 481–94.

Hughes, Helen. "Industrialization and Development: A Stocktaking". *Industry and Development*, no. 2 (1979): 1–27.

Huntington, Samuel P. "Social and Institutional Dynamics of One-Party Systems". In *Authoritarian Politics in Modern Society: The Dynamics of Established One-Party Systems*, edited by Samuel P. Huntington and Clement H. Moore, pp. 3–47. New York: Basic Books, 1970.

———. "How Countries Democratize". *Political Science Quarterly* 106, no. 4 (1991–92): 579–616.

"Industrial Policy of the Union of Burma". *Burma's Freedom: The Second Anniversary*, pp. 113–18. Rangoon: Ministry of Information, 1950.

Jayasuriya, S. K. "Technical Change and Revival of the Burmese Rice Industry". *Developing Economies* XXII, no. 2 (1984): 137–54.

Jei Guk Jeon. "The Comparative Politics of Economic Development in East Asia: A Conceptual Mapping". *Pacific Focus* IX, no. 1 (1994): 69–54.

"The Jewel in Thailand's Contraband Empire". *SOUTH* (December 1987), p. 15.

Johnson, Chalmers. "The Developmental State: Odyssey of a Concept". In *The Developmental State*, edited by Meredith Woo-Cummings, pp. 32–60. Ithaca and London: Cornell University Press, 1999.

Johnson, Harry G. "The Ideology of Economic Policy in the New States". In *Economic Nationalism in Old and New States*, edited by Harry G. Johnson, pp. 124–41. London: George Allen & Unwin, 1967.

Jomo, K. S. "Southeast Asian Developmental States in Comparative Perspective". In *Developmental States: Relevancy, Redundancy or Reconfiguration?* edited by Linda Low, pp. 57–77. New York: Nova Science Publishers, 2004.

Kalecki, M. "Outline of a Method of Constructing a Perspective Plan". In *Socialist Economics*, edited by Alec Nove and D. M. Nuti, pp. 213–22. Harmondsworth: Penguin, 1972.

Khin Kyi Kyi, Daw. "The Contribution of Banks to Economic Development". In *A Collection of Papers Prepared by the Research & Training Department*, vol. 1, pp. 64–86. Rangoon: Union of Burma Bank, 1985.

———. "The Role of Central Banks in Development Finance (Burma)". In *A Collection of Papers Prepared by the Research & Training Department*, vol. 1, pp. 56–63. Rangoon: Union of Burma Bank, 1985.

Khin Maung Kyi. "Western Enterprise and Economic Development in Burma". *Journal of the Burma Research Society* LIII, no. i (1970): 25–51.

———. "Modernization of Burmese Agriculture". In *Southeast Asian Affairs 1982*, pp. 115–31. Singapore: Heinemann/Institute of Southeast Asian Studies, 1982.

Khin Maung Oo. "Myanmar's Market Policy and External Economic Relations Policy". In *Myanmar-Korea Economic Cooperation*, edited by Than Nyun and Dalchoong Kim, pp. 101–20. Seoul: Institute of East and West Studies, Yongsei University, 1993.

Khin Maung Win. "Myanmar Road Map to Democracy: The Way Forward". In *Seminar on Understanding Myanmar*, Yangon, 27–28 January 2004, pp. 6–26. Yangon: Myanmar Institute of Strategic and International Studies, n.d.

Khin Saw Oo. "Domestic Resource Mobilization in Myanmar". In *Domestic Resource Mobilization in SEACEN Countries,* edited by Y. M. W. B. Weerasekera, pp. 231–73. Kuala Lumpur: SEACEN Centre, 1993.

Khin Than Kywe. "Financing the Small Manufacturing Establishments of Burma". *Burma Research Society Fiftieth Anniversary Publication,* vol. 1 (1960), pp. 125–42.

Killick, Tony. "Relevance, Meaning and Determinants of Flexibility". In *The Flexible Economy: Causes and Consequences of the Adaptability of National Economies,* edited by Tony Killick, pp. 1–33. London: Routledge, 1995.

———. "Economic Inflexibility in Africa: Evidence and Causes". In *The Flexible Economy: Causes and Consequences of the Adaptability of National Economies,* edited by Tony Killick, pp. 154–96. London: Routledge, 1995.

——— and Christopher Stevens. "Eastern Europe: Lessons on Economic Adjustment from the Third World". *International Affairs* 67, no. 4 (1991): 689–90.

Kiryu, Minoru. "Introduction". In *Industrial Development and Reforms in Myanmar: ASEAN and Japanese Perspectives,* edited by Minoru Kiryu, pp. 1–8. Bangkok: White Lotus, 1999.

———. "The Role of Small and Medium-Sized Enterprises in the Industrial Development of Myanmar". In *Industrial Development and Reforms in Myanmar: ASEAN and Japanese Perspectives,* edited by Minoru Kiryu, pp. 9–30. Bangkok: White Lotus, 1999.

Koh Hui Chuan et al. "Myanmar's Foreign Investment Law." In *Business Opportunities in Myanmar,* edited by Tan Teck Meng et al., pp. 125–42 Singapore: Prentice Hall, 1996.

Krasner, Stephen D. "Approaches to the State: Alternative Conceptions and Historical Dynamics". *Comparative Politics* 16, no. 2 (1984): 223–46.

Krueger, Anne O. "The Political Economy of Rent-Seeking Society". *American Economic Review* 64, no. 3 (1974): 291–303.

Kudo, Toshihiro. "Industrial Policy in Myanmar: Lessons from the Past". In *Industrial Development and Reforms in Myanmar: ASEAN and Japanese Perspectives,* edited by Minoru Kiryu, pp. 209–38. Bangkok: White Lotus, 1999.

Kyaw Myint, U. "Drift". *Burma Digest* 1, no. 3 (1946): 45–51.

Kyaw Thu. "Myanmar Biggest Gas Exporter in Asia, Says Minister". *Asia Times,* 29 November–5 December 2004, p. 7.

Kyaw Yin Hlaing. "Reconsidering the Failure of the Burma Socialist Programme Party Government to Eradicate Internal Economic Impediments". *South East Asia Research 11,* no. 1 (2003): 5–58.

———. "Burma: Civil Society Skirting Regime Rules". In *Civil Society and Political Change in Asia,* edited by Muthiah Alagappa, pp. 389–418. Stanford CA: Stanford University Press, 2004.

———. "Myanmar in 2004: Why Military Rule Continues". In *Southeast Asian Affairs 2005*, pp. 231–56. Singapore: Institute of Southeast Asian Studies, 2005.

Kyi May Kaung. "Theories, Paradigms, or Models in Burma Studies". *Asian Survey* (November 1995): 1030–41.

"Labour Administration in Burma". *Burma: The Fourth Anniversary* II, no. 2 (1952): 49–50.

Lal, Deepak. "Nationalism, Socialism and Planning: Influential Ideas in the South". *World Development* 13, no. 6 (1985): 749–59.

———. "Industrialization Strategies and Long-Term Resource Allocation". In *Development Strategies for the 21st Century*, edited by Teruyuki Iwasaki, Takeshi Mori, and Hiroichi Yamaguchi, pp. 480–507. Tokyo: Institute for Developing Economies, 1992.

Leftwich, Adrian. "Governance, the State and the Politics of Development". *Development and Change* 25, no. 2 (1994): 363–86.

———. "Bringing Politics Back In: Towards a Model of the Developmental State". *Journal of Development Studies* 31, no. 3 (1995): 400–27.

Leipziger, Danny M. and Vinod Thomas. "Roots of East Asia's Success". *Finance and Development* (March 1994): 6–9.

Lentner, Howard H. "The Concept of the State: A Response to Stephen Krasner". *Comparative Politics* 16, no. 3 (1984): 367–77.

Liddle, R. William. "Soeharto's Indonesia: Personal Rule and Political Institution". *Pacific Affairs* 58, no. 1 (1985): 68–90.

———. "The Relative Autonomy of the Third World Politician: Soeharto and Indonesian Economic Development in Comparative Perspective". *International Studies Quarterly* 35, no. 4 (1991): 403–27.

Loungani, Prakash and Assaf Razin. "How Beneficial is Foreign Direct Investment for Developing Countries". In *Finance & Development* (June 2001): 6–9.

Megginson, William L. "The Impact of Privatization". *Economic Reform Today* 1 (1998): 11–15.

Maung Maung. "State Socialism in Burma". *The Guardian*, December 1953, pp. 26–27.

Maung Maung Hla. "Some Aspects of Central Banking in Burma". In *Burma Research Society Fiftieth Anniversary Publication*, vol. 1 (1960), pp. 147–55.

———. "The Coordination of Monetary and Fiscal Policies with Special Reference to the Balance of Payments Adjustment (Burma)". In *A Collection of Papers Prepared by the Research & Training Department*, vol. 1, pp. 1–25. Rangoon: Union of Burma Bank.

Migdal, Joel S. "The State in Society: An Approach to Struggles for Domination". In *State Power and Social Forces: Domination and Transformation in the Third World*, edited by Joel S. Migdal, Atul Kohli and Vivienne Shue, pp. 7–34. Cambridge: Cambridge University Press, 1994.

Min Zin. "Sanctions Revisited". *Irrawaddy* (May 2001), pp. 15–16.

Mutebi, Alex. "'Muddling Through' Past Legacies: Myanmar's Civil Bureaucracy and the Need for Reform". In *Myanmar: Beyond Politics to Societal Imperatives*, edited by Kyaw Yin Hlaing, Robert H. Taylor and Tin Maung Maung Than, pp. 140–60. Singapore: Institute of Southeast Asain Studies, 2005.

Mya Maung. "Burma's Economic Performance under Military Rule". *Asian Survey* (June 1997): 503–24.

Mya Than. "Burma in 1986: The Year of the Snake". In *Southeast Asian Affairs 1987*, pp. 105–28. Singapore: Institute of Southeast Asian Studies, 1987.

———. "Agriculture in Myanmar: What Has Happened to Asia's Rice Bowl?". In *Southeast Asian Affairs 1990*, pp. 240–54. Singapore: Institute of Southeast Asian Studies, 1990.

———. "Recent Developments in Myanmar: Impact and Implications of ASEAN Membership and Asian Crisis". In *Burma/Myanmar: Strong Regime Weak State?* edited by Morton B. Pederson, Emily Rudland and Ronald J. May, pp. 138–63. Adelaide: Crawford House, 2000.

———. "Recent Economic Developments: Little Change in Myanmar". In *The Illusion of Progress: The Political Economy of Reform in Burma/Myanmar*, edited by David S. Mathieson and R. J. May, pp. 39–64. Adelaide: Crawford House, 2004.

——— and Myat Thein. "Mobilization of Financial Resources for Development in Myanmar". In *Financial Resources for Development in Myanmar: Lessons form Asia*, edited by Mya Than and Myat Thein, pp. 1–22. Singapore: Institute of Southeast Asian Studies, 2000.

Mya Than and Nobuyoshi Nishizawa. "Agricultural Policy Reforms and Agricultural Development in Myanmar". In *Myanmar Dilemmas and Options: The Challenge of Economic Transition in the 1990s*, edited by Mya Than and Joseph L. H. Tan, pp. 89–116. Singapore: Institute of Southeast Asian Studies, 1990.

Myat Thein. "Monetary and Fiscal Policies for Development". In *Myanmar Dilemmas and Options: The Challenge of Economic Transition in the 1990s*, edited by Mya Than and Joseph L. H. Tan, pp. 53–88. Singapore: Institute of Southeast Asian Studies, 1990.

Myint Myint Tin, Daw. "Financial Structure and the Effectiveness of Monetary Policy". In *A Collection of Papers Prepared by the Research & Training Department*, vol. 1, pp. 133–59. Rangoon: Union of Burma Bank, 1985.

———. "Creating Domestic Investment via the Banking System in Myanmar". In *Financial Resources for Development in Myanmar: Lessons form Asia*, edited by Mya Than and Myat Thein, pp. 72–92. Singapore: Institute of Southeast Asian Studies, 2000.

Naing Oo. "Urbanization and Economic Development in Burma". *SOJOURN* 4, no. 2 (1989): 233–60.

Nam Chong-Hyun. "Trade Policy and Industrial Development in Korea". In *Strategies for Industrial Development: Concepts and Policy Issues*, edited by Suk Jang-Won, pp. 60–79. Kuala Lumpur: Asia and Pacific Development Centre, 1989.

Narongchai Akrasanee. "The Role of Policy Research in the Trade and Industrial Reforms of Thailand". In *Authority and Academic Scribblers: The Role of Research in East Asian Policy Reform*, edited by Sylvia Ostry, pp. 7–21. San Francisco: ICS Press, 1991.

Nelson, Joan M. "The Politics of Economic Transformation: Is Third World Experience Relevant in Eastern Europe?". *World Politics* 45, no. 3 (1993): 433–63.

Nelson, Michael A. and Ram D. Singh. "The Deficit Growth Connection: Some Recent Evidence from Developing Countries". *Economic Development and Cultural Change* 43, no. 1 (1994): 167–91.

Neuber, Alexander. "Adapting the Economies of Eastern Europe: Behavioral and Institutional Aspects of Flexibility". In *The Flexible Economy: Causes and Consequences of the Adaptability of National Economies*, edited by Tony Killick, pp. 111–53. London: Routledge, 1995.

Nu, Thakin. "Foreign Capital in Burma". In *Burma's Freedom: Second Anniversary*, pp. 70–73. Rangoon: Directorate of Information, 1950.

Nu Nu Yin. "A Survey of Selected Manufacturing Firms in Myanmar". In *Industrial Development and Reforms in Myanmar: ASEAN and Japanese Perspectives*, edited by Minoru Kiryu, pp. 31–88. Bangkok: White Lotus, 1999.

Nyi Nyi. "The Development of University Education in Burma". *Journal of the Burma Research Society* XLVII, no. i (1964): 11–76.

Nyi Nyi Aung. "Golden Export Outlook for Natural Gas". *Myanmar Times*, 22–28 March 2004, p. 1.

Odom, William E. "Durable Democracy Requires a State That Works". *International Herald Tribune*, 14 February 1992.

Pack, Howard. "Industrial Policy: Growth Elixir or Poison?". *World Bank Research Observer* 15, no. 1 (2000): 47–67.

Pangestu, Mari. "Managing Economic Policy Reforms in Indonesia". In *Authority and Academic Scribblers: The Role of Research in East Asian Policy Reform*, edited by Sylvia Ostry, pp. 93–120. San Francisco: ICS Press, 1991.

Park, Phillip Hookon. "A Reflection on the East Asian Development Model; Comparison of the South Korean and Taiwanese Experiences". In *The East Asian Development Model: Economic Growth, Institutional Failure and the Aftermath of the Crisis*, edited by Frank-Jurgen Richter, pp. 141–68. Basingstoke: Macmillan, 2000.

Pedersen, Morten B. "The World According to Burma's Military Rulers". In *The Illusion of Progress: The Political Economy of Reform in Burma/Myanmar*, edited by David S. Mathieson and R. J. May, pp. 85-136. Adelaide: Crawford House, 2004.

Peiris, Denzil. "Socialism without Commitment". *Far Eastern Economic Review*, 13 September 1974, pp. 27–30.

———. "Where Survival is Tied to the Blackmarket". *Far Eastern Economic Review*, 20 September 1974, pp. 34–35.

Pfanner, M. Ruth. "Burma". In *Underdevelopment and Economic Nationalism in Southeast Asia*, edited by Frank H. Golay, Ralph Anspach, M. Ruth Pfanner, and Eliezer B. Ayal, pp. 203–65. Ithaca: Cornell University Press, 1969.

"Privatising in Myanmar". *Myanmar Times and Business Review*, 4–10 September 2000.

Quick, Stephen A. "The Paradox of Popularity: 'Ideological' Program Implementation in Zambia". In *Politics and Policy Implementation in the Third World*, edited by Merilee S. Grindle. Princeton, N.J.: Princeton University Press, 1980, pp. 40–63.

Rana, Pradumna and Wilhelmina Paz. "Economies in Transition; The Asian Experience". In *From Reform to Growth: China and Other Countries in Transition in Asia and Central and Eastern Europe*, edited by Chung H. Lee and Helmut Reisen. Paris: OECD, 1994, pp. 119–40.

Ranis, Gustav. "Another Look at the East Asian Miracle". In *The World Bank Economic Review* 9, no. 3 (1995): 509–34.

Reynolds, Lloyd G. "Government and Economic Growth". In *From Classical Economics to Development Economics*, edited by Gerald M. Meier, pp. 226–41. Basingstoke and London: Macmillan, 1994.

Richter, H. V. "The Impact of Socialism on Economic Activity in Burma". In *Opportunity and Response: Case Studies in Economic Development*, edited by T. Scarlett Epstein and David H. Penny, pp. 216–39. London: C. Hurst, 1972.

Roemer, Michael. "Resource-Based Industrialization in the Developing Countries: A Survey". *Journal of Development Economics* 6, no. 2 (1979): 163–202.

Rosenstein-Rodan, Paul. "International Aid for Underdeveloped Countries". *Review of Economics and Statistics* XLIII, no. 2 (1961): 107–38.

Rudner, Martin. "Japanese Official Development Assistance to Southeast Asia". *Modern Asian Studies* 23, no. 1 (1989): 73–116.

Rueschemeyer, Dietrich and Peter B. Evans. "The State and Economic Transformation: Toward an Analysis of the Conditions Underlying Effective Intervention". In *Bringing the State Back In*, edited by Peter B. Evans, Dietrich Rueschmeyer, and Theda Skocpol, pp. 44–77. Cambridge: Cambridge University Press, 1985.

San Khup. "Macroeconomic Policies with Special Emphasis on Infrastructural Development". In *Business Opportunities in Myanmar*, edited by Tan Teck Meng et al., pp. 69–70. Singapore: Prentice Hall, 1996.

Schmitt, Hans O. "Decolonisation and Development in Burma". *Journal of Development Studies* 4, no. 1 (1967): 97–108.

Schneider, Ben Ross. "The *Desarrollista* State in Brazil and Mexico". In *The Developmental State*, edited by Meredith Woo-Cummings, pp. 276–305. Ithaca and London: Cornell University Press, 1999.

Schweitzer, Julian. "Transition in Eastern Europe: The Social Dimension". *Finance and Development* (December 1990): 6–8.

Seddon, David and Tim Belton-Jones. "The Political Determinants of Economic Flexibility, with Special Reference to the East Asian NICs". In *The Flexible*

Economy: Causes and Consequences of the Adaptability of National Economies, edited by Tony Killick, pp. 325–64. London: Routledge, 1995.

Seekins, Donald M. "The North Wind and the Sun: Japan's Response to the Political Crisis in Burma, 1988-1998". *Journal of Burma Studies* 4(1999): 1–33.

"Self-Sufficiency is Key to Success". Perspective, *The New Light of Myanmar, 19 January 2000.*

Senghaas, Dieter. "The Case for Autarky". In *The Political Economy of Development and Underdevelopment*, edited by Charles K. Wilber, 3rd ed., pp. 208–18. New York: Random House, 1984.

Shambaugh, David. "Losing Control: The Erosion of State Authority in China". *Current History* (September 1993): 253–59.

Shaw, G. K. "Policy Implications of Endogenous Growth Theory". *Economic Journal* 102, no. 412 (1992): 611–21.

Shue, Vivienne. "State Power and Social Organization in China". In *State Power and Social Forces: Domination and Transformation in the Third World*, edited by Joel S. Migdal, Atul Kohli and Vivienne Shue, pp. 65–88. Cambridge: Cambridge University Press, 1994.

Silverstein, Josef. "Burma". In *Governments and Politics in Southeast Asia*, edited by George McTurnan Kahin, 2nd ed., pp. 75–179. Ithaca: Cornell University Press, 1964; reprint, 1966.

———. "Introduction". In *The Political Legacy of Aung San*, compiled by Josef Silverstein. Cornell University Southeast Asia Program, Data Paper no. 86, pp. 1–12. Ithaca: Cornell University Southeast Asia Program, 1972.

Simmons, Colin. "Economic Development and Economic History". In *Development Studies and Colonial Policy*, edited by Barbara Ingham and Colin Simmons. London: Frank Cass, 1987, pp. 3–99.

Smith, Martin. "Ethnic Conflict and the Challenge of Civil Society in Burma". In *Strengthening Civil Society in Burma: Possibilities and Dilemmas for International NGOs*, edited by Tom Kramer and Pietje Vervest, pp. 15–53. Chiangmai: Silkworm Books, 1999.

Soe Myint. "Financing the Deficit Since Independence". *Journal of the Burma Research Society* XLIV, no. ii (1961): 183–95.

Soesastro, Hadi. "Governance and the Crisis in Indonesia". In *Reform and Recovery in East Asia: The Role of the State and Economic Enterprise*, edited by Peter Drysdale, pp. 120–46. London: Routledge, 2000.

"Specific Characteristics of BSPP Party". *Forward*, 13 September 1964, pp. 4–6.

"State Lottery Introduces a K30 Million Monthly Prize". *Myanmar Times and Business Review*, 29 May–4 June 2000.

Steinberg, David I. "Burma Under the Military: Towards a Chronology". *Contemporary Southeast Asia* 3, no. 3 (1981): 244–85.

———. "Economic Growth with Equity? The Burmese Experience". *Contemporary Southeast Asia* 4, no. 2 (1982): 124–52.

———. "Japanese Economic Assistance to Burma: Aid in the 'Tarenagashi' Manner?". *Crossroads* 5, no. 2 (1990): 51–107.

———. "A Void in Myanmar: Civil Society in Burma". In *Strengthening Civil Society in Burma: Possibilities and Dilemmas for International NGOs*, edited by Tom Kramer and Pietje Vervest. Chiangmai: Silkworm Books, 1999, pp. 1–14.

———. "Myanmar: The Roots of Economic Malaise". In *Myanmar: Beyond Politics to Societal Imperatives*, edited by Kyaw Yin Hlaing, Robert H. Taylor and Tin Maung Maung Than, pp. 86–116. Singapore: Institute of Southeast Asian Studies, 2005.

Stern, Nicholas. "The Economics of Development". *Economic Journal* 99, no. 397 (1989): 597–685.

Stiglitz, Joseph E. "Some Lessons from the East Asian Miracle". *World Bank Research Observer* 11, no. 2 (1996): 151–77.

Streeten, Paul. "Against the Minimalist State". *World Development* 21, no. 8 (1993), n.7, p. 1296

Sutcliffe, Bob. "Industry and Underdevelopment Re-examined". *Journal of Development Studies* 21, no. 1 (1984): 121–33.

Syrquin, Moshe. "Flexibility and Long-Term Economic Development". In *The Flexible Economy: Causes and Consequences of the Adaptability of National Economies*, edited by Tony Killick, pp. 34–63. London: Routledge, 1995.

Tarling, Nicholas. "'A New and a Better Cunning': British Wartime Planning for Post-War Burma, 1942–1943". *Journal of Southeast Asian Studies* 13, no. 1 (1982): 33–59.

Taylor, Robert H. "Burma in the Anti-Fascist War". In *Southeast Asia under Japanese Occupation*, edited by Alfred W. McCoy, pp. 159–90. Yale University Southeast Asia Studies Series no. 22. New Haven: Yale University, 1980.

———. "Perceptions of Ethnicity in the Politics of Burma". *Southeast Asian Journal of Social Science* 10, no. 1 (1982): 7–22.

———. "The Burmese Communist Movement and Its Indian Connection: Formation and Factionalism". *Journal of Southeast Asian Studies* 14, no. 1 (1983): 95–108.

———. "Burmese Concepts of Revolution". In *Context Meaning and Power in Southeast Asia*, edited by Mark Hobart and Robert H. Taylor, pp. 79–92. Ithaca: Cornell University Southeast Asia Program, 1986.

———. "Change in Burma: Political Demands and Military Power". *Asian Affairs* XXII, Part II (1991): 131–42.

———. "Myanmar in 1990: New Era or Old?". *Southeast Asian Affairs 1991*. Singapore: Institute of Southeast Asian Studies, 1991.

———. "Disaster or Release? J. S. Furnivall and the Bankruptcy of Burma". *Modern Asian Studies* 29, no. 1 (1995): 45–63.

Tekkatho Tin Kha. "Victories of the State, the People and the *Tatmadaw*". *New Light of Myanmar*, 16 July 2000.

Than Nyun. "Myanmar's Policy on Natural Resources and Industrial Development". In *Myanmar-Korea Economic Cooperation*, edited by Than Nyun and Dalchoong Kim, pp. 147–70. Seoul: Institute of East and West Studies, Yongsei University, 1993.

Thawnghmung, Ardeth Maung. "Agricultural Implementation Processes in Burma/ Myanmar: Problems and Limitations". In *The Illusion of Progress: The Political Economy of Reform in Burma/Myanmar*, edited by David S. Mathieson and R. J. May, pp. 200–22. Adelaide: Crawford House, 2004.

"The 1998/99 Budget". *Myanview* 4, no. 2 (1998): 7–11.

"The 1999/2000 Budget". *Myanview* 5, no. 2 (1999): 8–11.

Theimm Htut. "To Exert All-Out Efforts for Industrial Development". *New Light of Myanmar*, Sunday Supplement, 5 September 1999.

———. "UMFCCI to Work with Patriotism and National Outlook". *New Light of Myanmar*, 6 May 2001.

Thein, U. "Economic Development of New Burma". *Burma* 1, no. 1 (1944): 57–66.

Thet Khaing. "Korean Firms Doubles Staff to 2000 in Search of Profits". *Myanmar Times and Business Review*, 1–7 May 2000.

Thet Tun. "Outline of a Socialist Economy for Burma". *Journal of the Burma Research Society* XXXVII, no. i (1954): 59–76.

———. "A Review of Economic Planning in Burma". In *Burma Research Society Fiftieth Anniversary Publication*, vol. 1 (1960), pp. 485–527.

———. "Organization of Planning Machinery: Lessons from Burmese Experience". *Journal of the Burma Research Society* XLVI, no. i (1963): 27–34.

Thet Tun. "A Critique of Louis J. Walinsky's Economic Development in Burma, 1951-1960". *Journal of the Burma Research Society* XLVII, no. i (1964): 173–81.

Thomson, John Seabury. "Marxism in Burma". In *Marxism in Southeast Asia: A Study of Four Countries*, edited by Frank N. Trager, pp. 14–57. The Rand Corp., 1959; reprint, Stanford: Stanford University Press, 1965.

Tin, U. "Commentary on the New Order Plan". *Burma* 1, no. 1 (1944): 17–23.

Tin Maung Maung Than. "Burma's Energy Use: Perils and Promises". In *Southeast Asian Affairs 1986*, pp. 68–95. Singapore: Institute of Southeast Asian Studies, 1986.

———. "Burma in 1987: Twenty-Five Years after the Revolution". In *Southeast Asian Affairs 1988*, pp. 73–93. Singapore: Institute of Southeast Asian Studies, 1988.

———. "Burma's National Security and Defence Posture". *Contemporary Southeast Asia* 11, no. 1 (1989): 40–60.

———. "Myanmar (Burma) in 2000: More of the Same?". *Asian Survey* (January/ February 2001): 148–55.

———. "Myanmar: Military in Charge". In *Government and Politics in Southeast Asia*, edited by John Funston, pp. 203–51. Singapore: Institute of Southeast Asian Studies, 2001.

———. "Myanmar's Energy Sector: Banking on Natural Gas". In *Southeast Asian Affairs 2005*, pp. 257–89. Singapore: Institute of Southeast Asian Studies, 2005.

Tin Soe and Brian S. Fisher. "An Economic Analysis of Burmese Rice-Price Policies". In *Myanmar Dilemmas and Options: The Challenge of Economic*

Transition in the 1990s, edited by Mya Than and Joseph L. H. Tan, pp. 117–66. Singapore: Institute of Southeast Asian Studies, 1990.

Tsiang, S. C. and Rong-I Wu. "Foreign Trade and Investment as Boosters for Take-of: The Experiences of the Four Asian Newly Industrializing Countries". In *Foreign Trade and Development in the Newly Industrializing Asian Countries*, edited by Walter Galenson, pp. 301–32. Madison: University of Wisconsin Press, 1985.

Tun Wai, U. "Outlook for Burma's Balance of Payments". *Journal of the Burma Research Society* XXXVII, no. ii (1954): 35–40.

———. "Burma". In *Asian Economic Development*, edited by Cranley Onslow, pp. 3–27. New York: Praeger, 1965; reprint, 1967.

———. "Myanmar". In *From Centrally Planned to Market Economies: The Asia Approach — Volume 3, Lao PDR, Myanmar and Vietnam*, edited by Pradumna B. Rana and Naved Hamid, pp. 151–331. Hong Kong: Oxford University Press, 1996.

——— and Chorng-huey Wong. "Determinants of Private Investment in Developing Countries". *Journal of Development Studies* 19, no. 1 (1982): 19–36.

Turnell, Sean. "Myanmar's Banking Crisis". Research Notes, *ASEAN Economic Bulletin* 20, no. 3 (2003): 272–82.

Vokes, Richard. "Burma and Asia-Pacific Dynamism: Problems and Prospects of Export-Oriented Growth in the 1990s". In *Myanmar Dilemmas and Options: The Challenge of Economic Transition in the 1990s*, edited by Mya Than and Joseph L. H. Tan, pp. 219–47. Singapore: Institute of Southeast Asian Studies, 1990.

Wade, Robert. "The Role of the Government in Overcoming Market Failure: Taiwan, Republic of Korea and Japan". In *Achieving Industrialization in East Asia*, edited by Helen Hughes, pp. 129–63. Cambridge: Cambridge University Press, 1988.

———. "The Reprinting of Governing the Market: A Dinner Table Conversation". *Issues & Studies* 40, no. 1 (2004): 103–34.

Wajima, Takinori. "Recent Banking Sector Developments and Current Monetary Status in Myanmar". In *Industrial Development and Reforms in Myanmar: ASEAN and Japanese Perspectives*, edited by Minoru Kiryu, pp. 239–70. Bangkok: White Lotus, 1999.

Walinsky, Louis J. "The Role of the Military in Development Planning in Burma". *The Philippine Economic Journal* 8, IV (1965): 310–26.

Warr, Peter G. "The Failure of Myanmar's Agricultural Policies". In *Southeast Asian Affairs 2000*, pp. 219–38. Singapore: Institute of Southeast Asian Studies, 2000.

Waterbury, John. "The Long Gestation and Brief Triumph of Import-Substituting Industrialization". *World Development* 27, no. 2 (1999): 323–41.

Wellisz, Stanislaw and Ronald Findlay. "Protection and Rent-Seeking in Developing Countries". In *Neoclassical Political Economy: The Analysis of Rent-Seeking and DUP Activities*, edited by David C. Colander, pp. 141–53. Cambridge, MA: Ballinger, 1984.

Wiant, Jon A. "The Vanguard Army: The *Tatmadaw* and Politics in Revolutionary Burma". In *The Armed Forces in Contemporary Asian Societies*, edited by Edward A. Olsen and Stephen Jurika, Jr., pp. 241–67. London and Boulder, CO: Westview Press, 1986.

Win Kyaw Oo. "More Inputs are Needed to Power a Hydro Future". *Myanmar Times and Business Review*, 4–10 June 2001.

———. "Eight Government Properties listed for Privatisation". *Myanmar Times and Business Review*, 19–25 August 2002.

———. "Minister Urges Gradual Pace with Privatisation Process". *Myanmar Times and Business Review*, 10–16 March 2003.

Woo-Cummings, Meredith. "Introduction: Chalmers Johnson and the Politics of Nationalism and Development". In *The Developmental State*, edited by Meredith Woo-Cummings, pp. 1–31. Ithaca and London: Cornell University Press, 1999.

"Workers Affairs: A Decade of Socialism". *Forward*, 1 March 1972, pp. 12–13.

Yi Feng. "Political Foundations of Economic Management: An Interpretation of Economic Development and Economic Crisis in East Asia". In *The East Asian Development Model: Economic Growth, Institutional Failure and the Aftermath of the Crisis*, pp. 71–96. Basingstoke: Macmillan, 2000.

Yoshimatsu, Hidetaka. "Japanese Policy in the Asian Economic Crises and the Developmental State Concept". *Journal of the Asia Pacific Economy* 8, no. 1 (2003): 102–25.

Young, Peter. "The Lessons of Privatization". *Economic Reform Today* 1 (1998): 1–7.

Zin Min. "Over 300 Vehicles Denied Registration". *Myanmar Times and Business Review*, 13–19 June 2005, p. 4.

OFFICIAL PUBLICATIONS

Burma Communist Party's Conspiracy to Take Over State Power. Yangon: News and Periodicals Enterprise, 1989.

Burma Independence Celebration. Rangoon: Department of Information and Broadcasting, 1948.

Burma and the Insurrections. Rangoon: Ministry of Information, 1949.

"Burmese Way to Socialism". In *The System of Correlation of Man and His Environment*. 3rd ed., pp. 43–52. Rangoon: Burma Socialist Programme Party, 1964.

"The Constitution of the Burma Socialist Programme Party". In *The System of Correlation of Man and His Environment*. 3rd ed, pp. 53–77. Rangoon: Burma Socialist Programme Party, 1964.

The Constitution of the Socialist Republic of the Union of Burma. Rangoon: Ministry of Information, 1974.

The Fourth Party Congress 1981: Party Chairman's Speech and Political Report of the Central Committee. Rangoon: Burma Socialist Programme Party, 1985.

Index of Laws and Rules, Enacted and Promulgated by the State Law and Order Restoration Council and The State Peace and Development Council (1988–1999). Yangon: Attorney-General Office, 2000.

Is It a People's Liberation? A Short Survey of Communist Insurrection in Burma. Rangoon: Ministry of Information, 1952.

Is Trust Vindicated? Rangoon: Director of Information, 1960.

KNDO Insurrection. Rangoon: Government Printing and Stationery, 1949.

Nation-Building Endeavours, Volume III: Historical Records of Endeavours Made by the State Law and Order Restoration Council (From 1 April 1995 to 14 November 1997). Yangon: Printing and Publishing Sub-Committee, Historical Records of Endeavours made by the State Law and Order Restoration Council: Yangon, 1999.

The National Ideology and the Role of the Defence Services. 3rd ed. Rangoon: Ministry of Defence, 1960.

Party Seminar 1965: Speeches of Chairman General Ne Win and Political Report of the General Secretary. Rangoon: Burma Socialist Programme Party, 1966.

Pyidawtha: The New Burma. Rangoon: Economic and Social Board, 1954.

The Pyidawtha Conference: Resolutions and Speeches. Rangoon: Ministry of Information, 1952.

Second Four-Year Plan for the Union of Burma (1961–62 to 1964–65). Rangoon: Government Printing and Stationary, 1961.

The System of Correlation of Man and His Environment. 3rd ed. Rangoon: Burma Socialist Programme Party, 1964.

Taingkyo Pyipyu [Nation-Building Endeavours], 1988–1991. Yangon: Printing and Publishing Sub-Committee on the Historical Records of Endeavours made by the State Law and Order Restoration Council, 1991.

Two-Year Plan of Economic Development for Burma. Rangoon: Government Printing and Stationery, 1948.

UNPUBLISHED SOURCES

Badgley, John. H. "Survey of Burma's Foreign Economic Relations, 1948-58". Mimeographed. Rangoon: The Rangoon-Hopkins Center for Southeast Asian Studies, 1959.

———. "Progress and Polity in Burma". Ph.D. dissertation, University of California, Berkeley, 1962.

Badgley, John, et al. "Reconciling Burma/Myanmar: Re-examining U.S. Relations with Burma". Asian Voices Seminar Series Transcript. Washington, D.C.: Sasakawa Peace Foundation, 25 March 2004.

Chao-Tzang Yaunghwe. "Ne Win's Tatmadaw Dictatorship". Master thesis, University of British Columbia, 1990.

"Conference Papers on Current Economic Problems". Mimeographed. Rangoon, 1951.

"Country Commercial Guide, Burma (Myanmar)—Fiscal Year 2000". Prepared by the United States Embassy, Rangoon, Burma (Yangon, Myanmar), September 2000.

"Current Situation of the Myanmar Economy and Its Future Development Strategy". Study Group on the Myanmar Economy, Institute of Fiscal and Monetary Policy, Ministry of Finance, Japan, June 1999.

Daniel, C. E. W. "Some Aspects of Organization and Administration of State Enterprises: The Burmese Experience as Compared with that of the United Kingdom, Saskatchewan, and Chile". Seminar paper, Harvard University Graduate School of Public Administration, Cambridge, MA, April 1959.

Economic and Social Commission for Asia and the Pacific (ESCAP). "Main Trends and Issues in Industrialization of the ESCAP Region". Bangkok, 9 November 1983. IHT/HLE/1.

"Economic and Social Indicators". Yangon, Ministry of Planning and Finance, March 1990.

"The Financial Sector Development in Myanmar". Yangon: Ministry of Finance and Revenue, 23 March 1998.

"Guidelines for Operating on Commercial Lines to be Used by State Economic Organizations in the Various Ministries". Rangoon, Ministry of Planning and Finance, 1975.

Htein Lynn. "The Role of Small and Medium Enterprises (SMEs) in Myanmar". Unpublished research paper, Institute of Economics, Yangon, n.d.

Institute of Asian Economic Affairs (Tokyo). "Economic Development in Burma". Translated by U.S. Joint Publications Research Service. Washington, D.C.: Joint Publications Research Service, 1962; New York, CCM Information Corporation, n.d.

International Labour Office. "Report to the Government of the Union of Burma on the Further Development of Social Security". Geneva, International Labour Office, 1964. ILO/TAP/Burma/R.28.

International Monetary Fund (IMF). "Burma: Recent Economic Developments". Washington, D.C., 20 May 1987.

———. "Burma: Recent Economic Developments". Washington, D.C., 16 June 1988.

Khin Maung Kyi. "Patterns of Accommodation to Bureaucratic Authority in a Transitional Culture (A Sociological Analysis of Burmese Bureaucrats with Respect to Their Orientations Toward Authority)". Ph.D. dissertation, Cornell University, 1966.

———. "Political Economy of Agricultural Modernization in Burma". Discussion paper, Singapore, 1987.

———. "Problems of Socialist State Enterprise in International Economy: A Case Study of Competitiveness of Public Enterprise in a Trade-Dependent Developing Country". Discussion paper, Singapore, n.d.

Khin Maung Myint, U. "Burma, Country Paper". Paper presented at the Regional Seminar on Import Management, Pattaya, Thailand, 19–20 February 1981.

Khin Maung Nyunt. "Some Aspects of Public Finance in Burma: 1964–65 to 1979–80." Master thesis, Institute of Economics, Rangoon, 1980.

Knappen Tippetts Abbett Engineering Co. "Comprehensive Report, Economic and Engineering Development of Burma. Prepared for the Government of the Union of Burma" by Knappen Tippetts Abett McCarthy, Engineers, in Association with Pierce Management, Inc., and Robert R. Nathan Associates, Inc., 2 Vols., August 1953.

Kyaw Htin, Dr. "SME Development in Myanmar-Policies and Strategies". Unpublished working paper, Yangon, *c.*1999.

———. "Myanmar's Industrialization". Unpublished working paper, Yangon, December 1999.

Kyaw Myint. "Industrialization in Burma". Master thesis, University of Sydney, 1978.

Kyaw Yin Hlaing. "The Political Economy of Hmaung-kho in Socialist Myanmar". Unpublished working paper, Yangon, n.d.

Kyaw Yin Hlaing, Tin Maung Maung Than and Zaw Oo. "Contested Legitmacies and Governance in Burma/Myanmar". Asian Voices Seminar Series Transcript. Washington, D.C.: Sasakawa Peace Foundation, 26 October 2004.

Maung Maung Gyi. "An Analysis of the Social and Political Foundations of the Burmese Executive (1948-1956)." Ph.D. dissertation, Yale University, 1958.

Maung Maung Yi, U. "Trade and Investment Situation in Myanmar". Unpublished paper presented at the Workshop on Myanmar-Japan Cooperation for the Structural Adjustment of the Myanmar Economy, 25–26 June 2000, Yangon, Myanmar.

Maung Myint. "Agriculture in Burmese Economic Development". Ph.D. dissertation, University of California, Berkeley, 1966.

Mya Maung. "The Genesis of Economic Development in Burma: The Plural Society". Ph.D. dissertation, Catholic University of America, Washington, 1961.

Mya Than. "A Brief Survey on Burma's Textiles Industry". Mimeographed. Institute of Economics, n.d.

"Myanmar Export/Import Rules and Regulations for Private Business Enterprises 1997". Yangon: Ministry of Commerce, 1997.

Myat Thein. "A Preliminary Note on Smuggling between Burma and Her Neighbours". Mimeographed. Discussion paper. Rangoon, Institute of Economics, 23 October 1975.

———. "Economic Growth, Poverty, and Development Policy in Myanmar". Unpublished paper presented at the Symposium on Food Policy in Indochina and Myanmar, Hanoi, March 1999.

———. "Thoughts on New Rice Trading Policy". Unpublished discussion paper, Yangon, *c. 2003*.

———. "Banking Crisis in Myanmar: A Matter of Fundamentals". Unpublished seminar paper, Yangon, 15 July 2003.

Myo Myint. "The Politics of Survival in Burma: Diplomacy and Statecraft in the Reign of King Mindon, 1853–1878". Ph.D. dissertation, Cornell University, 1987.

Nyun Han, Norman. "Burma's Experiment in Socialism". Ph.D. dissertation, University of Colorado, 1970.

"An Outline of the Discussion for the Twenty-Year Plan and the Second Four-Year Plan". Rangoon, Ministry of Planning and Finance, 13 December 1973.

"An Outline of the Second Four-Year Plan Adopted at the First Pyithu Hluttaw". Rangoon, Planning Department, 26 October 1974.

"An Outline of the Five Year Plan of Union of Myanmar (1996/97 to 2000/2001)". Yangon: Ministry of National Planning and Economic Development, May 1996.

Palis, R. K. and O. J. S. Lazo. "Position Paper on Rice Production in Myanmar". Yangon, 19 September 1992.

Parchelo, Joseph J. "Recruitment of the Burmese Political Elite in the Second Ne Win Regime: 1962–1967". Master thesis, University of British Columbia, 1969.

"Planning Procedures in Burma". Rangoon, Planning Department, 23 April 1984.

"Report on the Second Four Year Plan". Presented to the Pyithu Hluttaw on 11 March 1974, Rangoon, Ministry of Planning and Finance.

Sang Khup. "Diversification of Economy with Special Reference to Burma". Diploma paper for the Advanced Course in National Economic Planning, Central School of Planning and Statistics, Warsaw, 1963.

Sundrum, R. M. "Census Data on the Labour Force and the Income Distribution in Burma, 1953-54". Mimeographed. Rangoon, n.d.

Taylor, Robert H. "The Relationship between Burmese Social Classes and British Indian Policy on the Behavior of the Burmese Political Elite". Ph.D. dissertation, Cornell University, 1974.

Than Toe, Dr Daw. "Human Resources Development in Myanmar with Special Reference to Vocational Training for Industrial Development". Unpublished working paper, Yangon, c. 1998.

Tun Wai, U. "Economic Reform in Myanmar". Draft report, Yangon, August 1991.

———. "Agricultural Sector Reforms". Draft report, Yangon, n.d.

"The Union of Burma: A Group Study". Joint International Business Ventures, Country Study no. 4, New York, Columbia University, 1959.

Union of Myanmar Federation of Chambers of Commerce and Industry. "Myanmar: Demand Survey on Automotive Components". Yangon, November 2002.

United Nations Development Programme (UNDP). "Burma: A Brief Review of the External Trade Sector". Paper prepared for Burma Donors' Co-ordination Meeting, Rangoon, UNDP, 2 August 1988.

United Nations Industrial Development Organization (UNIDO). "Industrial Development Series: Burma". Vienna, 16 December 1987. PPD.65.

———. "UNIDO Industry Sector Review Mission to Myanmar, 12–19 June 1989: Report". Vienna, Regional and Country Studies Branch, 12 October 1989. PPD/R.30.

World Bank. "Chairman's Report of Proceedings". Meeting of the Burma Aid Group, Tokyo, 14 September 1986.

———. "The Economy of the Union of Burma". Washington, D.C., South Asia Regional Office, 10 November 1972. SA-34.

———. "The Current Situation and Prospects of the Union of Burma". Vol. 1, Main Report. Washington, D.C., Asia Region, 1 June 1973. 168-BA.

———. "Development in Burma: Issues and Prospects". Washington, D.C., South Asia Regional Office, 27 July 1976. 1024-BA.

———. "Burma: Domestic and External Resource Prospects". Washington, D.C., South Asia Programs Department, 10 October 1980. 3098-BA.

———. "Burma: Policies and Prospects for Economic Adjustment and Growth". Washington, D.C., South Asia Programs Department, 18 November 1985. 4814-BA.

———. "Myanmar: A Current Assessment". Washington, D.C., Country Department 2, Asia Region, 30 May 1991. 9209.

———. "Myanmar: Energy Sector Investment and Policy Review Study". Washington, D.C., Country Department 2, Asia Region, 16 March 1992. 10394-BA.

———. "Myanmar: An Economic and Social Assessment". Washington, D.C., Poverty Reduction and Economic Management Unit, East Asia and Pacific Region, 18 August 1999.

Zaw Min Win. "An Analysis of FDI in Myanmar". Paper presented at the Third Myanmar-Japan Economic Conference, Yangon, 6–7 December 1999.

BOOKS AND MONOGRAPHS IN MYANMAR

Aung Than Tun, U. *Tawhlanyei Khit Oopadei Myar* [Laws of the Revolutionary Era]. Vol. 1. Yangon: Aunglandaw, 1974.

———. *Tawhlanyei Khit Oopadei Myar* [Laws of the Revolutionary Era]. Vol. 2. Yangon: Aunglandaw, 1975.

Ba Nyein, U. *Gyapun Sit Yawkyei* [Japanese War Reparations]. Yangon: Ahthit Sarpay, 1962.

Bo Thanmani. *Bah Gyaunt Sterling Ngwekyei Neipei Hma Myanmar Naingngan Hnote Htwet Khe Thalei Bah Dway Gayet Yite Khe Thalei* [Why did Myanmar Withdrew from the Sterling Area and What Was the Impact?]. Yangon: News and Periodical Enterprise, 1991.

Hpo Kyaw San. *Myanma Leiyar Sipwayei Sittan* [Survey of Myanmar Agricultural Economy]. Yangon: Yamona, 1968.

———. *Parliman Demokraysi Sanit Hnint Myanmar Naingan* [Myanmar and the Parliamentary Democracy System]. Yangon: Sanpya, 1970.

Kyaw Win, Mya Han, and Thein Hlaing. *1958–1962 Myanma Nainganyei* [Myanmar's Politics]. Vol. 3. Yangon: Universities Press, 1991.

Maung Soo San. *Bama Sipwayei Sittan* [Survey of Myanmar's Economy]. Yangon: n.p., 1954.

Mya Han, Khin Hla Han, Kyaw Nyein, Than Lwin, and Sein Myint. *Myanma Nainganyei Sanitpyaung Karla (1962–1974)* [Myanmar's Politics in the Period of Systemic Change]. Vol. 1. Yangon: Universities Press, 1993.

Mya Han and Thein Hlaing. *1958–1962 Myanma Nainganyei* [Myanmar's Politics]. Vol. 4. Yangon: Universities Press, 1991.

Myint Kyi and Naw Angelene. *1958–1962 Myanma Nainganyei* [Myanmar's Politics]. Vol. 2. Yangon: Universities Press, 1991.

Ngwe Than Naing. *Sipwayei Simungain Akyaung Thigaungzayar* [Facts about Economic Planning]. Yangon: Sarpay Beikman, 1985.

San Nyein and Mya Han. *Myanma Nainganyei Sanitpyaung Karla (1962–1974)* [Myanmar's Politics in the Period of Systemic Change]. Vol. 2. Yangon: Historical Research Department, 1993.

San Nyein and Myint Kyi. *1958–1962 Myanma Nainganyei* [Myanmar's Politics]. Vol. 1. Yangon: Universities Press, 1991.

Tatmadaw Thar Thutaythi Tit Oo. *1948 Khu Hnit Hma 1988 Khu Hnit Atwin Hpyat Than Lar Thaw Myanma Thamaing Akyin Hnint Tatmadaw Ghanda* [A Concise History of Myanmar and the Role of the Armed Forces from 1948 to 1988]. 2 vols. Yangon: News and Periodicals Enterprise, 1990.

Thein Hlaing and Khin Hla Han. *Myanma Nainganyei Sanitpyaung Karla (1962–1974)* [Myanmar's Politics in the Period of Systemic Change]. Vol. 3. Yangon: Historical Research Department, 1993.

Thein Pe Myint. *Kyaw Nyein*. With Introduction by U Kyaw Nyein. Yangon: Shwe Pyi Dan, 1961.

Tin Soe (Bawgagon). *Bogyoke Aung San Ei Sipwayei Amyin* [General Aung San's Economic View]. Yangon: Pyithu Sa-oke Taik, 1974.

Tu Maung, U. *Myanma Bun Lokengan Thamaing* [History of Myanmar's Banking]. Yangon: Sabei Oo Sarpay, 1983.

ARTICLES IN MYANMAR

Aung Khin, U. "Myanma Yeinan Lokengan" [Myanmar's Oil Industry]. In *Presidential Addresses 1966: Burma Research Congress*, pp. 1–20. Yangon: Research Policy Direction Board, 1966.

Aye Thida, Daw. "1930 Matainghmi Myanmar Naingan Twin Tho Hsoshelit Sarpay Pyant Hnant Largyin" [Diffusion of Socialist Literature into Myanmar before 1930]. *Tekkatho Pyinnyar Padeithar Sarsaung* 14, no. 1: 47–53.

Ba Chit, U. "Myanmar Naingan Pyithu Paing Ghanda Hma Sethmu Lokengan Tihsaukhmu Atwe Akyon Hnint Twaykhaw Mhyawmyinhmu Myar" [Experiences in and Ideas on the Development of State-Sector Industries in Myanmar]. In *Presidential Addresses 1972: Burma Research Congress*, pp. 67–114. Yangon: Research Policy Direction Board, 1972.

Chin Gyar. "Made in Myanmar Pi Pho Yar" [To be a True Made in Myanmar]. *Kyemon*, 19 March 2001.

Kyan, Daw. "Yadanabon Setyon Myar" [Factories of Yadanabon]. *Pyidaungsu Myanmar Naingan Sarpay Hnint Luhmuyei Theikpan Jarnei* I (1968): 140–79.

Kyi May Kaung, Daw. "Ayin Ahni Hnint Konhtwet Achoe Myar" [Capital-Output Ratios]. *Tekkatho Pyinnyar Padeithar Sarsaung* 2, no. 1 (1967): 227–39.

Kyi Myint Hein. "*Naignant Ah Mahn Hse Taman-2* [Reservoirs and Dams, the Strength of the Country]. *Kyemon*, 19 February 2001.

Saw Htoo Sein. "Mathudaw Myar Paunghpet Thi Akhar" [When Dissolute People Associate]. *Lokethar Pyithu Neizin*, 28 November 1985.

Soon Sein, U. "Myanma Thattu Tuphawyei Lokengan" [Myanmar's Mining Industry]. In *Presidential Addresses 1971: Burma Research Congress*, pp. 53–61. Yangon: Research Policy Direction Board, 1971.

Than Maung, U. "Pyanlei Know Hta Lar Thaw Puggliga Bangyi Myar [Revival of the Big Private Banks]". *Living Color* (March 2004), pp. 72–73

Thet Tun, U. "Sethmu Lethmu Phuntbyoyei Mahar Byuhar" [Industrial Development Strategy]. In *Presidential Addresses 1971: Burma Research Congress*, pp. 29–35. Yangon: Research Policy Direction Board, 1971.

Thurein Nyunt. "Lanzin Parti Parti Unit Myar Ei Akhan Ghanda" [Role of Party Units]. *Botahtaung*, 7 August 1988.

Tun Aung. "Thwinkon Htokekon Lokengan Myar Euro Phyint Asinpyay" [Convenience with Euro for Imports/Exports Business]. *Living Color* (October 2003), pp. 23–24.

Ye Min. "Parti Oohsaunghmu Hnint Pyithu Tatmadaw" [Party's Leading Role and People's Armed Forces]. *Botahtaung*, 25 October 1987.

Yebaw Than Hlaing. "Ahnuak Ashet Ahant Atar Myar Goh Hpeishar Hpyayshin Yei" [Removing Obstacles and Hindrances]. *Botahtaung*, 20 September 1987.

Wint Kyaw, U. "Ban Akyaung Ngwe Akyaung" [On Banks and Money]. *Dhana* (January 2002), pp. 30–34.

OFFICIAL PUBLICATIONS IN MYANMAR

Alokethamar Aseeayone Thamaing [History of the Worker's Union]. Vol. 1. Yangon: Burma Socialist Programme Party, 1982; reprint, 1984.

———. Vol. 2. Yangon: Burma Socialist Programme Party, 1983.

Alokethamar Hnihnawbwe Hmattan [Workers' Seminar Record]. Yangon: Burma Socialist Programme Party, 1965.

Alokethamar Yeiyar [Worker's Affairs]. No. 4. Yangon: Burma Socialist Programme Party, 1968.

Alokethamar Yeiyar [Worker's Affairs]. No. 5. Yangon: Burma Socialist Programme Party, 1969.

1973 Khu Hnit Dutaya Akyein Parti Nyilargun Parti Baho Kommiti Okahta Gyi Ei Maintgun Myar Hnint Parti Baho Kommiti Ei Nainganyei Asiyinkhanzar [Second Party Congress, 1973: Speeches of the Central Committee Chairman and the Political Report of the Party Central Committee]. Yangon: Burma Socialist Programme Party, 1974.

1971 Khu Hnit Pahtama Akyein Parti Nyilargun Parti Baho Kommiti Okahta Gyi Ei Maintgun Myar Hnint Parti Siyoneyei Baho Kommiti Ei Nainganyei Asiyinkhanzar [First Party Congress, 1971: Speeches of the Central Committee Chairman and the Political Report of the Party Central Organizing Committee]. Yangon: Burma Socialist Programme Party, 1971.

Myanma Hsoshelit Lanzin Parti Ei Hnit-Shei Hnit-Toh Sipwayei Muwada Myar [Long-Term and Short-Term Economic Policies of the Burma Socialist Programme Party]. Yangon: Burma Socialist Programme Party, 1972.

Myanma Hoshelit Lanzin Parti Okahta Gyi Ei Khitpyaung Tawhlanyei Thamaingwin Maintgun Baungyoke [Compendium of Historic Revolutionary Speeches by the Chairman of the Burma Socialist Programme Party], No. 1. Yangon: Burma Socialist Programme Party, 1985.

Myanma Leiyar Myei Thamaing [History of Myanmar's Agricultural Land]. 2 vols. Yangon: Burma Socialist Programme Party, 1971.

Myanma Yeinan Lokengan [Myanmar's Oil Industry]. Yangon: Burma Socialist Programme Party, 1978.

Myanmar Naingan Thattu Twin Myar [Myanmar's Mines]. Yangon: Burma Socialist Programme Party, 1976.

Pahtama Akyein Pyithu Hluttaw Hsahtama Aseeawei Hmattan [Record of the First Pyithu Hluttaw, Sixth Session]. Yangon: n.p., 1976.

Pahtama Akyein Pyithu Hluttaw 1977 Khu Hnit Oopadei Myar Nioopadei Myar Hnint Lokehtone Lokeni Myar [First Pyithu Hluttaw, Laws, By-laws and Procedures, 1977]. Yangon: n.p., 1978.

Pahtama Akyein Pyithu Hluttaw Thatama Aseeawei Hmattan [Record of the First Pyithu Hluttaw, Seventh Session]. Yangon, n.p., 1977.

1968 Parti Hnihnaw Phaleibwe [Party Seminar, 1968]. Yangon: Burma Socialist Programme Party, 1968.

Pyinsama Akyein Parti Nyilargun Tho Tinthwin Thi Baho Kommiti Ei Naiganyei Asiyinkhanzar [Political Report of the Central Committee to the Fifth Party Congress]. Yangon: Burma Socialist Programme Party, 1985.

Pyitwin Yeiyar [Internal Affairs], No. 3, part 2. Yangon: Burma Socialist Programme Party, 1967.

———, No. 7. Yangon: Burma Socialist Programme Party, 1972.

Pyiyei Ywahmu: Pyidaungsu Myanmar Naingandaw Asoeya Ei Hsuangywetchet Myar (1/11/58–6/2/60) [National Affairs: Undertakings of the Government of the Union of Burma]. Yangon: Directorate of Information, 1960.

Sethmu Lethmu Hnyunkyaryeiwun Htarna Ei 1959-60 Bandardaw Hnit Atwet Hnitpatlei Asiyinkhanzar [Annual Report of the Directorate of Industries for the Fiscal Year 1959–60]. Yangon: Government Printing and Stationary, 1963.

Sipwa Yeiyar [Economic Affairs]. No. 4. Yangon: Burma Socialist Programme Party, 1969.

———, No. 7. Yangon: Burma Socialist Programme Party, 1972.

Taingyinthar Lumyo Myar Arlone Ei Sipwayei Goh Simungain Hpyint Akaung Ahtei Phawyei Simungyet [Planned Implementation of the Economy for All Nationalities]. Yangon: Burma Socialist Programme Party, 1971.

Tawhlanyei Kaungsi Ei Alokethamar Yeiyar Hsaungywetchet Myar [Revolutionary Council's Actions on Workers' Affairs]. Yangon: Burma Socialist Programme Party, 1977.

Tawhlanyei Kaungsi Ei Lokehsaungyek Thamaing Akyingyoke [Historical Summary of the Actions of the Revolutionary Council]. Yangon: Printing and Publishing Corporation, 1974.

Thabawtayar Yeiyar [Theoretical Affairs], No. 11. Yangon: Burma Socialist Programme Party, 1977.

UNPUBLISHED SOURCES IN MYANMAR

Baho Yeiyar Kommiti Myar Ei Phwezibon Hnint Lokengan Tarwun Myar [Organization and Tasks of the Central Affairs Committees]. Yangon: Burma Socialist Programme Party, January 1971.

"Hnit-Shei Hnit-Toh Sipwayei Muwada Myar Hnint Simungain Lunhyunhmu Myar." [Long-Term and Short-Term Economic Policies and Plan Guidelines]. Yangon: Planning Department, October 1983.

Myanmar Naingan Sethmu Lokengan Thamaing Apaing 2: Coloni Khit Sethmu Lokengan Thamaing [History of Myanmar's Industry, Part 2: Colonial Era]. Yangon: Ministry of No. 1 Industry, n.d.

Myanmar Naingan Sethmu Lokengan Thamaing Apaing 3: Pyanlehtudaungyei Khit Sethmu Lokengan Thamaing [History of Myanmar's Industry, Part 3: Rehabilitation Era]. Yangon: Ministry of No. 1 Industry, n.d.

Myanmar Naingan Sethmu Lokengan Thamaing Apaing 4: Tawhlanyei Kaungsi Karla Sethmu Lokengan Thamaing [History of Myanmar's Industry, Part 4: Revolutionary Period]. Yangon: Ministry of No. 1 Industry, n.d.

Myat Thein, U, U Than Aung Yin, and U Maung Maung Lwin. "Sitpyikhit Myanma Sethmu Htudaungyei Hnint Pyipa Konthweiyei" [Post-War Myanmar's Industrialization and External Trade]. Paper presented at the Burma Research Congress, Yangon, April 1971.

Naingandaw Ei Sipwayei Hsaingyar Muwada Myar Hnint Lunhnyunhmu Myar Pyupyin Pyaungleiyei Hnint Pathet Ywei Tinpyagyek [Report on Reforming National Economic Policies and Guidelines]. Yangon: Burma Socialist Programme Party, 1988.

Pyidaungsu Myanmar Naingan Sipwayei Simungain Lunhnyunhmu Myar Hnint Asiyinkhanzar [Union of Burma Economic Plan Guidelines and Report]. Yangon: Burma Socialist Programme Party, 1971.

Su Su Khin. "Puggliga Tho Hlwepyaung Lokekain Ne Thaw Setyon Mya Ei Lokengan Hsaungywet Hmu Achei Anay Goh Leilar Sisit Chin" [Analysis of Operational Situation at Factories Transferred to the Private Sector]. Unpublished Master thesis. Commerce Department, Institute of Economics, Yangon, June 1996.

Tin Aung Hein, U. "Myanmar Naingan Ei Nainganyei Sipwayei Simunkhantgweyei Luhmuyei Hnint Tayasiyinyei Keissa Myar Hnint Sutthlyin Ywei Akyanpyu Tinpyagyet Sardan" [Advisory Report on Myanmar's Political, Economic, Administrative, Social, and Judicial Matters]. Yangon, 2 October 1987.

Thein Tun, U. *Myanmar Naingan Hnint Sethmu Lokengan Yeizeegyaung* [Myanmar and Industrial Current]. Paper presented at the economic education seminar organized by the Myanmar Women Entrepreneurs Association, Yangon, 18 December 1999.

UNTITLED AND UNPUBLISHED SOURCES IN MYANMAR

Open letter from retired Brigadier Aung Gyi to President San Yu, six retired senior army officers, and former members of the Revolutionary Council. Yangon, 9 May 1988, 39 pp.

Report submitted to the Working Group for Compiling Guidelines to Harmonize Domestic Production and External Trade. Yangon, *c.* 1987.

Report submitted by the Ministry of No. 1 Industry in response to the Party Chairman's Speech of 10 August 1987. Yangon, *c.* 1987.

INTERNET SOURCES

BurmaNet News. An Internet newspaper providing comprehensive coverage of news and opinion on Myanmar for subscribers. It is posted from editor@burmanet.org. Also available at www.burmanet.org.

Soc.culture.burma. A newsgroup on Myanmar, which is available on the Internet as a topic in the Usenet news system.

Index

N

T

U

V

W

Y

www.ingramcontent.com/pod-product-compliance
Lightning Source LLC
LaVergne TN
LVHW102103300926
849161LV00001B/5
* 9 7 8 9 8 1 2 3 0 3 7 1 4 *